HOUSING AMERICA IN THE 1980s

HOUSING AMERICA IN THE 1980s

John S. Adams

for the
National Committee for Research
on the 1980 Census

RUSSELL SAGE FOUNDATION / NEW YORK

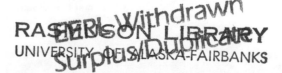

The Russell Sage Foundation

The Russell Sage Foundation, one of the oldest of America's general purpose foundations, was established in 1907 by Mrs. Margaret Olivia Sage for "the improvement of social and living conditions in the United States." The Foundation seeks to fulfill this mandate by fostering the development and dissemination of knowledge about the political, social, and economic problems of America. It conducts research in the social sciences and public policy, and publishes books and pamphlets that derive from this research.

The Board of Trustees is responsible for oversight and the general policies of the Foundation, while administrative direction of the program and staff is vested in the President, assisted by the officers and staff. The President bears final responsibility for the decision to publish a manuscript as a Russell Sage Foundation book. In reaching a judgment on the competence, accuracy, and objectivity of each study, the President is advised by the staff and selected expert readers. The conclusions and interpretations in Russell Sage Foundation publications are those of the authors and not of the Foundation, its Trustees, or its staff. Publication by the Foundation, therefore, does not imply endorsement of the contents of the study.

Library of Congress Cataloging-in-Publication Data

Adams, John S., 1938–
    Housing America in the 1980s.

    (The Population of the United States in the 1980s)
    "For the National Committee for Research on the 1980 Census."
    Bibliography: p.
    Includes index.
    1. Housing—United States.   I. Title.   II. Series.
HD7293.A625   1987   363.5'0973   86-42950
ISBN 0-87154-003-7

Cover and text design: HUGUETTE FRANCO

10 9 8 7 6 5 4 3 2 1

Foreword

Housing America in the 1980s is one of an ambitious series of volumes aimed at converting the vast statistical yield of the 1980 census into authoritative analyses of major changes and trends in American life. This series, "The Population of the United States in the 1980s," represents an important episode in social science research and revives a long tradition of independent census analysis. First in 1930, and then again in 1950 and 1960, teams of social scientists worked with the U.S. Bureau of the Census to investigate significant social, economic, and demographic developments revealed by the decennial censuses. These census projects produced three landmark series of studies, providing a firm foundation and setting a high standard for our present undertaking.

There is, in fact, more than a theoretical continuity between those earlier census projects and the present one. Like those previous efforts, this new census project has benefited from close cooperation between the Census Bureau and a distinguished, interdisciplinary group of scholars. Like the 1950 and 1960 research projects, research on the 1980 census was initiated by the Social Science Research Council and the Russell Sage Foundation. In deciding once again to promote a coordinated program of census analysis, Russell Sage and the Council were mindful not only of the severe budgetary restrictions imposed on the Census Bureau's own publishing and dissemination activities in the 1980s, but also of the extraordinary changes that have occurred in so many dimensions of American life over the past two decades.

The studies constituting "The Population of the United States in the 1980s" were planned, commissioned, and monitored by the National Committee for Research on the 1980 Census, a special committee appointed by the Social Science Research Council and sponsored by the Council, the Russell Sage Foundation, and the Alfred P. Sloan Foundation, with the collaboration of the U.S. Bureau of the Census. This committee includes leading social scientists from a broad range of fields—demography, economics, education, geography, history, political science, sociology, and statistics. It has been the committee's task to select the main topics for research, obtain highly qualified specialists to carry out that research, and provide the structure necessary to facilitate coordination among researchers and with the Census Bureau.

The topics treated in this series span virtually all the major features of American society—ethnic groups (blacks, Hispanics, foreign-born); spatial dimensions (migration, neighborhoods, housing, regional and metropolitan growth and decline); and status groups (income levels, families and households, women). Authors were encouraged to draw not only on the 1980 Census but also on previous censuses and on subsequent national data. Each individual research project was assigned a special advisory panel made up of one committee member, one member nominated by the Census Bureau, one nominated by the National Science Foundation, and one or two other experts. These advisory panels were responsible for project liaison and review and for recommendations to the National Committee regarding the readiness of each manuscript for publication. With the final approval of the chairman of the National Committee, each report was released to the Russell Sage Foundation for publication and distribution.

The debts of gratitude incurred by a project of such scope and organizational complexity are necessarily large and numerous. The committee must thank, first, its sponsors—the Social Science Research Council, headed until recently by Kenneth Prewitt; the Russell Sage Foundation, under the direction of president Marshall Robinson; and the Alfred P. Sloan Foundation, led by Albert Rees. The long-range vision and day-to-day persistence of these organizations and individuals sustained this research program over many years. The active and willing cooperation of the Bureau of the Census was clearly invaluable at all stages of this project, and the extra commitment of time and effort made by Bureau economist James R. Wetzel must be singled out for special recognition. A special tribute is also due to David L. Sills of the Social Science Research Council, staff member of the committee, whose organizational, administrative, and diplomatic skills kept this complicated project running smoothly.

The committee also wishes to thank those organizations that contributed additional funding to the 1980 Census project—the Ford Foundation and its deputy vice president, Louis Winnick, the Na-

tional Science Foundation, the National Institute on Aging, and the National Institute of Child Health and Human Development. Their support of the research program in general and of several particular studies is gratefully acknowledged.

The ultimate goal of the National Committee and its sponsors has been to produce a definitive, accurate, and comprehensive picture of the U.S. population in the 1980s, a picture that would be primarily descriptive but also enriched by a historical perspective and a sense of the challenges for the future inherent in the trends of today. We hope our readers will agree that the present volume takes a significant step toward achieving that goal.

CHARLES F. WESTOFF

Chairman and Executive Director
National Committee for Research
on the 1980 Census

This book is dedicated to
Fred E. Lukermann and John R. Borchert—my teachers, colleagues, and friends.

Acknowledgments

The U.S. decennial Census of Population tells us who we Americans are as people, while the companion Census of Housing, taken decennially since 1940, gives us a profile of the way we live and the settlements we create.

Our houses, as historian Fernand Braudel reminds us, endure. They bear "witness to the essential slowness of civilizations, of cultures bent on preserving, maintaining and repeating."* One set of forces wants to keep it that way, while another tries to make housing a battleground of social change. No wonder that many of our domestic policy disputes seem to involve housing.

When we look at our housing, a large part of our national life is reflected. Not the market production part, with people at work for pay, but our production and consumption life at home, which forms the essential fabric of American civilization. Housing anchors us to the land and to our neighbors. Our housing is a document describing our settlement pattern on the land. We read it to learn something about our lives at home, our individual and group ambitions, our achievements—and some of our failures. In this book, I try to capture and frame part of that document.

Support for the research and writing of this book was provided by the Russell Sage Foundation through the National Committee for Research on the 1980 Census. I was pleased to be asked by the committee to prepare this book, for housing analysis is inevitably geographical analysis. I cannot imagine how patterns of housing supply, demand, and use can be understood without central attention to the spatial distribution of housing and the local environments that it creates.

I appreciate the valuable advice and enthusiastic support from fellow members of the National Advisory Committee, and the espe-

cially memorable insistence of Marshall Robinson, then president of the Russell Sage Foundation, that I wrestle with the housing subareas of New York. The special treatment of that city, with Los Angeles and Chicago thrown in for good measure, is the result. In a national-scale comparative analysis, these places are large points on the map. On another scale, they are gargantuan areas of immense complexity.

Kenneth Prewitt and David L. Sills of the Social Science Research Council showed great enthusiasm for the project from the start. I thank them for their support. Charles F. Westoff has been a stern but always helpful series editor. An advisory panel consisting of Anthony Downs, John L. Goodman, Jr., Robert Gutman, and Arthur F. Young received the manuscript in draft stage and made numerous suggestions for improvement. Donald C. Dahmann, a geographer at the U.S. Bureau of the Census, read the entire manuscript twice and provided valuable comments and suggestions.

I am grateful that Brian J. L. Berry suggested to the National Committee that I might be interested in the project, and for the support of my colleagues at the University of Minnesota—in the Center for Urban and Regional Affairs, in the Humphrey Institute of Public Affairs, and in the Department of Geography. In the planning and execution of the work I have been ably assisted by Yeong-ki Beck, Hee-bang Choe, and Greg Chu, who had principal responsibility for map design and production, and by Judith E. Adams, Lori Brown, Richard Greene, Hee-yeon Lee, Lynn Newman, Neil Saxton, John Tocho, and John M. Weiss. Barbara J. VanDrasek typed the manuscript. She and David J. C. Adams also helped with the photographs. I accept responsibility for errors of fact, omission, or interpretation.

JOHN S. ADAMS
University of Minnesota

---

*Fernand Braudel, *Capitalism and Material Life: 1400–1800* (New York: Harper & Row, 1975), p. 193.

Contents

List of Tables

List of Figures

HOUSING, PEOPLE, AND SETTLEMENT IN THE UNITED STATES

THIS BOOK describes and analyzes the housing portion of the U.S. settlement landscape during the early 1980s. The facilities that we as a nation construct to carry out our daily production and consumption of goods and services are dominant elements in the settlement patterns that portray how we live, at the same time that they regulate the way we live.[1]

Like our language, our weather, our food, and other features of everyday life and experience, housing is such a fundamental, pervasive yet diverse element of the American scene that it is hard to discuss it in a systematic and comprehensive way. How can a decrepit apartment in the South Bronx be compared with a shack in a Louisiana bayou? Or a Montana ranch house with a Gold Coast condo in Chicago?

This book, based largely on data from the 1980 Census of Housing, provides one answer. This introductory chapter examines part of the recent history of U.S. housing, especially since 1960. Chapter 2 explores the meaning of housing in America—as shelter, as home, as store of wealth for households, as tax base for local governments, as

status symbol for the middle class, and as an element of inclusion and weapon of exclusion in neighborhood and community life.

Chapter 3 describes the U.S. housing stock—its volume, composition, and geographical distribution. Chapter 4 treats the nature of housing demand, giving special attention to the ways that demographic changes affect housing demand and financial institutions help support the housing industry.

Chapter 5 explores how households of various types are matched with housing units throughout the United States. This national and regional treatment is followed by small-area analysis in Chapter 6, presenting tract-level portrayals of housing use patterns in selected central cities and urbanized areas across the country. Chapter 7 reviews some persistent contemporary housing policy questions and related governmental responses.

Housing in America

To the average adult American, the question "What do you do?" is an inquiry about the source of one's livelihood. It means "Where do you work?" or "What kind of job do you hold to earn your living?"

---

[1]See James E. Vance, Jr., *This Scene of Man: The Role and Structure of the City in the Geography of Western Civilization* (New York: Harper & Row, 1977), for perhaps the most original and thorough geographical treatment of the emergence of urban settlement form in Western civilization.

The emphasis is on the person's role as an economic production unit within society.

The question "Where do you live?" is for some people a more personal query. It asks about one's private life and private consumption at home in contrast to the employment question, which focuses on the public self.

During the first century and a half of our republic, private and publicly generated data systems focused on economic production and trade, but paid little attention to distribution and consumption. It is easy to find out how many barrels of salt pork passed through Cincinnati or New Orleans in 1850, but it is hard to learn what people in those times and places ate for lunch or how they spent their money or leisure time. It was not until the Great Depression of the 1930s, while the giant production machine known as the U.S. economy was flagging badly, that serious national attention turned to measuring spending habits, consumption patterns, and the American housing system.[2]

To note that production statistics have received more attention than consumption and housing is not to say that the two areas of concern are unrelated. As a society, we build our houses in the vicinity of our jobs. But when mobility becomes cheaper and more convenient, the distance between home and work can widen. If we have the financial means to live without working at a paying job, we often can live in pleasant locations without regard to job considerations.

Unlike some parts of the world where housing is often built simply and only for temporary occupancy, or inexpensively for low-income occupants, new housing in the United States usually is built durably, rather expensively, and for middle- and upper-income households.[3] It becomes available for low-income groups only after the initial occupants have moved on. This tradition means that American housing forms a relatively permanent feature of the U.S. settlement landscape. Once we build houses, we use them virtually indefinitely. They almost always outlast their builders and the households who first occupy them. The large amount of real capital stored up in housing and the high real value of services provided annually by housing

slow down the geographical adjustment to production demands elsewhere in the economy, thereby making regional economies and populations much more stable, inflexible, and immobile than they would otherwise be.

Housing provides an important clue to society at the local level. Households come and go from a neighborhood, but the social relationships that are fostered and nurtured by the design and spatial arrangements of the housing stock help to define the local societies that constitute the nation.

The history and geography of a people are revealed in its settlements. Within nucleated settlements—hamlets, villages, towns, and cities—housing forms the predominant land use element. Housing is seldom the most vivid feature of our settlement fabric, but socially and culturally it is one of the most fundamental in the services it provides for people and in the formative impact it has on them.

What Housing Means in the United States

The activity that we call housing involves households using dwellings. Housing activity forms a central feature in the human occupancy of the earth. A house considered by itself is merely a structure. A home, on the other hand, is a household living in a house; the word "home" implies an experience (Figures 1.1– 1.4).

Housing is an interactive process that carries meanings at several levels. It is a symbol of status in American society, a mark of social position, a store of household wealth, a statement of household aspirations, and an expression of identity for the household as a unit as well as for individual household members.

The familiar housing and neighborhood environments of one's youth help shape later ideas of one's place in society. In certain crucial respects one's place in the housing landscape defines and channels one's participation in social networks and social structures.

An urban household's decision about where to live reflects social forces encouraging congregation and segregation within cities. The housing landscapes that we create help to make social and cultural categories of urban society visible, understandable, and somewhat stable. On the other hand, housing landscapes in American urban areas are constantly assaulted by the destabilizing effects of changing population age structures, the withdrawal of wealth and real estate values from one set of neighborhoods and their transfers elsewhere, domestic migration and residential mobility, foreign immigration, and interregional wealth shifts.

---

[2]It was only after World War II that national housing concerns could be addressed using comprehensive and consistent national housing data. For a set of excellent representative writings on housing from the 1940s, 1950s, and 1960s, see William L. C. Wheaton, Grace Milgram, and Margi Ellin Meyerson, eds., *Urban Housing* (New York: Free Press, 1966).

[3]For national practices that contrast sharply with the United States, see Irving H. Welfeld, *European Housing Subsidy Systems: An American Perspective*, U.S. Department of Housing and Urban Development Report (Washington, DC: U.S. Government Printing Office, 1972).

FIGURE 1.1 City-owned apartment houses on South State Street in Chicago, with neighborhood shopping facilities and parking lot in the foreground. Public housing serves the lowest-income households in the city.

FIGURE 1.3 Comfortably spaced middle-class houses in Minneapolis, built in the 1920s on 40-foot lots, with alleys and garages behind.

FIGURE 1.2 Working-class single-family housing in the Brooklyn borough of New York City, built during the streetcar era, on narrow lots without alleys behind houses. Trash cans are carried by residents to the street for weekly pickup.

FIGURE 1.4 Upper-middle-class houses on Russian Hill in San Francisco. Population pressure on the peninsula raises land prices, and sites on the hills are still more expensive, forcing builders to use small parcels for large, expensive houses.

Vigorous legal and social policy initiatives have been launched over the years to help break down neighborhood class barriers. Equal opportunity housing laws have been passed and enforced as efforts to create color-blind and class-neutral housing markets. Yet despite strong and persistent initiatives to erode neighborhood class barriers, strong zoning laws and firm court decisions have staunchly protected middle-class single-family housing areas by curtailing entry into them by low-income and nonfamily households. Certain kinds of neighborhoods are evidently understood by society as important means for nurturing and reproducing selected lifestyles. Attempts to disrupt these conservative strongholds are fought, perhaps as an expression of a basic instinct to protect and nurture human life itself.

Valiant efforts have been made in the United States to modify zoning laws and to expand the number of good-quality housing opportunities for the less affluent classes. But it has proved difficult to enhance the housing position of the poor without simultaneously undermining the tenuous sense of control that is shared by the working class and lower middle class.[4] Trying to help the less fortunate classes without threatening the position of the better off is a social policy dilemma, but the American utopian tradition stimulates the nation's continuing effort.

Social Meanings and Market Realities for Housing in the 1980s

In most years following World War II American builders put up over 1 million units of new housing per year. Some years production exceeded 2 million—an extraordinary volume of new high-quality housing. This construction boom extended through the 1960s and 1970s until a combination of forces driven by inflation, real estate speculation, and record-high mortgage interest rates ended it in the early 1980s.

The long, postwar building binge of cheap and high-quality housing went a long way toward eroding the importance of high-quality single-family housing as a symbol of social status in the United States. Because of what was readily available to the majority of postwar American families, and taken for granted by their children, belief developed among the middle class during the postwar years that a large share of them, perhaps a majority, were living a material existence well above average—at least when judged by the standards of the Depression and war years.

It is important to examine what happens to a society (1) when its feelings of well-being are both supported and symbolized by housing achievements that are thought to be "above average," (2) when it increasingly discovers that the definition of average has moved sharply upward, and (3) when its children discover that the residential environments they have been reared in are largely beyond their economic reach as they form their own households. In the face of harder economic times and necessarily diminished housing expectations, net new household formation in the 1980s became many fewer per year than the rates typical of earlier decades. We do not know exactly how all these trends are causally related, but we do know that during the 1980s ownership rates have risen and standard quality of housing has been higher than ever, even though housing has become more expensive, socioeconomic mobility seems harder, and real incomes of new households often have fallen far short of what is needed to match the sense of housing achievement realized by the new households of the 1950s, 1960s, and 1970s.[5]

Tracking Our Housing Situation

Counting housing units and households and measuring their characteristics are the main tasks of decennial censuses and periodic housing surveys. Although important national housing surveys were carried out during the Roosevelt Administrations of the 1930s, the first U. S. housing census was taken only in 1940.[6] It has been repeated decennially since 1940 and has been supplemented by the American Housing Survey and other sample surveys of housing finance, inventory change, and new construction.

The content and modes of presentation of the housing data series prepared by federal agencies are shaped by current and historical issues that demand public attention, as well as social science notions about the nature of society and about how and why people acquire,

---

[4]For numerous examples of housing problems and policy responses, see Daniel R. Mandelker and Roger Montgomery, eds., *Housing in America: Problems and Perspectives* (Indianapolis: Bobbs-Merrill, 1973).

[5]As Richard A. Easterlin has pointed out, large variations throughout the twentieth century in birthrates have wielded major consequences later in expectations and available economic opportunities for successive cohorts of young entrants into the economy. See his *Birth and Fortune: The Impact of Numbers on Personal Welfare* (New York: Basic Books, 1980).

[6] Homer Hoyt, *The Structure and Growth of Residential Neighborhoods in American Cities* (Washington, DC: Federal Housing Administration, 1939). I consider this to be the most important and influential book ever published on the nature of urban housing markets in the United States.

furnish, and use housing as they do. Public health concerns provoke questions about crowding, household water and sewer service, and plumbing facilities. The energy crisis of recent years has triggered questions about types of fuel used to heat housing, insulation, and other energy-related topics. Concern about adequate housing for low-income households prompts such questions as how much household income is devoted to meeting housing expenses. Concern for minority groups and the nature of their housing arrangements has led to detailed inquiry about these topics and extensive reporting of the statistical results.

On the other hand, some housing and neighborhood topics that might well be important to household and to national well-being are not examined systematically in our housing surveys and censuses. For example, we do not measure and report small-area data on housing density—that is, number of housing units per unit area. We fail to examine and report on visual environments, on the use of color, the vegetation around our houses, street congestion, ambient noise levels, air quality, toxic substances, or the smells that are part of everyday neighborhood life.

When basic research discloses a widespread problem, such as large amounts of lead in many neighborhoods of our cities, pressure mounts to monitor all neighborhoods systematically in order to document the problem and to support efforts to solve it. When a known problem, such as burglary, rises to a sufficiently high position on the public's list of concerns, households may be polled to assess the geographic incidence of crimes against property and against persons. Our data series are products of social theories, political agendas, economic interests, and scientific concerns. Every data series represents answers to questions thought to be important today or at some time in the past. Every classification system that is used to present the data represents an implicit theory.

U.S. Housing Stock in 1980: Paths to the Present

The decennial census of housing is the only comprehensive assessment of American housing that provides geographical details at the neighborhood and tract levels. The final results of the 1980 housing census became available in 1984; the accuracy and comprehensiveness of the census come at some cost in timeliness.

The 1980 census counted 226.5 million persons and 88.4 million housing units. During the 1970s the housing stock of the United States increased 28.7 percent. There was a net increase of nearly 20 million housing units—the largest 10-year increase in the history of the nation. Housing increases occurred in all regions and states. Only the District of Columbia experienced a slight decline in housing units during the decade. Growth was greatest in the South and West (Figures 1.5 and 1.6).

Some basic trends in housing growth have persisted in nearly every decade between 1940 and 1980. Pacific and southwestern states have had large increases in housing since the 1940s. States along the Atlantic seaboard and in the industrial Midwest experienced more moderate growth during this period. Great Plains states and states along the lower Mississippi River grew slowly. These trends continued during the 1950s and 1960s, although total growth in housing slowed during the 1960s across the United States. The huge jump in the housing stock during the 1970s highlighted a significant trend toward renewed growth in rural areas. States in New England, the South, and Rocky Mountain areas showed unusually rapid gains, along with the traditional fast-growth areas in the Pacific states and the Southwest. Florida was the only state east of the Mississippi River to experience very high growth in each decade since 1940.

Over the past 40 years, western states experienced large expansions of their housing inventories, although many of these states had relatively small numbers of housing units (Figure 1.7). Southern states had generally above-average growth, with states in the South Atlantic division and Texas growing more rapidly than Appalachia. Northeast and North Central states generally increased at a much slower pace than the nation.

Almost all of the 3,137 U. S. counties and county equivalents—about 98 percent—had increases in the number of housing units. Most of the counties with a net loss in housing were in a belt beginning in the Texas Panhandle and running north through Kansas and Nebraska to the Dakotas. A few counties along the Mississippi River also had housing losses. Many of these counties reached their maximum population early in the twentieth century. In contrast, most counties that doubled their housing stock in the 1970s were located in Florida, Texas, and western mountain states, demonstrating the strong attraction of these areas during the decade.

Recent Growth in Population and Changes in the Housing Stock

The 1980 census was the first in the twentieth century to show a divergence in the growth rates of population and housing. Although formerly the rates moved essentially in parallel, the growth rate for

FIGURE 1.5

Regions and Census Divisions of the United States, 1980

FIGURE 1.6
Percentage Change in Total Housing Units, by State, 1970–1980

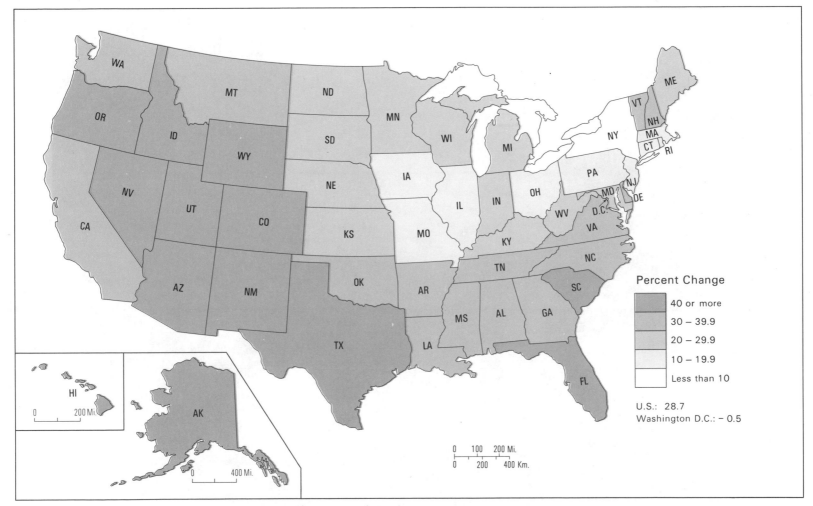

Percent Change

- 40 or more
- 30 – 39.9
- 20 – 29.9
- 10 – 19.9
- Less than 10

U.S.: 28.7
Washington D.C.: − 0.5

0 100 200 Mi.
0 200 400 Km.

SOURCE: U.S. Bureau of the Census, 1980 Census of Housing; vol. 1, *Characteristics of Housing Units, U.S. Summary*, pp. 1–2.

FIGURE 1.7

Percentage Change in Total Housing Units, by State, 1940–1980

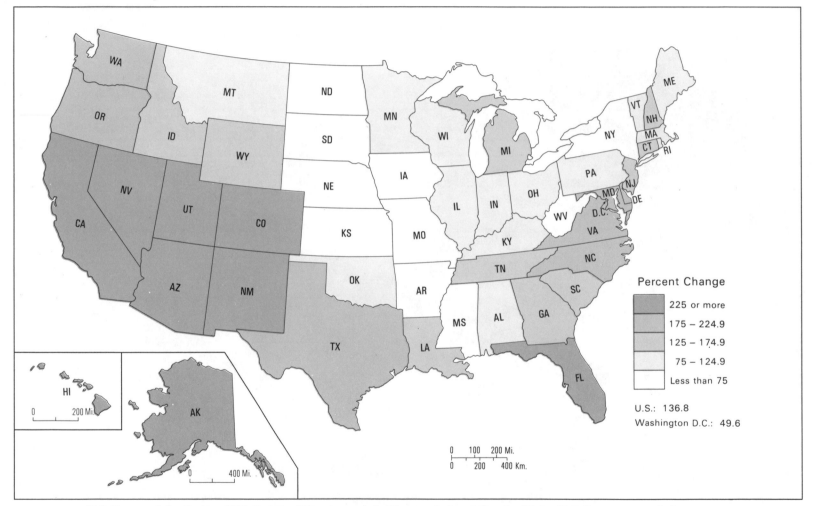

Percent Change

- 225 or more
- 175 – 224.9
- 125 – 174.9
- 75 – 124.9
- Less than 75

U.S.: 136.8

Washington D.C.: 49.6

SOURCE: U.S. Bureau of the Census, 1980 Census of Housing, vol. 1, *Characteristics of Housing Units, U.S. Summary*, pp. 1–4.

housing increased between 1970 and 1980 while that for population declined. As a result, a greater supply of housing units relative to total population existed at the close of the decade than ever before in U. S. history.

The homeownership rate increased substantially, from 43.6 percent of households in 1940 to 61.9 percent in 1960. Since 1960 homeownership has increased at a much slower pace. Homeownership rates among white households were greater than homeownership rates among other racial and ethnic groups throughout the period.

Declines in the percentage of units with more than 1 person per room and increases in the percentage of units with .5 person or less per room have resulted in an overall decline in persons per room, reflecting improvements in housing conditions. One-to-3-room housing units make up a declining percentage of all units. The percentage of 4-to-6-room units has remained constant after reaching its peak in 1960. The share of units with 7 rooms or more has increased in recent decades.

The lack of complete plumbing facilities for exclusive use was no longer a major housing problem by 1980. In 1940 44.6 percent of U.S. households lacked complete plumbing, while in 1980 only 2.2 percent were so classified. The few counties where inadequate plumbing remained a significant problem in 1980 were mainly in the rural South.

The median value of owner-occupied single-family houses increased roughly $5,000 per decade between 1940 and 1970 and $30,000 between 1970 and 1980, or an increase of 178 percent during the 1970s. The increase was 43 percent during the 1960s, 61 percent during the 1950s, and 208 percent during the 1940s. Median monthly contract rent increased steadily between 1940 and 1980, but the percentage increase was lower than that for median value of owner-occupied houses. During the 1970s median rent increased $109, or 122 percent—the largest increase reported in any housing census.

Most of the states with the greatest increase in median value during the 1970s were also the states with the largest percentage increase in population. Conversely, the slower-growing states were among those with the smallest change in median value. States with the smallest percentage of increase in median monthly contract rent had high median rent initially in 1970. Large percentages of increase were most common in states with below-average rent in 1970 and rapidly increasing population during the decade.

Counties with the highest median value of owner-occupied single-family housing were found in metropolitan areas—primarily on the West Coast, the Rocky Mountain areas, the Boston–Washington, D.C., corridor, and in southern Florida. The median value in over 85 percent of the counties was below the national median of $47,200 because these counties generally had substantially fewer owner-occupied housing units than densely populated metropolitan counties with high median values.

Median contract rent was highest in metropolitan counties, with only approximately 10 percent of all counties having median rent higher than $198—the median contract rent for the United States. Low rent was still common outside large urban areas in 1980. Fifty percent of counties had median contract rent of $125 or less.

Almost three fourths of America's housing units in 1980 were in single-unit structures. The quality of the housing stock, measured in such terms as completeness of plumbing facilities, age of structures, structural quality, and equipment and furnishings available, improved in every major respect during the decade of the 1970s.

Urban housing contained better plumbing on the average than rural housing, but otherwise the condition of occupied units differed little by location (for example: urban, rural, central city, suburban) or by census region. The South and the West received a disproportionate share of new construction in the 1970s, thereby raising the measures of average housing quality in the areas where the new housing was built. In terms of sheer volume of new construction, nonmetropolitan housing stocks grew faster in the 1970s than metropolitan stocks.

The average number of rooms per housing unit rose during the 1960s and 1970s. The number of owner-occupied units grew at a faster rate than rental units. Thus, despite recessions, migration, disrupted financial markets, and unusual demographic trends during the decades, the U.S. housing stock expanded in size and quality essentially in all locations except inner cities and in all regions.

Housing Demand and the Forces Behind It

Population increase provides the principal impetus for additional housing demand. Between 1920 and 1950 the nation added almost 45 million people, and between 1950 and 1980 over 75 million more. Besides the expansions in sheer numbers, the American population changed in age composition as birthrates fluctuated and life expectancy rose. Living styles changed and housing preferences adjusted as average household sizes steadily dropped.

Obsolete houses have had to be replaced, adding to the demand for new units. And people have moved from city to suburb, from rural to metro regions and back again, and from long-settled areas of the

North and East into the boom regions of the West and South. Since it is physically and economically difficult to move housing units from places where they are unwanted to other locations where they are needed, housing left behind must be replaced at migration destinations, adding more demand for new units.

As life expectancy in the United States has been extended, the number of elderly households has abruptly enlarged. Single-parent families became increasingly common in the 1960s and 1970s, as did nonfamily households. A steadily increasing percentage of adult Americans choose to live alone. When these trends unfold across the United States, their initial consequence is to raise the demand for housing units even faster than the rate of increase in the overall population. But then these general trends are magnified in their impact by migration flows, and the consequences are severe for local housing markets.

Fast-growth areas have trouble responding to the housing wants and needs of an increasingly heterogeneous mix of additional households. Stagnant regions have trouble keeping their existing housing stock in good repair when real incomes drop and real deflation strikes a blow to the local base of real estate wealth.

Another major source of flux in housing demand has been the reorganization of the housing finance system. The continuous post–World War II housing boom had been nurtured by government-sponsored mortgage insurance and mortgage guarantee programs that protected mortgage lenders and by a highly regulated savings and loan system that ensured a steady supply of loanable funds for the construction and purchase of new housing. But this boom was abruptly terminated in 1978–1979 as a result of a series of government measures, backed by certain business interests, and aimed at curtailing the residential real estate speculation and the inflation excesses of the previous decade. Housing lost its sheltered credit market, construction of new housing became more expensive and lower in volume, and historically high housing ownership rates showed signs of dipping. Changes in the financial frameworks for housing brought about by federal legislation in 1980 had the effect of sharply raising mortgage interest rates, which raised the price of housing relative to other consumer goods and services and alternative investments. The upward adjustment in relative price levels cut into the effective demand for owned housing.

A final source of changing demand for housing is the introduction of new fashions, tastes, and outlooks. Americans like new things, and they generally prefer new housing to used housing. They are attracted not only to new design features, interior arrangements, appointments, and materials; they also like novel site plans and in-novative arrangements of housing on the land. In every period of city building, Americans have consistently expressed a preference for lower-density housing than they currently consumed. Fashions in taste are heavily influenced by what the upper-income groups consume, with their superior mobility and greater discretionary time.

In housing, the wealthy were first to escape the high densities and congestion of the industrial-commercial city (Figures 1.8 and 1.9). Until the streetcar and finally the automobile released the average family from its high-density neighborhood in the city, the high cost

FIGURE 1.8 Housing in large cities before the introduction of the electric streetcar in the late 1880s was built on small lots at high density. Most people moved about only by foot, restricting the spatial extent of the city and promoting a compact form, as in central Baltimore.

FIGURE 1.9 As streetcar lines were extended away from downtowns in the decades after 1890, apartment houses were built on high-value sites along the lines, while single-unit houses were built on lots just half a block from the line.

FIGURE 1.10 Several blocks from streetcar lines, low land prices permitted generous use of land per house before World War I in Minneapolis.

FIGURE 1.11 During the 1920s and 1930s in fast-growing urban areas of the Midwest and West developers subdivided land using a 5-acre (2-hectare) rectangle of land, bisected lengthwise with an alley providing access to garages, and divided into 50 (25-foot lots), 40 (30-foot lots), 30 (40-foot lots, shown here), or fewer lots, depending on the development pressure at the time.

of urban land, plus the expense in time and money of long distance commuting, kept suburbia or small town and rural life beyond the reach of urban workers and their families. But when mobility did improve, new construction and new demand were stimulated at all the locations added to each urban housing market (Figures 1.10–1.12).

Publicly sponsored housing programs try to affect the demand for housing by adding to the purchasing power of low- and moderate-income households. But direct federal and state housing subsidy programs as a percentage of all housing market activity have had only modest impact in the United States during the past 50 years.

Households Using Housing

Almost every person in the United States has a place to live, and almost every housing unit is in use by a household (Figure 1.13). On the demand side are households of diverse tastes, needs, and ability to pay. On the supply side is the stock of housing units. The housing market in each community and neighborhood continuously mediates

FIGURE 1.12 In the post–World War II era, with universal use of private cars in newly developing areas, low densities are constrained mainly by the cost of supplying roads, water, sewer, and other services, paid by the developer and added to the sale price of the new houses.

FIGURE 1.13 Inexpensive rural housing in Washburn County, Wisconsin. An all-weather highway provides access to nearby towns. Discarded equipment is ignored by residents. There are no near neighbors to object to the unkempt appearance.

the forces of housing supply and the elements of housing demand in that locale. As the market clears, patterns of housing use emerge and are altered.

The central questions in the investigation of the housing situation of Americans are which *households* obtain what kind of *housing* at what *locations* and under what *terms*? Type of household is considered with respect to race of householder, income, age of members, household composition, ethnic origins, and so forth. Each household type presents a different array of wants, needs, tastes, and ability to achieve its goals.

The kind of housing that is obtained by a household can be described by the type of structure and the facilities available within it. The stock is dispersed into four census regions and smaller subareas and diverse locational settings ranging from the heart of the central city to the rural farms (Figure 1.14). The terms of housing use include the type of tenancy (whether renter or owner), the levels of rents, the prices of owned housing, and the monthly costs of occupancy.

FIGURE 1.14 Unpretentious but solidly constructed housing built for wartime factory workers in Maple Grove Park, near Ravenna, Ohio, in the early 1940s survives as privately owned but very low-rent (1-bedroom unit, $105 in 1983; 2-bedroom, $115; 4-bedroom, $129) housing in the 1980s. Recently some buildings containing three or four housing units have converted to condominium ownership.

Sources of Change in Housing Use Patterns

Patterns of housing use change constantly because of the dynamics underlying housing demand and housing supply. On the demand side the structure and performance of the U.S. economy are always changing. As they change, some households prosper and others are left behind. The adjustments in expectations, income, and wealth that flow from economic adjustments have direct consequences in the form of stepped-up or reduced housing demands and changes in patterns of housing use.

Migration and natural population change affect housing demand and housing use patterns. In addition, since each age group has different housing needs, patterns of housing use are disrupted when the average age of the population rises or falls because of migration and natural change.

Households attempt to translate their social and economic achievements into correspondingly better housing: the greater the degree of advance and consequent geographical mobility, the more flux in demand patterns and eventually in patterns of housing use.

There is also the matter of housing fashions or styles (Figures 1.15 and 1.16). Since people generally prefer the new to the old, as

FIGURE 1.16 New mobile homes used as year-round residences next to Shell Lake, Wisconsin.

FIGURE 1.15 Late nineteenth-century double houses, in Quincy, Illinois. They were fine houses when built, but below average in quality and price a hundred years after construction.

new styles of housing are added to the stock, they are sought out and acquired. New housing use patterns result. When certain kinds of old-style houses return to favor, what had been scorned earlier can once again attract interest and premium prices (Figures 1.17 and 1.18). Expanded recognition of and tolerance for lifestyles that differ from traditional ones have added new sources of flux to housing demand and patterns of housing use.

Besides changes on the demand side there are continued adjustments to the housing stocks in each census region and at each type of location. New construction attracts households into newly developing areas and out of their old residences (Figures 1.19 and 1.20). Use patterns change in both places. Government intervention into the housing stock, aimed at specific locations and groups of households, produces significant changes in use patterns over the years.

It is hard to form a complete and accurate picture of housing use patterns in the United States, because there are so many diverse arrangements in thousands of separate local housing markets and submarkets. Each local situation is unique, to be sure, but using small-area data to view housing use patterns within each census region (see Chapter 6) helps to reveal what are fairly common patterns from

FIGURE 1.17 Century-old frame houses in excellent repair in Millheim, Pennsylvania.

FIGURE 1.19 Apartment houses built in the late 1960s in St. Louis, Missouri, on old industrial land cleared in an urban renewal effort.

FIGURE 1.18 Early twentieth-century townhouses in the South Bronx, New York City. After passing through several generations of use, these houses are being refurbished and rehabilitated.

FIGURE 1.20 Farmhouse, barn, and outbuildings on dairy farm in Barron County, Wisconsin.

FIGURE 1.21 Apartment buildings from the 1920s crowding close to Lake Michigan (just beyond the farthest building) on the south side of Chicago, Illinois.

place to place, as well as what is distinctive about separate locales (Figure 1.21).

Housing Policy and Government Involvement in Housing

Housing serves the private purposes of shelter, privacy, savings, social standing, and access to neighborhoods, school systems, community services, and facilities. But there is a public concern for

housing as well. Most Americans believe that each household is entitled to some minimum amount and quality of living space. The national goal as articulated by the federal government has been "a decent home and a suitable living environment for every American family."

The interdependence of activities inside confined spaces and areas provides other reasons for government involvement in housing. Public health considerations demand attention to safety and sanitation in housing. Inside urban areas and in many nonurban jurisdictions the use of land for housing is closely regulated because the way a person uses or misuses property can affect the safety, livability, and value of neighboring properties. Thus, whenever people have established permanent nucleated settlements, they have turned to the governing authority to protect the housing of those who live close together. Zoning laws, building codes, housing codes, traffic regulations, and neighborhood or areawide approaches to renewal and rehabilitation of older housing have been directed by government authority.[7]

Government uses housing as a means of redistributing wealth or capital through various tax and subsidy measures. It also acts through housing to affect local economies. Increases in housing production have major multiplier effects that percolate throughout other sectors and regions of the economy. When the economy becomes overheated, monetary policy is often used to curb inflation, but tight money and higher interest rates also put the brakes on housing production. Thus, housing policies in the United States have the goal of ensuring the provision of adequate shelter for all households. Meanwhile monetary policy, as it addresses macroeconomic issues such as stabilizing the business cycle, affects housing construction and the provision of mortgage credit to different classes of households and throughout various regions of the country.

Besides the use of its regulatory powers government housing policies intervene in the housing market through supply-side subsidies to encourage expansion of new construction, supplies of certain types of housing units at specific locations, and demand-side subsidies that make it easier for selected groups to buy the housing they otherwise would not be able to afford.

---

[7] See Morton J. Schussheim, "Housing: An Overview," and Grace Milgram, "Housing the Urban Poor: Urban Housing Assistance Programs," in *Housing—A Reader*, prepared by the Congressional Research Service, Library of Congress, for the 98th Congress, 1st Session, Committee Print 98-5 (Washington, DC: U.S. Government Printing Office, 1983).

Housing Policy at the Local Government Level

While federal housing policy is made at the national level, it is implemented at local levels. Federal policy in the late 1970s tried to induce the dispersal of the poor and minority households throughout metropolitan communities. But residents of many suburban communities do not want poor neighbors, so they erect restrictions to frustrate federal objectives.[8] The tactics used take many forms: high and costly standards for residential development that screen out low- and moderate-income households; large minimum lot sizes and high minimum floor areas per housing unit; expensive street and utility requirements, or dedication by the developer or builder of land for public purposes; and low-growth or no-growth policies ostensibly to protect existing environments. Some communities decide to go it alone—foregoing participation in federal aid programs of various kinds in order to avoid the need to comply with federal rules that participation would require. There is a never-ending tug-of-war between national objectives centered on efficiency, equity, and equal opportunity as seen from Washington and the desire of local officials for local control and flexibility.

[8]See Milgram, "Housing the Urban Poor."

HOUSING AND SOCIETY: GOALS, POLICIES, AND MEASUREMENT

HOUSING and society are best understood when examined together. Society creates housing and then uses it in ways that subdivide and segregate some elements of society while uniting others. Public policy intervenes to remedy abuses and deficiencies, but society responds with initiatives that include new construction, migration, and abandonment of unwanted units. Society acts to create housing landscapes and then reacts to their creation.[1]

The decennial census of housing measures in detail the nation's housing stock and patterns of housing use. For the years between censuses the nation's social scientists, planners, and policy analysts rely mainly on the Census Bureau's periodic sample surveys to learn what is happening to our housing stock and how it is being used nationally and regionally. They use assessment listings, records of real estate transactions, and related data sources for local measurement.

[1]See Larry S. Bourne, *The Geography of Housing* (New York: Halsted Press, 1981), and James E. Vance, Jr., "The American City: Workshop for a National Culture," in John S. Adams, ed., *Contemporary Metropolitan America*, vol. 1 (Cambridge, MA: Ballinger, 1976), pp. 1–49. An earlier version of the first part of this chapter appeared as "The Meaning of Housing in America," Association of American Geographers, *Annals* 74, no. 4 (1984): 515–26.

The Meaning of Housing in the United States

One of the central inquiries in human geography is into how the earth provides a home for humankind. The inhabited places on the surface of the earth take on various meanings as people encounter them, learn about them, and eventually come to know them, use them, and transform them. As places are settled, houses are built, homes are established, and the housing process is set in motion. Housing forms a central activity in the human use of the earth.

In discussions of the housing process, preliminary inquiry often revolves around the words "house," "home," and "housing." These words, along with their counterparts in other languages, are laden with multiple meanings. As a noun, the word "house" means a building in which people live, a structure used as a dwelling or a residence. As a verb, "to house" means to remove from exposure, to put in a safe place, or to provide with a house or dwelling.

In its traditional meaning, "home" means a residence, but with connotations of family ties and domestic comforts—the place where one's domestic affections are centered. One of the Gothic roots of the word "home" (haims) means a village, implying *social* bonds as well. Thus, one's home is a place where one properly belongs; it is a setting where one finds refuge, rest, and satisfaction.

In everyday usage, housing is the stock of houses, apartments, and other shelters that provide the usual residences of persons, families, and households. Housing is also the process that converts houses into homes.

Housing: Fact and Hidden Meanings

How does the housing process work, and what does housing mean in the United States? To begin with, there are 88.4 million dwelling units, almost all of them being used by households—that is housing. Housing represents the largest single use of urban land and touches virtually every person in profound ways. To be homeless in America is to be at the edge of personhood, with a status below even that of prison inmate.[2]

The equity in owned housing represents the dominant financial asset of the typical household in America, where 64 percent own the houses they live in. Buying a house is usually the most important financial commitment that a family makes, and for many households—maybe most—housing decisions are highly emotional and intensely personal.

Like sex, death, and religion, housing has multiple hidden meanings. In the case of housing, the meanings concern status, position, power, and personal identity and are continually reflected in things that are said, argued about, fought over.

Consider residential real estate taxes, for example. Americans object to all forms of taxation to some degree—but have a special antagonism toward taxes levied on homes. We object to increases in property taxes as though they were taxes on our life itself. Sometimes the words we use suggest the deeper meanings. People speak of renting an apartment or a house, but when they own it, they call it their home.

Houses are relatively easy to study, as useful buildings, as cultural artifacts, or as events on the land whose structural features and topographical arrangements can be measured and recorded, inside and out. The emphasis here is on people buying, building, and using houses as they make their homes in the United States, especially households living beyond levels of basic need. This housing process forms part of the core subject matter of geography, sociology, and eco-nomics. Yet the social sciences in general tell us little about how and why households acquire and use housing units in the ways that they do.[3]

What People Get When They Buy or Rent

The housing economist approaches the question of housing by asking what is wanted, what is offered, what is paid, and what is received as the market clears. A central question for the land economist and the appraiser is why housing prices vary from place to place. The direct answer is that when people buy or rent a housing unit they pay for a bundle of services provided by the housing unit and by the lot on which it stands.

The housing unit itself includes a basic structure plus improvements that have been added to the structure. The structure provides floor area, room volume, and a basic design style. Improvements include fireplaces, air conditioning, garages, built-in appliances, and extra bathrooms. Each increment to the structure and each improvement increases the price.

The price of the lot can be viewed separately from the structure and has three main components: a location, which determines its accessibility to other places; the physical environment of the lot and surroundings; and the social setting in the vicinity of the lot—what the neighbors are like. Good locations close to desirable places raise prices, while remote locations lower them. Lake views and ocean frontage drive prices up, while noise, soot, smells, bad drainage, and objectionable views reduce them. Socially desirable, high-status neighbors elevate prices, while low-status neighbors depress them.[4]

In this *à la carte* view of housing value, you get what you pay for. This hedonic price approach, as it is called (from the Greek *hedonikos*, meaning pleasure), accounts for house price variations from place to place, but it ignores the fact that housing means much more than simple shelter. Why do people want housing in the first place? Or, put another way, why do people value goods in general, and housing in particular?

[2]Mary Ellen Hombs and Mitch Snyder, *Homelessness in America: A Forced March to Nowhere* (Washington, DC: Committee for Creative Non-Violence, 1982).

[3]Peter Gould and Gunnar Olsson, *A Search for Common Ground* (London: Pion, 1982).

[4]Brian J. L. Berry, "Ghetto Expansion and Single Family Housing Prices: Chicago, 1968–1972," *Journal of Urban Economics* 3 (1976): 297–423; A. C. Goodman, "Hedonic Prices, Price Indices and Housing Markets," *Journal of Urban Economics* 5 (1978): 471–84; and Risa Palm, "Spatial Segmentation of the Urban Housing Market," *Economic Geography* 54 (1978): 210–21.

Why People Want Housing and Other Goods

People want housing for individual reasons and social reasons.[5] Housing satisfies the simple physical need for shelter, and shelter is a crucial element in material welfare and personal security. Housing satisfies important emotional wants as well.

Housing also provides a social stage in which competitive display forms a part. Housing choice and use are ways for renters and owners to communicate to society about where they feel they deserve to fit within the social fabric. The awareness of the status that accompanies their tenure reinforces those feelings.

Housing is used to make social and cultural categories visible and stable; zoning laws help to formalize the categories. Housing choices, like any deliberate or habitual consumptive acts, are social acts. Thus, housing landscapes in neighborhoods, in cities, in suburbs, and beyond the metropolitan fringe become social documents for us to read and study.

A household's choice of housing forms part of its effort to impose identity and sense on the environment.[6] We can best understand housing consumption by setting it into the larger social process because consumption is part of the same social system that accounts for our role in production and our motivation to work. Consumption and production behavior both provide ways to relate to other people, and both involve the use of materials to mediate the relationships.[7] In order to think and to behave rationally, people need an intelligible universe, and that intelligibility needs some visible expression. Abstract ideas are easier to understand when they take on physical appearance.[8] Housing landscapes in the United States, in their assemblage, provide households with a set of meanings, more or less coherent, more or less intentional—that can be read and understood by all who know the code.[9] In the acquisition and the use of housing, people participate in a live information system.[10] The housing units themselves are neutral, but their uses become social. Americans use housing to hold onto their wealth, to state who they are, to build social bridges and fences, to join groups, and to exclude others from their groups.

Americans generally subscribe to a theory of distributive justice that accepts the notion that inequalities of wealth are acceptable when they result from unequal loads of responsibility to the group.[11] It is acceptable to receive more than your share provided that you contribute more than your share. A corollary of this view seems to be that the more one gets, the more one feels it is deserved. Similarly, the less one gets, the more one may tend to blame oneself. Thus, the wildly inflationary and deflationary swings in the real values of housing wealth—as occurred during the 1970s and 1980s in the United States—produced serious individual and social consequences by the way the economic swings affected national moods while they alternately promoted and discouraged consumption and production behavior at the household level and the national level.

The theory of permanent income tells us why. Within this theory, income is the amount that a household "believes it could consume while maintaining its wealth intact."[12] But housing has become the major wealth holding of a sizable percentage of middle-class Americans. Large inflationary gains in house value in the 1970s were interpreted as wealth gains, so that when they occurred consumption could be stepped up even with unchanged income. But consumption of what? Normally, a household's discretionary consumption agenda is heavily influenced by the displays of the rich, with their retinue of artists and designers. The rich generate a vivid social environment by their consumption behavior, and that behavior is imitated as followers try to duplicate the favored environment.[13] It has been that way for a long time. For example, taking their lead from the ostentatious displays of recently deposed kings and nobles, the wealthy classes built suburbs outside Paris before the 1840s that were much noticed

---

[5]Yi-Fu Tuan, *Segmented Worlds and Self: Group Life and Individual Consciousness* (Minneapolis: University of Minnesota Press, 1982).

[6]Mary T. Douglas and Baron Isherwood, *The World of Goods* (New York: Basic Books, 1972), p. x; see also Clare Cooper, *The House as Symbol of Self*, Working Paper no. 120 (Berkeley: Institute of Urban and Regional Development, University of California, 1971).

[7]Conceptual frameworks for examining the built environment as a cultural object that encapsulates "meaning" are provided by Geoffrey Broadbent, *Signs, Symbols, and Architecture* (New York: Wiley, 1980); Henry H. Glassie, *Folk Housing in Middle Virginia: A Structural Analysis of Historical Artifacts* (Knoxville: University of Tennessee Press, 1975); and Amos Rapoport, *The Meaning of the Built Environment: A Non-Verbal Communication Approach* (Beverly Hills, CA: Sage, 1982). All appear to be based on structural principles developed by Claude Lévi-Strauss in *Structural Anthropology* (New York: Basic Books, 1963), which were refined by Mary T. Douglas in *Implicit Meanings: Essays in Anthropology* (London: Routledge & Kegan Paul, 1975).

[8]Douglas and Isherwood, *The World of Goods*, pp. 4–5.

[9]Ibid., p. 5.

[10]Ibid., p. 10.

[11]Robert Nozick, *Anarchy, State, and Utopia* (New York: Basic Books, 1974).

[12]Milton Friedman, *A Theory of the Consumption Function* (Princeton, NJ: Princeton University Press, 1957), p. 10. See also Benjamin J. Stevens, "Employment, Permanent Income and the Demand for Housing," *Journal of Urban Economics* 6, no. 4 (1979): 480–500.

[13]Douglas and Isherwood, *The World of Goods*, p. 53.

in England. Inevitably, housing and landscape tastes of the English gentry were widely imitated in the United States, whence they trickled down to the Restons and the Levittowns.

The prosperous *nouveau riche* have regularly sought to emulate the quasi-rural existence of the aristocracy, leading to the question: What lies behind this aping of style in general and of housing style in particular by the upwardly mobile of yesteryear and by today's young urban and upwardly mobile professionals? Instead of supposing that housing is primarily for shelter and mere competitive display, why not assume that housing is used as a principal means for making visible and stable some of today's categories of American culture?[14] If all material possessions carry social meanings and are used as communicators, this assumption makes perfect sense.

No persons or families exist except as steeped in the culture of their time and place.[15] Housing analysis forms part of our inquiry in social science and especially in human geography. Households interacting impose their constructions on the social reality that they create in their world of housing.[16]

Housing is a special kind of commodity, and commodities that are purchased by the consumer "are for the most part means to the attainment of objectives, not objectives in themselves."[17] According to anthropologists Douglas and Isherwood, "goods are the hardware and the software of an information system whose principal concern is to monitor its own performance."[18] It is false to conclude that the choice of food or drink or clothing or housing carries less meaning than ballet or poetry. But no good carries a meaning all by itself. The question of why a *particular* good is valued cannot be answered. The meaning of housing is in its relation to all goods used in both a social and a regional setting, just as the meaning of music is in the arrangement of sounds, and not in any one note.[19]

Disagreements about housing choice and housing use reveal metaphysical differences that can be seen only indirectly. We should understand housing as major social signposts or markers, as visible tips of the iceberg that is the whole social process. Housing is used for classifying social categories. It is endowed with value by the unspoken agreement of its consumers. Households come together to grade events and to uphold their judgments about housing or to reverse them. Each person becomes a source of judgments and a subject of judgments by others. Each household is in the social classification scheme whose discrimination it is helping to establish.

People must be present at other people's rituals of consumption to be able to circulate their own judgments.[20] When the new homeowners ask their guests, "Would you like to see the rest of the house?" it is safely assumed that the guests really want to see it, and the hosts really want to show it. In the process both sides reveal envy and competitiveness, which are said to be basic to unredeemed human nature. But both sides also restate their positions with respect to one another and their locations on the social landscape.[21]

From what source comes a person's power to attract and hold the collaboration of others in this exchange of information and of judgments? It is hard for economics to provide an answer to this question because economics is a method of analysis that prefers theory that is morally neutral and empty of social judgment. Yet no serious consumption theory can remain morally neutral and avoid the responsibility of social criticism. Ultimately, a theory of choice and consumption of housing is a theory about power. When we see how power is related to the choices of housing and other goods, we can see why a sound theory of consumption can illuminate social policy. We see why income is a means of access to a social system, why low income restricts such access, and why homelessness has the effect of stripping persons or families of their place in the social system.[22]

There will always be luxuries because every society has its ranks, and rank must be marked.[23] Luxury housing in the United States, like luxuries in tribal societies, tends to be used as a weapon of exclusion. "One way to maintain a social boundary is to demand an enormous fee for admission."[24] As a weapon of social exclusion, housing normally works extremely well.

To be rich is to be well integrated in a rich community. A poor person who wins a lottery is a different case altogether. It is a socioeconomic anomaly for which we have no immediate response. Deep

---

[14]Douglas and Isherwood, *The World of Goods*, p. 59.
[15]Ibid., p. 63.
[16]P. Berger and T. Luckmann, *The Social Construction of Reality: A Treatise on the Sociology of Knowledge* (Garden City, NY: Doubleday, 1966).
[17]John R. Hicks, *A Revision of Demand Theory* (Oxford: Oxford University Press, 1965).
[18]Douglas and Isherwood, op. cit., p. 72.
[19]Ibid., pp. 72–73.

[20]Ibid., p. 81.
[21]Cooper, *The House as Symbol of Self*.
[22]Douglas and Isherwood, *The World of Goods*, pp. 89–90.
[23]Ibid., p. 118.
[24]Ibid., p. 140.

down we feel we know that the money does not necessarily mean rich. Being rich means that credit will be forthcoming if wanted, as it is for those who are able to buy housing with mortgage money; that minor short-term losses can readily be absorbed; that there is a web of continuing mutual involvement and support. To be poor in the United States is to be isolated and excluded.[25]

What Happens
When People Build, Buy, and Use Housing

On the supply side the housing process begins when developers and builders determine that it is worth their while to construct additional dwellings. New units, which (except for mobile homes) are usually rather expensive, come to be built and occupied. The vacancies that are created by new construction are filled mainly by households moving up socioeconomically and from outside the community. As households occupy new units, they leave behind their former housing for others to use. The chains of vacancies created by a series of such moves percolate through the housing inventory in one direction—from the high value ranks downward—while the households move in the other direction. The process relocates people and population densities on the ground and reordered patterns of settlement emerge on our maps.[26]

Through the process of new construction and residential mobility, housing demand is withdrawn from some areas—often in the inner city—and transferred toward other, more desirable houses and neighborhood settings.[27] The steady relocation of effective demand for housing—away from the less desirable stock and toward the more desirable—produces several outcomes. It stimulates above-average price rises in the growing, high-demand areas; but the relocation of households depresses real prices in low-demand areas, which are usually areas of heavy net out-migration.[28]

As a result of the disparity between the high real appreciation rates in the value of houses in fast-growth districts of urban areas and the low or negative rates in other neighborhoods, equity values are extracted from declining areas and injected into boom areas.[29] The households caught up in this urban housing process are consciously or unconsciously competing for relative positions in a dynamic social landscape in which there are big financial gainers as well as losers. Like the day bugs and the night bugs that live off the same fixed feed source but remain unaware of the actions and consequences of the other, the winners and losers are in serious competition. But because each group is unaware of the existence of the other, and they do not know of the incompatibility of their goals of mutual prosperity, open conflict seldom occurs. Yet one group of households makes significant equity gains, and those gains are largely at the expense of others who slip behind.

By means of their moving and staying behavior, households are able to define certain aspects of their relative positions with respect to other households. But because of the dynamic and competitive quality of much of the urban housing market, households are forced to move occasionally in order to maintain their relative social and financial position with respect to other households in their housing submarket. If they do not move, they will lose their rank.[30]

Yet, by moving from one housing unit to another, a household often reorders the social context of housing use for their new neighbors and creates a threatening instability in the old neighborhood left behind. Since households try to move quickly to improve their housing to match improved circumstances (but seldom backslide quickly when fortunes reverse), it tends to be the better-off and upwardly mobile neighbors who leave the neighborhood first, while the newcomers to the neighborhood tend to be on the lower end of the neighborhood scale. The newcomers normally buy all the housing they can afford—and perhaps more—and then maintain a tenuous hold for several years while their circumstances improve. Meanwhile, the neighborhood's old-timers tend to be comfortably secure.

The demand for existing housing at each location, compared with the local supply there, gives housing its market value and determines

[25]See Lee Rainwater, *What Money Buys: Inequality and the Social Meanings of Income* (New York: Basic Books, 1974); and Richard P. Coleman and Lee Rainwater, *Social Standing in America: New Dimensions of Class* (New York: Basic Books, 1978).

[26]John S. Adams and James D. Fitzsimmons, "Planning for the Geography of Metropolitan America," in Charles M. Christian and Robert A. Harper, eds., *Modern Metropolitan Systems* (Columbus: Merrill, 1981), pp. 457–80.

[27]Bourne, *The Geography of Housing.*

[28]James D. Fitzsimmons, John S. Adams, and David J. Borchert, "Recent U.S. Population Redistribution: A Geographical Framework for Change in the 1980s," *Social Sciences Quarterly* 61(1980): 485–507.

[29]George Sternlieb, James W. Hughes, et al., *America's Housing: Prospects and Problems* (New Brunswick, NJ: Center for Urban Policy Research, Rutgers University, 1980).

[30]James T. Little, "Residential Preferences, Neighborhood Filtering, and Neighborhood Change," *Journal of Urban Economics* 3 (1976): 68–81.

its contribution as a consumption expenditure in the gross national product (GNP).[31] For rental units, the contribution to GNP is the rental paid. For owner-occupied units, it is the imputed rentals that the owner-occupants pay to themselves. Construction expenditures for new houses are treated separately in GNP accounts and account for about 4 percent of GNP.

Housing demand at desirable locations—along with the resulting market values of housing at those locations—and eventual consumption patterns there are all related in part to social exclusion. The market value of the housing, then, depends in part on who is allowed to live there and who is kept out. In an immigrant society like the United States, a society that lacks a visible and established class or caste structure, other markers are introduced to establish and maintain social order and to communicate its meanings. In many ways housing has become one of the central means for serving this function *in* American society and *on* the American landscape.

The Sources and the Significance of Flux in the Housing Landscape

Housing landscapes are never stable. They are disrupted by new construction, by chains of vacancies that wend their way through the housing stock, by the consolidation of smaller units into larger ones, by the subdivision of large units into small ones, and eventually by the removal of units by demolition. Behind these disruptions are four main sources of flux: variations in fertility and the different sizes of age cohorts that result, wealth shifts among neighborhoods, foreign immigration, and redistribution of wealth among United States regions.

First, each population age group differs in its housing needs and its ability to pay. The effects on the housing market of these differences are magnified by the sizes of those groups and by the amounts of wealth and income that they control. For example, the present generation of older Americans is the wealthiest such generation in the nation's history. Their wealth accumulated by means of postwar real estate appreciation, high wages, better pensions, savings, as well as Social Security and social insurance benefits. The things they own provide solid affirmation of lives lived according to the rules. For many of them—perhaps most—the American dream came true.[32] Meanwhile, the crowded postwar baby boom generation of the late 1940s and 1950s has had a sharply contrasting experience—large numbers in competition with one another, pessimistic in outlook, slow to finish school, reluctant to enter the economy, and uncertain about the prospects for marriage and family life.[33] Thus, opportunities—including housing opportunities—differ markedly among age cohorts.

Second, inside every urban region wealth constantly shifts from a set of stagnant and declining neighborhoods toward fast-growing locales of superior status and desirability, predominantly but not exclusively in the suburban ring. The desire of households to leave one setting and to dwell in another, in combination with their ability to pay, helps to create patterns of market demand that are different in each neighborhood. Housing prices adjust in each locale in response to the differentials. Paradoxically, the result has been ever cheaper housing for the rich—as capital gains offset interest and taxes and the wealth accumulates—and more expensive housing for lower-income groups, who never catch up. Their lowly place on the housing map marks their lowly rung on the socioeconomic ladder.

Third, more immigrants probably entered the United States in the 1970s than in any other decade in U.S. history—perhaps 10 million persons. They settled largely in the Sunbelt boom areas of the West and South, injecting new vigor into those places, producing more than they consumed, saving more than they spent, and adding to the vitality that attracted domestic migrants who expanded further the cycle of boom in the growth areas—while intensifying the contractions and recessions elsewhere in the North and Northeast. As boom areas accumulate wealth, the share of national wealth within them expands disproportionately.

Fourth, there have been major absolute and relative shifts in wealth from stagnant areas to growth regions. As further migration

[31]Simon Kuznets was one of the most influential figures in the design of national income and product estimates, within which the rental value of owned and rented housing is reckoned, and in setting high standards for the preparation and publication of federal statistics. See "Simon Kuznets and the Early Development of National Income and Product Estimates," *Survey of Current Business*, July 1985, pp. 27-28. Paul Starr—citing Aaron Wildavsky, *The Politics of the Budgetary Process* (Boston: Little, Brown, 1964)—noted that it was a coalition of special interests that fought successfully for the introduction of the housing census. See "The Sociology of Official Statistics," in William Alonso and Paul Starr, *The Politics of Numbers*, The Population of the United States in the 1980s: A Census Monograph Series (New York: Russell Sage Foundation, 1987).

[32]John Oliver Wilson, *After Affluence: Economics to Meet Human Needs* (San Francisco: Harper & Row, 1980).

[33]Richard A. Easterlin, *Birth and Fortune: The Impact of Numbers on Personal Welfare* (New York: Basic Books, 1980).

and investment have moved in to catch a share of the boom, they have added a further stimulus to push the boom still higher.

What Zoning Laws Accomplish

We have looked at goods and housing as social markers, and we saw how population and wealth are rearranged on the land. In this fluid situation, we try to establish some order by drawing land use classification boundaries on our maps. We call it zoning.[34] Modern zoning practice began in Germany near the end of the nineteenth century, and then moved to the United States in 1909 when Los Angeles adopted a zoning ordinance splitting the city into residential and industrial districts. New York adopted a zoning law in 1916 that was widely copied elsewhere.

The early zoning laws restricted property uses supposedly to control nuisances, but other goals were intended as well—mainly the protection of family-oriented residential neighborhoods from uses that threatened the quality and attractiveness of neighborhood surroundings. This goal has usually been understood to mean excluding any change in the social or physical environment that would threaten property values. But the phrase "property values" is a code word with several meanings.[35]

Traditionally, the higher-class residential area of single-family detached dwellings has been most preferred and most protected.[36] Understandably, households of lesser means often wish to share these attractive areas, if possible without paying full market price. Paradoxically, if they succeed, what they want and what they thought they were getting begins to disappear. Zoning thus helps the elite and middle classes to affirm their claims to membership in particular strata of society while simultaneously repudiating their membership in a lower class. Their desire to stake such claims is probably an expression of a primordial competitive drive for power over others in a society where bonds of family and village may not exist and where a hereditary status or class system has been constitutionally prohib-

ited.[37] Yet most people crave security, and family-oriented households press hard to secure the means to protect, to nurture, and to perpetuate their lifestyles in family-oriented settings.

What one group has already achieved, other groups also desire. The efforts of weaker social and economic classes to secure access to the higher-status neighborhoods and their steadily appreciating property values have been supported recently by government attitudes and aggressive actions.[38] A growing judicial and legislative view in some parts of the United States—that these environments and the wealth they contain must be shared—carries an implicit judgment that such environments of exclusivity should not exist at all. This view also holds that zoning laws and subdivision regulations should not be used to establish or to perpetuate the differentiation of residential neighborhoods along socioeconomic class lines.[39]

Insiders in Competition Against Outsiders

The debate about who should be permitted access into geographically defined, high-status communities is repeated at the international and national level, at the state level, and at the local level. At each level an in-group sets about using its power to keep others out. At the national level the debate centers on immigration policy—who should be allowed to enter and on what terms.[40] At the state level, for example, is Alaska's effort to discourage inmigrants from other states by passing laws distributing oil royalties to residents according to length of tenure in the state.

The most common examples of geographical insiders pitted against outsiders occur at the local level and arise because areas with expensive houses have relatively few cheap houses or low-income households, while areas with mostly inexpensive houses have few upper-income households. In addition, since most black Americans receive below-average incomes, the segregation of housing by value—and the freezing of housing patterns by zoning—contribute to residential segregation by race. Of course, overt discrimination in the selling or renting of housing on the basis of race, religion, or national origin

[34]Robert H. Nelson, *Zoning and Property Rights: An Analysis of the American System of Land-Use Regulation* (Cambridge, MA: MIT Press, 1980).

[35]See Constance Perin, *Everything in Its Place: Social Order and Land Use in America* (Princeton, NJ: Princeton University Press, 1977); and Nelson, *Zoning and Property Rights*.

[36]Gwendolyn Wright, *Building the Dream: A Social History of Housing in America* (Cambridge, MA: MIT Press, 1983).

[37]Bertrand Russell, *Power: A New Social Analysis* (New York: Norton, 1938).

[38]Lawrence Gene Sager, "Insular Majorities Unabated: Warth v. Seldin and City of Eastlake v. Forest City Enterprises, Inc.," *Harvard Law Review* 91 (1978): 1373–425.

[39]"Developments in the Law: Zoning," *Harvard Law Review* 91 (1978): 1427–708.

[40]C. Mills, ed., "Illegal Immigration and U.S. Obligation." *Philosophy and Public Policy* 1 (1981): 1–5.

is illegal in the United States, but segregation continues, due in part to the continued segregation of housing by value.[41]

These issues arise from fundamental conflicts in American society in which laws and administrative rule-making move in one direction while a substantial percentage of the population continues to act in a contrary manner. Thus, it is inevitable that questions related to zoning and its exclusionary effects eventually reach the U.S. Supreme Court. Two court decisions of the 1970s illustrate the complexity of deciding who may join a geographically defined community, and these cases highlight much of the meaning of housing in America today. The case of *Warth* v. *Seldin* raised a challenge to the zoning ordinances of the town of Penfield, a suburb of Rochester, New York, on the grounds that existing laws and their administration had both the purpose and the effect of excluding lower-income persons and members of racial minorities from residence within the town. The plaintiffs, who argued that the town was using exclusionary land use zoning practices, included five groups: (1) a nonprofit citizens action group working for low- and moderate-income housing in the town, (2) five property owners in the city of Rochester who claimed that their taxes were higher than they would be if Penfield did not exclude low-income and minority households, (3) minority residents of Rochester, (4) an association of house building companies, and (5) a housing council made up of persons and firms working for low- and moderate-priced housing in Penfield.

In a 5-to-4 decision, the Court denied standing to the plaintiffs, stating that they had failed to show that relaxing the zoning laws would in fact be followed by (1) construction of low- and moderate-income housing and (2) its occupation by low-income plaintiffs. By its decision the Court ruled, in effect, that Penfield could decide who could enter and live there and left the zoning law in the hands of that community.

The question of who exactly should decide zoning issues was raised in the case of *City of East Lake* v. *Forest City Enterprises, Inc.* In that case, the U.S. Supreme Court upheld a city charter amendment that required a 55 percent referendum vote of the city's voters to bring about any zoning change that had been approved by the city council. This decision raises the threat of a popular veto of any city's effort to accommodate unpopular but necessary uses of city land, such as low-income housing. Chief Justice Burger commented that a referendum is not a delegation of power, but a reservation of power in the hands of the electorate. As a result of this decision, intrusion on the liberty and property interests of landowners is seen as arbitrary and unjust, however responsive it might be to continuing social problems. Critics of the Court's rulings see these two decisions as a direct message that the federal judiciary, except in the most egregious cases, is unlikely to respond to those who seek redress from injustice and inequality created by the zoning process. To Court supporters, the two cases reflect the equating of the local zoning process with the joint exercise of the prerogatives of unfettered private ownership. The municipality therefore is like a club, which enjoys the mandatory and exclusive membership of its residents and landowners. Its majority decisions—however insular, irrational, or unjust they may appear to outsiders—will prevail.[42]

Owning Versus Renting: The Meaning of Tenure

The form of tenure is taken as a primary social sign. Tenure is used to classify and evaluate people in a shorthand way, much as people come to use race, income, and occupation as predictors of other traits. The categories—owner and renter — are symbolic as well as real.

The two forms of tenure are widely viewed as inherently distinctive because they distinguish people in their personal attributes, in their social esteem, in the spatial arrangements of new housing developments, in zoning district classifications, in building codes governing occupancy, and even in their differing rights under the law.[43] Our interpretation of tenure categories flows from our understanding of the family life cycle, which is composed of a sequence of phases that in the ideal case would be lived out in a certain order. Each stage has an appropriate marital status, income level, presence and ages of children, school years completed, leisure tastes, tenure form, and housing type.[44]

Social order is reflected in the proper sequence of life cycle phases and appropriate housing to match. The prevailing view is that there is a single, normal chronology of life events. Each stage should be perfectly attained, and movement to the next stage should

[41]Mary A. Brauer and John S. Adams, "Useful Goal Achievement Measures: Zelder's Segregation Indices," *Journal of the American Institute of Planners* 40 (1974): 430–39.

[42]See John S. Adams, "Post–World War II Urban Development in the United States," vol. 5, *Americana-Austriaca* (Vienna: Wilhelm Braumuller, 1980), pp. 151–68.
[43]Perin, *Everything in Its Place*, p. 32.
[44]Ibid., p. 32.

be smooth. One should not be stuck at a stage, skip a stage, or get trapped between stages.

Apartments can be understood as serving specific stages of the life cycle. Homeowners accept the idea of people living in apartments, but want them located someplace other than next door. What lies behind this objection?

Just as a tree taking root acts in ways that modify the soil texture and chemistry to maximize its chances to survive and reproduce, it is likely that the instincts of the human group and the families within it are to survive, to thrive, and to reproduce. Exceptional effort is expended to ensure our children's survival, health, education, training for life—amid plenty of evidence of failure. Thus, any intrusion that appears to threaten those goals will be fought—tenaciously and often without a clearly articulated logic.

Family-oriented neighborhoods are protected and quickly defended from threats, perhaps as an expression of a basic conservative instinct to protect and nurture the life therein. In the American system of urban land use classification, this instinct is expressed in a hierarchy of land use types—and traditionally at the apex of the hierarchy is the single-family detached house. Other kinds of land may cost more—but none other is as highly valued socially, or as staunchly protected legally.[45]

Zoning caught on in America as an effective technique for protecting the neighborhood of detached single-family houses. Despite subsequent embellishments, that objective remains paramount. And notice that we say "single-family," not "single-household."[46]

The hierarchy of residential land uses mirrors the ladder of life. One moves from renting an apartment or townhouse, to renting a duplex or attached row house, to owning one of them, to the ultimate rung—owning a single-family detached house. In climbing the ladder, rung by rung, the movement is sensed as forward and upward.[47]

The anonymity of contemporary society promotes intense support for zoning. With our relatives scattered, with friendships shallow and specialized, with impermanent professional and social associations—the continuity of local community support is hard to find. In its absence, single-family detached property areas promise the implicit support offered by a shared rung on the ladder of life. In this context the rung seriously devoted to childbearing and childrearing takes on an added and vital significance.

In the famous case of *Village of Euclid* v. *Ambler Realty Co.* (1926)—which upheld zoning laws—and in subsequent cases such as *Village of Belle Terre* v. *Boraas* (1974), the U.S. Supreme Court set single-family detached housing areas constitutionally apart as a legitimate classification under the First Amendment—distinguishing such areas from those from which more than two unrelated persons living together could be properly excluded—and defending the distinction.[48] The U.S. Census of Population and Housing measures single-family detached housing areas, and the Court defends the segregation of them.

In defending the distinction between *families* and groups of *unrelated* persons, the courts classify intrusions as "disorderly conduct"—in effect, nuisances. What is out of place spatially is out of place chronologically and socially and is therefore seen as a threat.[49]

Middle-Class Opposition to Low-Income Housing

Insecurity on the part of many in America's middle class about their hard-won social and economic status probably accounts for a large part of their opposition to low-income housing in their midst. Their concern, though, is probably different from the concerns that underlie their opposition to nonfamily housing. Housing is about wealth and status and power, and maybe in an uncertain world, where community support is hard to achieve even with the protection of a zoning law, these are felt to be needed to foster family life—a profane base for a sacred goal.

The phrase most commonly used by homeowners in land use objections about low-income renters is that "they will lower our property value." The main concern is spatial proximity of renters. The accumulation of wealth is future-oriented conscientious behavior—as are childbearing and childrearing. The threat to the house asset is interpreted as a threat to family life extended into the unseen future.[50]

In certain nations and in many working-class American neighborhoods where folk traditions and family-oriented values persist rel-

[45]Daniel R. Mandelker, *The Zoning Dilemma* (Indianapolis: Bobbs-Merrill, 1971), pp. 32, 84.
[46]Richard F. Babcock, *The Zoning Game: Municipal Practices and Policies* (Madison: University of Wisconsin Press, 1966), p. 115; and Perin, *Everything in Its Place*, p. 46.
[47]Perin, op. cit., p. 47.

[48]Charles M. Haar, *Land Use Planning: A Casebook on the Use, Misuse and Re-Use of Urban Land* (Boston: Little, Brown, 1959), p. 163; and Perin, *Everything in Its Place*, p. 48.
[49]Perin, op. cit., p. 50.
[50]Ibid, p. 50.

atively unthreatened, housing and related land use disputes are un-common. If family values are socially and legally reinforced, there can be a corresponding reduction of anxiety about mixed land uses and less concern about transitional stages in the life cycle and the transi-tional areas needed to accommodate them.

This argument explains why Anthony Downs's influential pro-posal to "open up the suburbs" to low-income owners and renters runs directly counter to what families in "closed" suburbs desire.[51] The concern of social science is not just to argue Downs's case and others like it, but to understand the argument and the nerve that it touches.

Adroit politicians try to sidestep the "equal opportunity housing" issue, and sometimes they succeed. For example, the President's An-nual Housing Report focuses on expanding the supply of low- and moderate-income housing, but its concern appears to be merely the provision of shelter. This series of reports routinely skips over the social and political issue of where the new units should be located.

The history of this issue runs long and deep. The Founding Fa-thers worried about it. The U.S. Constitution makes explicit refer-ence to protecting people in their homes. The Bill of Rights prohibits quartering soldiers without owner consent and protects the right of people to be secure in their houses.

Recent assaults on zoning laws and on development control or-dinances are valiant efforts to extend to poorer groups the same rights to life and liberty enjoyed by the privileged and secure. The trick is to extend protection to additional groups without seriously threaten-ing the already protected classes. But this may be a logically and po-litically impossible goal—to eliminate a power differential, yet leave all feeling equally secure.

It is an old problem, and it is unlikely to be resolved. The Amer-ican tradition is to imagine utopias and push to create them, all the while anxious that we might backslide into anarchy. Meanwhile, we are now witnessing the creation of the geography of a de-urbanizing postindustrial America. The emerging housing landscape tells us much about ourselves and our progress toward national and house-hold goals if we penetrate its hidden meanings.[52]

American Housing Policy in the 1980s: Looking Back and Looking Ahead

A quiet revolution in the way Americans build, buy, and use housing has been under way since the late 1970s. The nation has been dismantling its existing specialized housing institutions—especially those involved in savings and lending for construction and pur-chase—that formed the foundation of housing improvement for 50 years. The very role of housing as a unique anchor of American soci-ety is questioned as housing comes to be viewed by some observers merely as one of a variety of economic goods and occasionally as a negative input into the country's economic future.[53]

The Construction Boom of the 1960s and 1970s

The decades of the 1960s and 1970s formed the most productive housing era in American history.[54] Despite the fluctuations of the boom-and-bust construction cycles that followed one another in rapid succession, overall housing production was unprecedented. There was also a record volume of housing demolitions, which brought down to modest levels the nation's stock of seriously blighted housing that was common across the United States after World War II.

From 1960 to 1970, the U.S. housing inventory increased by over 10 million units. In the 1970s, spurred first by a variety of govern-ment initiatives, the net gain in housing units soared by almost 20 million, or 29 percent. Thus, in only 20 years the nation added about 30 million housing units, or one for every two that existed in 1960. Most new units were single detached dwellings for owner occupancy, but the construction of rental units also flourished.

The financial foundation for this boom in production was the availability of low-cost, long-term, fixed-rate, amortizing mortgages. The long term (up to 35 years) and fixed rate were made possible by lenders' faith in the stability of the dollar and by the dominant posi-tion of the United States in the world economy. The low cost re-flected the low rates of return paid to small savers, who supplied

[51]Anthony Downs, *Opening Up the Suburbs: An Urban Strategy for America* (New Haven: Yale University Press, 1973).

[52]See Yi-fu Tuan, "Landscape as Text," in *The Paradigm Exchange* (Minneapolis: College of Liberal Arts, University of Minnesota, 1981), pp. 3–9; and David Ley, "Cul-tural/Humanistic Geography," *Progress in Human Geography* 5 (1981): 252.

[53]George Sternlieb, "The Evolution of Housing and Its Social Compact," *Urban Land* 41, no. 12 (December 1982): 17–20.

[54]Leo Grebler, "The Growth of Residential Capital Since World War II," *Journal of the American Real Estate and Urban Economic Association* 7, no. 4 (Winter 1979): pp. 539–80.

much of the money to the savings banks and savings and loan institutions—the "thrifts"—which were the dominant lenders for home mortgages.

Inflation, Speculation, Financial Deregulation, and the End of the Boom

Tradition kept this system operating through the 1960s and into the 1970s until rapid inflation began to undermine it.[55] Increasingly serious bouts of high inflation, beginning in the final years of the Vietnam war and aggravated by the OPEC oil price shocks starting in 1973, disrupted the small savers and the institutions that catered to them. As prices in general and house prices in particular began a steep rise, interest rates rose unevenly. Both were expressions of inflation throughout the economy. Commercial lending rates rose rapidly, following the prime rate. Mortgage interest rates rose more slowly, held down by federal rules on insured mortgages, by competition, and by their low cost of funds. Rates paid to small savers were kept low by federal regulation well into the 1970s.

Meanwhile, in the face of generally escalating prices and interest rates, housing began to assume the role of a speculative investment and hedge against inflation. It took several years for the gap to close between the net interest rate (after taxes) at which mortgage money could be borrowed and the rate at which (untaxed capital gain) residential real estate values were rising. In the interim huge amounts of U.S. savings flowed into housing, both as direct savings and as investments through the secondary mortgage market.

Both 1978 and 1979 were years of record single-family house construction. By 1979 housing equity constituted over a third of the total personal wealth of Americans. But the flight of the dollar into housing—and away from cash, commercial uses, industrial investment, and public infrastructure—could not be sustained. Changes in laws and financial regulations beginning in the late 1970s eventually raised the limits on the interest rates that could be paid to savings, thus adjusting the priority previously given to spending on material goods, especially housing.

The rise of money market funds produced stiff competition for the conventional savings and loan industry. These funds paid high

interest and attracted much of the money that the savings industry formerly had drawn to itself at low cost. Certificates of deposit offered by the savings industry and paying market rates of interest eventually stemmed the flow of savings out of the thrifts, but the result was a much higher cost of funds for them. The difference between what the thrifts were earning on their assets (long-term, low-interest mortgage loans) and what they were paying on their liabilities (short-term passbook savings and certificates of deposit as well as federal home loan bank loans and other borrowings) produced net losses and resulted in bankruptcy, merger, or acquisition for many thrifts.

The stable relationship between house prices and interest rates was shattered in the 1970s, as mortgage interest rates moved to a level double those of a decade earlier. The deregulation of interest rates paid by thrifts to small savers allowed housing to compete for funds while moderating the earlier boom-and-bust cycles in housing attributable to disintermediation when market interest rates would rise above regulated levels paid to savers. The two separate financial markets—small savings in thrifts, which supported lending for housing, and demand and time deposits in commercial banks, which supported short-term lending to businesses, government, and households—had become one market, and housing now competed squarely with other uses, including payment of interest on a burgeoning national debt.

Fewer New Households, Lower Incomes, and Expensive Housing

These economic and financial changes produced a sharp drop in housing production after 1978. From 1970 to 1979 the nation averaged over 1.7 million new units annually as the effects of inflation interacted with the effects of the Internal Revenue Code to spur housing construction. From 1980 through 1983 the average was below 1.3 million, with a post–World War II low set in 1982. Nevertheless, 1980–82 would have been worse for housing had interest rate deregulation not already begun.

As a result, housing increasingly plays a new role in American society. The beginning of the 1970s was a period during which the rate of new housing supply was in tune with the exuberant rate of net new household formations. During the 1970s fewer than one new household in four assumed the classic configuration of married-cou-

[55]Richard F. Muth, "Is the Housing Price Bubble About to Burst?" Regional Science Association, *Papers* 48 (1981): 7–24.

ple families. More than half were nonfamily households, with nearly four households in five of this group composed of persons living alone. Among families, the growth of female householders (no husband present) nearly equaled that of married couples.

According to the U.S. Bureau of the Census definitions, the term "family household" applies to households composed of two or more related persons. Nonfamily households consist of persons living alone or two or more unrelated persons living together. Family households are of three types: married couple families, female householders, and male householders. Because the recent mix of new household types and their economic circumstances differ from the 1950s and 1960s, the volume and type of demand for new housing differ as well.

Much of the recent change in the volume and type of households reflects the maturing of the baby boom birth cohort as persons born in the 1950s and 1960s form households of their own. This trend alone accounts for a large share of the single-person households. But even more, the apparent economic optimism of young middle-class households in the 1950s and 1960s and their house-buying power are far different from the sense of economic disadvantage combined with high expectations of the young adults of the 1980s.

This outcome was not anticipated 15 or 20 years ago. Instead, based on the headship rates (the proportion of any age group that heads a household) of the late 1960s and early 1970s, Census Bureau projections estimated an average net annual growth of 1.7 million households through the 1980s. That expectation went unrealized in the early 1980s. Household formation rates steadily declined, from 1.6 million in the year ending March 1981 to 1.2 million in March 1982, and under 400,000 the following year. But as the economy recovered by mid-decade, rates had risen to 1.5 in 1984 and 1.4 in 1985.

The average gain in number of households in the early 1980s resembles that of the 1960s when the U.S. population was much smaller: It is little more than half of what was expected just a few years earlier. It is striking that the largest decline has been in nonfamily households, particularly persons living alone—the very group that had the largest absolute growth in the earlier decade.

Besides demographic changes, basic changes in the U.S. economy and in average household incomes are producing major adjustments in the production, marketing, and use of new and used housing. Median family income in the United States in constant 1982 dollars just about doubled between 1950 and 1973, from $13,318 to $26,175. But in the succeeding two years, real median income dropped by over $1,500, a decline that was matched by a near halving of the rate of new housing starts. Between 1975 and 1979 real income

growth resumed, although falling below the 1973 high, and housing starts soared. After 1979 real family income and housing starts dropped again: The median income of $23,433 in 1982 was more than $2,700 below the 1973 level.

The inescapable conclusion is that without the incentive of inflation in housing values, with mortgage interest rates likely to remain high during periods of economic boom when people are eager to buy houses, and with a decline in real housing buying power, many Americans—and most first-time buyers—will probably get less housing in the 1980s than they expected or feel they deserve. The poor will get less, too. There are fewer dollars for subsidized new units and slower rates of existing units filtering down. The post–World War II success of the filter-down process, revealed in census tabulations of the sharp decline in housing units that lacked plumbing and were overcrowded, occurred not so much from purposeful public housing policy as from the enormous additions of new housing units. Thus, constrictions of the housing market in the private, middle-class sector inhibit the middle-class lifestyle, but eventually have harsh consequences for the low-income groups as well.

The Political Economy of Housing Statistics

The Major Statistical Series

The decennial census of housing supplies the most extensive assessment of housing in the United States by providing the greatest amount of geographical detail—down to the city block. In addition to the decennial census, the Bureau of the Census conducts several periodic and current surveys. Two periodic national surveys are conducted in conjunction with the decennial census of housing: The Components of Inventory Change Survey provides data on the sources of the current inventory and the disposition of a previous inventory between two points in time and furnishes housing characteristics data on the various components; the Residential Finance Survey obtains data on the financing of nonfarm homeowner and rental properties.

Current surveys include the American (formerly Annual) Housing Survey, which provides information on the size and composition of the housing inventory and related topics for the nation, census regions, and selected SMSAs; and two quarterly surveys used by the construction and residential finance industries—the Housing Vacancy Survey and the Survey of Market Absorption of Apartments—

which obtain, respectively, data on selected characteristics of new apartments that are absorbed 3, 6, 9, and 12 months after construction.

The construction statistics program of the Bureau of the Census conducts current surveys to obtain housing-related data such as housing starts and completions, characteristics of new one-family houses, and residential alterations and repairs.

The Forces That Shape Statistical Series

It is tempting to believe that the population and housing statistics that flow from the U.S. Census of 1980 or from other official censuses and surveys are neutral observations, like a weatherman's report of the day's temperature and precipitation. But this view is too simple. Official statistical series are not merely a mirror reflecting reality; they are a product of social, political, economic, and scientific interests that often conflict with one another.[56] Their conduct and modes of presentation are shaped by theories about the nature of society. Their structure and coverage depend on methodological and operational decisions made within the statistical agencies that produce the numbers under tight time and budget constraints and on the bureaucracies that use them. Moreover, official data series, especially continuing series, are often slow to respond to changing realities. Instead, they continue to echo the past of their origins, much as the surface of the land reflects its underlying geology.

Federal statistical series have always been subject to these influences, but the stakes are higher now. Substantial amounts of federal aid to states and to local units of government are allocated according to formulas that use federal statistical series such as the Census of Population and Housing. Goals and achievements for neighborhood and school desegregation programs rely on official statistics. Eligibility of cities and counties to participate in federal programs such as Urban Development Action Grant (UDAG) depends on series reporting such measures as unemployment rates, poverty rates, and housing vacancy rates.

Silences in data series also carry meanings. Sometimes the silence is due to political pressure. Such pressure keeps questions about religion off the U.S. population census, for instance. Sometimes the silence is due to custom or to lack of sufficient pressure from business, scientific, or political interests that would lead to their collection, such as what foods, beverages, and drugs people ingest each day. Political judgments are implicit in the choice of what to measure, how to measure it, how often to measure it, and how to present and interpret the results.

Our national self-image is confirmed or challenged by numbers that describe changes in the family, in the structure of households, in the geographical redistribution of population from one region to another, or in the recent reversal of certain rural-to-urban migration flows. Our priorities about what to measure may be faulty, and our selection of variables to measure change may not be apt, but even when our data series miss their mark they have the advantage of standardizing our perceptions of what is happening. We shape our statistical series, and then they shape us. The political economy of official statistics means an interplay of forces—political, economic, social, and scientific—that shape institutions and define the assumptions, the agenda, and the choices of government.[57]

What to Measure to Understand the Housing Situation

Among the myriad of possible questions that could be asked, only a handful can be selected. The U.S. Constitution requires that a decennial population census be conducted, but no mention is made of a housing census. The first census of housing had its roots in a series of "real property inventories" conducted during the depression years of the 1930s. At that time the federal government became involved in providing housing assistance to needy families in urban and rural areas, and it hoped to stimulate the depressed economy by promoting housing construction in places where demand would absorb new units.

The first focus of the national housing surveys during the 1930s was on standards of health, comfort, and safety. Measures of crowding (persons per room), sanitation (plumbing facilities), age (year built), type (housing units per structure), and comfort (electricity, telephone) were eventually defined and used to portray the housing landscape and to defend public interventions in housing questions at the local level.

The second focus was on forms of tenure, on the value of housing (value, rent levels), and on the composition (singles, apartments) and

---

[56]William Alonso and Paul Starr, "The Political Economy of National Statistics," Social Science Research Council, *Items* 36, no. 2 (September 1982): 29–35.

[57]Ibid.

use of housing at the neighborhood level. Through block and neighborhood scale analysis of rent levels in over 100 cities, the dynamics of residential real estate markets were described and linked to patterns of urban residential structure and change.[58]

Once the theoretical importance of rent levels and property values was established, the 1940 census proceeded to collect data on value (rent, price), tenure (own, rent), and occupancy (occupied, vacant). The census also collected and published uniform data for selected cities by census tract and by block for the first time. City planners, urbanists, and public health officials had argued the relevance of a neighborhood scale statistical unit. The real property inventories had demonstrated the economic importance of small-area data, and the tract was introduced in 1940—with local census advisory committees helping to define appropriate tract boundaries. There had been census population data published by wards for selected large cities before 1940, but the 1940 census introduced the census tract as a nationally uniform small-area data unit.

In the time that has elapsed since 1940, the public's attention has been drawn to the inferior economic position of certain racial and ethnic groups, especially blacks, American Indians, Eskimos, and persons of Spanish-Hispanic origin. The Census of Housing has responded by providing separate tabulations for these groups so that their progress toward full participation in the economic, social, and geographical mainstream can be monitored.

In the 1970s, while many apartment buildings were converted to condominium ownership and a large share of newly constructed housing took condominium form, the census responded with a new reporting category for 1980—"condominiums."

When the first housing census was taken, 45 percent of American households lived in housing units that lacked complete plumbing facilities for their exclusive use. By 1980 only 2 percent of the households were so classified. The few counties where the measure revealed a housing quality problem were mainly in the rural South. By 1980 satisfactory plumbing had virtually ceased to be a housing issue.

On the other hand, new goals had been established for which new measures of housing quality were needed to evaluate the position of households in lower-quality housing—goals such as "racial integration of the neighborhood," "presence of low- and moderate-priced housing in middle-priced areas," and "minority households in new housing in the suburbs."

[58]Homer Hoyt, *The Structure and Growth of Residential Neighborhoods in American Cities* (Washington, DC: Federal Housing Administration, 1939).

What Classification Systems to Use

The central elements in a housing census are the housing unit, the household that lives in it, and its location. The census can count only within categories, so the construction of categories is as much a social as a technical and scientific process. The census uses five headings to describe the categories of housing units and their use.

Living Quarters

Living quarters are either housing units or group quarters. They are usually in structures intended for residence (house, apartment, condominium, mobile home, convent, hotel, and so forth). However, living quarters may also be in structures intended for nonresidential use (rooms in warehouses, boats, tents, vans, and so forth).

Occupancy and Vacancy Characteristics

A housing unit is classified as occupied if it is the usual place of residence of the household living in it at the time of enumeration. A household includes all the persons occupying a housing unit as their usual place of residence.

A housing unit is vacant if no one is living in it at the time of enumeration, unless its occupants are only temporarily absent. "Seasonal and migratory" vacant units are intended for occupancy only during certain seasons of the year. "Year-round" vacant units include those for sale, for rent, rented or sold and awaiting occupancy, for occasional use, and others, including boarded up. Since vacant units often affect their neighborhood and the expectations and behavior of their neighbors, the vacancy status is important.

Homeowner vacancy rates and the rental vacancy rates measure the amount of demand for housing in an area and index what a local housing market might be able to absorb in the way of newly constructed housing units.

Tenure describes the legal and socially relevant distinction between homeowners and renters. For many decades tenure has been taken as a primary socioeconomic marker that on the average distinguishes households on the upper rungs of the socioeconomic ladder (mainly owners, with adequate access to mortgage credit) from those on the lower rungs (mainly renters, who normally lack access to mortgage credit). In recent tabulations census data on tenure have been further subdivided routinely to distinguish white, black, and Spanish-Hispanic householders by their tenure status. This is a convenient and readily understood way to measure socioeconomic progress of the major minority groups.

Utilization Characteristics

The number of persons per room in a housing unit has long been used as a measure of crowding. Other measures such as floor area per person or interior room volume per person, which might seem to promise useful measures of crowding, have failed to gain favor. They are harder to calculate reliably and do not seem to have the theoretical and empirical usefulness of the persons-per-room measure, which emphasizes the importance of privacy rather than living area per person. The measure is based on the number of *whole* rooms used for living purposes (living rooms, dining rooms, kitchens, bedrooms, finished recreation rooms, enclosed porches suitable for year-round use, and lodgers' rooms).

Structural Characteristics

Structural characteristics focus on the completeness of plumbing and on the number of housing units at the same address. Plumbing facilities have been used as an index of housing quality since the first housing census. Type of residential structure, as revealed by "units at address" and "units in structure," is important in classifying land uses locally. Most zoning laws distinguish several classes of residential area based on the type of structures and the size of the lots on which they are located.

Financial Characteristics

Value is the estimate of how much a property (house and lot) or condominium unit would sell for if it were for sale. Value statistics are gathered and reported for "specified owner-occupied" units—conventional condos and single-family houses on less than 10 acres, without a commercial establishment or medical office on the property.

Contract rent is the monthly rent agreed to, or contracted for, regardless of any furnishings, services, or utilities that may be included. The relevance of value and rent questions is determined by local governments that tax real estate, by agencies that try to maintain or to reduce the homogeneity of housing market areas, by planning agencies that monitor the economic health of local market areas by following price and rent movements, and by society in general for which "value in exchange" in the market is the unquestioned arbiter of value.

Assigning Numbers to Clearly Defined Categories

The production of numbers requires definitions that have sharp edges. Geographical divisions and subdivisions must have clear boundaries that place a housing unit and a household on one side of the boundary or the other. In reality, the boundaries of urbanized areas, poverty neighborhoods, and ethnic areas are not sharp, but to count means to define a set and to attach numbers to it. The mathematical logic of counting is joined with the bureaucratic regimen of classification and procedures. Both of these imperatives tend to count and to classify more rigidly and mechanically than would be warranted from intuitive concepts of the census categories or from the disposition of individual cases.[59]

Consistency in Data Series

There is a strong argument in favor of statistical series that are comparable over time—so that change can be studied. But the desire for comparability is often in conflict with changing emphases and new realities. We retain measures of inadequate plumbing facilities in housing despite the fact that there often is almost no variation today in this measure from unit to unit or from place to place. On the other hand, in the case of ethnicity and housing no time series exists for Hispanics because censuses prior to 1980 used categories such as "Spanish-surname" that cannot be compared with the 1980 categories.

National statistics must also be comparable from one locality to another, although local circumstances may be misrepresented by such standardization. Consider the definition of the Standard Metropolitan Statistical Area (SMSA), which attempts to combine a central employment core with surrounding counties that send significant numbers of daily commuters to the core job centers. It is easier to define and discuss such a Daily Urban System in theory than in practice. In some areas of the South and New England where certain large centers have no major neighboring competitors, the surrounding SMSA counties (in the South) and towns and cities (in New England) are small in area and can often be identified and assembled with precision to form the SMSA. In the Midwest, where major centers are often widely spaced, there is relatively less overlap of commutersheds around employment cores, but the frequently large-sized counties

[59]Alonso and Starr, op. cit.

means assembling SMSAs with oversized building blocks. But that problem seems pale beside the problem of SMSA definition for many East Coast and California cities whose commuter hinterlands have frequent and intensive interpenetration; yet each county can be assigned to only one SMSA even though it may be functionally linked to several. The definitions are necessary to permit tabulations of the census data, but in their reporting they state patterns and imply processes that do not exist in the forms reported. The tension between local individuality that demands exceptionalism and centralized standardization of censuses has been a political issue for two centuries, and will continue to be.

1980 Census of Housing-Enumeration and Processing Procedures

Usual Place of Residence

Following census practice dating back to the first U.S. census in 1790, each person enumerated in the 1980 census was counted as an inhabitant of his or her "usual place of residence," which means the place where the person lives and sleeps most of the time. This place is not necessarily the same as the person's legal residence or voting residence. In the vast majority of cases, however, the use of these different bases of classification would produce substantially the same statistics.

This practice has resulted in the establishment of residence rules for certain categories of persons whose usual place of residence is not immediately apparent. Furthermore, this practice means that persons are not always counted as residents of the place where they happen to be staying on Census Day (April 1). Persons without a usual place of residence, however, are counted where they happen to be staying.

Data Collection Procedures

The 1980 census was conducted primarily through self-enumeration. A census questionnaire was delivered by postal carriers to each household several days before Census Day, April 1, 1980. This questionnaire included explanatory information and was accompanied by an instruction guide. Spanish-language versions of the questionnaire and instruction guide were available on request. The questionnaire was also available in narrative translation in 32 languages.

In most areas of the United States, altogether containing about 95 percent of the population, the householder was requested to fill out and mail back the questionnaire on Census Day. Approximately 83 percent of these households returned their forms by mail. Households that did not mail back a form were visited by an enumerator. Households that returned a form with incomplete or inconsistent information that exceeded a specific tolerance were contacted by telephone or, if necessary, by a personal visit, to obtain the information.

In the remaining (mostly sparsely settled) areas of the country, which contain about 5 percent of the population, the household received a questionnaire in the mail. The householder was requested to fill out the questionnaire and return it when an enumerator visited the household. Incomplete and unfilled forms were completed by interview during the enumerator's visit. In all areas of the country vacant units were enumerated by a personal visit and observation.

Each household in the country received one of two versions of the census questionnaire: a short-form questionnaire containing a limited number of basic population and housing questions, or a long-form questionnaire containing these basic questions as well as a number of additional questions. (See census questionnaire facsimiles in the Appendix.) A sampling procedure was used to determine the households that were to receive the long-form questionnaire. Two sampling rates were employed. For most of the country, one household in every six (about 17 percent) received the long-form or sample questionnaire; in areas estimated to have fewer than 2,500 inhabitants, every other household (50 percent) received the sample questionnaire to enhance the reliability of sample data in small areas.

Special questionnaires were used for the enumeration of persons in group quarters such as colleges and universities, hospitals, prisons, military installations, and ships. These forms contained the same population questions that appeared on either the short form or the long form but did not include any housing questions. In addition to the regular census questionnaire, a Supplementary Questionnaire for American Indians was used in conjunction with the short form on federal and state reservations and in the historic areas of Oklahoma (excluding urbanized areas) for households that had at least one American Indian, Eskimo, or Aleut household member.

Processing Procedures

The 1980 census questionnaires were processed in a manner similar to that used for the 1960 and 1970 censuses. The questionnaires were designed to be processed electronically by the Film Optical Sensing Device for Input to Computer (FOSDIC). For most items on the questionnaire the information supplied by the respondent or obtained by the enumerator was indicated by marking the answers in predesignated positions that would be "read" by FOSDIC from a microfilm copy of the questionnaire and transferred onto computer tape with no intervening manual processing. The computer tape did not include information on individual names and addresses.

Sources of Data Error

In any large-scale statistical operation such as a decennial census, human and mechanical errors occur. Such errors include failure to enumerate every housing unit or person in the population, to obtain all required information from respondents, to obtain correct and consistent information, and to record information correctly. Errors can also occur during the field review of the enumerators' work, the clerical handling of the census questionnaires, or the electronic processing of the questionnaires.

In an attempt to reduce various types of nonsampling error in the 1980 census, a number of new quality-control and review measures were used throughout the data collection and processing phases of the census to minimize undercoverage of the population and housing units and to keep the errors at a minimum. There were programs after the 1980 census—as after the 1950, 1960, and 1970 censuses—to measure various aspects of the quality achieved in the 1980 census.

A major component of the evaluation work is to ascertain, insofar as possible, the degree of completeness of the count of persons and housing units. The Census Bureau has estimated that the 1970 census did not count 2.5 percent of the population.

Editing Unacceptable Data

The objective of the processing operation is to produce a set of statistics that describes the nation's housing as accurately and clearly as possible. To meet this objective, certain unacceptable entries were edited.

In the field, questionnaires were reviewed by a census clerk or an enumerator for omissions and certain inconsistencies and, if necessary, a call was made to obtain missing information. A similar review of questionnaires was performed in the central processing offices.

As one of the first steps in editing, the configuration of marks on the questionnaire column was scanned electronically to determine whether it contained information for a housing unit or merely spurious marks. If any characteristic for a housing unit was still missing when the questionnaires reached the central processing offices, it was supplied by a procedure called "allocation." Allocations, or assignments of acceptable codes in place of unacceptable entries, were needed most often when an entry for a given item was lacking or when the information reported for a housing unit on that item was inconsistent with other information for the housing unit or with information reported for a similar housing unit in the immediate neighborhood. As in previous censuses, the general procedure for changing unacceptable entries was to assign an entry for a housing unit that was consistent with entries for other housing units with similar characteristics. For example, if the unit was reported as rented but the amount of rent was missing, the computer automatically assigned the rent that was reported for the preceding renter-occupied unit.

The editing process also includes another type of correction, namely, the assignment of a full set of characteristics for a person or a housing unit, which occurs when no housing information is available. If the housing unit is occupied, the housing characteristics are assigned from the previously processed occupied unit; if vacant, from the previously processed vacant unit. When a housing unit was occupied but the questionnaire contained no information for all or most of the occupants, although persons were known to be present, a previously processed household was selected as a substitute and the full set of characteristics for each substitute person was duplicated. These duplications fall into two classes: (1) "persons or housing units substituted due to non-interview," for example, when a housing unit was indicated as occupied but the occupants or the housing unit characteristics were not listed on the questionnaire, and (2) "persons or housing units substituted due to mechanical failure," for example, when the questionnaire page was not properly microfilmed.

The American Housing Survey

The American Housing Survey (AHS) was designed to provide a current series of information on the size and composition of the housing inventory, the characteristics of its occupants, the changes in the inventory resulting from new construction and from losses, the indicators of housing and neighborhood quality, and the characteristics of recent movers. The survey is performed for the Department of Housing and Urban Development.

AHS statistics are based on information from a sample of housing units in 69 SMSAs and Standard Consolidated Statistical Areas (SCSAs). Original plans called for one third of the areas to be surveyed each year, and each area in the sample to be surveyed every three years. A separate report is issued jointly by the Department of Housing and Urban Development and the Bureau of the Census for each SMSA in the surveys. Each report has five parts: Part A presents statistics on general housing characteristics, part B on indicators of housing and neighborhood quality, part C on financial characteristics, part D on recent mover households, and part F on financial characteristics cross-classified by indicators of housing and neighborhood quality. (Part E is published only for the national sample.)

The content and procedures of the American Housing Survey were determined after consultation with users of housing data and by field pretesting. The data for many of the subjects covered are the same as those collected in the Census of Housing; in general, the AHS data are comparable to those in census reports. In addition, the AHS covers subjects such as breakdowns in equipment, the physical condition of the structure, neighborhood conditions and services, distance and travel time from home to work for the householder, storm windows and doors, and insulation.

Sample Size

The statistics presented in AHS reports are based on samples of housing units and are, therefore, subject to sampling variability. The larger areas are each represented by a sample of about 8,500 designated housing units, which are evenly divided between the central city or cities and the balance of the respective area, that is, the area not in central cities. Remaining SMSAs are each represented by samples of about 4,250 designated housing units, which are divided between the central city or cities and the balance of the respective area based on the proportionate distribution of all housing units in the entire area.

The Quality of the Data

Since the estimates in AHS reports are based on samples, they may differ somewhat from the figures that would have been obtained from a complete census using the same questionnaires, instructions, and interviews. As in any survey work, the results are subject to errors of response and nonreporting and to sampling variability.

The concepts and definitions are essentially the same for those items that appear both in AHS reports and in the census reports. The SMSA and SCSA boundaries are the same as those used in the census. In making comparisons between AHS and Census of Housing results, differences in the data may reflect such factors as the use of direct interview in the AHS contrasted with the extensive use of self-enumeration in the census, the sample design, the estimation procedure used, the sampling variability of the estimates, and the processing procedures.

The AHS data on housing and neighborhood quality are intended to serve as broad indicators of housing quality and not as precise measurements. A housing unit, for example, that is reported as having signs of a leaking roof or a breakdown in plumbing facilities is not necessarily inadequate or poor housing. Conversely, a housing unit that is reported as not having such defects is not necessarily housing of good quality. The data presented for items such as neighborhood conditions and neighborhood services are based on the individual respondent's opinion of conditions in the neighborhood, which may or may not reflect a consensus view of the situation.

Care should be exercised in making comparisons between the American Housing Survey data and the 1970 and 1980 Censuses of Housing results. Differences in the data may reflect the time periods during which the data were collected (possible seasonal effects), sample designs, estimation procedures used, sampling variability of the estimates, and the processing procedures.

The national Annual Housing Survey and the 1980 Census of Housing produced significant differences for several key characteristics. For example, the April 1980 census had a homeownership rate for the United States of 64.4 percent; the October 1979 AHS national, 65.4 percent; and the October 1980 AHS national, 65.6 percent. The 1980 census showed that 18 percent of the housing units were in multiunit structures (5 housing units or more); both the 1979 and 1980 surveys reported 15 percent. In the 1980 census 26 percent of the housing inventory was reported built since January 1970; the October 1979 AHS, 21 percent since March 1970; and the 1980 AHS, 23 percent since March 1970.

The Reliability of the Estimates

There are two types of possible error associated with estimates based on data from sample surveys—sampling and nonsampling errors. In general, nonsampling errors can be attributed to many sources: inability to obtain the information about all cases; definitional difficulties; differences in the interpretation of questions; inability or unwillingness of respondents to provide correct information; mistakes in recording or coding the data; other errors of collection, response, processing, and coverage; and estimation for missing data. Nonsampling errors are not unique to sample surveys since they can, and do, occur in complete censuses as well.

Obtaining a measurement of the total nonsampling error associated with estimates from a survey is difficult, considering the number of possible sources of error. However, an attempt was made to measure some of the nonsampling errors associated with the estimates for the 1970 Census of Population and Housing and the 1977 AHS-SMSA sample.

1970 Census

A number of studies were conducted to measure two types of general errors associated with 1970 census estimates—"coverage" and "content" errors. The "coverage" errors determined how completely housing units were counted in the census and the extent to which occupancy status was erroneously reported. The "content" errors measured the accuracy of the data collected for enumerated housing units. These errors were measured by reinterviews, record checks, and other surveys.

The detailed results of these studies, as well as the methodology employed, are presented in the 1970 Census of Population and Housing Evaluation and Research Program Reports, series PHC(E)-5, the Coverage of Housing in the 1970 Census, and PHC(E)-10, Accuracy of Data for Selected Housing Characteristics as Measured by Reinterviews.

The AHS-SMSA Sample

A study was conducted for the 1977 AHS-SMSA sample, and the results are presented in the Census Bureau memorandum "Reinterview Results for Annual Housing Survey—SMSA Sample: 1977." A 1981 AHS-SMSA sample reinterview program was also carried out.

Coverage Errors

In errors of coverage and estimation for missing data, the AHS new construction sample had deficiencies in the representation of conventional (non-mobile-home) new construction. Because of time constraints, only those building permits issued more than five months before the survey ended were eligible to be sampled to repre-

sent conventional new construction in permit-issuing areas for the SMSAs. However, the permits issued during the last five months of the survey do not necessarily represent missed housing units. Because of the relatively short time span involved, it is possible that construction of these housing units was not completed at the time the survey was conducted, in which case they would not have been eligible for interview. In addition to these deficiencies, new construction in special places that do not require building permits, such as military bases, are also not adequately presented.

The Census Bureau's Coverage Improvement Program was not very effective in finding nonresidential conversions. Such conversions were primarily in business districts, whereas the listing procedure started from a residential unit.

Rounding Errors

For errors associated with processing, the rounding of estimates introduces another source of error in the data, the severity of which depends on the statistics being measured. The effect of rounding is significant relative to the sampling error only for small percentages or small medians when these figures are derived from relatively large bases (for example, median numbers of persons per household). This means that confidence intervals formed from the standard errors given may be distorted, which should be taken into account when considering the results of the survey.

Sampling Errors for the AHS-SMSA Sample

The particular sample used for the AHS is one of a large number of possible samples of the same size that could have been selected using the same sample design. Even if the same questionnaires, instructions, and interviews were used, estimates from each of the different samples would differ. The sampling error of a survey estimate provides a measure of the variation among the estimates of all possible samples and thus is a measure of the precision with which an estimate from a sample approximates the average result of all possible samples.

One common measure of the sampling error is the standard error. The standard error reflects the variation in the estimates due to sampling and nonsampling errors, but it does not measure as such any systematic biases in the data. Therefore, the accuracy of the estimates depends on the standard error, biases, and any additional nonsampling errors not measured by the standard error.

The reliability of an estimated percentage, computed by using the sample data for both numerator and denominator, depends on both the size of the percentage and the size of the total on which the percentage is based. Estimated percentages are relatively more reliable than the corresponding estimates of the numerators of the percentages, particularly if the percentages are 50 percent or more.

Summary and Conclusions

Housing activity—households using dwellings—is a central feature in the human use of the earth. A house is merely a structure, but a home is an experience. Housing is an interactive process with meanings tied to status, social position, wealth, power, aspirations, and personal identity. Housing decisions reflect social drives for congregation and segregation within U.S. cities, thus making social and cultural categories of urban society visible, intelligible, and stable. Urban housing landscapes in the United States are destabilized by changing population age structure, wealth transfers among neighborhoods, immigration, and interregional wealth shifts. Despite vigorous initiatives to break down neighborhood class barriers, zoning laws and court decisions staunchly protect single-family housing areas, perhaps as an expression of a basic conservative instinct to protect and nurture human life. Valiant efforts to modify zoning laws to improve the position of weaker classes without threatening the stronger present a dilemma, but the American utopian tradition urges us to keep trying.

During the construction boom of the 1960s and 1970s, an enormous quantity of high-quality new housing was built in the United States, but inflation, speculation, and sharply higher mortgage interest rates brought an end to the boom. There were many fewer net new household formations per year in the early 1980s than in previous decades, although levels were rising again during the middle years of the decade. Housing is more expensive and real incomes of new households fall far short of what would be needed to repeat the housing experience of new households of the 1960s and 1970s.

The first U. S. decennial housing census was taken in 1940. It is supplemented by the American Housing Survey and other current surveys of housing finance, inventory change, and new construction. The content and modes of presentation of federal housing data series are shaped by theories about the nature of society. The series are products of social, political, economic, and scientific interests that are often in conflict, but that is the nature of housing and society in the United States. Housing is a scarce and valuable resource. There are winners and losers as the resource is allocated. It comes as no surprise, then, that there would be disputes about what to measure and how.

HOUSING STOCK LOCATION AND COMPOSITION

Housing Units in 1980

THE 1980 Census of Population and Housing counted 226.5 million persons and 88.4 million housing units during the April 1 enumeration.[1] The Annual (now American) Housing Survey conducted on a sample basis later in the same year estimated the total U.S. housing inventory as 88.2 million units. The difference between the two totals highlights the difficulty in producing an accurate count. Enumeration methods and imperfections, sampling variability, plus new construction, demolition, and modification of housing units by consolidation and by subdivision between the census and survey dates all contribute to the difference.[2]

There were 29 million housing units in the South at census time, 23 million in the Midwest, 19 million in the Northeast, and 17 million in the West. Within the census regions, the housing inventory is unevenly distributed by state, with the top 10 states—led by California, New York, and Texas—accounting for 54 percent of the nation's housing (Table 3.1).

There were 64.9 million units in urban areas and 23.5 million in rural settings. These totals are close to the counts of 65.1 million in Standard Metropolitan Statistical Areas (SMSAs) and 23.3 million outside SMSAs, but there are differences between the definitions and their underlying concepts (Table 3.2).

---

[1]The housing sector in the U.S. economy can be viewed as comprising four markets: the flow of housing services from the available stock of housing; the flow of residential construction, that is, real estate production that includes structure and land; the flow of mortgage credit; and the flow of construction inputs. Each market is tied to others. This chapter treats only the housing inventory and its characteristics. See J. Eric Fredland and C. Duncan MacRae, *Econometric Models of the Housing Sector* (Washington, DC: Urban Institute, 1978). Market considerations are treated in later chapters. For comprehensive treatments of the social and economic contexts of the U.S. housing stock, see Glenn H. Beyer, *Housing: A Factual Analysis* (New York: Macmillan, 1965); Wallace F. Smith, *Housing: The Social and Economic Elements* (Berkeley: University of California Press, 1970); and Earl W. Morris and Mary Winter, *Housing, Family, and Society* (New York: Wiley, 1978).

[2]For comprehensive accounts, see U.S. Department of Housing and Urban Development, *Housing in the Seventies: Working Papers* (Washington, DC: U.S. Government Printing Office, 1976), 2 vols.; and Office of Policy Development and Research, *1982 National Housing Production Report* (Washington, DC: U.S. Department of Housing and Urban Development, 1983).

TABLE 3.1

Housing Units, by State, 1980 (in millions)

	Units	Rank	Percentage of United States
California	9.28	1	10.5%
New York	6.87	2	7.8
Texas	5.55	3	6.3
Pennsylvania	4.60	4	5.2
Florida	4.38	5	5.0
Illinois	4.32	6	4.9
Ohio	4.11	7	4.6
Michigan	3.59	8	4.1
New Jersey	2.77	9	3.1
North Carolina	2.27	10	2.6
Massachusetts	2.21	11	2.5
Indiana	2.09	12	2.4
Georgia	2.03	13	2.3
Virginia	2.02	14	2.3
Missouri	1.99	15	2.2
Wisconsin	1.86	16	2.1
Tennessee	1.75	17	2.0
Washington	1.69	18	1.9
Minnesota	1.61	19	1.8
Maryland	1.57	20	1.8
Louisiana	1.55	21	1.7
Alabama	1.47	22	1.7
Kentucky	1.37	23	1.5
Oklahoma	1.24	24	1.4
Colorado	1.19	25	1.3
Connecticut	1.16	26	1.3

TABLE 3.1 *(continued)*

	Units	Rank	Percentage of United States
South Carolina	1.15	27	1.3
Iowa	1.13	28	1.3
Arizona	1.11	29	1.3
Oregon	1.08	30	1.2
Kansas	.95	31	1.1
Mississippi	.91	32	1.0
Arkansas	.90	33	1.0
West Virginia	.75	34	.8
Nebraska	.62	35	.7
New Mexico	.51	36	.6
Maine	.50	37	.6
Utah	.49	38	.6
New Hampshire	.39	39	.4
Idaho	.38	40	.4
Rhode Island	.37	41	.4
Nevada	.34	42	.4
Hawaii	.33	43	.4
Montana	.33	44	.4
South Dakota	.28	45	.3
Washington, DC	.28	46	.3
North Dakota	.26	47	.3
Delaware	.24	48	.3
Vermont	.22	49	.2
Wyoming	.19	50	.2
Alaska	.16	51	.2

SOURCE: U.S. Bureau of the Census, 1980 Census of Housing, vol. 1; *Characteristics of Housing Units*, table 2.

Urban and Rural Housing

As defined for the 1980 census, urban housing comprises all housing units in urbanized areas and in places of 2,500 persons or more outside urbanized areas. Places are of two types: those incorporated under the laws of their respective states—cities, boroughs, towns, villages, and so forth; and closely settled population centers without corporate limits. Housing units not classified as urban are rural.

The Census Bureau defines urbanized areas to provide a better separation of urban and rural housing in the vicinity of large cities. An urbanized area consists of a central city or cities, plus the surrounding closely settled "urban fringe" territory that together have a population of at least 50,000.[3] There were 54.0 million housing units inside urbanized areas in 1980 and 11.0 million housing units in small places outside urbanized areas (Table 3.2). The 23.5 million

[3]The analysis of the nation's urban and rural housing stock often occurs in connection with policy issues that center on selected regions or classes of user groups. See B. A. Smith, "The Supply of Urban Housing," *Quarterly Journal of Economics* 90 (1976):389–405; U.S. Senate, Committee on Agriculture and Forestry, *The Provision of Housing for the Rural Elderly* (Washington, DC: U.S. Government Printing Office, 1973); U.S. Department of Housing and Urban Development, *Low Rise Housing for Older People: Behavioral Criteria for Design* (Washington, DC: U.S. Government Printing Office, 1977); Housing Assistance Council, *The Politics of Rural Housing: A Manual for Building Rural Housing Coalitions* (Washington, DC: Housing Assistance Council, 1980); U.S. Congress, Congressional Budget Office, *Rural Housing Programs: Long-Term Costs and Their Treatment in the Federal Budget* (Washington, DC: U.S. Government Printing Office, 1982).

TABLE 3.2
Housing Units, by Location, 1980 (in millions)

	Housing Units
United States	88.4
Urban	64.9
Inside urbanized areas	54.0
Central cities	27.2
Urban fringe	26.8
Outside urbanized areas	11.0
Places of 10,000 or more	5.2
Places of 2,500 to 10,000	5.7
Rural	23.5
Places of 1,000 to 2,500	2.9
Other rural	20.6
Inside SMSAs	65.1
Urban	56.3
Central cities	27.4
Not in central cities	28.9
Rural	8.8
Outside SMSAs	23.3
Urban	8.6
Rural	14.7

SOURCE: U.S. Bureau of the Census, 1980 Census of Housing, vol. 1, *Characteristics of Housing Units*, table 1.

units of rural housing in 1980 were located in small incorporated and unincorporated places, 1,000 to 2,500 in population; in places below 1,000; and in other configurations including farm housing (Table 3.2).

Standard Metropolitan Statistical Areas

The general concept of a metropolitan area is one of a large population nucleus together with surrounding territory containing persons who are employed in the area's core region. Each SMSA normally has one central county or more containing the area's main population concentration: an urbanized area with at least 50,000 inhabitants. An SMSA may also include outlying counties that have close ties with the central counties as measured by the level of daily commuting to the central counties and that meet certain standards regarding metropolitan character, such as population density, urban population, and population growth. In New England SMSAs are composed of cities and towns rather than whole counties. In some parts of the United States metropolitan development has progressed to the point that adjoining SMSAs are themselves socially and economically integrated. These areas are designated Standard Consolidated Statistical Areas (SCSAs).

Since SMSAs are composed of whole counties, they can include rural as well as urban housing. In 1980, 8.8 million SMSA units were in rural areas, while 56.3 million were in urban areas. Outside SMSAs 14.7 million units were found in rural settings—such as places under 2,500 population, isolated homesteads, and farm housing. The rest of the non-SMSA housing was 8.6 million units in urban places (2,500 and over) too small to qualify for SMSA status.

Urbanized areas and metropolitan areas differ significantly. An urbanized area consists of the physically continuously built-up territory around a large city and corresponds generally to the core of high and medium population density at the heart of the metropolitan area. In concept a metropolitan area is larger than its core urbanized area, even if the metropolitan area is defined using small areal building blocks, because it incorporates the daily commuter hinterland of one or more core counties.

Metropolitan areas nationwide include considerable rural territory whose residents commute to work in the city or its suburbs, while the urbanized area excludes such territory. In practice, because the SMSA definitions normally use counties as building blocks, considerable rural territory with few commuters is included. Sometimes, because of boundary anomalies, a portion of an urbanized area extends across the SMSA boundary into a nonmetropolitan county or another SMSA. Such overlap portions are usually small in area and population. Each SMSA is associated with an urbanized area, but the reverse is not true because an urbanized area may not qualify for SMSA status. Some SMSAs contain more than one urbanized area, such as when two or more urban concentrations not far apart and of similar size have separate urbanized areas but qualify as a single SMSA (for example, Greensboro–High Point and Raleigh–Durham, North Carolina), or when a large SMSA includes a large urbanized area and one or more smaller urbanized areas within its boundaries (for example, Joliet, Aurora, and Elgin within the Chicago SMSA).

Structural Characteristics of American Housing

In the 1980 stock of 86.7 million year-round housing units, 61.7 million (71 percent) were in single-unit structures (Table 3.3). The ratio of singles was lower in urban areas (68 percent) and higher in rural areas (81 percent). Among the four census regions, the ratio of singles was greatest in the South (76 percent) and lowest in the Northeast (60 percent).

There were 12.0 million units in groups of 2 to 9 at the same address, with 89 percent of them in urban areas. Another 8.7 million units were in groups of 10 or more at the same address, but only 3 percent of these units were in rural areas. Despite vigorous rates of production of mobile homes and trailers in the 1960s and 1970s, by 1980 the 4.3 million units in this class accounted for barely 5 percent of the total stock of year-round units, but still formed a basic element in the American housing stock.[4] Of the national total over 2 million (47 percent) were located in the South—which had the greatest ratio of mobile homes to conventional houses in the new construction of the 1960s and 1970s—while the Northeast had just under .4 million (9 percent). Over 60 percent nationwide were in rural areas. In 1980 and 1981 about one fourth of all new mobile homes were placed in Texas and Florida. California, with its preponderance of new multi-section mobile homes placed, had the highest averages sales price in both 1980 ($31,100) and 1981 ($32,900).[5]

The market for mobile homes has broadened over the years as the size and quality of the units have improved. Mobile homes have changed in average size from an average of 8 feet wide in 1940 and 10 feet in 1960 to 12 feet in the 1970s. The most popular size in the mid-1980s was 14 feet by 70 feet. (The maximum dimensions are 16 feet by 80 feet.) Average prices in the Midwest ranged from $20,000 to $25,000 new and about $15,000 used.

Plumbing Facilities

The quality of plumbing facilities in housing units has been measured in successive censuses as a central index of housing quality.[6] The census category "complete plumbing for exclusive use" consists of housing units that have hot and cold piped water, a flush toilet, and a bathtub or shower for the exclusive use of the occupants of the unit. "Lacking complete plumbing for exclusive use" means that (1)

all three facilities are present inside the unit, but are shared by another household; (2) some but not all three facilities are present; or (3) none is present (Table 3.3).

By census time in 1980 only 2.3 million year-round units (under 3 percent) lacked complete plumbing for exclusive use, a drop of 2.4 million from the 4.7 million reported in 1970. Previous censuses reported that 84 percent of occupied units had complete plumbing in 1960 and 95 percent in 1970.[7] Rural areas, with just over 25 percent of the nation's year-round units, had 56 percent of the units lacking complete, exclusive plumbing. The deficient units were found disproportionately in the South, where 59 percent of the nation's units with no plumbing were located—almost all of them (87 percent) in rural areas.

Units completely lacking in plumbing were rare in the Midwest (.7 percent of all units in the Midwest) and the West (.6 percent of all units in the West) where the levels of household income have usually been much higher than in the rural South. In five states the proportion of housing units lacking complete private plumbing was less than 1.5 percent: Utah (1.1 percent), Florida (1.2), and California, Connecticut, and Nevada (all 1.4). There were 130 counties—three fourths of them in metropolitan areas—in which less than 1 percent of the housing units lacked complete private plumbing.[8]

Problems of Aging Units

Mid-twentieth-century population movements at the national scale have been largely from the Northeast and Midwest into the West and South. A simultaneous net movement has occurred outward from central cities into suburban areas. New housing has been constructed in disproportionately large volumes in areas of heavy net inmigration, so that those areas today have much of the newer housing while places of steady net outmigration are left with an aging housing stock (Table 3.4). For central cities problems identified by various housing and neighborhood conditions (other than crowding) are usually two to four times as intense in pre-1940 housing as in housing built in 1940 or later. Some Annual Housing Survey data suggest that SMSA housing conditions vary less between pre-1940 and

[4]Arthur D. Bernhardt, *Building Tomorrow: The Mobile/Manufactured Housing Industry* (Cambridge, MA: MIT Press, 1980); and Margaret J. Drury, *Mobile Homes: The Unrecognized Revolution in American Housing* (New York: Praeger, 1972).

[5]U.S. Bureau of the Census, *Data User News*, December 1982, p. 8.

[6]U.S. Bureau of the Census, *Measuring the Quality of Housing: An Appraisal of Census Statistics and Methods*, Working Paper no. 25 (Washington, DC: U.S. Department of Commerce, 1967); and Jeanne E. Goedert and John L. Goodman, Jr., *Indicators of the Quality of U.S. Housing* (Washington, DC: Urban Institute, 1977).

[7]U.S. Bureau of the Census, *Statistical Abstract of the United States, 1984*, p. 753.

[8]U.S. Bureau of the Census, *Data User News*, February 1982, pp. 1–2.

TABLE 3.3

Year-Round Housing Units at an Address, and Plumbing Facilities, 1980 (in millions)

	United States	Urban	Rural	Northeast	Midwest	South	West
All Types	86.7	64.6	22.1	18.5	22.3	29.0	16.8
1 Unit at Address	61.7	43.8	17.9	11.2	16.7	21.9	11.9
2-9 Units at Address	12.0	10.7	1.3	4.2	3.1	2.7	1.9
10 Units or more at Address	8.7	8.5	.3	2.7	1.6	2.3	2.0
Mobile Home or Trailer	4.3	1.7	2.6	.4	.9	2.0	1.0
Urban				.1	.3	.7	.6
Rural				.3	.5	1.3	.4
Complete Plumbing for Exclusive Use	84.4	63.6	20.8	18.1	21.8	27.9	16.5
Lacking Complete Plumbing for Exclusive Use	2.3	1.0	1.3	.5	.5	1.1	.3
Complete, shared	.6	.5	(-)	.2	.2	.1	.1
Incomplete	.9	.3	.6	.1	.2	.5	.1
No plumbing	.8	.2	.7	.1	.2	.5	.1

NOTE: Care should be taken in using "units at address" as a proxy for "units in structure" because some multiunit buildings have more than one street address; (-): 50,000 or fewer; rounds to zero.
SOURCE: U.S. Bureau of the Census, 1980 Census of Housing, vol. 1, *Characteristics of Housing Units*, tables 3, 16, 29, 42, and 55.

1940-and-later housing for stock outside the central city than for stock inside.[9]

Half of the year-round housing units in the Northeast were built before 1940, while only 19 percent of the units in the South and West are of that vintage. Well over half the housing in the South and West was built after 1959. Within metropolitan areas 42 percent of central city housing was built before 1940, while 70 percent of suburban housing was built after 1949.

Major structural defects—exposed wiring, water leakage through the roof, open cracks and holes in walls, broken plaster, peeling interior paint, holes in floors—affect about 2 to 6 percent of housing units nationwide (Table 3.5). Wiring defects and leaking roofs are more common outside of SMSAs than inside, but maintenance of interior walls and floors is worse inside central cities than outside. Newer housing (and owner-occupied housing) is generally in better condition than older housing, so that suburban housing usually reveals fewer structural problems than older central city and rural structures. The Northeast and the South, with large concentrations of old, rental, and rural units, have a larger incidence of problem structures than the Midwest. The West, where most of the housing is quite new, has the fewest problem units (Table 3.5).

Telephones are present in 92 percent of the nation's housing units, with the ratio rising to 93 percent in SMSAs and 94 percent in

[9]Marilyn A. Brown, "Do Central Cities Have Similar Dimensions of Need?" *Professional Geographer* 32, no. 4 (1980):pp. 400–11.

TABLE 3.4

Age of Year-Round Housing Units, 1980

	Year Structure Built				
	Pre-1940	1940–1949	1950–1959	1960–1969	April 1970 or later
United States	31%	9%	16%	20%	23%
SMSA	30	9	18	21	22
Central city	42	10	16	17	15
Balance	21	9	19	24	27
Outside SMSA	33	9	14	19	25
Northeast	50	8	14	16	12
Midwest	39	8	15	18	19
South	19	11	17	23	30
West	19	10	19	23	29

NOTE: 1970 SMSA definitions are used here.
SOURCE: Annual Housing Survey, pt. A.

TABLE 3.5

Condition of Occupied Housing Units, 1980

Condition	United States	SMSA	Central City	Balance	Non-SMSA	NE	Midwest	South	West
Some or all Wiring Exposed	3%	3%	NA	NA	4%	3%	3%	3%	3%
Signs of Water Leakage in Roof	6	6	NA	NA	8	6	7	7	6
Open Cracks or Holes in Wall[1]	6	6	8	4	5	7	5	6	4
Broken Plaster[1]	4	4	5	2	3	5	4	3	2
Peeling Paint on Interior Walls[1]	4	4	7	3	4	6	4	4	3
Holes in Floor[1]	2	2	3	1	2	2	1	3	1
Telephone	92	93	90	94	90	93	94	89	92
Air Conditioning	57	59	55	61	55	46	60	77	34
Central system	26	28	23	32	23	8	27	42	20
Public Sewer[2]	73	92	99	86	67	76	75	65	83
Basement	46	50	NA	NA	39	84	70	18	21
Signs of Mice or Rats	11	10	NA	NA	14	10	10	14	9

NOTE: NA = not available.

[1]Generally rental housing units, which are more than twice as likely as owned units to exhibit this problem.

[2]Percentage of all year-round units.

SOURCE: Annual Housing Survey, pts. A and E.

suburban and exurban portions of SMSAs. Among the census regions only the South is conspicuously low, with 89 percent of housing units served by telephone.

Air conditioning is available in 57 percent of occupied housing units, but this share varies sharply among census regions—from 77 percent in the South to 34 percent in the West. Newer housing is more likely to feature central air conditioning. Older, high-density, and rental housing that is harder to retrofit with new central systems relies on window units. Thus, central systems are relatively uncommon in the Northeast.

Over one fourth of U.S. housing units are not served by public sewers. Service is highest in central cities of SMSAs (99 percent) and in SMSAs generally (92 percent). Service is lowest outside SMSAs (67 percent) and falls to 65 percent throughout the South.

Another housing feature that varies widely by region is the presence of basements beneath the housing units. An average of 46 percent of occupied housing units have basements. In the colder areas of the Northeast (84 percent have basements) and Midwest (70 percent) where construction costs are higher than other regions and central heating is customary, the basements can provide additional low-cost living space plus space for storing bulky heating equipment and

fuel—usually oil and coal for houses built before World War II. In urban locations where land prices are high, basements can add living space without proportional increases in construction costs.

If houses are well constructed and carefully maintained inside and out and public garbage disposal and sanitation programs work effectively, problems with vermin can be minimized. Nationwide there is evidence of mice and rats in 11 percent of occupied housing units. Metropolitan areas reveal fewer signs of these rodents than do nonmetro areas. The housing in the West has the lowest proportion (9 percent), while the South has the highest (14 percent).

Structure Size, Rooms, and Facilities

In 1960 renter-occupied housing units were smaller than owned units: 65 percent of renter-occupied units had 1 to 4 rooms, and 77 percent of owner-occupied units had 5 rooms or more. In the 20 years that followed, the renter-occupied mix of housing units by type remained the same, but the share of small owner-occupied units dropped from 23 to 16 percent (Table 3.6).

Well over 90 percent of owner-occupied units have been in sin-

TABLE 3.6

Rooms in Housing Unit and Types of Structure, 1960–1980

	1960		1980	
	Owner-Occupied	Renter-Occupied	Owner-Occupied	Renter-Occupied
Rooms in Unit				
1–2		14%	1%	12%
3–4	23%	51	15	53
5	29	19	25	19
6	26	10	26	10
7 or more	22	6	33	6
Units in Structure				
1	94	48	93	31
2–4		25	4	24
5–9	6	9	3	45
10 or more		18		

		In Urbanized Areas	
		Central Cities	Urban Fringe
Year-Round Units (in millions)	86.8		
Structures with four			
or more stories	4.4	3.3	1.0
With elevators	3.3	2.4	.8

SOURCES: U.S. Bureau of the Census, 1980 Census of Housing, vol. 1, *Characteristics of Housing Units*, table 80; *Statistical Abstract of the United States, 1984*, table 1346, p. 753.

gle-unit structures. Between 1960 and 1980 the share of renter-occupied units that were single-unit structures dropped from 48 to 31 percent, while the share of all rental units that were found in structures of 5 units or more rose from 27 to 45 percent, a consequence no doubt of the high volume of apartment building construction in the 1960s and 1970s.

In 1980, 4.4 million housing units were in structures with four stories or more. Almost all of these units (4.3 million) were in urbanized areas. There were 34,000 units in tall structures in rural areas, and 117,000 in urban places that had populations under 10,000. Only 75 percent of the total were in structures with elevators (Table 3.6). The tall structures lacking elevators are concentrated in old districts of central cities of urbanized areas.

Kitchen Facilities, Water Supply, Heating Fuel, and Motor Vehicles

Over 97 percent of the nation's year-round housing units contain complete kitchen facilities; that is, an installed sink with piped water, a range or cook stove, and a mechanical refrigerator are all available. A water supply is available in almost 99 percent of the year-round units (Table 3.7). Public systems and private companies serve housing units in urbanized areas and other smaller concentrations. Wells are typical in some low-density suburbs and in most scattered site housing in rural areas.

The most popular house heating fuel is gas supplied by a utility company (42.7 million occupied units), followed by electricity (14.8 million) and by fuel oil or kerosene (14.7 million). Bottle, tank, and LP gas (4.5 million) and wood (2.6 million) fall far behind the major fuels. Coal and coke have almost disappeared except in a few areas close to mines where delivery is convenient.

TABLE 3.7

Kitchen Facilities, Water Supply, Heating Fuel, and Motor Vehicles at Housing Units, 1980 (in millions)

	Number of Units
Year-Round Housing Units	86.8
Complete kitchen facilities	84.6
Public water system or private company	72.5
Individual drilled or dug well	13.1
Occupied Housing Units	80.4
Heating fuel	
Utility gas	42.7
Bottle, tank, or liquid petroleum gas	4.5
Electricity	14.8
Fuel oil, kerosene, etc.	14.7
Coal or coke	.5
Wood	2.6
Other	.2
None	.5
Motor Vehicles (cars, trucks, vans)	
Available	
None	10.4
1 or 2	55.9
3 or more	14.1

SOURCE: U.S. Bureau of the Census, 1980 Census of Housing, *Detailed Housing Characteristics*, tables 81 and 82.

Over 10 million occupied housing units have no motor vehicle available for use by the household. At the other extreme, over 14 million occupied units have three or more vehicles available (Table 3.7).

The geographical distribution of the housing stock in relation to the location of employment opportunities and the availability of motor vehicles and transit services determines the patterns of journey to work. The average American householder took 22.5 minutes to go 11.1 miles to work in 1979. The average one-way commuting travel time and distance ranged from 10.8 minutes and 0.7 miles for pedestrians to 60.1 minutes and 34.2 miles for rail commuters. The distance of the typical trip to work increased slightly between 1975 and 1979, but there was no corresponding increase in average travel time. Within central cities of metropolitan areas, commuters on the average spent 23.1 minutes going 8.8 miles to their jobs. Persons outside central cities in metro areas took 24.2 minutes to go 12.6 miles to work. In nonmetropolitan areas, commuters spent 19.7 minutes going 11.3 miles to their jobs.[10]

The proportion of those who carpooled rose from 14 percent in 1974 to 17 percent in 1979. The percentages of those who drove to work alone and those who used public transportation remained unchanged at 69 percent and 6 percent, respectively. Of all U.S. householders who used public transportation to get to work in 1979, half lived in the Northeast.

Median family income for householders who used a car or truck to get to work was about $19,400 in 1979 compared with $14,000 for those who used public transportation. Male householders were more likely to drive to work alone or with a carpool than female householders. Women were more likely than men to use public transportation.[11]

Changes in the National Housing Stock

Residential construction in the United States has been highly cyclical for at least a century (Figure 3.1). It also varies by season of the year. During economic good times and periods of rapid population expansion, construction rates rise, and during economic recession and the world wars, construction levels drop sharply.

Construction Cycles

Since 1950 there have been eight separate residential building cycles, varying in length and in the amplitude of their swings from high to low and back again, but averaging 50 months in length. The last two cycles of the 1970s were the most severe since 1950: The seventh cycle began in January 1970, reached a peak in October 1972, and then declined until February 1975.The eighth cycle started in February 1975, reached a peak in June 1978, and then declined into 1982. The decline was interrupted briefly in the late spring and early summer of 1979 and again in the spring of 1980, but fell to low levels not seen since the end of World War I. By the end of 1982 it appeared that the great post–World War II building boom had ended.[12]

The yearly record of new housing units started since 1960 averaged over 1.5 million units per year, showing a high of almost 2.4 million units in 1972 and a low of just over 1 million units in 1982 (Table 3.8). Privately owned single-unit structures accounted for 77 percent of new housing starts in 1960, but this proportion dropped to a low of 54 to 55 percent during the height of the suburban apartment boom from 1969 through 1973. Publicly owned new units have never formed a large percentage of the total. A peak construction volume of 52,000 in 1961 was achieved during the post-1960 period, but the volume dropped steadily to 10,000 units in 1982 as federal housing assistance increasingly emphasized rent supplement programs for low- and moderate-income housing.

The Modifications of Existing Units

Housing units are added to the housing stock in three ways: by construction of new conventionally built housing, by production of new manufactured housing, and by conversions of existing structures (Figure 3.2). Information on the number of units supplied annually by new construction and new production is well reported and widely known. However, the extent of supply by conversion has not been well reported, and it appears that its importance has been underestimated significantly.[13] Its importance is exceptional in certain locales where conversions can account for the largest proportion of new housing units.

---

[10]U.S. Bureau of the Census, *Data User News*, March 1983, p. 7.
[11]Ibid.

[12]Resources for the Future, *Resources*, March 1982, p. 12.
[13]U.S. Department of Housing and Urban Development, Office of Policy Development and Research, *Additions to the Housing Supply by Means Other Than New Construction* (Washington, DC: U.S. Government Printing Office, 1983), p. v.

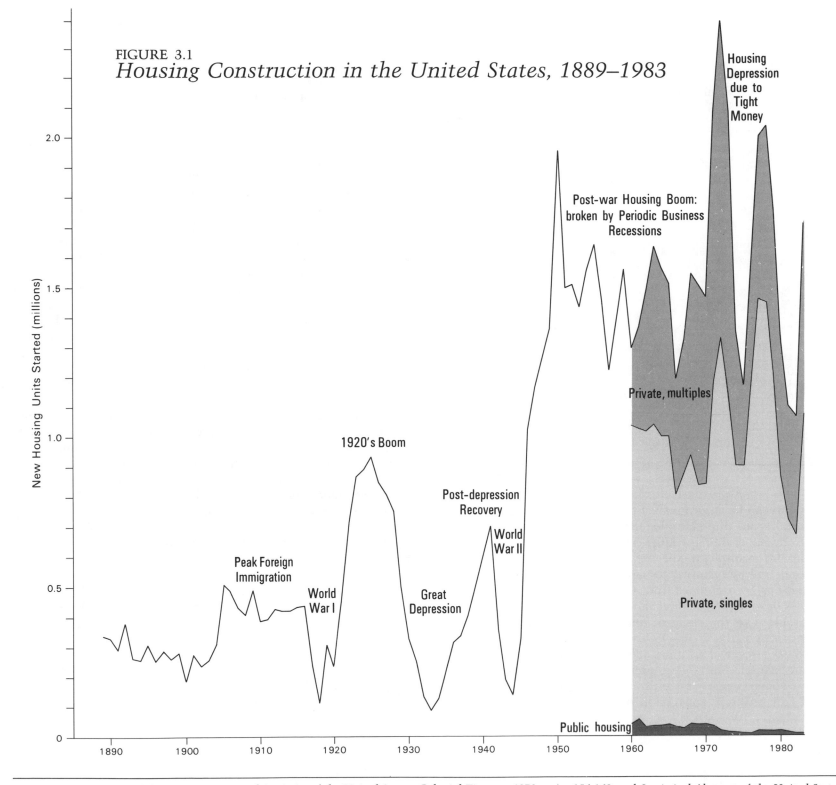

FIGURE 3.1
Housing Construction in the United States, 1889–1983

New Housing Units Started (millions)

2.0

1.5

1.0

0.5

0

Peak Foreign
Immigration

World
War I

1920's Boom

Great
Depression

Post-depression
Recovery

World
War II

Post-war Housing Boom:
broken by Periodic Business
Recessions

Housing
Depression
due to
Tight
Money

Private, multiples

Private, singles

Public housing

1890   1900   1910   1920   1930   1940   1950   1960   1970   1980

SOURCES: U.S. Bureau of the Census, *Historical Statistics of the United States: Colonial Times to 1970*, series 156-169; and *Statistical Abstract of the United States, 1985,* p. 726.

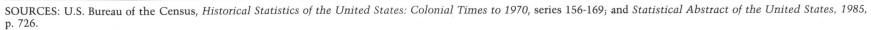

TABLE 3.8

New Housing Units Started, 1960–1982 (in thousands)

Year	Housing Units	Privately Owned Single-Unit Structures	Percentage of Total	Publicly Owned Units
1960	1,296	995	77%	44
1961	1,365	974	71	52
1962	1,492	991	66	30
1963	1,635	1,012	62	32
1964	1,561	970	62	32
1965	1,510	964	64	37
1966	1,196	779	65	31
1967	1,322	844	64	30
1968	1,545	899	58	38
1969	1,500	811	54	33
1970	1,469	813	55	35
1971	2,085	1,151	55	32
1972	2,379	1,309	55	22
1973	2,057	1,132	55	12
1974	1,353	888	66	15
1975	1,171	892	76	11
1976	1,548	1,162	75	10
1977	2,002	1,451	72	15
1978	2,036	1,433	70	16
1979	1,760	1,194	68	15
1980	1,313	852	65	20
1981	1,100	705	64	16
1982	1,072	663	62	10

SOURCE: U.S. Bureau of the Census, *Statistical Abstract of the United States, 1984*, table 1328, p. 743.

Conversion can be accomplished by turning nonresidential space into residential space (for example, an old warehouse or school into apartments), by subdividing a large housing unit into two or more smaller units (for example, modifying a one-family house into a two-unit structure); and by restoring to habitable condition an uninhabitable unit that has been dropped from the housing inventory.

In the 1950s and 1960s, conversions supplied roughly 10 percent of the units added to the stock of housing. The importance of this source increased greatly in the 1970s. Since 1973 conversions supplied almost 28 percent of all units added to the stock. Between 1973 and 1980, for example, units were added to the stock of various locations by new construction (13.1 million), moving in of houses or mobile homes (2.8 million), conversion of existing structures to more

units (.5 million), change from nonresidential use (.6 million), change from group quarters (.3 million), rehabilitation of defective housing (.1 million), and other additions (.3 million). Meanwhile, units counted in 1973 at various locations were lost by 1980 because of demolition or disaster (1.8 million), moving out of houses or mobile homes (2.2 million), consolidation or merger of existing housing to fewer units (.4 million), conversion to nonresidential use (.5 million), change to group quarters (.1 million), condemnation or damage (.6 million), and losses from other sources (under 39,000). Units removed from the inventory—both inside and outside SMSAs—tend to be old, relatively lacking in basic services, often overcrowded, and of low market value.[14]

The number of housing units supplied from conversions varied each year from fewer than 200,000 to almost 850,000 during the 1973-80 period. On average, 150,000 more units (both single and multifamily) were supplied each year by conversions than by new multifamily construction—that is, 670,000 conversions compared with 520,000 new multifamily units. Moreover, conversions appear to be countercyclical to new production; that is, additions from sources other than new production increase when new production declines and decrease when new production increases. Moreover, losses from the existing inventory tend to decrease when new production decreases, because there is more intensive conservation of land investment in existing units, so that less new construction is required. The increase in conversions and investment in existing units in the 1970s was due both to the growth in real income—which enabled households to satisfy their housing demand even during periods of low housing production levels—and to the increasing value of housing investment relative to other investment opportunities for households.[15]

The potential for future conversions seems high. Over a long period housing units have become larger while households have become smaller, so there is far more dwelling space per person. Over 60 percent of households now have two rooms or more per person. Much of this extra space can be converted into separate units as market conditions and other considerations warrant. It is probable that only a small percentage of the possible conversions of existing residential and nonresidential structures have taken place. Experience in the

[14]Donald C. Dahmann, *Housing Opportunities for Black and White Households: Three Decades of Change in Supply of Housing* (Washington, DC: U.S. Government Printing Office, 1982).

[15]Dahmann, *Housing Opportunities*, fn. 13, p. v.

FIGURE 3.2

Changes in the United States Housing Inventory, 1973-1980

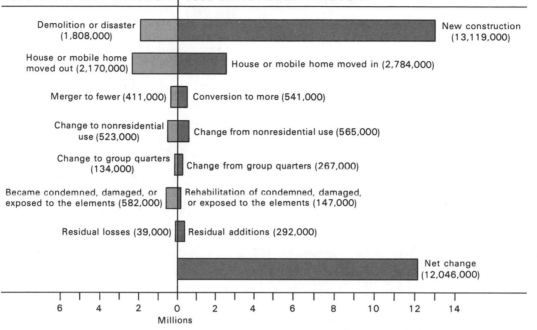

SOURCE: U.S. Bureau of the Census, *Data User News*, October 1983, p. 4, based on *Components of Inventory Change Survey*, HC 80-51-2.

1970s demonstrated that conversions are compatible with the continually improving quality of housing in the United States.[16]

New construction occurs in response to net new household formations. It also provides for replacements for accidental losses (fire,

flood, earthquake, violent weather, and so forth) and public action leading to demolition (road construction, urban renewal, and so forth). Some new construction replaces physically obsolete mobile homes, which have shorter useful lives than conventionally built residential structures. There is a continuing demand for second houses and a desire on the part of the rental industry to maintain normal vacancy rates. Finally, newly constructed housing units permit American households to upgrade their housing and living environments.[17]

The net gain from these additions and subtractions was 12 million units. Housing unit growth rates were 23 percent in the West, 21

[16]Dahmann, *Housing Opportunities*. See also Mayor's Mid-Town Action Office, *Residential Re-Use of Non-Residential Buildings in Manhattan* (New York: Department of City Planning, City of New York, 1977); David Listokin, ed., *Housing Rehabilitation: Economic, Social, and Policy Perspectives* (Piscataway, NJ: Center for Urban Policy Research, 1983), which reviews three decades of public and private efforts; and Martin Gellen, *Accessory Apartments in Single Family Housing* (Piscataway, NJ: Center for Urban Policy Research, 1985), which discusses such apartments as a genuine housing form, their potential in a period of altered housing standards, and changing family and household structures.

[17]Bernard J. Frieden and Arthur P. Solomon, *The Nation's Housing: 1975–1985* (Cambridge, MA: Joint Center for Urban Studies, 1977).

percent in the South, 11 percent in the Midwest, and 8 percent in the Northeast. Although the West had only 19 percent of the nation's housing inventory in 1980, it had 25 percent of all units built between 1973 and 1980. In contrast, the Northeast had 22 percent of the stock in 1980, but had only 11 percent of the construction between 1973 and 1980.

Owned and Rented Units

Housing losses during the 1970s were fewer than had previously been thought. Additions to the housing inventory from unconventional sources such as the conversion of school buildings, warehouses, and commercial properties to residential use were fewer than had previously been estimated.[18] During the decade of the 1970s the housing inventory expanded much faster than did the population. The inventory increased by almost 20 million units, a growth of 29 percent (Table 3.9). Owner-occupied units increased by 12 million (30 percent) and renter-occupied units by 5 million (21 percent). Meanwhile, the population grew by only 11 percent.

In 1980 almost two thirds of U.S. households were homeowners, continuing the steady growth in homeownership associated with the 1960s and 1970s, but the rate of increase slowed significantly toward the end of the 1970s (Table 3.9). Owner-occupied units in 1980 continued to outnumber renter-occupied units (52 million versus 29 million). Rental units were heavily concentrated in the most highly populated counties. In 1980 half the nation's rental units were concentrated in only 84 of the over 3,100 counties and independent cities (that is, cities not located in counties) in the United States. These 84 counties contained 34 percent of the nation's owner-occupied units and 39 percent of the population. Fully 10 percent of the nation's rental units were located in only three counties: Cook (Chicago), Los Angeles, and New York.[19]

Unit Size and Vacancy Rate

A significant indicator of the steady improvement in the quality of American housing is the growth of living space in the average unit. The median number of rooms per year-round housing unit was 5.0 in

[18]U.S. Bureau of the Census, *Components of Inventory Change Survey*, HC 80-51-2.
[19]U.S. Bureau of the Census, *Data User News*, February 1982, p. 1.

TABLE 3.9
Selected Housing Characteristics, 1960–1980 (in millions)

	1960	1970	1980
All Housing Units	58.3	68.7	88.4
Year-Round Units	56.6	67.7	86.7
Occupied	53.0	63.4	80.4
Owner-occupied	32.8	39.9	51.8
Renter-occupied	20.2	23.6	28.6
Vacant	3.6	4.3	6.3
Vacant, Seasonal, and Migratory Units	1.7	1.0	1.7

SOURCE: U.S. Bureau of the Census, *Statistical Abstract of the United States, 1984*, table 1339, p. 748.

1970. Occupied units were slightly larger than vacant units. Occupied units in 1980 had 5.2 rooms, an average between the 5.1 for urban units and 5.4 for rural units. This increase, when combined with the marked decline in average number of persons per household—from 3.11 in 1970 to 2.75 in 1980—resulted in roughly a 15 percent increase in housing space per person during the 1970s.

Nationwide the homeowner vacancy rate was 1.8 percent at census time in 1980. All states in the Northeast had vacancy rates below the national average, while all states in the West, except Hawaii, had vacancy rates above 1.8 percent.[20]

The U.S. rental vacancy rate was 7.1 percent in 1980. In the Northeast, 7 of the 9 states had vacancy rates below 7.1 percent, and in the West 12 of the 13 states had vacancy rates above the national average. States with rental vacancy rates of 11 percent or more were Alaska, Arizona, Montana, and New Mexico. States with rental vacancy rates below 5 percent were New York, New Jersey, and Connecticut.[21]

Changes in the Housing Stock, by Census Region, 1960–1980

The nationwide housing stock grew faster in the 1970s than in the 1960s (28 percent versus 18 percent), and in both decades the

[20]U.S. Bureau of the Census, *Data User News*, p. 2.
[21]U.S. Bureau of the Census, *Data User News*, p. 2. Based on U.S. Bureau of the Census, 1980 Census of Housing, *Selected Housing Characteristics by States and Counties, 1980*, HC 80-51.

TABLE 3.10

Housing Units, by Census Region, 1960–1980 (in millions)

	All Units	Year-Round Units	Occupied Units	Owner-Occupied	Percentage of All Occupied	Renter-Occupied	Percentage of All Occupied	Units Vacant Year-Round	Percentage of Year-Round Units
United States									
1960	58	57	53	33	63%	20	37%	3	6%
1970	69	68	63	40	63	24	37	4	6
1980	88	86	80	53	66	28	35	6	7
Change 1960–70	18%	19%	19%	20%		18%		25%	
Change 1970–80	28%	27%	26%	32%		17%		40%	
Northeast									
1960	15	14	14	8	57	6	43	1	4
1970	17	16	15	9	58	7	42	1	4
1980	19	18	17	10	61	7	39	1	6
Change 1960–70	12%	14%	13%	13%		12%		29%	
Change 1970–80	16%	13%	12%	18%		3%		52%	
Midwest									
1960	17	16	16	10	67	5	33	1	6
1970	19	19	18	12	68	6	32	1	6
1980	23	22	21	15	70	6	30	1	7
Change 1960–70	13%	13%	13%	14%		10%		18%	
Change 1970–80	20%	19%	19%	23%		11%		27%	
South									
1960	17	17	16	10	64	6	36	1	7
1970	21	21	19	12	65	7	35	2	8
1980	29	29	26	18	68	8	32	2	8
Change 1960–70	22%	25%	24%	25%		21%		33%	
Change 1970–80	38%	37%	37%	44%		23%		38%	
West									
1960	10	9	9	5	60	3	40	1	7
1970	12	12	11	7	59	5	41	1	6
1980	17	17	16	9	60	6	40	1	7
Change 1960–70	26%	31%	31%	30%		33%		16%	
Change 1970–80	42%	41%	40%	44%		36%		51%	

NOTE: 1970 census figures do not agree with 1970 figures in the 1970 Annual Housing Survey.

SOURCES: 1970 and 1980 data are from U.S. Bureau of the Census, Current Housing Reports, series H-150-80, *General Housing Characteristics for the U.S. and Regions: 1980,* which presents 1970 data drawn from the 1970 Census of Housing and 1980 data drawn from the 1980 Annual Housing Survey, pt. A. The 1960 data come from the 1970 Census of Housing, *Components of Inventory Change,* Final Report HC(4)-1, United States and Regions.

growth in the South and West was much faster than in the Northeast and Midwest (Table 3.10).[22] The Northeast especially fell behind the other census regions in the 1960s and 1970s in the replenishment and expansion of its housing stock. Owner-occupied housing grew at a rate slightly ahead of the total stock, while the growth of rental hous-

[22]Part of the increase was due to new construction and part to conversion of rental units. See U.S. Department of Housing and Urban Development, Office of Policy Development and Research, *The Conversion of Rental Housing to Condominiums and Cooperatives: A National Study of Scope, Courses and Impacts,* 4 vols.; and U.S. Department of Housing and Urban Development, *The Conversion of Rental Housing to Condominiums and Cooperatives: Annotated Bibliography* (Washington, DC: U.S. Government Printing Office, 1980).

ing fell behind the total growth rate in the 1970s after slightly exceeding it in the 1960s.

The rate of owner occupancy nationwide rose steadily from the start of the 1960s (63 percent) to the end of the 1970s (66 percent). The Midwest and the South had consistently higher rates of owner occupancy than the Northeast and the West, while these latter two regions maintained higher than average renter occupancy rates from 1960 to 1980.

The number of vacant year-round units was distributed fairly evenly among the four census regions, but their volume increased

TABLE 3.11

Housing Units and Type of Structure, by Region, 1960–1980 (in millions)

	Units in Structure			Mobile Homes and Trailers	Cooperatives and Condominiums
	1	2–4	5 or More		
United States					
1960	43	8	6	1	(—)
1970	47	9	10	2	NA
1980	58	11	13	4	2
Change 1960–70	8%	11%	57%	184%	
Change 1970–80	25%	20%	34%	82%	
Northeast					
1960	9	3	3	(—)	(—)
1970	9	4	4	(—)	NA
1980	10	4	4	(—)	(—)
Change 1960–70	2%	7%	28%	315%	
Change 1970–80	17%	8%	7%	39%	
Midwest					
1960	13	2	1	(—)	(—)
1970	13	3	2	(—)	NA
1980	16	3	3	1	(—)
Change 1960–70	6%	5%	59%	105%	
Change 1970–80	19%	9%	29%	43%	
South					
1960	15	1	1	(—)	(—)
1970	16	2	2	1	NA
1980	21	2	4	2	(—)
Change 1960–70	11%	23%	132%	311%	
Change 1970–80	30%	28%	73%	100%	
West					
1960	7	1	1	(—)	(—)
1970	8	1	2	(—)	NA
1980	11	2	3	1	(—)
Change 1960–70	15%	25%	70%	114%	
Change 1970–80	31%	74%	48%	111%	

NOTES: Co-op and condo totals are included in other totals; (—): under half million; rounds to zero.
SOURCES: 1970 and 1980 data are from U.S. Bureau of the Census, Current Housing Reports, series H-150-80, *General Housing Characteristics for the U.S. and Regions: 1980,* which presents 1970 data drawn from the 1970 Census of Housing and 1980 data drawn from the 1980 Annual Housing Survey, pt. A. The 1960 data come from the 1970 Census of Housing, *Components of Inventory Change,* Final Report HC(4)-1, United States and Regions.

sharply in the 1970s (40 percent growth) compared with the 1960s (25 percent growth). The percentage of year-round housing that was vacant fell between 6 and 8 percent during the two decades, but these average figures mask major variations from time to time and from place to place.

Changes in Type of Structure

About three fourths of the nation's housing units in 1960 were in single-unit structures, but that percentage dropped to 69 in 1970 and to 68 percent in 1980 as new construction increasingly favored double- and multiple-unit structures (Table 3.11). In the South and the West—the regions that grew fastest in population during the 1960s and 1970s—the rate of change in the number of units in each kind of structure stayed well above the corresponding national averages, except for mobile homes in the West in the 1960s.

In each census region the share of housing units in structures of 5 units or more rose sharply in the 1960s and again (except for the Northeast) in the 1970s. Meanwhile, the share of units in structures with 2 to 4 units dropped on the national level between 1960 and 1980, and all regions followed this pattern, except for the West in the 1970s, where the percentage rose because of exceptionally vigorous construction.

The census counted almost 1 million mobile homes in 1960, over 2 million in 1970, and almost 4 million in 1980. Among the regions absolute increases were greatest in the South in both the 1960s (+.7 million) and the 1970s (+.9 million), and the West in the 1970s (+.5 million). Relative gains in the Northeast in the 1960s were impressive, mainly because the 1960 base was so small (58,000 units). Condominium and cooperative units were relatively unimportant in almost all areas before 1970. By 1980 the approximately 2 million units were distributed fairly evenly among the four regions, where they constituted between 1 and 3 percent of the year-round units.

Changes in Unit Size

American housing units increased in size on the average each year until 1980 when the trend apparently reversed. The median number of rooms per housing unit was 4.9 in 1960, 5.0 in 1970, and 5.1 in 1980 (Table 3.12). About two thirds of the housing stock has 4 to 6 rooms, a proportion that is fairly stable through time and among

TABLE 3.12
Size of Housing Units, by Region, 1960–1980

	Rooms in Unit			Median Rooms
	1–3	4–6	7 or More	
United States				
1960	19%	65%	15%	4.9
1970	16	66	18	5.0
1980	15	63	22	5.1
Northeast				
1960	17	63	20	5.1
1970	18	60	22	5.2
1980	17	58	25	5.2
Midwest				
1960	16	66	18	5.0
1970	13	68	19	5.1
1980	12	64	24	5.3
South				
1960	19	68	12	4.7
1970	15	70	15	4.9
1980				
West				
1960	27	63	10	4.5
1970	21	64	15	4.8
1980	19	62	19	4.9

SOURCES: 1970 and 1980 data are from U.S. Bureau of the Census, Current Housing Reports, series H-150-80, *General Housing Characteristics for the U.S. and Regions: 1980*, which presents 1970 data drawn from the 1970 Census of Housing and 1980 data drawn from the 1980 Annual Housing Survey, pt. A. The 1960 data come from the 1970 Census of Housing, *Components of Inventory Change*, Final Report HC(4)-1, United States and Regions.

the regions of the country. Smaller units of 1 to 3 rooms have diminished as a proportion of the total, from 19 to 15 percent, although their absolute number rose from 11 million in 1960 to 13 million in 1980. Large units with 7 rooms or more rose steadily as a share of the total, from 15 percent in 1960 (9 million units) to about 22 percent in 1980 (19 million units).

The average floor area of new, privately owned single-family houses completed in 1970 was 1,500 square feet (median: 1,385); in 1980, 1,740 square feet (median: 1,595); but in the recession year 1982, 1,710 square feet (median: 1,520).[23]

[23]U.S. Bureau of the Census, *Statistical Abstract of the United States, 1984*, p. 744.

Housing units in the Northeast and the Midwest have been larger on the average than those in the West and South. The growth of large units of 7 rooms or more averaged 32 percent nationwide in the 1960s and 56 percent in the 1970s. Growth rates of large units were greatest in the South (50 percent in the 1960s and 76 percent in the 1970s) and the West (85 percent and 81 percent). Smaller units of 1 to 3 rooms actually declined by over 100,000 units nationwide during the 1960s, due in large part to urban highway construction, slum clearance, and redevelopment activity. In the 1970s small units increased in number by a modest 16 percent nationwide, with regional extremes marked by 5 percent in the Midwest and 28 percent in the West.

Plumbing, Telephones, and Air Conditioning

Certain household conveniences and appliances are evidence of overall housing quality and access to the local community. Each has a relationship to health and comfort (plumbing facilities, air conditioning), access to information (telephone, television), or employment and services (automobile). Complete plumbing facilities for the exclusive use of the occupants of a housing unit have been a major index of housing quality for over four decades. New housing and urban housing have traditionally been furnished with complete plumbing for private use at higher rates than old housing and rural housing. In 1960, 85 percent of the occupied units in the United States contained complete and private plumbing facilities (Table 3.13). The Northeast (93 percent) and the West (94 percent) enjoyed much higher rates, but the South, with only 73 percent, pulled down the national average. Since 1960 all regions have improved to the point where there is little variation among the regional averages of 96 to 99 percent. In 1960 the South had over 3 million units with private plumbing incomplete or lacking altogether; by 1980 the total of deficient units had dropped below 1 million, while a 20-year construction boom had increased the total number of year-round units in the South from 17 million to 29 million.

In 1960 only two thirds of the occupied housing units in the South had telephones (Table 3.13). In other regions over 80 percent had telephones, and the national average stood at 78 percent. Since 1960 the regional disparities have mostly been eliminated. The 1980 national average of 92 percent was little different from the regional averages, which varied between 89 and 94 percent.

There are dramatic differences in the availability of air condition-

TABLE 3.13
Housing Equipment, by Region, 1960–1980

	Complete Plumbing Within Unit	Telephone	Air Conditioning	Central Air Conditioning
United States				
1960	85%	78%	12%	2%
1970	94	87	37	11
1980	98	92	57	26
Northeast				
1960	93	84	10	1
1970	97	90	30	4
1980	98	93	46	8
Midwest				
1960	86	84	11	2
1970	96	91	34	9
1980	98	94	60	27
South				
1960	73	66	18	3
1970	90	81	52	18
1980	96	89	77	42
West				
1960	94	81	9	3
1970	98	89	24	10
1980	99	92	34	20

SOURCES: U.S. Bureau of the Census, *Components of Inventory Change, 1970* (1960 plumbing data), from 1960 Census of Housing, Final Report HC(1)-1, States and Small Areas (1963), pp. 1-28, 29 (1960 telephone and air conditioning data); *Annual Housing Survey*, 1980 (1970 and 1980 data).

ing from place to place and through time. In 1960 only 12 percent of the occupied housing units nationwide had air conditioning, and only 2 percent had central air conditioning. By 1980 the percentage of air conditioned housing units had risen to 57 percent, and 26 percent of the units had central air conditioning. The South started with a higher percentage in 1960 (18 percent of units air conditioned) and rose higher than the other regions by 1980 (77 percent). The rise is due to the steady improvement in household incomes, steady rates of new construction, and the fact that the South suffers the highest levels of temperature with humidity of any of the census regions. Central air conditioning is least common in the Northeast, where new housing construction has been most limited in the 1960s and 1970s compared with the other regions and where summer temperatures generally are more tolerable than in other regions.

Changes in the Housing Stock by Location, 1960–1980

During the 1960s and 1970s, approximately two thirds of the national housing stock was located inside SMSAs (using constant 1970 SMSA definitions), but important shifts were underway that would redistribute population from inside SMSAs to outside, and from central cities of SMSAs outward to the suburbs and the balance of the metropolitan areas. During the 1960s the housing stock inside metropolitan areas rose 21 percent while the stock outside rose only 12

percent. But in the 1970s the lead reversed when metropolitan area housing stocks rose 26 percent while nonmetropolitan stock rose 33 percent (Table 3.14). In the 1960s renter- and owner-occupied units grew at about the same rate inside SMSAs, but outside SMSAs owner-occupied units grew at a rate for the decade over twice that of rental units (15 versus 6 percent). In the 1970s the growth of owner-occupied units far outpaced the growth of renter-occupied units inside (29 versus 18 percent) as well as outside metropolitan areas (37 versus 14 percent) (Table 3.14). There was a significant relative increase in the number of vacant units outside SMSAs in the 1960s (57 percent) and

TABLE 3.14

Housing Units, by Type of Location, 1960–1980 (in millions)

| | | | | Year-Round Housing Units | | | | | |
| | | | Occupied | | | | | Vacant | |
	All Units	Total	Owner-Occupied	Percentage	Renter-Occupied	Percentage	Number	Percentage of Total
Inside SMSAs								
1960	38.4	37.9	21	60%	14	40%	2	6%
1970	46.3	46.1	26	59	18	41	2	5
1980	58.5	58.0	34	62	21	39	3	6
Change 1960–70	21%	22%	22%		23%		5%	
Change 1970–80	26%	26%	29%		18%		55%	
Central City								
1960	20.9	20.8	10	49%	10	51%	1	5%
1970	22.6	22.6	10	48	11	52	1	5
1980	25.5	25.5	12	50	12	50	2	9
Change 1960–70	8%	9%	7%		11%		6%	
Change 1970–80	13%	13%	15%		8%		87%	
Balance of SMSA								
1960	17.5	17.1	12	72%	4	28%	1	6%
1970	23.7	23.5	16	70	7	30	1	4
1980	33.0	32.5	22	71	9	29	2	6
Change 1960–70	35%	37%	35%		49%		4%	
Change 1970–80	39%	38%	38%		34%		76%	
Outside SMSAs								
1960	20.0	18.8	12	69%	5	31%	1	7%
1970	22.4	21.6	14	70	6	30	2	9
1980	29.7	28.0	19	74	7	26	3	9
Change 1960–70	12%	15%	15%		6		57%	
Change 1970–80	33%	30%	37%		14%		24%	

NOTE: 1970 SMSA definitions are used here.

SOURCES: U.S. Bureau of the Census, *Components of Inventory Change, 1970*, pp. 1-17–1-21; 1980 Annual Housing Survey, pt A.

inside metropolitan areas in the 1970s (55 percent), although the absolute number of units involved is not great.

Inside the SMSAs, the housing stock rose slowly in the central cities during both decades (8 percent in the 1960s and 13 percent in the 1970s). Outside the central cities in the suburbs and exurban areas beyond, where developable land was cheaper and effective demand for new housing was greater, the housing stock rose fast—35 percent in the 1960s and 39 percent in the 1970s. Throughout the SMSAs in the 1960s renter-occupied units increased in number more rapidly than owner-occupied units. In the 1970s the growth in owner-occupied units took the lead at all locations (Table 3.14). In the 1960s the leading edge of the post–World War II baby boom was having effects nationwide as newly formed households began entering the rental portion of the housing market in significant numbers. By the 1970s they were making their presence felt in a disproportionate way in the owner-occupied portion of the market.

Changes in Type of Structure

During the 1960s and 1970s, the 4.6 million housing units added to SMSA housing stocks had minor effects on the composition of the central city stock in terms of structure types. About half of the central city stock was in single units, with the share in structures of 5 units or more rising from 23 percent in 1960 to 29 percent in 1980 (Table 3.15). Mobile homes—excluded from many cities and suburbs—accounted for only 1 percent of the central city housing stock during this period.[24] Condominium and cooperative units formed 2 percent of central city units, following rapid growth in the 1970s, although comparisons with 1970 and 1960 are difficult.

In the suburban and exurban areas of the nation's SMSAs, the rapid expansion of multiple-unit structures compared with the construction of singles led to a sharp drop in their share of singles from 82 percent in 1960 to 72 percent in 1980, while the share of units in multiples (5 units or more) rose from 6 to 14 percent. Mobile homes doubled from 2 to 4 percent, and condominiums and cooperatives reached 3 percent in 1980, higher than the 2 percent rate in central cities (Table 3.15).

Outside SMSAs, single-unit housing is more common than within, but the proportion dropped from 89 percent in 1960 and 82

[24]Daniel R. Mandelker and Roger Montgomery, eds., *Housing in America: Problems and Perspectives* (Indianapolis: Bobbs-Merrill, 1973), pp. 135–38.

TABLE 3.15
Housing Units and Type of Structure, by Type of Location, 1960–1980

	Units in Structure			Mobile Homes and Trailers	Cooperatives and Condominiums
	1	2–4	5 or More		
Inside SMSAs					
1960	67%	17%	15%	1%	NA
1970	63	16	19	2	NA
1980	62	15	20	3	2
Central City					
1960	54	22	23	1	NA
1970	51	21	28	1	NA
1980	50	21	29	1	2
Balance of SMSA					
1960	82	11	6	2	NA
1970	75	10	12	3	NA
1980	72	10	14	4	3
Outside SMSAs					
1960	89	7	3	2	NA
1970	82	8	4	5	NA
1980	79	8	5	8	(-)

NOTES: Coop and condo totals are included in other totals; 1970 SMSA definitions are used here; (-): under .5 percent; rounds to zero.
SOURCES: U.S. Bureau of the Census, *Components of Inventory Change, 1970*, pp. 1-17–1-21; 1980 Annual Housing Survey, pt. A.

percent in 1970 to 79 percent in 1980. Meanwhile, mobile homes—the lowest-cost new housing option—jumped from only 2 percent of the non-SMSA stock in 1960 to 8 percent in 1980. Condominiums and cooperatives were unimportant outside SMSAs, numbering only 100,000 in 1980, or under .5 percent of the non-SMSA total.

Changes in Unit Size

As the quality of the U.S. housing stock improved, the average housing unit increased in median number of rooms—from 4.9 in 1960 and 5.0 in 1970 to 5.1 in 1980 (Table 3.16). About two thirds of the nation's housing stock has between 4 and 6 rooms. The share with 1 to 3 rooms has steadily dropped, although the rate of decline seems to have slowed, while the share with 7 rooms or more has risen briskly, reaching 22 percent both inside and outside SMSAs in 1980.

TABLE 3.16
Size of Housing Units, by Type of Location, 1960–1980

	1–3	4–6	7 or More	Median Rooms
Inside SMSAs				
1960	21%	65%	14%	4.9
1970	18	65	17	5.0
1980	17	62	22	5.1
Central City				
1960	26	62	11	4.6
1970	24	63	13	4.7
1980	23	61	15	4.8
Balance of SMSA				
1960	14	68	18	5.1
1970	12	66	22	5.3
1980	11	62	27	5.4
Outside SMSAs				
1960	16	66	18	4.9
1970	13	69	18	5.1
1980	11	67	22	5.2

Rooms in Unit header spans 1–3, 4–6, 7 or More.

SOURCES: U.S. Bureau of the Census, *Components of Inventory Change, 1970; 1980;* and 1960 Census of Housing, Final Report HC(1)-1, States and Small Areas, U.S. Summary.

TABLE 3.17
Housing Equipment by Type of Location, 1960–1980

	Complete Plumbing Within Unit	Telephone	Air Conditioning	Central Air Conditioning
Inside SMSAs				
1960	92%	83%	14%	2%
1970	98	90	40	12
1980	99	93	59	28
Central City				
1960	91	81	14	2
1970	97	87	39	11
1980	99	90	55	23
Balance of SMSA				
1960	93	86	14	2
1970	97	92	40	13
1980	99	94	61	32
Outside SMSAs				
1960	72	70	10	1
1970	89	83	30	8
1980	96	90	55	23

NOTE: 1960 data are based on 1960 SMSA definitions; other data are based on 1970 SMSA definitions.
SOURCES: U.S. Bureau of the Census, *Components of Inventory Change, 1970; 1980;* and 1960 Census of Housing, Final Report HC(1)-1, States and Small Areas, U.S. Summary.

Central city housing is smaller on the average than housing units in the suburbs and beyond, but the averages have been rising in both settings. Housing units outside SMSAs tend to be larger than inside.

Plumbing, Telephones, and Air Conditioning

Complete and exclusive plumbing became almost universal within SMSAs between 1960 and 1980 (Table 3.17). Central cities with their generally older housing stock were somewhat behind the suburban and exurban areas in 1960 in the share of units fully equipped, but the gap was closed during the 1960s and 1970s, as obsolete and inferior units were removed and replaced and as sound units were remodeled to bring their plumbing up to contemporary standards. In areas outside the SMSAs in 1960 over one quarter of the housing units had incomplete plumbing or none at all, but rapid improvements in nonmetropolitan areas—abandonment of the worst units, improvement of others, and steady rates of new construction

of fully equipped units—raised the proportion of units with complete plumbing to 96 percent by 1980.

Telephone availability has also improved steadily. The record inside the SMSAs is better than outside, and the suburban and exurban portions of the SMSAs stayed ahead of the central cities—but all areas improved after 1960. By 1980, between 90 and 94 percent of the occupied housing units had telephone service (Table 3.17).

Inside SMSAs, 59 percent of the households in 1980 reported air conditioning within their housing units up from 14 percent in 1960 (Table 3.17). Almost half of the 1980 SMSA units with air conditioning had central air conditioning systems—a reflection of the popularity of this feature in newly built housing and of the share of new housing in the 1960s and 1970s that has been built in warm parts of the United States. Inside or outside SMSAs air conditioning and central air conditioning systems seem about equally popular. Central air conditioning is somewhat more common in suburban and exurban portions of the SMSAs (32 percent in 1980) than in their central city portions (23 percent in 1980).

Summary

In 1980 over two thirds of the American housing stock was in single-unit structures. The quality of the housing stock—measured in terms of completeness of plumbing facilities, age of structure, structural quality, and equipment available—had improved in all major respects during the 1970s.

At census time in 1980, urban housing generally had better plumbing than rural housing, but the condition of occupied units did not differ much by location or by census region. The South and the West received a disproportionate share of new construction in the 1970s, thereby pulling up the average-quality measures in areas that gained the most new housing. Meanwhile, nonmetropolitan housing stocks in the 1970s grew faster than metro stocks.

The average number of rooms per unit rose during the 1960s and 1970s. Owner-occupied units expanded at a faster relative rate than rental units. Thus, despite recessions, migrations, disrupted financial markets, and unusual demographic trends during the decades, housing stock continued to expand and generally to improve in quality at all locations and in all regions.

4

THE SOURCES OF FLUX IN HOUSING DEMAND AND USE

A<small>T CENSUS</small> time in April 1980, when almost two thirds of American households owned their own housing, the nation appeared to be entering an era that would see an overhauling of the financial apparatus that had helped shape its social and political fabric since the Great Depression of the 1930s.[1] In the half century following 1930 the United States moved from a nation of renters to a nation of owners, living in housing envied by the world. But the share of households that owned their homes seemed to peak around 1980 as a result of an implicit public policy shift that raised the cost of housing and increasingly diverted American savings to nonhousing expenditures and investments.[2]

The continuous post–World War II housing boom abruptly ended in 1978–79, bringing to a close the residential real estate speculation and inflation excesses of the preceding decade. Housing lost its sheltered credit market, dimming the nation's chances for sustaining historically high ownership rates. But more may have been lost to the nation than the chance to produce and consume relatively inexpensive high-quality housing. Since the early Depression years widespread home ownership has been promoted and defended in the United States as an essential—the tangible evidence of belonging to and succeeding in the American socioeconomic system. President Herbert Hoover established a planning committee on housing in 1931, and in his charge to the committee he stressed that "nothing contributes more to happiness or sound social stability than . . . homes." He earlier had announced his intention to recommend to Congress the creation of ". . . a system of home loan discount banks." The Home Owners' Loan Act passed in 1933, creating the Federal Home Loan Bank System and setting in motion a savings and residential investment framework that transformed the United States from a nation of renters to a nation of homeowners.[3]

Changes in the financial frameworks for housing have the effect of increasing the relative price of housing. This adjustment upward in relative price levels changes the amount of effective demand for

[1]George Sternlieb and James W. Hughes, *The Evaluation of Housing and Its Social Compact* (Washington, DC: Urban Land, 1982), pp. 17–20.

[2]In the most fundamental sense, it is the existence of the household that underlies the demand for shelter, and it is the family unit that forms the typical household. See Earl W. Morris and Mary Winter, *Housing, Family, and Society* (New York: Wiley, 1978). For a general review of the forces that affected housing demand in the 1970s, see David L. Birch, *America's Housing Needs: 1970–1980* (Cambridge, MA: MIT and Harvard University Press, 1973); and Frank de Leeuw, "The Demand for Housing: A Review of Cross-Section Evidence," *Review of Economics and Statistics* 53 (1971): 1–10.

[3]Sternlieb and Hughes, *The Evaluation of Housing*, p. 17.

owned housing. Other sources of flux in housing demand include trends in birth and deaths, domestic migration, foreign immigration, changing household composition, trends in the value of housing in regional markets and local submarkets, opportunities for mortgage finance, changing fashions and outlooks, and governmental housing assistance programs. Taken together, these forces underlie demand and patterns of housing use.[4]

Population Change and Housing Demand

Population increase in the United States is the principal engine that drives the demand for additional housing units. Between 1920 and 1950 the nation added almost 45 million people, and in the next 30 years it added over 75 million more. Besides the expansions in raw numbers, the population changed its age composition as birthrates fluctuated and life expectancy rose. Living styles changed as average household sizes dropped. Obsolete houses had to be replaced, adding to the demand for new units. And people relocated, from central city to suburbs, from rural to metro areas and back again, and from one region of the country to another. Since it is difficult to move most housing units, houses left behind often must be replaced at migration destinations, adding still more demand for new units.

Changes in the Resident Population, 1920–1980

The United States is the fourth largest country in the world (after China, India, and the USSR) in terms of population, with over 227 million persons counted in the 1980 census (Table 4.1). Much is made of the post–World War II baby boom that contributed to the 48 million persons added to the U.S. population between 1940 and 1960—

[4]There are numerous sources of variation in the structure of demand from time to time and from place to place. See Edgar Olsen, "A Competitive Theory of the Housing Market," *American Economic Review* 59 (1969): 612–22; Kenneth T. Rosen, *Seasonal Cycles in the Housing Market: Patterns, Costs, and Policies* (Cambridge, MA: MIT Press, 1979); John C. Weicher, Lorene Yap, and Mary S. Jones, *Metropolitan Housing Needs for the 1980s* (Washington, DC: Urban Institute Press, 1982); Charles L. Senn and David Yentis, "Defining and Measuring the National Housing Needs," *American Journal of Public Health*, vol. 61 (September 1971): 2341–47; Charles F. Manski, *The Implication of Demand Instability for the Behavior of Firms: The Case of Residential Construction*, Working Paper no. 17 (Cambridge, MA: Joint Center for Urban Studies, 1973); and Richard L. Florida, ed., *Housing and the New Financial Markets* (Piscataway, NJ: Center for Urban Policy Research, 1985).

TABLE 4.1
Population and Population Change, 1920–1980
(in millions)

Year	Population	Decade	Change
1920	106.5		
1930	123.1	1920–30	15.6%
1940	132.0	1930–40	7.2
1950	151.2	1940–50	14.6
1960	180.0	1950–60	19.0
1970	203.8	1960–70	13.2
1980	227.2	1970–80	11.5

SOURCE: U.S. Bureau of the Census, *Statistical Abstract of the United States, 1982*, p. 12.

an increase similar to the entire population of France, Great Britain, or Italy. But the increase of another 47 million between 1960 and 1980 was equally remarkable—and it meant that additional housing units were needed to accommodate the growth.

The rates of population expansion were high in the good times of the 1920s and low in the Depression years of the 1930s. Postwar immigration and the baby boom (1947–64) caused expansion rates to double in the 1940s compared with the Depression decade. After the peak decade of the 1950s produced a 19 percent population expansion, rates of growth trailed off. But since the United States is such an enormous country, even modest rates of growth in population mean big requirements for additions to the housing stock.

Rates of Birth and Death

American population totals change because of births, deaths, emigration, and foreign immigration. Most of the adjustment is due to natural change—the difference between births and deaths—and most of the variation in natural increase is due to fluctuations in births from decade to decade (Table 4.2).

Births numbered under 3 million per year before World War II, but then rose sharply after the war to an all-time high of about 4.3 million per year at the peak of the baby boom (1959–62). When persons born after World War II reached the family formation and childbearing ages, they produced children of their own in large numbers. This "echo boom" kept the number of births relatively high from the

TABLE 4.2

Births and Deaths in the United States, Selected Years, 1920–1980 (in thousands)

Year	Live Births	Births per 1,000 Population	Deaths	Deaths Per 1,000 Population	Natural Increase
1920	2,950	27.7	1,118	13.0	1,832
1930	2,618	21.3	1,327	11.3	1,291
1940	2,559	19.4	1,417	10.8	1,142
1950	3,632	24.1	1,452	9.6	2,180
1960	4,258	23.7	1,712	9.5	2,546
1965	3,760	19.4	1,828	9.4	1,932
1970	3,731	18.4	1,921	9.5	1,810
1975	3,144	14.8	1,893	8.9	1,251
1980	3,598	16.2	1,986	8.9	1,612

NOTES: 1920 and 1930 data exclude states that lack death registration. Natural increase is computed.

SOURCE: U.S. Bureau of the Census, *Statistical Abstract of the United States, 1982*, p. 60.

TABLE 4.3

Foreign Immigration and Natural Increase, Selected Years, 1920–1980 (in thousands)

Year	Natural Increase	Foreign Immigration	Immigration as a Percentage of Natural Increase
1920	1,832	430	23%
1930	1,291	242	19
1940	1,142	71	6
1950	2,180	249	11
1960	2,546	265	10
1965	1,932	297	15
1970	1,810	373	21
1975	1,251	386	31
1980	1,612	531	33

NOTE: 1920 and 1930 data exclude states that lack death registration.

SOURCES: U.S. Bureau of the Census, *Statistical Abstract of the United States, 1982*, p. 60; *1981*, p. 84; *Historical Statistics of the United States: Colonial Times to 1970*, p. 105; *Immigration and Naturalization Service Yearbook, 1980*, p. 6.

late 1960s and through the 1970s, producing steady pressure on the demand for additional housing units.

Just under 2 million persons die each year in the United States (Table 4.2). Both the number of deaths per year and the death rate per 1,000 population are fairly stable. On the average in recent years there are about 6 deaths for every 10 births. The difference yields a natural increase of 1.5 million to 2.5 million persons each year. With average household size of 2 to 3 persons, a natural population increase of this magnitude implies eventual additional housing requirements each year of half a million to over 1 million units.

Foreign Immigration and New Housing Demand

Foreign immigration has risen fast in recent years—in absolute volume and in the share of total population increase (and new housing demand) that it represents. The years immediately following World War I were important immigration years, until restrictive federal immigration laws curtailed the flow to a trickle. Depression and war cut into the flows still further so that foreign immigration was almost negligible compared with the population added by natural increase (Table 4.3).

In the 1960s, immigration began increasing steadily in volume, and as a proportion of U.S. population increase. In 1950 immigration—mainly from Europe—accounted for only about 10 percent of the nation's population increase that year. By 1980 legal immigration—largely from Pacific Basin and Caribbean origins—was over 25 percent of that year's increase. Estimates of the volume of illegal immigration place the flow at 50 to 100 percent of the legal immigration, which means that in recent years foreign immigration may account for as much as 33 to 40 percent of the nation's total population increase. In the states that are closest to the principal sources of recent immigrants—California, Arizona, Texas, and Florida—the effects of immigration on housing demand are especially vivid.

The Redistribution of Population and Households

Births, deaths, and foreign immigration combine with domestic migration to bring about relative shifts in population that redistribute housing demand among the various regions of the United States. Since 1950 the states of the Northeast and Midwest regions have lost part of their share, and most parts of the South and West have steadily gained (Table 4.4).

TABLE 4.4

*Relative Population Shifts, 1950–1980, and Absolute Change
in Number of Households, 1970–1980 (in thousands)*

	Percentage of U.S. Population				Net New Households to be Housed, 1970–1980
	1950	1960	1970	1980	
Northeast					
New England	6.2%	5.9%	5.8%	5.5%	717
Middle Atlantic	19.9	19.1	18.3	16.2	1,272
Midwest					
East North Central	20.1	20.2	19.8	18.4	2,268
West North Central	9.3	8.6	8.0	7.6	1,052
South					
South Atlantic	14.0	14.5	15.1	16.3	3,716
East South Central	7.6	6.7	6.3	6.5	1,182
West South Central	9.6	9.5	9.5	10.5	2,322
West					
Mountain	3.4	3.8	4.1	5.0	1,467
Pacific	10.0	11.8	13.1	14.0	2,933
Total	100%	100%	100%	100%	16,927

SOURCE: U.S. Bureau of the Census, *Statistical Abstract of the United States, 1981*, pp. 10 and 44.

About 17 million net new households were created in the United States in the 1970s (Table 4.4), and all of them needed a place to live. Almost 7 net new American households in 10 were added to the South and West regions in the 1970s, putting severe pressure on the existing housing stock, on the inventory of vacancies, and on the house-building industry in those areas. Surplus housing in slow growth or declining states in the Northeast and Midwest—for example, New York and Rhode Island actually lost population in the 1970s—cannot satisfy housing demand added in other parts of the country.

Declines in Persons per Household and Added Housing Demand

Population changes that come about from births, deaths, and migration direct upward or downward effects on local housing demand. But the ways that local populations divide into household units affect housing demand as well. A hundred persons living alone will require a hundred housing units. The same hundred living in households of 2 to 4 persons will need only 25 to 50 units. The price of housing and its availability exert some influence on household formation. Young people may delay leaving their parents' houses and forming their own households if suitable housing is in short supply or too expensive. Single persons may prefer the privacy and freedom that come from living alone, but may decide to share the rent with a roommate when privacy carries too high a price.

Elderly couples and elderly single persons usually choose to live by themselves as long as they are physically and financially able. In recent years general improvements in the health of the elderly and their superior wealth and income positions compared with earlier decades have made it possible for an increased proportion of elderly couples and singles to retain the independence they prefer.

Still other sources of decline in the average size of households in recent years are delays in childbearing and continued reductions in the average family size. These declines in average household size mean that the effective demand for additional housing units rose faster than the rate of population increase in the nation at large and in the various regional submarkets where demand and supply come together.

Between 1970 and 1980, the average size of household dropped from 3.11 to 2.75 persons, a decline of almost 12 percent. Statewide averages vary from highs in Hawaii (3.15), where housing is expensive, and Utah (3.20), where large families are favored by many residents, to lows in the District of Columbia (2.39), with its large numbers of single persons and childless couples, and Florida (2.55), where retired populations bring down the average for the state. All states participated in the decline in average household size. The biggest drop was Alaska's 16.8 percent decline from 3.52 to 2.93. The smallest was California's drop from an already low 2.95 in 1970 to 2.68 in 1980, a reduction of 9.2 percent.

Changing Population Age Structure and the Demand for Housing

After formation, households pass through a series of stages during their life cycle. Young childless couples move to larger and better appointed units when their income rises and becomes more secure. If children arrive, families typically want more interior living area, more rooms, and the lower housing densities that make it easier for children to play safely out of doors. Teenage and older children introduce additional needs and wants for housing space and facilities that households will try to provide if income and wealth positions permit. When children leave home and parents decide that excessive housing has become an unwelcome burden, they may move to smaller quarters that are easier to maintain. Finally, as elderly persons are left alone, they may move to housing that can alleviate housekeeping chores and supply the special forms of assistance that may be needed during the final years of life.

This "conventional sequence" of stages in the household life cycle matches a more or less typical sequence of housing options that households seem to prefer at each stage of life. Inexpensive apartments are usually the first choice of the new household. Families in the middle of the childbearing and childrearing years prefer single-unit housing in neighborhoods dominated by households like themselves. Elderly persons beyond the family years usually return to rental units or condominiums to minimize the physical demands for housing maintenance and perhaps to enhance their sense of personal security.[5]

There are several reasons why the smooth movement of households through successive well-defined stages in the household life cycle fails to occur in many cases.

1. When young households enjoy exceptionally favorable economic opportunity, as they did from the late 1940s through the early 1960s, they marry younger, bear children earlier, and move quickly into the family housing market—stimulating heavy demand for new housing and the ability and willingness to pay for it.[6]

2. When young people enter the labor force at a rate that seriously exceeds the rate of retirements, as happened from the mid-1960s through the 1970s, they must compete for scarce jobs; rates of pay stay low, savings rates decline, labor is substituted for increasingly expensive capital, young people are disheartened, marriage is delayed, childbearing is postponed, and extra heavy demand is generated for apartments as young persons extend their stay in the apartment life.

3. Some persons remain single their entire life and prefer to live alone. Their housing requirements in the middle years will normally be quite different from those of childless couples or families with children.

4. Some couples never have children. They may, however, choose to live in single-unit housing in family-oriented neighborhoods, or they may favor the adults-only environment of apartments and condominiums.[7]

5. A significant number of households begin their life cycle in a conventional way, but divorce or death of one partner forces an adjustment in housing. In the case of divorce, one household becomes two households needing housing, and the income per household usually drops sharply. The single parent (usually the mother) left alone with childrearing responsibilities—a large group and expanding in the 1970s—has a significant need for good-quality, family-oriented housing, which in most housing market areas is expensive.

6. Major extensions of life expectancy in recent decades, coupled with sharp rises in the income and wealth positions of the elderly, have dramatically expanded the demand for specialized housing for them—publicly assisted housing for the elderly, retirement communities, and nursing homes—in ad-

[5]To the degree that residential satisfaction for a household depends on matching (a) the structure of the household and (b) its tastes and preferences with (c) the features of the housing unit it occupies and (d) the characteristics of the neighborhood where the housing unit is located, dissatisfaction can arise from changes in any or all of the four aspects of housing demand (a and b) and supply (c and d). When levels of dissatisfaction rise to a degree that produces unacceptable levels of stress, the household decides to move. If the household is unable to move, the stress is resolved in other ways. See John L. Goodman, Jr., "Housing Consumption Disequilibrium and Local Residential Mobility," *Environment and Planning* 11, no. 2 (1979): 175–83. The main cause of disequilibrium appears to be changes in the structure of the household. See S. L. Nock, "Family Life Cycle Transitions: Longitudinal Effects on Family Members," *Journal of Marriage and the Family* 43, no. 3 (1981): 703–14; S. L. Nock, "The Family Life Cycle: Empirical or Conceptual Tool," *Journal of Marriage and the Family* 41, no. 1 (1979): 15–38; Paul C. Glick, "Updating the Life Cycle of the Family," *Journal of Marriage and the Family* 39, no. 1 (1977): 5–13; and M. Inman, "Family Social Climate and Attitudes Toward Living Space in Four Stages of Family Life Cycle," *Housing and Society* 5, no. 2 (1978): 74–76. On the analysis of how disequilibrium leads to residential mobility, see Kevin F. McCarthy, "The Household Life Cycle and Housing Choice," Regional Science Association, *Papers* 37 (1976): 55–80; and Clare M. Stapleton, "Reformulation of the Family Life Cycle Concept: Implications for Residential Mobility," *Environment and Planning A*, vol. 1–2, no. 10 (October 1980), pp. 1103–18; William A. V. Clark and Martin Cadwallader, "Location Stress and Residential Mobility," *Environment and Behavior* 5 (1973): 29–41; and William A. V. Clark and Lun A. Anoka, "Life Cycle and Housing Adjustment as Explanations of Residential Mobility," *Urban Studies* 20 (1983): 47–57. Today's trends in residential mobility and the forces that drive them have a long history. See John Martin Weiss, "Patterns of Residential Mobility in Edinburgh, 1775–1800," doctoral dissertation, University of Minnesota, 1985.

[6]Richard A. Easterlin, *Birth and Fortune* (New York: Basic Books, 1980).

[7]Max Neutze, *The Suburban Apartment Boom* (Washington, DC: Resources for the Future, 1968); J. E. Veevers, "Voluntary Childless Wives: An Exploratory Study," *Sociology and Social Research* 57, no. 3 (April 1973), pp. 356–66; J. R. Wilkie, "The Trend Toward Delayed Parenthood," *Journal of Marriage and the Family* 43 (1981): 583–89; Pierre DeVise, "The Expanding Singles Housing Market in Chicago: Implications for Reviving City Neighborhoods," *Urbanism Past and Present* 9 (Winter 1979–80): 30–39; and Barbara Anderson Flannery, "Housing Characteristics and Constraints of Adult Households," doctoral dissertation, University of Minnesota, 1985.

dition to the increased ability of the elderly to remain in conventional housing many years after their children have grown and moved away.

During the decade of the 1970s, the number of persons under age 15 dropped from 58 million to 51 million (Table 4.5). Meanwhile the group aged 15 to 34 jumped by about 19 million persons. Of course there was a corresponding change downward in demand for housing for families with young children, but a major jump upward in the demand for additional housing units suitable for young adults and childless households. The number of persons aged 35 to 55 was almost stable.

Some of the highest rates of increase in population during the 1970s were for persons aged 25 to 34 (up 49 percent), and for persons aged 65 and over (up 28 percent)—especially those aged 75 and over (up 32 percent), who are mainly women, with special housing requirements to be met.

Population Redistribution and Its Effect on Housing Demand

Between 1920 and 1980 the U.S. population more than doubled, and additional housing was needed to handle the growth. Most of the new growth was in urban areas—their populations growing from 54 million to 167 million compared with rural area advance from 52 million to just 59 million (Table 4.6). The Bureau of the Census defines urban population to include persons living in nucleated settlements of 2,500 or more. Although this definition includes some population that is tied directly to traditional rural pursuits like farming and forestry, persons living in towns and villages below the 2,500 threshold commonly are directly supported by traditional urban pursuits like manufacturing, retail trade, business services, and administration. Thus, the urban population expansion reported for the 1920–80 period is a minimum figure.

Another perspective on the location of new population growth and new demand for housing comes from the definition of Standard Metropolitan Areas (1950) and Standard Metropolitan Statistical Areas (1960 and later). Just over half the U.S. population lived in the nation's 212 SMSAs in 1960, but three quarters lived in the 318 metro areas in 1980 (Table 4.6). Yet while American population has been

TABLE 4.5

Age Structure of the U.S. Population, 1970–1980
(in millions)

	Resident Population by Age Cohort		
Age	1970	1980	Percentage Change, 1970–1980
0–4 Years	17	16	−5%
5–14 Years	41	35	−14
15–24 Years	35	42	20
25–34 Years	25	37	49
35–44 Years	23	26	11
45–54 Years	23	23	−2
55–64 Years	19	22	17
Males	9	10	15
Females	10	12	18
65 and Over	20	26	28
Males	8	10	23
Females	11	15	31
65–74	12	16	25
Males	5	7	24
Females	7	9	26
75 and Over	8	10	32
Males	3	4	20
Females	5	6	40

NOTE: The percentage is calculated before rounding.

SOURCE: U.S. Bureau of the Census, *Statistical Abstract of the United States, 1982,* p. 27.

TABLE 4.6

U.S. Population Distribution and the Demand for Housing, Urban and Rural, 1920–1980 (in millions)

	1920	1940	1960	1980	Percentage Change 1920–1980
Urban Population	54	74	125	167	12%
Percentage of U.S.	51%	57%	70%	74%	
Rural Population	52	57	54	59	10
Percentage of U.S.	49%	43%	30%	26%	
SMSA Population		70	113	169	22
Percentage of U.S.		53%	63%	75%	
SMSA Population in Central Cities			58	68	7
Percentage of SMSAs			51%	40%	
Percentage of U.S.			32%	30%	

NOTE: Before 1950, urban population did not include unincorporated places; 1950 SMSA definitions apply to 1940 county populations.

SOURCES: U.S. Bureau of the Census, *Historical Statistics of the United States,* pp. 11 and 39; *Statistical Abstract of the United States, 1969,* p. 17; *1979,* p. 17; *1981,* p. 14; *1982,* pp. 14–5.

TABLE 4.7

Resident Population and Metropolitan Area Population, Rates of Change, 1970–1980

	Resident Population: Percentage Change, 1970–1980	Metropolitan Area Population: Percentage Change, 1970–1980
United States	11.4%	10.1%
Northeast	.2	−1.9
New England	4.2	1.0
Middle Atlantic	−1.1	−2.7
North Central	4.0	2.7
East North Central	3.5	1.9
West North Central	5.2	5.5
South	20.0	21.5
South Atlantic	20.4	20.8
East South Central	14.5	14.0
West South Central	22.9	26.3
West	23.9	21.9
Mountain	37.2	37.6
Pacific	19.8	18.6

SOURCE: U.S. Bureau of the Census, *State and Metropolitan Area Data Book, 1982,* pp. lxxx–lxxxi.

concentrating inside metro regions, it has been redistributing itself within them.[8] Total SMSA central city population rose rapidly between 1960 and 1980 as the number of SMSAs rose 50 percent, but the share of SMSA population living in central cities dropped sharply after 1960 (51 to 40 percent), while the share of the entire population in central cities dropped from 32 to 30 percent. These declines mean that the long-term trend of new housing demand located predominantly in suburban areas and in SMSA territory beyond the fringe of the urbanized area persisted throughout the 1960s and 1970s.

Regional Changes and Housing Demand

At an intermediate geographical scale of analysis, new housing demand was strongest in the West and South, where all census divisions gained resident population and metropolitan area population at rates above the national averages between 1970 and 1980 (Table 4.7). Meanwhile, in the Northeast and Midwest all census divisions experienced corresponding rates of change below the national averages. The Middle Atlantic division (New York, New Jersey, and Pennsyl-

[8]Martin T. Cadwallader "A Unified Model of Urban Housing Patterns, Social Patterns, and Residential Mobility," *Urban Geography* 2, no. 2 (1981): 115–30.

vania) actually lost population because of big losses in New York. The only other areas to lose population were Ohio and the District of Columbia. Metro area populations declined in Massachusetts, New York, New Jersey, Pennsylvania, and the District of Columbia, and as population dropped, an effect was felt in housing demand.

Meanwhile, spectacular increases occurred elsewhere in the 1970s. The biggest percentage increases were in Nevada (64 percent), Arizona (53 percent), Florida (44 percent), and Wyoming (42 percent). The largest absolute gains in resident population were in California (3.7 million), Texas (3.0 million), and Florida (3.0 million).

Movers and Nonmovers

Although mobility rates of Americans were showing signs of decline in the 1970s, almost half of the 1980 population aged 5 and over had changed their residence during the previous five years. Since the flows into and out of each region are seldom equivalent in terms of the number and type of persons and households entering and leaving, population movements produce major redistributions of housing demand.

The Northeast and Midwest experienced heavy net outmigration during the 1970s while the South and the West enjoyed net inmigration. These net flows left the Northeast with 63 percent of its 1980 population (age 5 and over) as nonmovers and the Midwest with 56 percent—both above the U.S. average of 54 percent nonmovers. The net outflows from these two regions contributed to generally softer housing markets and somewhat lower average price inflation within them because of the muted demand for housing (Table 4.8).

Meanwhile in the South and West, the net inflows of new population raised the proportion of movers to 48 percent in the South and 56 percent in the West. Outside the South the nonmovers are concentrated in the suburbs. In the South the greatest stability seems to lie outside the SMSAs—in smaller urban places and rural areas (Table 4.8). When they do occur, most moves are short and are house- or neighborhood-related rather than job-related, with households expanding or contracting their housing consumption in response to changes in household size and composition or to changes in financial circumstances.[9] Thus, the largest share of moves occur within the same SMSA. Movers from abroad represent only 2 percent of the total population, but their settlement is relatively concentrated in major metropolitan centers of the Northeast, South, and West. Some of the movers from abroad are citizens returning to the United States, while the others are immigrants, visitors, students, and foreign guest workers.

Migration by Type of Place

The nation's SMSAs have been experiencing net outmigration since the mid-1960s, while areas outside the SMSAs have had net inmigration (Table 4.9). The net shifts are relatively small and have been dispersed throughout the United States, so the effects on housing demand have been minimal compared with other forces.

Inside the SMSAs, inmigrants by the millions entered the nation's suburbs, and although there was movement out as well, the net suburban inflow for the 1970s was over 10 million persons. The central cities gained almost 13 million inmigrants in the 1970s, but lost over 26 million through outmigration. The net flow outward brought about a general reduction in demand for central city housing. The softer market that was created by reduced demand in the face of a relatively fixed supply in general meant lower house price inflation for the central cities and even real price reductions in some areas, which stimulated many households to head for the suburbs where the reverse was occurring.

Foreign Immigration and Housing Demand

As rates of natural increase declined during the 1970s in the United States, the rate of foreign immigration rose to account for an increasingly significant share of population increase and of additional

TABLE 4.8
Mobility Status, 1975–1980,
of Population Aged 5 and Older in 1980 (in millions)

	United States	Northeast	Midwest	South	West
Total Population Aged 5 and Over, 1980	198	45	53	65	36
Nonmovers: Same House, 1975–1980	107	28	30	34	16
Nonmovers: Percentage of Total	54%	63%	56%	52%	44%
In central cities	14	19	14	12	13
In balance of SMSAs	22	31	23	15	21
Outside SMSAs	18	13	19	25	10
Movers: Percentage of Total	46%	37%	44%	48%	56%
Within same SMSA	21	21	22	17	26
Between SMSAs	7	6	5	7	13
From Outside to SMSAs	3	2	3	4	4
From SMSAs to outside	4	2	3	5	4
From outside to outside	11	6	11	15	9
Movers from Abroad: Percentage of Total	2%	2%	1%	2%	4%

NOTE: Total population excludes persons who moved from abroad or failed to report mobility status.

SOURCE: U.S. Bureau of the Census, *Statistical Abstract of the United States, 1982*, p. 14.

[9]The classic treatment on the subject of residential mobility is Peter H. Rossi, *Why Families Move* (Beverly Hills, CA: Sage, 1980). This topic has been studied extensively by geographers and sociologists who view residential mobility as a principal engine of urban transformation. See John S. Adams, "Directional Bias in Intra-Urban Migration" *Economic Geography* 45 (1969): 302–23; Avery M. Guest and C. Cluett, "Workplace and Residential Location: A Push-Pull Model," *Journal of Regional Science* 16 (1976): 399–410; John M. Quigley and D. H. Weinberg, "Intra-Metropolitan Residential Mobility: A Review and Synthesis," *International Regional Science Review* 2 (1977): 41–66; and Martin T. Cadwallader, "Neighborhood Evaluation in Residential Mobility," *Environment and Planning A* 11 (1979), pp. 393–401.

TABLE 4.9

Mobility by Type of Place, 1965–1980
(in thousands)

	1955–1960	1965–1970	1970–1975	1975–1980
Total Population Aged 5 and Over in End Year	156,519	176,354	179,489	198,403
Movers Over the 5 Years	49%	44%	44%	46%
SMSAs				
Inmigrants		5,457	5,127	5,993
Outmigrants		5,809	6,721	7,337
Net migration		−352	−1,594	−1,344
Central Cities				
Inmigrants			5,987	6,891
Outmigrants			13,005	13,237
Net migration			−7,018	−6,346
Suburbs (Balance of SMSAs)				
Inmigrants			12,732	13,628
Outmigrants			7,309	8,627
Net migration			5,423	5,001
Non-SMSA				
Inmigrants		5,809	6,721	7,337
Outmigrants		5,457	5,127	5,993
Net migration		352	1,594	1,344

NOTES: Figures for 1955–60 and 1965–70 exclude those who failed to report mobility status; 1970–75 and 1975–80 figures exclude those who failed to report mobility status and movers from abroad; 1970 SMSA definitions are used here.

SOURCES: U.S. Bureau of the Census, *Statistical Abstract of the United States, 1969*, p. 34; *1976*, p. 30; *1982*, p. 14; *Current Population Reports*, series P-20, no. 368 (1981), p. 2.

housing requirements. Legal immigration averaged over 413,000 per year during the decade, while estimates of additional illegal immigration often exceeded the legal count.

The fastest-growing states and metropolitan economies offer the widest array of new job opportunities, as well as a flexibility in expanding businesses that makes it easier to match up the talents and interests of workers with the new jobs that need to be done. Unsatisfactory workers can be let go in a fast-growth region by employers who are confident that the fired workers can find other jobs. Dissatisfied workers can quit an unsatisfactory job with reasonable assurance that another job will be quickly forthcoming. Morale is higher in fast-growth regions than in stagnant ones. A better match between employer needs and worker wants and talents can mean higher

worker productivity and enhanced job satisfaction, which lead immigrants to send back positive reports about economic prospects and to encourage additional immigration to fuel the boom.

California, with net inmigration of 2.1 million during the 1970s, Florida with 2.7 million, and Texas with 1.8 million led all other states in net inmigration. In Minnesota and Wisconsin, the number of immigrants admitted (28,000 and 24,000, respectively) exceeded the net inmigration (including immigrants). Thus, without foreign immigration, net domestic migration would have been negative for the decade. In other states such as New York, New Jersey, and Illinois the high rates of immigration kept the net outmigration rates from falling to levels even more serious than those recorded (Table 4.10).

One of the hidden consequences of immigration is the effects

TABLE 4.10

Net Migration, 1970–1980, and Foreign Immigrants Admitted by Intended State of Residence, 1969–1979, Selected States (in thousands)

	Total (Legal) Immigrants Admitted, 1969–1979	Net Migration, 1970–1980
California	957	+2,078
Connecticut	67	−52
District of Columbia	29	−150
Florida	623	+2,722
Illinois	258	−402
Indiana	26	−87
Kansas	13	−19
Massachusetts	139	−136
Michigan	102	−294
Nebraska	8	−12
New Jersey	271	−114
New York	942	−1,542
North Dakota	3	−17
Ohio	75	−543
Pennsylvania	101	−292
Rhode Island	26	−33
South Dakota	2	−26
Texas	271	+1,780

NOTES: 1969–1979 = July 1, 1969, through September 30, 1979; selected states = leading states in net inmigration, plus all states with net outmigration; net migration includes immigration.

SOURCES: Immigration and Naturalization Service, *Statistical Yearbook, 1979*, p. 30; U.S. Bureau of the Census, *Statistical Abstract of the United States, 1984*, p. 14.

that it produces on natural changes and on subsequent demand for housing. Immigrants tend to be young, healthy, ambitious, upwardly mobile, and in the first stages of the household life cycle. Once they are settled and established in the economy, family formation and childbearing follow. When they enter a state like New York, Illinois, Florida, or Texas in large numbers, they bring along their reproductive potential. Population gains from immigration are followed by additional gains from births. Meanwhile, outmigrants from the old industrial Northeast and Midwest include a significant number of elderly persons. Sometimes the housing that is given up by persons leaving the state is different from the styles, prices, and locations sought by the newcomers.

These crosscurrents in the migration streams cause effective demand for housing to fluctuate from one submarket to another. High-priced housing given up by elderly New Jersey suburbanites cannot satisfy the buildup in demand for low- and moderate-income housing for immigrants to the central city. A surplus of family housing cannot readily meet the needs of young singles and couples. And surplus housing in areas of heavy outmigration does not alleviate shortages in booming areas, except when the contrast between low housing prices in declining areas and high prices in growing areas retards the rate of migration and sometimes invites migrants to return to their origins.

Changing Household Composition and Its Effect on Housing Demand

The composition of U.S. households has steadily changed since World War II. Life expectancy has been extended, enlarging the number of elderly households. Families have changed in average size and composition. Single-parent families have become increasingly common, as have nonfamily households. A steadily increasing proportion of adult Americans live alone. When these trends unfold across the United States, and are magnified in some regions by migration flows, the consequences include serious strains on the local housing markets. Fast-growth areas have trouble meeting the needs of an increasingly heterogeneous mix of additional households. Stagnant regions have trouble maintaining the existing housing stock in good repair as real income sags and deflation strikes at the local base of real estate wealth.

The Living Arrangements of Older Americans

Better health, longer lives, and more money meant that older Americans could adjust their living arrangements during the 1960–80 period more according to their preferences and less according to their infirmities and financial limitations.

Between 1970 and 1983 average monthly Social Security benefits for retired workers rose 46 percent in real terms, while wages and salaries for the nonelderly fell 7 percent.[10] Five elderly men in six live in families, that is, with relatives (Table 4.11). Elderly women are more likely to live alone or with nonrelatives, a tendency that has increased steadily since 1960. By 1980 almost half the elderly women (42 percent) lived in nonfamily households. Older women outnumbered older men by about 3 to 2 in 1980. On the basis of these numbers, then, it would appear easier for a widowed or divorced man to remarry and reestablish a family, and many do so. Older women, left alone and usually possessed of better-developed homemaking skills and the interest in using them than men their age, maintain or establish independent households outside a family setting. The economic security provided by Social Security and other pensions, Medicare, life insurance benefits from deceased spouses, and savings provide the financial base that has supported the continued increases in independent living by elderly women since 1960.[11]

How do these changes in living arrangements of the elderly translate into recent adjustments in housing demand? As elderly persons live longer, they stay in the housing market longer. Housing units remain in use rather than being released for reuse. As average levels of retirement income and wealth levels of the elderly edged upward for large numbers of them, they remained in their houses, able to pay the bills, or they moved to retirement housing. Continued use of post–World War II suburban family housing by elderly couples and singles whose children are grown and gone has delayed the entry of young families into those houses. The houses are held by the elderly

---

[10]The decision by the elderly to stay or to move has important consequences for the available supply of housing units for younger households and for the vitality of neighborhoods. See Michael Gutowsia and Tracy Field, *The Graying of Suburbia* (Washington, DC: Urban Institute, 1979); Jordan L. Louviere, *Analysis of Housing Choices of the Elderly* (Iowa City: Institute of Urban and Regional Research, 1982); Raymond J. Struyk, *Improving the Elderly's Housing: A Key to Preserving the Nation's Housing Stock and Neighborhoods* (Cambridge, MA: Ballinger, 1980); Phyllis Meyers, *Aging in Place: Strategies to Help the Elderly Stay in Revitalizing Neighborhoods* (Washington, DC: Conservation Foundation, 1982); and M. Powell Lawton and Sally L. Hoover, eds., *Community Housing for Older Americans* (New York: Springer, 1981).

[11]*The Wall Street Journal*, June 21, 1985, p. 20.

TABLE 4.11

Persons Aged 65 and Older by Family Status and Living Arrangements, 1960–1980
(in millions)

	1960		1970		1980	
	Male	Female	Male	Female	Male	Female
Total	7.5	9.0	8.3	11.5	9.8	14.0
Family Status						
In families	82%	68%	79%	58%	83%	57%
Nonfamily households	13	27	15	35	16	42
Secondary individual	2	3	2	2	2	1
Resident of institution	2	3	4	4	NA	NA
Living Arrangements						
Living in household	97%	97%	96%	95%	100%	100%
Living alone	11	23	14	34	15	41
Spouse present	73	37	70	34	76	38
Living with someone else	13	38	12	27	10	21
Not living in household (group quarters, institutions)	3	3	4	5	(…)	(…)

NOTES: "Living alone" (1960) is estimated by using Current Population Survey data in source, p. 49 ("persons living alone by sex"), divided by census cohort figures; "Living with someone else" (1960) is estimated by subtracting other categories from 100 percent; (…) = under .5 percent.

SOURCE: U.S. Bureau of the Census, *Statistical Abstract of the United States, 1981*, pp. 31 and 49.

as a store of wealth, a place to store possessions, a familiar environment, a set of neighborhood and community relations, and a symbol of middle-class achievement. Many elderly remain in their houses as long as they are physically and financially able. Often they would prefer a move to something smaller and easier to manage, but zoning laws in most urban areas have prohibited small owner-occupied units and small rental units in neighborhoods designated for low-density single-unit housing. As a result, elderly persons must stay in family housing in order to retain their neighborhood setting. Experiments in the early and mid-1980s with accessory apartments in exclusively single-family housing areas provide one type of response to this recently expanded demand for housing by elderly, at the same time that the demand for family housing continued almost unabated.

The rural farm elderly encounter special risks from accident or illness if they are left alone, a problem that has traditionally been resolved by living with children who take over the farming business or by moving to town where transportation problems are minimized. Thus, extended longevity of the rural elderly, plus somewhat greater financial security, has stepped up demand for housing for the elderly in small towns and cities in agricultural areas. Public housing programs in such areas have been well received.

The changes in housing demand brought about by changes in household composition include small and inexpensive units for the elderly, specially fitted with door handles easy to grasp; light switches easy to find and use; convenient bathroom fixtures that minimize the chance of accidents; extra hand rails and grab bars to compensate for failing strength, coordination, and eyesight; warning systems to alert the elderly householder when something needs attention, and alarm systems that facilitate a call for help. A general expansion in the number of retired people has expanded the demand for retirement housing in the warm and dry parts of the country, where the bright light and dry weather make life more comfortable for many, with less risk of accident.

The widespread availability of home nursing care and physical therapy services has allowed handicapped persons to remain at home while receiving specialized short-term or long-term care. Social service agencies that prepare and deliver well-balanced, nutritious hot meals each day ("Meals on Wheels") to elderly and handicapped shut-ins not only encourage these persons to remain in their houses, but contribute to their health and longevity. The knowledge that these services are available and used encourages many elderly couples and singles to live alone, which encourages their children and other relatives and friends to accept or even promote this independence—but the outcome for housing demand is that more housing units are needed, especially in areas that the elderly find to be secure and agreeable.

Marital Status and Housing Demand

Between 1950 and the start of the 1980s, the proportion of all adults who were married dropped from almost three fourths to under two thirds (Table 4.12). Meanwhile, the single and divorced population more than doubled, from 20 million in 1950 to 41 million in 1980, as they expanded their share from 19 to 26 percent of the adult population.

The causes of these changes are found partly in the postwar baby boom, which loaded the population of the late 1960s and 1970s with disproportionately large numbers of young adults who themselves normally account for higher than average numbers of single and divorced persons. The hardships encountered by young adults were ag-

gravated by the slow-growing economy of the 1970s with its labor market glutted by young entrants whose wages remained low, whose advancement up the income and responsibility ladder was slow, and who therefore delayed marriage and family formation until better times arrived, as they did in the late 1970s and 1980s for many of the baby boomers.

During the 1950s the main additions to the adult population took the form of 9 million married persons. The population of singles actually declined, while the widowed and divorced rose by 1 million each (Table 4.13). But the 1970s were a sharp contrast to the 1950s—singles added 10 million and divorced, 6 million more. Married persons added only 8 million—fewer than in the 1950s, even though the pool of singles in the 1970s was much larger than it had been 20 years earlier.

The housing needs of this vast number of new singles and divorced put extreme pressure on the low-income rental markets and, in the case of divorced persons with dependent children, pressure on the low-income family housing market. Sixteen million additional adults had to be housed in the 1970s. They exerted exceptional pressure on the available rental units, driving up the rents and stimulating conversions to condominiums so that owners could reap capital gains, and stimulating new construction of modest apartment houses. For single parents on limited incomes but with difficult financial obligations, the 1970s ushered in a grim era. Low-income family-oriented housing in satisfactory living environments is seldom abundant

TABLE 4.12

Marital Status of the Population Aged 18 and Older, 1950–1980 (in millions)

	1950	1960	1970	1980	Percentage Change, 1970–1980
Total	103	115	132	156	18%
Single	18	17	21	31	47
Married	76	85	95	103	8
Widowed	9	10	12	12	6
Divorced	2	3	4	10	126
Percentage Distribution					
Single	17%	15%	16%	20%	
Married	74	74	72	66	
Widowed	9	9	9	8	
Divorced	2	3	3	6	

NOTE: Percentage change is calculated using unrounded data.

SOURCES: U.S. Bureau of the Census, *Historical Statistics of the United States*, p. 20; *Statistical Abstract of the United States, 1981*, p. 37.

TABLE 4.13

Marriage and Divorce in the United States, 1920–1980, Selected Years (in thousands)

Year	Marriages	Per 1,000 Population	Divorces	Per 1,000 Population
1920	1,274	12.0	171	1.6
1930	1,127	9.2	196	1.6
1940	1,596	12.1	264	2.0
1950	1,667	11.1	385	2.6
1960	1,523	8.5	393	2.2
1965	1,800	9.3	479	2.5
1970	2,159	10.6	708	3.5
1975	2,153	10.1	1,036	4.9
1980	2,413	10.9	1,182	5.3

SOURCE: U.S. Bureau of the Census, *Statistical Abstract of the United States, 1982*, p. 60.

in good times, and in the period of excess demand of the 1970s, when new supplies were aimed mainly at upper-income families and childless singles, single-parent families—usually headed by low-income women—faced a special burden.

Marriage, Divorce, and Housing Demand

Variations in the rate of marriages and divorces produce important variations in effective demand on different segments of the national and local housing markets. When two persons join to form a single household, they usually leave behind their former living quarters. Marriage of single persons living alone creates demand for a smaller number of larger and more completely furnished housing units than the partners normally would have required as single persons. On the other hand, when a marriage is dissolved the former partners must be separately housed.[12] Since the expense of running the two separate households can easily exceed the former cost of running one together, the separated couple—usually with little additional income but with higher expenses—often must enter the lower-priced housing market following a divorce.

Marriage rates were high in the good times of the 1920s and low in the years of depression and war before 1945 (Table 4.13). Divorce rates in absolute and percentage terms stayed low through the 1950s, but rose steadily after 1960 as the baby boom generation (and some of their parents) were divorced in ever greater numbers. By 1980 the divorce rate was almost half the marriage rate, but as a steadily larger percentage of the baby boom generation got on their feet occupationally and financially, marriage rates began to rise and divorce rates showed strong signs of dropping.

The consequences for housing demand in the United States have been rapidly changing. For a long time after the mid-1960s there was a chronic shortage of small, modestly priced rental units for single and divorced persons. By the end of the 1970s and into the early 1980s the family housing market was seriously short of new and used units at prices and monthly payments that couples and young families felt they could afford.

TABLE 4.14

Changes in Family Composition by Number of Own Children Under Age 18, 1950–1980 (in millions)

	1950	1960	1965	1970	1975	1980
All Families	38	45	48	52	56	58
Percentage with						
No children	48%	43%	43%	44%	46%	48%
1 child	21	18	18	18	20	21
2 children	16	18	17	17	18	19
3 children	} 14	} 20	11	11	9	8
4 children			11	10	7	4

NOTE: In 1980, unrelated subfamilies were no longer considered separate families.
SOURCE: U.S. Bureau of the Census, *Statistical Abstract of the United States, 1981*, p. 46.

Family Composition and Housing Demand

The emphasis on family housing reached a high point at the end of the 1950s and in the early 1960s when the proportion of families without children in the household reached a postwar low of about 43 percent (Table 4.14). Large families—those with 3 children or more at home—peaked as a share of the total in 1965, just after the peak of the baby boom and just before the children began to leave home in large numbers. By the early 1980s almost half the families had no children at home, and those with 3 or more children were becoming rare.

The abruptness of these changes in family composition produced strains in the 1950s and 1960s when large and growing families needed large housing units.[13] A generation later the incremental demand arises mainly from childless and small households. On the other hand, the change in housing needs as a family grows from 1 child to 2 children is probably greater than the change from 2 to 3 or from 3 to 4 children. If this is so, then the recent shift to smaller average family size will not have a dramatic effect on changing patterns of housing demand. Families have an easier time confronting modest increases in per capita living space than modest decreases.

---

[12]Gerda R. Wekerle, Rebecca Peterson, and David Morley, *New Space for Women* (Boulder, CO: Westview Press, 1980); Eugenie Ladner Birch, ed., *The Unsheltered Woman: Women and Housing in the '80s* (Piscataway, NJ: Center for Urban Policy Research, 1985); and Tamar Gavrielli, "Single Parent Female-Headed Families: Patterns of Residential Mobility," master's thesis, University of Minnesota, 1985.

[13]Cecile Smull, *Housing Our Families* (Washington, DC: U.S. Department of Housing and Urban Development and U.S. Government Printing Office, 1980).

Other Changes in Household Composition

The volume and character of new housing demand change steadily as the number and type of households in each locale change from decade to decade. In 1920 the Census Bureau reported 24 million families in just under 21 million dwelling units, with an average of 4.3 persons per family and 5.1 persons per dwelling.[14] By 1950 the number of households had almost doubled, while average household size had dropped to 3.37 (Table 4.15). In the next three decades the number of households almost doubled again, pushed along by population increase, but also boosted by average household size continuing its downward trend, reaching 2.75 in 1980.

Family households contain 2 persons or more related by blood or marriage. After World War II, about 9 households in 10 were families, but by 1980 the proportion had fallen to below three fourths. In the 1970s nonfamily households grew in number at five times the rate of family households (Table 4.15). A few family households are headed by a male with spouse absent—for example, a man whose elderly parents live with him, a man with brothers and sisters who live with him, or a man alone with his children.

Female family householders were five times more common in 1980 than their male counterparts, and their numbers jumped over 50 percent in the 1970s. Almost half of the black families with children under age 18 were headed by women with spouse absent in 1980, and their numbers rose 70 percent during the 1970s.

Most of the nonfamily households are single persons living alone. The desire for privacy, young adults delaying marriage, older persons who never married or who live alone following a divorce, and elderly persons in good health with the financial means to live alone all contribute to the rapid rise in single-person households, from 7 million in 1960 and 11 million in 1970 to 18 million in 1980 (Table 4.16).

Much has been noted and discussed concerning the recent rise in the number of multiperson nonfamily households, which range in style from young working people sharing a house or apartment to elderly persons of the same or opposite sex living together. The number of such households rose 142 percent in the 1970s to 2.9 million in 1980, but the numbers are not large. A major component of this group of nonfamily households is composed of persons of the opposite sex sharing living quarters. This type of household grew fastest in the

[14]U.S. Bureau of the Census, *Statistical Abstract of the United States, 1925* (Washington, DC: U.S. Government Printing Office, 1925), p. 29.

TABLE 4.15
Household Composition, 1950–1980 (in millions)

	1950	1960	1970	1980	Percentage Change 1970–1980
Total Households	43.6	52.8	63.4	79.1	25%
Average size	3.37	3.33	3.14	2.75	−12
Family Households	38.8	44.9	51.5	58.4	14
Male family householder, spouse absent	1.2	1.2	1.2	1.7	15
Female family householder, spouse absent	3.6	4.4	5.6	8.5	53
White	NA	3.3	4.2	6.0	43
Percentage of all white families with children under age 18	NA	6%	8%	13%	
Black	NA	.9	1.4	2.4	76
Percentage of all black families with children under age 18	NA	21%	31%	47%	
Unrelated Individuals	9.1	11.1	15.0	25.8	72
Nonfamily Households	4.7	7.9	11.9	20.7	73
Single person households					
Male	1.5	2.3	3.5	6.8	94
Female	2.5	4.6	7.2	11.0	53
Multiperson nonfamily households	.7	1.0	1.2	2.9	142
Persons of opposite sex sharing living quarters	NA	NA	.3	1.1	244

NOTES: The 1950 figure for household size includes only related persons in the household; all nonfamily households are assumed to have one related person—thus, 3.37 is probably an underestimate; *Statistical Abstract of the United States, 1969*, p. 35, reports total persons: total households equals 3.52 in 1950.

Statistical Abstracts use female "householders," while *Current Population Reports* use the same numbers for female-headed "families," presumably including unrelated subfamilies. NA = not available.

SOURCES: U.S. Bureau of the Census, *Historical Abstract of the United States, 1982*, pp. 43–4; *1981*, pp. 41 and 48; private communication from the Census Bureau.

TABLE 4.16

Persons Living Alone, by Age and Sex, 1960–1980 (in thousands)

Age	1960	1970	1980	Percentage Change, 1970–1980
Total	7.1	10.9	17.8	64%
Males	2.6	3.5	6.8	92
14–24 years	.1	.3	.9	235
25–44 years	.7	.9	2.8	203
45–64 years	1.0	1.2	1.6	38
65+ years	.9	1.2	1.4	22
Females	4.4	7.3	11.0	51
14–24 years	.1	.3	.8	166
25–44 years	.5	.7	1.8	162
45–64 years	1.8	2.5	2.8	14
65+ years	2.0	3.9	5.7	46

NOTES: 1960 census and Current Population Survey data differ slightly. There is a slight discrepancy with *Statistical Abstract of the United States, 1982*, p. 43, for unknown reasons.

In 1980 the age category 14–24 years was changed to 15–24 years.

SOURCE: U.S. Bureau of the Census, 1960 Census of Population; *Statistical Abstract of the United States, 1981*, p. 49, from Current Population Survey, March 1970 and 1980.

1970s, but still accounted for only slightly over 1 million by census time in 1980 (Table 4.15).

How do changes in household composition affect the demand for housing? Smaller households need less space and fewer rooms, but higher disposable income per capita in the smaller households may mean greater outlays for better-quality construction and finer appointments and furnishings. As household size drops, the demand for additional units rises faster than the population. Single parents of dependent children may need large amounts of interior and exterior activity space, but may not be able to afford housing aimed at middle-income and two-income households.

Single persons living alone often spend a much higher than average percentage of their leisure time outside their housing unit and prefer living in small and inexpensive units. But since the cost per square foot of housing space typically rises sharply as the units diminish in size, the desire to live alone often confronts the financial reality that it is too expensive—especially during the 1970s when the number of single-person households rose by almost two thirds. Shar-

ing the housing with nonrelatives was a popular alternative in the 1970s. The cost of small units appropriate for singles living alone is hard to bring down. The production cost per square foot is a much better bargain in large housing units, new or used, than in small. For existing units the heavy demand generated by young singles and elderly relatives keeps the price of small units beyond the reach of many who might otherwise prefer it to shared housing.

The consequences of changing household composition on the demand for additional housing units are revealed by the details of net household formations (total newly formed households minus households dissolved) during the 1970s, when the net annual increment of households ranged between 973,000 and 2.3 million (Table 4.17). Through 1975 family households were the clear majority, except between 1973 and 1974. After 1975 the balance shifted sharply to a preponderance of nonfamily households until 1980, when approximate parity was achieved. The record of the 1970s is partly an artifact of large numbers of young people, born in the peak years of the baby boom (1959–61), coming into the housing market in large numbers, partly a result of independent living by the elderly, and partly a measure of delayed marriage by young adults entering a troubled economy. But the large numbers of new households meant steady upward pressure on housing demand and a need for larger numbers of non-family units.

TABLE 4.17

Net Household Formations in the 1970s (in thousands)

	Net Household Formations Since Prior Year	Family Households	Nonfamily Households
1971	973	367	606
1972	2,302	1,340	962
1973	1,575	1,101	474
1974	1,608	653	955
1975	1,261	646	615
1976	1,747	493	1,254
1977	1,275	416	858
1978	1,888	505	1,383
1979	1,300	540	760
1980	1,778	928	850

NOTE: Figures are computed from published annual estimates.

SOURCES: U.S. Bureau of the Census, *Statistical Abstract of the United States, 1973*, p. 40; *1976*, p. 39; *1979*, p. 44; *1981*, p. 42.

National Changes in Population and Household Numbers

National trends since 1950 toward a steadily larger population and ever smaller average household sizes were played out unevenly across the map of the United States. In each census region during the 1960s and 1970s the number of households advanced at rates that vastly exceeded the rate of population growth (Table 4.18). When population rose over 13 percent in the 1960s, households rose almost 20 percent; when population growth slowed to 11 percent in the 1970s, households rose almost 27 percent. The Northeast and Midwest lost millions of people through migration in the 1970s, but their household numbers still rose briskly. The South and the West were on the receiving end of the national net migration streams of the 1970s, boosting their population growth to about twice the national rate and expanding their household numbers at rates almost twice the rate of population expansion. Excess demand for housing built up steadily in the South and West in the 1960s and 1970s, stimulating construction booms, real estate price inflation, initiatives for growth control laws, pressures to contain real estate property taxes, overtaxed water and sewer systems, and local rent control ordinances that tried to protect existing renters from the market consequences of steeply escalating housing costs. Meanwhile, in the slow-growth Northeast and Midwest, especially in the 1970s, the brisk expansion in the number of households supplied some vitality to an otherwise bleak demographic growth picture. Population was not rising much, but there was significant need for additional housing units.

Housing Prices and Housing Finance

During the 1970s, the median sales prices of new and existing (used) single-unit houses almost tripled (Table 4.19). At the start of the decade sales prices on the average were highest in the Northeast; by 1980, due to the market consequences of industrial restructuring in the Northeast and the redistribution of effective demand to other regions, the West reported the highest sales prices of both new and existing houses. Average new house prices in the West in 1980 were over three times what they were in 1970 ($72,400 versus $24,000), while used houses approached four times their 1970 level ($89,300 versus $24,300).

The median sales price for used housing is traditionally lower than for new housing. During the peculiar housing market conditions of the 1970s the combination of high inflation rates and low mortgage interest rates encouraged new construction and new house sales at steadily higher prices. In the first half of the decade price inflation rates for new houses in most areas stayed well above the inflation rates for used houses. But by the end of the decade, after new house prices and related housing costs had risen sharply, builders began to scale back severely the average size and quality of new units to help make them affordable, which resulted in tipping a sizable part of the potential new house market back into the used house market—where large and high-quality prewar and postwar units appeared to be relative bargains in terms of their neighborhood settings, number of rooms, cost per room, cost per square foot, cost per 1,000 cubic feet of interior space, interior and exterior fittings, and other adornments.

TABLE 4.18

Population and Household Change, by Region, 1960–1980 (in thousands)

	Population Change		Household Change		Intercensual Migration	
	1960–1970	1970–1980	1960–1970	1970–1980	1970–1975	1975–1980
United States	13.4%	11.4%	19.7%	26.7%		
Northeast	9.8	0.2	14.5	12.8	−1,342	−1,486
Midwest	9.6	4.0	14.0	18.9	−1,195	−1,173
South	14.3	20.0	24.2	37.5	1,829	1,764
West	24.2	23.9	29.6	39.4	708	893

SOURCES: U.S. Bureau of the Census, *Statistical Abstract of the United States, 1981*, pp. 10–11, 44; *1982*, p. 14.

TABLE 4.19

Median Sales Price of New and Existing (Used) Single Unit Houses, by Region, 1970–1980 (in thousands of dollars)

Year	United States	Northeast	Midwest	South	West
1970					
New	$23.4	$30.3	$24.4	$20.3	$24.0
Existing	23.0	25.2	20.1	22.2	24.3
1975					
New	39.3	44.0	39.6	37.3	40.6
Existing	35.3	39.3	30.1	34.8	39.6
1980					
New	64.5	69.0	63.2	59.8	72.4
Existing	62.2	60.8	51.9	58.3	89.3
Percentage Change					
New: 1970–75	68%	45%	62%	84%	69%
1975–80	64	57	60	60	78
Existing: 1970–75	53	56	50	57	63
1975–80	76	55	72	68	126

SOURCES: U.S. Department of Housing and Urban Development, *HUD Statistical Yearbook, 1974*, p. 250; *1979*, p. 286; *1980*, p. 356; U.S. Bureau of the Census, *Statistical Abstract of the United States*, 1981, pp. 769–70.

In the locations where demand was most intense in the late 1970s the bargains disappeared quickly, and in most areas existing house sales prices rose faster than new house sales prices between 1975 and 1980 (Table 4.19).

During the days of market turmoil in the late 1970s, the financial markets, the households that were buying or trying to buy housing, and the builders of new units were each adjusting quickly to the changes presented by the other two sides. As the average monthly payment for all new mortgages written (new and existing housing units, condos, and multifamily structures) rose from $329 in 1976 to $599 in 1980, this payment as a proportion of income rose steadily from 24 percent to over 32 percent. The source of the downpayment changed as many young households discovered that owner-occupied housing was beyond their reach without extraordinary measures. About 71 percent of the first-time buyers in 1976 financed their downpayments entirely from savings and investments, while 20 percent had help from relatives. Four years later in 1980 only 51 percent managed the downpayment from their own resources, while almost 33 percent received help from relatives.

During this difficult period, the average age of the first-time buyer remained stable at just over 28 years, but the share of all sales made to first-time buyers dropped from 45 percent in 1976 to 33 percent in 1980. Even with help from family members, with new houses being more modestly built, and with a larger share of their income devoted to housing, young, first-time buyers were increasingly handicapped from achieving ownership status. Thus, by the mid-1980s, after a long period of steady increase among households of all age groups, it was clear that overall homeownership rates had peaked at just over 65 percent of all American households during the last half of the 1970s.

The subsequent decline occurred at the very time when the baby boom generation might have been expected to raise homeownership rates by making their initial "starter home" purchases. Younger households in particular were falling behind in the race for homeownership. Homeownership rates for households with adult members in their early 40s or younger peaked during the latter half of the 1970s. The subsequent decline was so precipitous that if 1984 homeownership rates for this group had equaled those of the peak 1978–79 years, an additional 7.9 million households (of the nation's 1984 total of 85.4 million households) would have been homeowners. Among middle-aged households, homeownership rates remained more or less constant from the mid-1970s through the mid-1980s, while homeownership rates among the elderly continued to increase.[15]

Higher Prices and Smaller New Houses in the 1970s

In the last half of the 1970s, the rapid rise of house prices, the sharply higher interest rates, the peak of the post–World War II baby boom entering the market, and changing product mixes by house builders all yielded significant changes in the types of housing that were bought (Table 4.20). House prices rose as a consequence of population redistributions at local and national scales that put added pressures on existing stocks in areas receiving net inmigration. Prices also rose in response to generally higher rates of net household formation as the peak of the post–World War II baby boom entered the housing market. These demand pressures were augmented by specu-

[15]For this information, based on 1960 and 1970 Census of Population and Housing microdata files, 1973 to 1981 Annual Housing Survey microdata files, and 1982 to 1984 Current Population Survey microdata files, I am indebted to Donald C. Dahmann, U.S. Bureau of the Census, personal communication, May 23, 1985. See also U.S. Bureau of the Census, *Statistical Abstract of the United States, 1982* (Washington, DC: U.S. Government Printing Office, 1982), p. 762; and Leo Grebler and F. Mittelbach, *The Inflation of House Prices* (Lexington, MA: Heath, 1979).

TABLE 4.20

Type of Housing Bought, 1976–1980

	1976	1977	1978	1979	1980
Percentage of All Buyers Buying					
New houses	15%	13%	14%	18%	22%
Existing houses	85	87	86	82	78
In single-unit houses	89	90	87	88	82
In multiunit buildings	5	6	8	5	6
Condominiums	6	4	6	7	12

SOURCE: U.S. Bureau of the Census, *Statistical Abstract of the United States, 1982,* p. 762.

lative buying of housing in anticipation of continued high rates of price inflation, which was probably the main reason for the relative increase in housing prices in the mid- to late 1970s.

Faced with so much demand pressure, the existing stocks failed to meet housing needs in many areas of the country. As prices rose, builders added to the housing stock. But because purchasing power of new and relocating households often fell far short of what was needed to buy what had become the standard new housing unit, builders scaled back the average size of units, which meant higher costs per square foot of interior space but less per housing unit than the larger units of the early 1970s would have cost. Builders also supplied less land per housing unit by building at higher densities, which meant more units per acre but less land cost per unit. So new housing units rose as a share of all sales, but single-unit houses dropped as a share of the total, and the proportion accounted for by condominiums doubled from 6 percent in 1976 to 12 percent in 1980 (Table 4.20).

A Savings and Loan System Born in the Depression

Savings societies were organized in the nineteenth century to facilitate house purchases by members of immigrant groups, and savings banks and commercial banks regularly made short-term loans for house purchases by established, upper-middle-class families. But long-term amortized mortgages did not exist before the 1930s, and access to mortgage credit was simply beyond the reach of the average American family. These restrictive financial frameworks fell away after Congress passed the Homeowners' Loan Act of 1933. The new financial environment was conceived broadly and simply to have two

functions: to create a secure means to accumulate long-term savings of families and single persons, thereby encouraging savings; and to invest the savings thus accumulated back into housing in the form of first-mortgage loans for building or buying houses. The savings and mortgage loan institutions conceived in this plan were to be different from commercial banks holding demand deposits (checking accounts) and making primarily short-term business loans. The new institutions were founded on the propositions that the encouragement of long-term savings and habits of thrift was in the best interests of people and the stability of the country, and that long-term individual savings were an especially appropriate source of funds for house mortgages.[16]

The 1933 legislation making possible specialized lending institutions for housing marked the beginnings of the thrift industry. The new law granted tax exemptions to these institutions in exchange for their focus on housing. The Federal Housing Administration (FHA) insured lenders against defaults by borrowers, bolstering the confidence of depositors and lenders. Meanwhile, the self-amortizing mortgage loan, in which each monthly payment by the borrower included a partial payment to reduce the loan principal, quickly became the standard for both government-insured mortgage loans and for uninsured loans. Before the Homeowners' Loan Act of 1933, it was customary for the buyer of a house to obtain two or three separate mortgage loans. This practice was the consequence of low levels of coverage of the first mortgages, which typically ran five years or less and covered much less than the purchase price of the house.

During the darkest days of the Great Depression, both major political parties moved to strengthen and revitalize an ideal as old as the nation—the ownership of real property. The focus shifted from the rural scene to urban and suburban settings, but carried forward the Jeffersonian ideal of the independent farmer as the backbone of the nation. The recovery from the Depression and the conclusion of World War II generated a remarkably homogeneous set of shared values and outlooks, including family formation and home ownership.

Savings of returning veterans following the war, combined with the enormous volume of domestic savings during the war, provided a solid financial base to launch the postwar housing era. The specialized housing savings and lending institutions, the political support for home ownership, the apparently insatiable demand for new family housing, the large pool of savings available for housing, the develop-

[16]Sternlieb and Hughes, op. cit., and J. C. Weicher, "New Home Affordability, Equity and Market Behavior," *Journal of the American Real Estate and Urban Economics Association* 6, no. 4 (1979): 395–416.

ment of secondary financial markets to provide greater liquidity to the thrifts, and the self-amortizing mortgage—each of these promoted record levels of housing production and an immense demand for construction and mortgage loans.

The America of the late 1940s and 1950s believed in newer and better housing, in growth, and in development. Without such a shared view there would never have been the rise of the large-volume house builders and land developers who overcame the nation's urban housing shortages and delivered housing that most American households could afford. Steadily higher real incomes and substantially expanded borrowing power encouraged Americans to enlarge the housing inventory by 50 percent between 1950 and 1970, adding 21 million units (Table 4.21). Greater affluence of the white households as well as of black and other households pushed owner-occupancy rates for all groups steadily upward (Table 4.22).[17]

Following the remarkable rates of production and sales of the 1950s and 1960s, the 1970s saw even more frenetic activity—before the financial rules began to change. Between 1970 and 1980 the nation added almost 20 million new units, almost duplicating in one decade the achievement of the previous two. Not only were production rates unsurpassed, but quality levels reached heights unimagined by earlier generations.

The trends began to reverse in 1973, the year of the oil embargo, following the sharp rise in oil prices by the Organization of Petroleum Exporting Countries (OPEC). Median family income in constant dollar terms reached a peak in 1973, then dropped (Table 4.21). By 1981 the real median family income in America had dropped almost $2,300 below the 1973 high. Yet housing production accelerated, driven forward by a combination of inflationary expectations and financial support systems. Land costs began adding to house cost inflation, moving from 12 percent of total house costs to 20 to 30 percent and even more. Restrictive zoning practices and the introduction of development management controls had made developable land a relatively scarce item in many communities.[18]

The increases in raw land prices were compounded by locally mandated requirements for infrastructure, with sewer hookup charges in some jurisdictions reaching $3,000 to $5,000 per unit. Increasingly developers were obligated to dedicate land for parks, schools, and other public purposes, with the cost added to the inflation in housing prices.

[17]Ibid.
[18]Fred Bosselman and David Callies, *The Quiet Revolution in Land Use Control* (Washington, DC: U.S. Government Printing Office, 1971).

TABLE 4.21
Median Family Income, 1950–1981

Year	Current Dollars	Constant 1981 Dollars	Gains in Real Income (Constant 1981 Dollars)		
1950	$3,310	$12,549	1950–		
1955	4,418	15,003	1960	$4,710	37.5%
1960	5,620	17,259	1960–		
1965	6,957	20,054	1970	5,852	33.9
1970	9,867	23,111	1970–		
1973	12,051	24,663	1973	1,552	6.7
1980	21,023	23,204	1973–		
1981	22,388	22,388	1981	−2,275	−9.2

SOURCE: U.S. Bureau of the Census, "Money Income and Poverty Status of Familes and Persons in the United States, 1981." *Current Population Reports*, series P-60, no. 134. (Advance data from the March 1982 Current Population Survey.)

Thus, lagging real incomes, record inflation levels, higher real tax rates as inflation-driven earnings increases pushed taxpayers into higher tax brackets, and startlingly rapid advances in house prices reinforced the traditional sentiments favoring housing as a safe haven for assets. Housing in the 1970s came to be seen by consumers as a refuge in an increasingly uncertain and hostile economic environment. Driven to this sanctuary by forces beyond their control, households committed themselves to paying unprecedented shares of their income for housing in order to get aboard the housing train, anxious that they would be permanently left behind with ownership beyond their reach. During this frantic episode housing in America became

TABLE 4.22
House Ownership Rates, 1920–1980

	Share of All Households Who Are Owners		
	Total	White	Black and Others
1920	46%	48%	24%
1930	48	50	25
1940	44	46	24
1950	55	57	35
1960	62	64	38
1970	63	65	42
1979	65	68	44
1980	64	68	44

SOURCE: U.S. Bureau of the Census, *Statistical Abstract of the United States, 1981*, 1986.

more important as a form of investment, of forced savings, of tax avoidance, and as a hedge against inflation than as a refuge from the elements.[19]

In seeking refuge from a tumultuous and inflationary economic environment, households used the residential finance industry in ways that made matters worse. Access to the refuge was provided by mortgage instruments and borrowing terms that were designed during the New Deal years of the 1930s and 1940s. They had been designed for use in stable noninflationary economic environments, but were still available for use in the inflationary 1970s. The guaranteed low interest rates over the life of the mortgage loan and the apparently unending rise in the market value of good-quality residential real estate combined to make housing borrowing an unprecedented bargain for house buyers. Rapid expansions in real estate borrowing in the 1970s fed an already insatiable housing demand and helped to escalate further the surge in housing outlays.[20]

During most of the chaotic 1970s the housing finance industry failed to provide new mortgage loan products for easy use by first-time buyers during a time of rapid inflation and sharp declines in real median family incomes. Thus, only those who already owned a house could easily enter the market, trading it in as a down payment as they traded up to a more expensive house.

Additional stresses on the economy and the housing finance industry developed as the inflation-driven increases in housing values were tapped through additional loans made possible by mortgage refinancing. The additional money borrowed became a vehicle for maintaining consumption of diverse goods and services in the face of stagnating incomes. House ownership had not only become a symbol of the good middle-class life, but had become a means for financing its continuation. Who needed a savings account when appreciation of house values produced far grander returns than any passbook balance? The consumption ethic had overcome the habits of thrift that had been so carefully nurtured by the residential savings and loan institutions. The housing finance industry was actually producing outcomes that were the opposite of those intended. Government policy as it worked its way through the thrift industry "made losers of savers and winners of speculators."[21]

[19]Bosselman and Callies, *The Quiet Revolution*, fn. 1.

[20]See Raymond J. Struyk, *Urban Homeownership: The Economic Determinants* (Lexington, MA: Lexington Books, 1976); John A. Tucillo, *Housing and Investment in an Inflationary World: Theory and Evidence* (Washington, DC: Urban Institute, 1980); and John A. Tucillo and Kevin E. Villani, eds., *House Prices and Inflation* (Washington, DC: Urban Institute, 1981).

[21]Sternlieb and Hughes, op. cit., p. 19.

The Collapse of the New Deal Thrift Institutions

The thrift industry was in trouble. Faced with an unabating demand for cheap mortgage money, the demand was met by depositors—who earned little—and by the secondary mortgage market, where the cost of funds began to rise. Disintermediation—the flow of savings out of thrift institutions into more rewarding uses—is an important regulator of the total economic system. As funds move out of the thrifts, housing and related industries should slow down, thereby putting the brakes on those parts of the economy.

The response of the thrifts to disintermediation was to press federal regulators to permit paying higher interest to savers and a broadening of their deposit-gathering activities. During the Carter Administration the certificate of deposit (CD), which had been used for many years, became available in small denominations, paying market rates of interest. These new CDs allowed the thrifts to attract more deposits by paying higher interest on time deposits—at the same time removing the wall that had existed since the 1930s separating general market interest rates from the low-interest housing market that had persisted for decades.

Within a short time the bulk of the thrifts' loanable funds came not from traditional low-interest passbook sources, but from high-interest CDs and from other borrowings in the money market. The nation had traded low-cost funds and low-cost housing and had received in return high-cost money, which raised the cost of housing. On the other hand, the new CDs assured the availability of mortgage money because disintermediation was no longer a threat. A nondifferentiated homogeneous financial market emerged. Housing had lost much of its protected status, and the financial costs of housing now put it beyond the reach of many households that in previous decades would have enjoyed easy access to housing.

The transition occurred quickly and was neither gradual nor orderly. Mortgage interest costs soared, with long-term rates rising to 18 percent. Few prospective house buyers could qualify for mortgage loans at those interest levels. Thus, housing starts during 1981 and 1982 dropped to about half the annual levels of about 2 million starts achieved in both 1977 and 1978.[22]

These adjustments have made big winners of those who already owned houses, which were bought on easy terms before 1980. These owners are living so cheaply that the tide of housing finance events does not affect them much—unless they try to sell their houses.

[22]Ibid., pp. 19–20.

Meanwhile, first-time prospective buyers find their access to housing substantially curtailed. High expectations and a sense of entitlement to cheap high-quality housing provide the ingredients for political discontent. The vast middle market for housing has been segmented into the affluent "haves" and the distressed "have nots." It will take a long time for adjustments in public policy, connecting new sources of higher-priced mortgage money, to meet adjustments in consumer expectations and behavior. The issue touches many households of persons born after World War II.[23]

FHA-Guaranteed Mortgages

The Federal Housing Administration (FHA) was created by the National Housing Act of 1934, which has been amended several times and charges the FHA to operate housing loan insurance programs, to facilitate sound housing finance on reasonable terms, and to help stabilize the mortgage market. The FHA does not lend much mortgage money directly, nor plan and build houses. It insures loans and sets underwriting conditions that must be met by lenders, borrowers, and the property involved in the loan.

In the early 1980s, the majority of FHA-insured loans originated under either Section 203(b) or Section 245 of the National Housing Act. The 203(b) program covers loans on single-family houses where the loan limits as a percentage of FHA-appraised value are 97 percent on the first $25,000 and 95 percent on the balance, up to a maximum set by Congress. The secretary of the U.S. Department of Housing and Urban Development (HUD) administers the program and sets the maximum interest rate that can be charged on a Section 203 FHA-insured mortgage. The newer Section 245 program covers graduated payment and adjustable rate mortgages, which differ from the level payment mortgages covered by Section 203(b). The maximum interest rates for the various graduated payment plans are also set initially by the secretary of HUD.

Sometimes the setting of maximum interest rates for FHA-insured mortgages produces a gap between the FHA rate and the conventional lending rate. If the FHA rate is lower than the conventional rate, it is often necessary for the seller of the property that is to be financed by an FHA-insured loan to pay the lender a discount inducement, called discount points, to make the loan at the lower FHA rate.

Borrowers are charged .5 percent of the loan amount annually to support the cost of the FHA mortgage program, which has generally been self-sufficient through the years. In the mid-1980s the premium was changed to 3.8 percent of the loan amount payable at the outset, but the amount could be financed by adding it to the loan total. In case the borrower defaults, the lender is entitled to receive from the FHA debentures equivalent to the amount of the remaining unpaid mortgage debt. The interest and principal payments on the debentures are guaranteed by the U.S. government.[24]

In 1960 the median sale price of new houses sold with Section 203 FHA-guaranteed mortgages was $14,324 (Table 4.23). The average mortgage loan term was 29.2 years, and the ratio of housing expense to expected income in the early years of the mortgage had a median value of 22.2 percent. Section 203 mortgages on existing houses in 1960 had shorter terms (25.8 years), covered lower-priced houses ($12,975 median), and involved a lower median ratio of housing expense to income (21.9 percent).

During the two decades following 1960 the median sales price of new houses rose from $14,324 to $54,524, an increase of 281 percent. Used houses with FHA-insured mortgages in 1980 had average values 226 percent above the 1960 average. Effective incomes rose at rates similar to the advance in average sales prices, but total median monthly housing expense for new houses rose from $129 in 1960 to $669 in 1980, a rise of 419 percent, while the monthly expense on used houses rose from $121 to $576, or 377 percent in the same period. By 1980 there was little difference in average mortgage term between new houses (29.9 years) and used houses (29.5 years). Median closing costs have been slightly above 2 percent of median sales prices of used houses and below 2 percent on new houses. These costs can include fees for title insurance, appraisal, survey, recording of legal documents, tax stamps, and other items, depending on the state in which the sale occurs.

Logically, the premiums paid for FHA mortgage default insurance should reflect the riskiness of the loans that are insured. In fact, the FHA has changed the same premium on all its insured mortgages, regardless of the size of the downpayment, the loan repayment schedule, and whether or not payments could rise unexpectedly.[25] It is estimated that graduated-payment mortgages (GPMs) with large down

[23]Wilhelmina Leigh, *The Housing Finance System and Federal Policy: Recent Changes and Options for the Future*, U.S. Congress, Congressional Budget Office (Washington, DC: U.S. Government Printing Office, 1983).

[24]Charles H. Wurtzebach and Mike E. Miles, *Modern Real Estate* (New York: Wiley, 1984), p. 341.

[25]Donald F. Cunningham and Patric H. Hendershott, *Pricing FHA Mortgage Default Insurance*, Working Paper no. 1382 (Cambridge, MA: National Bureau of Economic Research, 1985).

TABLE 4.23
Section 203 FHA-Guaranteed Mortgages on Single-Family Houses, 1960–1980

	1960	1965	1970	1975	1978	1979	1980
NEW HOUSES							
Median Family Effective Income, Monthly[1]	$597	$652	$1,029	$1,411	$1,697	$2,036	$2,256
Average Mortgage Term (Years)	29.2	31.7	29.9	30.0	29.9	29.9	29.9
Median Mortgage Payment, Including Taxes and Insurance	$104	$114	$207[2]	$284	$369	$469	$568
Total Median Monthly Housing Expense[3]	129	144	246[2]	347	454	566	669
Median Ratio: Housing Expense/Effective Income	22.2%	22.5%	23.9%	24.9%	27.2%	28.2%	30.1%
Median Sale Price	$14,324	$16,190	$22,460	$31,627	$39,736	$48,819	$54,524
Median Closing Costs	286	376	513	690	746	824	941
EXISTING HOUSES							
Median Family Effective Income, Monthly[1]	$565	$635	$903	$1,284	$1,526	$1,769	$2,064
Average Mortgage Term (Years)	25.8	28.6	28.8	29.3	29.5	29.5	29.5
Median Mortgage Payment, Including Taxes and Insurance	$97	$111	$164	$245	$300	$368	$466
Total Median Monthly Housing Expense[3]	121	141	200	306	386	464	576
Median Ratio: Housing Expense/Effective Income	21.9%	22.4%	23.0%	24.2%	26.0%	26.8%	28.2%
Median Sales Price	$12,975	$14,733	$17,459	$25,612	$32,127	$37,297	$42,300
Median Closing Costs	275	322	417	572	731	810	900

[1]Effective income: "The FHA-estimated amount of the mortgagor's earning capacity (before federal income tax deductions) likely to prevail during approximately the first third of the mortgage term." See *HUD Statistical Yearbook, 1973.*

[2]Arithmetic mean.

[3]Mortgage principal and interest, taxes, insurance, and utilities.

SOURCE: U.S. Department of Housing and Urban Development, *HUD Statistical Yearbook, 1980*, pp. 160–65.

payments are generally two to three times more likely to default than traditional 30-year level-payment mortgages (LPMs). Owners with GPMs with small downpayments are estimated to be four to six times more likely to default. A small downpayment and slowly (or negatively for a time) amortizing mortgages increase the likelihood that the value of the house will fall below the mortgage balance. A primary benefit to the borrower of default, then, is escaping from a mortgage that exceeds the value of the house. Another benefit is free rent from the date of default to the date of foreclosure. Thus, al-though .5 percent FHA mortgage insurance premium is sufficient to cover default risks for 30-year LPMs with 5 percent downpayments, it is estimated to be too low for most GPMs and too high for shorter-term LPMs or for LPMs with large downpayments.

The disruptions in the housing finance industry that began in the late 1970s have touched every aspect of housing. The new GPMs that were created to respond to new financial realities have brought problems of their own. Mortgage insurance premiums that closely reflect the risks of default for different kinds of mortgages reduce future losses by the FHA and reduce or eliminate implicit subsidies from one class of borrowers who pay premiums that are too high to another class who should pay more.[26]

VA Mortgage Underwriting and Private Mortgage Insurance

The Veterans Administration (VA), created in 1944, helps veterans and their widows obtain house financing by guaranteeing their house loans. In case of default on a VA-guaranteed mortgage, the VA becomes liable for a percentage of the outstanding principal (for example, 60 percent) or a maximum amount (say, $27,500), whichever is less. The VA also provides a loan insurance program, but it is inconsequential. The VA's major impact on housing finance has been through loan guarantees. By reducing the risk of mortgage lending, VA and FHA programs have directly facilitated the operation of a secondary mortgage market.

Indirectly, federal mortgage insurance and guarantee programs have affected original lending terms, building designs, and uniform loan documentation. The FHA and VA provide underwriting guidelines to mortgage loan originators. By following the guidelines the loan originators can expand their loan activity while maintaining acceptable risk levels. Building requirements have worked to upgrade and standardize the quality of the houses pledged as mortgage collateral. The requirement of uniform loan documentation enhances the marketability of mortgages.

Prior to the introduction of mortgage insurance by the federal government in the 1930s, this field was covered exclusively by private companies. These firms disappeared in the Depression, but reemerged in 1957 when the Mortgage Guarantee Insurance Corporation (MGIC) was organized and licensed by the Wisconsin Commissioner of Insurance. By the mid-1980s more than a dozen American and Canadian private mortgage insurers had been approved by the Federal National Mortgage Association (FNMA) and the Federal Home Loan Mortgage Corporation (FHLMC). The FNMA, called "Fannie Mae," is a privately owned, government-sponsored agency that buys and sells FHA-insured, VA-guaranteed, and conventional mortgage loans.

When a mortgage loan is foreclosed, the policyholder (the lender) takes title to the property and then files a claim against the mortgage

[26]Cunningham and Hendershott, *Pricing FHA Mortgage Default Insurance.*

insurance company. The company either takes the property and pays the lender's claim or pays the lender a percentage of the coverage on the loan. Unlike the FHA (which offers insurance up to 100 percent of the loan principal) or the VA (which guarantees up to perhaps $27,500 of the loan), the mortgage insurance companies provide insurance coverage up to a maximum of 20 to 25 percent of the loan amount, depending on the loan-to-value ratio and the coverage wanted by the lender. This limited coverage, even though it is on the riskiest part of the loan, has meant that private mortgage insurance often costs less than the FHA or VA insurance, except for high loan-to-value loans. Moreover, private insurance coverage can be canceled after the top 20 or 25 percent of the loan is paid off or when property's value rises enough to lower the loan-to-value ratio. In contrast, FHA insurance lasts for the life of the loan, but the actual differences in default risk are small.

In 1970 almost two thirds of the total originations of mortgage loans were conventionally financed. Mortgage insurance companies wrote insurance for under 10 percent of the conventional mortgage originations (Table 4.24). By the early 1980s over 80 percent of the mortgage originations were conventionally financed, and private mortgage insurance was covering about half of the originations.

Housing Finance: 1970–1980

Savings and loan associations originated about half of the residential mortgage loans on structures with one to four units in the 1970s (Table 4.25). Most of the remainder was split between commercial banks and mortgage companies. As the volume of long-term mortgage loan originations more than tripled from the early 1970s to the later years of the decade—exceeding $184 billion in 1979 before declining to $132 billion in 1980—the shares accounted for by the various sources of housing loans remained reasonably stable.

After the loans are made, many of them are resold in the secondary mortgage market, which is simply a mechanism for buying and selling already-existing mortgages. In the primary market, savings and loan associations and other lenders make mortgage loans directly to borrowers. In the secondary market the thrift institutions and other primary lenders take the loans they have made and sell them to long-term investors. The proceeds from the sale replenish the capital of the primary lenders who now can lend again in the primary market.

During the 1970s outstanding mortgage loans tripled to almost a trillion dollars (Table 4.25). The savings and loan associations have

TABLE 4.24

Mortgage Loans, Insurance, and Guarantees, One- to Four-Unit Structures, 1970–1981
(in billions of dollars)

Year	Mortgage Loans Originated	Conventional	FHA	VA	Percentage of Originations Insured	MICs	MIC Percentage of Insured Originations
1970	$36	$23	$9	$4	39%	$1	8%
1975	78	63	6	9	32	10	40
1980	134	107	15	12	34	19	41
1981	97	79	10	8	38	19	51

NOTE: MICs are conventional mortgages insured by private mortgage insurance companies.

SOURCE: Mortgage Insurance Companies of America, *Factbook and Directory, 1982–83*; quoted in Charles H. Wurtzebach and Mike E. Miles, *Modern Real Estate* (New York: Wiley, 1984), p. 344.

TABLE 4.25

Mortgage Loans Originated and Long-Term Mortgage Debt Outstanding, 1971–1980 (in billions of dollars)

Loan Organizations for Houses (1–4 Units)	1971	Percentage	1980	Percentage
Total	$58	100%	$132	100%
Savings and loan associations	27	46	61	46
Mutual savings banks	4	6	5	4
Commercial banks	13	22	27	20
Life insurance companies	–	1	2	1
Noninsured pension funds	–	–	–	–
State and local retirement funds	–	–	–	–
State and local credit agencies	–	–	2	2
Mortgage companies	12	22	30	22
Federal credit agencies	2	3	4	3
Credit unions	–	–	–	–
Mortgage investment trusts	–	–	–	–
Mortgage Loans Outstanding, Held by:				
Total	328	100	960	100
Savings and loan associations	141	43	419	44
Mutual savings banks	43	13	65	7
Commercial banks	48	15	160	17
Life insurance companies	25	8	18	2
Federal agencies	30	9	183	19
Other	40	12	114	12

NOTE: (–): rounds to zero.

SOURCES: United States League of Savings Institutions, *Savings and Loan Fact Book, 1980*, p. 32; U.S. Department of Housing and Urban Development, *HUD Statistical Yearbook, 1973*, p. 297; *HUD Statistical Yearbook, 1980*, p. 327; United States League of Savings Associations, *Savings and Loan Source Book 1982*, p. 26.

held just under half of this total while mutual savings banks have lost half of their share. Life insurance companies have reduced their holdings while commercial banks and federal agencies have expanded their holdings and their shares of the total.

Mortgaged Houses and Interest Rates, 1920–1980

Between 1920 and 1980 the United States changed from a nation of predominantly renters to a nation composed mainly of households who owned the housing units they occupied. Prior to the 1930s the lending terms of the banking and thrift industries were so strict that only households of substantial means could qualify for mortgage loans. Wealthy households could pay cash for their housing, upper-income households could borrow to buy, but most remained renters (Table 4.26).

As the percentage of nonfarm housing carrying mortgages rose from under two fifths in 1920 to almost two thirds in 1980, interest rates dropped slightly and then rose. The low interest rates in the 1940s and 1950s were partly the result of healthy personal savings rates coupled with low risk to the mortgage lenders because of federal mortgage insurance and mortgage guarantee programs.

By the 1970s the rate of increase in the percentage of houses with mortgages had leveled off, and interest rates had started their steep climb. The steadily worsening inflation of the 1970s encouraged households to buy ever-larger and more expensive houses, not as shelter but as hedges against inflation and as speculative investments. This collective response to inflation put added pressure on the de-

TABLE 4.26

Mortgaged Housing Units and Mortgage Interest Rates, 1920–1980

Year	Percentage of Nonfarm Housing Units Mortgaged	Median Interest Rate on First Mortgage, Single-Unit Houses		
		New	All	Existing
1920	39.8%		NA	
1940	45.3		6.0%	
1950	44.0		5.0	
1960	56.8		5.1	
1970 (1971)	(60.6)	8.3%		8.2%
1980	64.7	12.3		12.5

NOTES: 1920: all units; 1940 and 1950: owner-occupied, 1–4 units; 1960: all 1–4 units; 1970: all single-unit housing; 1980: specified single-unit housing on lots under 10 acres. NA = not available.

SOURCES: U.S. Bureau of the Census, *Historical Statistics of the United States*, p. 651; *Statistical Abstract of the United States, 1982*, pp. 762, 765; *1969*, p. 705; U.S. Department of Housing and Urban Development, *HUD Statistical Yearbook, 1979*, p. 259.

mand for mortgage credit and helped make the inflation even worse.[27] Steadily higher mortgage interest rates during the 1970s were one of the outcomes (Table 4.26).

The Ability of American Households to Afford Housing

American housing policy discussion in the nineteenth century emphasized the adequacy of supply, safe construction and maintenance, and protection from fire and disease. Health threats and other hazards were eventually brought under control by means of clean piped water, sanitary sewers, fire codes, laws governing building designs and materials (building codes), and laws governing occupancy rates to prevent crowding (housing codes). During the Depression years of the 1930s, new policy issues had moved to the fore, including the question of whether families of modest means could afford to buy and maintain the kind of housing that they felt they deserved. This question was primarily posed as an urban question since the majority of Americans were living in cities after World War I, but small town

and farm families of the 1920s and 1930s also demanded government response to their housing aspirations and unmet housing needs.

The fact that every household needs some minimum shelter is not debated in the United States. Instead, debate focuses on the definition of minimal housing and on how the poorest urban and rural households should be helped in obtaining it. Housing assistance programs for the poor started with philanthropic, fraternal, and benevolent societies and local poorhouses in the early years of the nation. They followed older traditions from England and the Continent. The federal government promoted housing for the poor with the public housing programs begun by the Roosevelt Administration during the late 1930s. In current programs low- and moderate-income households are helped by cash transfers, by low-interest loans, and by subsidized rents.

The affordability question, however, long ago moved beyond the plight of the poorest of the poor households that are unable to afford a decent minimum community standard of safe and sanitary housing. Today, the affordability question focuses on the vast middle-income, middle-class American households, on what they want in the way of housing, what they feel they need, and what they assert that they deserve. The intensity of their feelings in this matter and their large numbers elevate the affordability issue to the status of significant public policy questions.[28]

Housing Expenditures Within the Household Budget

American households divide their personal consumption expenditures among durable goods (mainly motor vehicles and parts, furniture, and household equipment), nondurable goods (mainly food, fuel, clothing), and services (housing, household operation, and transportation are among the most important). The outlays for durable goods, as a percentage of all consumer spending, varied between 11 and 15 percent after 1960 (Table 4.27). Despite major price hikes in the cost of oil, gasoline, and natural gas after 1960, the share of consumer spending on fuels remained stable. General inflation accompanied the

[27]Access to mortgage credit has varied from place to place and from one borrower group to another. See David Listokin and Stephen Casey, *Mortgage Lending and Race* (New Brunswick, N.J.: Center for Urban Policy Research, 1980).

[28]Raymond J. Struyk and Susan A. Marshall, *Urban Homeownership. The Economic Determinants* (Lexington, MA: Lexington Books, 1976); H. S. Rosen, "Owner-Occupied Housing and the Federal Income Tax: Estimates and Simulations," *Journal of Urban Economics* 6, no. 2 (1979): 247–66; Michael W. Andreassi and C. Duncan MacRae, *Homeowner Income Tax Provisions and Metropolitan Housing Markets: A Simulation Study* (Washington, DC: Urban Institute, 1981); and J. Khadduri and R. J. Struyk, "Housing Vouchers for the Poor," *Journal of Policy Analysis and Management* 1, no. 2 (1982): 196–208.

TABLE 4.27

Personal Consumption Expenditures by Persons and Nonprofit Institutions, in Constant 1972 Dollars, 1960–1982 (in billions of dollars)

	1960		1970		1980		1982	
Durable Goods	$51	11%	$89	13%	$138	15%	$140	14%
Motor vehicles and parts	24	5	38	6	54	6	57	6
Furniture and household equipment	20	4	36	5	60	6	60	6
Nondurable Goods	208	46	284	42	356	38	364	38
Gasoline and oil	14	3	23	3	25	3	26	3
Services	192	42	299	44	439	47	466	48
Housing	64	14	102	15	160	17	171	18
Household operation	28	6	42	6	62	7	64	7
Transportation	17	4	25	4	33	4	32	3
Total	$452	100%	$672	100%	$932	100%	$970	100%

NOTE: Totals include items not shown separately.

SOURCE: U.S. Bureau of the Census, *Statistical Abstract of the United States, 1984,* p. 452.

fuel price rises, and fuel conservation measures controlled the expansion of per capita and per household fuel consumption in the expanding economy. Food, clothing, and alcoholic beverage prices rose less rapidly than many other durable goods and services prices, permitting the share of consumer spending devoted to nondurables to drop significantly after 1960.

It was housing and related costs—furniture, household equipment, and household operations (maintenance insurance, utilities)—that absorbed a sharply rising share of consumer spending, especially after 1970. Rental levels grew relatively slowly, but the cost of financing, house taxes, and house insurance, plus the higher than average inflation in the prices of house heating fuels and other utilities, rose at exceptionally rapid rates (Table 4.28). In 1960 these categories of spending absorbed 24 percent of the total. By 1970 the total was 26 percent; by 1980, 30 percent; and by 1982, 31 percent.

Part of the steady rise can be traced to the efforts of households to maintain a housing standard in the face of prices that rose faster in the housing realm than in other areas. The other part of the explanation is found in the efforts of households to expand their spending on housing compared with other outlays. During the late 1960s and most of the 1970s the financial circumstances facing house buyers, coupled with the inflationary gains of house values, stimulated an expansion of housing consumption relative to other goods and services, which is reflected vividly in the large diversion of consumer spending into housing and out of other areas (Table 4.27). Households entering the market were consuming larger average amounts of housing of steadily higher quality and were laying out larger shares of their income for the housing that they bought or rented.

The presence of so much speculative investment in housing after the mid-1960s clouds the issues surrounding the affordability question. The high-quality, higher-priced new houses, which were built mainly in the more attractive suburbs, experienced higher rates of

TABLE 4.28

Consumer Price Index, Changes, 1970–1980 (1967 = 100)

	1970	1975	1980
All Items	116.3	161.2	246.8
Housing Items	118.9	166.8	263.3
Rentals			
House purchase	118.3	160.3	254.3
Financing, taxes, and insurance	142.3	201.9	396.0
Maintenance and repairs	124.0	187.6	285.7
Fuel and other utilities	107.6	167.8	278.6

NOTE: Definitions of goods and services included changed in 1980 to reflect changed consumption patterns.

SOURCES: U.S. Department of Housing and Urban Development, *HUD Statistical Yearbook, 1979,* p. 279; *1980,* p. 349; U.S. Bureau of the Census, *Statistical Abstract of the United States, 1981,* p. 468.

TABLE 4.29

Proportion of American Families Able to Afford the Median-Priced New House, 1965–1980

Year	Median Sales Price	Average Mortgage Interest Rate[1]	After Tax Total Expenses[2]	Percentage of Families Meeting Requirements[3]	Median Family Income	Sales Price ÷ Median Family Income
1965	$20,000	5.82%	$1,708	51%	$6,957	2.9
1966	21,400	6.25	1,883	51		
1968	24,700	6.97	2,263	47		
1970	23,400	8.44	2,288	55	9,867	2.4
1972	27,600	7.60	2,710	52	11,116	2.5
1974	35,900	8.92	3,664	42	12,836	2.8
1976	44,200	NA	NA	NA	14,958	3.0
1978	55,700	NA	NA	NA	17,640	3.2
1980	64,600	NA	NA	NA	21,023	3.1

NOTE: NA = not available.

[1]25-year conventional mortgage on 75 percent of sales price.

[2]Annual interest, principal payment, property tax, insurance, maintenance, and utilities.

[3]Required income equals four times annual housing expense.

SOURCES: U.S. Department of Housing and Urban Development, *HUD Statistical Yearbook, 1977*, p. 348; *1980*, p. 329; United States League of Savings Institutions, *Savings and Loan Sourcebook, 1982*, p. 35; U.S. Bureau of the Census, *Statistical Abstract of the United States, 1982*, p. 432.

price appreciation than did the more modest new and used houses in local housing markets and submarkets. Consumer knowledge that expensive new houses—because of their exceptionally high appreciation rates—were the best buys in terms of their net cost after appreciation put added pressure on the existing supply of fine houses and encouraged developers and builders to emphasize the production of steadily higher-priced and larger houses rather than smaller, more modest units. The more expensive houses were bought by upper-income households whose marginal income tax rates were quite high. For such families, the deductibility of mortgage interest and real estate taxes from their taxable incomes meant that the U.S. Treasury paid part of the extra housing cost—and the higher the household taxable income, the larger the share of interest and taxes the Treasury paid.

Thus, the median sales price of new houses rose from $20,000 in 1965 to $23,400 in 1970 and $64,600 in 1980 (Table 4.29). In the stable 1950s the income required to be able to afford a new house was usually quoted as four times the annual housing expense. In the 1950s over 50 percent of the families met this criterion, but by 1974 the proportion had dropped to 42 percent. Another way to show the

relation between changing new house prices and changing family incomes is to compare the average sales price of new housing units each year as a multiple of the median family income in that year. That multiple stayed below 3.0 until the early 1970s, and then rose above 3.0 as housing prices advanced faster than incomes rose (Table 4.29).

Affordability and Renters

The affordability question affects renters as well as owners, and the national averages also mask the surpluses and shortages that develop in local rental housing markets and submarkets.[29] On the supply side, what is available in the stock of rental units constantly changes as new and usually high-priced units are added at the top of

[29]See John C. Weicher, Kevin E. Villani, and Elizabeth A. Roistacher, eds., *Rental Housing: Is There a Crisis?* (Washington, DC: Urban Institute, 1981); Fred E. Case, "Housing Demand Characteristics of Underhoused Families in the Inner City," *Annals of Regional Science* 3, no. 2 (1969): 15–26. Each of the underhoused groups has its own special set of problems. See, for example, Margaret S. Treuer, *Indian Housing: Worst in the Nation* (Boulder, CO: Native American Rights Fund, 1981).

TABLE 4.30

Proportion of Gross Income of Renter Households Used for Rent, 1960–1977

	1960	1970	1976	1977
Less than 25 Percent	64.7%	60.4%	53.5%	51.3%
25 to 34 Percent	13.9	14.3	17.9	18.4
35 Percent and More	21.4	25.3	28.6	30.3

SOURCE: U.S. Department of Housing and Urban Development, *HUD Statistical Yearbook, 1980*, p. 330.

the line in growth areas while older, cheaper, and usually deteriorated units are demolished at the bottom of the line. Thus, the rental housing stock steadily improves, but the average price rises.

On the demand side, the quality of what people want rises as community standards rise, and as higher average incomes make higher rental outlays possible for households that want better housing. Faced with higher disposable incomes and higher average rental levels, households in each local market decide on their patterns of income disposal for durable goods, nondurable goods, and services.

In 1960 almost two thirds of renter households in the United States paid less than 25 percent of their gross income for rent (Table 4.30). The ease of buying new and used housing after 1945 had the effect of muting the demand for rental units, keeping the prices low. By the late 1970s almost half of the renter households were paying over 25 percent of their income for rent and almost a third were paying 35 percent or more. The sharp rise in the percentage of income devoted to rentals was partly due to changes in demand (rapid rise in rates of net household formations by members of the postwar baby boom generation and rising housing aspirations), by changes in supply (conversion of existing rental units to condominiums), by renting becoming more selective of the lowest-income households, and by heavy rates of interstate migration that sharply expanded demand for rentals in areas of significant net inmigration.

How Changing Fashions, Tastes, and Outlooks Affect Housing Demand

Consumption is a social act. People attempt to join certain consumption and taste communities and to avoid others by their deci-

sions about what to buy and consume. Housing is an especially vivid arena of consumption behavior in which prevailing fashion trends wield an important influence on housing preferences.[30]

For most of the nineteenth century (and in fact right up to the present day), U.S. cities were built at densities that were much higher than prevailing technologies would have required or that residents would have preferred. Prevailing transportation and communication technologies were more consistently applied to long-distance links between cities than to easing the congestion and communication problems within cities.

The introduction of the electric streetcar at the end of the 1880s permitted new residential areas to spill outward in every direction served by the streetcar lines. The new, low-density subdivisions and streetcar suburbs invited upper-middle-class families to relocate outward. Most households certainly preferred the newer, greener, lower-density housing areas, but only a few had the financial wherewithal to get what they wanted.

In every era of city building, Americans have consistently expressed a preference for lower-density housing than they currently consume. High fashions are set by what the upper-income groups consume. The high cost of urban land, plus the expense in time and money of long-distance commuting, kept suburbia or small town and rural life beyond the reach of workers tied to the city by the employment provided by the urban-industrial economy.

The high-density pre-1889 city based on "pedestrian and horsecar" movement added rings of lower-density developments during the "electric street-car era," extending from 1889 through World War I.[31] The introduction of widespread automobile ownership and use by upper-middle-income households in the 1920s and 1930s meant that suburban increments to the housing stock could be erected at still lower densities. The car-owning families who provided the market for the new housing were merely following fashions and tastes set for them by the rich of a generation earlier.

In the "freeway automobile era" of post–World War II the garden

[30]Dolores Hayden, *Redesigning the American Dream: The Future of Housing, Work, and Family Life*, (New York: Norton, 1984).

[31]John S. Adams, "Residential Structure of Midwestern Cities," Association of American Geographers, *Annals* 60, no. 1 (March 1970): 37–62. For a thorough geographical account of the emergence of American metropolitan regions within the constraints imposed by transportation and communications technologies set within a sequence of economic development eras, see John R. Borchert, "American Metropolitan Evolution," *Geographical Review* 57, no. 3 (1967): 301–32; and "America's Changing Metropolitan Regions," Association of American Geographers, *Annals* 62, no. 2 (June 1972): 353–73.

cities and suburban estates that had been dreamed about by utopian visionaries, enjoyed by the nobility and landed aristocracy in preindustrial Europe and America, favored by the rich before World War I, and consumed by the upper middle class in the 1920s and 1930s became available to most households after World War II. Single-family houses on large, landscaped suburban lots were brought into the reach of most households as all the previous constraints to ownership were relaxed. Widespread ownership of private cars, cheap gasoline, and good roads produced an increase in the supply of urban land of several orders of magnitude—and the price of land dropped sharply to low levels.

Historically Prominent Housing Styles in the United States

Several distinctive housing styles have appeared on the American landscape since colonial times. Some—like the seventeenth-century Puritan houses or antebellum planters' mansions—contained features that have been admired and imitated, while others—such as tenement houses and slave quarters—have been disdained and even feared. But all have supplied our present generation with ideas, examples, and attitudes that shape contemporary housing demand.[32]

The seventeenth-century Puritan houses in New England expressed attitudes of order and solemnity. Architecture, theology, and ways of daily life came together in the layout of towns, in the austere design of houses, and in subtle forms of adornment added to well-tended house exteriors. Other early styles included the typical small cottages for the independent farm households, on scattered rural farm sites—a sharp departure from the housing arrangements of the traditional European farm villages.

Shortly after independence, there developed an urban tradition favoring plain, uniform row houses drawn from patterns and models in builders' books. They became an established style, and remnants persist in Boston, Philadelphia, Baltimore, and other significant cities of the early nineteenth century. The row house style also persists in some contemporary urban and suburban developments of which Reston, Virginia, is among the most celebrated examples.

Enterprising factory owners in the early nineteenth century built industrial towns near waterpower sites, erecting boardinghouses and cottages for their workers. This factory housing became a distinctly American style during a time when industrialists were coming under increased fire for their rapacious ways and factory labor was frequently in short supply as frontier towns and free farmland continually drew factory workers westward. Other American housing styles from the nineteenth century include varieties of modest slave quarters built on southern plantations, not far from the grand colonnaded mansions that documented the social and economic position of the planter's household and the social distance from his slaves and the poor whites in the community.[33]

After the Civil War, steadily increasing rates of foreign immigration and the rapid growth of industrial cities brought on a clash of cultures and classes in the cities. The urban poor and working classes abruptly emerged as a source of shame and fear for the better-established middle and upper classes. Although the rich had always had their country homes and retreats, the middle and upper middle classes had no such safe havens. These latter groups, while trying to imitate the lifestyles of the rich and to isolate themselves from the poor, discovered the style of the planned Victorian suburb to be an attractive solution to their problem.

In the middle of the nineteenth century, poorer people in the city often lived in factories, warehouses, breweries, and large old houses that had been adapted for low-income, high-density residential use. By the last quarter of the century, increased numbers lived in multiple-unit tenements erected by philanthropists or speculative investors, under conditions overcrowded, unsanitary, and often unsavory.

At the other end of the socioeconomic spectrum, elegant inner city apartment buildings and apartment hotels served a small elite able and willing to pay high rents and eager to enjoy the latest technological advances in domestic heating, ventilation, plumbing, lighting, and electrical conveniences. This heavily touted and extravagantly urban style delivered less than its promoters promised, and although it remains a permanent feature of American housing styles, it has never been a dominant one.

Other housing styles that were introduced into the United States with varying success included the late nineteenth-century and early twentieth-century planned company towns. Industrialists and social reformers felt that radical union and political movements could be diluted by professional planning of total work and home environ-

---

[32]Gwendolyn Wright, *Building the Dream: A Social History of Housing in America* (Cambridge, MA: MIT Press, 1981), pp. 4–16; and United States League of Savings Associations, *Realizing the American Dream* (Chicago, 1978).

[33]Wright, *Building the Dream*, pp. 22–3.

ments. Early and smaller prototypes like Lowell, Massachusetts, had been famous since the 1820s, but the later wave of large, welfare-oriented industrial town developments—heavily influenced by George Pullman's $8 million, 4,000-acre model town at the edge of Chicago—set a style that was followed in many parts of the country.

By census time in 1920 the majority of Americans were classed as urban or suburban, and the suburban areas were adding housing faster than the central cities. A broad coalition—including developers, realtors, planners, architects, builders, scholars, government officials, social reformers, and others—designed and promoted the fully planned low-density suburban single-family detached residential development during the housing boom of the 1920s. This style persisted in various permutations throughout the post–World War II period suburbanization boom.

Another distinctive style started during the Hoover Administration (1929–32) as the federal government began to turn attention to the housing needs of the urban and rural poor. There followed a range of programs and publicly sponsored housing projects that in the public's eye are distinctively "public housing." A widely held sentiment in favor of helping the worst off has been muted by another widely shared view that public housing should avoid looking too attractive. It should have less visual appeal than market rate housing, and its individual housing units should be small and spare, consciously to discourage the idea that poverty and dependency or residency in public housing are permanent conditions.[34]

Contemporary Trends in Housing Styles

The prominent housing styles represented by new construction in the United States at the end of the twentieth century include the single-family detached house on a large suburban lot, suburban low-rise garden apartments, high-rise inner city apartment and condominium buildings on land redeveloped with public assistance, and high-density townhouses featuring condominium ownership and management of such common areas as lawns, sidewalks, and building exteriors. Some members of the upper middle class disdain mass, supply-directed suburban subdivisions and tract housing. They favor instead restored older housing that captures the elegance of another era. The historic preservation movement, under way since the

[34]Wright, *Building the Dream*, p. 218.

TABLE 4.31

Cooperative and Condominium Housing Units, Built in April 1970 or Later, 1980 (in thousands)

	Owner-Occupied		Vacant, for Sale
	Coop	Condo	
United States	36	811	102
Inside SMSAs	27	739	92
Central city	25	210	27
Balance	2	529	65
Outside SMSAs	8	72	10
Northeast	22	99	12
Midwest	11	178	6
South	2	261	33
West	1	273	51

SOURCE: U.S. Bureau of the Census, Annual Housing Survey, *General Characteristics*, Tables A-4, B-4, C-4, D-4, and E-4.

1920s but emerging as a full-fledged boom since the early 1970s, has an important place in the contemporary menu of styles.

Despite the novelty and subtle gradations of style that historic preservation of old houses introduced, it is the condominium style that deserves extra attention. In a significant way, the conversion of apartment buildings to condominiums in the 1970s, and the construction of many new condominium buildings since 1970, reflect a major change in housing wants and needs of childless households (or child-free, as some of the ads term it). The diminished affordability of conventional suburban housing, a reorientation of certain tastes toward inner city living and away from the suburban life, and the rapidly rising cost and diminished reliability of apartment house maintenance and management all contributed to the condominium boom of the 1970s and 1980s (Table 4.31).[35]

Almost a million condominium and cooperative housing units were built in the 1970s. In a cooperative arrangement the building is owned and operated by the co-op, and a member household owns shares in the co-op as well as rights to occupy a specific housing unit in the building. In a condominium arrangement the household owns its housing unit, plus an undivided share of the building exterior and grounds, and incurs an obligation to belong to the condominium as-

[35]See William Wheaton, "Income and Urban Residence: An Analysis of Consumer Demand for Location," *American Economic Review* 67 (1977): 620–31.

sociation and to pay a prescribed share of upkeep and maintenance expenses. In condo and co-op housing the household assumes a share of certain collective responsibilities to care for the building, but avoids the external maintenance, neighborhood participation, and limited privacy that usually accompany single-family detached housing. Delayed-marriage and childless households often prefer this style, as do older couples whose children are gone and for whom house and yard upkeep has lost its charm.

Conclusions

Changes in the supply and demand for mortgage money in the United States since 1980 have raised the interest rates on mortgage loans, which has cut down the effective demand for new and used housing. Other sources of flux in the effective demand for housing include the steadily rising U.S. population, population migration within the country, variations in rates of price appreciation of housing that encourage sales in some regions and purchases elsewhere, variations from place to place in the price of mortgage credit, and changing tastes in housing styles and neighborhood settings. Modifications in government housing assistance programs also affect housing demand. Selected programs will be discussed in Chapter 7.

When housing supplies (Chapter 3) and housing demand (Chapter 4) come together within each submarket, housing units are occupied by households, the market clears, and patterns of housing use unfold. The next chapter examines contemporary patterns of housing use in the United States.

5

THE USE OF NATIONAL AND REGIONAL HOUSING STOCKS

VIRTUALLY every American household has a place to live, and almost every housing unit in the United States is in use by one or more households. What patterns are formed when households match themselves with available housing? On the demand side are households of varying tastes, needs, and ability to pay. On the supply side is the stock of housing units. The housing market in each locale continuously mediates the forces of housing supply and the elements of demand in that locale. As the market clears, the stage is set for diverse patterns of housing use.[1]

[1]Major treatments of how households are matched with their housing units, and the ways that residential satisfaction is achieved with respect to specific housing and neighborhood norms, include Richard F. Muth, "The Allocation of Households to Dwellings," *Journal of Regional Science* 18 (1978); 159–78; Earl W. Morris and Mary Winter, *Housing, Family, and Society* (New York: Wiley, 1978); and William H. Michaelson, *Environmental Choice, Human Behavior, and Residential Satisfaction* (New York: Oxford University Press, 1977). Housing selection reflects social norms and personal characteristics of the household, as well as the nature of the available stock and its geographic distribution among the submarkets within which selections are made. See William H. Michaelson, *Man and His Urban Environment: A Sociological Approach* (Reading, MA.: Addison-Wesley, 1976); D. A. Dillman, K. R. Tremblay, Sr., and J. J. Dillman, "Influence of Housing Norms and Personal Characteristics on Stated Housing Preferences," *Housing and Society* 6, no. 1 (1979): 2–19; Wendel Bell, "Social Choice, Life Styles, and Suburban Residence," in W. M. Dobriner, ed., *The Suburban Community* (New York: Putnam, 1958), pp. 225–47; and Avery M. Guest, "Patterns of Family Location," *Demography* 9, no. 1 (1972); 159–71.

In this chapter we examine who gets what kind of housing and under what terms. The question of *who* can be answered in terms of racial composition, income levels, age of household members, household composition, ethnicity, and other traits. The question of *what kind* of housing involves the type of structure, density, number of rooms, setting, and structural features. Important *terms* of housing occupancy and use include tenure arrangements, cost, persons per unit, and persons per room.

Persons per Housing Unit, 1980

About one owner-occupied housing unit in seven in 1980 had just one household member; in rental housing over a third were single-person households (Table 5.1). Well over half of the owned and rental housing units had two to four household members. Large households of seven members or more were rare in 1980.

Households that own their housing are generally more prosperous than renters and are more likely to have dependent children; thus, the median number of persons per unit in owner-occupied housing in 1980 was 2.6 compared with only 2.0 in rented units.

TABLE 5.1

Persons per Occupied Housing Unit, by Tenure, Location, and Region, 1960–1980

Persons per Unit	United States	SMSA	Central City	Balance of SMSA	Non-SMSA	North-east	Mid-west	South	West
Owner-Occupied									
1	15%	15%	18%	13%	16%	14%	15%	16%	16%
2	32	32	33	31	34	30	32	33	35
3–4	37	38	34	40	36	38	37	37	36
5–6	13	13	12	14	13	15	13	12	12
7 or more	2	2	3	2	2	3	2	2	2
Median: 1980	2.6	2.7	2.4	2.8	2.5	2.8	2.7	2.6	2.5
Median: 1960	3.2	3.3	3.1	3.5	2.9	3.3	3.1	3.1	3.1
Renter-Occupied									
1	36%	36%	40%	32%	33%	37%	38%	32%	36%
2	29	30	28	31	27	29	30	29	28
3–4	26	25	24	28	29	25	25	28	26
5–6	7	7	7	7	8	7	6	8	8
7 or more	2	2	2	2	2	1	1	3	2
Median: 1980	2.0	2.0	1.9	2.1	2.1	1.9	1.9	2.1	2.0
Median: 1960	2.7	2.5	2.3	2.9	3.3	2.6	2.6	3.1	2.4

SOURCES: Annual Housing Survey, *Inventory of Housing, 1980*, part E; 1960 data from 1970 Census of Housing, *Components of Inventory Change, Final Report HC (4)-1, United States and Regions*. 1970 data from this source do not agree with 1970 data in the 1980 Annual Housing Survey, so comparisons are made between 1960 and 1980. The *Statistical Abstract of the United States, 1984*, table 1339, p. 748, based on the 1980 Census of Housing, gives median persons per occupied unit as follows: owner-occupied—1960, 3.1; 1970, 3.0; 1980, 2.6; and renter-occupied—1960, 2.6; 1970, 2.3; 1980, 2.0.

Persons per housing unit reaches its highest average in owned housing in the suburbs, especially in the Northeast. The lowest averages appear in rental units in the Northeast and Midwest. New housing is built mainly in prosperous, growing areas. Suburban areas and the South and West regions added new housing in the 1960s and 1970s faster than other locations. The new units are larger, on the average, than pre-1960 housing, and are occupied by larger-than-average households, many of whom are immigrants with above-average incomes. There are variations in persons per unit from location to location moving outward from central cities, and from region to region throughout the country, but the variations are small. Americans' preferences regarding persons per unit and their ability to consume the type of housing unit they want appear to be quite uniform from place to place. The big differences flow from tenure status, and the income, wealth, and unit size differences that lie behind variations in tenure status.

Changes in Persons per Housing Unit, 1960–1980

Between 1960 and 1980, persons per housing unit continued its long-term decline by dropping sharply in all types of locations and all regions (Table 5.1). The drop in median persons per unit over the two decades was greater for renter-occupied housing (down from 2.7 to 2.0) than for owner-occupied housing (3.2 to 2.6).

In owner-occupied housing declines in median number of persons per unit were sharpest in central cities of metropolitan areas (3.1 to 2.4, a drop of almost 23 percent) and in the West (3.1 to 2.5). In renter-occupied housing the declines were greatest in nonmetropolitan areas (3.3. to 2.1) and in the South (3.1 to 2.1). Rapid rates of net additions to the housing stock during the 1960–80 period made it easier for households to disaggregate and to spread out into the larger stock, but there was a simultaneous decline in average household size preference and in average family size, as described in Chapter 4. Demand

and supply changes thus worked together to lower the intensity of use of housing units.

Persons per Room and Crowding, 1980

Another variable that tells us something about the intensity of housing use in the United States is persons per room. Almost 97 percent of owner-occupied units have a person per room ratio of 1.0 or lower; almost 94 percent of renter-occupied units have a ratio of 1.0 or less (Table 5.2). If moderate crowding of a housing unit is defined as occurring when the person per room ratio exceeds 1.0, then about one owned unit in 33 and one rental unit in 16 was crowded, twice the rate of crowding in owned housing. The lower incomes of renters restrict their housing choices to smaller units, and crowding is one of the consequences. Owner-occupied housing units in 1980 had a median of 5.8 rooms, while renter-occupied units had a median of 4.0 rooms.[2] When incomes rise, households like to spread out into units with more rooms.

Changes in Crowding, 1960–1980

In 1960 the nation had 707,000 owner-occupied housing units with over 1.5 persons per room crowded into them. Over half of these housing units (401,000) were in the South, and over half (364,000) were located outside SMSAs. Twenty years later, the total number of crowded owner-occupied units was down to 326,000. The South still had the bulk of these crowded units, with half the national total (163,000), but there had been a big improvement since 1960. Non-SMSA areas contained more crowded owner-occupied units in 1980 (118,000) than either central cities (76,000) or suburban areas (94,000).

The crowding problem was worse in rental housing than in owned housing in 1960; 1,273,000 units had more than 1.5 persons per room, but the total dropped sharply to 461,000 in 1980. The South again accounted for over half the 1960 total (680,000), but that region reduced its number of crowded rental units (down 519,000) by a faster absolute rate and relative rate than any other region. In metro areas the number of crowded rental units was cut almost in half between 1960 and 1980 (724,000 to 351,000); in nonmetro areas, only one in

[2]U.S. Bureau of the Census, 1980 Census of Housing, *General Housing Characteristics: U.S. Summary*, vol. 1, chap. A, table 4.

TABLE 5.2
Persons per Room, by Tenure, 1980 (in thousands)

Persons per Room	Number	Percentage
Owner-Occupied		
0.50 or fewer	32,843	62.5%
0.51 to 1.00	18,042	34.3
1.00 to 1.50	1,305	2.5
1.51 or more	326	0.6
Renter-Occupied		
0.50 or fewer	15,483	56.2%
0.51 to 1.00	10,368	37.6
1.00 to 1.50	1,244	4.5
1.51 or more	461	1.7

SOURCE: Annual Housing Survey, *Inventory of Housing, 1980*, pt. E.

seven remained. Whether in relatively low-density owner-occupied housing or in the generally higher-density rental housing, crowding of housing units interferes with privacy needs and desires of household members and is said to contribute to stress in the home. Thus, it is generally good news that of the almost 2 million crowded housing units at the height of the postwar baby boom in America, more than 6 units in 10 were eliminated by declines in household size or moves to larger units by 1980.

The Age and Sex of Householders, by Tenure Status, 1980

Four owner-occupied housing units in five reported a male householder in 1980, while the ratio was three units in five in rental housing (Table 5.3). For householders under age 45, male or female, renters predominated although females were significantly more likely to be renting than were males. Rental status for male householders drops steadily with advancing age, but for females it drops in the middle years, ages 45–64, only to rise for the elderly because of divorce, widowhood, and the generally inferior income and wealth positions of female householders. Households with dependent children under age 18 are more likely to be owners than renters.[3]

[3]See Peter S. K. Chi, *Population Redistribution and Changes in Housing Tenure Status in the U.S.*, U.S. Department of Housing and Urban Development (Washington, DC: U.S. Government Printing Office, 1979).

TABLE 5.3
Age and Sex of Householders, by Tenure Status, 1980

Age of Householder	Owner-Occupied	Renter-Occupied
Male		
Under 45 years	36%	41%
45–64 years	31	12
65 years and over	14	7
Female		
Under 45 years	5	23
45–64 years	7	8
65 years and over	8	11
With Own Children		
Under age 18	41	33

SOURCE: Annual Housing Survey, *Inventory of Housing, 1980*, pt. E.

Year Householder Moved into Present Housing

The mobility of Americans makes it rare for homeowners to stay at the same address for more than two decades and almost unheard of for renters to take root at one address for that long. Over half the renter households had lived elsewhere before 1979, with the most stable renters located in the central cities and in the Northeast (Table 5.4). The greatest rates of instability, as measured by the percentage of renters who moved in during 1979 or later, occurred in the suburbs (56 percent), and in the fast-growth South (57 percent) and West (59 percent).

Over 43 percent of owner householders nationwide had moved into their housing unit before April 1970. By this measure of owner stability, central cities (48 percent) are more stable than suburbs (41 percent), and the Northeast (55 percent) and Midwest (45 percent) are much more stable than the South (41 percent) or West (33 percent).

Black and Spanish-Origin Householders

Black and Spanish-origin households own significantly less housing than their share of the U.S population might imply. In 1980 the black population constituted almost 12 percent of the U.S. total, and over 10 percent of all families (6.2 million of 59.6 million families), but only 7 percent of the owner-occupant householders were black

(Table 5.5).[4] Meanwhile, Spanish-origin families made up 6 percent of the 1980 population and over 5 percent (3.0 million) of American families, but only 3 percent of them were owner-occupants.

On the basis of national averages, black owner-occupants are overrepresented in the central cities and in the South, while Spanish-origin households are overrepresented in the central cities, in the South, and especially in the West, where Spanish owner-occupants outnumber black owner-occupants by 8 to 3.

Below-average economic status for black and Spanish households, on the average, leads to their above-average representation among renter households. Black and Spanish households compose over a fourth of all renter households, and over a third of central city renters. They make up 17 percent (9 percent for blacks; 8 percent for Spanish) of suburban renters, which is well below the black 12 percent share of total population, but significantly ahead of the Spanish 6 percent. By these measures Spanish households appear to be penetrating suburban renter-occupied housing faster than are blacks, but their penetration of suburban owner-occupied housing (3 percent of the total), while close behind that of blacks (4 percent), remains well behind their share of total population and of families.

Housing Use by Spanish-Origin Populations

Over 4 million housing units were occupied by a Spanish-origin householder in 1980.[5] Their origins were diverse, with the largest group reporting Mexican roots (55 percent), followed by Puerto Ricans (15 percent), Cubans (7 percent), and others (Central and South America, Caribbean lands, Philippines, and Europe) (Table 5.6).

The majority of the Spanish-origin householders reported their race as white (57 percent). A few reported as black (under 3 percent), and the remainder were Indians or Asians.

The owner occupancy rate of 43 percent for the Spanish-origin population is well below the U.S. average of 64 percent. In addition, the units occupied by Spanish-origin population have fewer rooms on the average, and persons per unit ratios are almost 50 percent higher than national averages (Table 5.6).

[4]U.S. Bureau of the Census, *Statistical Abstract of the United States, 1984* (Washington, DC: U.S. Government Printing Office, 1984), pp. 36 and 53.

[5]For analysis of residential patterns of Spanish-origin populations in the 29 largest SMSAs in the 1970s, see D. S. Massey, "Residential Segregation of Spanish Americans in U.S. Urbanized Areas," *Demography* 16, no. 4 (1979): 553–63.

TABLE 5.4

Year Householder Moved In, by Tenure, Location, Region, 1980

Year	United States	SMSA	Central City	Balance of SMSA	Non-SMSA	North-east	Mid-west	South	West
Owner-Occupied									
1979 or later	15%	15%	14%	15%	15%	11%	13%	17%	20%
April 1970–78	42	41	39	43	42	35	42	43	47
1960–March 1970	22	23	24	22	21	25	22	22	19
1950–59	12	13	14	12	11	17	13	11	9
1949 or earlier	9	8	10	7	11	13	10	8	5
Renter-Occupied									
1979 or later	52%	51%	47%	56%	55%	39%	53%	57%	59%
April 1970–78	37	38	40	36	34	44	37	34	36
1960–March 1970	7	8	9	6	7	12	7	7	4
1950–59	2	2	2	1	2	3	1	2	1
1949 or earlier	1	1	1	1	2	3	2	1	–

NOTE: (–): rounds to zero.

SOURCE: Annual Housing Survey, *Inventory of Housing*, pt. E.

TABLE 5.5

Racial and Spanish-Origin Status of Householder, by Tenure, Location, and Region, 1980

Status	United States	SMSA	Central City	Balance of SMSA	Non-SMSA	North-east	Mid-west	South	West
Owner-Occupied									
White and other	93%	92%	84%	96%	94%	95%	95%	88%	97%
Black	7	8	16	4	6	5	5	12	3
Spanish origin	3	4	6	3	2	1	1	4	8
Renter-Occupied									
White and other	82	81	73	91	88	84	84	74	91
Black	18	19	27	9	12	16	16	26	9
Spanish origin	9	10	11	8	4	10	3	8	15

NOTE: Spanish-origin percentages are included in other groups.

SOURCE: Annual Housing Survey, *Inventory of Housing, 1980*, pt. E.

Over half of the Mexican-based population in this group live in the West. Their nationwide rate of owner occupancy is 49 percent, which is higher than the other Spanish-origin groups.

Householders of Puerto Rican origin have the lowest rate of owner occupancy, and three out of four live in the Northeast. About two thirds of the householders with Cuban origins lived in the South in 1980, and at 44 percent owner occupancy was close behind the Mexican-origin households.

Household Income and Tenure Status, 1960–1980

The median annual income of owner households in 1980 was almost twice the income of renter households (Table 5.7). Only in nonmetropolitan areas was the income gap between owners and renters appreciably smaller. Among owner households median income inside SMSAs ($22,200) is far above the non-SMSA median ($16,100). Inside SMSAs the suburbs and exurban areas beyond concentrate the high-

TABLE 5.6

Housing Use by Spanish-Origin Population, 1980 (in thousands)

		Type				Race		
	Total	Mexican	Puerto Rican	Cuban	Other Spanish	White	Black	Other
Occupied Housing								
Units	4,008	2,227	599	279	903	2,276	116	1,616
Owner-occupied	1,739	1,089	124	123	403	1,104	37	598
Renter-occupied	2,269	1,138	475	157	500	1,172	79	1,018
Median Rooms/Unit								
Own [U.S. 5.8]	5.3	5.2	5.7	5.4	5.6	5.4	5.5	5.3
Rent [U.S. 4.0]	3.7	3.7	3.9	3.4	3.6	3.7	3.8	3.7
Median Persons/ Unit								
Own [U.S. 2.60]	3.67	3.84	3.73	3.42	3.26	3.50	3.29	3.98
Rent [U.S. 1.99]	2.89	3.15	2.89	2.24	2.54	2.71	2.57	3.10
Northeast								
Occupied units	789	26	448	64	251	408	45	335
Owner-occupied	156	9	67	18	62	106	8	42
Midwest								
Occupied units	343	211	58	11	63	185	12	146
Owner-occupied	150	96	18	5	31	91	4	55
South								
Occupied units	1,224	792	52	179	201	824	46	354
Owner-occupied	662	441	23	90	108	468	20	173
West								
Occupied units	1,652	1,198	41	25	388	859	12	781
Owner-occupied	772	543	16	10	203	439	4	329

SOURCE: U.S. Bureau of the Census, 1980 Census of Housing, *General Housing Characteristics: U.S. Summary*, vol. 1, chap. A, tables 15, 28, 41, 54, 67.

income owners (median: $23,500) while the central city housing units, older and usually lower in value, are home to lower-income owner occupancy ($19,500). Owner occupants in the Northeast and West have much higher incomes than those in the Midwest and South. In general, homeownership is preferred over tenant status. Although some households do prefer tenant status and the freedom from house and yard maintenance that tenancy can provide, most tenants remain renters because their incomes are too low or too unpredictable to satisfy the lending terms of institutions that extend mortgage credit. For the large majority of American households a mortgage loan is necessary to finance a house purchase.

Between 1960 and 1980 the median income of owner households rose 236 percent, significantly faster than the 156 percent rise posted by renter households. Since the percentage of households that were owners in 1960 (62 percent) was not appreciably different from the percentage in 1980 (64 percent), the sharp differences in income gains of owners compared with renters reflect a widening during the 1960s and 1970s of the average economic circumstances of the two classes of households.[6]

The rifts in average economic circumstances of owners and renters widened most rapidly in the Midwest (owner incomes up 341 per-

[6]U.S. Bureau of the Census, *Statistical Abstract of the United States, 1984* (Washington, DC: U.S. Government Printing Office, 1984), pp. 463, 753.

TABLE 5.7

Household Income and Tenure, by Location and Region, 1960–1980

| | Median Household Income | | | | | |
| | Owner-Occupied Housing | | | Renter-Occupied Housing | | |
	1960	1980	Percentage Change	1960	1980	Percentage Change
United States	$5,900	$19,800	236%	$4,100	$10,500	156%
SMSA	6,600	22,200	236	4,500	10,900	142
Central city	6,400	19,500	205	4,300	9,800	128
Balance of SMSA	6,800	23,500	246	4,900	12,400	153
Non-SMSA	4,200	16,100	283	3,000	9,100	203
Northeast	6,500	21,200	226	4,800	10,600	121
Midwest	5,800	19,800	241	4,400	10,100	130
South	4,800	17,600	267	3,000	10,200	240
West	6,700	22,700	239	4,500	11,200	149

NOTE: 1970 SMSA definitions are used here.

SOURCES: Annual Housing Survey, *Inventory of Housing, 1980.* pt. E; 1960 data from 1970 Census of Housing, *Components of Inventory Change*, Final Report HC(4)-1, United States and Regions. 1970 data from this source do not agree with 1970 data in the 1980 Annual Housing Survey, so comparisons are made between 1960 and 1980.

cent; renter incomes up only 130 percent) and the Northeast (226 percent versus 121 percent). At the other extreme, median owner income in the South advanced 267 percent in the 1960s and 1970s, while renter income advanced 240 percent.

The large influx of new young households into the nation's housing market during the 1960s and 1970s flooded job markets and kept wages low, as explained in earlier chapters. Young households with low incomes usually enter the rental segment of the housing market first. Ordinarily such a large increment to housing demand would have put an extra strain on the market and driven rents up even faster than actually occurred. But the exceptionally high rates of production of new housing during the 1960s and 1970s prevented shortages and serious rent inflation.

Housing Value, 1980

The value of housing from place to place across the United States depends on the pressures of supply and demand at each place.[7] Housing values are below average in the central cities of metropolitan

areas. They rise well above average in suburban areas with their concentrations of larger, higher-quality, newer houses, and then drop to very low average levels outside metropolitan areas. The variations from place to place in house values due to differences in supply are compounded by variations from place to place in households' ability and willingness to live in one kind of setting or another.

Constructing constant quality indexes of the price or value of housing is a difficult problem because housing is a heterogeneous commodity. Differences in the rents or values of two housing units can result from differences not only in the prevailing level of prices from place to place, but also from differences in the size, quality, and location of the units within a place. For example, if one house is twice as large as another and sells for twice as much, does the larger house have a higher price? Not necessarily. The larger house costs

[7]See John F. Kain and John M. Quigley, "Measuring the Value of Housing Quality," *Journal of the American Statistical Association* 65 (1970): 532–48; D. M. Grether and P. Mieszkowski, "Determinants of Real Estate Values," *Journal of Urban Economics* 1 (1974): 127–46; and S. A. Goodwin, "Measuring the Value of Housing Quality: A Note," *Journal of Regional Science* 17 (1977): 107–15.

more, but one gets more for the extra money. The "amount of house" purchased per dollar of expenditures may be the same for both units. It is this notion—the amount of house per dollar of expenditures—that housing price indexes try to measure. Our problem is that neither the price per unit of housing services nor the quantity of services is directly observable. Both must be inferred from data on the rents and values of housing units.

Two standard methods allow inferences to be made about the price per unit of housing services. One is the method of hedonic indexes (see Chapter 2), which is based on two key assumptions: (1) A housing unit is not a single heterogeneous unit but rather a bundle of housing unit characteristics—number of rooms, type of heating system, and so forth; (2) Each of these characteristics has its own price which, although not directly observable, can be estimated via multivariate regression analysis for each metropolitan market or any other larger or smaller housing market area. For example, the regression results might indicate that an additional room adds 10 percent to monthly rent in a particular metropolitan area.

Equipped with sets of these characteristic prices, any particular type of housing bundle—one for renter-occupied units and another for owner-occupied homes—is specified and then priced for each housing market area. The ratio of the predicted rents (or values) between any two metro areas corresponds to the ratio of the relative price per unit of housing services (or housing stock) between the two areas.

In a second method used by the Bureau of Labor Statistics (BLS), a particular type of housing bundle is specified. For example, a five-room rental unit with central heating might be selected. Then, all dwellings within a particular metro area (or a sample of these units) with such characteristics are selected, and the average rent of the selected units is computed. The procedure is repeated in other SMSAs using the same set of selected housing characteristics. The resulting schedule of average rents constitutes the BLS-type rental price index. An index of house values can be constructed analogously by specifying a particular type of owner-occupied housing and calculating its average value in each metro area.[8]

Using these methods on a large sample of U.S. metro areas in the late 1970s disclosed that significant variation exists under both index procedures in the price of housing among different metro areas. It is not unusual for some metro areas to be twice as expensive as others.

The variance in prices is substantial for both renter- and owner-occupied housing.[9]

The two indexes generally agree on which metro areas have more expensive housing and which have less expensive housing. For example, Paterson and Newark are expensive areas according to both indexes, while Kansas City and Wichita are inexpensive. The overall correlation between the two rent indexes is .61, and between the two house value indexes it is .75. However, the price differences between the most expensive and least expensive SMSAs tend to be smaller using the BLS-type index rather than the hedonic index. Both indexes are sensitive to changes in the reference bundles, which suggests that separate indexes are needed for low- and high-income families.[10]

Owner-occupied housing in the Northeast is average in value ($51,300). While it is more expensive to build there than in warmer climates, housing is older than average and, in the American way of looking at things, somewhat less desirable than newer housing. The older stock of the Midwest (median value $48,000) and the cheaper construction costs in the South (median value $43,700) keep housing values below average; while in the West heavy and sustained demand pressures brought about by steady net inmigration and a newer stock of larger and relatively more desirable housing stock have propelled the median value of owner-occupied housing to the highest in the country ($77,700) (Table 5.8).

Changes in Housing Values, 1960–1980

The median value of owner-occupied housing rose over 42 percent in the 1960s, from $12,000 to $17,000, but in the 1970s it rose 200 percent to $51,300, partly due to the larger, more expensive new units added to the stock in the 1970s, but mainly due to the runaway inflation in house prices during the decade. The places that were exposed to the greatest demand pressures—from natural change, foreign immigration, or domestic migration—had the biggest price advances. In the 1960s, the Northeast (up 48 percent) and the West (up 46 percent) led the other regions, while the suburbs (up 44 percent) and locations outside the metropolitan areas (up 51 percent) led other locations. Meanwhile, because of severe drops in what had been high positive rates of natural increase that had helped maintain higher demand levels in the Northeast and Midwest, plus stepped-up immigration and redirection of domestic net migration flows into the West

---

[8]Based on James R. Follain, Larry Ozanne, and Verna M. Alburger, *Place to Place Indexes of the Price of Housing: Some New Estimates and a Comparative Analysis* (Washington, DC: Urban Institute, 1979).

[9]Ibid., p. xi.
[10]Ibid., p. xii.

and South and into nonmetropolitan areas, median values of owner-occupied housing rose most rapidly in the South (up 221 percent) and West (up 277 percent), and in the suburbs (up 201 percent) and non-metropolitan areas (up 237 percent).

The Costs of Home Ownership

In 1980 housing costs climbed to new highs for owners and renters, reflecting increases in housing prices, mortgage payments, utility costs, real estate taxes, and rents. Homeowners in mortgaged houses experienced an increase of 9 percent in their median monthly housing costs, from $337 in 1979 to $367 in 1980. Monthly costs of nonmortgaged houses rose 13 percent to $131 in 1980, while median gross rents (rent plus utilities) rose 11 percent to $241.[11]

The most important cost of housing is the rent paid for rental units or the implicit or imputed rent that owner-occupants pay to themselves. This cost is equal to the fair market rental of the house.

Almost two thirds of owner-occupied housing serves as collateral on mortgage loans that were used to buy the housing. In areas of significant net inmigration, such as suburban areas or the West, much higher than average shares of their owner-occupied houses are mortgaged. Just 30 percent of the mortgages in 1980 were covered by insurance and guarantees provided by FHA, the VA, and the Farmers Home Administration. The rest of the mortgages were conventional loans (uninsured or privately insured) or were contracts for deed (Table 5.8).

The second major cost of owner-occupied housing is the monthly mortgage payment, containing a payment on the loan principal amount, plus a monthly interest charge. In 1980 the average monthly payment was $240, with higher-than-average levels occurring in the fast-growth areas where a large share of the loans are recent and carry high interest rates (the suburbs and the West).

A third major cost of homeownership is real estate taxes levied by local units of government (county, municipality, school district, and other special districts). These taxes averaged $460 per year in 1980 (Table 5.8). Median real property taxes are significantly higher in metropolitan areas ($582) than outside ($261). Most of the expenditures of local governments and special districts are for personnel, and wage levels and labor costs are lower outside metro areas. Moreover, much less complex governance systems are provided to non-metropolitan areas.

There are also significant differences from region to region in the levels of compensation and fringe benefits provided to public employees, as well as in the range and quality of public services provided. These differences in pay levels and services explain much of the difference between median real estate taxes of $909 in the Northeast and $197 in the South.

A fourth major housing cost for owner-occupants in mortgaged housing is a bundle that includes casualty insurance (fire, theft, earthquake, flood, storm, and so forth), utilities, fuel, water, and garbage and trash collection. These costs, combined with payment of principal and interest on mortgage loans, averaged $367 per month in 1980 (Table 5.8). The medians of these costs are fairly uniform across the United States. For houses with a mortgage, these selected monthly costs were 19 to 20 percent of household gross monthly income in 1980, and for houses without a mortgage, 10 to 15 percent (Table 5.8).

Rent Levels, 1980

For rental units all costs are direct and easily added to a gross rent total, which includes the contract rent plus all heat and utilities. The national median gross rent including subsidized units in 1980 was $241. Like many other measures of housing cost, gross rents were higher in metro areas than outside; higher in suburbs than central cities; higher than average in the colder, higher utility cost Northeast and the predominantly newer housing of the West; and a bit below average in the Midwest and South (Table 5.8).[12] But since households' disposable incomes vary roughly with the cost of living, which includes the cost of rental housing, median gross rent as a percentage of household income falls in a fairly narrow range of between 25 and 28 percent from one location to another inside and outside metro areas and from one region to another across the country.

Changes in Rent Levels, 1960–1980

Rents in the 1970s rose 123 percent, well over twice the 52 percent rate of the 1960s. The South (up 55 percent) and West (57 percent) were the leaders in rent increases in the 1960s, but the other

---

[11]Bureau of the Census, 1980 Census of Housing, vol. 5, *Residential Finance*, HC 80-5 (Nov. 1983).

[12]Rent control ordinances interfere with the market. See D. Keifer, "Housing Deterioration, Housing Codes and Rent Control," *Urban Studies* 17 (1981): 53–62.

TABLE 5.8

Value of Housing and Costs of Occupancy, by Location and Region, 1960–1980

	United States	SMSA	Central City	Balance of SMSA	Non-SMSA	North-east	Mid-west	South	West
Median Value of ("Specified" in 1980)[1] Owner-Occupied Housing Units:									
1980	$51,300	$57,700	$48,000	$62,700	$41,100	$51,300	$48,000	$43,700	$77,700
1970	17,100	19,000	16,400	20,800	12,200	19,500	16,700	13,600	20,600
1960	12,000	13,500	12,300	14,400	8,100	13,200	12,000	9,600	14,100
Mortgage Status of Owner-Occupied Housing, 1980:[2]									
No mortgage	35%	31%	35%	29%	44%	40%	37%	37%	25%
Mortgage	65	69	65	71	56	60	63	63	75
FHA/VA/FmHA[3]	30	31	NA	NA	79	21	23	36	64
Median Monthly Mortgage Payment (Principal and Interest) of Those with Mortgages, 1980[2]	$240	$260	$226	$280	$196	$241	$232	$218	$297
Median Annual Real Estate Taxes on Owner-Occupied Units, 1980	460	582	456	657	261	909	527	197	506
Median Selected Monthly Housing Costs,[4] Units with Mortgage, 1980[2]	367	387	342	412	321	405	359	335·	398
Median Selected Monthly Owner-Occupied Housing Costs, 1980, as a Percentage of Household Gross Income:[2]									
With mortgage	19%	19%	19%	19%	20%	20%	19%	19%	20%
Without mortgage	13	13	13	14	13	15	13	12	10
Median Gross Rent, Including Subsidized Units									
1980	$241	$254	$234	$283	$198	$246	$230	$227	270
1970	108	114	107	130	84	110	110	93	119
1960	71	74	72	82	58	72	76	60	76

TABLE 5.8 (*continued*)

	United States	SMSA	Central City	Balance of SMSA	Non-SMSA	North-east	Mid-west	South	West
Gross Rent as a Percentage of Household Income, Median of All Rental Units[2]									
1980	27%	27%	28%	26%	25%	27%	26%	25%	28%
1970	20	21	21	20	19	20	20	20	22

[1]Single-unit structures on less than 10 acres; no business on property.
[2]Based on data supplied by those reporting, which was significantly less than the total AHS, household sample.
[3]Percentage of all mortgages.
[4]Monthly mortgage payment (principal and interest), real estate taxes, insurance, utilities, fuel, water, and garbage and trash collection.
NOTE: 1970 SMSA definitions are used here.
SOURCES: 1970 and 1980 data from U.S. Bureau of the Census, *General Housing Characteristics for the United States and Regions: 1980, Current Housing Reports,* series H-150-80, and Annual Housing Survey, *Inventory of Housing, 1980,* pt. A. 1970 data in latter source are from 1970 Census of Housing, and 1980 data are from 1980 Annual Housing Survey. 1960 data are from U.S. Bureau of the Census, 1970 Census of Housing, *Components of Inventory Change,* Final Report HC(4)-1, United States and Regions. 1970 Census figures do not agree with 1970 figures reported in the 1980 Annual Housing Survey.

regions were close behind (Table 5.8). During the 1970s, the South jumped well ahead of other regions (up 144 percent), and the stable Midwest (up 109 percent) was far below the national average increase.[13]

The major pattern of rent increases changed among locations as well as among regions. In the 1960s the suburbs were the rent increase leaders, with average rents up 59 percent. By the end of the 1960s the suburban apartment boom was well under way, and areas of greatest relative rental demand pressures moved outside metro areas driving rents up an average of 136 percent, while rent inflation in central cities fell below the national average.

As rent levels escalated sharply in the 1970s, the share of renter household income allocated for rent rose steeply as well. In 1970 rent took 19 to 22 percent of renter households' income on the average. But in 1980 the proportion was 25 to 28 percent (Table 5.8).

[13]See Donald McAllister, "The Demand for Rental Housing: An Investigation of Some Demographic and Economic Determinants," *Annals of Regional Science* 1, no. 1 (1967): 127–42.

The Use of Mobile Homes

About one single-unit house in 14 in 1980 was a mobile home or trailer (Table 5.9). Since many of these movable units are used only seasonally, just 3.9 million of the total 4.3 million were occupied at census time. Mobile homes are usually smaller than conventional single-unit houses, but they may be as large as 16 feet wide and 80 feet long. Rooms can also be added. Some models have expansion walls that can be pushed out to enlarge interior space, and many models can be paired to double the size of the house. They can come fully furnished for immediate occupancy and use and are much cheaper than conventional single-unit houses.

Six mobile homes in 10 in use in America are in rural areas. On rural farm sites they provide extra or replacement housing that is easily connected to existing waste supply, on-site sewage disposal, electricity, and telephone service. On rural nonfarm sites mobile homes provide for seasonal recreation and for permanent occupancy in places where materials and building trades are unavailable, unsatisfactory, or too expensive. They are also popular as temporary housing at major

TABLE 5.9

Type of Occupied Housing, by Unit, Tenure, and Location, 1980 (in millions)

	Owner-Occupied			Renter-Occupied		
	Total	1 Unit	Mobile Home or Trailer	Total	1 Unit	Mobile Home or Trailer
United States	51.8	45.6	3.1	28.6	12.5	.8
Inside Urbanized Areas						
Central cities	12.4	10.8	.2	12.9	4.5	.1
Urban fringe	17.0	15.4	.6	8.2	3.4	.1
Urban, Outside Urbanized Areas						
Places 10,000 and over	3.0	2.7	.1	1.9	.9	—
Places 2,500 to 10,000	3.5	3.1	.2	1.7	.9	.1
Rural Places 1,000 to 2,500	1.9	1.7	.1	.7	.4	—
Other Rural	14.0	11.9	1.7	3.3	2.4	.4
Inside SMSAs	37.3	33.0	1.6	23.2	9.3	.4
Outside SMSAs	14.5	12.6	1.5	5.4	3.2	.4

	Year-Round Housing Units (Mobile Homes)		
	United States	Urban	Rural
United States	4.3	1.7	2.6
Northeast	.4	.1	.3
Midwest	.9	.3	.5
South	2.0	.7	1.3
West	1.0	.6	.4

NOTE: (–): rounds to zero.

SOURCE: U.S. Bureau of the Census, 1980 Census of Housing, *General Housing Characteristics: U.S. Summary*, HC 80-1-A1, tables 3, 16, 29, 42, and 55.

but isolated construction sites such as in the oil, gas, and mineral boom towns of the northern Great Plains and the mountain West.

There are a few mobile homes in small towns, but since there is often a surplus of low-priced conventional housing in stable or declining small towns, mobile homes do not compete well there. Suburban areas sometimes accommodate mobile homes and trailers, but they are more often unwelcome, especially in middle- and upper-middle-class communities. Residential land that is devoted to mobile home parks and scattered sites is seen by local officials as an opportunity foregone to develop these parcels with conventional housing, which pays real estate taxes at normal rates—something that mobile homes and trailers usually avoid because they are not usually permanently attached to the land.

Mobile homes are rare in central cities. There are relatively few in the Northeast, where restrictions and a surplus of housing in many areas push them out. Almost half are in the South, where two thirds are in rural areas. In the West 6 homes in 10 are urban. A large percentage of the mobile homes in the Sunbelt states of the South and West serve as retirement and seasonal homes for vacationers and occasionally for migrant workers.

Vacant Housing Units

Vacant units (6.3 million) include those for sale only (.9 million) or for rent (2.2 million), but also units that are rented or sold and

TABLE 5.10

Vacant Housing Units and Duration of Vacancy, 1980 (in millions)

	United States	Urban	Rural	North-east	Mid-west	South	West
Vacant Units	6.3	4.1	2.2				
Homeowner vacancy rate	1.8%	1.8%	1.7%	1.3%	1.7%	1.9%	2.4%
Rental vacancy rate	7.1	6.8	9.0	5.0	7.4	8.7	6.7
Duration of Vacancy							
Units for sale	.9	.7	.3				
6 months or more	.3	.2	.1				
Units for rent	2.2	1.8	.4				
6 months or more	.4	.3	.1				

SOURCE: U.S. Bureau of the Census, 1980 Census of Housing, *General Housing Characteristics: U.S. Summary*, HC 80-1-A1, tables 2 and 3.

awaiting occupancy, held for occasional use, boarded up, and so on (Table 5.10).

Homeowner vacancy rates are generally lower than rental vacancy rates because owned units turn over less often than rental units. The time vacant between occupancies is similar for the two kinds of housing. In a soft local housing market a net flow of households from rental housing into owned housing, taking advantage of low prices for owned housing, will lower the vacancy rate for owned housing and raise it for rental.

In tight housing markets, such as the South and West experienced in many places during the 1970s, steady demand pressures brought about by high rates of net domestic inmigration and foreign immigration stimulated rapid price inflation and attracted developers to expand the housing supply. By 1980 there was something of a surplus of owner-occupied and renter-occupied housing in the South and West—not because demand was weak, but because new supplies were not yet occupied. The higher-than-average vacancy rates for owner-occupied and renter-occupied housing was the result (Table 5.10)

Condominium Use

In the late 1960s and early 1970s, the costs of maintaining and managing middle- and upper-bracket rental property began to rise dramatically, cutting into profits of building owners. Meanwhile, the steadily increasing tax benefits and attractive speculative gains from home ownership presented serious competition to landlords, making it hard for them to raise rents to levels needed to recover all their costs and return a profit consistent with their investment. Speculators and apartment house owners in the 1970s began exploiting the gap between the flagging demand for high-quality renter-occupied units and increased demand for owner-occupied units by converting apartment buildings to condominium ownership.[14] New construction of condominiums added to the supply so that by 1980 there were over 2 million condo units in the United States (Table 5.11).

Some condo units are located in vacation and recreation sites in the mountains, ski areas, lake districts, and the seashore, and are used only seasonally. Yet despite their popularity in these kinds of settings, condo units are relatively rare outside urbanized areas. About one condo unit in five is owned by an investor and is renter-occupied. Well over half the units are located in suburban areas, where the bulk of the new construction occurred during the 1970s.

Condos are higher priced than average for owner-occupied housing. In central cities condos are much higher priced than the median for all owner-occupied housing there. In the suburban fringe condos are a bit cheaper than the average for owned housing (Table 5.11). Condos evidently serve two different ends of the middle-class income

[14]U.S. Department of Housing and Urban Development, Office of Policy Development and Research, *The Conversion of Rental Housing to Condominiums and Cooperatives: Impacts on Housing Costs* (Washington, DC: U.S. Government Printing Office, 1982).

TABLE 5.11

Condominiums by Location, Tenure, and Value, 1980 (in millions)

	United States	Inside Urbanized Areas		Rural Areas
		Central City	Urban Fringe	
Year-Round Condominium Units	2.1	.7	1.2	.1
Owner-occupied	1.2	.4	.7	—
Renter-occupied	.4	.2	.2	—
Median Value				
Specified owner-occupied housing units	$47,200	$43,100	$58,700	$40,200
Owner-occupied condominium units	$59,600	$64,200	$58,100	$60,500

NOTE: (–): under 50,000 units.

SOURCE: U.S. Bureau of the Census, 1980 Census of Housing, *General Housing Characteristics: U.S. Summary*, HC 80-1-A1, table 5.

distribution—an upper end inside central cities and a lower end in the suburbs for households who want to own and live in suburban property but do not want, do not need, or cannot afford conventional single-unit suburban housing. In rural areas the contrast between the value of condos and all owner-occupied housing is greatest. The condo median value is 50 percent higher than the median for all owned units, probably reflecting the income and tax positions of owners and investors in condos at expensive vacation and recreation sites.[15]

Housing and the Elderly

There were almost 17 million housing units with householder or spouse aged 65 and over in 1980. Almost three fourths of these elderly households lived in urban areas and SMSAs (Table 5.12). About 3 elderly households in 10 have no vehicle available, but for those inside SMSAs and other urban areas transit services provide a partial replacement. In addition, proximity to services is usually better in urban and metro areas than in rural areas outside towns and villages.

About 1.6 million elderly families, nearly 10 percent of the nation's elderly, occupy housing that contains inadequate plumbing, faulty heating, or some other defect. About 8.5 million elderly families—46 percent of the total—would have to pay over 25 percent of their income to obtain adequate housing in the areas where they currently live. Elderly people in rural areas have special problems: Over 12 percent are in physically deficient housing, and nearly 48 percent do not have access to housing costing under 25 percent of their income.[16]

Like people of other ages, most elderly adjust to their housing and report general satisfaction until an abrupt change in the household (for example, death of a spouse, illness, or incapacity) or the housing (for example, threats to security, sharply higher costs, damage to the housing unit, or conversion of rental housing to condominiums) brings on a decision to move, followed by the trauma of the move itself.[17] Elderly persons often feel more secure in a rented apartment in a building with a good security system than living alone in an owned single-unit detached house, provided that the other persons in the apartment building are not seen as threatening or disruptive in unpredictable or unmanageable ways.

The trauma of moving is ameliorated for the elderly if they can exchange large single-unit housing for a more agreeable housing unit

[15]Condo owners, even if organized, have special legal and neighborhood problems that traditionally renters and homeowners have been able to avoid. See Gregory Longhini, *Homeowners' Associations: Problems and Remedies* (Chicago: American Planning Association, Planning Advisory Service Report no. 337, 1978).

[16]Iric Nathanson, *Housing Needs of the Rural Elderly and Handicapped*, U.S. Department of Housing and Urban Development Report, HUD-PDR-633 (Washington, DC: U.S. Government Printing Office, 1980).

[17]Ibid., fn. 14.

TABLE 5.12

Housing Units with Householder or Spouse Aged 65 and Over, 1980 (in millions)

	United States	Urban	Rural	Rural Farm	Inside SMSAs	Outside SMSAs
Occupied Housing Units	16.9	12.5	4.3	.5	11.9	5.0
Owner-occupied	11.9	8.3	3.7	.4	7.9	4.0
No Vehicle Available	4.9	4.0	.8	–	3.7	1.2
No Telephone	.8	.5	.4	–	.5	.4

NOTE: (–): under 50,000 units.

SOURCE: U.S. Bureau of the Census, 1980 Census of Housing, *General Housing Characteristics: U.S. Summary*, HC 80-1-B1, table 81.

but remain in the familiar neighborhood.[18] Vacating family housing in this way makes it available for another household and contributes to neighborhood revitalization.

Housing for the severely disabled can be provided by institutions, but there are enormous community and personal benefits that accompany living in the community. Specialized housing can be provided by retrofitting existing housing with the special floor coverings, grab rails, elevators, ramps, switches, handles, bathroom equipment, locks, alarms, and other special home appliances that are needed for independent living. Adult boardinghouses and shared housing can also provide satisfactory alternatives for the elderly and the disabled. There may be a higher risk of fire in boardinghouses. Partially disabled rural elderly, both farm and nonfarm, face housing difficulties different from those occurring in urban neighborhoods.[19] Residents of small towns may be fortunate to have low-rise rental housing available, perhaps sponsored by a public authority, church, or other private for-profit or not-for-profit organization. If not, they may have to abandon their home area for the city or remain at home in increasingly unsatisfactory housing. In the case of farm households, leaving the family home almost certainly requires leaving the immediate area because most farm housing is located on dispersed farmsteads rather than in the farm villages that are customary throughout most of the world.[20] For those rural elderly who prefer to continue working part

time or full time, there is a chronic shortage of convenient paid jobs. Even with the small share of the U.S. population, rural areas contain a third of the poverty-level households, yet programs addressed to the poor focus disproportionately on urban areas.

Rural elderly are relatively inexperienced at dealing with public offices and public officials and often do not take advantage of existing programs devoted to their problems and needs. Their high rates of home ownership in weak real estate market areas contribute to their low mobility rates. Where would they go? How could the poor among them afford to buy or rent elsewhere?

Finally, the rural elderly often have strong family ties and a deep commitment to their land and local community. Despite serious problems, many rural elderly report a high degree of satisfaction and contentment. They cannot imagine a housing arrangement superior to what they currently enjoy. Many have known worse times, so they accept what they have even though it often falls short of contemporary national, regional, and urban standards.[21]

Household Income and New Housing

It is generally assumed that since new housing is more expensive on the average than existing housing, the new housing goes mainly to the wealthy. At the same time it is usually understood that the

[18]See David P. Varady, "Housing Problems and Mobility Plans Among the Elderly," *Journal of the American Planning Association* 46 (1980): 301–14.

[19]See U.S. Department of Housing and Urban Development, *Report of the Task Force on Rural and Non-Metropolitan Areas* (Washington, DC: U.S. Government Printing Office, 1978).

[20]George R. Sternlieb et al., eds., *America's Housing: Prospects and Problems* (New Brunswick, NJ: Center for Urban Policy Research, Rutgers University, 1980).

[21]See Raymond T. Coward and Gary R. Lee, eds., *The Elderly in Rural Society* (New York: Springer, 1985); and U. S. Senate, Special Committee on Aging, *Rural Elderly—The Isolated Population: A Look at Services in the 1980s* (Washington, DC: U.S. Government Printing Office, 1980).

wealthy have high incomes, and they normally do—but not necessarily.[22]

First of all, the chances of living in a new house (built in 1970 or later) are much greater if a household lives in the West or South than in other parts of the country. Seven American households in 10 in new housing units in 1980 lived in the South and West. Only 3 households in 10 were in the slow-growth Northeast and Midwest (Table 5.13).

Minority households had better chances of acquiring new housing in the Sunbelt than in the older settled regions. Nonwhite minorities in the Northeast had only 9 percent of the new units in 1980, while in the Midwest they had only 6 percent. In the South they had 14 percent, and in the West 12 percent.

The data are perturbed a bit by the way that some household heads answered the census race question. When asked to specify their race, some Spanish-origin householders wrote in "Spanish," a language-cultural description, rather than acknowledge one of the Census Bureau's race categories: black, white, Asian, Indian, and so forth. Most Spanish-origin householders, however, specified their race following Census Bureau rules and are included in the other four classes in the table.

One household in 10 in new housing units reported its 1979 income as under $5,000. There are at least three reasons for this result. Some wealthy households have many assets but very little income. They may own land that is not rented, own securities that defer interest or dividends, or even hold large amounts of cash. Their income may be low, but they can afford new housing.

Some households understate their income, which includes money from earnings, self-employment, dividends, interest, rents, and such transfer payments as Social Security. The Census Bureau definition of income excludes "in kind" income such as food stamps, Medicare and medical payments, and housing subsidies, but it does not exclude taxes. The Census Bureau, using survey data, and the Bureau of Economic Analysis, using data from government agencies, banks, corporations, and others about payments to individuals, suggest that people reported almost 90 percent of their money income in 1980. Thus, we have some assurance that 23 percent of the 1980 households in new housing had incomes under $10,000 in 1979, 43 percent had incomes between $10,000 and $24,999, and only 34 percent received $25,000 or more.

[22]See E. A. Hanushek and J. M. Quigley, "The Dynamics of the Housing Market: A Stock Adjustment Model of Housing Consumption," *Journal of Urban Economics* 6, no. 1 (1979): 90-111.

Household Income and the Value of Owned Housing

There is a rough correlation between the level of owner-occupant households' income in 1979 and the reported value of their housing unit in 1980. Low-income households tend to live in less valuable housing, and upper-income households predominate in the high-priced units. But the relationship is far from systematic and uniform (Table 5.14). There were many hundreds of thousands of upper-income households in very low-value units (under $25,000), and many hundreds of thousands of households in high-value units ($80,000 or more) who reported 1979 incomes under $10,000. Within these various combinations of income levels and housing values, high-income households in cheap housing are much more prevalent than low-income households in expensive housing.

What accounts for the general patterns and the deviations from them? To begin with, housing is what economists call a positive, normal good. Unlike distasteful goods that yield positive results (medicines), or distasteful goods that produce harmful results (poisons), or even sought-after goods that produce harmful results (addictive substances), housing is commonly viewed as a desirable consumer durable good that yields valuable services.

The income elasticity of demand for housing is positive, which means that as a household's income rises by some percentage, the household's outlay for housing also rises by some percentage. Whether the elasticity (that is, the percentage change in housing outlay divided by the percentage change in income) is high or low depends on households' attitudes toward housing compared with their preferences for other goods, services, and savings. If they value housing above other goods and services, or see it as a vehicle for savings or investment, they will make above-average outlays compared with others in their income class. If they see housing mainly as shelter and put extra money into food, clothing, cars, education for their children, or travel, the housing outlays and corresponding housing values will be below average for their income class.

Quite a few elderly households in 1980 found themselves in expensive housing despite the fact that their incomes had dropped sharply as they moved from full employment to retirement. For such households, housing expenses (taxes, insurance, utilities, maintenance, and perhaps a mortgage payment) often absorbed a large percentage of their annual income. Elderly households may make these payments because they have few other goods and services that they prefer more than housing, because they are slow to make and carry out the decision to move to smaller and more economical quarters,

TABLE 5.13

Households in New Housing Units, by Household Income in 1979, Region, and Race of Householder (in thousands)

	<$5,000	$5,000– 7,499	$7,500– 9,999	$10,000– 14,999	$15,000– 19,999	$20,000– 24,999	$25,000– 34,999	$35,000– 49,999	$50,000+	Total
				Household Income						
Northeast										
White	232	152	136	272	337	355	488	234	129	2,335
Black	32	26	14	22	19	15	29	2	2	161
American Indian	6	4	3	5	6	6	8	4	7	49
Spanish origin	4	3	–	4	1	3	2	1	–	18
Other	1	–	1	1	2	–	–	–	1	6
Total										2,569
Midwest										
White	408	240	245	519	606	618	850	498	242	4,226
Black	34	15	22	28	32	16	18	10	2	177
American Indian	15	5	3	8	4	3	11	8	4	61
Spanish origin	4	1	1	2	3	3	–	–	–	14
Other	1	–	–	–	1	–	–	–	–	2
Total										4,480
South										
White	647	489	506	1,183	1,116	1,069	1,335	706	372	7,423
Black	199	101	111	201	145	100	108	42	17	1,024
American Indian	18	6	4	16	10	14	15	9	7	99
Spanish origin	17	8	4	16	13	6	10	3	2	79
Other	4	1	–	3	7	2	3	–	1	21
Total										8,646
West										
White	341	264	261	609	596	593	831	509	273	4,277
Black	19	14	13	27	13	20	23	14	4	147
American Indian	33	16	14	37	38	47	51	31	27	294
Spanish origin	20	11	14	31	22	13	20	5	2	138
Other	2	2	–	4	2	1	3	3	1	18
Total										4,874
United States	2,037	1,358	1,352	2,988	2,973	2,884	3,805	2,079	1,093	20,569

NOTE: (–) = no household in the 1980 sample of 20,569 living in housing built in 1970 or later had this combination of attributes.

SOURCE: U.S. Bureau of the Census, 1980 Census of Population and Housing, Public Use Microdata Sample A.

TABLE 5.14

Households, by Value of Owned Units, Household Income, and Race of Householder, 1979 (in thousands)

Value of Unit		Household Income								
	<$5,000	$5,000–7,499	$7,500–9,999	$10,000–14,999	$15,000–19,999	$20,000–24,999	$25,000–34,999	$35,000–49,999	$50,000+	%
WHITE										
<$15,000	538	311	248	358	249	172	104	26	6	5.5
15,000–24,999	609	383	372	692	576	471	363	109	34	10.0
25,000–34,999	459	390	429	850	902	763	727	259	77	13.4
35,000–49,999	483	401	453	1,160	1,413	1,482	1,714	718	175	22.0
50,000–59,999	166	159	187	512	665	828	1,276	622	189	12.7
60,000–79,999	173	151	182	495	723	1,016	1,916	1,250	446	17.5
80,000–99,999	70	56	70	173	225	382	838	796	428	8.4
100,000–149,999	48	32	44	106	155	221	618	714	612	7.0
150,000–199,999	16	9	19	18	30	28	133	191	294	2.0
200,000+	19	5	8	12	21	28	49	106	347	1.6
Total White	2,581	1,897	2,012	4,376	4,959	5,391	7,738	4,791	2,608	100.0%
BLACK										
<$15,000	204	79	71	88	57	41	34	15	2	20.2
15,000–24,999	122	70	64	119	98	82	92	24	14	23.4
25,000–34,999	75	41	51	71	89	86	83	38	13	18.7
35,000–49,999	48	24	41	100	72	85	132	49	12	19.2
50,000–59,999	14	6	15	27	22	25	51	26	9	6.7
60,000–79,999	11	9	12	19	29	41	47	44	6	7.5
80,000–99,999	2	1	1	3	5	10	19	15	11	2.3
100,000–149,999	1	1	2	2	1	5	11	20	4	1.6
150,000–199,999	1	–	–	–	–	–	2	1	2	0.2
200,000+	–	1	–	–	1	–	–	1	1	0.1
Total Black	478	232	257	429	374	375	471	233	74	100.0%
Total Indian	45	21	23	67	66	97	139	102	66	
Total Spanish Origin	27	28	24	70	59	62	70	18	9	
Total Other	6	5	5	8	11	4	12	5	5	
Total All Races	3,137	2,183	2,321	4,950	5,469	5,929	8,430	5,149	2,762	

NOTE: (–) = zero households appeared in the sample.

SOURCE: U.S. Bureau of the Census, 1980 Census of Population and Housing, Public Use Microdata Sample A.

or because they are drawing down savings and have disposable incomes much higher than the household income reported to the census.

Another source of deviation from expected correspondence of household income and housing value is the changed value of residen-tial real estate. Almost identical houses can have widely varying values from one setting to another. A 2,500-square-foot, two-and-a-half-story house, built in 1915, in good condition on a 60-foot lot, may have a market value of $40,000 in a small midwestern town, $140,000 in a thriving midwestern city, and $240,000 in certain neighborhoods in Washington, D.C., or Los Angeles. If the escalation in values occurred while the owners lived in the houses, and without any corresponding income adjustment, it can easily produce situations in which the owners could ill afford to buy the houses that they occupy.

There is a rough correspondence between blacks and whites in their patterns of household incomes and housing values (Table 5.14). Close inspection of the table reveals, however, that although upper-income black households often live in extremely modest houses, it is rare for expensive houses to be occupied by low-income black households. Certainly discrimination in real estate markets curtails the free movement of blacks into the neighborhoods of expensive houses, most of which are largely or exclusively white neighborhoods. There are also ties with the black community that some black households are reluctant to loosen or break by moving away. But it is also true that at each level of household income black households on the average have fewer assets, less access to financial resources, and less predictable income streams than white households at the same income levels. This difference makes it hard for low-income blacks to own and consume housing at above-average rates, while permitting many whites to do so. The Indian, Spanish-origin, and other racial groups had too few households to permit constructing income-house value cross-tabulations that could be interpreted with much confidence.

Household Income and Contract Rents

Many of the same generalizations and explanations that were advanced to account for the correlation and other relationships between income levels and owner-occupied housing values also apply to income levels and contract rents paid for rental units (Table 5.15). The main difference is that rents seem to be more easily adjusted in response to rises or declines in income, and these prompt adjustments lead to a much closer correspondence between income and value. Within each income category for whites, the three rent intervals with the largest number of households occur together in the distribution and contain the median rent for the income category. The median rent rises steadily from the lowest income class to the highest. There are no discontinuities or bimodalities.

Some renting households pay no cash rent. They may live rent-free in housing owned by relatives or friends. Sometimes they exchange service for rent, as do house caretakers, farm employees, sharecroppers, migrant workers, medical personnel, college and university personnel, staff of correctional institutions, and others.

Renter households with a black householder are concentrated in the low-income, low-rent categories. Almost 57 percent of the sample householders were in the bottom three income classes, under $10,000. Yet among black households, compared with white, there are proportionately more higher-income households in cheap rental housing and proportionately fewer modest-income black households in upper-priced rental housing. Whites in the top three income classes ($25,000 and over) and the bottom four rent classes (under $200) were only 2.4 percent of the white households, but blacks in the same matrix cells totaled 3.0 of all black households. At the opposite corner of the cross-tabulation matrix, low-income whites (under $10,000) in high-priced rentals ($250 or more) were 7.1 percent of all white households, but only 4.3 percent of all black households.

These imbalances in the matrices and the differences in patterns of outlays between blacks and whites have many causes, some of which were discussed in the previous section. In some areas of the country, such as in low-growth regions of the South, upper-income blacks are able to acquire decent housing at prices that are low by national standards. In many relatively segregated housing market areas of the Northeast, upper-income black households live in ghetto housing and pay modest rents and spend the large bulk of their disposable incomes on goods and services other than housing. White households that spend above-average amounts for rents are much more likely than black households of the same income level to have wealth accumulation that can be drawn down to maintain housing and lifestyles that are more expensive than low incomes alone could sustain.

The distribution of incomes among households with an Indian householder has two modes, one under $5,000 and the other between $10,000 and $14,999, suggesting that two separate distributions might be superimposed. One distribution could be a desperately poor non-assimilated group including many of those living on reservations, while the other could be the urban group, generally with low incomes but with significant numbers in the upper-income categories as well. Even though a large share of all Indian households is included in this sample of renters, there are too few cases to make strong inferences from a large cross-tabulation. Almost the same observations apply to the Spanish-origin householders.

The Types of Housing Structures, by Race and Place

The housing stock in each region of the country has a distinctive composition. The old high-density areas of the northeastern part of the country are different in many respects from the new low-density

TABLE 5.15

Households, by Contract Rent of Rental Units, Household Income, and Race of Householder, 1980 (in thousands)

Monthly Contract Rent	Household Income									
	<$5,000	$5,000–7,499	$7,500–9,999	$10,000–14,999	$15,000–19,999	$20,000–24,999	$25,000–34,999	$35,000–49,999	$50,000+	%
WHITE										
<$60	479	107	63	84	34	27	14	8	–	3.9%
60–99	664	218	158	190	113	59	49	12	6	7.1
100–149	691	500	407	542	330	196	118	37	9	13.7
150–199	760	526	566	975	599	326	178	56	20	19.4
200–249	519	398	410	931	684	392	311	93	29	18.2
250–349	394	358	367	940	915	657	632	229	69	22.0
350–499	102	93	93	238	252	287	354	195	81	8.1
500+	25	10	24	49	52	71	105	77	87	2.4
No cash rent	254	138	124	197	137	84	92	34	18	5.2
Total White	3,888	2,348	2,212	4,146	3,116	2,099	1,853	741	319	100.0%
BLACK										
<$60	350	62	42	36	17	6	7	1	2	11.9
60–99	284	109	78	66	41	10	16	3	5	13.9
100–149	298	135	102	155	89	42	25	9	3	19.6
150–199	261	122	107	195	114	53	52	8	2	20.8
200–249	98	94	64	163	97	51	49	8	4	14.3
250–349	68	48	51	113	118	70	80	17	2	12.9
350–499	9	7	7	20	18	18	28	10	–	2.6
500+	1	–	–	–	3	1	5	3	3	0.4
No cash rent	70	18	10	20	18	11	6	1	3	3.6
Total Black	1,439	595	461	768	515	262	268	60	24	100.0%
Total American Indian	165	70	69	153	92	78	62	29	6	
Total Spanish Origin	216	108	97	180	107	63	43	14	3	
Total Other	25	15	14	28	22	9	11	–	1	
Total All Races	5,733	3,136	2,853	5,275	3,852	2,511	2,237	844	353	

NOTE: (–) = there were no households in the sample that reported this combination of attributes.

SOURCE: U.S. Bureau of the Census, 1980 Census of Population and Housing, Public Use Microdata Sample A.

areas of the West and South and from the small town and rural areas of the South and Midwest. Mobile homes for white householders are common in the low-density, retirement, recreational, seasonal vacation, and occasionally permissively zoned regions of the South and West, but are infrequent in the other regions (Table 5.16). White householders in multiple-unit structures are relatively common in the Northeast, but somewhat scarce elsewhere. When the proportion of white householders in single detached houses drops to a low of 54 percent in the congested areas of the Northeast, the share in single attached units (6 percent), duplexes (12 percent), and apartment houses (26 percent) rises to levels exceeded nowhere else.

The smaller the size of an urban center, or the more recently a metro region came into existence and attained large size, the lower is its residential density and the greater its share of housing in single detached units. All regions but the South have large percentages of their white-occupied housing in SMSA suburbs, typically about a fourth of the total. In the South almost two housing units in three lie in lower-density settings outside the big SMSAs, and four housing units in five are mobile homes or single detached units.

The kinds of housing occupied are sharply different for black and white householders. Blacks in single detached houses (16 percent) are unusual in the Northeast compared with whites (54 percent). The differences in the shares are much less in the Midwest (27 percent), the West (16 percent), and the South (11 percent), but the small differences do not necessarily imply minimal quality disparities. There are quite a few poor-quality single detached houses occupied by blacks throughout the small towns and rural areas of the South.

Almost a third of the blacks in the Northeast live in large apartment buildings (10 units or more) in central city locations (Table 5.16), while less than 8 percent of white householders live that way. The best chance for blacks to live in single detached housing in the suburbs of a large SMSA appears to be in the West (15 percent of black householders) and the Midwest (10 percent). Chances are significantly lower in the Northeast and the South (7 percent each).

Over half the Indian householders reported living in single detached housing, but some is low-quality rural and reservation housing, while the rest is distributed by region, location, and type of structure. Unfortunately, the small number of nationwide sample cases does not allow a detailed discussion that can be defended with much confidence. Even the total number of Indian householders in the microdata sample seems high at almost 1.6 million when the 1980 census reported only 1.4 million Indians, Eskimos, and Aleuts.[23] The remaining groups are equally hard to interpret.

Owning Versus Renting: Variations Across the Country

Home ownership is a highly prized goal in the United States, but the degree to which it is achieved appears to depend on the region of the country and the race of the householder (Table 5.17). In the Northeast white owners outnumber white renters in each locational setting except the central cities of large SMSAs. For black and Indian householders renters outnumber owners, except in the case of Indians

[23]U.S. Bureau of the Census, *Statistical Abstract of the United States, 1984*, p. 18.

in small SMSAs and blacks in mixed SMSA/non-SMSAs; however, the small numbers and small differences make it hard to draw certain conclusions about these apparent exceptions.

In the Midwest the majority of white householders had achieved ownership in all locational settings by census time, as did the small numbers of blacks and Indians who have made it into the suburbs or blacks who live in the softer housing markets of the smaller metro areas. Outside midwestern metro areas a majority of Indians apparently own their housing.

In the South home-owning householders appear to outnumber renters in most situations, except for nonwhites in the central cities of large SMSAs, most of whom are renters. Blacks and Indians in small southern metro areas are about evenly divided between owners and renters.

Most whites in the West are owners, as are most Indians in suburbs and other residents of the mixed SMSA/non-SMSA areas and the places outside the metro settings.

Persons and Rooms, 1980

One of the most widely used measures of housing adequacy, and a central topic in the 1950 SSRC-sponsored census monograph on housing, is the ratio of persons per room in housing units. The average number of rooms per housing unit rose at the same rate in the 1970s as in the 1960s, but the number of people per unit fell faster in the 1970s; thus, the number of rooms per person rose more in the later period. The census makes no distinction between adults and children in its data presentations on persons per room. Four adults have housing needs different from a couple with two small children or a single parent with three small children.

The intent of the census question on rooms is to count the number of whole rooms used for living purposes. For each housing unit the count of rooms includes living rooms, dining rooms, kitchens, bedrooms, finished recreation rooms, enclosed porches suitable for year-round use, and lodgers' rooms. Excluded are strip or pullman kitchens, bathrooms, open porches, balconies, halls, half rooms, utility rooms, unfinished attics or basements, or other unfinished space used for storage. A partially divided room is counted as a separate room only if there is a partition from floor to ceiling.

In the 1980 microdata sample, almost three fourths of the housing units had 4 to 7 rooms, with 5-room units the most common. Almost three fourths of the households had 1 to 3 household members, with 2 persons the most common number. In general, therefore,

TABLE 5.16

Households, by Units in Structure, Location Type, Region, and Race of Household Head, 1980 (in thousands)

	Mobile Home	Single Detached	Single Attached	Duplex	3–4 Family	5–9 Family	10+ Family	Boat, Tent, Van, etc.	%
WHITE									
Northeast									
Central city of SMSA	2	505	383	588	357	235	1,203	–	21.4%
SMSA suburbs	91	3,977	247	573	337	209	646	1	39.7
Small SMSAs	52	1,265	129	291	190	103	222	1	14.7
Mixed SMSA/ Non-SMSA	84	1,292	41	237	117	80	117	1	12.9
Outside SMSA	124	1,218	69	140	73	43	70	1	11.3
Percentage	2.3%	53.9%	5.7%	11.9%	7.0%	4.4%	14.7%	0.0%	100.0%
Total									15,314
Midwest									
Central city of SMSA	16	1,240	48	386	241	144	501	–	13.7
SMSA suburbs	180	4,510	152	269	227	251	590	1	32.9
Small SMSAs	133	2,307	60	214	125	107	267	–	17.1
Mixed SMSA/ Non-SMSA	160	1,590	31	80	68	53	112	–	11.1
Outside SMSA	331	3,798	47	191	115	89	162	–	25.2
Percentage	4.4%	71.5%	1.8%	6.1%	4.1%	3.4%	8.7%	0.0%	100.0%
Total									18,796
South									
Central city of SMSA	45	1,583	209	163	142	141	596	1	13.3
SMSA suburbs	308	3,664	282	133	140	204	838	1	25.7
Small SMSAs	338	3,032	122	189	150	157	508	–	20.8
Mixed SMSA/ Non-SMSA	376	2,556	51	101	74	59	135	1	15.5
Outside SMSA	614	4,161	62	161	100	77	157	1	24.7
Percentage	7.8%	69.3%	3.4%	3.5%	2.8%	2.9%	10.3%	0.0%	100.0%
Total									21,632
West									
Central city of SMSA	72	1,812	150	149	182	210	790	3	25.5
SMSA suburbs	247	3,071	256	135	234	221	692	1	36.7
Small SMSAs	189	1,555	77	66	95	70	227	2	17.3
Mixed SMSA/ Non-SMSA	72	375	13	24	25	19	30	–	4.2
Outside SMSA	357	1,443	45	65	63	56	124	2	16.3
Percentage	7.1%	62.5%	4.1%	3.3%	4.5%	4.4%	14.1%	0.1%	100.0%
Total									13,219

TABLE 5.16 (continued)

| | Type of Structure | | | | | | | | |
	Mobile Home	Single Detached	Single Attached	Duplex	3–4 Family	5–9 Family	10+ Family	Boat, Tent, Van, etc.	%
BLACK									
Northeast									
Central city of SMSA	1	89	162	179	118	78	511	—	70.1
SMSA suburbs	1	113	39	37	28	21	60	—	18.4
Small SMSAs	—	43	27	16	15	10	33	—	8.9
Mixed SMSA/ Non-SMSA	1	10	3	1	—	1	3	—	1.2
Outside SMSA	3	10	2	1	2	1	4	—	1.4
Percentage	0.4%	16.3%	14.4%	14.4%	10.0%	6.8%	37.6%	—	100.0%
Total									1,623
Midwest									
Central city of SMSA	1	436	45	219	115	111	209	—	66.0
SMSA suburbs	2	170	13	24	28	17	41	—	17.1
Small SMSAs	2	124	12	19	17	11	28	—	12.4
Mixed SMSA/ Non-SMSA	—	11	2	4	3	1	4	—	1.5
Outside SMSA	5	29	3	4	2	4	5	—	3.0
Percentage	0.6%	44.7%	4.4%	15.7%	9.6%	8.4%	16.7%	—	100.0%
Total									1,721
South									
Central city of SMSA	5	538	168	115	91	114	242	—	29.9
SMSA suburbs	25	310	38	18	37	41	111	—	13.6
Small SMSAs	22	555	41	63	56	63	108	—	21.4
Mixed SMSA/ Non-SMSA	30	287	12	18	15	12	16	—	9.2
Outside SMSA	105	791	22	53	34	51	44	—	25.9
Percentage	4.4%	58.4%	6.6%	6.3%	5.5%	6.6%	12.3%	—	100.0%
Total									4,251
West									
Central city of SMSA	—	208	30	28	50	40	116	—	60.7
SMSA suburbs	2	117	17	8	20	20	47	—	29.7
Small SMSAs	1	26	2	5	4	3	10	—	6.6
Mixed SMSA/ Non-SMSA	1	5	1	—	—	—	4	—	1.4
Outside SMSA	1	7	—	—	1	1	3	—	1.7
Percentage	0.6%	46.7%	6.4%	5.3%	9.6%	8.2%	23.1%	—	100.0%
Total									778
Total American Indian	58	797	67	79	106	105	349	—	1,561
Total Spanish origin	35	554	67	100	120	112	337	—	1,325
Total Other	2	79	15	16	21	20	55	—	208

NOTE: (−) = there were no households in the sample that reported this combination of attributes.

SOURCE: U.S. Bureau of the Census, 1980 Census of Population and Housing, Public Use Microdata Sample A.

TABLE 5.17

Households, by Tenure, Location, Region, and Race of Householder, 1980 (in thousands)

	Owner-Occupied					Renter-Occupied				
	SMSA Central City	SMSA Suburbs	Small SMSA	Mixed SMSA/ Non-SMSA	Outside SMSA	SMSA Central City	SMSA Suburbs	Small SMSA	Mixed SMSA/ Non-SMSA	Outside SMSA
Northeast										
White	1,257	4,382	1,448	1,410	1,296	2,016	1,699	805	559	442
Black	310	144	53	11	11	828	155	91	8	12
American Indian	22	34	7	6	1	86	36	5	6	1
Spanish origin	22	6	2	2	–	222	16	11	–	–
Other	2	3	3	1	1	25	3	1	1	1
Total										17,463
Midwest										
White	1,427	4,688	2,274	1,577	3,582	1,149	1,492	939	517	1,151
Black	476	154	110	9	25	660	141	103	16	27
American Indian	15	43	9	8	24	52	20	14	13	14
Spanish origin	17	9	4	1	4	48	11	7	8	4
Other	7	1	1	–	1	8	5	–	2	–
Total										20,867
South										
White	1,681	4,052	3,089	2,534	4,065	1,199	1,518	1,407	819	1,268
Black	510	317	451	231	671	763	263	457	159	429
American Indian	18	49	15	19	39	29	39	19	16	16
Spanish origin	38	18	57	18	13	55	26	39	12	14
Other	7	6	9	2	3	12	6	7	3	2
Total										26,489
West										
White	1,787	3,152	1,537	380	1,509	1,581	1,705	744	178	646
Black	173	109	23	6	7	299	122	28	5	6
American Indian	173	196	31	13	91	187	104	32	10	49
Spanish origin	76	100	33	17	38	175	117	40	15	30
Other	8	14	4	4	2	24	24	2	1	2
Total										15,609
United States										80,428

NOTE: (–) = there were no households in the sample that reported this combination of attributes.

SOURCE: U.S. Bureau of the Census, 1980 Census of Population and Housing, Public Use Microdata Sample A.

TABLE 5.18

Housing Units, by Persons in Household and Number of Rooms, 1980 (in thousands)

Persons per Household	Rooms in Housing Unit									Total	%
	1	2	3	4	5	6	7	8	9 or more		
1	923	1,595	4,293	4,560	3,468	2,061	812	328	218	18,258	22.7%
2	180	535	2,186	5,537	6,698	5,304	2,671	1,283	805	25,199	31.4
3	63	170	597	2,493	3,433	3,323	2,011	996	770	13,856	17.2
4	26	97	260	1,366	2,841	3,077	2,159	1,346	1,096	12,268	15.3
5	15	46	143	517	1,375	1,564	1,135	808	745	6,348	7.9
6	3	26	70	188	517	612	511	350	417	2,694	3.4
7	5	18	33	104	226	292	229	162	183	1,252	1.6
8	2	2	9	25	46	83	47	37	46	297	0.4
9	1	–	1	11	13	29	21	19	25	120	0.1
10 or More	–	1	2	5	15	11	5	9	15	63	0.1
Total	1,218	2,490	7,594	14,806	18,632	16,356	9,601	5,338	4,320	80,355	
Percentage	1.5%	3.1%	9.5%	18.4%	23.2%	20.4%	11.9%	6.6%	5.4%		100.0%

NOTE: 73,000 cases are missing; (–) = there were no households in the sample that reported this combination of attributes.

SOURCE: U.S. Bureau of the Census, 1980 Census of Population and Housing, Public Use Microdata Sample A.

the majority of people lived in housing units where the number of rooms was equal to or greater than the number of people in the household; in other words, the persons per room ratios were 1.0 or less (Table 5.18). Ratios greater than 1.0 are usually considered to be gross evidence of a crowding problem.

The lower left portion of the cross-tabulation of persons and rooms discloses a disturbingly large number of households— 656,000—in cells indicating person per room ratios of 2.0 or more (Table 5.18). About 180,000 are 2-person households in a single room, efficiency apartment, or 1-room house. The household dynamics of this pattern will probably differ from that of 4 persons in 2 rooms or 6 persons in 3 rooms. There will also be effects caused by the ages of the household members (small children have fewer space needs than adults) and the floor areas and room volumes in the housing units.

On the positive side, almost 89 percent of American households in 1980 enjoyed persons per room ratios below 1.0.

Household Income and the Type of Structure Occupied

While there is a fairly clear correspondence between household income and type of housing occupied by the household, there are significant deviations from the general patterns as well. For example, low-income households (under $10,000) made up 29 percent of all households, but occupied almost half (44 percent) of the units in the largest apartment buildings (50 units or more). They also had 40 percent of the units in buildings with 10 to 49 units. These buildings are disproportionately in the congested older parts of the inner city. They form much of the older parts of the housing stock and cost less than newer units. They also include many of the large public housing projects built with federal assistance, especially in the 1950s and 1960s (Table 5.19).

The low-income households have only 23 percent of the single detached housing units. Some of these houses are old and decrepit inner city houses worth very little, some are good houses with low values in declining small cities and towns, some are inexpensive houses of varying quality and value in rural and farm areas, and some are of average or above-average quality and value owned by households with modest to high assets but low incomes. The same observations can be made about the 38 percent of the nation's more than 4 million mobile homes that are occupied by low-income households. They are an economical variant of single detached housing usually found in suburban, small town, and rural areas, especially in the South and West, where satisfactory low-priced alternatives are hard to find.

At the other end of the income ladder are the 29 percent of the households reporting 1979 incomes of $25,000 or more and occupying over 36 percent of the single detached housing units. Since these up-

TABLE 5.19

Households, by Income in 1979, Units in Structure, and Type of Building, 1980 (in thousands)

Household Income	Type of Structure										
	Mobile Home	Single Detached	Single Attached	Duplex	3–4 Family	5–9 Family	10–19 Family	20–49 Family	50+ Family	Boat, Tent, Van, etc.	%
<$5,000	627	4,922	470	924	794	696	665	556	983	5	13.2%
$5,000–7,499	447	3,206	265	541	454	419	352	298	476	3	8.0
$7,500–9,999	500	3,295	263	513	427	356	363	255	358	–	7.9
$10,000–14,999	855	6,683	513	894	790	653	746	580	668	2	15.4
$15,000–19,999	682	6,858	459	760	586	459	543	384	515	2	14.0
$20,000–24,999	447	6,985	436	614	345	297	354	262	377	1	12.6
$25,000–34,999	371	9,625	441	554	346	321	296	226	402	2	15.6
$35,000–49,999	117	5,651	290	260	149	107	121	76	216	1	8.7
$50,000+	48	3,038	125	102	47	57	47	54	154	1	4.6
Total	4,094	50,263	3,262	5,162	3,938	3,365	3,487	2,691	4,149	17	
Percentage	5.1%	62.5%	4.1%	6.4%	4.9%	4.2%	4.3%	3.3%	5.2%	0.0%	100.0%

NOTE: (–) = there were no households in the sample that reported this combination of attributes.

SOURCE: U. S. Bureau of the Census, 1980 Census of Population and Housing, Public Use Microdata Sample A.

per-income householders have the greatest freedom to choose where to live, they generally avoid large apartment blocks, smaller multiple units of all kinds, and mobile homes and favor single detached houses.

Household Income and Housing Affordability

There are two main costs of home ownership: the direct monthly cost of mortgage payments, taxes, insurance, utilities, and maintenance; and the opportunity cost equal to what the net equity value in the house could have earned if invested elsewhere. When a household buys a house using money borrowed from a financial institution, the ability to make the monthly payments is usually assessed by calculating the monthly payment (interest, principal, taxes, insurance) as a percentage of monthly gross income. A percentage between 25 and 30 percent is usually judged manageable by the lender and tolerable by the borrower.[24] A percentage under 25 percent is usually

rather comfortable for the borrower and seen as a safe bet by the lender. Strain and risks normally rise when the ratio exceeds 30 percent.

The rules and averages that apply at the time of purchase often do not appropriately describe the reality long after the loan is made and the sale is completed. Moreover, new house sales plus sales of used houses in any given year compose only a small percentage of the total stock. In 1980, for example, there were 545,000 new single-family houses sold, 2,973,000 used houses sold, and 233,700 new mobile homes placed for use, for a total of 3.8 million units, or something over 6 percent in a stock of 61.6 million single-unit houses and mobile homes.[25] As a result, the relation between income and housing values bears little resemblance to mortgage loan rules, and monthly owner costs depart significantly from the 25 to 30 percent guideline.

Although there is a rough correlation between household income levels and value of owned houses, there is a substantial dispersion within each row and column of the cross-tabulation (Table 5.20). Each income class is well represented in each housing value class. Households may have bought their houses when their incomes were low, and then remained in the same houses while their incomes rose. The reverse happens when older workers retire and experience a sig-

[24]See U.S. Department of Housing and Urban Development, *The Affordable Community: Growth, Change, and Choice in the 1980s*, Report of the Council on Development Choices for the 1980s (Washington, DC: U.S. Government Printing Office, 1981); Larry S. Bourne, *Access to Housing and the Affordability Issue: Concept and Empirical Reality* (Toronto: Center for Urban and Community Studies, University of Toronto, 1982); and Frank Schmidman and Jane A. Silverman, *Housing, Supply, and Affordability* (Washington, DC: Urban Land Institute, 1983).

[25]U.S. Bureau of the Census, *Statistical Abstract of the United States*, 1984, pp. 745–46, 748.

TABLE 5.20

Households, by Income in 1979, and Value of Owned Houses (in thousands)

Value of Owned Houses	<$5,000	$5,000–7,499	$7,500–9,999	$10,000–14,999	$15,000–19,999	$20,000–24,999	$25,000–34,999	$35,000–49,999	$50,000+	%
					Household Income					
<$10,000	410	176	177	187	126	78	45	17	3	3.0%
$10,000–14,999	353	225	154	277	190	142	97	25	6	3.6
$15,000–19,999	363	210	214	334	280	218	186	48	23	4.7
$20,000–24,999	383	255	232	503	411	343	285	89	26	6.3
$25,000–29,999	301	226	246	449	443	400	332	121	34	6.3
$30,000–34,999	245	214	239	494	568	469	489	181	57	7.3
$35,000–39,999	210	171	189	486	522	526	526	220	48	7.2
$40,000–49,999	330	266	318	801	992	1,067	1,355	559	144	14.5
$50,000–59,999	187	167	205	549	698	872	1,348	657	202	12.1
$60,000–79,999	193	164	197	536	782	1,100	2,014	1,319	459	16.8
$80,000–99,999	73	59	73	185	239	413	897	837	451	8.0
$100,000–149,999	52	34	49	116	164	240	662	762	635	6.7
$150,000–199,999	18	10	19	20	32	31	142	201	309	1.9
$200,000+	19	6	9	13	22	30	52	113	365	1.6
Percent	7.8%	5.4%	5.8%	12.3%	13.6%	14.7%	20.9%	12.8%	6.8%	100.0%

SOURCE: U.S. Bureau of the Census, 1980 Census of Population and Housing, Public Use Microdata Sample A.

nificant drop in income, yet remain in their relatively expensive housing. For older householders, whose house is fully paid for, the direct costs of remaining in the house may be low, although the indirect costs may be quite high. Householders whose house is not fully paid for may decide to devote an unusually large proportion of their income to housing because their outlays for other goods and services might be already low or easily contracted. Still others may draw down savings and other assets in order to maintain housing outlays and other expenditures at levels considerably above their income.

The Census Bureau asks a sample of householders in specified single-family houses on less than 10 acres, without a commercial establishment or medical office on the property, to report selected monthly owner costs, which are the sum of payments for mortgages, deeds of trust, or similar debts on the property, real estate taxes, fire and hazard insurance on the property, utilities (electricity, gas, water), and fuels (oil, coal, kerosene, wood, and so forth). The specified owner-occupied housing units from which the sample was drawn exclude owner-occupied condominium units, mobile homes, trailers, boats, tents, or vans occupied as a usual residence, as well as owner-occupied noncondominium units in multifamily buildings—for example, cooperative housing.

In the sample of specified owner-occupied units, the median monthly owner cost was about $275 monthly in 1980, while the median household income was almost $22,000 (Table 5.21). In other words, the median monthly owner cost ($275) was about 15 percent of the median owner-occupant household income in 1979 ($1,833). In terms of monthly financial burdens, getting into owner-occupied housing is evidently harder on the average than staying in. But the averages can be misleading. Most of the cells in the lower left portion of the cross-tabulation of monthly housing cost and household income involve costs equal to or exceeding half of income—close to 2 million households. At the opposite corner of the matrix is a much larger group of households paying only a small percentage of their monthly income in housing costs.

Household Types and Housing Types

The typical household in 1980 was a married couple family of two or more persons. Six households in 10 were of this type (Table 5.22). Nonfamily households, which include single-person households and households of two or more persons unrelated by blood or mar-

TABLE 5.21
Households, by Income in 1979, and Selected Monthly Owner Costs (in thousands)

Monthly Owner Costs	Household Income										
	<$5,000	$5,000–7,499	$7,500–9,999	$10,000–14,999	$15,000–19,999	$20,000–24,999	$25,000–34,999	$35,000–49,999	$50,000+	Total	%
$1–49	189	62	43	43	26	8	11	3	1	386	1.0%
$50–99	944	567	484	664	393	288	253	85	25	3,703	9.5
$100–149	681	507	493	918	743	624	634	298	90	4,988	12.7
$150–199	387	366	385	696	666	584	715	407	159	4,365	11.2
$200–299	403	317	430	1,134	1,309	1,279	1,758	931	419	7,980	20.4
$300–399	177	124	198	687	1,051	1,202	1,587	893	402	6,321	16.2
$400–499	95	61	102	310	581	857	1,305	746	337	4,394	11.2
$500–599	51	35	40	136	267	486	844	567	292	2,718	6.9
$600–749	33	23	30	82	141	270	697	555	322	2,153	5.5
$750–999	25	11	10	33	48	89	301	351	313	1,181	3.0
$1,000–1,999	11	–	3	6	12	21	54	127	248	482	1.2
$2,000+	76	44	31	67	56	60	52	38	40	464	1.2
Percentage	7.8%	5.4%	5.7%	12.2%	13.5%	14.7%	21.0%	12.8%	6.8%	39,135	100.0%

NOTE: (–) = there were no households in the sample that reported this combination of attributes.

SOURCE: U.S. Bureau of the Census, 1980 Census of Population and Housing, Public Use Microdata Sample A.

TABLE 5.22
Households, by Type and Units in Structure, 1980 (in thousands)

Units	Married Couple Family, Head of Household	Family, Male Head of Household, No Wife	Family, Female Head of Household, No Husband	Nonfamily Household
Mobile Home	2,523	116	332	1,123
Single Detached	36,516	1,122	4,317	8,308
Single Attached	1,691	105	561	905
Duplex	2,431	152	801	1,778
3–4 Family	1,461	136	615	1,726
5–9 Family	1,141	92	523	1,609
10–19 Family	1,075	90	475	1,847
20–49 Family	805	84	321	1,481
50+ Family	1,159	82	405	2,503
Boat, Tent, Van, etc.	6	–	–	11
Total	48,808	1,979	8,350	21,291
Percentage	60.7%	2.5%	10.4%	26.5%

NOTE: (–) = there were no households in the sample that reported this combination of attributes.

SOURCE: U.S. Bureau of the Census, 1980 Census of Population and Housing, Public Use Microdata Sample A.

riage, accounted for over a quarter of all households. Family house-holds headed by a woman (no husband present) were more than four times as prevalent as family households headed by a man (with no wife present).

Single-unit houses—detached, attached, and mobile homes—are the most sought-after options, and five married couples in six are successful in achieving this goal. Male-headed families are next at 68 percent, followed by female-headed families at 62 percent. Nonfamily households usually live in duplexes or multiple-unit buildings.

It is hard to draw any general conclusions from these data. The nonfamily households are a mixed group of singles of all ages, unmarried couples of the same and of opposite sex, and groups of working people living together. Thus, several distinctive groups are aggregated into one column of data. It is widely reported that single-parent families encounter special housing problems, especially those families headed by women, whose earning power is lower on the average than that of men. The data show little difference between the housing patterns of these two groups of families, except that there are over four times as many headed by women as by men. If anything, compared with the male-headed families, the female-headed families seem present in above-average numbers in all the attached and multiple-unit housing types except the 20-to-49-unit buildings and in below-average numbers in the expensive single detached units and mobile homes.

Children and Their Housing

When the census classifies households according to the presence or absence of children, it uses five categories, each having distinctive housing, neighborhood, and schooling implications. Families with children under age 6 (9 percent of all 1980 sample households) need less room per person than households of the same size with only older members. Schools and outdoor play areas are not as urgent a priority as they are for families with children aged 6 to 17 (22 percent of households). These households with older children need large amounts of interior room, plus play access outside, and neighborhood schools. The third census class of family has children under age 6 as well as children aged 6 to 17. These families compose only 7 percent of all households but generate complex housing and neighborhood requirements (Table 5.23).

Families without children (36 percent of all 1980 households) and nonfamily households (27 percent of all households) have housing needs unrelated to children, except for those who prefer child-free residential settings. Mobile homes compose only 5 percent of the housing units, but house over 8 percent of the family households with small children. The same households are overrepresented in duplexes and small apartment houses as they obtain small, inexpensive units at low and moderate densities so that their children can play out of doors. Single detached houses compose over 62 percent of the occupied housing units in the sample, but significantly larger proportions of families with children aged 6 to 17 and families with children both under age 6 and aged 6 to 17 live in such housing (Table 5.23).

Families without own children are mainly of three kinds: married couples whose children are grown and gone, married couples without children, and adult relatives. These families are also overrepresented in single detached houses. Meanwhile, nonfamily households are overrepresented in duplexes and apartments. These non-child, nonfamily households evidently select lower-cost, smaller-unit, more transient housing arrangements than do those with dependent children.

When the number of rooms in the housing unit is evaluated with respect to household presence of children, we observe first that the modal number of rooms per housing unit is 5. Nonfamily households cluster in units with 3 to 5 rooms, while families with children under age 6 only cluster in units with 4 to 6 rooms. Families with older children only are concentrated in large units with 5 to 7 rooms, while those with children of all ages—which probably are larger families on the average—are concentrated in the 5-to-7-room units, but are relatively underrepresented in the largest units compared with the families with older children only. Families without own children are heavily concentrated in the smaller 4-to-6-room units (Table 5.23).

The Race and Sex of Householders in Terms of Housing Age

Whites throughout the United States occupy a slightly larger share of the post-1960 housing stock (88 percent) than their share of householders in the census microdata sample (85.7 percent) (calculated from data in Table 5.24). Within the white householder group, males outnumber females by almost 3 to 1. In the expensive new late-1970s housing, male householders outnumber females by over 4 to 1, a reflection of the superior purchasing power of the males and the likelihood that in a husband-wife family the husband will be listed as the householder. In the pre-1950 housing the ratio of male household-

TABLE 5.23

Households, by Presence and Age of Own Children, Units in Structure, and Rooms in Unit, 1980 (in thousands)

| | Children | | | | | | |
	Nonfamily, Vacant, and Group Quarters	Family with Own Children Under Age 6 Only	Family with Own Children Aged 6–17 Only	Family with Own Children Ages 6–17 and Under Age 6	Family Without Own Children	Total	%
Units in Structure							
Mobile home	1,123	593	666	313	1,399	4,094	5.1%
Single detached	8,308	4,264	13,317	4,204	20,170	50,263	62.5
Single attached	905	340	667	233	1,117	3,262	4.1
Duplex	1,778	544	800	352	1,688	5,162	6.4
3–4 family	1,726	440	530	229	1,013	3,938	4.9
5–9 family	1,609	356	430	190	780	3,365	4.2
10–19 family	1,847	351	365	125	799	3,487	4.3
20–49 family	1,481	188	246	99	677	2,691	3.3
50+ family	2,503	207	319	116	1,004	4,149	5.2
Boat, tent, van, etc.	11	2	1	—	3	17	—
Total	21,291	7,285	17,341	5,861	28,650	80,428	
Percentage	26.5%	9.1%	21.6%	7.3%	35.6%	100.0%	100.0%
Rooms in Unit							
1	979	63	31	12	133	1,218	1.5
2	1,730	159	99	62	443	2,493	3.1
3	4,803	520	379	175	1,720	7,597	9.4
4	5,479	1,792	1,795	727	5,020	14,813	18.4
5	4,132	1,727	3,832	1,440	7,519	18,650	23.2
6	2,419	1,381	4,222	1,416	6,893	16,371	20.4
7	1,002	873	3,110	904	3,721	9,610	11.9
8	413	451	2,012	600	1,871	5,347	6.6
9 or more	294	319	1,861	525	1,330	4,329	5.4
Total	21,291	7,285	17,341	5,861	28,650	80,428	100.0
Percentage	26.5%	9.1%	21.6%	7.3%	35.6%	100.0%	

NOTE: (–) = there were no households in the sample that reported this combination of attributes.

SOURCE: U.S. Bureau of the Census, 1980 Census of Population and Housing, Public Use Microdata Sample A.

ers to female drops to 2.3 and below, reflecting in part the concentration of low-income female-headed households in the older, cheaper housing stock.

Just as whites are overrepresented on a per capita basis in the newer segments of the housing stock, black households, with 10.4 percent of the total households, occupy above-average shares of the pre-1960 housing stock (Table 5.24); the older the housing, the greater the concentration of black households. Slightly above 45 percent of the black householders in the microdata sample were female, producing an overall male-to-female ratio of black householders of 1.2. That

TABLE 5.24

Households, by Race, Sex of Householder, and Year Residential Structure Built, 1980 (in thousands)

| | Year Built | | | | | | | | |
	1939 and Earlier	1940–1949	1950–1959	1960–1969	1970–1974	1975–1978	1979–March 1980	Total	%
White	85.4%	79.6%	85.3%	86.1%	87.0%	90.7%	90.7%		
Male	12,125	4,949	9,099	10,548	6,948	5,597	1,711	50,977	63.4%
Female	5,560	2,112	2,857	3,450	2,227	1,361	417	17,984	22.4
M/F ratio	2.2	2.3	3.2	3.1	3.1	4.1	4.1	2.8	
Black	11.4%	15.7%	10.9%	9.8%	9.2%	5.3%	5.5%		
Male	1,226	732	828	911	568	248	83	4,596	5.7
Female	1,137	657	694	679	402	161	47	3,777	4.7
M/F ratio	1.1	1.1	1.2	1.3	1.4	1.5	1.8	1.2	
American Indian	1.4%	1.7%	1.7%	2.3%	2.3%	2.6%	2.4%		
Male	204	118	192	283	182	169	47	1,195	1.5
Female	89	35	53	84	61	34	10	366	.5
M/F ratio	2.3	3.4	3.6	3.4	3.0	5.0	4.7	3.3	
Spanish Origin	1.6%	2.6%	1.8%	1.6%	1.3%	1.2%	1.0%		
Male	217	157	183	202	98	77	18	952	1.2
Female	107	75	72	63	36	14	6	373	.5
M/F ratio	2.0	2.1	2.5	3.2	2.7	5.5	3.0	2.6	
Other	0.3%	0.4%	0.3%	0.2%	0.3%	0.2%	0.3%		
Male	37	20	34	20	21	12	6	150	.2
Female	16	14	9	11	7	1	–	59	.1
Total	20,718	8,869	14,021	16,251	10,550	7,674	2,345	80,429	100.0%

NOTE: (–) = there were no households in the sample that reported this combination of attributes.

SOURCE: U.S. Bureau of the Census, 1980 Census of Population and Housing, Public Use Microdata Sample A.

ratio ranges from a high of 1.8 in the newest and most expensive housing, wherein a large percentage of the households are likely to be formed around a married couple with income well above average, to lows of 1.1 in housing dating from the period before 1970. In the older and cheaper housing, low-income households, headed by black females, are common in many places and occasionally are typical.

Indian householders compose just 2 percent of the total, but they occupy significantly more than 2 percent of the sample housing units built after 1960 (Table 5.24). These numbers include some immigrant Spanish-origin householders who answered the race question correctly (that is, they designated a race rather than recording Spanish or an equivalent cultural term other than a race) and have acquired sub-sidized or market-rate housing. If it is subsidized, it may well be in urban areas, built since 1960 under federally assisted programs. If it is market rate, the householder may simply have bought or rented housing, perhaps in the South or West, where a large share of the units are relatively new. A significant amount of government-assisted housing has been built on reservations since 1960, but much of it is modest in quality and low in market value. Whether the housing is older or new, the male-to-female ratio among Indian householders is almost always well above the ratios for blacks and for whites in each housing age class.

The Spanish-origin householders accounted for over 1.6 percent of the total and live disproportionately in early post–World War II housing. Very few show up in the newest units. As might be expected, the male-to-female ratios for householders stand well above the overall ratio of 2.6 in the segments of the housing stock built since 1960. Male householders usually have higher-than-average household incomes, making new housing more readily affordable.

Spanish-Origin Households, and the Age and Value of Their Housing

The story of the entry into the United States of the Spanish-origin population and its settlement in various regions has several major chapters plus some important minor themes. The major movements include Puerto Rican settlements in and around New York City, Cuban settlements in Miami and the Southeast, and Mexican settlements in the West, Midwest, and South. The remaining groups include the Hispanos of southern Texas and New Mexico, whose ancestors are said to have descended from the early Spanish settlers and lived in the area when it was still part of Mexico; immigrants from the Philippines; newcomers from Hispaniola (Dominican Republic and Haiti) and the rest of the Caribbean; persons from Central and South America; and a few from Spain. In many ways these groups are as diverse as their origins, but their common language origins, supplemented occasionally by cultural, political, and religious traditions and outlooks, have worked successfully to define them as an ethnic group for census purposes. The data that have been gathered according to the Spanish-origin definition nurture the concept and give it political significance, since the enumerated group defined this way numbered almost 15 million in 1980.

The census microdata samples tell us where each major group lives and in what kind of housing. Spanish-origin owner-occupant households in the South on the average live in the newest housing compared with those living in other regions. The South is followed by the West, the Midwest, and the Northeast. The fact that the Spanish-origin population in the South occupies relatively new housing compared with the other regions is due to the generally newer housing stock in the places that received them, such as Miami and the fast-growth cities of coastal Florida, but it is also due to the presence of large numbers of Cubans and others who are often well-educated professionals and business people whose high incomes and good housing pull up the averages for the South (Table 5.25).

In the West almost three Spanish-origin home-owning householders in four are of Mexican origin; since the economy has been generally strong in the states of the West, the newcomers have entered the economy and worked with some degree of success. The West's housing stock is relatively new. This situation has facilitated the immigrants placing themselves into the housing stock in units that on the average were built after 1950, relatively new by national standards.

In the Midwest all Spanish-origin populations are well represented, although almost 6 householders in 10 are of Mexican descent. The entire owner-occupant group is distributed in a regional housing stock that is older on the average than that in the West and South. Within the group the Mexican and Puerto Rican households are in housing that is distinctly older, and presumably lower in price and quality, than that used by the Cubans and others.

Over half the Spanish-origin owner-occupants in the Northeast are of Puerto Rican origin. Since they began to arrive in the New York area in large numbers in the 1950s, many have had several decades to settle into the economy and to achieve some means of economic success that normally translates into better housing. To the extent that age of housing corresponds roughly with quality, the Puerto Rican and other Spanish-origin owner-occupant households in the Northeast had better housing than did those with Mexican and Cuban roots (Table 5.25).

The census microdata sample classifies almost 6.2 million Spanish-origin households according to place of origin, region of residence, and tenure. In 1980 65 percent of these householders were owners and 35 percent were renters. In the Northeast, where the housing stock has a much higher share of rentals and the costs of home ownership are higher than elsewhere, the Spanish-origin ownership rate was a low 55 percent. In the South, where prosperous Cubans and others pull up the averages, the rate reached 69 percent.

Among the renting households, those of Mexican origin in the South had the lowest median rents, while Cubans and the "other" class generally had the highest median rents in each region (Table 5.26). Except for a few thousand households in the South and West, almost none of the sample renter households were living in units in the top price range, $500 per month or more; but at the same time there were relatively few in the cheapest units. Most were in the middle price ranges. Their asset position may have been modest, but their ability and willingness to occupy rental housing in the middle price ranges describe a minority group that has already taken long steps toward full participation in the economy and the society at large.

When Spanish-origin households purchase houses for owner occupancy, it appears that they enter mainly at the bottom of the price

TABLE 5.25
Spanish-Origin Householders, by Region, Origin, and Year Structure Built, 1980 (in thousands)

	Year Built							
	1939 and Earlier	1940–1949	1950–1959	1960–1969	1970–1974	1975–1978	1979–March 1980	Total
Northeast								
Mexican	18	4	1	1	1	2	–	27
Puerto Rican	201	84	62	54	17	6	6	430
Cuban	45	13	7	7	5	3	–	80
Other	116	36	39	32	13	3	4	243
Total	380	137	109	94	36	14	10	780
Midwest								
Mexican	86	25	27	29	14	9	5	195
Puerto Rican	22	14	3	7	4	4	–	54
Cuban	4	2	3	4	3	–	–	16
Other	22	9	11	11	9	4	2	68
Total	134	50	44	51	30	17	7	333
South								
Mexican	99	126	202	158	116	73	22	796
Puerto Rican	3	8	4	12	10	6	1	44
Cuban	17	20	33	33	43	21	6	173
Other	18	20	42	48	43	21	8	200
Total	137	174	281	251	212	121	37	1,213
West								
Mexican	216	195	259	277	123	83	29	1,182
Puerto Rican	3	5	6	9	7	–	2	32
Cuban	3	7	8	5	7	–	1	31
Other	70	63	77	94	47	39	13	403
Total	292	270	350	385	184	122	45	1,648
Total Owner-Occupied Units, All Regions								3,974

NOTE: Some missing cases yield a discrepancy between totals in tables 5.25 and 5.27; (–) = there were no households in the sample that reported this combination of attributes.

SOURCE: U.S. Bureau of the Census, 1980 Census of Population and Housing, Public Use Microdata Sample A.

range (Table 5.27) According to microdata samples, slightly more than two houses in three owned by Spanish-origin households were in the lowest (under $15,000) value category. To be sure, the distribution in each region is skewed upward into the high-priced houses, worth $100,000 or more, but the typical case is an extremely modest house. Households of Mexican origin, many of whom have been well established in the region for a long time, plus those in the "other" category, showed the greatest variation in the values of their owned

housing. But even in those cases, the majority of the houses were in the lowest value class.

Summary and Conclusions

This analysis of the use of the national and regional housing stocks, based on the data from the 1980 Census of Population and

TABLE 5.26

Households, by Spanish Origin, Region, and Contract Rent, 1980 (in thousands)

	Monthly Contract Rent								No Cash Rent	Total
	<$60	$60–99	$100–149	$150–199	$200–249	$250–349	$350–499	$500+		
Northeast										
Mexican	1	4	4	3	1	5	1	–	2	21
Puerto Rican	8	25	81	113	84	46	6	–	4	367
Cuban	–	2	5	20	15	4	3	1	1	51
Other	3	6	22	50	43	50	7	–	6	187
Total	12	37	112	186	143	105	17	1	13	626
Midwest										
Mexican	3	12	23	33	15	9	3	–	4	102
Puerto Rican	2	–	8	11	6	9	–	–	1	37
Cuban	–	–	1	3	4	–	–	–	–	8
Other	–	2	3	9	10	7	–	–	–	31
Total	5	14	35	56	35	25	3	–	5	178
South										
Mexican	30	60	69	64	36	43	11	–	21	334
Puerto Rican	1	–	4	10	4	6	2	–	–	27
Cuban	2	1	14	21	21	21	3	1	–	84
Other	2	9	5	17	20	22	7	2	5	89
Total	35	70	92	112	81	92	23	3	26	534
West										
Mexican	15	40	98	141	121	128	49	2	17	611
Puerto Rican	–	–	3	6	7	4	–	1	1	22
Cuban	–	1	2	5	4	7	2	–	1	22
Other	9	9	17	33	37	56	21	6	6	194
Total	24	50	120	185	169	195	72	9	25	849
Total Renter-Occupied Units, All Regions										2,187

NOTE: (–) = there were no households in the sample that reported this combination of attributes.

SOURCE: U. S. Bureau of the Census, 1980 Census of Population and Housing, Public Use Microdata Sample A.

Housing, asked: *Which households* obtain *what kind* of housing at *what locations* and under *what terms?* Type of household is described in terms of race of householder, income, age of members, composition, ethnic origins, and so forth. Each household type has a different constellation of wants, needs, and ability to achieve its goals.

The kind of housing obtained varies by type of structure and facilities available within it. The stock exists in each of four census regions and at different kinds of locations from central cities to rural farm settings. The terms of use include the type of tenancy, the levels of rents, the prices of owned housing, and the monthly costs of occupancy.

When just a few attributes are used to discuss each of the four questions, the variety of patterns generated is enormous. There are typical arrangements and numerous regularities in housing use pat-

TABLE 5.27

Households, by Spanish Origin, Region, and Value of Owned Housing, 1980 (in thousands)

					Value of Unit					
	<$15,000	$15,000–24,999	$25,000–34,999	$35,000–49,999	$50,000–59,999	$60,000–79,999	$80,000–99,999	$100,000–149,999	$150,000–199,999	$200,000+	Total
Northeast											
Mexican	22	–	1	–	1	2	1	–	–	–	27
Puerto Rican	406	4	3	4	4	3	4	2	–	–	430
Cuban	67	–	1	2	3	2	3	1	1	–	80
Other	209	2	4	4	5	6	8	3	–	2	243
Total	704	6	9	10	13	13	16	6	1	2	780
Midwest											
Mexican	135	6	15	9	13	5	7	2	2	1	195
Puerto Rican	47	–	1	1	3	1	–	–	1	–	54
Cuban	10	1	–	–	–	1	2	1	1	–	16
Other	41	3	5	4	6	2	2	3	2	–	68
Total	233	10	21	14	22	9	11	6	6	1	333
South											
Mexican	491	89	88	44	35	21	24	3	1	–	796
Puerto Rican	30	1	4	3	2	1	2	–	–	–	43
Cuban	99	1	8	8	14	13	19	5	5	1	173
Other	114	9	11	16	17	9	11	7	4	1	199
Total	734	100	111	71	68	44	56	15	10	2	1,211
West											
Mexican	720	25	37	61	53	53	126	54	42	9	1,180
Puerto Rican	25	–	–	–	1	–	3	1	2	–	32
Cuban	23	–	–	–	1	2	1	2	2	–	31
Other	241	4	17	14	19	19	34	26	17	6	397
Total	1,009	29	54	75	74	74	164	83	63	15	1,640
Total Owner–Occupied Units, All Regions											3,964

NOTE: (–) = there were no households in the sample that reported this combination of attributes.

SOURCE: U.S. Bureau of the Census, 1980 Census of Population and Housing, Public Use Microdata Sample A.

terns across the United States, and it has been our purpose here to present and interpret many of those typical patterns.

Patterns of housing use are in constant flux because of the dynamics that underlie both housing demand and housing supply. On the demand side, as discussed in Chapter 4, the structure and performance of the U.S. economy are always changing. As they change, some households prosper and others are left behind. The expectations and the income and wealth changes that flow from economic adjustments have direct effects on stepped-up and cut-back housing demands, and then on patterns of housing use.

Migration (moves in and moves out) and natural change (births and deaths) affect housing demand and housing use patterns. Regions that receive immigrants and net domestic inmigration need more housing to accommodate the newcomers. When households move, the origin loses and the destination gains. Natural change can amplify or mute the effects of migration depending on the balance between births and deaths. In addition, patterns of housing use are disrupted when the average age of the population in a local housing market rises or falls under the impact of migration and natural change.

Socioeconomic advances bring adjustments in housing demand. Households try to translate their social and economic achievements into adjustments in their housing. The more they succeed in doing so, the more flux is added to patterns of housing demand and eventually to housing use.

Then there is the matter of fashion or style. Many Americans—perhaps most—like new things, and they generally like new housing better than old housing. As new styles of housing are added to the stock, they are sought out and acquired, and new housing use patterns emerge. On the other hand, in the 1970s several kinds of old-style houses came back into favor, and what had been scorned a generation earlier was able to command premium prices. Styles are hard to predict, but they always affect demand, and eventually they have their influence on housing use patterns as well.

Finally, we should observe how expanded recognition and acceptance of diverse lifestyles that depart from traditional stages and sequences in the household life cycle have added new sources of flux in housing demand and patterns of housing use.

Besides changes in the demand side, there are constant adjustments to the housing stocks in each census region and at each type of location. New construction draws households into new areas and away from their former residences. Use patterns change in both places. Government interventions into the housing stock targeted at specific locations and groups of households have produced major changes in use patterns through the decades.

It is hard to get a complete picture of housing use patterns, because there are so many different patterns in thousands of separate housing submarkets—each with its distinctive expressions of the forces of supply and demand. In the next chapter we will examine the geographical structure of local housing markets in 46 different cities and urban regions. Each pattern is unique, but viewing them in certain regional ensembles helps us understand how generalized patterns of demand, supply, and use discussed here take expression in distinctive ways in each locale.

6

THE USE OF HOUSING INSIDE URBAN AREAS

The Social Geography of Urban Housing

IT IS CUSTOMARY and convenient to consider the dynamic U.S. national housing stock as a whole and to examine how various subgroups of the nation's households make use of their share of the stock. But this macro approach to the study of housing use patterns cannot illuminate the social and physical attributes of neighborhood settings in the household's choice and use of housing. Nor can it consider in informative ways the geographic structure of housing market forces and trends that control demand, supply, real estate values, and ultimately the fate of each urban neighborhood within each metropolitan housing market and the geographically defined submarkets that constitute the total metro housing fabric.[1] The previous chapter examined groups of households and how they use segments of the national and regional housing stocks. This chapter examines the subareas of the nation's principal urban regions and the significant patterns of housing use within them that can be gleaned from census data. The analysis focuses on a sample of 27 urbanized areas, supplemented by profiles of the nation's three largest cities and by 19 additional large cities from all parts of the country (Figure 6.1).

Selecting 27 Sample Urbanized Areas

In the 1980 Census of Population and Housing there were 16 New England County Metropolitan Areas and 289 Standard Metropolitan Statistical Areas. From this vast array of nucleated settlements, it was necessary for practical reasons to select a small sample of representative places in order to study the geographic structure of housing use at the local level inside urban areas. The decision to focus on metropolitan areas rather than other kinds of geographical areas in the detailed study of local areas was based on the fact that metro areas accounted for three fourths of the 1980 population, on the similarity in structure between small metro areas and large urban areas that had not achieved metro status, and on the difficulty of constructing a manageable number of useful profiles of geographic patterns of housing use in small urban places, in rural nonfarm (under 2,500 population) towns and villages, and in rural farm areas, in a project of limited scope.[2]

---

[1]See Risa I. Palm, "Spatial Segmentation of the Urban Housing Market," *Economic Geography* 54 (1978): 210–21; and Ronald J. Johnston, *Urban Residential Patterns: An Introductory Review* (New York: Praeger, 1972).

[2]See Curtis C. Roseman, "Metropolitan Areas as Redistributors of Population," *Urban Geography* 3, no. 1 (1982): 22–33.

FIGURE 6.1
Metropolitan Areas Included in Tract-Level Analysis

1980 SMSAs included in analysis

■ Central city

● Urbanized area

Note: see Figure 1–5 for census region and division names

We selected 27 SMSAs for analysis of selected aspects of housing use, but our focus is restricted to their urbanized areas (Table 6.1). The urbanized areas are the continuously built-up parts of metro areas. Metro areas are normally made up of one or more whole counties, so that the central city of the metro area, plus the contiguous built-up suburban areas around it, often leave substantial territory that lies outside the built-up area but still within the officially defined metro area (Table 6.1).

The 27 urbanized areas that were selected for study vary systematically from large to small, from fast-growth to slow-growth (or decline), and from new (twentieth-century boom areas) to old (already prominent in the eighteenth century). The 27 urbanized areas contain 42 central cities and are located in all four census regions.

The sample includes urban areas from all parts of the nation, old colonial centers from the Northeast, places that rose to national prominence during the nineteenth century, and places in the West and South that have had exceptional growth since 1920. Eleven of the metro areas had more than 1 million population in 1980, and 8 had under 600,000. In 10 of the areas household counts expanded less than 25 percent in the 1970s (slow growth), while in 9 areas the number of households expanded by 40 percent or more (fast growth). Households nationwide increased in number by 27 percent during the decade, while population increased by only 11 percent, but it is the expansion in household numbers that provides the basis for new housing demand.

Once the selection of the 27 areas was completed, we identified the 10 largest SMSAs in 1980. In order of population size they are:

1. New York
2. Los Angeles
3. Chicago
4. Philadelphia
5. Detroit
6. Boston–Lowell–Brockton–Lawrence–Haverhill
7. San Francisco-Oakland
8. Washington, D.C.
9. Dallas–Fort Worth
10. Houston

We set aside New York, Los Angeles, and Chicago for special analysis. The urbanized area of San Francisco was already included in the 27 areas. Philadelphia and Detroit were bypassed for detailed analysis because they are too large to be accommodated within the time

TABLE 6.1
Twenty-Seven Urbanized Areas:
Size in 1980 and Change in Number of Households, 1970–1980

	Population (in thousands), 1980	Change in Number of Households, 1970–1980
NORTHEAST		
Albany–Schenectady–Troy	795	15%
Allentown–Bethlehem–Easton	635	20
Hartford (NECMA)	1,052	17
Paterson–Clifton–Passaic	448	4
Providence–Warwick–Pawtucket (NECMA)	866	16
Springfield–Chicopee–Holyoke (NECMA)	582	14
MIDWEST		
Grand Rapids	602	29
Indianapolis	1,167	21
Madison	324	36
Minneapolis–St. Paul	2,114	27
Omaha	570	23
Wichita	411	23
SOUTH		
Atlanta	2,030	47
Birmingham	301	26
Memphis	913	28
Orlando	700	76
Oklahoma City	834	36
Raleigh–Durham	531	51
San Antonio	1,072	39
WEST		
Denver–Boulder	1,621	54
Las Vegas	463	98
Phoenix	1,509	80
Portland	1,243	40
Salt Lake City–Ogden	936	47
San Diego–Chula Vista	1,862	58
San Francisco	3,251	18
Seattle–Everett	1,607	31

NOTE: SMSAs as defined in June 1981; data as of April 1, 1980.

SOURCE: U.S. Bureau of the Census, *State and Metropolitan Area Data Book, 1982*.

and budget constraints of our study. The remaining four largest metro areas were put on the list for a limited central city analysis.

It is contended here that housing submarkets within each type of metro area operate with considerable uniformity and predictability. In the urban regions of the old Northeast, central cities are often small and underbound their metro cores. Suburban municipalities often have become exclusive enclaves that are difficult or impossible for low- and moderate-income households and most minorities to enter. In contrast, in many parts of the Midwest, and particularly in the South and West, central cities have annexed vast stretches of territory and have brought within areally extensive municipalities the newer subdivisions that often lie outside the cities of the Northeast.

In the cities that were already large in the nineteenth century there is a legacy of old and often decrepit housing. When an underbounded central city has housing from only the least attractive and least desirable segments of the metro housing stock, the city loses much of its potential community leadership to the suburbs. It also loses the disposable income and purchasing power that a city needs to support its downtown and neighborhood retail sector, plus the tax base to support its public sector. These negative economic and demographic trends put a central city at a disadvantage compared with its suburbs and weaken the city's ability to take control of its future.

In the cities that rose to prominence in the twentieth century, the central city housing stocks are relatively new. The current mix of population types, income ranges, locally owned wealth, and locally produced purchasing power usually sustains central city and metro vitality. Growth can produce new wealth. It also can—and usually does—deplete stores of wealth at older settled locations and move them to newly developing areas.[3] Significant amounts of income can be generated and wealth accumulated merely in the process of building an urban area at a sustained pace over a number of decades. The new wealth in the form of profits, new real estate developments, and commercial and industrial facilities may have high value because of the effects of favorable tax treatment of new investments compared with old, the higher rates of return on new investments in expanding areas, or speculative outlooks. Then, the areas that suffered the losses and the outmigration of people and capital discover that their remaining resources are undervalued and capable of carrying out new forms of work, so they set out on a new course of development that can feed on its successes as it moves into the future. The economy

enters a new phase and new housing is needed. This atmosphere of boom in certain areas provides the context for housing market forces and patterns of housing use. It is hard to understand patterns of local housing use without considering the various contexts within which housing markets operate—the age and condition of the stock, the size of the metro area, and the rates of expansion of the population and the number of households.[4]

Finally, regardless of their age, size, and rates of growth, urban areas differ significantly in the attractiveness of their settings and in the share of the local housing stock that has direct access to desirable physical amenities. Lakes, streams, wooded and natural areas, ocean frontage, and terrain that affords pleasant views are all highly prized in local housing markets. In cities like San Francisco and Seattle a large proportion of the housing stock is located on sites that take advantage of ocean and bay views.[5] For many households in these cities the view is the most desirable feature of their house and neighborhood. In Minneapolis and Chicago households pay high premiums to live by lakes. Ocean frontage in Miami and mountainside vistas in Los Angeles and Boulder are highly valued site amenities. Because the central cities in these cases offer amenities that many suburbs cannot, the central city housing markets can compete successfully with the suburbs for prosperous and self-sufficient residents. Patterns and dynamics of these sorts are explored in the map sets that follow.

[4]See Thierry J. Noyelle and Thomas M. Stanback, Jr., *The Economic Transformation of American Cities* (Totowa, NJ: Rowman and Allenheld, 1984); and Edgar J. Dunn, Jr., *Concepts, Structures, Regional Shifts*, The Development of the U.S. Urban System, vol. 1 (Baltimore: Resources for the Future and Johns Hopkins University Press, 1980); and *Industrial Shifts: Implications*, The Development of the U.S. Urban System, vol. 2 (Baltimore: Resources for the Future and Johns Hopkins University Press, 1983).

[5]For detailed discussion of the geographical structures within leading U.S. metro regions, see John S. Adams, ed., *Cities of the Nation's Historic Metropolitan Core* (Boston, New York, Philadelphia, Hartford); *Nineteenth Century Ports* (Baltimore, New Orleans, San Francisco); *Nineteenth Century Inland Centers and Ports* (Pittsburgh, St. Louis, Cleveland, Chicago, Detroit, Minneapolis–St. Paul, Seattle); and *Twentieth Century Cities* (Dallas–Fort Worth, Miami, Houston, Atlanta, Los Angeles, Washington DC), Contemporary Metropolitan America, vols. 1–4 (Cambridge, MA: Ballinger, 1976). Perhaps the most useful theoretical treatments of the spatial structure of urban residential land uses, from an economic analysis point of view, are William Alonso, *Location and Land Use: Toward a General Theory of Land Rent* (Cambridge, MA: Harvard University Press, 1964); Richard F. Muth, *Cities and Housing: The Spatial Pattern of Urban Residential Land Use* (Chicago: University of Chicago Press, 1969); Alan W. Evans, *The Economics of Residential Location* (London: Macmillan, 1973); Martin J. Beckmann, "Spatial Equilibrium in the Housing Market," *Journal of Urban Economics* 1 (1974): 99–107; William C. Wheaton, "Income and Urban Residence: An Analysis of Consumer Demand for Location," *American Economic Review* 67 (1977): 620–31; and Gregory K. Ingram, *Residential Location and Urban Housing Markets* (Cambridge, MA: Ballinger, 1977).

[3]Barry Bluestone and Bennett Harrison, *The Deindustrialization of America* (New York: Basic Books, 1982).

Measures of Housing Use in 27 Urbanized Areas

Six measures of housing use are examined for the 27 urbanized areas. (1) The median value of a census tract's owner-occupied housing is the best single measure of housing desirability. (2) The proportion of households in a tract with children under age 18 is a good index of the degree of family orientation present in the neighborhood. (3) The percentage of households that lived in the same house in 1980 as they had in 1975 is a good measure of neighborhood stability. (4) The proportion of black owner-occupant households as a percentage of all owner-occupants tells us about the locations and the degrees of success achieved by equal opportunity housing programs. (5) The percentage of children who speak a language other than English at home is a measure of the location and intensity of immigrant settlements and ethnic character in cities and suburbs. (6) Finally, the percentage of the housing units that are single attached or single detached units helps explain the geographic distribution of the local housing stock, which regulates in turn where wealthy and upper-income households are likely to want to live.

Other Important Cities

The analysis of housing characteristics at the census tract level in 27 SMSAs focuses on the continuously built-up areas around 42 central cities in all parts of the country. The selection of only 27 areas based on size, age, recent growth rate, and location meant that some of the most important places in the country were bypassed. In order to provide a more comprehensive treatment of housing use patterns within American urban areas 19 additional metro areas were identified for a close look at selected housing characteristics within their 23 central cities. These 19 places were selected because of their size and significance and because they could be treated in some detail within our page and map formats and time and budget constraints.

The 19 SMSAs, named for the central cities within them, include:

Midwest	Northeast
Cincinnati, Ohio	Boston, Massachusetts
Cleveland, Ohio	Buffalo, New York
Columbus, Ohio	Newark, New Jersey
Kansas City, Missouri–Kansas	Pittsburgh, Pennsylvania
Milwaukee, Wisconsin	
St. Louis, Missouri	

West	South
Anaheim–Santa Ana–Garden Grove, California	Baltimore, Maryland
Riverside–San Bernardino–Ontario, California	Dallas, Texas
Sacramento, California	Houston, Texas
	Miami, Florida
	New Orleans, Louisiana
	Washington, D.C.

The attributes of housing use that are examined in the central city analysis include three that also form part of the urbanized area analysis: (1) black homeowners as a share of all homeowners, (2) the proportion of children whose mother tongue is non-English, and (3) the share of housing units that are single. Besides these three, an additional three variables are examined solely within the central city analysis: (1) the amount and location of new housing in central cities—a measure of central city housing stock renewal; (2) the rate of change in central city housing values between 1970 and 1980—a measure of the city neighborhood's ability to compete with the suburbs for residents; and (3) the proportion of elementary school children who attended nonpublic schools in 1980—a measure of how families with school-age children discharge a central childrearing responsibility that is affected by their choice of a place to live.

A significant amount of research in urban sociology and urban geography in the last two generations has suggested that there are three prominent and largely independent geographical patterns of household distribution and housing use in American cities and suburbs, based on (1) income, wealth, and social class—and housing to match; (2) stage in the family or household life cycle—with housing appropriate to the stage; and (3) race or ethnicity, in which forces of congregation and segregation carve out a patchwork of subareas within an urban area. "Independent geographical patterns" means that a map expressing one of them does not usually resemble a map of another. Knowing the value of housing in a tract does not reveal whether there are children present. Knowing that there are children present does not reveal their race or their mother tongue.

Changes in the Number of Households and Housing Units in the Largest SMSAs

About one resident in seven lived in the five leading metropolitan areas—New York, Chicago, Los Angeles, Philadelphia, and Detroit—at census time in 1980. During the 1960s and 1970s these areas added households and housing units at varying rates, except for the

New York area, which suffered a slump in the 1970s (Table 6.2). Except for Los Angeles, the big central cities saw declines in the number of households in the 1970s. For New York and Philadelphia the central city household declines of the 1970s were a reversal of gains made during the 1960s.

The aggregate net population and household changes over a decade or two depend on four kinds of demographic events: births, deaths, moves in, and moves out (see Chapter 4). For example, the Chicago area gained over 300,000 households in the 1970s, but the central city lost 45,000: migrants who were added to the central city from the suburbs, outside the metropolitan area, and abroad, plus births to residents of the central city, minus those who moved out and those who died.

The Socioeconomic Status of Households

The characteristics of the households within a metro area, and their decisions about where to live, establish the social geography of the area. Within the Chicago area, as in other major urban regions, there are three main patterns of spatial variation from place to place.[6] The first is the variation in the average socioeconomic status of householders and related value of the housing units they occupy. The map of social status and housing value usually shows distinct sectors, radiating outward from the downtown. The sectors are often bounded by and aligned with major radial transport corridors linking the city center with areas outside the metropolitan area. One sector or more is upper middle class, others are middle class, and the rest are distinctly working class in their measures of income, occupation, education levels, housing values, rent levels, and lifestyles. Each sector reveals a tendency to project outward the general social class character of its inner city neighborhoods.[7] Working-class central city neighborhoods project their outlooks and behaviors outward into what become working-class suburbs. Upper-class inner city areas carry their affluence, life outlooks, and styles outward into exclusive suburbs. Middle- and upper-middle-class sectors are usually the most dynamic; they generate the most vigorous and rapidly expanding suburban extensions and leave the largest number of vacancies at their inner precincts near the downtown, which lure immigrants and native minority households who are eager to try to repeat the upward-mobility success story of those who have already achieved the comfortable suburbs. Unlike the middle class, neither the rich nor the poor consider that their status has changed or will change soon. It is the mobile middle class that supplies most of the energy that transforms the map of social status.

Stage in the Household Life Cycle

A second geographical pattern is formed by the spatial segregation of households according to stage in the household life cycle (see Chapter 4). Small housing units built at high densities and favored by single persons and small households at the beginning and ending stages of the household life cycle are located mainly near the core of the central city, along transit routes, near outlying commercial centers, and in suburban apartment districts, often adjacent to transport corridors and commercial land.[8] At the other extreme of the unit size and housing density continuum are large single-unit houses on large lots, catering to family households at their stage of maximum involvement with family life and child rearing. The family status of a household is largely independent of a household's socioeconomic status, so the geographic patterning of an urban area in terms of social status variations—usually sectoral—is different from and largely unrelated to the geographic patterning of an urban area in terms of the life cycle stage of households and corresponding unit size and housing density—which usually forms a roughly concentric pattern around the city center.

[6]Brian J. L. Berry and John D. Kasarda, *Contemporary Urban Ecology* (New York: Macmillan, 1977). See especially pp. 108–58. Michael White's book in the Social Science Research Council's series based on the 1980 census focuses on census tracts and how they change through time with respect to the variables underlying these patterns. See also J. R. Pinkerton, "City-Suburban Residential Patterns by Social Class: A Review of the Literature," *Urban Affairs Quarterly* 4, no. 4 (1969): 499–519; and J. R. Pinkerton, "The Changing Class Composition of Cities and Suburbs," *Land Economics* 49, no. 4 (1973): 462–69.

[7]A leading early discussion of this process appears in Robert E. Park, Ernest W. Burgess, and Roderick D. McKenzie, *The City* (Chicago: University of Chicago Press, 1925), especially pp. 47–79. The most complete treatment appears in Homer Hoyt, *The Structure and Growth of Residential Neighborhoods in American Cities* (Washington, DC: Federal Housing Administration, 1939), especially pp. 96–104.

[8]On the location preferences of young unmarried persons and households without children and their willingness to pay high prices to be near goods and services they want, see R. H. Nelson, "Accessibility and Rent: Applying Becker's Time-Price Concept to the Theory of Residential Location," *Urban Studies* 10, no. 1 (1973): 83–86. For locational requirements of single and childless women in the labor force, see E. A. Roistacher and J. S. Senyoung, "Working Women and City Structure: Implications of the Subtle Revolution," *Signs* 5, no. 3 (1980): 220–25. On the general problem of family change and the impact on the city, see William H. Frey and Frances E. Korbin, "Changing Families and Changing Mobility: Their Impact on the Central City," *Demography* 19, no. 3 (1982): 261–75.

TABLE 6.2

Population and Housing, Selected Large SMSAs, 1960–1980 (in thousands)

	1980			Change in Number of Households			
	Population	Households	Housing Units	1960–1970	%	1970–1980	%
Chicago							
SMSA	7,104	2,487	2,653	286	15%	303	14%
Central city	3,005	1,093	1,174	−19	−2	−45	−4
Suburbs	4,099	1,393	1,462	305	41	347	33
Detroit							
SMSA	4,353	1,509	1,588	186	17	242	19
Central city	1,203	434	471	−16	−3	−64	−13
Suburbs	3,150	1,076	1,117	202	36	307	40
Los Angeles–Long Beach							
SMSA	7,478	2,731	2,854	216	10	299	12
Central city	2,967	1,135	1,189	150	17	50	5
Suburbs and other	4,511	1,596	1,665	66	5	260	19
New York							
SMSA	9,120	3,499	3,669	403	13	−357	−9
Central city	7,071	2,789	2,941	166	6	−32	−1
Suburbs and other	2,049	710	728	237	30	−325	−31
Philadelphia							
SMSA	4,717	1,639	1,757	213	17	159	11
Central city	1,688	620	685	26	4	−22	−3
Suburbs	3,029	1,020	1,072	187	29	182	22

NOTE: Data are based on SMSA definitions current at census dates.

SOURCES: U.S. Bureau of the Census, *County and City Data Book, 1962*, tables 3 and 6, pp. 433–55 and 476–575; *Statistical Abstract of the United States, 1971*, pp. 830–80; *State and Metropolitan Area Data Book, 1982*, pp. 356–445; *County and City Data Book, 1972*, pp. 642–53.

Race and Ethnicity

The third basic pattern of geographical variation within metro areas is an expression of race and ethnicity. The maps of racial and ethnic patterns are significantly different from maps of family status and socioeconomic status, except in the cases where social class is due in part to racial or ethnic characteristics or family status flows in some measure from cultural practices based on ethnic roots or on practices rooted in religious belief (for example, the number of children or the persistence of extended families).

Maintaining the Social Status and Housing Value of Central City Neighborhoods

Over time, most residential neighborhoods of central cities decline in relative attractiveness or desirability compared with their suburban counterparts. The suburbs offer newer houses, lower densities, easier movement, and the more exclusive socioeconomic environments that many households seem to prefer if they have the financial means to achieve them. Suburban development usually begins with land speculators and developers anticipating that new, high-priced houses can be built and sold for a profit at a specific suburban location. After the houses are built, sold, and occupied, the process is repeated, this time with less uncertainty. If the development fails or is slow to succeed, it is not repeated unless adjustments in project scale or housing styles and prices are made.

The construction, sale, and occupation of new suburban housing draws population out of the central city and softens the housing submarkets in the inner segments of markets that were developed during earlier periods (see the Chapter 4 discussion of vacancy chains).[9] Over time, the average income levels of central city households and average market values of central city houses fall behind these measures in the suburbs. The movement of upper-income households from city to suburb sharply raises aggregate suburban income and drops the city average income and usually its aggregate personal income as well. Withdrawing effective demand for housing from the central city to the suburbs will cause housing prices to slide in the city, where housing supply remains roughly the same as demand is reduced, and to rise in the suburbs, where supply is rising slowly but strong demand continues.

The evidence that certain portions of central cities seem to resist these forces of housing market decline and decay is the persistence of above-average housing values and above-average rents within a fast-changing metropolitan housing market. The normal life cycle course of a housing unit runs through a succession of stages from new and expensive to old and cheap. The process is interrupted when the physical structures after construction are maintained or improved in ways that maintain or enhance their relative desirability in the midst of a regularly updated and improved housing stock.

The obsolescence, deterioration, and eventual dilapidation process can be averted, slowed, or reversed if the neighborhood attractiveness is maintained or improved even though houses within the neighborhood continue to age. The value of a housing unit depends on the structure itself, but also on the lot on which it stands. The value of the lot depends on the neighborhood social environment, the quality of the physical environment and attitudes toward physical features, and the location of the lot with respect to the principal nodes of interaction within the local metropolitan system (see Chapter 2).[10] These three aspects of metropolitan structure are revealed in the central cities of the nation's three leading metropolitan areas: Chicago, New York, and Los Angeles.

Housing Patterns in the Nation's Three Largest Metropolitan Regions

Housing Values and Rent Levels in Chicago, 1980

In the city of Chicago the median value of owner-occupied housing (in tracts where owner-occupied housing predominates) and the median contract rent (in tracts where renter-occupied housing predominates) were above the respective metro averages in 1980 at locations along Lake Michigan and in selected neighborhoods at the north edge of the city and in the far south side (Figure 6.2). The lake provides a natural scenic and recreational amenity of great desirability. Houses with a view of the lake command high premiums when rented or sold. The value of this amenity diminishes with increasing distance from the lake unless some other factors interrupt the decline. South of downtown Chicago there are four well-defined zones of above-average housing prices along the lake. The first runs from the south edge of downtown, north and south of Roosevelt Road, along waterfront parks to McCormick Place (the Chicago Exhibition Center). The second includes the neighborhood of the Illinois Institute of Technology (between 31st and 35th Streets). The third surrounds the University of Chicago–Hyde Park Area (from 47th to 63rd Streets) and extends back from the lake almost a mile. The fourth runs from the 67th Street Beach to Rainbow Park Beach (79th Street).

North of downtown the high prices run in an unbroken string of tracts to the northern city boundary with Evanston and westward across the north end of the city in newer, high-quality housing.

---

[10]For specific examples from an increasingly rich literature using this method of estimating the contribution of various elements to the value of housing, see Patricia Apps, "An Approach to Urban Modelling and Evaluation: 1. A Residential Model; 2. Implicit Prices for Housing Services," *Environment and Planning* 5 (1973); 705–17; C. B. Daniels, "The Influence of Racial Segregation on Housing Prices," *Journal of Urban Economics* 2 (1975): 105–22; William T. Bielby, *Evaluating Measures of Neighborhood Quality in the Annual Housing Survey* (Washington, DC: U.S. Government Printing Office, 1980); D. G. Bagby, "The Effects of Traffic Flow on Residential Property Values," *Journal of the American Planning Association* 46 (1981): 88–94; J. R. Jackson, "Intraurban Variation in the Price of Housing," *Journal of Urban Economics* 6, no. 4 (1979):464–79; and David Dale-Johnson, "An Alternative Approach to Housing Market Segmentation Using Hedonic Price Data," *Journal of Urban Economics* 11 (1982): 311–32.

[9]See also John B. Lansing, Charles W. Clifton, and James N. Morgan, *New Homes and Poor People: A Study of Chains of Moves* (Ann Arbor: Institute for Social Research, University of Michigan, 1969).

These highly priced areas feature attractive neighborhoods, open space and other physical amenities, and excellent access to the downtown, lake, parks, industrial centers, and shopping opportunities on the West Side. They are relatively remote from the noise, pollution, and social environment of the South Side and West Side poor minority areas.

When developers sense that the housing market in these above-average inner city neighborhoods is strong and likely to remain so, new housing is often added at market rates, which holds the tracts' average housing price high or raises it higher. It is the desire of above-average-income households to live in them that holds up their house prices, but it is the above-average structures and environmental attributes (social, physical, locational) that attract those households from other places and in the process hold up the value of housing.

Changes in Housing Values and Rent Levels in Chicago, 1970–1980

The 1980 median contract rent in the Chicago SMSA was $214, which was 65 percent higher than the median of $130 in 1970.[11] The consumer price index of residential rents in the Chicago SMSA stood at 172.2 (1967 = 100) in 1980, up over 60 percent from 107.6 in 1970.[12]

Within a general metropolitan climate of rising rents, certain city tracts that had a majority of rental units had rent increases above the SMSA average. Sometimes the above-average rise accompanied changes in the tracts' rental stock due to rehabilitation, remodeling, or clearance and replacement. Sometimes tracts were abruptly exposed to intensified demand without a corresponding expansion of the supply at prevailing prices, such as in newly fashionable areas, around schools and hospitals that expanded in the 1970s, or at the leading edges of expanding minority neighborhoods.

The same observations can be made about owner-occupied housing in the city of Chicago and how it maintained its relative value in the metropolitan housing market in the 1970s. The median value of owner-occupied housing in the Chicago SMSA in 1980 was $65,000, up 167 percent from $24,360 in 1970. Again, as in the case of new rental units, some new construction on vacant and cleared sites supplied some new owner-occupied units in the largely built-up central

city. But since most of the new housing in the metropolitan area was built in the suburbs in the 1970s, and since most newly built housing carries prices well above the metropolitan median, it is a struggle for central city housing to retain its value relative to the entire metropolitan housing stock, which is constantly improving in quality and advancing in price.

Most of the tracts in the city of Chicago in which median rents and median values rose faster than average in the 1970s were located in the northeastern quadrant of the city (Figure 6.2). Since these areas have not generally been the locations of major redevelopment activity, the higher-than-average price inflation for housing must be traceable to strong demand in those neighborhoods for a relatively fixed supply of rental and owned housing units.

New York City, 1980

New York City is a constellation of five boroughs (Figure 6.3). The city forms the core of an enormous metropolitan region of between 10 million and 20 million persons, but each of the boroughs is a place in its own right. Manhattan Island (New York County, 22 square miles) stands functionally, symbolically, and visually as the capital of the city and serves as the headquarters for the entire metropolitan region. New York's colonial origins as an independent city on Manhattan Island took root at the southern end of the island, from where it expanded and suburbanized steadily northward in the eighteenth and nineteenth centuries.[13]

The Borough of Brooklyn (seat of and coextensive with Kings County, 70 square miles) is separated by the East River from Manhattan. First settled in 1645, and linked to Manhattan by the Brooklyn Bridge in 1883, it became a borough of New York City in 1898. It grew outward south and east from its original site on the East River near Manhattan and the bridge.

The Borough of Queens (Queens County, 109 square miles), on the west end of Long Island, is the largest of the boroughs. First settled by the Dutch in 1635, and chartered as a borough of New York City in 1898, it is mainly a residential area that has absorbed much of the twentieth-century suburban growth generated by Manhattan and Brooklyn. Brooklyn and Queens form the western end of Long Island and are connected to the other boroughs and the mainland by ten bridges and tunnels.

[11]Data sources: U.S. Bureau of the Census, 1980 and 1970 Census of Population and Housing, *Census Tracts*, Chicago SMSA, table H1.
[12]U.S. Bureau of the Census, *Statistical Abstract of the United States, 1984*, p. 499.
[13]Areal data from U.S. Bureau of the Census, *County and City Data Book, 1983*, p. 382.

FIGURE 6.2 *Housing Values and Rent Levels, 1980, and Changes in Values and Rent Levels, 1970–1980*

Los Angeles/ Chicago

Median value of owner occupied housing (where owner occupied units predominate), or median contract rent (where rental units predominate) exceeds 1980 SMSA median.

• Median value of owner occupied housing percentage increase, 1970 to 1980 (where owner occupied units predominate), or median contract rent percentage increase, 1970 to 1980 (where rental units predominate) exceeded SMSA percentage increase.

(Maps based on sample of one-third of all tracts. Condominiums excluded from value calculations.)

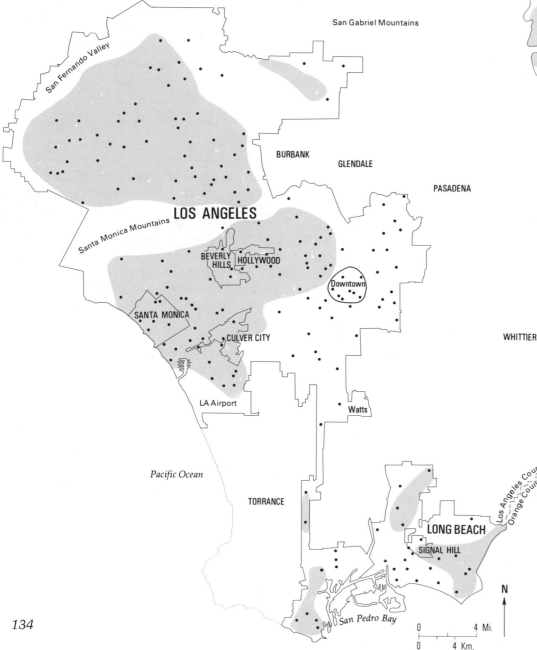

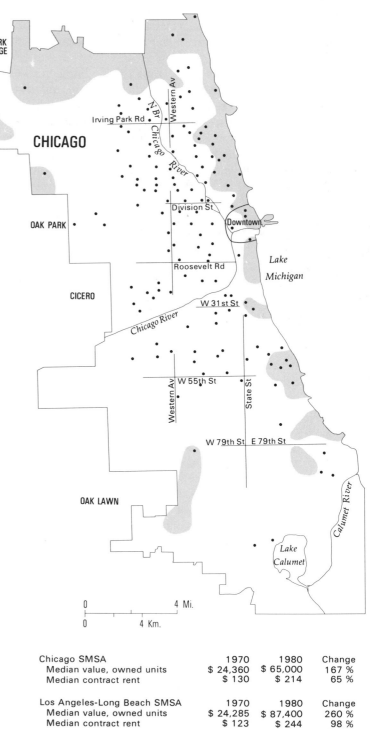

134

Chicago SMSA	1970	1980	Change
Median value, owned units	$ 24,360	$ 65,000	167 %
Median contract rent	$ 130	$ 214	65 %
Los Angeles-Long Beach SMSA	1970	1980	Change
Median value, owned units	$ 24,285	$ 87,400	260 %
Median contract rent	$ 123	$ 244	98 %

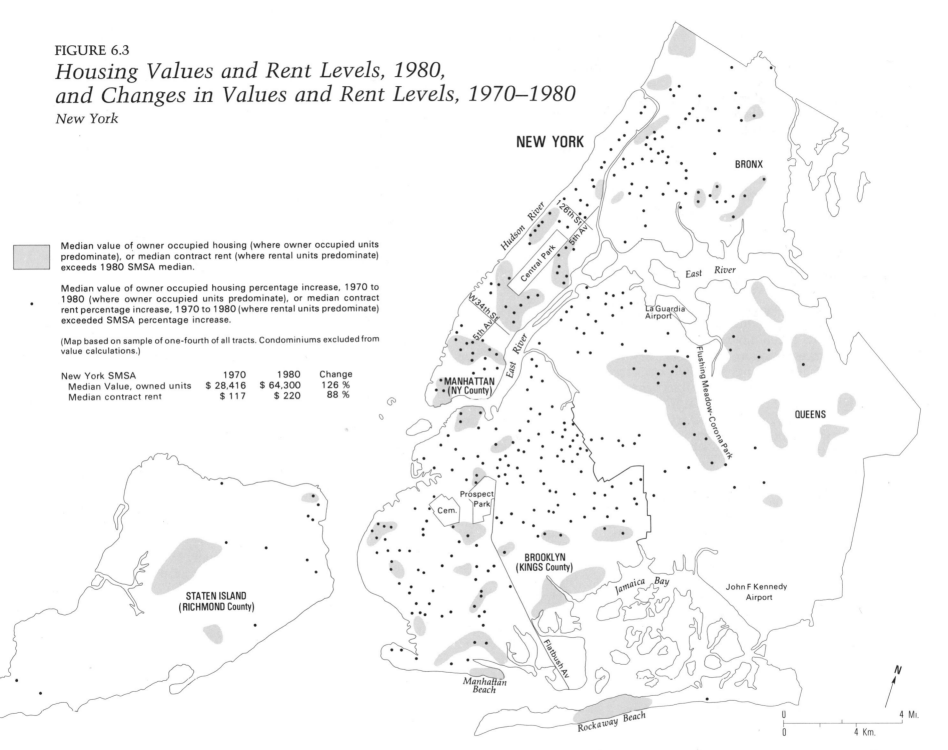

FIGURE 6.3
Housing Values and Rent Levels, 1980,
and Changes in Values and Rent Levels, 1970–1980
New York

Median value of owner occupied housing (where owner occupied units predominate), or median contract rent (where rental units predominate) exceeds 1980 SMSA median.

Median value of owner occupied housing percentage increase, 1970 to 1980 (where owner occupied units predominate), or median contract rent percentage increase, 1970 to 1980 (where rental units predominate) exceeded SMSA percentage increase.

(Map based on sample of one-fourth of all tracts. Condominiums excluded from value calculations.)

New York SMSA	1970	1980	Change
Median Value, owned units	$ 28,416	$ 64,300	126 %
Median contract rent	$ 117	$ 220	88 %

NEW YORK

BRONX

Hudson River

126th St

5th Av

Central Park

East River

La Guardia Airport

W 34th St

5th Av

East River

Flushing Meadow-Corona Park

MANHATTAN (NY County)

QUEENS

Prospect Park

Cem.

BROOKLYN (KINGS County)

Jamaica Bay

John F Kennedy Airport

STATEN ISLAND (RICHMOND County)

Flatbush Av

Manhattan Beach

Rockaway Beach

N

4 Mi.

4 Km.

The Bronx (Bronx County, 42 square miles) is a residential borough north of Manhattan which received a large share of Manhattan's first waves of upper-middle-class suburbanization in the nineteenth and early twentieth centuries. All other routes of suburban expansion away from lower and midtown Manhattan were relatively inconvenient because of water barriers or congested bridges, tunnels, and ferries.

Richmond Borough (Staten Island, which is Richmond County, 59 square miles) has been settled since 1661 with industrial activity, shipbuilding, and low-density residential activity. Connected to Brooklyn and the mainland by bridges, and to Manhattan by ferry, its relative isolation from the core of the city and the rest of the boroughs has held down its population to 352,000 in 1980.

Housing Values and Rent Levels in New York City, 1980

The median value of owner-occupied housing (in tracts where owned housing predominated) and the median contract rent (in tracts where rentals predominated) were above the respective 1980 metropolitan averages in many parts of the city at census time. The median value of specified owner-occupied housing units in the SMSA was $64,300; the SMSA median contract rent was $220.[14]

There is significant variation from borough to borough in housing values and costs (Table 6.3). Rents in Richmond and Manhattan are higher than the metro averages, while those in the other boroughs are lower. Meanwhile the average value of owner-occupied housing in the central city boroughs, with the exception of Manhattan, is well below the metropolitan average.

The residential districts in New York City with rents (in tracts where rental housing predominates) and housing values (in tracts where owner-occupied housing units are in the majority) above the SMSA average are concentrated at the southern tip of Manhattan; north of Houston Street either side of Fifth Avenue in the vicinity of New York University; south, west, and east of Central Park; around the edges of The Bronx near the water; in Queens on either side of Flushing Meadow Park; and in scattered neighborhoods of Brooklyn near Jamaica Bay, Rockaway Beach, Manhattan Beach, park districts, and near the bridge to Manhattan (Figure 6.3). A few newly developed tracts in central Richmond County were above average.

[14]See Michael A. Stegman, *Housing in New York* (Piscataway, NJ: Center for Urban Policy Research, 1985).

TABLE 6.3
Median Value of Specified Owner-Occupied Housing Units, and Median Contract Rents, New York City Boroughs, 1980

Borough	Owner-Occupied Units	Median Value	Renter-Occupied Units	Median Rent
Bronx (The Bronx)	62,883	$48,200	366,374	$195
Kings (Brooklyn)	193,560	50,500	634,697	198
New York (Manhattan)	54,785	92,400	649,717	239
Queens (Queens)	271,072	51,400	440,868	237
Richmond (Staten Island)	69,805	60,000	44,769	229
SMSA		64,300		220

NOTE: Condominium values are excluded from published tables.
SOURCE: U.S. Bureau of the Census, 1980 Census of Population and Housing, *Census Tracts*, New York, New York–New Jersey SMSA, table H-1.

Changes in Housing Values and Rent Levels in New York City, 1970–1980

The median value of owner-occupied housing (excluding co-ops and condominiums) in the New York SMSA advanced from $28,416 in 1970 to $64,300 in 1980—a rise of 126 percent. During the same period median contract rent rose 88 percent, from $117 to $220 per month.[15]

Many tracts throughout the five boroughs had value and rent rises in excess of the metro averages. A systematic one-in-four sample of the census tracts in New York City revealed widespread inflation of rents and values in south, central, and north Manhattan; throughout The Bronx, much of Brooklyn, the older parts of Queens near Manhattan; and a few locations near the older, high-density rental areas of Staten Island (Figure 6.3). A substantial amount of new housing was constructed in New York City in the 1970s (213,000 structures in the five boroughs, and many with two or more housing units). There was also a boom in the formation of new households seeking housing, and the added demand for city rather than suburban living pushed up prices in both owner-occupied areas and in predominantly rental areas. Prices might have risen even faster if New York City had not had a strict rent control law. On the other hand, if there had been no rent control, faster inflation might have stimulated even more new construction than actually occurred.

[15]Data sources: U.S. Bureau of the Census, 1980 and 1970 Census of Population and Housing, *Census Tracts*, New York SMSA, table H1.

Los Angeles, 1980

The city of Los Angeles lies at the heart of the Los Angeles–Long Beach SMSA. It is the capital of southern California, the dominant metropolis of the western United States, and the nation's front door to the Pacific Basin and much of Latin America. In addition to the locational advantages that flow to a capital city in fast-growing regions of the nation and the world, the economy of southern California has received major stimulus from steady foreign immigration and net domestic inmigration during the twentieth century of bright, eager students and workers, often trained and educated elsewhere at others' expense; from persons who retire to the area bringing their Social Security, pensions, and savings accumulated elsewhere; from the U.S. government, which has for decades apparently spent more money in the region than it has withdrawn in taxes; from a remarkable agricultural, mineral, and climatic resource base; and from entrepreneurs who have moved into this region to direct and to exploit its economic opportunities.[16]

The Los Angeles area fills a lowland triangular site framed by the San Gabriel Mountains on the northern edge, the Santa Ana Mountains beyond Orange County to the southeast, and the Pacific Ocean to the southwest. A broad valley corridor east of downtown Los Angeles into San Bernardino County and Riverside County directed the southern transcontinental railroads into the region and pulled the suburbs eastward (Figure 6.2).

From its original site on a broad alluvial fan on the southern slopes of the San Gabriel Mountains, the city pushed southward past Watts to Los Angeles harbor at San Pedro Bay and directly westward to the passenger boat terminal at Santa Monica.

The most vigorous middle- and upper-middle-class residential expansion activity pushed south and southeast of downtown to an unbroken patchwork quilt of suburban-style cities, covering Orange County and extending into Riverside County. The working-class areas east of downtown were connected to the heavy industry and rail freight transport that linked the Los Angeles economy to the rest of the nation. Wealthy areas developed west of downtown, northwest to the San Fernando Valley, along the ocean front, and perched on the hills and climbing the mountainsides, with Beverly Hills and Hollywood protruding as especially prominent landmarks of gilded consumptive display by successful entrepreneurs, movie moguls, media legends—and their imitators.

[16]See Nathan Glazer, ed., *Clamor at the Gates: The New American Immigration* (San Francisco: Institute for Contemporary Studies, 1985), which has several pieces focused on recent immigration and economic change in the Los Angeles area.

Housing Values and Rent Levels in Los Angeles, 1980

The unrelenting demand pressure on the Los Angeles SMSA (Los Angeles County) housing stock, plus a continuing stream of high-priced additions to the stock, raised the median value of owner-occupied housing units from $24,285 in 1970 to $87,400 in 1980, an extraordinary rise of 260 percent. Recall that the parallel rise in the Chicago SMSA was 167 percent and in the New York SMSA was 126 percent. The median contract rent in the Los Angeles SMSA rose 98 percent, from $123 in 1970 to $244 in 1980.[17]

The median value of owner-occupied housing (in tracts where owned housing predominated) and the median contract rent (where rentals predominated) were above the corresponding metropolitan averages in northwestern Los Angeles in the direction of the San Fernando Valley, west of downtown to Santa Monica, through Hollywood and Beverly Hills to the foothills of the Santa Monica Mountains; on the far south side with a charming mixture of old and new on the hills near San Pedro Bay; and much of the coast and newer areas of Long Beach (Figure 6.2).

The two large districts of the city that are excluded from the regions of high values and above-average rents are the largely Hispanic east side of downtown and the region south and southwest of downtown, which has been the city's principal middle-class housing corridor for upwardly mobile newcomers. The first wave was transplanted from the Midwest, coming in large numbers in the decades before and after World War I. They prospered and moved south and east (continued movement southwest was blocked by the ocean), to be followed by blacks from the western regions of the Old South and from Texas. In the 1970s and 1980s newcomers south of downtown have included large numbers of Asians. The Korean population alone is said to number 250,000. As Los Angeles increasingly becomes the nation's premier immigrant city, the historic immigrant reception neighborhoods south and east of downtown Los Angeles continue to perform their traditional function, and on a grand scale.

Changes in Housing Values and Rent Levels in Los Angeles, 1970–1980

The city of Los Angeles appears to retain a large share of the metropolitan area's exclusive neighborhoods as well as low-income

[17]Data sources: U.S. Bureau of the Census, 1980 and 1970 Census of Population and Housing, *Census Tracts*, table H1.

FIGURE 6.4
Children and Poverty, 1979–1980
Los Angeles/Chicago

Percentage of families in 1980 with own children under 18 years of age exceeds 50 percent.

• Percentage of families reporting 1979 incomes below 1979 poverty levels exceeds 30 percent.

(Maps based on sample of one-third of all tracts.)

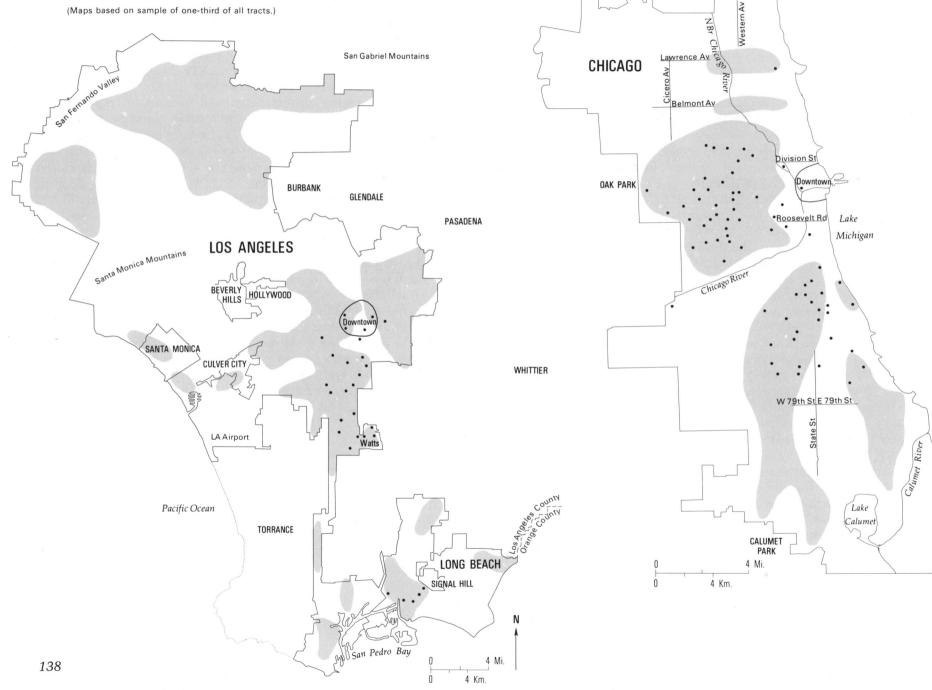

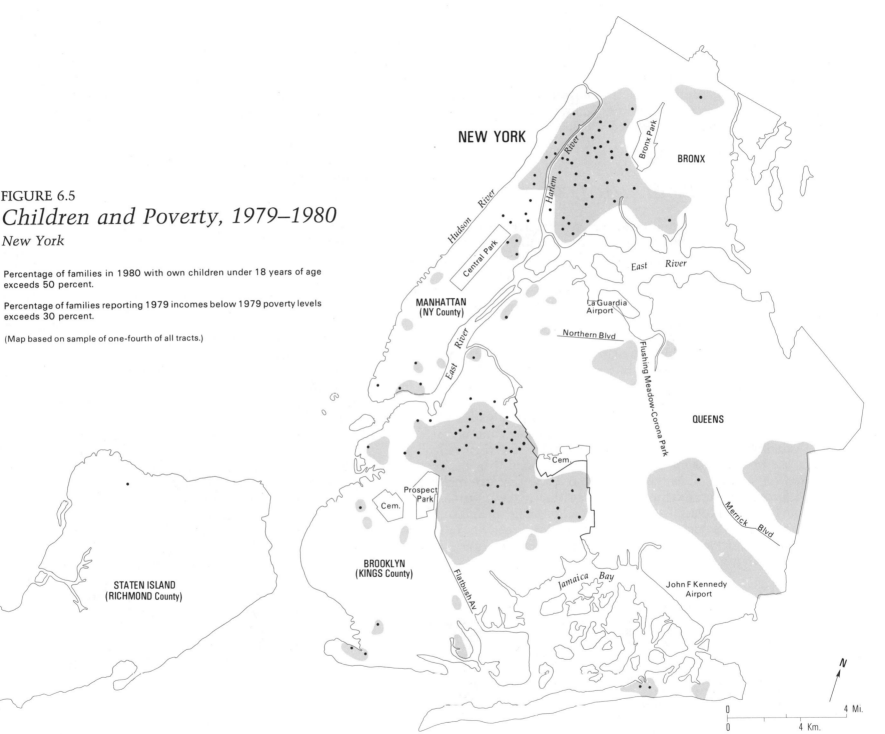

FIGURE 6.5
Children and Poverty, 1979–1980
New York

Percentage of families in 1980 with own children under 18 years of age exceeds 50 percent.

Percentage of families reporting 1979 incomes below 1979 poverty levels exceeds 30 percent.

(Map based on sample of one-fourth of all tracts.)

NEW YORK

BRONX

Bronx Park

Hudson River

Harlem River

Central Park

MANHATTAN
(NY County)

East River

La Guardia Airport

Northern Blvd

Flushing Meadow-Corona Park

QUEENS

East River

Cem.

Prospect Park

Cem.

BROOKLYN
(KINGS County)

Flatbush Av

Jamaica Bay

Merrick Blvd

John F Kennedy Airport

STATEN ISLAND
(RICHMOND County)

N

0   4 Mi.

0   4 Km.

minority areas. Housing in the exclusive areas appreciated faster than the SMSA average in the 1970s in the very areas that featured above-average values and rents (Figure 6.2). In addition, values and rents rose faster than metropolitan averages in selected regions of the lower-income areas south and west of downtown, which were straining to accommodate a large influx of newcomers during the 1970s, when the SMSA (the county) added 436,000 persons.

Children and Poverty
in Chicago's Residential Areas, 1979–1980

Most families with children under age 18 prefer low-density housing in family-oriented neighborhoods. Young childless households at the beginning of the family life cycle, along with older households whose children are grown, often prefer the smaller housing units found in large numbers near the core of the city. But the families with children push outward to the extent that they are able.

In Chicago the proportion of families with children under age 18 exceeds 50 percent in two vast regions that correspond roughly with Chicago's two principal black neighborhoods—one directly south of downtown and the other directly west of downtown (Figure 6.4). In these two ghetto areas high rates of low family income occurred in 1979.

Several forces operate to create and to sustain the spatial patterns on the Chicago map. To be sure, a force of congregation operates to bind minority racial and ethnic groups together, and their neighborhoods are one expression of the congregating bond.[18] In the case of blacks in American cities there can be no doubt that externally generated forces of discrimination and segregation make it virtually impossible for blacks to achieve full participation in urban and suburban housing markets. Some of the segregation is due directly to racial discrimination, and some is due to social class discrimination that uses race as a predictor of class.[19]

[18]James E. Vance, Jr., "The American City: Workshop for a National Culture," in John S. Adams, ed., *Cities of the Nation's Historic Metropolitan Core*, Contemporary Metropolitan America, vol. 1, pp. 1–49; Blair Badcock, *Unfairly Structured Cities* (Oxford: Basil Blackwell, 1984), especially pp. 169–205; and Risa I. Palm, *The Geography of American Cities* (New York: Oxford University Press, 1981), pp. 253–302.

[19]Brian J. L. Berry, Carole A. Goodwin, Robert W. Lake, and Katherine A. Smith, "Attitudes Towards Integration: The Role of Status in Community Response to Racial Change," in Barry Schwartz, ed., *The Changing Face of the Suburbs* (Chicago: University of Chicago Press, 1976), pp. 221–64.

Within black areas there is significant income and social class partitioning between the poor inner neighborhoods, the working-class midsections, and the white collar and professional areas on the outer edges. Young, upwardly mobile families with middle-class jobs, tastes, and incomes head for the newer lower-density neighborhoods at the edge of the city and in the suburbs. In these outer fringes of the black neighborhoods of Chicago, on both the West Side and the South Side, poverty is rare as moderately successful families put as much distance as they can between themselves and the inner city squalor that many have worked hard to escape.

Children and Poverty
in New York City's Residential Areas, 1979–1980

In New York City two prominent districts stand out on the map of children and poverty—Harlem, spilling over into the South Bronx, and the older parts of Brooklyn, centered on the Bedford-Stuyvesant neighborhood (Figure 6.5). Both areas first developed as streetcar suburbs for middle-class households, but were long ago left behind as early residents prospered and moved still farther out. From Manhattan the suburban thrust was northward. The extensive upscale suburbs of Westchester County pulled upper-income households northward and transmitted housing vacancy chains southward to The Bronx and across the Harlem River into Harlem, making them available to the low-income families who were there in 1979–1980.

The vast suburban developments east of Manhattan and Brooklyn during the twentieth century meant large numbers of families with children, concentrating first in Kings and Queens counties, and then later in Nassau County (east of Queens) and Suffolk County (east of Nassau County). Enormous rates of new construction to the east created housing vacancies that eventually percolated westward and accumulated within five miles east and southeast of downtown Brooklyn, attracting the poor and minority families who were concentrated there by census time. Besides the South Bronx and central Brooklyn, there are a few other significant patches of family concentrations with children in eastern and northern Queens and a few more scattered through Manhattan, Brooklyn, and Staten Island. The overall New York pattern resembles that of Chicago in that the families with young children appear disproportionately concentrated in impoverished city neighborhoods.

Children and Poverty
in the Los Angeles and Long Beach Residential Areas,
1979–1980

Most of the Los Angeles–Long Beach area was built up at low residential densities that look and feel like suburbs to inner city residents of Chicago and New York. But each metropolitan region evolves its own definitions of old and new housing, high densities and low, cheap and expensive, ugly and attractive. In Los Angeles and Long Beach there are three classes of areas where families with children tend to outnumber those without dependent children (Figure 6.4). The first is the heavily Spanish-language area east of downtown Los Angeles, where large families are common. The second is the area west and south of downtown, the inner portion of which houses many Asian immigrant families, while the farther-out reaches southward to the harbor are heavily black; the old parts of Long Beach by the bay are part of this class. The third includes the new and expensive suburban-type developments in the northwestern section of the city; coastal areas in the northwestern section of the city; and other coastal areas in and near Santa Monica, by San Pedro Bay, and the newer inland sections of Long Beach.

Los Angeles and Long Beach were prosperous areas in the 1970s and early 1980s, and concentrations of families with 1979 incomes below the poverty line occurred only in the inner black neighborhoods south of downtown and in the old inner city portions of Long Beach. Yet as limited in extent as the spatial pattern of poverty concentrations appears, it unfortunately coincides closely with the areas of black families with dependent children south of downtown.

Black, Spanish-Language, Asian Areas: Chicago 1980

Since its settlement and platting in the 1820s Chicago has been a vital, robust city that has attracted immigrants and transplants from all over the world and from all parts of the country. Native-born whites who founded the city north and south of the mouth of the Chicago River were joined by waves of foreign-born newcomers—especially from Eastern, Southeastern, and Southern Europe and Ireland—who entered the city in the decades just preceding and following 1900. Prosperity for the native white middle classes stimulated their outmigration first to the south and to the west of downtown, leaving behind vacancies and soft real estate markets in those inner

city areas which blacks occupied during the first large influx into Chicago, around the time of World War I (Figure 6.6). The initial geographical concentrations of blacks were due to a combination of large influxes, a spatial concentration of available housing opportunities, and the traditional forces of congregation that hold newcomer groups together. Later residential segregation of blacks was fortified by white community fears and suspicions and reinforced by legal discrimination against blacks and by conspiracies on the part of real estate interests to create and perpetuate a dual housing market.[20]

When heavy industrial developments expanded in the Lake Calumet, South Chicago, and South Shore areas in the 1890s and early years of the twentieth century, the middle-class drive to the south of downtown—documented, for example, by the selection of the Hyde Park site for the University of Chicago (1890), Jackson Park, and the monumental architecture remaining from the Chicago World's Fair—was severely curtailed. Expensive South Side suburbia had only a limited desire for coking plants and steel mills as neighbors. So the western suburbs got a boost in demand, as did the areas directly north of downtown. The center of downtown, which had been migrating southward away from the river, following the purchasing power that was concentrated in that direction, made a U-turn and started moving northward after the turn of the century, heading up Michigan Avenue, and finally crossing the river to its present location near Water Tower Place.

The white working-class areas to the southwest of downtown were largely unaffected by these major migration and real estate trends. The wedge of the city northwest of downtown had a similar history. Today's map documents the relative permanence of the South Side and West Side black neighborhoods. Spanish-language areas are concentrated in the inner precincts of the traditional white, Catholic, working-class and lower-middle-class southwest and northwest sectors. Except for Chinatown just southwest of downtown, the Asian populations—mainly from India, Korea, Japan, China, and the Philippines—are concentrated in the middle-class white strongholds at the north edge of the city near Evanston, Lincolnwood, and Skokie.

[20]Chicago Commission on Race Relations, *The Negro in Chicago* (Chicago: Arno Press, 1968); Stanley Lieberson, "Comparative Segregation and Assimilation of Ethnic Groups," doctoral dissertation, University of Chicago, 1960; Brian J. L. Berry, "Monitoring Trends, Forecasting Change, and Evaluating Goal Achievement in the Urban Environment: The Ghetto Expansion vs. Desegregation Issue in Chicago as a Case Study," in Michael Chisholm, Allan Frey, and Peter Haggett, eds., *Regional Forecasting* (London: Butterworth, 1971), pp. 93–117; Brian J. L. Berry, *The Open Housing Question: Race and Housing in Chicago, 1966–1976* (Cambridge, MA: Ballinger, 1980).

FIGURE 6.6 *Black, Spanish-Language, and Asian Areas, 1980*
Los Angeles/Chicago

Population over 50 percent black in 1980.

+ Sample tract with Spanish origin population of 400 or more persons in 1980.

• Sample tract with Asian origin population of 400 or more persons in 1980.

(Maps based on sample of one-third of all tracts.)

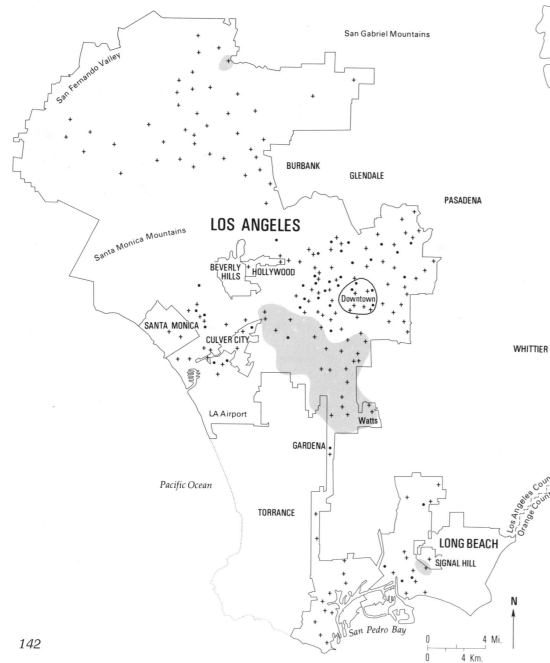

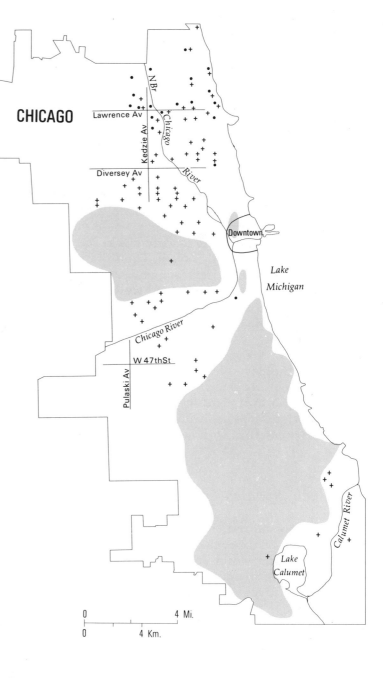

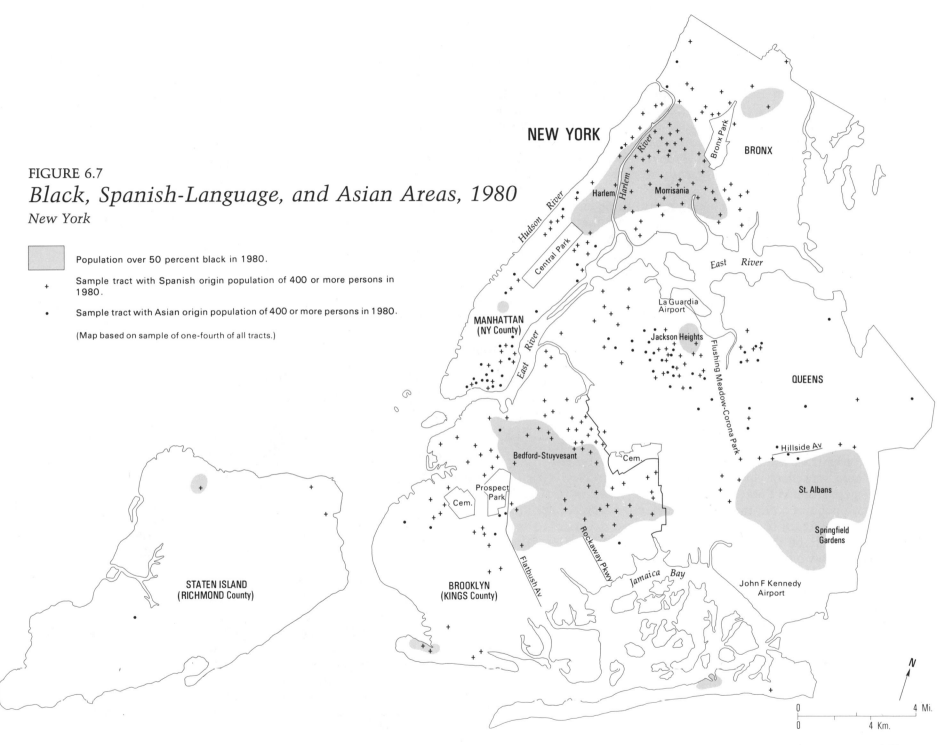

FIGURE 6.7
Black, Spanish-Language, and Asian Areas, 1980
New York

Population over 50 percent black in 1980.

Sample tract with Spanish origin population of 400 or more persons in 1980.

Sample tract with Asian origin population of 400 or more persons in 1980.

(Map based on sample of one-fourth of all tracts.)

NEW YORK

BRONX

Bronx Park

Harlem

Harlem River

Morrisania

Hudson River

Central Park

East River

La Guardia Airport

MANHATTAN
(NY County)

East River

Jackson Heights

Flushing Meadow-Corona Park

QUEENS

Hillside Av

St. Albans

Bedford-Stuyvesant

Cem.

Springfield Gardens

Prospect Park

Cem.

Rockaway Pkwy

STATEN ISLAND
(RICHMOND County)

Flatbush Av

BROOKLYN
(KINGS County)

Jamaica Bay

John F Kennedy Airport

N

0   4 Mi.

0   4 Km.

143

Black, Spanish-Language, Asian Areas: New York 1980

The dynamics of metropolitan development, as revealed in the sectoral structure of housing markets, show up in three ways in New York City. Manhattan developed from the southern tip and Battery Park northward through Midtown, Central Park, Harlem, and across the Harlem River into The Bronx and to Westchester County beyond. The Harlem–South Bronx ghetto formed in the wake of the upper-middle-class thrust to the north. Brooklyn grew to the southeast toward Jamaica bay, following the early middle- and upper-income expansions in that direction; the Brooklyn black ghetto, centered on the Bedford-Stuyvesant area, has been a result. Residents of working-class Brooklyn south of the Brooklyn Bridge to Manhattan stayed where they were, lacking either the financial means to leave, and be replaced by newcomers, or the desire to do so. In Queens a large and steady suburbanward movement out to Long Island from midtown Manhattan created the basis for a third large black concentration north of Kennedy Airport in the St. Albans–Springfield Gardens neighborhood. Today's coalescing of housing developments in the four largest boroughs makes it hard to trace the impacts of early streetcar lines into streetcar suburbs south, east, and north of Manhattan, or the amplification of those trends by later rail commuter lines and freeways; but the locations of the major black neighborhoods are largely the results of these movements and their accompanying urban growth dynamics. Since Staten Island was never part of these movement corridors, it was never abandoned in a significant way and never had the large volume of low-priced housing that is needed to attract low-income and minority newcomers.

There are several Spanish-language groups in New York City, but the largest group is Puerto Rican in origin (Table 6.4).[21] The Spanish-language population in the city is much less segregated than the black population (Figure 6.7). There are significant occurrences in several parts of each of the boroughs, with concentrations in the South Bronx, in the old parts of Queens by Flushing Meadow Park, and around the edges of the black ghetto of Brooklyn.

Asians of various origins are concentrated in Queens by the park, mixed with Spanish-language groups, and Chinese are concentrated on the lower East Side of Manhattan. Many Asian groups are relatively affluent compared with the average black or Spanish resident, so it is not surprising to find scattered locations in newer subdivisions of Queens where Japanese, Chinese, or Asian Indian households form conspicuous concentrations.

[21]The Commonwealth of Puerto Rico is a self-governing part of the United States. Puerto Ricans are U.S. citizens, but do not vote in national elections. Most federal taxes are not levied in Puerto Rico.

TABLE 6.4

Spanish-Origin Populations in the New York, Chicago, and Los Angeles Areas, by County, 1980 (in thousands)

County	Total Persons	White	%	Spanish	%
Cook	5,254	3,512	67%	499	9%
Bronx	1,169	554	47	396	34
Kings	2,231	1,249	56	392	18
New York	1,428	841	59	336	24
Queens	1,891	1,336	71	262	14
Richmond	352	314	89	19	5
Five boroughs	7,072	4,294	61	1,406	20
Los Angeles	7,478	5,074	68	2,066	28

SOURCE: U.S. Bureau of the Census, *State and Metropolitan Area Data Book, 1982.*

Black, Spanish-Language Asian Areas: Los Angeles 1980

Almost a third of the Los Angeles County population was non-white in 1980, and almost 3 residents in 10 identified themselves as Spanish-language or Spanish-origin. The black population is heavily concentrated in an inner city area south and southwest of downtown Los Angeles (Figure 6.6). The Spanish-origin population is much more dispersed. Low-income households and newcomers concentrate east of downtown Los Angeles and within a mile or two of downtown in other directions. The Spanish-origin population is relatively absent from the south-side black area. Significant numbers of Hispanic persons live in the new suburban areas in northwest Los Angeles west of Burbank, in the attractive Santa Monica–Culver City areas, and near the harbor at San Pedro Bay in Los Angeles and Long Beach. In sum, the Spanish-origin populations are relatively absent from the richest areas and the poor black neighborhoods, but are present in most other places.

Asian-origin populations are more concentrated geographically than are Spanish-origin persons. The main concentrations are near downtown, with Korean and Japanese especially prominent north of downtown and westward to Santa Monica, interspersed with Spanish; the Japanese concentration is south of the black region, spilling over into Gardena, and in several locations in Long Beach. Persons of Asian origin are scattered widely throughout the new middle- and upper-middle-class areas of northwest Los Angeles, but generally do not appear as significant ethnic concentrations as they do in older areas near the city core.

The Geography of Housing Use in Urban Areas
Large and Small, Old and New

The Estimated Value of Owner-Occupied Housing: An Index of Desirability

Almost two thirds of the occupied housing units in the United States in 1980 were owner-occupied. The median value of owner-occupied units was $47,200, but values ranged widely from below $10,000 to well above $200,000, depending on the attributes offered by house, lot and setting, and demand at the location. Newer houses are usually more expensive than older ones and are typically located in the suburbs, although there have been important new additions to central city and central business district housing stocks in the 1970s.[22]

Nationwide, the value of owner-occupied housing inside urbanized areas exceeded average values in rural areas in 1980 ($49,500 versus $40,200), and the values of urban fringe or suburban housing exceeded average values in central cities ($58,700 versus $43,100).

Just as there is variation of average housing values from rural to central city to suburban locations, based on differences in the houses, lots, settings, accessibility features, and the demand for these attri-

butes at each locale, there are patterns of price variation from neighborhood to neighborhood. The neighborhoods in central cities, for example, differ significantly from one another in their ability to maintain property values and to compete with the high-priced suburbs in attracting and holding onto upper-income residents. Thus, the average value of owner-occupied housing for a central city or its suburban ring fails to convey a sense of the wide variation in average property values from place to place in the urbanized area. The averages also ignore the price variations that usually exist within census tracts and other areal statistical units. Normally, the variation in housing values within census tracts increases as the median value increases.

When the median value of owner-occupied housing in a tract exceeds the median for the metro area, the tract can be said to be in a strong market position—that is, more households on the average want to enter the tract than want to leave it, and high prices are thereby sustained. If a tract is able to maintain or improve its ranking in the value hierarchy of tracts, its long-term vitality is likely.

In the accompanying map sets, tracts that have a median value of owner-occupied housing equal to or greater than 1.25 of the metro area median are marked "high" value and in 1980 were holding onto a strong market position. Tracts with medians less than or equal to .75 of the metro median are shaded "low" value. The remainder of the tracts have medians near the metro median.

[22]In the discussions of the map sets, the city and SMSA statistics are taken from the U.S. Bureau of the Census, 1980 Census of Housing, *General Housing Characteristics: U.S. Summary*, and from the *State and Metropolitan Area Data Book, 1983*, unless otherwise specified. The printed tract statistics books are the data source for all tract-level maps in chapter 6. Base maps were constructed from the sets of tract maps published with the tract statistics.

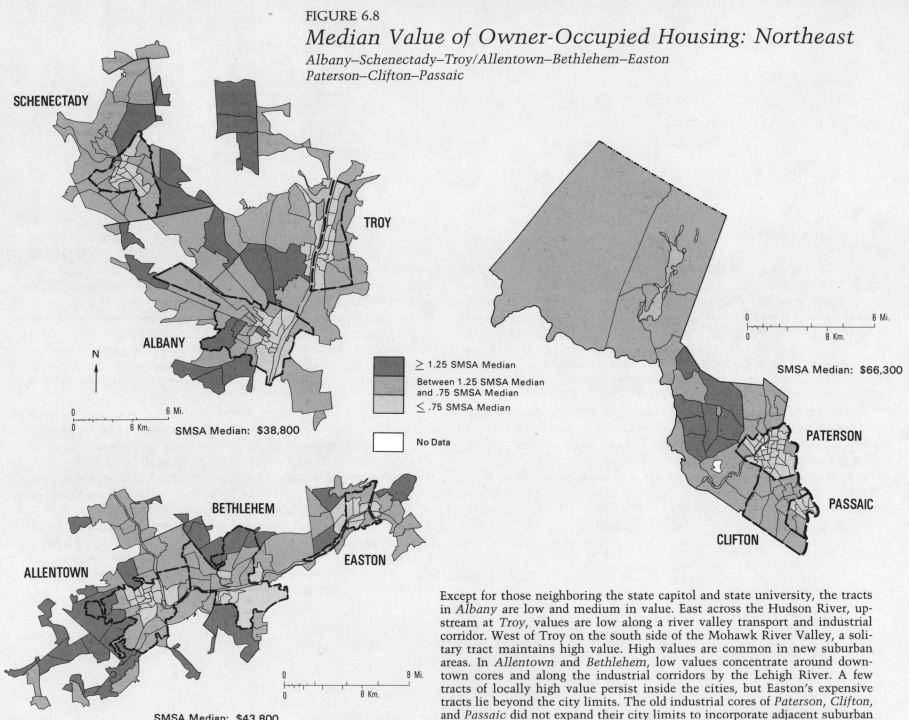

FIGURE 6.8
Median Value of Owner-Occupied Housing: Northeast
Albany–Schenectady–Troy/Allentown–Bethlehem–Easton
Paterson–Clifton–Passaic

SCHENECTADY

TROY

ALBANY

N

0   6 Mi.

0   6 Km.

SMSA Median: $38,800

≥ 1.25 SMSA Median

Between 1.25 SMSA Median
and .75 SMSA Median

≤ .75 SMSA Median

No Data

SMSA Median: $66,300

PATERSON

PASSAIC

CLIFTON

0   8 Mi.

0   8 Km.

BETHLEHEM

EASTON

ALLENTOWN

0   8 Mi.

0   8 Km.

SMSA Median: $43,800

Except for those neighboring the state capitol and state university, the tracts in *Albany* are low and medium in value. East across the Hudson River, upstream at *Troy*, values are low along a river valley transport and industrial corridor. West of Troy on the south side of the Mohawk River Valley, a solitary tract maintains high value. High values are common in new suburban areas. In *Allentown* and *Bethlehem*, low values concentrate around downtown cores and along the industrial corridors by the Lehigh River. A few tracts of locally high value persist inside the cities, but Easton's expensive tracts lie beyond the city limits. The old industrial cores of *Paterson, Clifton*, and *Passaic* did not expand their city limits to incorporate adjacent suburban areas, so they remain underbounded, with housing generally low in value compared with metro averages.

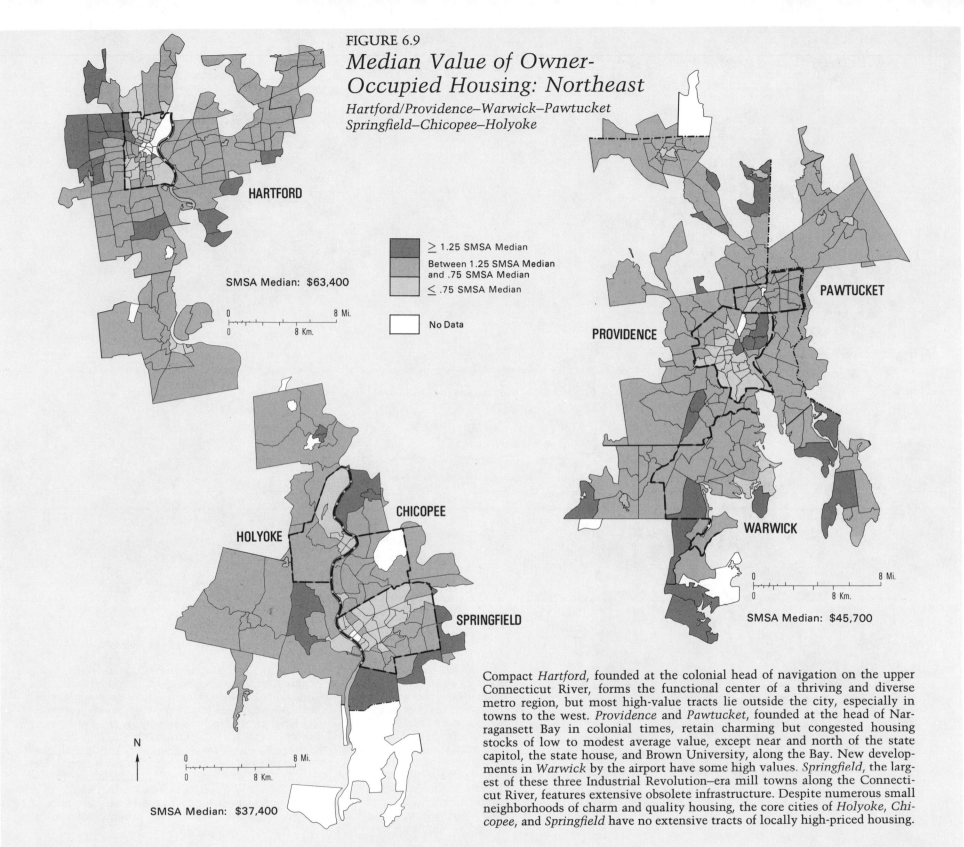

FIGURE 6.9
Median Value of Owner-Occupied Housing: Northeast
Hartford/Providence–Warwick–Pawtucket
Springfield–Chicopee–Holyoke

HARTFORD

SMSA Median: $63,400

≥ 1.25 SMSA Median

Between 1.25 SMSA Median
and .75 SMSA Median

≤ .75 SMSA Median

No Data

0   8 Mi.
0   8 Km.

PAWTUCKET

PROVIDENCE

WARWICK

0   8 Mi.
0   8 Km.

SMSA Median: $45,700

CHICOPEE

HOLYOKE

SPRINGFIELD

N

0   8 Mi.
0   8 Km.

SMSA Median: $37,400

Compact *Hartford*, founded at the colonial head of navigation on the upper Connecticut River, forms the functional center of a thriving and diverse metro region, but most high-value tracts lie outside the city, especially in towns to the west. *Providence* and *Pawtucket*, founded at the head of Narragansett Bay in colonial times, retain charming but congested housing stocks of low to modest average value, except near and north of the state capitol, the state house, and Brown University, along the Bay. New developments in *Warwick* by the airport have some high values. *Springfield*, the largest of these three Industrial Revolution–era mill towns along the Connecticut River, features extensive obsolete infrastructure. Despite numerous small neighborhoods of charm and quality housing, the core cities of *Holyoke*, *Chicopee*, and *Springfield* have no extensive tracts of locally high-priced housing.

FIGURE 6.10
Median Value of Owner-Occupied Housing: Midwest
Omaha/Wichita/Grand Rapids/Madison

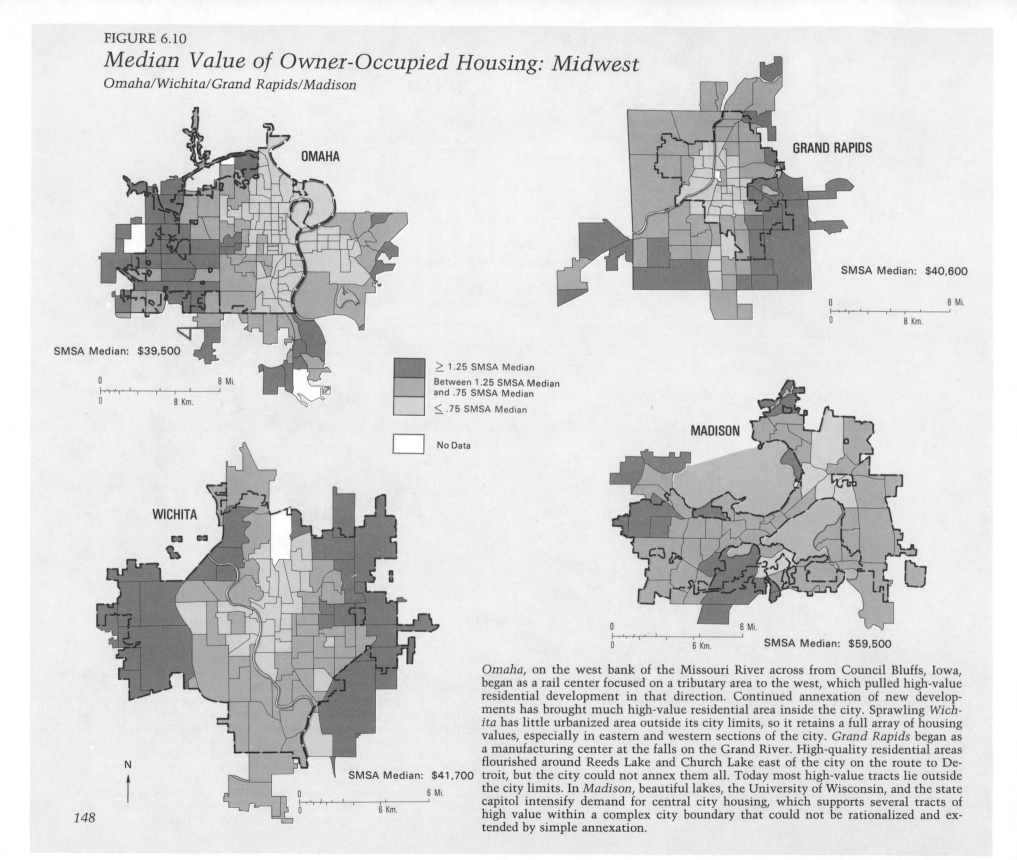

OMAHA

SMSA Median: $39,500

0 ___ 8 Mi.
0 ___ 8 Km.

GRAND RAPIDS

SMSA Median: $40,600

0 ___ 8 Mi.
0 ___ 8 Km.

≥ 1.25 SMSA Median

Between 1.25 SMSA Median
and .75 SMSA Median

≤ .75 SMSA Median

No Data

WICHITA

SMSA Median: $41,700

0 ___ 6 Mi.
0 ___ 6 Km.

N

MADISON

SMSA Median: $59,500

0 ___ 6 Mi.
0 ___ 6 Km.

148

Omaha, on the west bank of the Missouri River across from Council Bluffs, Iowa, began as a rail center focused on a tributary area to the west, which pulled high-value residential development in that direction. Continued annexation of new developments has brought much high-value residential area inside the city. Sprawling *Wichita* has little urbanized area outside its city limits, so it retains a full array of housing values, especially in eastern and western sections of the city. *Grand Rapids* began as a manufacturing center at the falls on the Grand River. High-quality residential areas flourished around Reeds Lake and Church Lake east of the city on the route to Detroit, but the city could not annex them all. Today most high-value tracts lie outside the city limits. In *Madison*, beautiful lakes, the University of Wisconsin, and the state capitol intensify demand for central city housing, which supports several tracts of high value within a complex city boundary that could not be rationalized and extended by simple annexation.

FIGURE 6.11

Median Value of Owner-Occupied Housing: Midwest
Minneapolis–St. Paul/Indianapolis

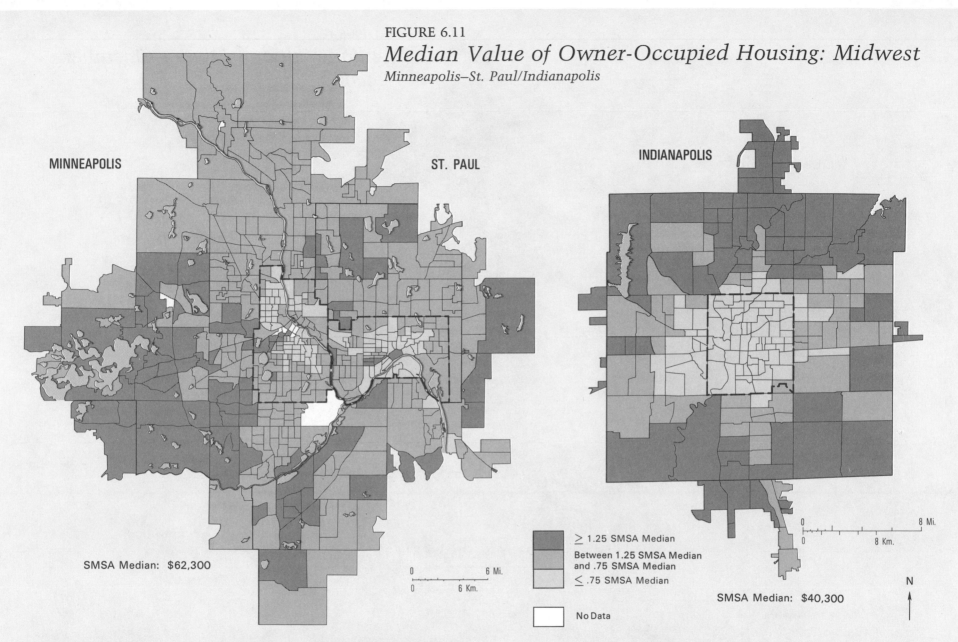

MINNEAPOLIS

ST. PAUL

INDIANAPOLIS

SMSA Median: $62,300

≥ 1.25 SMSA Median

Between 1.25 SMSA Median
and .75 SMSA Median

≤ .75 SMSA Median

No Data

0   6 Mi.
0   6 Km.

0   8 Mi.
0   8 Km.

SMSA Median: $40,300

N

The Twin Cities grew up around manufacturing at the falls of St. Anthony (*Minneapolis*) and trade at the head of early navigation on the upper Mississippi River (*St. Paul*). St. Paul, boxed in on the east side of the river, suffered restricted movement and developed a tributary area smaller than that of Minneapolis, but expanded its boundaries to retain high-value tracts. Minneapolis lakes, creeks, and river frontage add great value to nearby neighborhoods. Extensive high-value areas sprawl into western, southern, and southwestern suburbs. *Indianapolis* occupies a modest site on the White River, which proceeds southwest to the Mississippi. Situated to conduct business with the East, the Ohio Valley, Chicago, and the Great Lakes, the city has prosperous suburbs in all directions but a high concentration of low-value tracts inside the city.

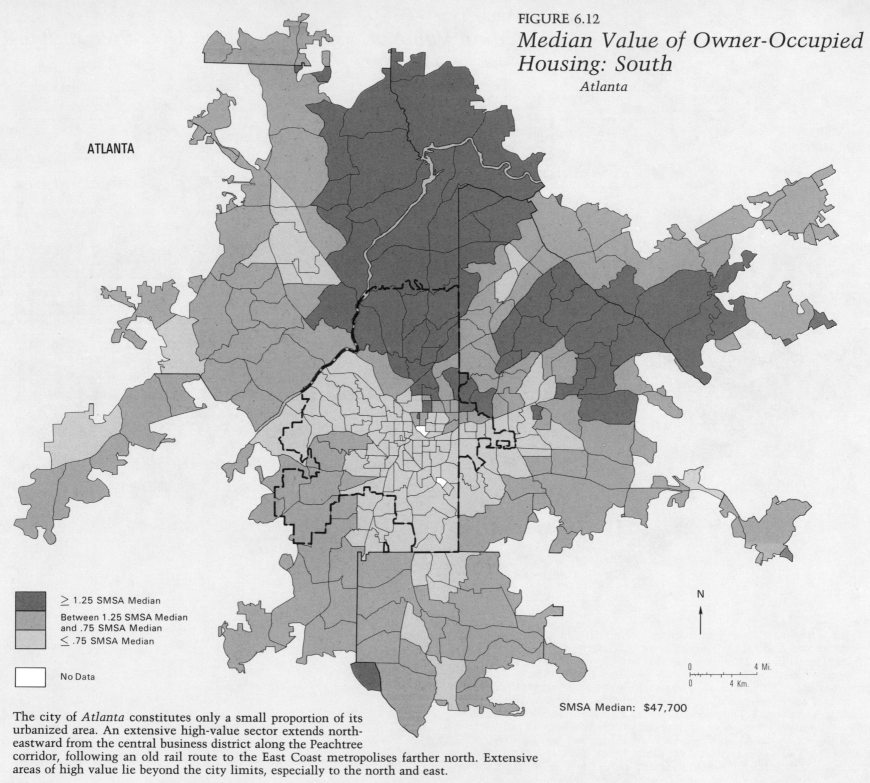

FIGURE 6.12
Median Value of Owner-Occupied Housing: South
Atlanta

ATLANTA

≥ 1.25 SMSA Median

Between 1.25 SMSA Median
and .75 SMSA Median

≤ .75 SMSA Median

No Data

N

0   4 Mi.

0   4 Km.

SMSA Median: $47,700

The city of *Atlanta* constitutes only a small proportion of its urbanized area. An extensive high-value sector extends northeastward from the central business district along the Peachtree corridor, following an old rail route to the East Coast metropolises farther north. Extensive areas of high value lie beyond the city limits, especially to the north and east.

FIGURE 6.13
Median Value of Owner-Occupied Housing: South
Raleigh–Durham/Orlando

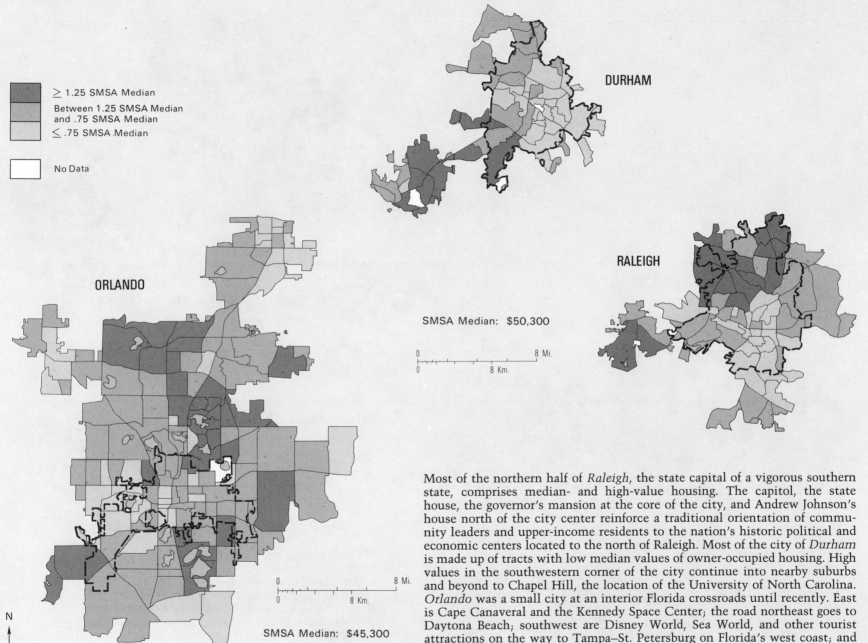

≥ 1.25 SMSA Median

Between 1.25 SMSA Median
and .75 SMSA Median

≤ .75 SMSA Median

No Data

DURHAM

SMSA Median: $50,300

0 ———————————— 8 Mi.
0 ———————————— 8 Km.

RALEIGH

ORLANDO

0 ———————————— 8 Mi.
0 ———————————— 8 Km.

SMSA Median: $45,300

N

Most of the northern half of *Raleigh*, the state capital of a vigorous southern state, comprises median- and high-value housing. The capitol, the state house, the governor's mansion at the core of the city, and Andrew Johnson's house north of the city center reinforce a traditional orientation of community leaders and upper-income residents to the nation's historic political and economic centers located to the north of Raleigh. Most of the city of *Durham* is made up of tracts with low median values of owner-occupied housing. High values in the southwestern corner of the city continue into nearby suburbs and beyond to Chapel Hill, the location of the University of North Carolina. *Orlando* was a small city at an interior Florida crossroads until recently. East is Cape Canaveral and the Kennedy Space Center; the road northeast goes to Daytona Beach; southwest are Disney World, Sea World, and other tourist attractions on the way to Tampa–St. Petersburg on Florida's west coast; and south-southeast Florida's turnpike runs to Miami. All high-value tracts lie outside the city, mostly in the northern suburbs.

151

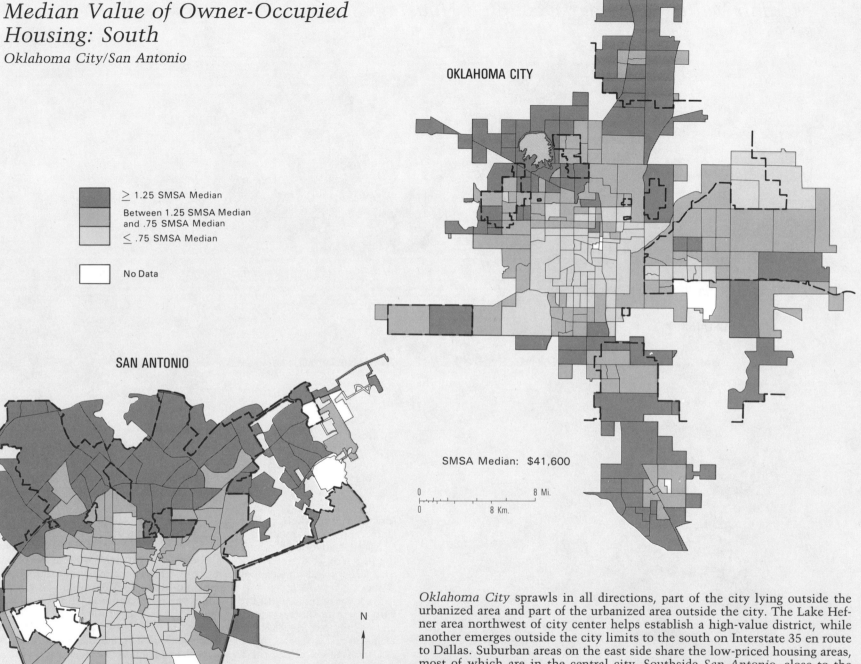

FIGURE 6.14
Median Value of Owner-Occupied Housing: South
Oklahoma City/San Antonio

OKLAHOMA CITY

≥ 1.25 SMSA Median

Between 1.25 SMSA Median and .75 SMSA Median

≤ .75 SMSA Median

No Data

SMSA Median: $41,600

0 — 8 Mi.
0 — 8 Km.

SAN ANTONIO

N

SMSA Median: $33,200

0 — 8 Mi.
0 — 8 Km.

Oklahoma City sprawls in all directions, part of the city lying outside the urbanized area and part of the urbanized area outside the city. The Lake Hefner area northwest of city center helps establish a high-value district, while another emerges outside the city limits to the south on Interstate 35 en route to Dallas. Suburban areas on the east side share the low-priced housing areas, most of which are in the central city. Southside *San Antonio*, close to the Mexican origins of many of its residents, forms the principal low-value residential area in the city. High-value neighborhoods jut outward to the northwest (El Paso), northeast (Austin, Dallas), and east (Houston). The city annexes almost all suburban development so it remains almost coterminous with the urbanized area.

152

FIGURE 6.15

Median Value of Owner-Occupied Housing: South

Birmingham/Memphis

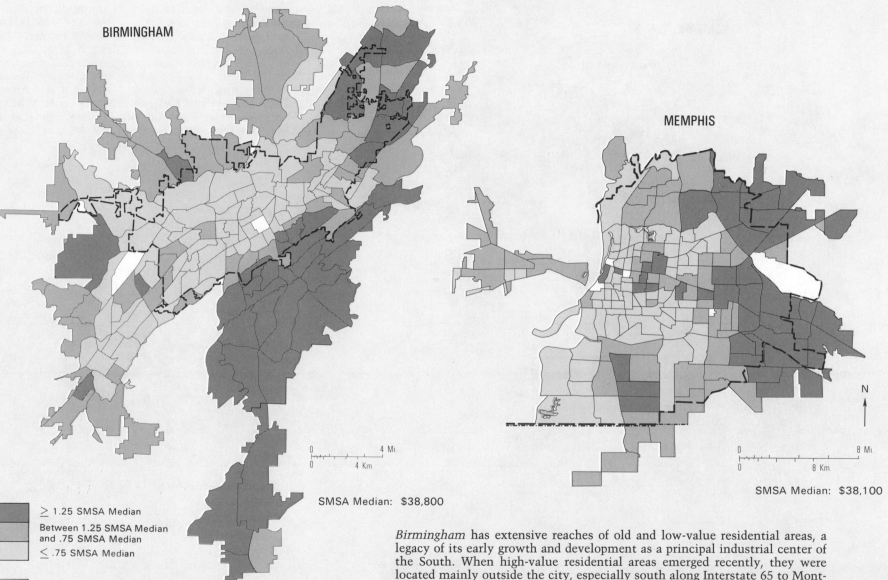

BIRMINGHAM

MEMPHIS

N

≥ 1.25 SMSA Median

Between 1.25 SMSA Median and .75 SMSA Median

≤ .75 SMSA Median

No Data

0   4 Mi.

0   4 Km.

SMSA Median: $38,800

0   8 Mi.

0   8 Km.

SMSA Median: $38,100

Birmingham has extensive reaches of old and low-value residential areas, a legacy of its early growth and development as a principal industrial center of the South. When high-value residential areas emerged recently, they were located mainly outside the city, especially south along Interstate 65 to Montgomery and the Gulf of Mexico and northeast past the airport along Interstate 59 to Chattanooga. The old city of *Memphis* served the antebellum South as a major cotton port on the Mississippi River, which bounds the city on the west. Old districts of wealth and fine houses grew up on the east side of the city, facing the source of the city's wealth and trade area and spilling into adjacent suburbs that were not annexed. Most of the urbanized area lies inside the city.

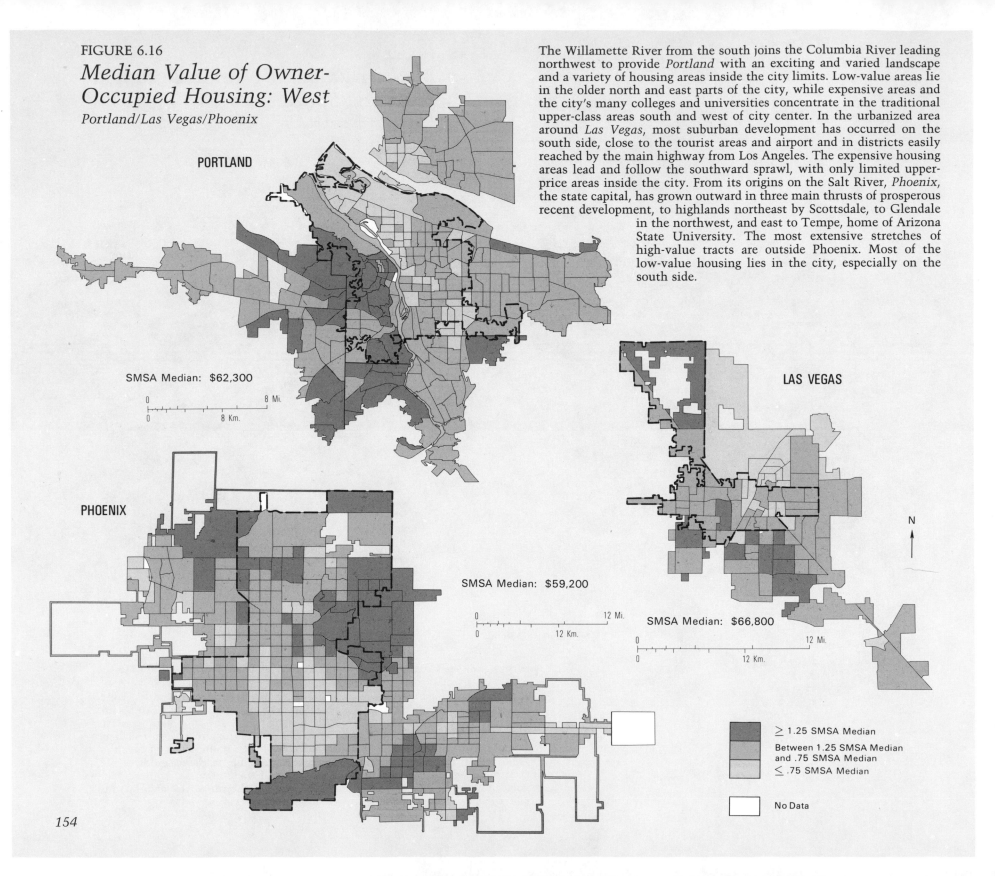

FIGURE 6.16
Median Value of Owner-Occupied Housing: West
Portland/Las Vegas/Phoenix

The Willamette River from the south joins the Columbia River leading northwest to provide *Portland* with an exciting and varied landscape and a variety of housing areas inside the city limits. Low-value areas lie in the older north and east parts of the city, while expensive areas and the city's many colleges and universities concentrate in the traditional upper-class areas south and west of city center. In the urbanized area around *Las Vegas*, most suburban development has occurred on the south side, close to the tourist areas and airport and in districts easily reached by the main highway from Los Angeles. The expensive housing areas lead and follow the southward sprawl, with only limited upper-price areas inside the city. From its origins on the Salt River, *Phoenix*, the state capital, has grown outward in three main thrusts of prosperous recent development, to highlands northeast by Scottsdale, to Glendale in the northwest, and east to Tempe, home of Arizona State University. The most extensive stretches of high-value tracts are outside Phoenix. Most of the low-value housing lies in the city, especially on the south side.

PORTLAND

SMSA Median: $62,300

0 — 8 Mi.
0 — 8 Km.

LAS VEGAS

PHOENIX

SMSA Median: $59,200

0 — 12 Mi.
0 — 12 Km.

SMSA Median: $66,800

0 — 12 Mi.
0 — 12 Km.

N

≥ 1.25 SMSA Median

Between 1.25 SMSA Median and .75 SMSA Median

≤ .75 SMSA Median

No Data

154

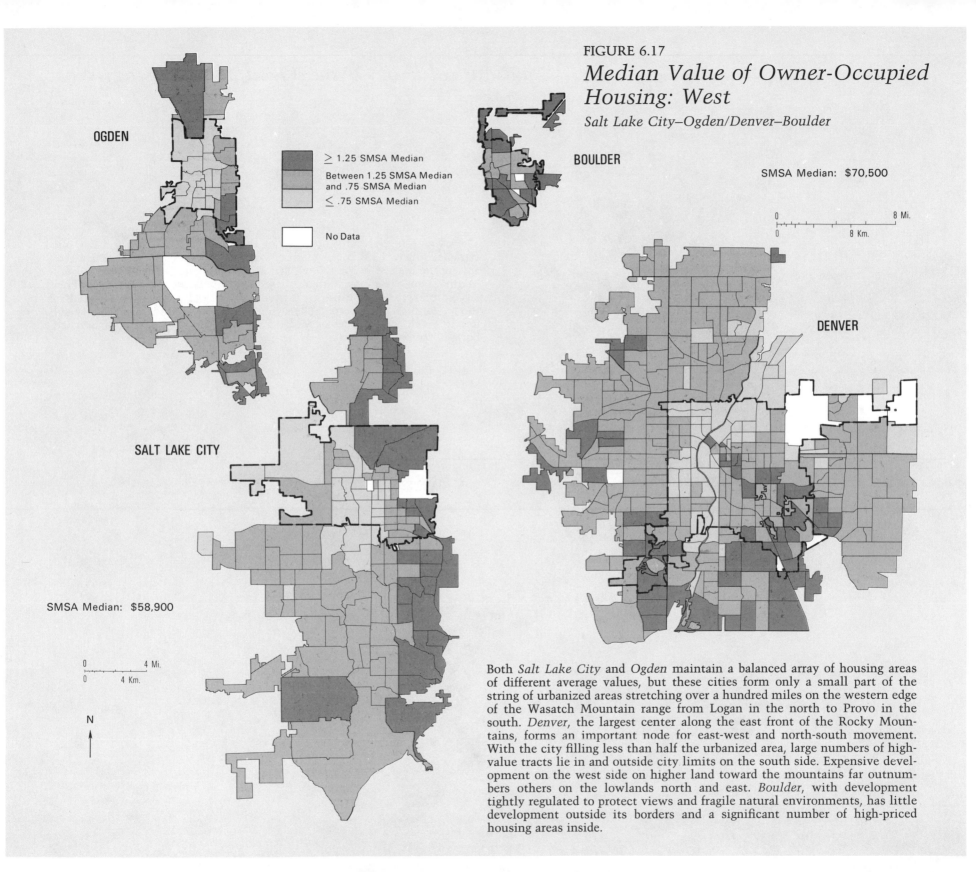

FIGURE 6.17
Median Value of Owner-Occupied Housing: West
Salt Lake City–Ogden/Denver–Boulder

OGDEN

BOULDER

SMSA Median: $70,500

≥ 1.25 SMSA Median

Between 1.25 SMSA Median
and .75 SMSA Median

≤ .75 SMSA Median

No Data

0   8 Mi.

0   8 Km.

DENVER

SALT LAKE CITY

SMSA Median: $58,900

0   4 Mi.

0   4 Km.

N

Both *Salt Lake City* and *Ogden* maintain a balanced array of housing areas of different average values, but these cities form only a small part of the string of urbanized areas stretching over a hundred miles on the western edge of the Wasatch Mountain range from Logan in the north to Provo in the south. *Denver*, the largest center along the east front of the Rocky Mountains, forms an important node for east-west and north-south movement. With the city filling less than half the urbanized area, large numbers of high-value tracts lie in and outside city limits on the south side. Expensive development on the west side on higher land toward the mountains far outnumbers others on the lowlands north and east. *Boulder*, with development tightly regulated to protect views and fragile natural environments, has little development outside its borders and a significant number of high-priced housing areas inside.

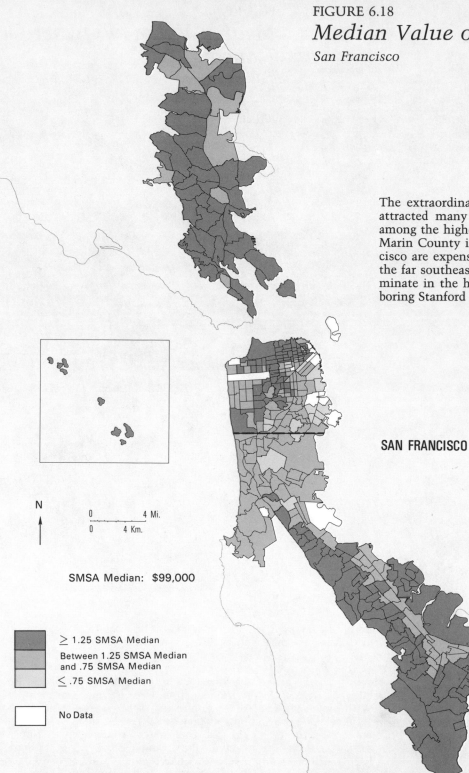

FIGURE 6.18

Median Value of Owner-Occupied Housing: West

San Francisco

The extraordinary beauty of much of the western *San Francisco* Bay area attracted many to a confined space, driving up housing prices that rank among the highest in the United States. North of the Golden Gate Bridge in Marin County is a large and exclusive area, but inside the city of San Francisco are expensive housing areas in all but the older industrial lowlands of the far southeastern quarter. The string of suburbs southeast of the city culminate in the high values of Menlo Park and Palo Alto in the tracts neighboring Stanford University.

SAN FRANCISCO

N

0   4 Mi.
0   4 Km.

SMSA Median: $99,000

≥ 1.25 SMSA Median

Between 1.25 SMSA Median
and .75 SMSA Median

≤ .75 SMSA Median

No Data

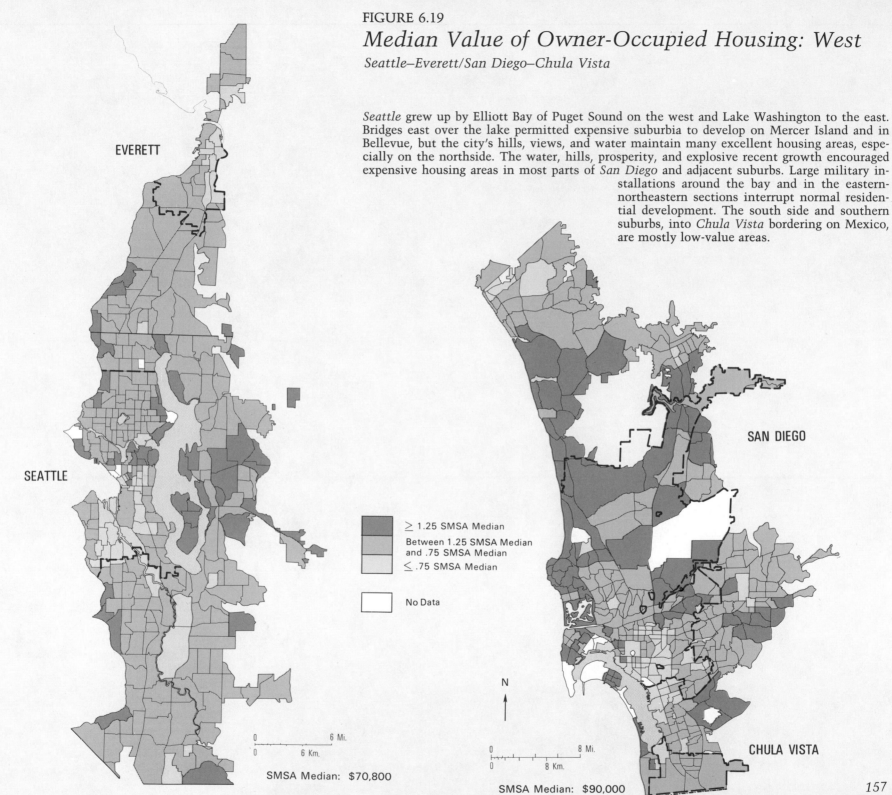

FIGURE 6.19
Median Value of Owner-Occupied Housing: West
Seattle–Everett/San Diego–Chula Vista

Seattle grew up by Elliott Bay of Puget Sound on the west and Lake Washington to the east. Bridges east over the lake permitted expensive suburbia to develop on Mercer Island and in Bellevue, but the city's hills, views, and water maintain many excellent housing areas, especially on the northside. The water, hills, prosperity, and explosive recent growth encouraged expensive housing areas in most parts of *San Diego* and adjacent suburbs. Large military installations around the bay and in the eastern-northeastern sections interrupt normal residential development. The south side and southern suburbs, into *Chula Vista* bordering on Mexico, are mostly low-value areas.

EVERETT

SEATTLE

SAN DIEGO

CHULA VISTA

≥ 1.25 SMSA Median

Between 1.25 SMSA Median and .75 SMSA Median

≤ .75 SMSA Median

No Data

N

0   6 Mi.
0   6 Km.

SMSA Median: $70,800

0   8 Mi.
0   8 Km.

SMSA Median: $90,000

157

Households with Children Under Age 18: Where the Young Families Are Concentrated

Where are the children housed in the urban area? Theory and empirical research tell us to expect concentrations in inmigrant reception areas, in newer low-density residential subdivisions near the edge of the urbanized area, and at the edges of expanding inner city ghetto areas. In the latter two settings young families attempt to provide large housing units and the maximum affordable open space for their children. Children in census tracts ensure a degree of vitality and at least short-term rejuvenation of the neighborhood population. Children mean new life in the area and imply vitality for the community.

In the 1980s, when easy sale and quick capital gains on housing have been harder to achieve than they were in the 1970s, many urban neighborhoods began to exhibit greater demographic stability and vitality than they did during the rush of construction, mobility, and housing abandonment that were common in the late 1960s and early 1970s. Starting in 1980 it became harder for middle-class householders to sell at prices they liked and harder for them to move on to more desirable housing in superior settings. Real interest rates for house purchase became prohibitively high for many—perhaps most—prospective movers, and the net cost of housing after tax benefits and capital gains rose briskly after 1980. Thus, areas with above-average numbers of children in 1980 had bright prospects for population stability or increase in the 1980s. When children are present, the costs to a household of moving rise fast, just as family living expenses rise steadily. Additional housing space may be needed by the growing family, but additions to existing housing or remodeling became economical alternatives when the costs and benefits of moving are considered carefully. And once a house is customized, it may be harder to sell at the same time that the family's desire to move has abated. So the rate of turnover drops and the children remain.

On the accompanying maps we calculated the number of families with children of their own under age 18 and divided this figure by the number of householders (this number is also the number of households) in the SMSA.[23] Then the same ratio was calculated for each tract and shaded dark when the tract ratio exceeded the SMSA ratio. The SMSA ratios are highest in Salt Lake City (.47), San Antonio (.43), and Grand Rapids (.42), and lowest in San Francisco–Oakland (.30), Minneapolis–St. Paul (.34), and San Diego (.34). In the darkly shaded portions of the urbanized areas, demand for schools, recreational facilities, and family-oriented goods and services is likely to be strong.

[23]See U.S. Bureau of the Census, 1980 Census of Population and Housing, *Census Tracts*, tables P-1 and P-11.

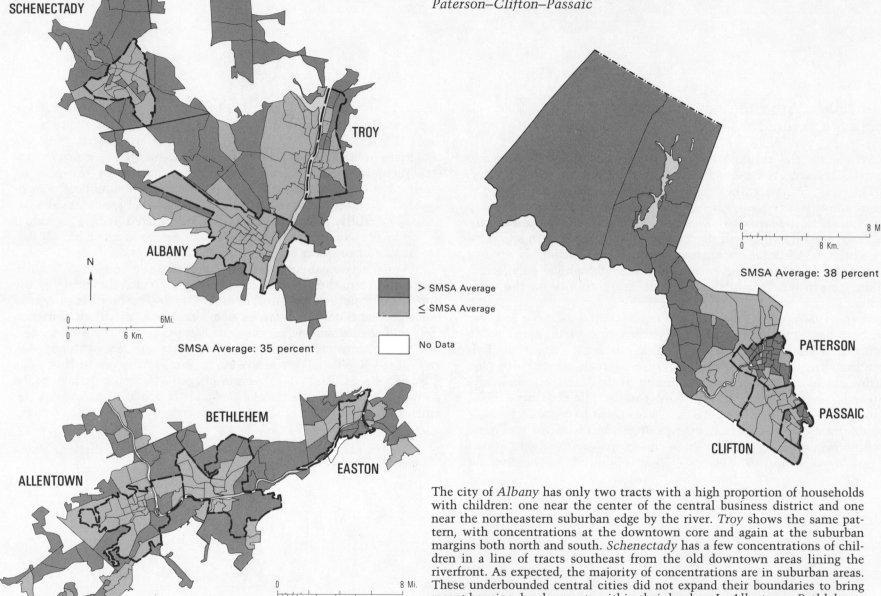

FIGURE 6.20
Proportion of Households with Children Under Age 18: Northeast

Albany–Schenectady–Troy/Allentown–Bethlehem–Easton
Paterson–Clifton–Passaic

SCHENECTADY

TROY

ALBANY

N

0   6Mi.

0   6 Km.

SMSA Average: 35 percent

> SMSA Average

≤ SMSA Average

No Data

0   8 Mi.

0   8 Km.

SMSA Average: 38 percent

PATERSON

PASSAIC

CLIFTON

BETHLEHEM

EASTON

ALLENTOWN

0   8 Mi.

0   8 Km.

SMSA Average: 35 percent

The city of *Albany* has only two tracts with a high proportion of households with children: one near the center of the central business district and one near the northeastern suburban edge by the river. *Troy* shows the same pattern, with concentrations at the downtown core and again at the suburban margins both north and south. *Schenectady* has a few concentrations of children in a line of tracts southeast from the old downtown areas lining the riverfront. As expected, the majority of concentrations are in suburban areas. These underbounded central cities did not expand their boundaries to bring recent housing developments within their borders. In *Allentown–Bethlehem–Easton* the cities and suburbs both maintain a mix of tracts with above- and below-average concentrations of children, but the concentrations remain higher in the suburbs than inside these small and slow-growth cities. In the *Paterson–Clifton–Passaic* area concentrations of children in new suburbs and around ancient downtown cores are separated by low points in the first-tier suburbs and in Clifton.

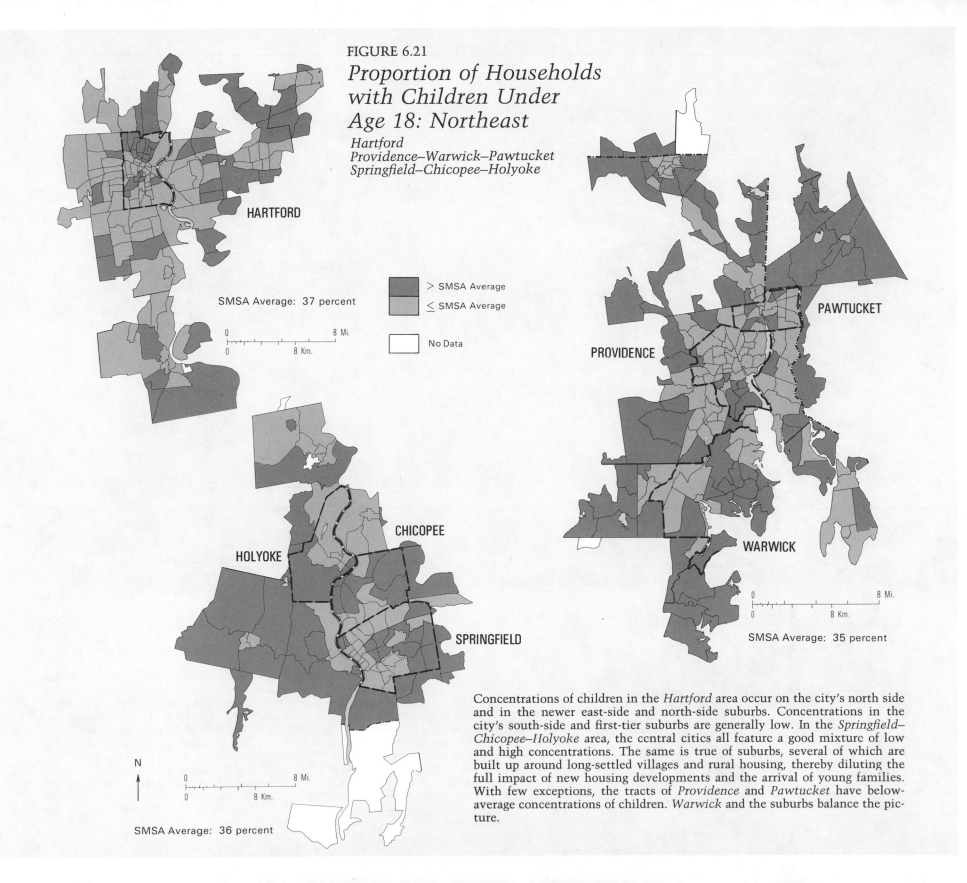

FIGURE 6.21

Proportion of Households with Children Under Age 18: Northeast

Hartford
Providence–Warwick–Pawtucket
Springfield–Chicopee–Holyoke

HARTFORD

SMSA Average: 37 percent

0 — 8 Mi.
0 — 8 Km.

> SMSA Average
≤ SMSA Average
No Data

PROVIDENCE   PAWTUCKET

WARWICK

SMSA Average: 35 percent

HOLYOKE   CHICOPEE

SPRINGFIELD

N

0 — 8 Mi.
0 — 8 Km.

SMSA Average: 36 percent

Concentrations of children in the *Hartford* area occur on the city's north side and in the newer east-side and north-side suburbs. Concentrations in the city's south-side and first-tier suburbs are generally low. In the *Springfield–Chicopee–Holyoke* area, the central cities all feature a good mixture of low and high concentrations. The same is true of suburbs, several of which are built up around long-settled villages and rural housing, thereby diluting the full impact of new housing developments and the arrival of young families. With few exceptions, the tracts of *Providence* and *Pawtucket* have below-average concentrations of children. *Warwick* and the suburbs balance the picture.

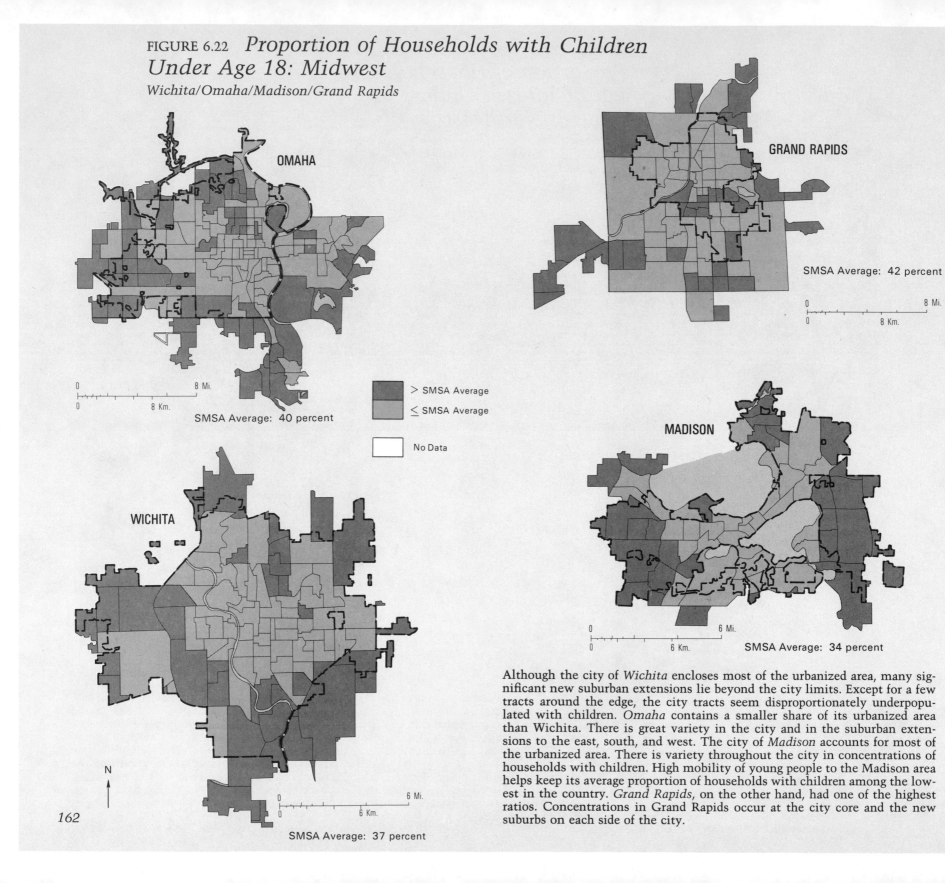

FIGURE 6.22 *Proportion of Households with Children Under Age 18: Midwest*
Wichita/Omaha/Madison/Grand Rapids

OMAHA

0   8 Mi.
0   8 Km.

SMSA Average: 40 percent

GRAND RAPIDS

SMSA Average: 42 percent

0   8 Mi.
0   8 Km.

> SMSA Average

≤ SMSA Average

No Data

WICHITA

N

0   6 Mi.
0   6 Km.

SMSA Average: 37 percent

MADISON

0   6 Mi.
0   6 Km.

SMSA Average: 34 percent

Although the city of *Wichita* encloses most of the urbanized area, many significant new suburban extensions lie beyond the city limits. Except for a few tracts around the edge, the city tracts seem disproportionately underpopulated with children. *Omaha* contains a smaller share of its urbanized area than Wichita. There is great variety in the city and in the suburban extensions to the east, south, and west. The city of *Madison* accounts for most of the urbanized area. There is variety throughout the city in concentrations of households with children. High mobility of young people to the Madison area helps keep its average proportion of households with children among the lowest in the country. *Grand Rapids*, on the other hand, had one of the highest ratios. Concentrations in Grand Rapids occur at the city core and the new suburbs on each side of the city.

162

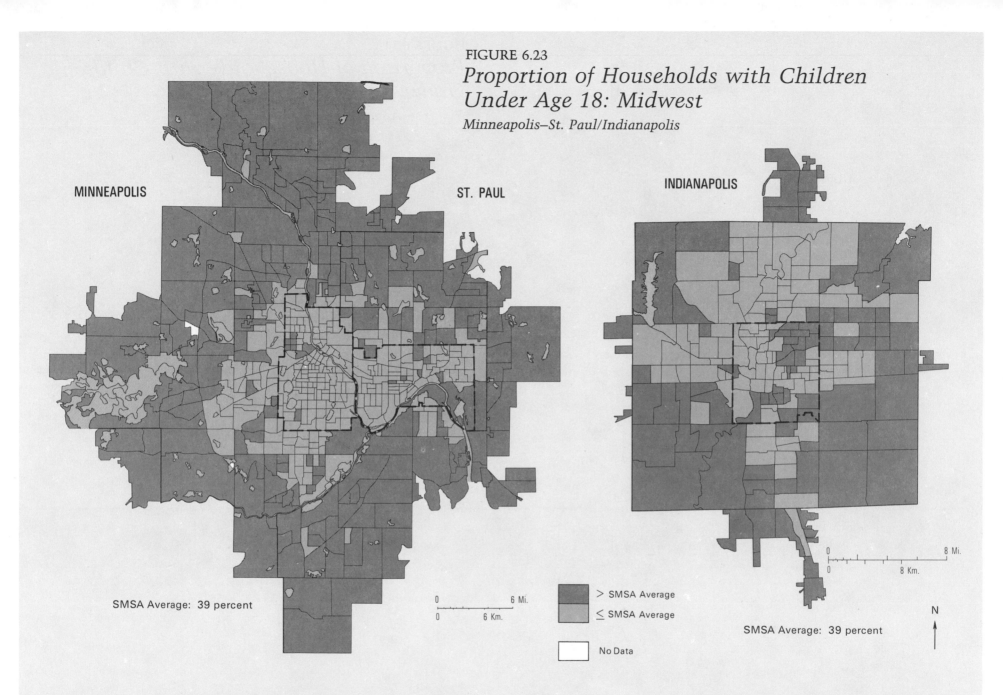

FIGURE 6.23

Proportion of Households with Children Under Age 18: Midwest

Minneapolis–St. Paul/Indianapolis

MINNEAPOLIS

ST. PAUL

INDIANAPOLIS

SMSA Average: 39 percent

0   6 Mi.

0   6 Km.

0   8 Mi.

0   8 Km.

> SMSA Average

≤ SMSA Average

No Data

SMSA Average: 39 percent

N

The central cities of *Minneapolis* and *St. Paul* cover less than 10 percent of this sprawling urbanized area, which features islands of child-centered family life in the low-income and black neighborhoods northwest of downtown Minneapolis and in an upper-income high-amenity area in the southwestern corner. In St. Paul minority areas west of downtown (black, Southeast Asian) and across the river south of the central business district (Mexican), plus new suburban-style housing in the far southeastern corner, contain significant concentrations of households with children. A ring of tracts with high concentrations defines the urbanized area. Most first-ring suburbs have low concentrations like the central cities. The *Indianapolis* area map resembles the Twin Cities pattern with high concentrations in outer suburbs, low in the first-tier suburbs, and below average in most central city tracts.

163

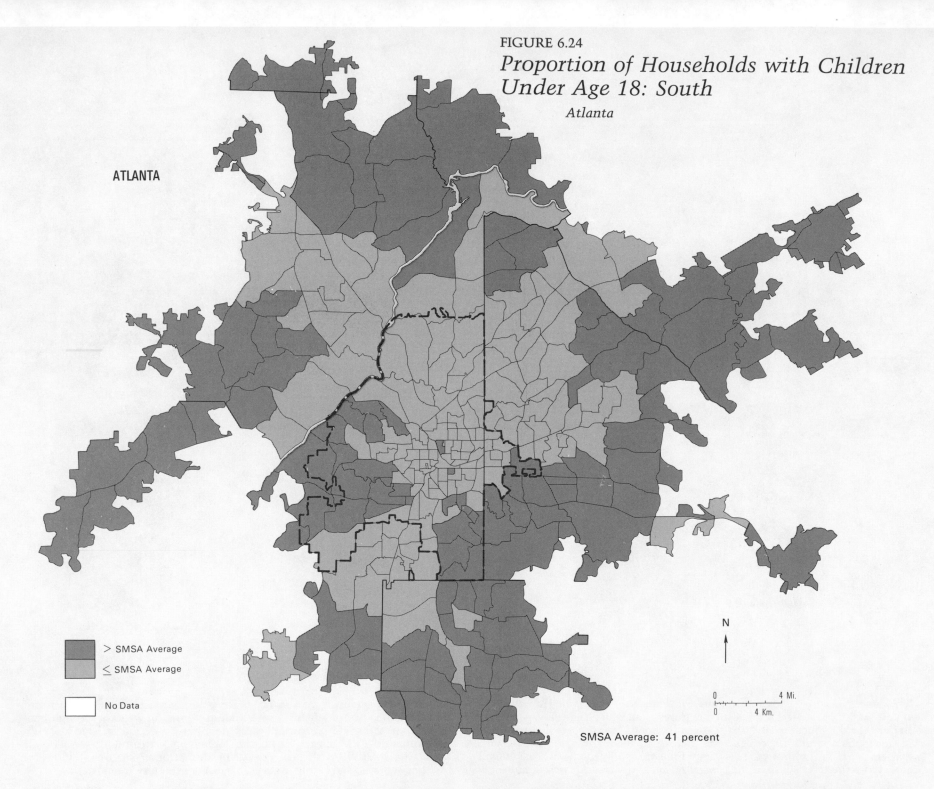

FIGURE 6.24

Proportion of Households with Children Under Age 18: South

Atlanta

ATLANTA

> SMSA Average

≤ SMSA Average

No Data

N

0   4 Mi.

0   4 Km.

SMSA Average: 41 percent

Most tracts in recently suburbanized *Atlanta* have a high percentage of households with children. Older suburbs close in and most tracts in the core of the city scored low, along with the northern wealthy quarter of the city.

The more prosperous black tracts on the outer west side of the city, spilling over into the black suburbs, have several concentrations of households with children.

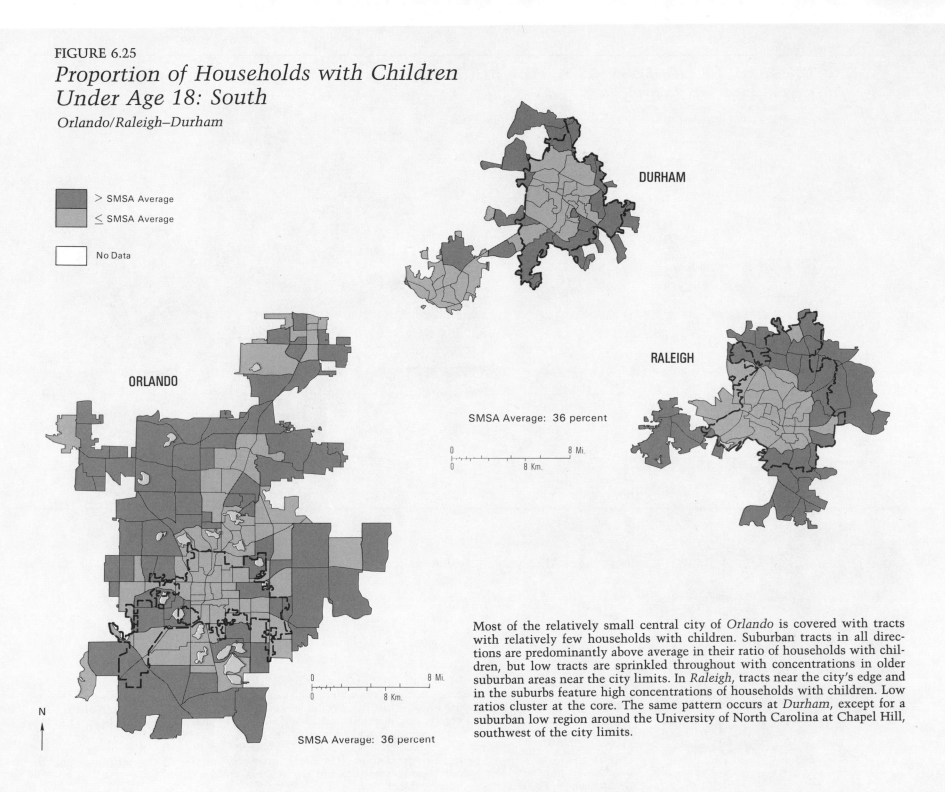

FIGURE 6.25
Proportion of Households with Children Under Age 18: South
Orlando/Raleigh–Durham

> SMSA Average

≤ SMSA Average

No Data

DURHAM

SMSA Average: 36 percent

0 ——— 8 Mi.
0 ——— 8 Km.

RALEIGH

ORLANDO

0 ——— 8 Mi.
0 ——— 8 Km.

SMSA Average: 36 percent

N

Most of the relatively small central city of *Orlando* is covered with tracts with relatively few households with children. Suburban tracts in all directions are predominantly above average in their ratio of households with children, but low tracts are sprinkled throughout with concentrations in older suburban areas near the city limits. In *Raleigh*, tracts near the city's edge and in the suburbs feature high concentrations of households with children. Low ratios cluster at the core. The same pattern occurs at *Durham*, except for a suburban low region around the University of North Carolina at Chapel Hill, southwest of the city limits.

165

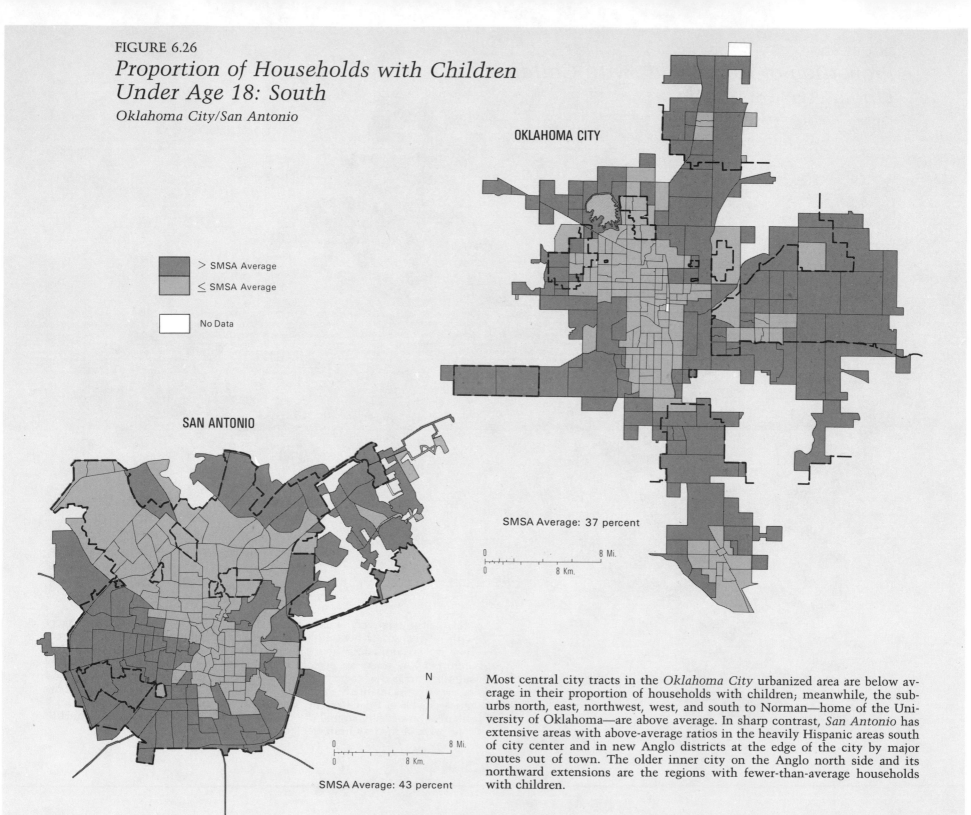

FIGURE 6.26
Proportion of Households with Children Under Age 18: South
Oklahoma City/San Antonio

> SMSA Average

≤ SMSA Average

No Data

OKLAHOMA CITY

SMSA Average: 37 percent

0   8 Mi.
0   8 Km.

SAN ANTONIO

N

0   8 Mi.
0   8 Km.

SMSA Average: 43 percent

Most central city tracts in the *Oklahoma City* urbanized area are below average in their proportion of households with children; meanwhile, the suburbs north, east, northwest, west, and south to Norman—home of the University of Oklahoma—are above average. In sharp contrast, *San Antonio* has extensive areas with above-average ratios in the heavily Hispanic areas south of city center and in new Anglo districts at the edge of the city by major routes out of town. The older inner city on the Anglo north side and its northward extensions are the regions with fewer-than-average households with children.

FIGURE 6.27
Proportion of Households with Children Under Age 18: South

Birmingham/Memphis

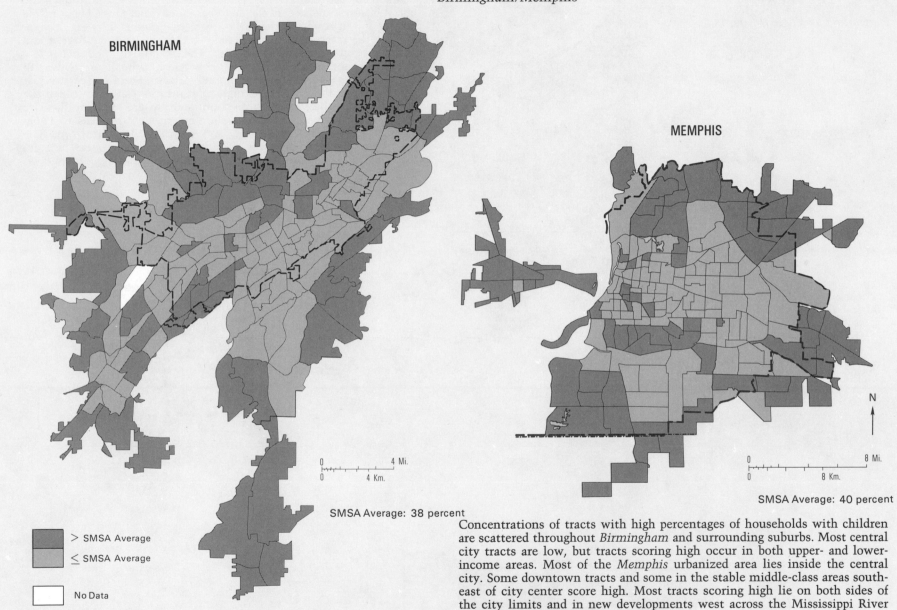

BIRMINGHAM

MEMPHIS

0   4 Mi.
0   4 Km.

0   8 Mi.
0   8 Km.

N

SMSA Average: 38 percent

SMSA Average: 40 percent

> SMSA Average

≤ SMSA Average

No Data

Concentrations of tracts with high percentages of households with children are scattered throughout *Birmingham* and surrounding suburbs. Most central city tracts are low, but tracts scoring high occur in both upper- and lower-income areas. Most of the *Memphis* urbanized area lies inside the central city. Some downtown tracts and some in the stable middle-class areas southeast of city center score high. Most tracts scoring high lie on both sides of the city limits and in new developments west across the Mississippi River adjacent to Interstate 40 in Arkansas.

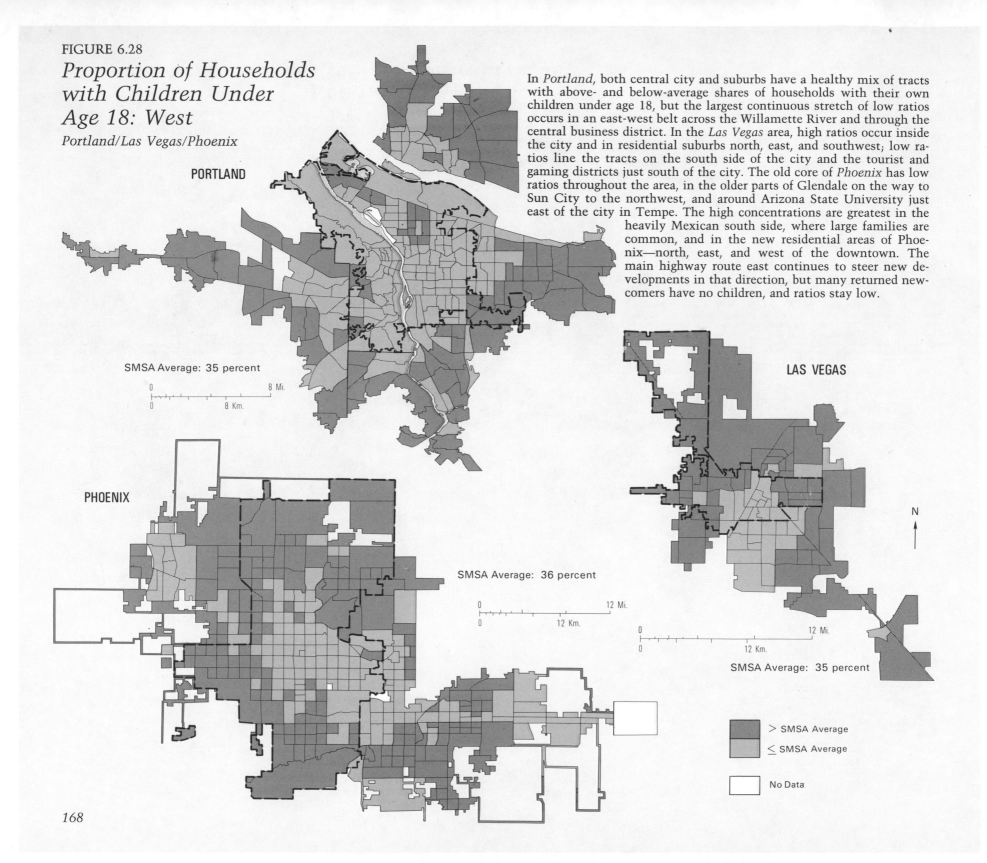

FIGURE 6.28

Proportion of Households with Children Under Age 18: West

Portland/Las Vegas/Phoenix

PORTLAND

SMSA Average: 35 percent

0   8 Mi.

0   8 Km.

In *Portland*, both central city and suburbs have a healthy mix of tracts with above- and below-average shares of households with their own children under age 18, but the largest continuous stretch of low ratios occurs in an east-west belt across the Willamette River and through the central business district. In the *Las Vegas* area, high ratios occur inside the city and in residential suburbs north, east, and southwest; low ratios line the tracts on the south side of the city and the tourist and gaming districts just south of the city. The old core of *Phoenix* has low ratios throughout the area, in the older parts of Glendale on the way to Sun City to the northwest, and around Arizona State University just east of the city in Tempe. The high concentrations are greatest in the heavily Mexican south side, where large families are common, and in the new residential areas of Phoenix—north, east, and west of the downtown. The main highway route east continues to steer new developments in that direction, but many returned newcomers have no children, and ratios stay low.

LAS VEGAS

N

PHOENIX

SMSA Average: 36 percent

0   12 Mi.

0   12 Km.

0   12 Mi.

0   12 Km.

SMSA Average: 35 percent

> SMSA Average

≤ SMSA Average

No Data

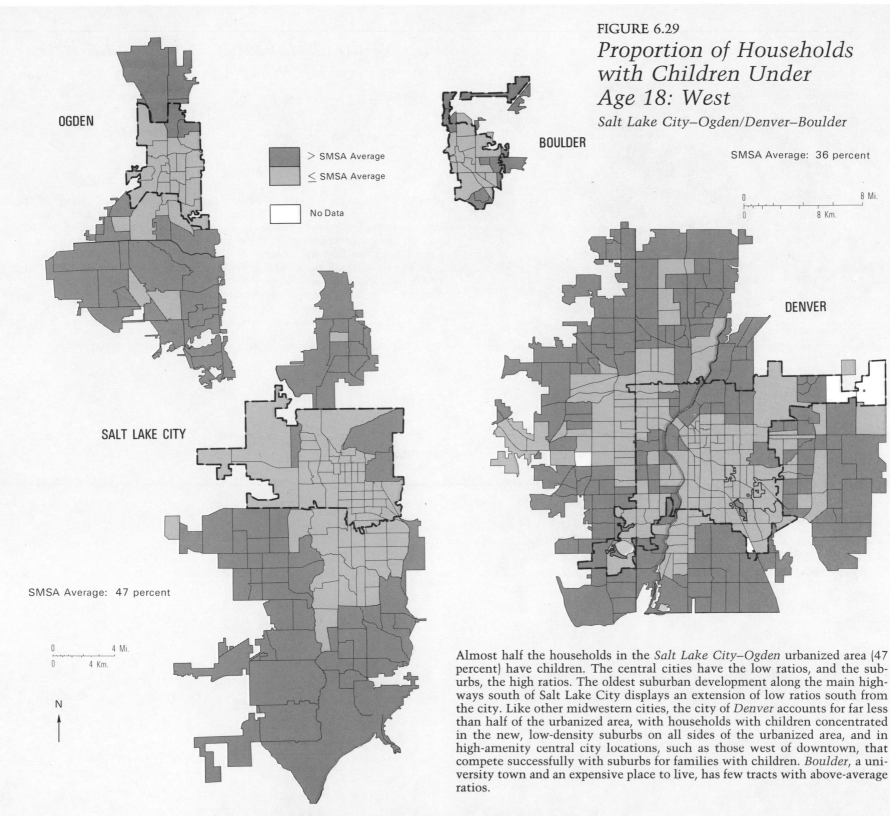

FIGURE 6.29

Proportion of Households with Children Under Age 18: West

Salt Lake City–Ogden/Denver–Boulder

OGDEN

BOULDER

> SMSA Average

≤ SMSA Average

No Data

SMSA Average: 36 percent

0 _____ 8 Mi.

0 _____ 8 Km.

DENVER

SALT LAKE CITY

SMSA Average: 47 percent

0 _____ 4 Mi.

0 _____ 4 Km.

N

Almost half the households in the *Salt Lake City–Ogden* urbanized area (47 percent) have children. The central cities have the low ratios, and the suburbs, the high ratios. The oldest suburban development along the main highways south of Salt Lake City displays an extension of low ratios south from the city. Like other midwestern cities, the city of *Denver* accounts for far less than half of the urbanized area, with households with children concentrated in the new, low-density suburbs on all sides of the urbanized area, and in high-amenity central city locations, such as those west of downtown, that compete successfully with suburbs for families with children. *Boulder*, a university town and an expensive place to live, has few tracts with above-average ratios.

FIGURE 6.30
Proportion of Households with Children Under Age 18: West

San Francisco

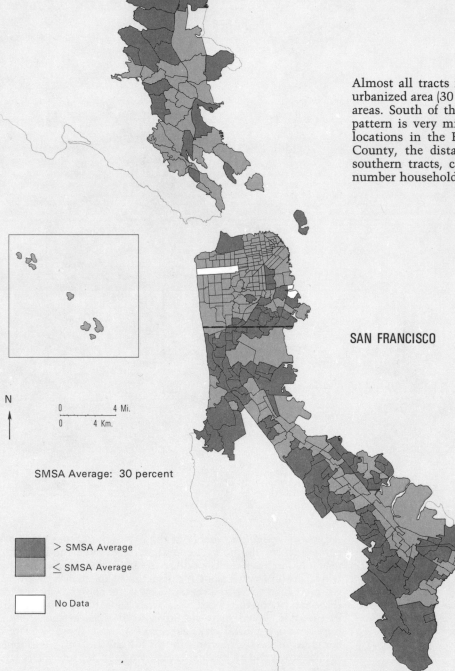

Almost all tracts in the city of *San Francisco* are below the average of the urbanized area (30 percent), which is the lowest average among our 27 sample areas. South of the city some areas have continuously high ratios, but the pattern is very mixed. Family living may be too expensive compared with locations in the East Bay. North of the Golden Gate in expensive Marin County, the distant tracts are above average and family-oriented. In the southern tracts, childless, single, and post-family and retired persons out-number households oriented toward childrearing and ratios are low.

SAN FRANCISCO

N

0   4 Mi.
0   4 Km.

SMSA Average: 30 percent

> SMSA Average

≤ SMSA Average

No Data

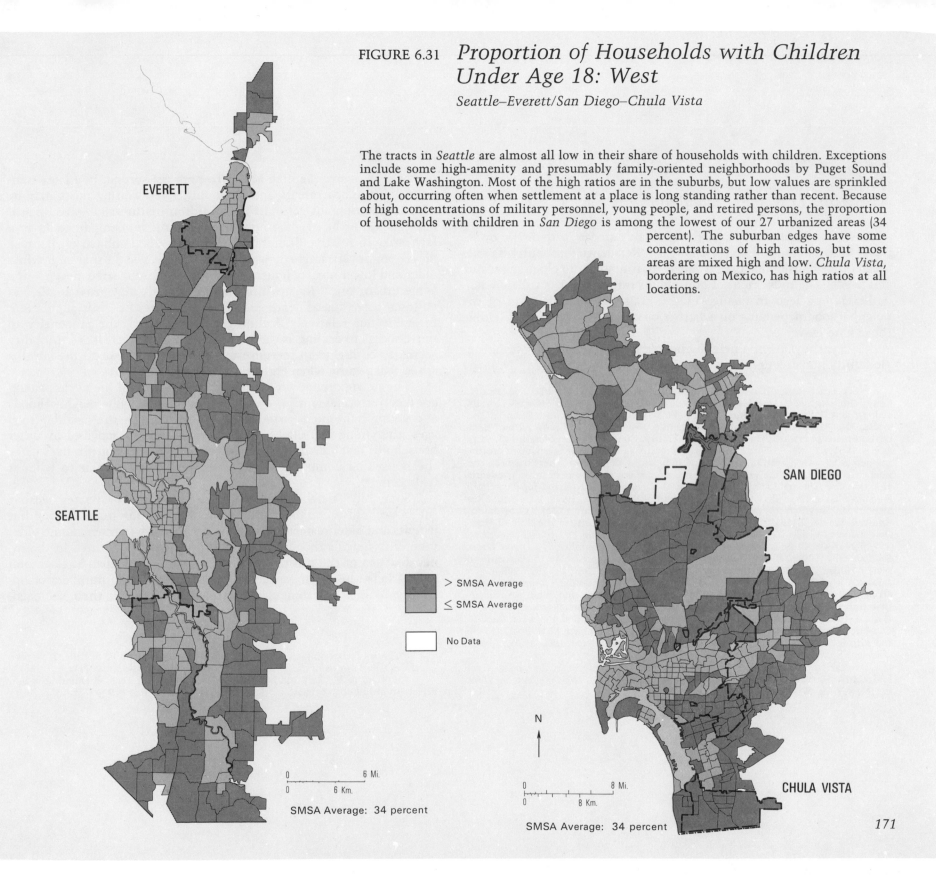

FIGURE 6.31 *Proportion of Households with Children Under Age 18: West*

Seattle–Everett/San Diego–Chula Vista

The tracts in *Seattle* are almost all low in their share of households with children. Exceptions include some high-amenity and presumably family-oriented neighborhoods by Puget Sound and Lake Washington. Most of the high ratios are in the suburbs, but low values are sprinkled about, occurring often when settlement at a place is long standing rather than recent. Because of high concentrations of military personnel, young people, and retired persons, the proportion of households with children in *San Diego* is among the lowest of our 27 urbanized areas (34 percent). The suburban edges have some concentrations of high ratios, but most areas are mixed high and low. *Chula Vista*, bordering on Mexico, has high ratios at all locations.

EVERETT

SEATTLE

SAN DIEGO

CHULA VISTA

> SMSA Average

≤ SMSA Average

No Data

0   6 Mi.

0   6 Km.

SMSA Average: 34 percent

N

0   8 Mi.

0   8 Km.

SMSA Average: 34 percent

171

Persons Aged 5 and Over Who Lived in the Same House in 1975 and 1980: A Measure of Neighborhood Stability

As households pass through successive stages in their life cycle, their housing requirements change.[24] Residential mobility is one means that households use to adjust their housing to changing wants and needs. The movement of households into and out of urban neighborhoods can lead to change in the household composition of the neighborhood depending on whether or not the newcomers resemble those who leave.

The early years of a neighborhood's life cycle normally bring single-family housing units and young families with children.[25] Housing turnover rates may be high as newcomers get settled. In a later transitional stage apartments and other multiple-dwelling units may be added as households get older and children mature and leave. In still later stages of the neighborhood life cycle the housing drops down a few ranks in relative desirability within its areal submarket because newer, more attractive houses have been added farther out while older and lower-quality houses have steadily disappeared closer to the aging urban core.[26] Meanwhile, the households may grow smaller as children leave and as death and divorce deplete the adult population. In stable but relatively declining neighborhoods, the propensity to move seems to decline as the length of residence increases.[27] Mobility seems to be higher in response to overcrowding than to the surplus space that results when children leave home.

The neighborhood life cycle and the household life cycle usually are nicely correlated for the early stages of each. New neighborhoods and young households usually occur together. As the neighborhood ages, the young households may move on and be replaced by other households just starting out. In this case, high rates of turnover leave the household composition of the neighborhood similar to what it had been.

Some older neighborhoods have very low turnover rates because the households are aging without moving. Children are leaving but parents and older residents are under no pressure to move. Some older inner city neighborhoods, especially those that are located in the inner districts of the most vigorously building and expanding sectoral submarkets, are often especially attractive for large numbers of upwardly mobile newcomers who are eager to mark their socioeco-

[24]See Peter Rossi, *Why Families Move* (Glencoe, IL: Free Press, 1955); Paul C. Glick, *American Families*, (New York: Wiley, 1957); Alden Speare, Sidney Goldstein, and William H. Frey, *Residential Mobility, Migration, and Metropolitan Change* (Cambridge, MA: Ballinger, 1975); and G. Sabagh, M. D. Van Arsdol, and E. W. Butler, "Some Determinants of Intra-Urban Residential Mobility: Conceptual Considerations," *Social Forces* 48 (1967): 88–98. Since intraurban mobility is a principal mechanism creating and perpetuating segregation patterns and in breaking them down, there has been considerable interest over the years in learning more about the nature of urban residential mobility. See Chester Rapkin and William G. Grigsby, *The Demand for Housing in Racially Mixed Areas* (Berkeley: University of California Press, 1960); J. O. Huff, "Residential Mobility Patterns and Population Redistribution Within a City," *Geographical Analysis* 11, no. 2 (1979): 133–48; R. J. Struyk, "Determinants of the Role of Home Ownership of Blacks Relative to White Households," *Journal of Urban Economics* 2 (1975): 291–306; D. Bell, "Indebtedness in Black and White Families," *Journal of Urban Economics* 1 (1974): 48–60; A. Anas, "A Probabilistic Approach to the Structure of Rental Housing Markets," *Journal of Urban Economics* 7, no. 2 (1980): 225–47; A. Anas, "A Model of Residential Change and Neighborhood Tipping," *Journal of Urban Economics* 7, no. 3 (1980): 358–70; T. A. Clark, "Race, Class, and Suburban Housing Discrimination: Alternative Judicial Standards of Proof and Relief," *Urban Geography* 2, no. 4 (1981): 327–38; D. J. Morgan, "Residential Housing Abandonment in the U.S.: The Effects on Those Who Remain," *Environment and Planning* 12 (1980): 1343–56; and Ann B. Schnare, "Trends in Residential Segregation by Race: 1960–1970," *Journal of Urban Economics* 7 (1980): 293–301.

[25]Edgar M. Hoover and Raymond E. Vernon, *Anatomy of a Metropolis* (Cambridge, MA: Harvard University Press, 1959); Larry S. Bourne, *The Geography of Housing* (New York: Wiley, 1981).

[26]Charles L. Leven, James T. Little, Hugh O. Nourse, and R. B. Read, *Neighborhood Change: Lessons in the Dynamics of Urban Decay* (New York: Praeger, 1976).

[27]William A. V. Clark and J. O. Huff, "Some Empirical Tests of Duration-of-Stay Effects in Intra-Urban Migration," *Environment and Planning A* 9 (1977): 1357–74.

nomic progress by moving outward in large numbers to better housing. Their increased presence in older, traditionally stable neighborhoods can eventually speed up the departure of overhoused older residents who, like the newcomers, are often part of the mobile middle class and are able and willing to make a move when the need arises. High turnover rates are the result. These events are common on the outer or leading edges of expanding immigrant and minority areas in cities.

The typical geographical pattern that develops in an urbanized area is a "donut of stability" surrounding an unstable core and bounded by unstable edges. The boundaries of some central cities enclose mainly the unstable, high-turnover metropolitan core. Other cities contain most of the urbanized area and all three zones. In debates about planning and local policy questions, the geographical patterning makes a big difference. For instance, if school districts correspond to municipalities, as they do in many northern urbanized areas, problems such as racial balance in schools or efficient management of school facilities can be solved within an overbounded city but would require municipal cooperation to resolve elsewhere.

Measuring Turnover and Stability

In the 1980 census persons aged 5 and older were asked whether or not they had lived in the same house in 1975. The percentage of persons in the same house both years reached the highest level of 63 percent in the slow-growth northeastern urbanized areas of Allentown–Bethlehem–Easton, Paterson–Clifton–Passaic, and Springfield–Chicopee–Holyoke. Places that undergo heavy net outmigration record great stability on the part of those who stay. The low rates of stability occurred in the fast-changing and expanding regional econ-

omies that experienced net inmigration: Denver–Boulder (40 percent), San Diego (37 percent), and Las Vegas (34 percent).

One source of neighborhood stability and strength is the expectation of long-term residence on the part of people living there. These expectations depend in part on social class outlooks and on the financial position of the households. Four kinds of situations arise as the forces underlying the neighborhood life cycle and the household life cycle are played out under constraints of class-based outlooks and finances.

For poor households—living on low and uncertain incomes and without a cushion of savings, wealth, or helpful financial connections—instability in residential arrangements is common and turnover is high. For working-class households of modest but steady income, long-term residence is desirable if it can be achieved. Ties of family, church, and community are important and are broken only with extreme reluctance. Work is locally based and real annual earnings potential of family breadwinners does not increase much over the working years. Workers at skilled trades and lower-level civil servants reach the peak of their buying power early in life. Their neighborhoods are stable because residents do not have to move and they do not want to. Death, divorce, or loss of employment with its financial reverses can force an unwanted move.

The upwardly mobile middle and upper middle classes move for job-related reasons—being transferred by their employers or moving voluntarily to better positions. In addition, when they can afford better housing in a more prestigious setting they try to move to it. Community and neighborhood ties may be strong while they live in a place, but they are quickly severed without remorse when the opportunity arises to move up—and move on.

A final group—very stable—is the rich, who neither want to move nor are required to move. In the accompanying map sets, the stable areas are those whose percentage of households in the same house in 1975 and 1980 is higher than the average for the SMSA.

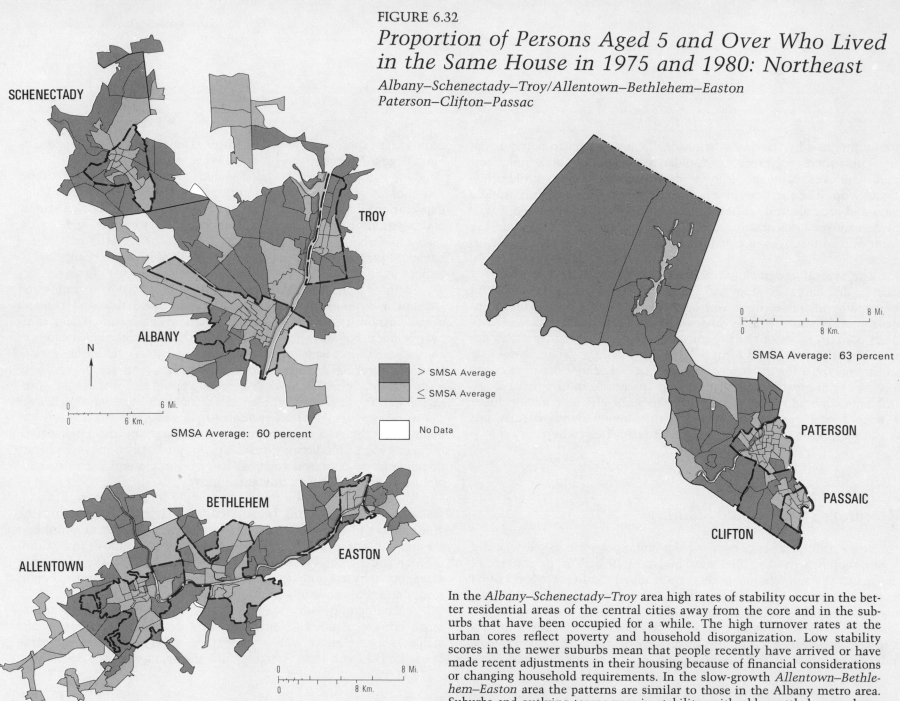

FIGURE 6.32

Proportion of Persons Aged 5 and Over Who Lived in the Same House in 1975 and 1980: Northeast

Albany–Schenectady–Troy/Allentown–Bethlehem–Easton
Paterson–Clifton–Passac

SCHENECTADY

TROY

ALBANY

N

0   6 Mi.
0   6 Km.

SMSA Average: 60 percent

> SMSA Average

≤ SMSA Average

No Data

0   8 Mi.
0   8 Km.

SMSA Average: 63 percent

PATERSON

PASSAIC

CLIFTON

BETHLEHEM

EASTON

ALLENTOWN

0   8 Mi.
0   8 Km.

SMSA Average: 63 percent

In the *Albany–Schenectady–Troy* area high rates of stability occur in the better residential areas of the central cities away from the core and in the suburbs that have been occupied for a while. The high turnover rates at the urban cores reflect poverty and household disorganization. Low stability scores in the newer suburbs mean that people recently have arrived or have made recent adjustments in their housing because of financial considerations or changing household requirements. In the slow-growth *Allentown–Bethlehem–Easton* area the patterns are similar to those in the Albany metro area. Suburbs and outlying towns vary in stability, with older settled areas showing greater stability. The cores of all three cities display the normal unstable pattern of high turnover rental areas. In the *Paterson–Clifton–Passaic* area, almost all central city tracts have low stability, while most suburban tracts show a high percentage of persons in the same house in 1975 and 1980.

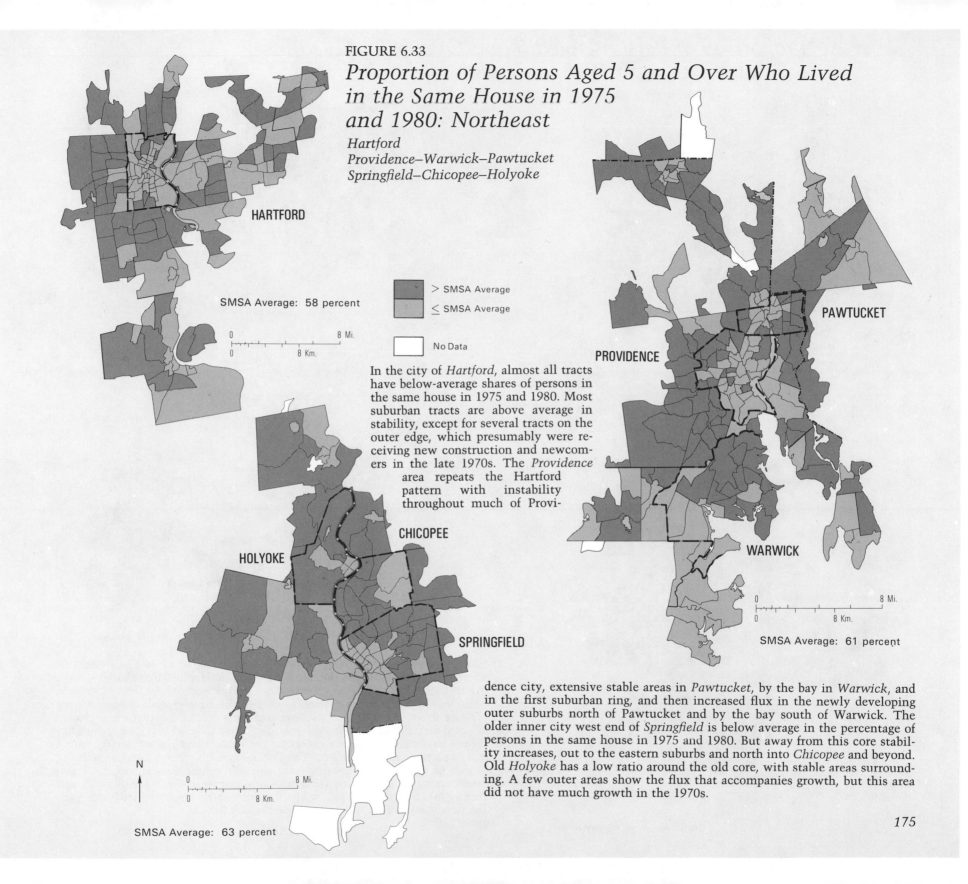

FIGURE 6.33

Proportion of Persons Aged 5 and Over Who Lived in the Same House in 1975 and 1980: Northeast

Hartford
Providence–Warwick–Pawtucket
Springfield–Chicopee–Holyoke

HARTFORD

SMSA Average: 58 percent

0 ——— 8 Mi.
0 ——— 8 Km.

> SMSA Average
≤ SMSA Average
No Data

PROVIDENCE

PAWTUCKET

WARWICK

SMSA Average: 61 percent

HOLYOKE

CHICOPEE

SPRINGFIELD

N

0 ——— 8 Mi.
0 ——— 8 Km.

SMSA Average: 63 percent

In the city of *Hartford*, almost all tracts have below-average shares of persons in the same house in 1975 and 1980. Most suburban tracts are above average in stability, except for several tracts on the outer edge, which presumably were receiving new construction and newcomers in the late 1970s. The *Providence* area repeats the Hartford pattern with instability throughout much of Provi-

dence city, extensive stable areas in *Pawtucket*, by the bay in *Warwick*, and in the first suburban ring, and then increased flux in the newly developing outer suburbs north of Pawtucket and by the bay south of Warwick. The older inner city west end of *Springfield* is below average in the percentage of persons in the same house in 1975 and 1980. But away from this core stability increases, out to the eastern suburbs and north into *Chicopee* and beyond. Old *Holyoke* has a low ratio around the old core, with stable areas surrounding. A few outer areas show the flux that accompanies growth, but this area did not have much growth in the 1970s.

175

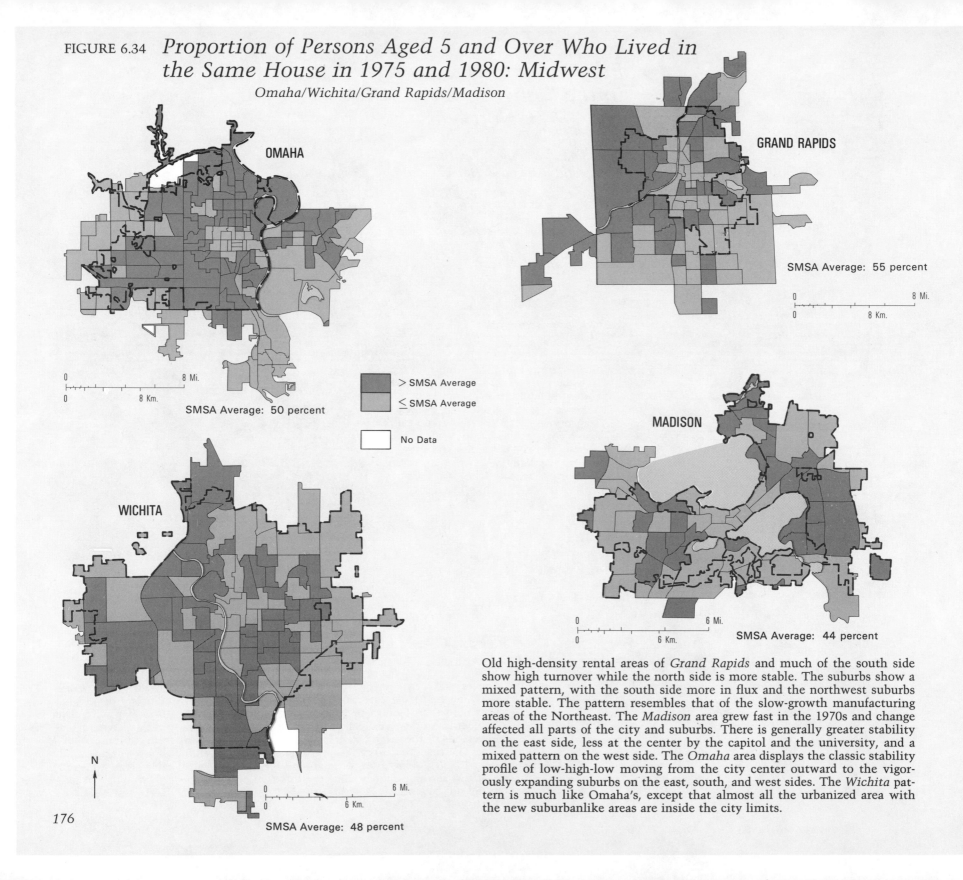

FIGURE 6.34 *Proportion of Persons Aged 5 and Over Who Lived in the Same House in 1975 and 1980: Midwest*

Omaha/Wichita/Grand Rapids/Madison

OMAHA

GRAND RAPIDS

SMSA Average: 55 percent

0   8 Mi.

0   8 Km.

0   8 Mi.

0   8 Km.

> SMSA Average

≤ SMSA Average

No Data

SMSA Average: 50 percent

MADISON

WICHITA

N

0   6 Mi.

0   6 Km.

SMSA Average: 48 percent

0   6 Mi.

0   6 Km.

SMSA Average: 44 percent

Old high-density rental areas of *Grand Rapids* and much of the south side show high turnover while the north side is more stable. The suburbs show a mixed pattern, with the south side more in flux and the northwest suburbs more stable. The pattern resembles that of the slow-growth manufacturing areas of the Northeast. The *Madison* area grew fast in the 1970s and change affected all parts of the city and suburbs. There is generally greater stability on the east side, less at the center by the capitol and the university, and a mixed pattern on the west side. The *Omaha* area displays the classic stability profile of low-high-low moving from the city center outward to the vigorously expanding suburbs on the east, south, and west sides. The *Wichita* pattern is much like Omaha's, except that almost all the urbanized area with the new suburbanlike areas are inside the city limits.

176

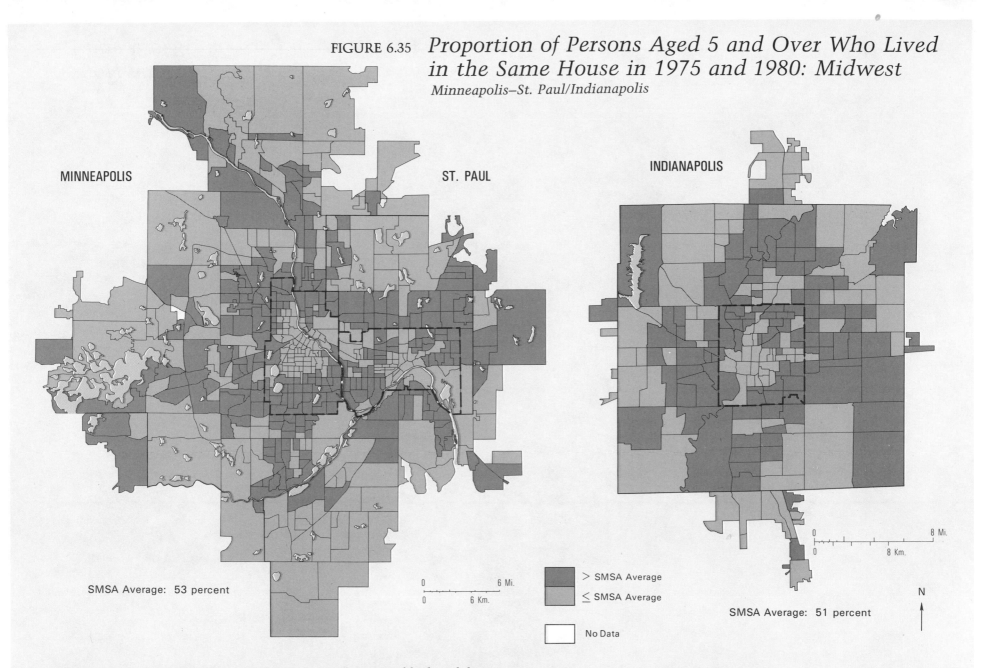

FIGURE 6.35 *Proportion of Persons Aged 5 and Over Who Lived in the Same House in 1975 and 1980: Midwest*
Minneapolis–St. Paul/Indianapolis

MINNEAPOLIS

ST. PAUL

INDIANAPOLIS

SMSA Average: 53 percent

6 Mi.
6 Km.

8 Mi.
8 Km.

> SMSA Average

≤ SMSA Average

No Data

SMSA Average: 51 percent

N

In the Twin Cities area (*Minneapolis* and *St. Paul*), a ring of high stability surrounds the cores of both central cities and covers their outer edges and first-tier suburbs. High turnover rates are common around the two downtowns and in the vigorous suburbs, especially in the south, north, and west. High-amenity neighborhoods in both central cities are very stable. The pattern is the same in the *Indianapolis* area except that the unstable core covers a larger share of the central city. Stable first-tier suburbs are ringed by new areas and newly arrived households.

177

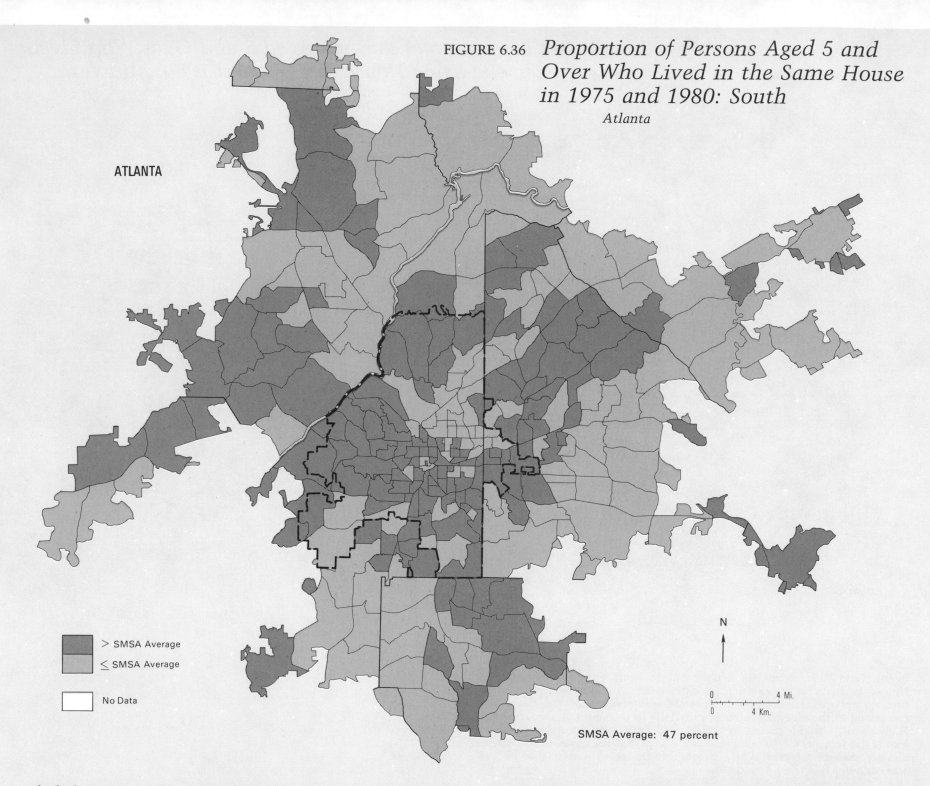

FIGURE 6.36 *Proportion of Persons Aged 5 and Over Who Lived in the Same House in 1975 and 1980: South*

Atlanta

ATLANTA

> SMSA Average

≤ SMSA Average

No Data

N

0   4 Mi.

0   4 Km.

SMSA Average: 47 percent

The high turnover core in *Atlanta* lies just at the north of downtown, the inner reaches of the white upper-middle-class growth sector that sprawls to the north-northeast. The ring of highly stable tracts includes most of the west-side black area and the first ring of suburbs. Outer suburbs on the east and north sides are below average in stability, while the south and west sides show mixtures of older settled areas and new subdivisions of the 1970s.

FIGURE 6.37

Proportion of Persons Aged 5 and Over Who Lived in the Same House in 1975 and 1980: South

Raleigh–Durham/Orlando

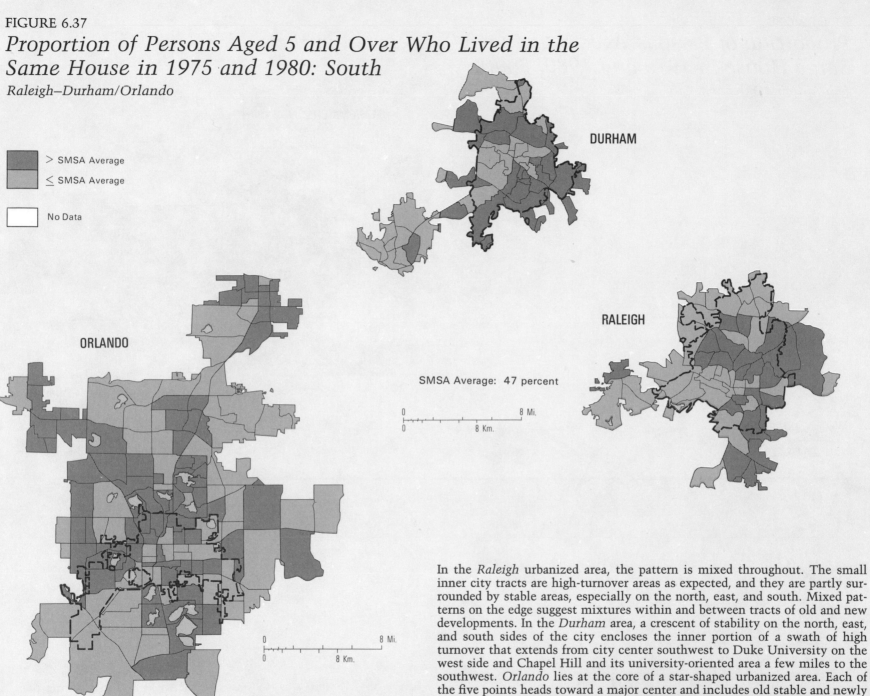

> SMSA Average

≤ SMSA Average

No Data

DURHAM

SMSA Average: 47 percent

0   8 Mi.

0   8 Km.

RALEIGH

ORLANDO

N

SMSA Average: 42 percent

0   8 Mi.

0   8 Km.

In the *Raleigh* urbanized area, the pattern is mixed throughout. The small inner city tracts are high-turnover areas as expected, and they are partly surrounded by stable areas, especially on the north, east, and south. Mixed patterns on the edge suggest mixtures within and between tracts of old and new developments. In the *Durham* area, a crescent of stability on the north, east, and south sides of the city encloses the inner portion of a swath of high turnover that extends from city center southwest to Duke University on the west side and Chapel Hill and its university-oriented area a few miles to the southwest. *Orlando* lies at the core of a star-shaped urbanized area. Each of the five points heads toward a major center and includes old stable and newly built-up areas. The largest developments protrude to the northwest (Gainesville), northeast (Daytona Beach), and east (Cape Canaveral). Extensions southwest (Disney World, Tampa–St. Petersburg) and southeast (Miami) are more muted. The city core is more mixed than normal.

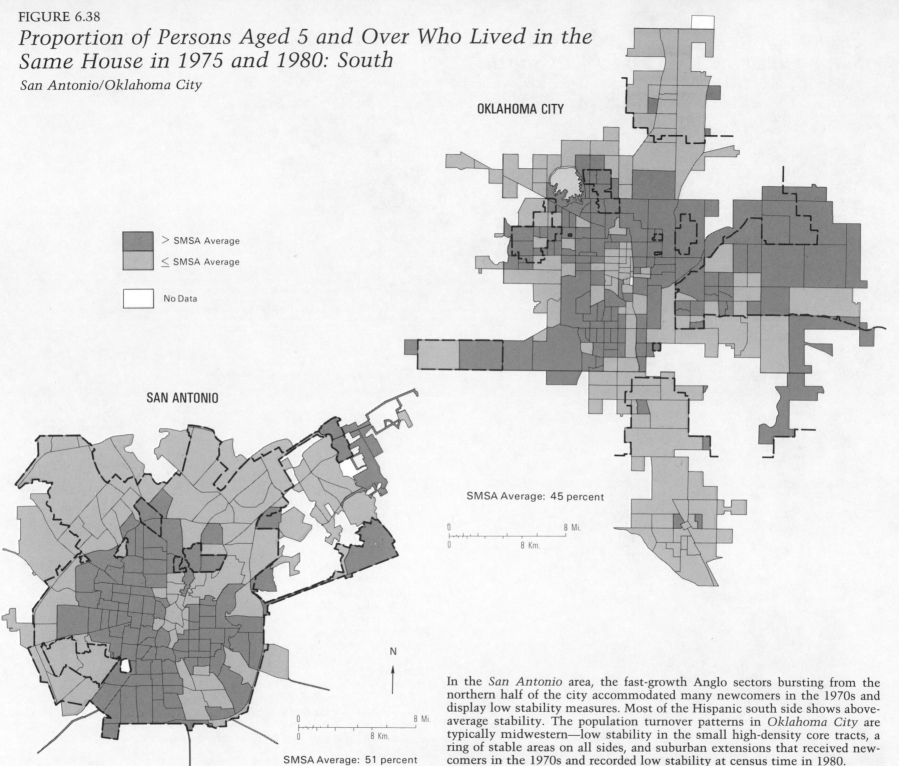

FIGURE 6.38

Proportion of Persons Aged 5 and Over Who Lived in the Same House in 1975 and 1980: South

San Antonio/Oklahoma City

OKLAHOMA CITY

> SMSA Average

≤ SMSA Average

No Data

SMSA Average: 45 percent

0   8 Mi.

0   8 Km.

SAN ANTONIO

N

0   8 Mi.

0   8 Km.

SMSA Average: 51 percent

In the *San Antonio* area, the fast-growth Anglo sectors bursting from the northern half of the city accommodated many newcomers in the 1970s and display low stability measures. Most of the Hispanic south side shows above-average stability. The population turnover patterns in *Oklahoma City* are typically midwestern—low stability in the small high-density core tracts, a ring of stable areas on all sides, and suburban extensions that received newcomers in the 1970s and recorded low stability at census time in 1980.

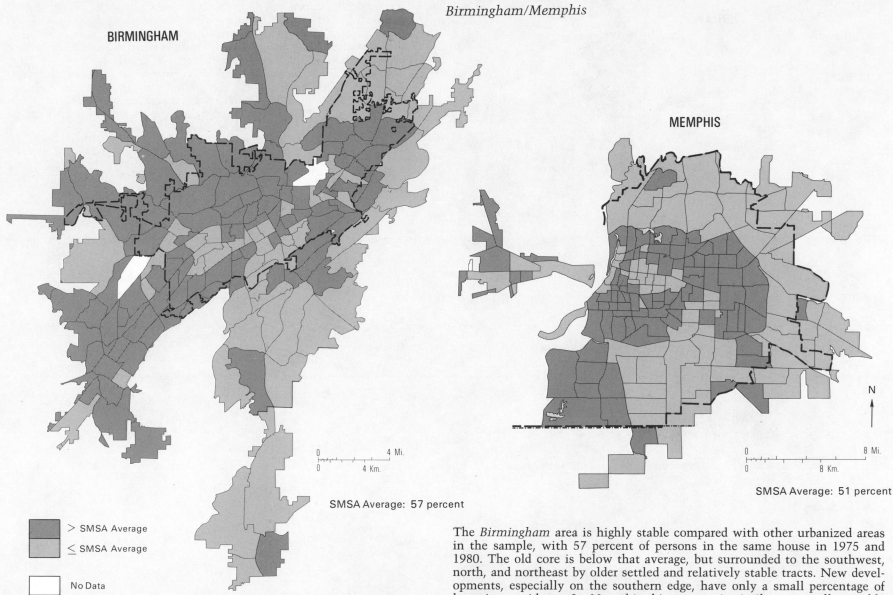

FIGURE 6.39

Proportion of Persons Aged 5 and Over Who Lived in the Same House in 1975 and 1980: South

Birmingham/Memphis

BIRMINGHAM

MEMPHIS

N

0   4 Mi.

0   4 Km.

0   8 Mi.

0   8 Km.

SMSA Average: 57 percent

SMSA Average: 51 percent

■ > SMSA Average

▨ ≤ SMSA Average

□ No Data

The *Birmingham* area is highly stable compared with other urbanized areas in the sample, with 57 percent of persons in the same house in 1975 and 1980. The old core is below that average, but surrounded to the southwest, north, and northeast by older settled and relatively stable tracts. New developments, especially on the southern edge, have only a small percentage of long-time residents. In *Memphis* this pattern is similar, as small unstable inner city tracts flank the old east-west corridor across the Mississippi River and through the city. Highly stable tracts surround the core; and because most of the urbanized area falls inside the city, many of the new residential developments with their low-stability indices lie inside the city limits.

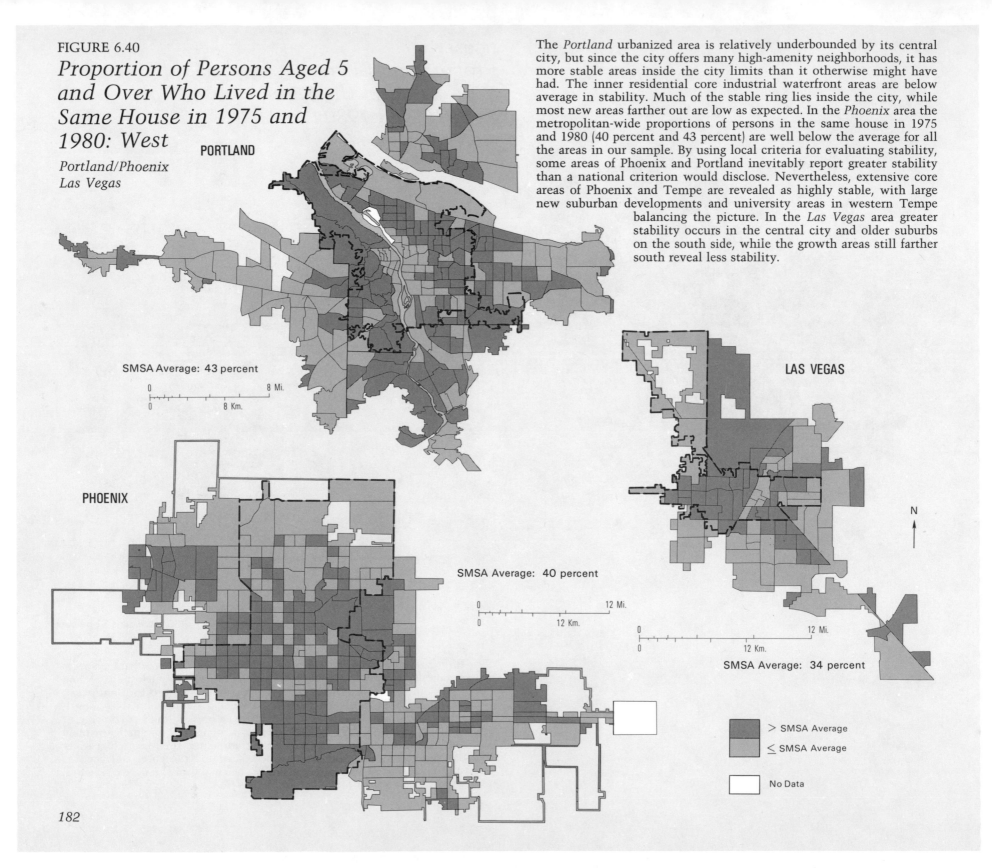

FIGURE 6.40

Proportion of Persons Aged 5 and Over Who Lived in the Same House in 1975 and 1980: West

Portland/Phoenix
Las Vegas

PORTLAND

SMSA Average: 43 percent

0 ——————————— 8 Mi.
0 ——————————— 8 Km.

LAS VEGAS

PHOENIX

SMSA Average: 40 percent

0 ——————————— 12 Mi.
0 ——————————— 12 Km.

0 ——————————— 12 Mi.
0 ——————————— 12 Km.

SMSA Average: 34 percent

N

> SMSA Average

≤ SMSA Average

No Data

The *Portland* urbanized area is relatively underbounded by its central city, but since the city offers many high-amenity neighborhoods, it has more stable areas inside the city limits than it otherwise might have had. The inner residential core industrial waterfront areas are below average in stability. Much of the stable ring lies inside the city, while most new areas farther out are low as expected. In the *Phoenix* area the metropolitan-wide proportions of persons in the same house in 1975 and 1980 (40 percent and 43 percent) are well below the average for all the areas in our sample. By using local criteria for evaluating stability, some areas of Phoenix and Portland inevitably report greater stability than a national criterion would disclose. Nevertheless, extensive core areas of Phoenix and Tempe are revealed as highly stable, with large new suburban developments and university areas in western Tempe balancing the picture. In the *Las Vegas* area greater stability occurs in the central city and older suburbs on the south side, while the growth areas still farther south reveal less stability.

182

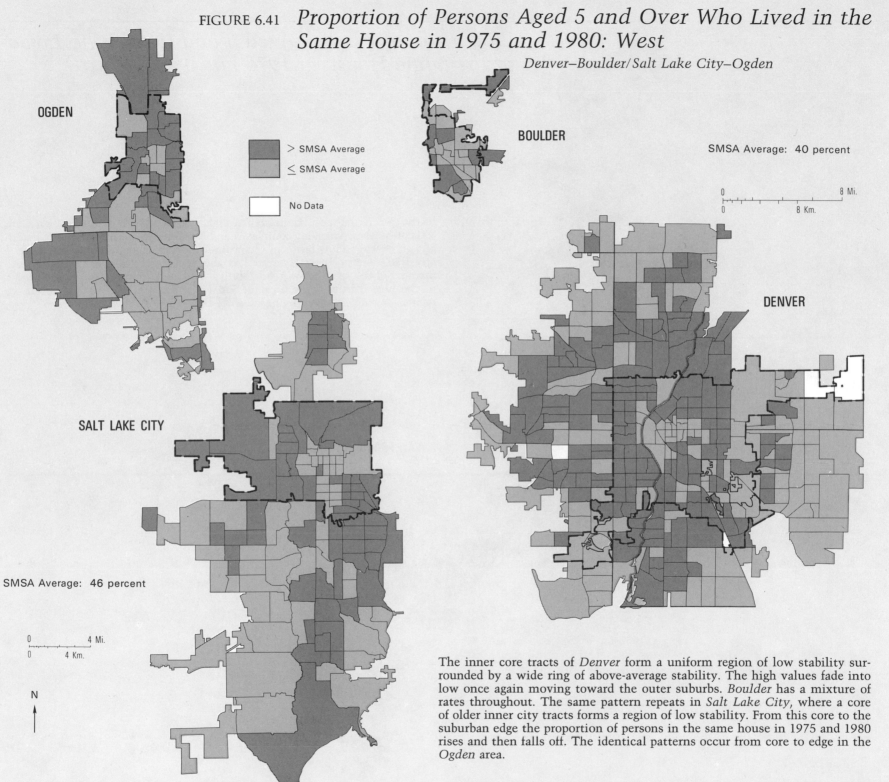

FIGURE 6.41 *Proportion of Persons Aged 5 and Over Who Lived in the Same House in 1975 and 1980: West*

Denver–Boulder/Salt Lake City–Ogden

OGDEN

> SMSA Average

≤ SMSA Average

No Data

BOULDER

SMSA Average: 40 percent

0   8 Mi.

0   8 Km.

DENVER

SALT LAKE CITY

SMSA Average: 46 percent

0   4 Mi.

0   4 Km.

N

The inner core tracts of *Denver* form a uniform region of low stability surrounded by a wide ring of above-average stability. The high values fade into low once again moving toward the outer suburbs. *Boulder* has a mixture of rates throughout. The same pattern repeats in *Salt Lake City*, where a core of older inner city tracts forms a region of low stability. From this core to the suburban edge the proportion of persons in the same house in 1975 and 1980 rises and then falls off. The identical patterns occur from core to edge in the *Ogden* area.

FIGURE 6.42

Proportion of Persons Aged 5 and Over Who Lived in the Same House in 1975 and 1980: West

San Francisco

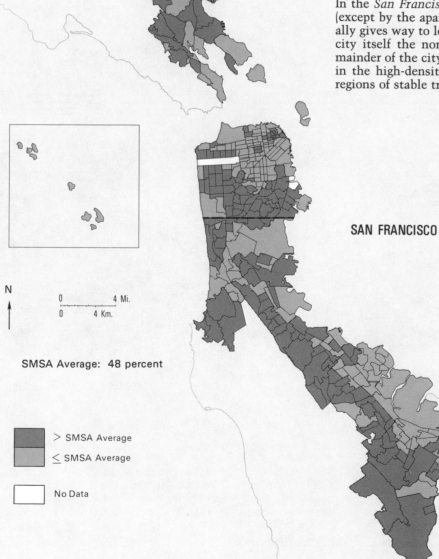

In the *San Francisco* urbanized area high stability north of the Golden Gate (except by the apartment complexes and tourist traps near the bridge) gradually gives way to low ratios in the northern new developments. In the central city itself the northeast quarter has above-average turnover, while the remainder of the city shows great stability. The large numbers of mobile people in the high-density inner areas of San Francisco are balanced by extensive regions of stable tracts ranging south of the city to Palo Alto.

SAN FRANCISCO

N

0   4 Mi.
0   4 Km.

SMSA Average: 48 percent

> SMSA Average

≤ SMSA Average

No Data

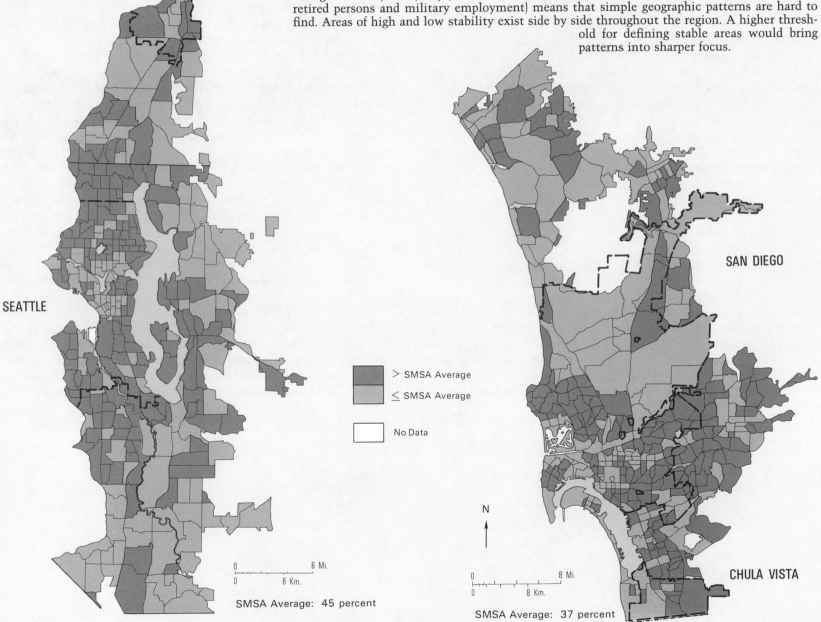

FIGURE 6.43

Proportion of Persons Aged 5 and Over Who Lived in the Same House in 1975 and 1980: West

Seattle–Everett/San Diego–Chula Vista

The peculiar site of the *Seattle-Everett* urbanized area makes the midwestern pattern of unstable core and edges, separated by a "donut of stability," harder to see, but it is present nonetheless. In *San Diego* the extremely low rate of stability (37 percent) combined with the highly variegated site (ocean, bays, and mountains) and unusual economy (significant presence of retired persons and military employment) means that simple geographic patterns are hard to find. Areas of high and low stability exist side by side throughout the region. A higher threshold for defining stable areas would bring patterns into sharper focus.

EVERETT

SEATTLE

> SMSA Average

≤ SMSA Average

No Data

SAN DIEGO

CHULA VISTA

N

0   6 Mi.

0   6 Km.

SMSA Average: 45 percent

0   8 Mi.

0   8 Km.

SMSA Average: 37 percent

Black Shifts from Inner City Rentals
to Owner Occupancy Farther Out

During the middle 1970s black households increasingly shifted away from the congested cores of the central cities and moved outward to owner occupancy and to suburbia. Some of the movement was direct intraurban migration, with households relocating from an inner city address to an outer city or a suburban one. The rest of the shift was due to natural change as elderly blacks died in old neighborhoods near the urban core while black children were born to peripheral central city and suburban families.

The greatest real and symbolic progress has been made by blacks in suburbia. Although the numbers of blacks in suburbia are still small, they are increasing steadily. Of those who moved to suburbs, approximately 40 percent went to white neighborhoods (defined as 90 percent or more white). In contrast, 99 percent of whites who moved to suburbs entered white neighborhoods. The suburbs to which blacks moved generally had lower socioeconomic levels than those that whites entered. Twice as many blacks as whites moved to low-income suburban neighborhoods.[28]

Blacks were less than 5 percent of suburban population as late as 1970, when central cities were over 20 percent black and several important cities had black majorities. Suburban blacks historically lived in marginal places, often in all-black towns, or outlying poverty pockets, or as pioneers in all-white areas. The social and economic distance between whites and suburban blacks was great in these early cases.[29] "More often than not, blacks were an accidental prior presence in areas that became suburbs—rather than participants in the upward residential mobility that suburbia stereotypically represented for whites."[30]

During the 1970s suburban black population increased 40 percent compared with a 10 percent increase for whites. As blacks have been moving into suburban settings and becoming owner occupants at rapid rates, several explanations for the trend have been advanced. First, improved black access to the suburbs suggests that the desire for social homogeneity on the part of persons already residents in suburbia is diminishing. Social contacts in suburbia, it is argued, are less neighborly and more extra-local, so that the race of neighbors has become less important than it was in earlier decades. This argument seems more valid for wealthy areas and for working-class suburbs where residents' sense of their social position is unambiguous. It seems less likely for insecure residents of middle- and upper-middle-class areas where it is hoped that geographical location will help to testify to socioeconomic achievement.

A second proposed explanation for rapid entry of blacks into suburbia is that suburban homogeneity persists as a desired state, but the increasing black suburbanization is evidence that race is losing its importance as a major status-differentiating criterion or as a predictor of social class.[31] This argument seems likely to hold in places of significantly increasing prosperity, where the economic gains of one group are generally not seen as achieved at the expense of others, and in places of heavy long-term inmigration, where population diversity is familiar rather than strange.

The third explanation is that the suburban desire for population homogeneity and the invidiousness of race persist as strong sentiments and outlooks, but that black suburbanization is synonymous

[28]Larry Long, *Black Movers to the Suburbs: Are They Moving to Predominantly White Neighborhoods?* (Washington, DC: U.S. Bureau of the Census, Center for Demographic Studies, 1980).

[29]Robert W. Lake, *The New Suburbanites* (New Brunswick, NJ: Center for Urban Policy Research, Rutgers University, 1981).

[30]Ibid., p. 3.
[31]Ibid., pp. 4–5.

with neither social nor spatial integration. According to this view, segregation persists in suburbia by means of black towns, black subdivisions, and black enclaves that are hard to see in geographical data series that are too coarse-grained.[32]

In the United States in 1980 black owner-occupied housing was 7.2 percent (over 3.7 million of almost 51.8 million), or one owner-occupied unit in 14. The average for urbanized areas of 5.2 percent varied sharply between 7.4 percent in central cities where most urban blacks live and only 2.9 percent in suburbs. Outside urbanized areas in towns and small cities with populations of 10,000 or more black owner occupancy averaged 3.8 percent; in urban places of 2,500 to 10,000, only 3.6 percent. Rural owner occupants, both farm and nonfarm, were 3.7 percent black, but those numbers (727,000 of 19.8 million) are a small proportion of the national totals.

In the comparative map series presented here, a tract is shaded dark if black owner-occupied housing units as a share of all owner-occupied units exceed 5 percent, or one in 20. When applied to all 27 urbanized areas (and to 19 additional central cities in the subsequent analysis), this criterion not only portrays the locations of significant black strides toward full residential achievement in these metro areas, but does so in a way that permits comparison of large differences from one metro area to another.

[32]Harold M. Rose, *Black Suburbanization: Access to Improved Quality of Life or Maintenance of the Status Quo?* (Cambridge MA: Ballinger, 1976).

FIGURE 6.44

Black Owner-Occupied Housing as a Share of All Owner-Occupied Housing: Northeast

Albany–Schenectady–Troy/Allentown–Bethlehem–Easton
Paterson–Clifton–Passaic

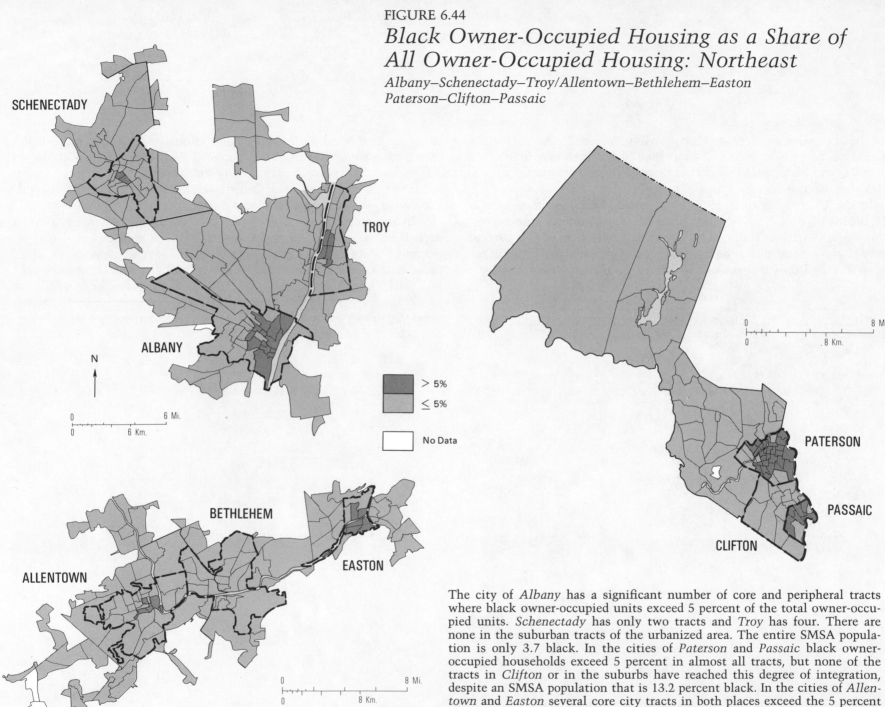

> 5%

≤ 5%

No Data

The city of *Albany* has a significant number of core and peripheral tracts where black owner-occupied units exceed 5 percent of the total owner-occupied units. *Schenectady* has only two tracts and *Troy* has four. There are none in the suburban tracts of the urbanized area. The entire SMSA population is only 3.7 black. In the cities of *Paterson* and *Passaic* black owner-occupied households exceed 5 percent in almost all tracts, but none of the tracts in *Clifton* or in the suburbs have reached this degree of integration, despite an SMSA population that is 13.2 percent black. In the cities of *Allentown* and *Easton* several core city tracts in both places exceed the 5 percent threshold, but none have reached 5 percent in *Bethlehem* or in the suburban tracts of the urbanized area. Yet with an SMSA population only 1.4 percent black, that any at all exceed 5 percent is due only to blacks being concentrated in certain neighborhoods.

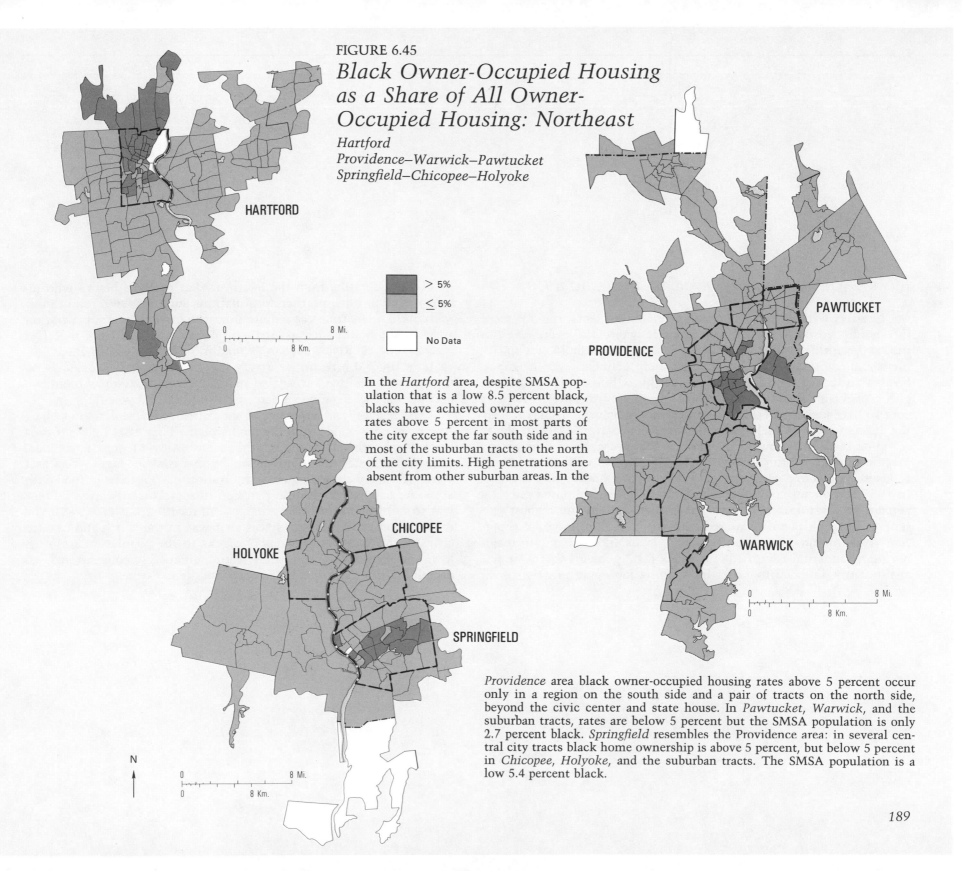

FIGURE 6.45

Black Owner-Occupied Housing as a Share of All Owner-Occupied Housing: Northeast

Hartford
Providence–Warwick–Pawtucket
Springfield–Chicopee–Holyoke

HARTFORD

> 5%

≤ 5%

No Data

0   8 Mi.

0   8 Km.

PAWTUCKET

PROVIDENCE

WARWICK

0   8 Mi.

0   8 Km.

CHICOPEE

HOLYOKE

SPRINGFIELD

N

0   8 Mi.

0   8 Km.

In the *Hartford* area, despite SMSA population that is a low 8.5 percent black, blacks have achieved owner occupancy rates above 5 percent in most parts of the city except the far south side and in most of the suburban tracts to the north of the city limits. High penetrations are absent from other suburban areas. In the

Providence area black owner-occupied housing rates above 5 percent occur only in a region on the south side and a pair of tracts on the north side, beyond the civic center and state house. In *Pawtucket*, *Warwick*, and the suburban tracts, rates are below 5 percent but the SMSA population is only 2.7 percent black. *Springfield* resembles the Providence area: in several central city tracts black home ownership is above 5 percent, but below 5 percent in *Chicopee*, *Holyoke*, and the suburban tracts. The SMSA population is a low 5.4 percent black.

Black Owner-Occupied Housing in the Central City

In cities with a high proportion of black residents, the 5 percent threshold is easier to exceed than in cities where blacks are few. But trial and error demonstrated that the 5 percent threshold was convenient and informative. It permitted a sharp delineation of neighborhoods that lacked significant numbers of black households because of either exclusionary practices or black hesitancy to enter. And in a comparative map series the uniform threshold helps to display starkly the differences in the relative presence of blacks from place to place.

A household is counted as black if the householder—the person in column one of the census questionnaire, who filled in the responses—is black, regardless of the race of other household members. In 1983 interracial couples in the United States composed only 1.4 percent of the total. The metro areas that contain the highest percentage of black population are southern cities (Baltimore, 25.6 percent; Washington, 27.9 percent; New Orleans, 32.6 percent) or major northern industrial centers like Newark (21.3 percent) that were not significantly shielded by other intervening job opportunities sought by blacks migrating from the South or that received blacks who remigrated from other northern destinations such as New York or Philadelphia. The metro areas remote from the major black outmigration areas in the South such as Anaheim–Santa Ana–Garden Grove (1.3 percent black), Riverside–San Bernardino–Ontario (5.0 percent), or Sacramento (6.0 percent) have very low percentages of blacks, as do the metro areas that lie beyond major intervening employment opportunities, like Boston (5.8 percent) or Buffalo (9.2 percent).

The maps reveal an aspect of the continued segregation of black American households from the mainstream. They also highlight how black neighborhoods in the Northeast and Midwest grew up at locations on the inner side of middle- and upper-middle-class sectors that were vigorously expanding outward to suburbia. Patterns in the South are more patchy because the tradition of social stratification by race was so well established that geographical location was not among the most important symbols of status as it was in the North and East. In cities of the West, proportions of blacks in the population are often low, but black owner occupancy seems remarkably concentrated, especially in the California cities portrayed here.

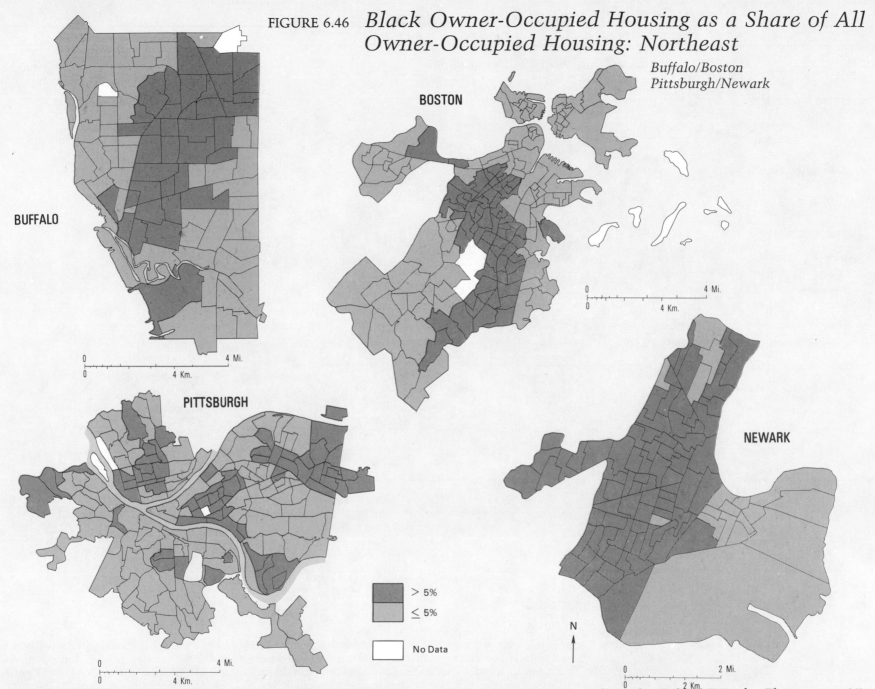

FIGURE 6.46 *Black Owner-Occupied Housing as a Share of All Owner-Occupied Housing: Northeast*

Buffalo/Boston
Pittsburgh/Newark

BUFFALO

BOSTON

PITTSBURGH

NEWARK

> 5%

≤ 5%

No Data

N

A wedge of black homeownership extends northeast and somewhat east and south from downtown *Buffalo*, matching closely the traditional black neighborhood in a metro area that is 9.2 percent black. In *Boston* the sector of black owner occupancy runs southwest of downtown to and through the Roxbury district, the traditional route of residential mobility to better neighborhoods farther out. The sector is small but dense, in a metro area that is 5.8 percent black.[33] *Pittsburgh* grew up where the Allegheny River (from the northeast) and the Monongahela River (from the southeast) join to form the

Ohio River running west from the Golden Triangle. The upper-middle-class residential corridor developed east of city center, and as it pushed farther eastward black newcomers filled in behind, defining today's major black district in a metro area only 7.8 percent black. Additional black settlement has developed in old and lower-priced housing, near industrialized river valleys. A high proportion of blacks in the *Newark* metro area (21.3 percent) means that most tracts in the central city exceed easily the "5 percent of owner-occupied housing" threshold—except for an exclusive extension on the west side and eastern tracts by Newark Bay.

[33]See R. Schafer, "Racial Discrimination in the Boston Housing Market," *Journal of Urban Economics* 6, no. 2 (1979): 176–96.

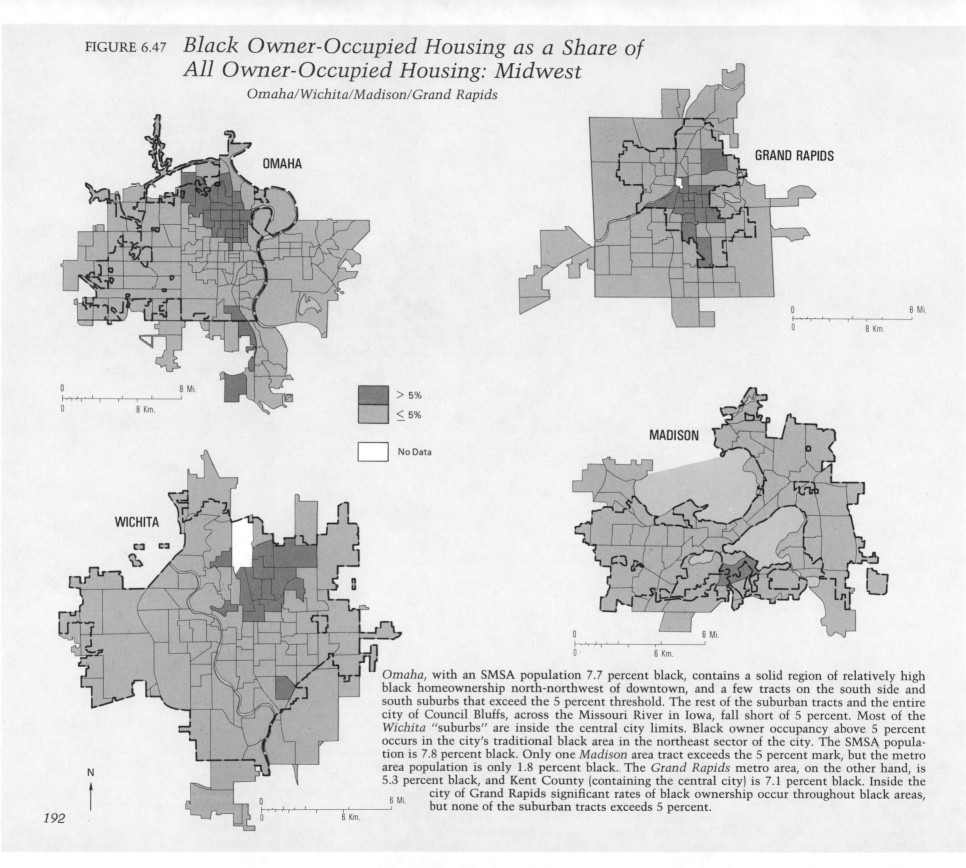

FIGURE 6.47 *Black Owner-Occupied Housing as a Share of All Owner-Occupied Housing: Midwest*
Omaha/Wichita/Madison/Grand Rapids

OMAHA

GRAND RAPIDS

0   8 Mi.
0   8 Km.

> 5%

≤ 5%

No Data

0   8 Mi.
0   8 Km.

MADISON

WICHITA

N

0   6 Mi.
0   6 Km.

0   6 Mi.
0   6 Km.

Omaha, with an SMSA population 7.7 percent black, contains a solid region of relatively high black homeownership north-northwest of downtown, and a few tracts on the south side and south suburbs that exceed the 5 percent threshold. The rest of the suburban tracts and the entire city of Council Bluffs, across the Missouri River in Iowa, fall short of 5 percent. Most of the *Wichita* "suburbs" are inside the central city limits. Black owner occupancy above 5 percent occurs in the city's traditional black area in the northeast sector of the city. The SMSA population is 7.8 percent black. Only one *Madison* area tract exceeds the 5 percent mark, but the metro area population is only 1.8 percent black. The *Grand Rapids* metro area, on the other hand, is 5.3 percent black, and Kent County (containing the central city) is 7.1 percent black. Inside the city of Grand Rapids significant rates of black ownership occur throughout black areas, but none of the suburban tracts exceeds 5 percent.

FIGURE 6.48 *Black Owner-Occupied Housing as a Share of All Owner-Occupied Housing: Midwest*

Minneapolis–St. Paul/Indianapolis

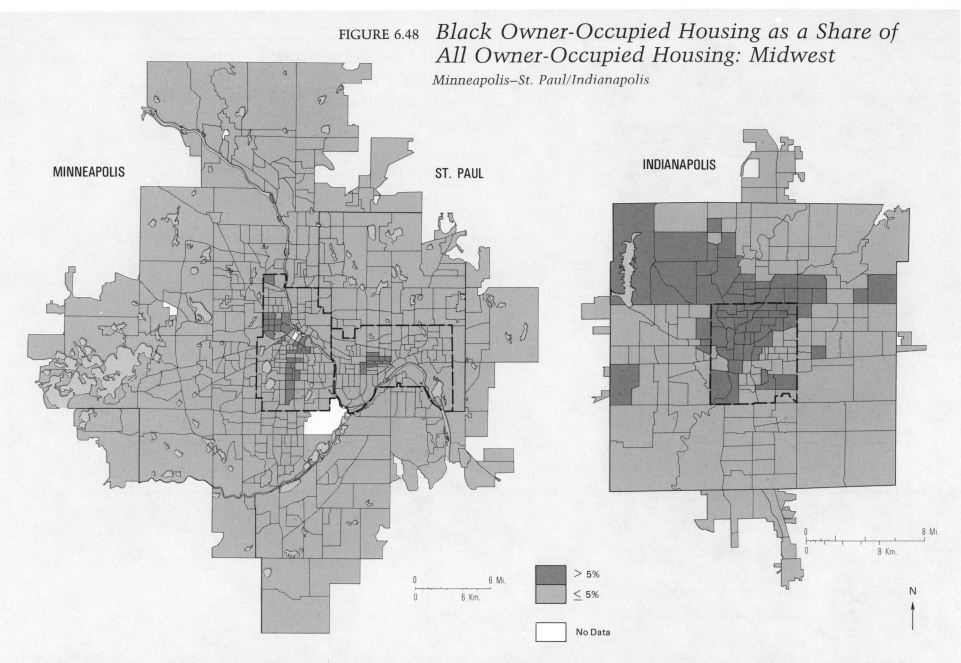

MINNEAPOLIS

ST. PAUL

INDIANAPOLIS

> 5%

≤ 5%

No Data

N

The 50,000 blacks in the *Minneapolis–St. Paul* metro area constitute 2.4 percent of the population, while the 157,000 blacks in the Indianapolis SMSA, a metro area about half as big in population and two thirds the area, are 13.5 percent of the total. In the Twin Cities black owner-occupied units exceed 5 percent in the north-side black area stretching west to the city limits, the south-side black area, and the St. Paul black neighborhood west of down-town. None of the suburban tracts have achieved the 5 percent mark. In the *Indianapolis* area, where blacks are proportionately a much bigger presence, they have not only exceeded the 5 percent threshold in all parts of the city, but have entered suburbs on the north, east, and west sides to a significant degree.

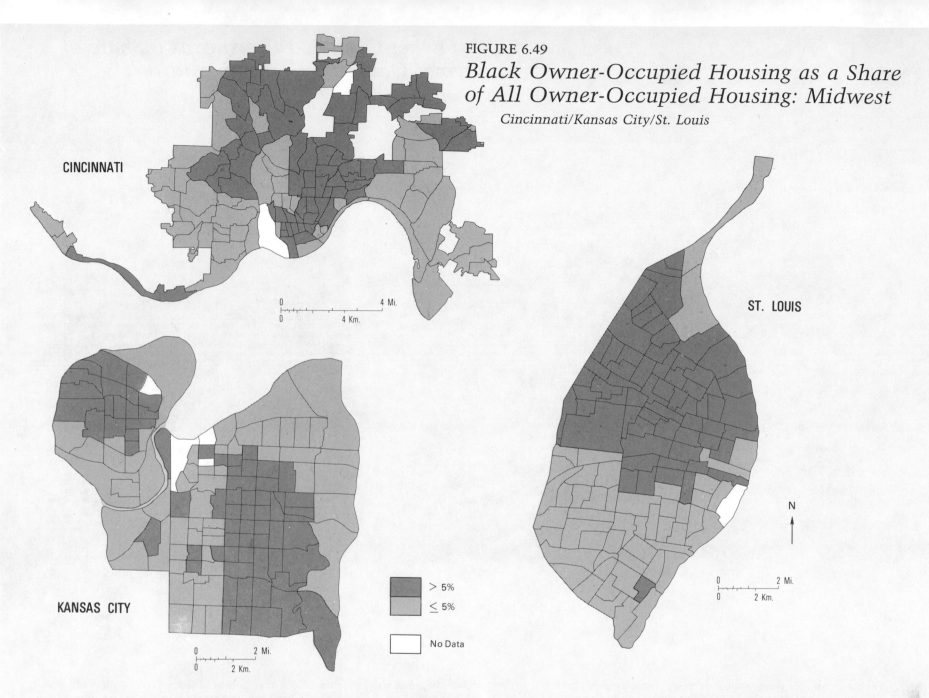

FIGURE 6.49

Black Owner-Occupied Housing as a Share of All Owner-Occupied Housing: Midwest

Cincinnati/Kansas City/St. Louis

CINCINNATI

ST. LOUIS

0   4 Mi.
0   4 Km.

N

KANSAS CITY

> 5%

≤ 5%

No Data

0   2 Mi.
0   2 Km.

0   2 Mi.
0   2 Km.

Cincinnati developed just beyond the north bend in the Ohio River, a convenient deep-water river port heavily used by settlers coming downriver from Pittsburgh and the East to settle southern Ohio in the early nineteenth century. Local urban development fanned out in all directions, with the vigorous middle-class wedge to the north eventually filling in with black newcomers (12.4 percent black in the metro area) and black owner occupants to the edge of the city. *Kansas City*, Missouri (east side), and Kansas City, Kansas (west), lie south of the Missouri River, just at the mouth of the Kansas River, which

enters from the southwest. The metro area is 13.0 percent black, with each city having its own black concentration extending from respective city centers outward to the suburban edges. Downtown *St. Louis* developed around the nation's first bridge over the lower Mississippi River carrying east-west rail traffic. Early road traffic northwest to St. Charles on the Missouri River pulled middle-class merchant trade, their homes, and eventually the black settled area in that direction, all the way into the suburbs and away from the white, blue collar, industrial south side. The metro area is 17.3 percent black.

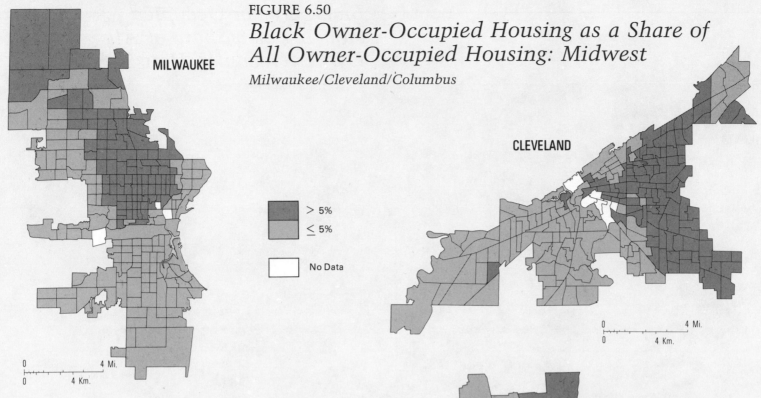

FIGURE 6.50

Black Owner-Occupied Housing as a Share of All Owner-Occupied Housing: Midwest

Milwaukee/Cleveland/Columbus

MILWAUKEE

CLEVELAND

> 5%

≤ 5%

No Data

0 — 4 Mi.

0 — 4 Km.

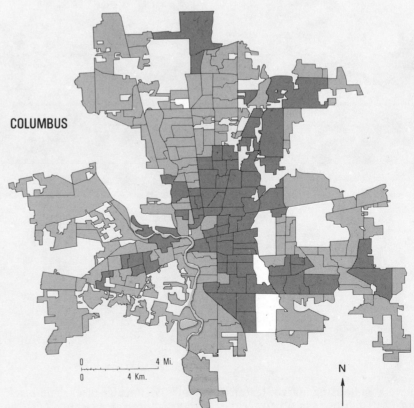

COLUMBUS

The pattern in *Milwaukee* is much like that in St. Louis, and for the same reasons. A wedge of black settlement extends northwest of downtown, on Lake Michigan. It filled in behind upwardly mobile whites who moved on, creating numerous vacancies taken by black newcomers. Tracts near the lake feature expensive housing and few black owner occupants. In the metro area the black population is 10.8 percent, but blacks are virtually absent from the half of the city south of downtown. Downtown *Cleveland* developed on the right bank where the Cuyahoga River empties into Lake Erie. Rail lines followed ancient lake beach ridges to cities to the east and New York, pulling middle-class housing—and eventually black settlement—eastward. A second, southeastern upper-middle-class thrust to suburban Shaker Heights produced a second spate of housing vacancies into which black newcomers settled. The stable white, blue collar west side has little of the area's 18.2 percent black population. The *Columbus* metro area is 12.3 percent black. The city developed on the east side of the Scioto River, just below its confluence with the Olentangy River from the north. Significant black homeownership occurs in a major sector to the northeast and a smaller sector east of downtown.

FIGURE 6.51 *Black Owner-Occupied Housing as a Share of All Owner-Occupied Housing: South*

Atlanta

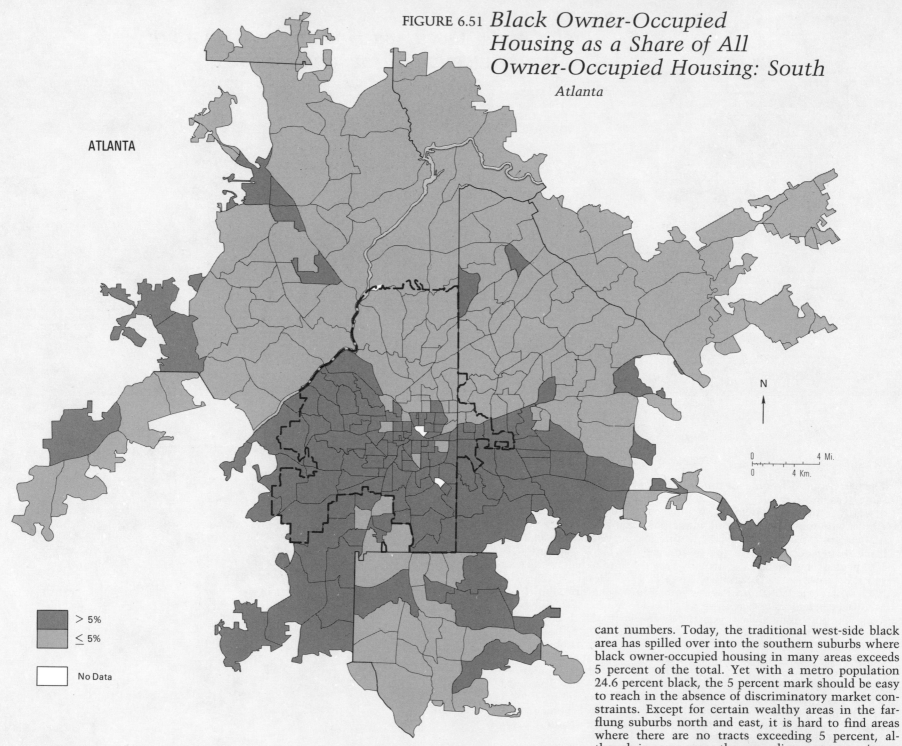

ATLANTA

> 5%

≤ 5%

No Data

N

0   4 Mi.
0   4 Km.

The *Atlanta* area housing market featured new subdivisions for blacks and black suburbs well before most other American urban regions. Although these areas were a creation and a legacy of a highly segregated housing market, they invited black owners into the suburbs in signifi-

cant numbers. Today, the traditional west-side black area has spilled over into the southern suburbs where black owner-occupied housing in many areas exceeds 5 percent of the total. Yet with a metro population 24.6 percent black, the 5 percent mark should be easy to reach in the absence of discriminatory market constraints. Except for certain wealthy areas in the far-flung suburbs north and east, it is hard to find areas where there are no tracts exceeding 5 percent, although in some cases the expanding metro area incorporated villages and small town populations that contain clusters of blacks who are not suburbanites in the conventional sense.

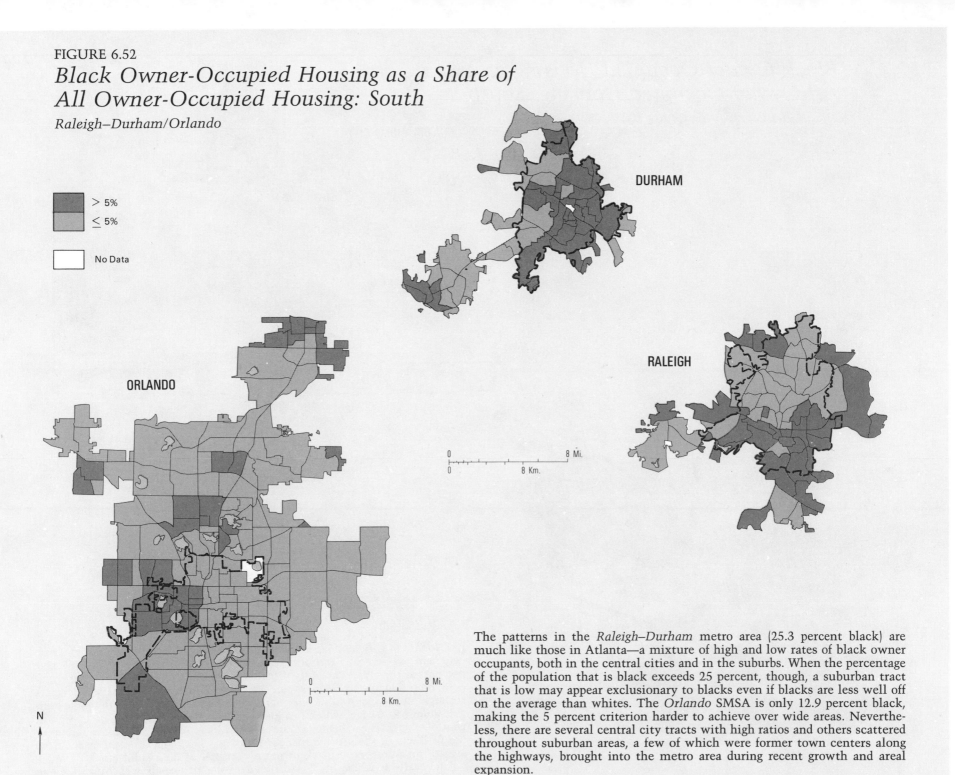

FIGURE 6.52

Black Owner-Occupied Housing as a Share of All Owner-Occupied Housing: South

Raleigh–Durham/Orlando

> 5%

≤ 5%

No Data

DURHAM

ORLANDO

RALEIGH

0 ——— 8 Mi.
0 ——— 8 Km.

0 ——— 8 Mi.
0 ——— 8 Km.

N

The patterns in the *Raleigh–Durham* metro area (25.3 percent black) are much like those in Atlanta—a mixture of high and low rates of black owner occupants, both in the central cities and in the suburbs. When the percentage of the population that is black exceeds 25 percent, though, a suburban tract that is low may appear exclusionary to blacks even if blacks are less well off on the average than whites. The *Orlando* SMSA is only 12.9 percent black, making the 5 percent criterion harder to achieve over wide areas. Nevertheless, there are several central city tracts with high ratios and others scattered throughout suburban areas, a few of which were former town centers along the highways, brought into the metro area during recent growth and areal expansion.

197

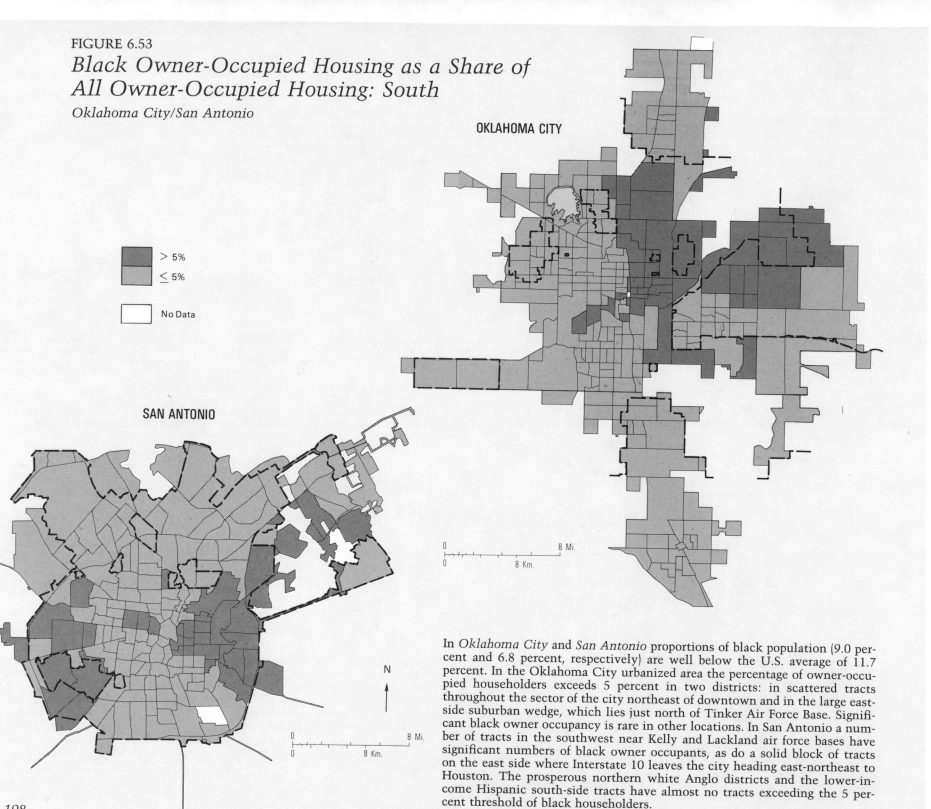

FIGURE 6.53
Black Owner-Occupied Housing as a Share of All Owner-Occupied Housing: South
Oklahoma City/San Antonio

> 5%

≤ 5%

No Data

OKLAHOMA CITY

SAN ANTONIO

N

0   8 Mi.

0   8 Km.

0   8 Mi.

0   8 Km.

In *Oklahoma City* and *San Antonio* proportions of black population (9.0 percent and 6.8 percent, respectively) are well below the U.S. average of 11.7 percent. In the Oklahoma City urbanized area the percentage of owner-occupied householders exceeds 5 percent in two districts: in scattered tracts throughout the sector of the city northeast of downtown and in the large east-side suburban wedge, which lies just north of Tinker Air Force Base. Significant black owner occupancy is rare in other locations. In San Antonio a number of tracts in the southwest near Kelly and Lackland air force bases have significant numbers of black owner occupants, as do a solid block of tracts on the east side where Interstate 10 leaves the city heading east-northeast to Houston. The prosperous northern white Anglo districts and the lower-income Hispanic south-side tracts have almost no tracts exceeding the 5 percent threshold of black householders.

FIGURE 6.54

Black Owner-Occupied Housing as a Share of All Owner-Occupied Housing: South

Birmingham/Memphis

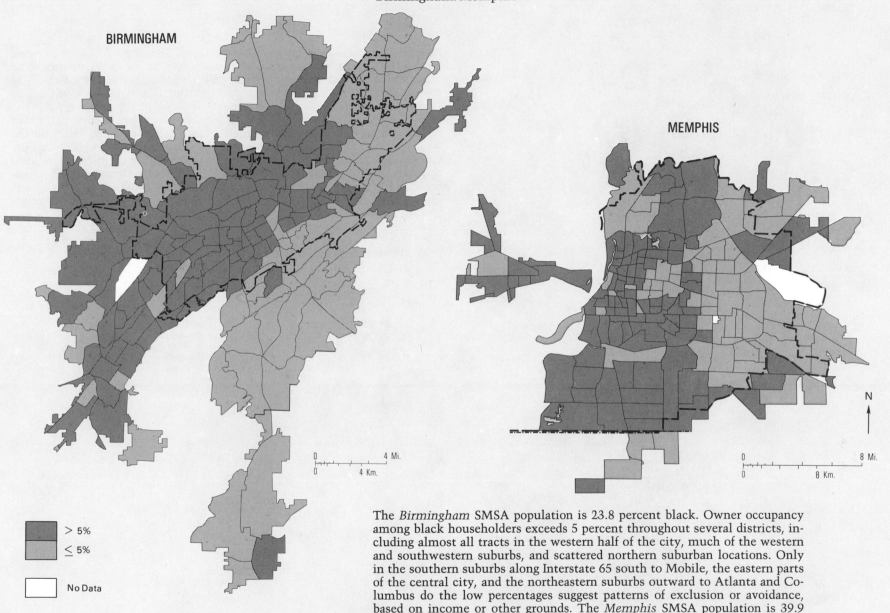

BIRMINGHAM

MEMPHIS

> 5%

≤ 5%

No Data

0 ——— 4 Mi.
0 ——— 4 Km.

0 ——— 8 Mi.
0 ——— 8 Km.

N

The *Birmingham* SMSA population is 23.8 percent black. Owner occupancy among black householders exceeds 5 percent throughout several districts, including almost all tracts in the western half of the city, much of the western and southwestern suburbs, and scattered northern suburban locations. Only in the southern suburbs along Interstate 65 south to Mobile, the eastern parts of the central city, and the northeastern suburbs outward to Atlanta and Columbus do the low percentages suggest patterns of exclusion or avoidance, based on income or other grounds. The *Memphis* SMSA population is 39.9 percent black, higher than that in the Birmingham area, but the tracts in which black owner occupants exceed 5 percent are confined to a region surrounding the downtown at the river and extending south to the city limits. Other sections of the city and suburbs display a significant presence of black owner occupancy above 5 percent. As in the Birmingham area, however, large stretches of low percentages in a metro area almost 40 percent black suggest patterns of exclusion or systematic avoidance.

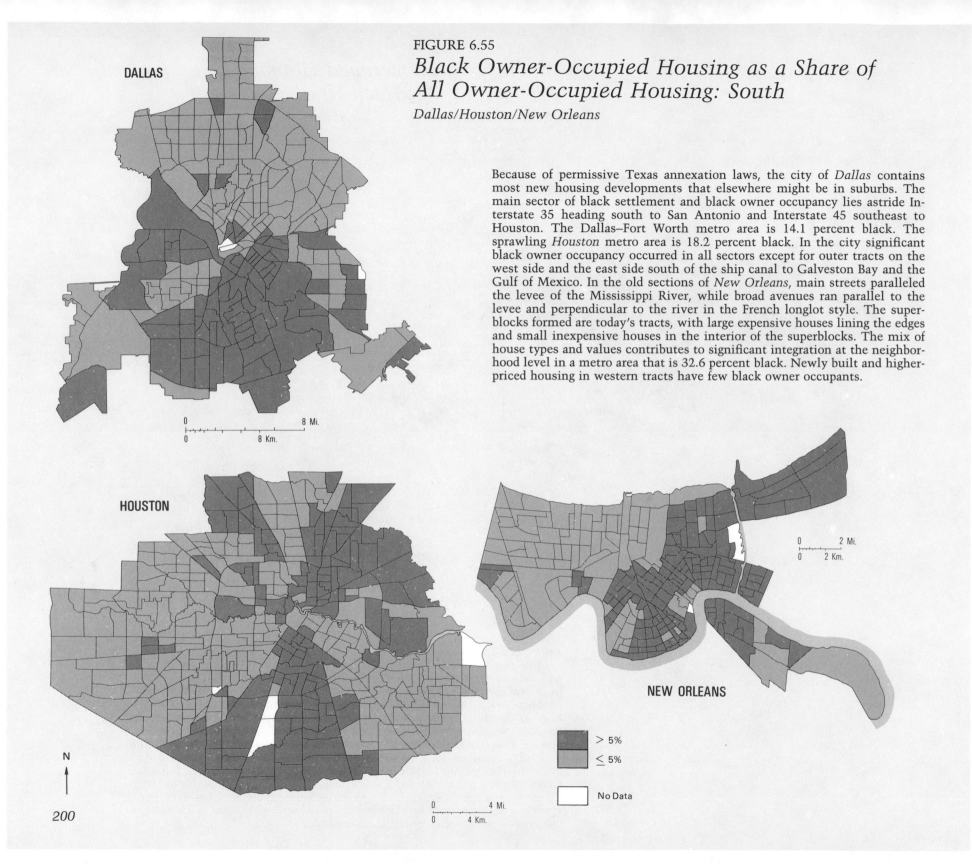

FIGURE 6.55

Black Owner-Occupied Housing as a Share of All Owner-Occupied Housing: South

Dallas/Houston/New Orleans

Because of permissive Texas annexation laws, the city of *Dallas* contains most new housing developments that elsewhere might be in suburbs. The main sector of black settlement and black owner occupancy lies astride Interstate 35 heading south to San Antonio and Interstate 45 southeast to Houston. The Dallas–Fort Worth metro area is 14.1 percent black. The sprawling *Houston* metro area is 18.2 percent black. In the city significant black owner occupancy occurred in all sectors except for outer tracts on the west side and the east side south of the ship canal to Galveston Bay and the Gulf of Mexico. In the old sections of *New Orleans*, main streets paralleled the levee of the Mississippi River, while broad avenues ran parallel to the levee and perpendicular to the river in the French longlot style. The superblocks formed are today's tracts, with large expensive houses lining the edges and small inexpensive houses in the interior of the superblocks. The mix of house types and values contributes to significant integration at the neighborhood level in a metro area that is 32.6 percent black. Newly built and higherpriced housing in western tracts have few black owner occupants.

DALLAS

HOUSTON

NEW ORLEANS

0   8 Mi.

0   8 Km.

0   2 Mi.

0   2 Km.

0   4 Mi.

0   4 Km.

N

> 5%

≤ 5%

No Data

FIGURE 6.56

Black Owner-Occupied Housing as a Share of All Owner-Occupied Housing: South

Baltimore/Washington/Miami

The *Baltimore* area is 25.6 percent black, and a disproportionate share of the black population lives in the central city. Only a few of the newer and the more exclusive districts along the Jones Falls in the northwest of city center, the northeast beyond Herring Run, and near Chesapeake Bay fail to exceed the threshold of 5 percent black owner occupants. The *Washington* metro area is 27.9 percent black, and the district percentage is much higher. Between the Potomac River on the southwest and Rock Creek running north lies Georgetown and Washington's most expensive residential area, where black owner occupants are few. In the rest of the city's east side, including the tracts southeast of the Anacostia River, black owner occupancy is common. In *Miami*, where blacks constitute 17.2 percent of the metro total, black owner occupancy is concentrated in a wedge north of downtown, but away from the expensive beachfront tracts. The map excludes the city of Miami Beach.

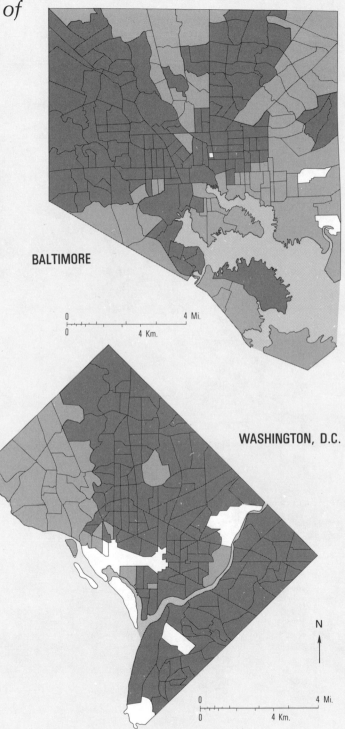

BALTIMORE

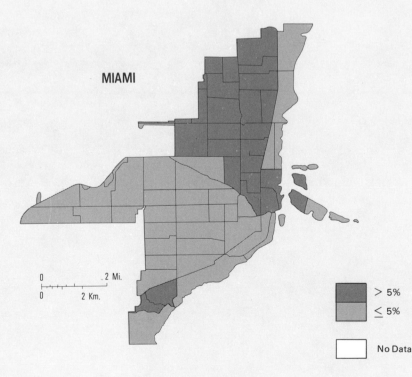

MIAMI

WASHINGTON, D.C.

> 5%

≤ 5%

No Data

N

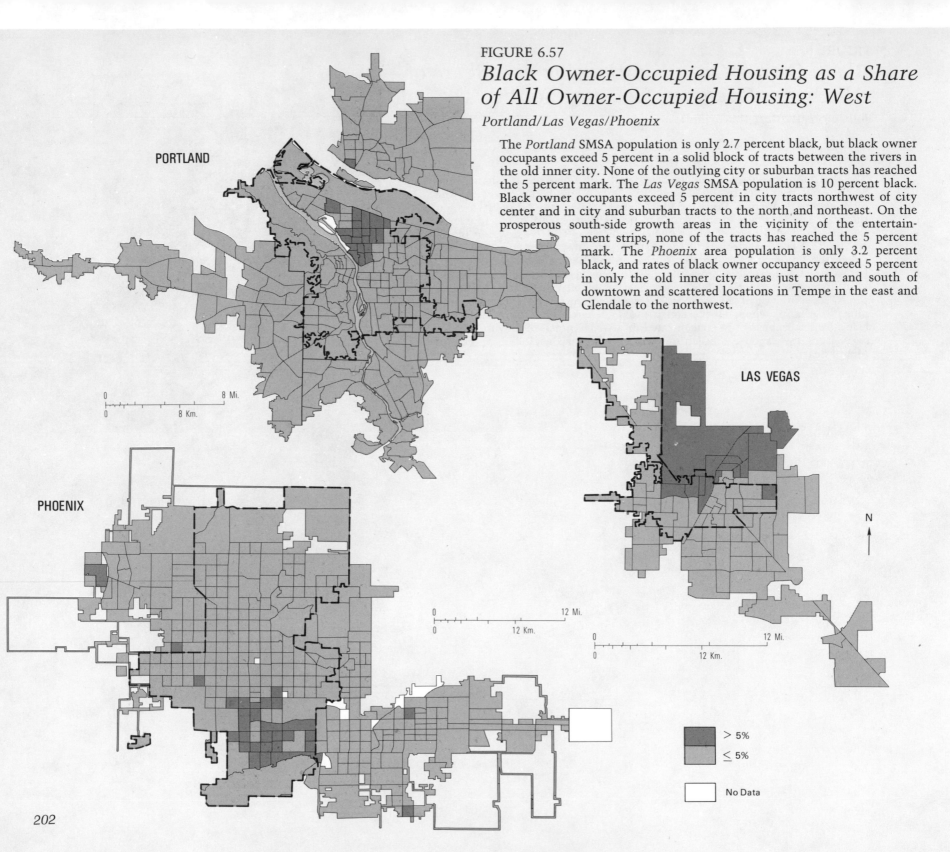

FIGURE 6.57

Black Owner-Occupied Housing as a Share of All Owner-Occupied Housing: West

Portland/Las Vegas/Phoenix

The *Portland* SMSA population is only 2.7 percent black, but black owner occupants exceed 5 percent in a solid block of tracts between the rivers in the old inner city. None of the outlying city or suburban tracts has reached the 5 percent mark. The *Las Vegas* SMSA population is 10 percent black. Black owner occupants exceed 5 percent in city tracts northwest of city center and in city and suburban tracts to the north and northeast. On the prosperous south-side growth areas in the vicinity of the entertainment strips, none of the tracts has reached the 5 percent mark. The *Phoenix* area population is only 3.2 percent black, and rates of black owner occupancy exceed 5 percent in only the old inner city areas just north and south of downtown and scattered locations in Tempe in the east and Glendale to the northwest.

PORTLAND

LAS VEGAS

PHOENIX

0   8 Mi.
0   8 Km.

0   12 Mi.
0   12 Km.

0   12 Mi.
0   12 Km.

N

> 5%

≤ 5%

No Data

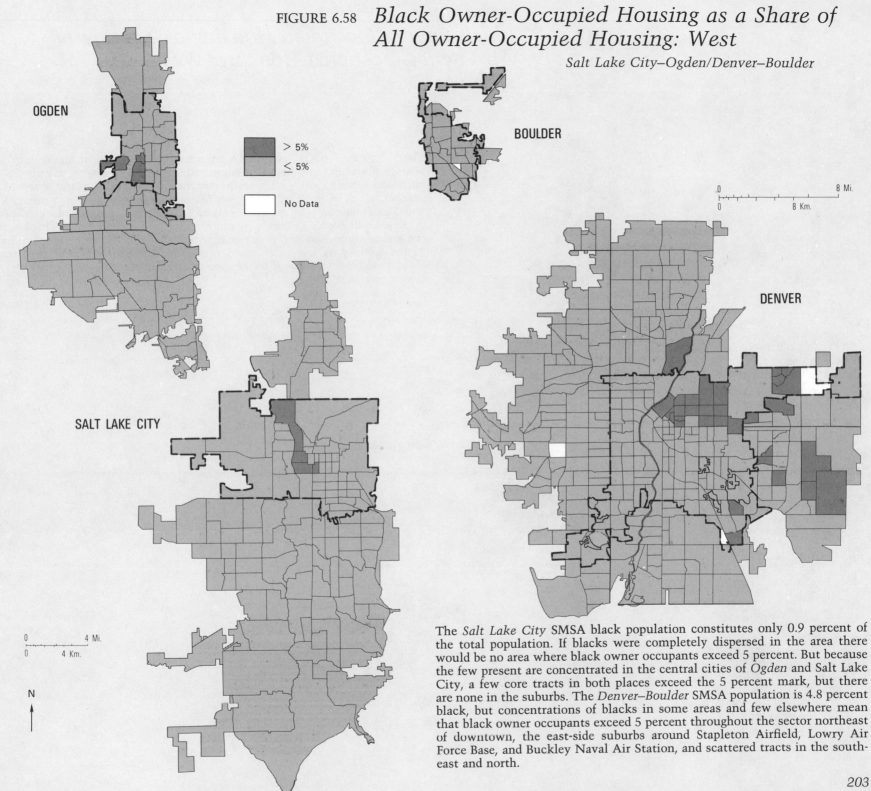

FIGURE 6.58 *Black Owner-Occupied Housing as a Share of All Owner-Occupied Housing: West*

Salt Lake City–Ogden/Denver–Boulder

OGDEN

> 5%

≤ 5%

No Data

BOULDER

DENVER

SALT LAKE CITY

0   8 Mi.

0   8 Km.

0   4 Mi.

0   4 Km.

N

The *Salt Lake City* SMSA black population constitutes only 0.9 percent of the total population. If blacks were completely dispersed in the area there would be no area where black owner occupants exceed 5 percent. But because the few present are concentrated in the central cities of *Ogden* and Salt Lake City, a few core tracts in both places exceed the 5 percent mark, but there are none in the suburbs. The *Denver–Boulder* SMSA population is 4.8 percent black, but concentrations of blacks in some areas and few elsewhere mean that black owner occupants exceed 5 percent throughout the sector northeast of downtown, the east-side suburbs around Stapleton Airfield, Lowry Air Force Base, and Buckley Naval Air Station, and scattered tracts in the southeast and north.

203

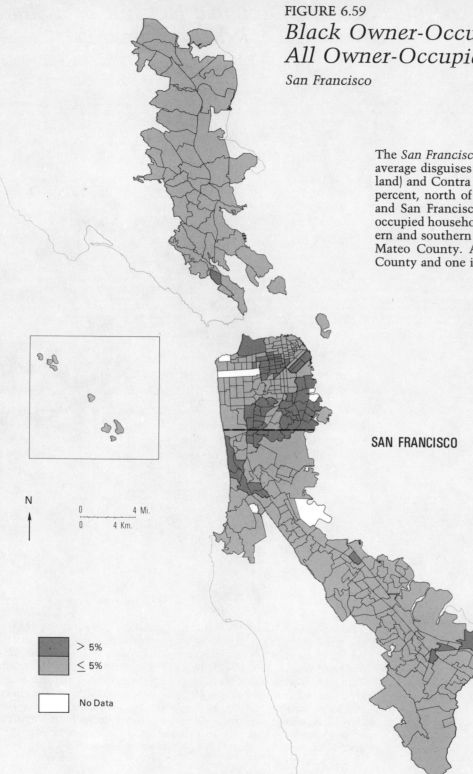

FIGURE 6.59
Black Owner-Occupied Housing as a Share of All Owner-Occupied Housing: West

San Francisco

The *San Francisco*–Oakland SMSA population is 12.0 percent black, but this average disguises big differences among Alameda (18.4 percent, mainly Oakland) and Contra Costa (9.2 percent) counties in the East Bay and Marin (2.5 percent, north of San Francisco), San Mateo (6.0 percent, south of the city), and San Francisco (12.7 percent) counties. Concentrations of black owner-occupied households above the 5 percent cutoff are scattered throughout eastern and southern sections of the city, with some spillover into suburban San Mateo County. A few older tracts beside the bay in southern San Mateo County and one in Marin County show additional spread.

SAN FRANCISCO

N

0   4 Mi.

0   4 Km.

> 5%

≤ 5%

No Data

FIGURE 6.60

Black Owner-Occupied Housing as a Share of All Owner-Occupied Housing: West

Seattle–Everett/San Diego–Chula Vista

Only 3.6 percent of the *Seattle–Everett* SMSA population is black, but concentrations of black owner-occupant households still emerge around downtown, east to the lake, and south along the lake to the city limits and just beyond. Tracts in which black owner occupants exceed 5 percent are totally absent from other city and suburban areas. The *San Diego* metro area has a 5.6 percent black population, but concentrations of black owner occupants above 5 percent occur around downtown, which is adjacent to several marine and naval bases, east of downtown in a concentration extending into the suburbs, and on the far northern edge of the urbanized area adjacent to the Camp Pendleton Marine Corps Base.

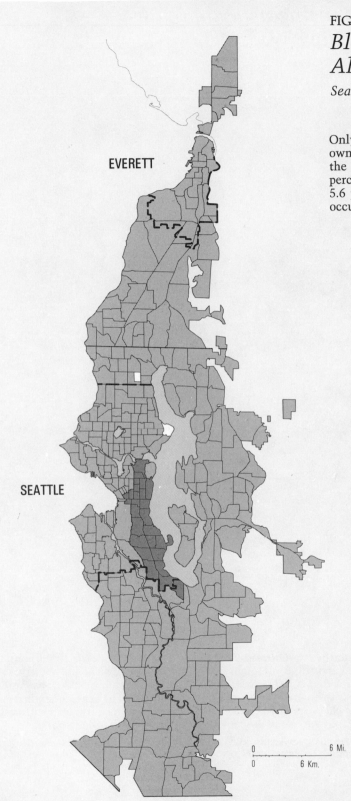

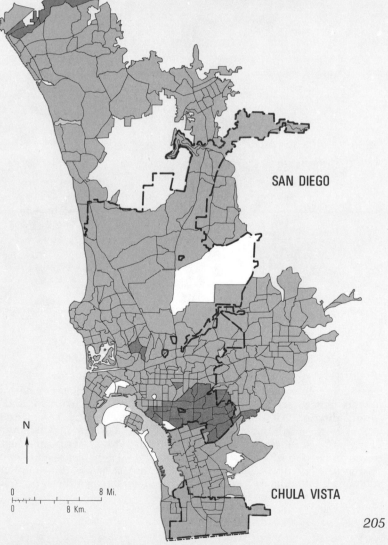

> 5%

≤ 5%

No Data

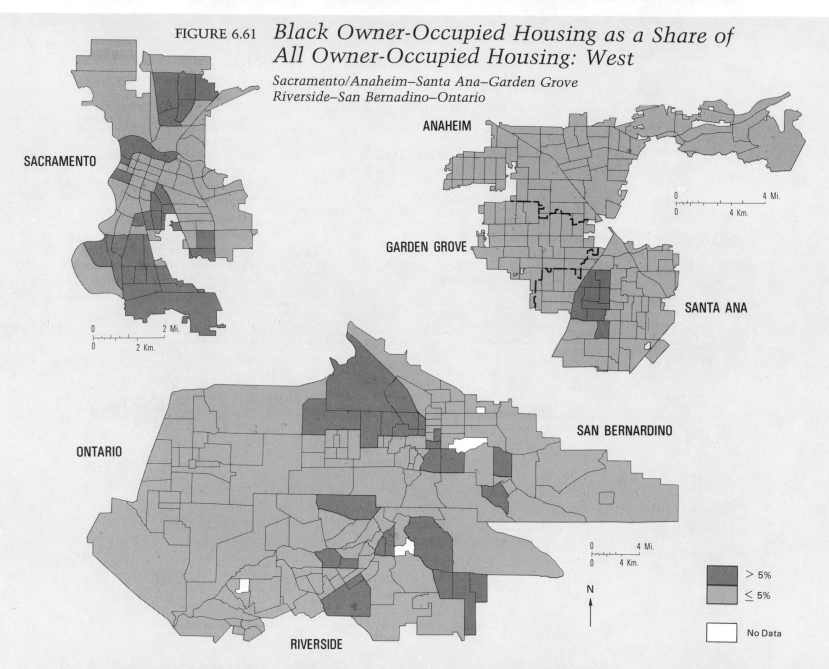

FIGURE 6.61 *Black Owner-Occupied Housing as a Share of All Owner-Occupied Housing: West*

Sacramento/Anaheim–Santa Ana–Garden Grove
Riverside–San Bernadino–Ontario

ANAHEIM

SACRAMENTO

GARDEN GROVE

SANTA ANA

ONTARIO

SAN BERNARDINO

RIVERSIDE

N

> 5%

≤ 5%

No Data

The *Sacramento* metro area has relatively few blacks (6.0 percent), but those few are concentrated in the city, well south of the downtown and the state capitol district. Another patch of tracts exceeding the 5 percent threshold occurs north-northeast of downtown, which borders McClellan Air Force Base.[34] The *Anaheim–Santa Ana –Garden Grove* metro area has an even lower proportion of blacks than Sacramento—1.3 percent—but their concentration in a few of the older tracts in Santa Ana makes this small group conspicuous by its relative segregation. The *Riverside* (southern tracts)–*San Ber-* *nardino* (northeast)–*Ontario* (west) area on the map, with some boundaries generalized and some suburban tracts included, forms the polycentric core of a metro area that is 5.0 percent black. Tracts in which blacks constitute over 5 percent of the owner occupants appear in clusters in central San Bernardino and in the old parts of Riverside. A cluster of tracts in the far southeast borders on March Air Force Base and houses some military personnel.

[34]See Dennis Dingemans, "Redlining and Mortgage Lending in Sacramento," *Annals, Association of American Geographers*, vol. 69, no. 2 (June 1979): 225–239.

Children with a Non-English Mother Tongue: Immigrant Areas and Ethnic Concentrations

Immigration into the United States reached record numbers during the 1970s according to many estimates, and most of the newcomers settled in cities. Although there are several ways to describe their presence, using the mother tongue of children not only identifies settlement patterns, but also amplifies the future significance of the newcomer group and the residential areas where they live in a way that attention to adults or the elderly foreign stock would not. In some areas children adopted from abroad augment the totals from conventional immigration.

The overall average proportion of children (aged 5 to 17) with a non-English mother tongue is small in most SMSAs and urbanized areas, but high in neighborhoods where they concentrate. Thus, the average value for the city or the urbanized area is not representative of specific living and housing environments, because children whose mother tongue is not English tend to live in areas surrounded by many others like themselves. For the sample of 27 urbanized areas the SMSA proportions ranged from highs of 22.5 percent in Wichita, 18.3 percent in Portland, and 17.4 percent in San Diego to lows of 9.4 percent in Indianapolis, 8.8 percent in Madison, 7.9 percent in Albany, and 5.9 percent in Birmingham.

Present geographical patterns of immigrant settlement in northeastern cities and midwestern manufacturing cities differ little in fundamental respects from the central city immigrant neighborhoods of the late nineteenth and early twentieth centuries. In each era these concentrations have made possible the participation in an economy in which the immigrant could usually find employment, as well as a residential environment that retained many familiar old country features of language, religion, custom, and kinship.[35]

As the scattered tracts with high concentrations of non-English-speaking children in many western and southern areas show, urbanized areas differ in important ways in how they serve as receiving areas for immigrants and in the extent that they do so. They also differ in the degree of concentration of their minorities from neighborhood to neighborhood within the cities. Generally speaking, the strong urban economies in boom regions that added many jobs in the 1970s attracted many more immigrants than did stable or declining areas. Moreover, urbanized areas located close to the major immigrant source regions in Latin America and Asia had a big advantage in attracting newcomers.

Sometimes an urban area in a fast-growth region (Birmingham in the South) has an economy that is growing more slowly than its regional competitors, so it attracts and retains only a small number of children with a non-English mother tongue. Sometimes an area has been able to attract and retain immigrants despite locations that are relatively remote from important source areas (Minneapolis–St. Paul, 15.7 percent; Wichita, 22.5 percent).

Although immigrants initially make new and occasionally complex demands on schools and public services, they quickly apply their talents and energy to the local economy and society, generally putting in more than they take out, saving and investing, and building for their future—which is part of the future of the community.[36]

---

[35]David Ward, *Cities and Immigrants: A Geography of Change in Nineteenth Century America* (New York: Oxford University Press, 1971).

[36]See George J. Borjas, *The Impact of Assimilation on the Earnings of Immigrants: A Reexamination of the Evidence*, Working Paper no. 1515 (Cambridge, MA: National Bureau of Economic Research, 1985).

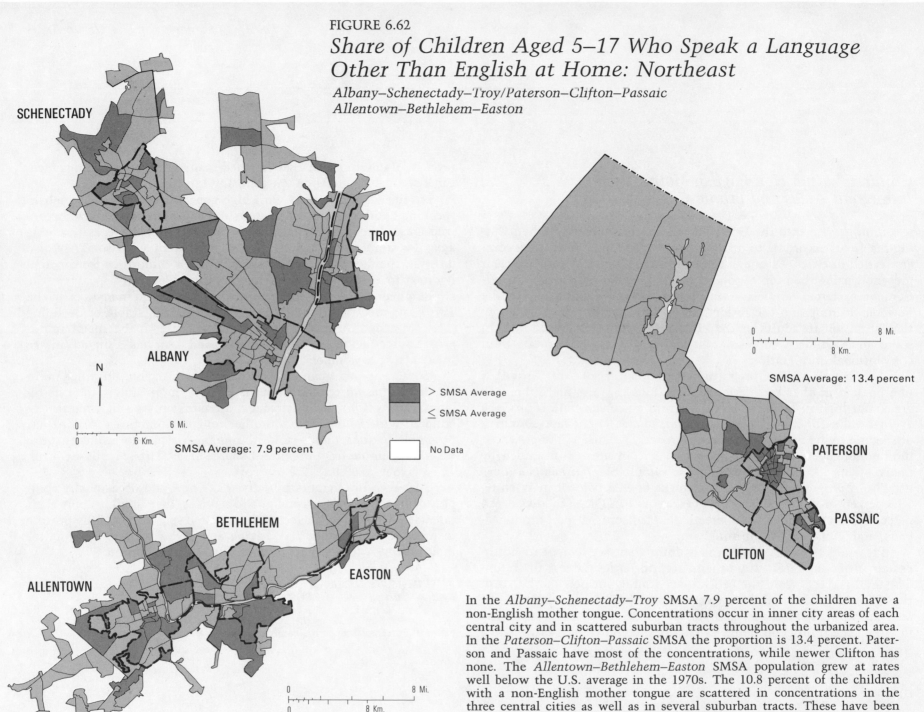

FIGURE 6.62

Share of Children Aged 5–17 Who Speak a Language Other Than English at Home: Northeast

Albany–Schenectady–Troy/Paterson–Clifton–Passaic
Allentown–Bethlehem–Easton

SCHENECTADY

TROY

ALBANY

N

0   6 Mi.
0   6 Km.

SMSA Average: 7.9 percent

> SMSA Average

≤ SMSA Average

No Data

SMSA Average: 13.4 percent

PATERSON

PASSAIC

CLIFTON

BETHLEHEM

EASTON

ALLENTOWN

0   8 Mi.
0   8 Km.

SMSA Average: 10.8 percent

In the *Albany–Schenectady–Troy* SMSA 7.9 percent of the children have a non-English mother tongue. Concentrations occur in inner city areas of each central city and in scattered suburban tracts throughout the urbanized area. In the *Paterson–Clifton–Passaic* SMSA the proportion is 13.4 percent. Paterson and Passaic have most of the concentrations, while newer Clifton has none. The *Allentown–Bethlehem–Easton* SMSA population grew at rates well below the U.S. average in the 1970s. The 10.8 percent of the children with a non-English mother tongue are scattered in concentrations in the three central cities as well as in several suburban tracts. These have been areas of net out-migration for native persons, so the presence of minority children is magnified in the statistics.

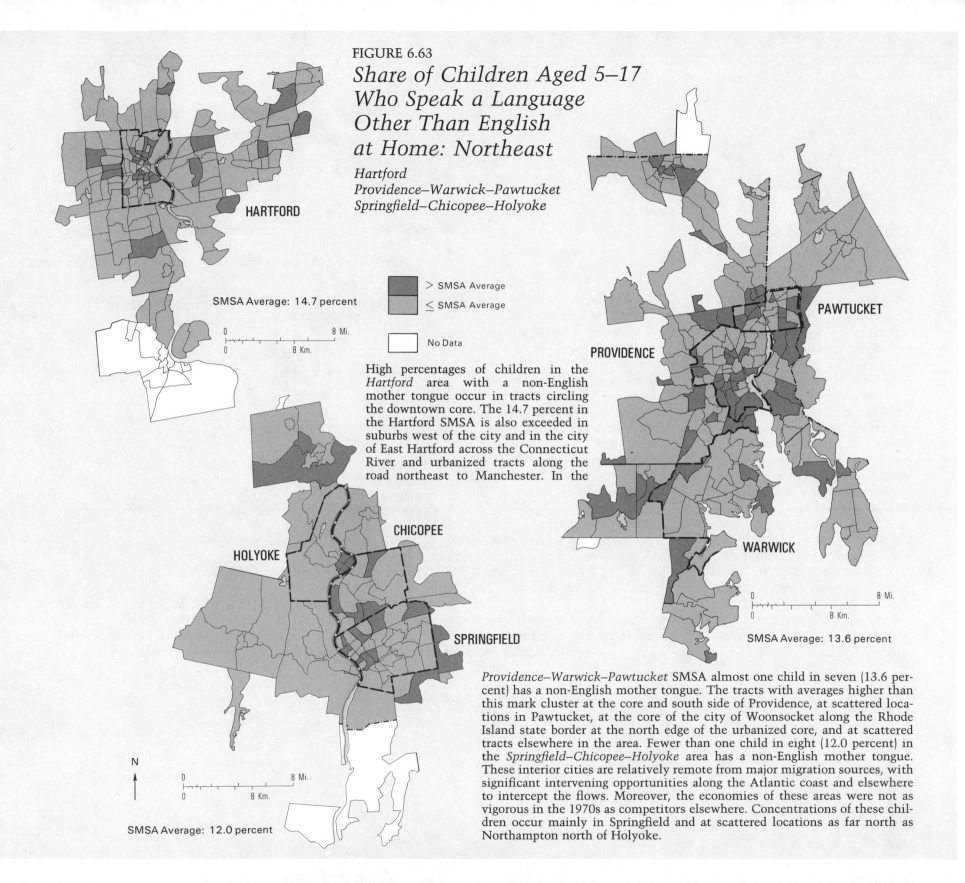

FIGURE 6.63

Share of Children Aged 5–17 Who Speak a Language Other Than English at Home: Northeast

Hartford
Providence–Warwick–Pawtucket
Springfield–Chicopee–Holyoke

HARTFORD

SMSA Average: 14.7 percent

0 — 8 Mi.
0 — 8 Km.

> SMSA Average

≤ SMSA Average

No Data

PROVIDENCE

PAWTUCKET

WARWICK

0 — 8 Mi.
0 — 8 Km.

SMSA Average: 13.6 percent

HOLYOKE   CHICOPEE

SPRINGFIELD

N

0 — 8 Mi.
0 — 8 Km.

SMSA Average: 12.0 percent

High percentages of children in the *Hartford* area with a non-English mother tongue occur in tracts circling the downtown core. The 14.7 percent in the Hartford SMSA is also exceeded in suburbs west of the city and in the city of East Hartford across the Connecticut River and urbanized tracts along the road northeast to Manchester. In the

Providence–Warwick–Pawtucket SMSA almost one child in seven (13.6 percent) has a non-English mother tongue. The tracts with averages higher than this mark cluster at the core and south side of Providence, at scattered locations in Pawtucket, at the core of the city of Woonsocket along the Rhode Island state border at the north edge of the urbanized core, and at scattered tracts elsewhere in the area. Fewer than one child in eight (12.0 percent) in the *Springfield–Chicopee–Holyoke* area has a non-English mother tongue. These interior cities are relatively remote from major migration sources, with significant intervening opportunities along the Atlantic coast and elsewhere to intercept the flows. Moreover, the economies of these areas were not as vigorous in the 1970s as competitors elsewhere. Concentrations of these children occur mainly in Springfield and at scattered locations as far north as Northampton north of Holyoke.

Children Aged 5 to 17 with a Non-English Mother Tongue: in Selected Central Cities

Our central city analysis closely parallels that of the 27 urbanized areas. Neighborhoods in central cities are internally knit together and separated from one another by language. Cities that receive a major influx of non-English-speaking immigrants benefit from the new vitality, skills, ambitions, and energies of those who arrive to make new lives, but the initial period of settlement and adjustment can be a difficult time, for both the newcomers and the host city.

One means used by immigrants for coping with the problems of entry into an alien environment is to cluster with others like themselves, with people who have been in America for a longer time and can help show the way. The central city maps pinpoint the places within our set of 19 cities where immigrant concentrations are especially notable. Again, we focus on children aged 5 to 17 with a non-English mother tongue.

The lowest metro averages among the 19 cities occurred in the Pittsburgh (7.0 percent) and Cleveland (7.2 percent) SMSAs, which had languishing economies during the 1970s, making them unattractive places for ambitious newcomers, as well as for many old residents who moved away, thereby magnifying the downward trends of their regional economic fortunes.

At the other extreme were a number of places that expanded vigorously in the 1970s, attracted large numbers of domestic migrants and foreign immigrants, and concluded the decade with significant shares of metropolitan-wide children aged 5 to 17 with a non-English mother tongue. Among the 19 sample cities the Anaheim–Santa Ana–Garden Grove SMSA was highest at 21.6 percent, and the Houston area was next at 19.0 percent:

Midwest SMSAs		Northeast SMSAs	
Cincinnati	10.1%	Boston	11.5%
Cleveland	7.2	Buffalo	8.4
Columbus	8.6	Newark	12.1
Kansas City	11.4	Pittsburgh	7.0
Milwaukee	11.5		
St. Louis	8.9	South SMSAs	
		Baltimore	9.2
West SMSAs		Dallas	16.0
Anaheim–		Houston	19.0
Santa Ana–		Miami	11.6
Garden Grove	21.6	New Orleans	15.7
Riverside–		Washington	10.6
San Bernardino–	14.9		
Ontario			
Sacramento	13.6		

Highest SMSA percentages are in fast-growing metro regions close to Latin America and Asia—the source of most of today's immigrants, but these are metropolitan-wide averages and are not very representative of specific neighborhoods. For detailed analysis we must look at the tract level of geographic detail. Specific central city tracts often have proportions well in excess of half.

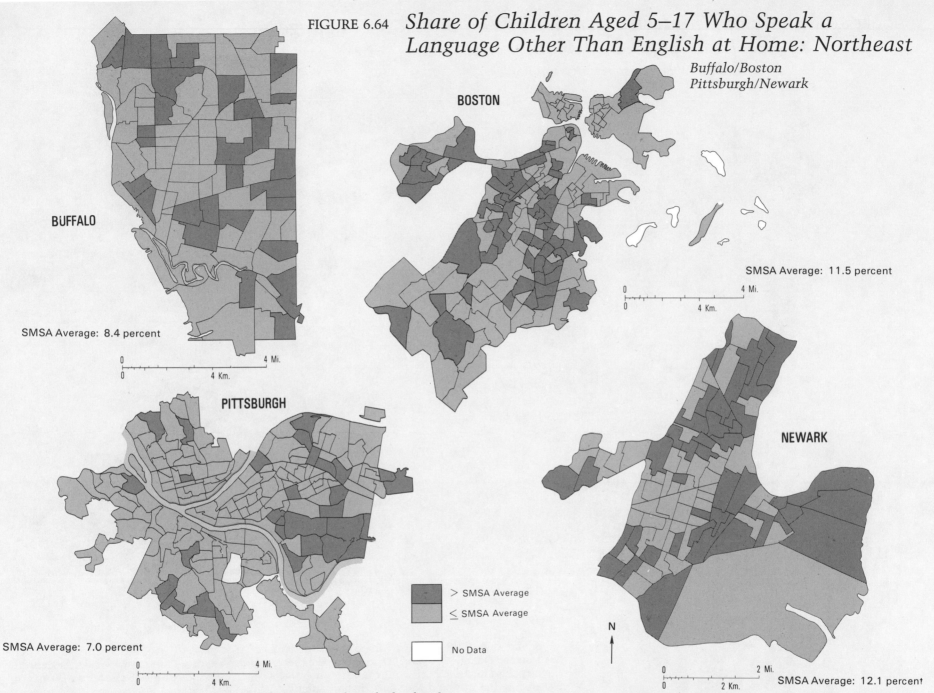

FIGURE 6.64 *Share of Children Aged 5–17 Who Speak a Language Other Than English at Home: Northeast*

Buffalo/Boston Pittsburgh/Newark

BOSTON

BUFFALO

SMSA Average: 8.4 percent

0   4 Mi.
0   4 Km.

SMSA Average: 11.5 percent

0   4 Mi.
0   4 Km.

PITTSBURGH

NEWARK

SMSA Average: 7.0 percent

0   4 Mi.
0   4 Km.

> SMSA Average

≤ SMSA Average

No Data

N

SMSA Average: 12.1 percent

0   2 Mi.
0   2 Km.

The *Buffalo* area was a vigorous heavy industrial area through the decades, but began losing ground relative to the West and South in the 1960s and 1970s. A steady trickle of immigrants from Europe, supplemented by others transplanted from other places and other ports of entry in the United States, creates pockets of children with a non-English mother tongue in diverse locations in the city. *Boston* has been a major immigrant city since colonial times, and children with a non-English mother tongue are scattered in most parts of the city, from old inner city to prosperous newer areas. Many are linked to academic institutions and to high-technology firms in the local economy. The *Pittsburgh* pattern resembles Buffalo's, as mixtures of Europeans, Latin Americans, and Asians, linked to several eras of U.S immigration history, continue to supply the city's neighborhoods with significant groups with a non-English mother tongue. The foreign-language children in *Newark* are heavily Hispanic and live scattered throughout the city, generally following a pattern different from that of blacks.

211

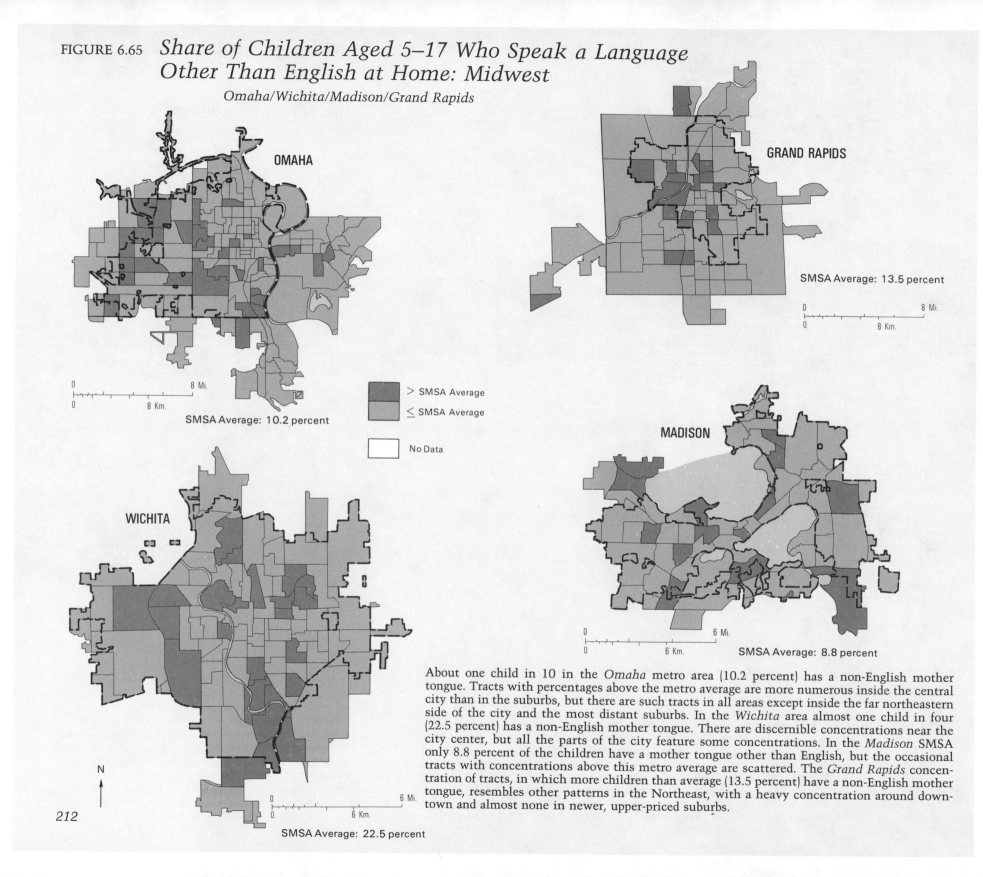

FIGURE 6.65 *Share of Children Aged 5–17 Who Speak a Language Other Than English at Home: Midwest*
Omaha/Wichita/Madison/Grand Rapids

OMAHA

GRAND RAPIDS

SMSA Average: 13.5 percent

0   8 Mi.
0   8 Km.

SMSA Average: 10.2 percent

> SMSA Average

≤ SMSA Average

No Data

MADISON

WICHITA

0   6 Mi.
0   6 Km.

SMSA Average: 8.8 percent

N

0   6 Mi.
0   6 Km.

SMSA Average: 22.5 percent

212

About one child in 10 in the *Omaha* metro area (10.2 percent) has a non-English mother tongue. Tracts with percentages above the metro average are more numerous inside the central city than in the suburbs, but there are such tracts in all areas except inside the far northeastern side of the city and the most distant suburbs. In the *Wichita* area almost one child in four (22.5 percent) has a non-English mother tongue. There are discernible concentrations near the city center, but all the parts of the city feature some concentrations. In the *Madison* SMSA only 8.8 percent of the children have a mother tongue other than English, but the occasional tracts with concentrations above this metro average are scattered. The *Grand Rapids* concentration of tracts, in which more children than average (13.5 percent) have a non-English mother tongue, resembles other patterns in the Northeast, with a heavy concentration around downtown and almost none in newer, upper-priced suburbs.

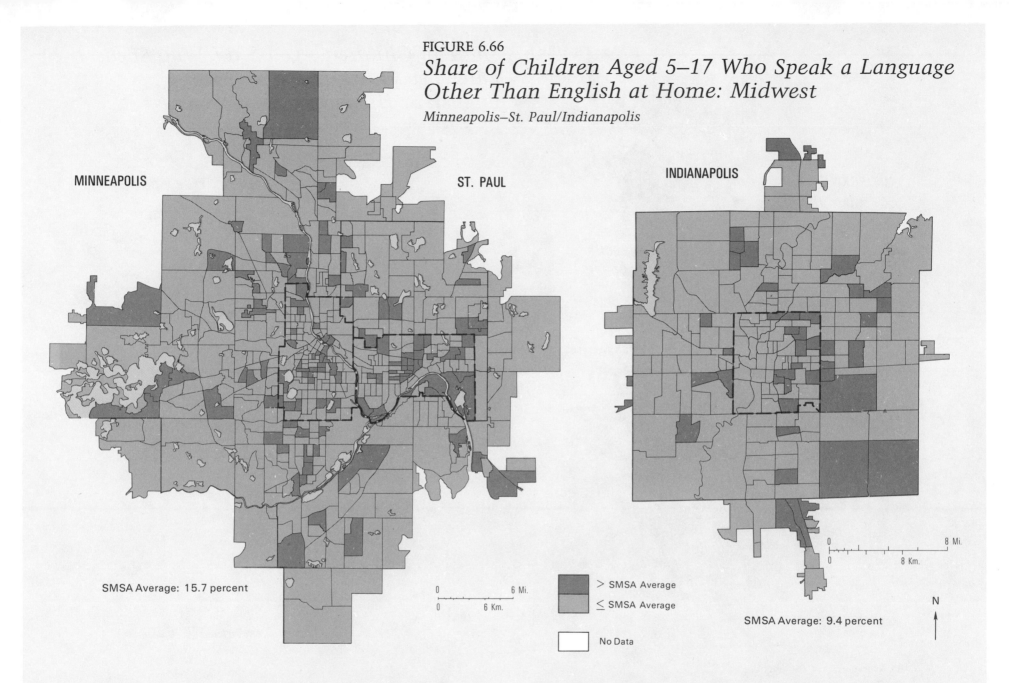

FIGURE 6.66

Share of Children Aged 5–17 Who Speak a Language Other Than English at Home: Midwest

Minneapolis–St. Paul/Indianapolis

MINNEAPOLIS

ST. PAUL

INDIANAPOLIS

SMSA Average: 15.7 percent

SMSA Average: 9.4 percent

0 ——— 6 Mi.

0 ——— 6 Km.

0 ——— 8 Mi.

0 ——— 8 Km.

> SMSA Average

≤ SMSA Average

No Data

N

The *Minneapolis–St. Paul* area received a major influx of immigrants from Southeast Asia in the 1970s, supplementing a significant Hispanic group in St. Paul. The result is that almost one child in six in the SMSA (15.7 percent) does not have English as a mother tongue. Major concentrations occurred west of downtown St. Paul—a traditional staging area for newcomers—and south of the river (a major Spanish-speaking concentration). Minneapolis has concentrations east of downtown by the Twin Cities campus of the Univer-sity of Minnesota and in traditional newcomer and minority areas west and south of downtown. Many other concentrations are scattered throughout central cities and suburbs. The *Indianapolis* metro area has a comparatively low percentage of children with a non-English mother tongue (9.4 percent). Most of the tracts with concentrations above the metro average are in the suburbs on all sides of the city. City tracts with concentrations are scattered.

213

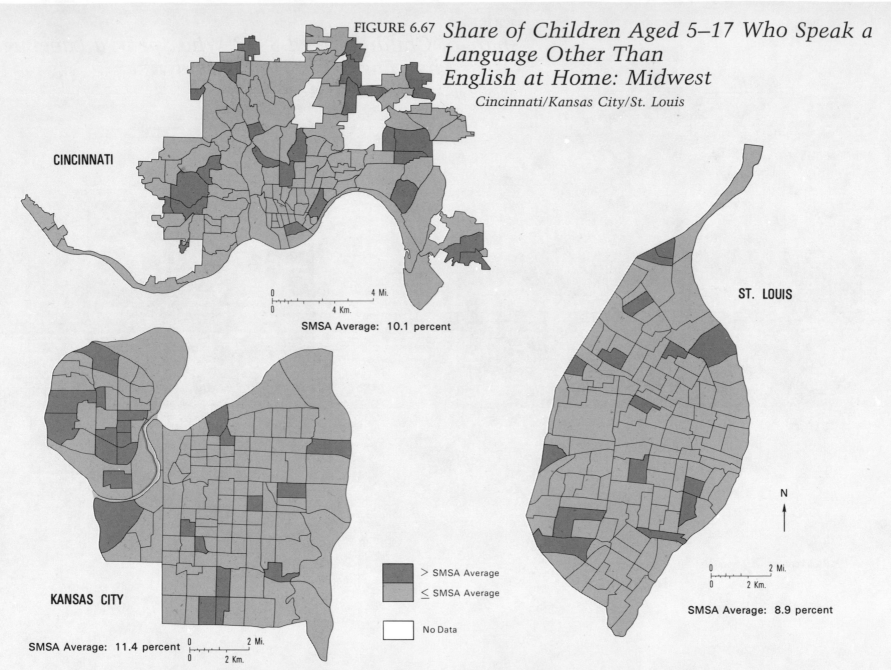

FIGURE 6.67 *Share of Children Aged 5–17 Who Speak a Language Other Than English at Home: Midwest*

Cincinnati/Kansas City/St. Louis

CINCINNATI

SMSA Average: 10.1 percent

ST. LOUIS

SMSA Average: 8.9 percent

KANSAS CITY

SMSA Average: 11.4 percent

> SMSA Average

≤ SMSA Average

No Data

About one child in ten in these metro areas has a non-English mother tongue. In *Cincinnati* clusters appear around the edges of the city on all sides, with relatively few in the core tracts and major black areas. Only a few tracts in *Kansas City*, Kansas, and Kansas City, Missouri, have percentages above the low metro average, which implies that these children are scattered, except for a few places by downtown Kansas City, Kansas, and scattered tracts in

Kansas City, Missouri, especially in the prosperous sector south of downtown to the city limits. The *St. Louis* metro area has been undergoing net out-migration for some time. The city lost population in each census since 1950. A few scattered minority-language areas occur in the white ethnic south side, where European roots are deep, and on the north side, where Hispanic and other concentrations appear.

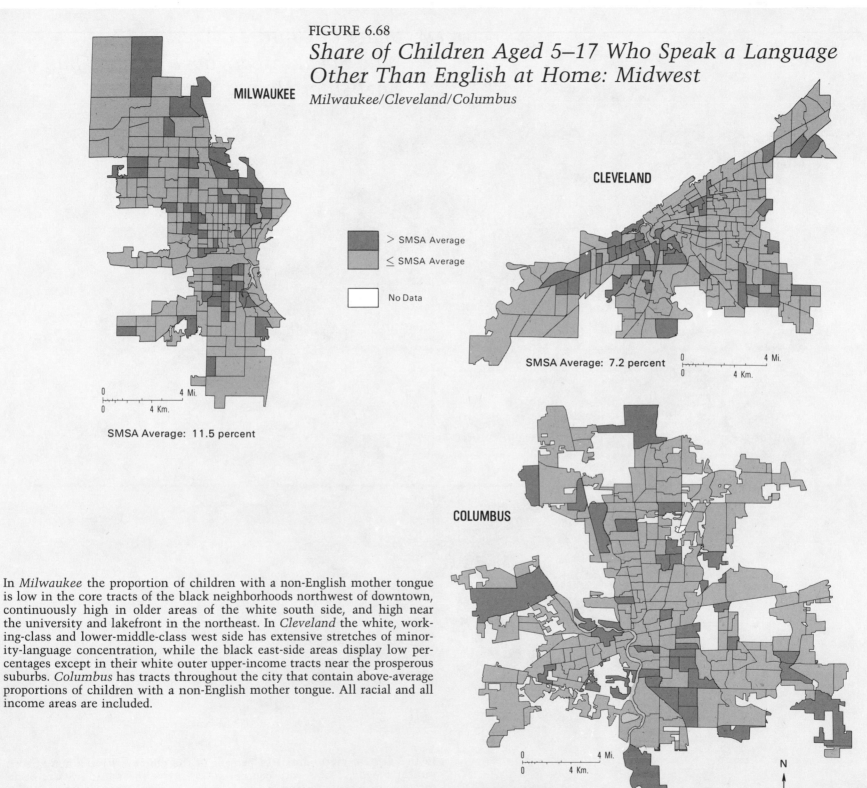

FIGURE 6.68
Share of Children Aged 5–17 Who Speak a Language Other Than English at Home: Midwest
Milwaukee/Cleveland/Columbus

MILWAUKEE

CLEVELAND

COLUMBUS

> SMSA Average

≤ SMSA Average

No Data

SMSA Average: 11.5 percent

SMSA Average: 7.2 percent

SMSA Average: 8.6 percent

N

0   4 Mi.
0   4 Km.

In *Milwaukee* the proportion of children with a non-English mother tongue is low in the core tracts of the black neighborhoods northwest of downtown, continuously high in older areas of the white south side, and high near the university and lakefront in the northeast. In *Cleveland* the white, working-class and lower-middle-class west side has extensive stretches of minority-language concentration, while the black east-side areas display low percentages except in their white outer upper-income tracts near the prosperous suburbs. *Columbus* has tracts throughout the city that contain above-average proportions of children with a non-English mother tongue. All racial and all income areas are included.

215

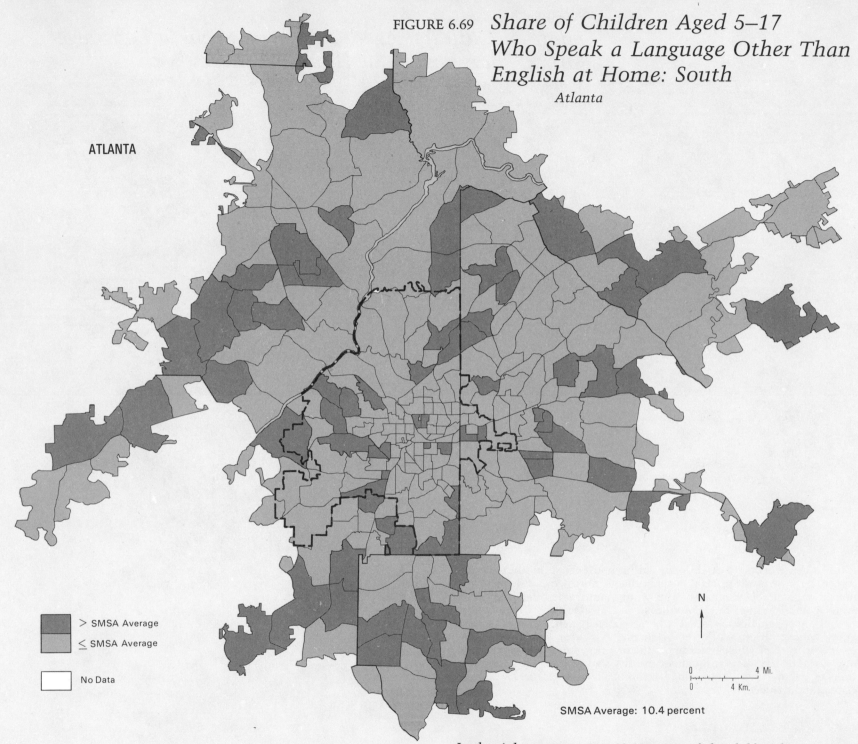

FIGURE 6.69 *Share of Children Aged 5–17 Who Speak a Language Other Than English at Home: South*

Atlanta

> SMSA Average

≤ SMSA Average

No Data

N

0   4 Mi.

0   4 Km.

SMSA Average: 10.4 percent

In the *Atlanta* metro area 10.4 percent of the children have a non-English mother tongue. Tracts with concentrations above the metro average occur throughout the suburbs and in a few scattered central city locations.

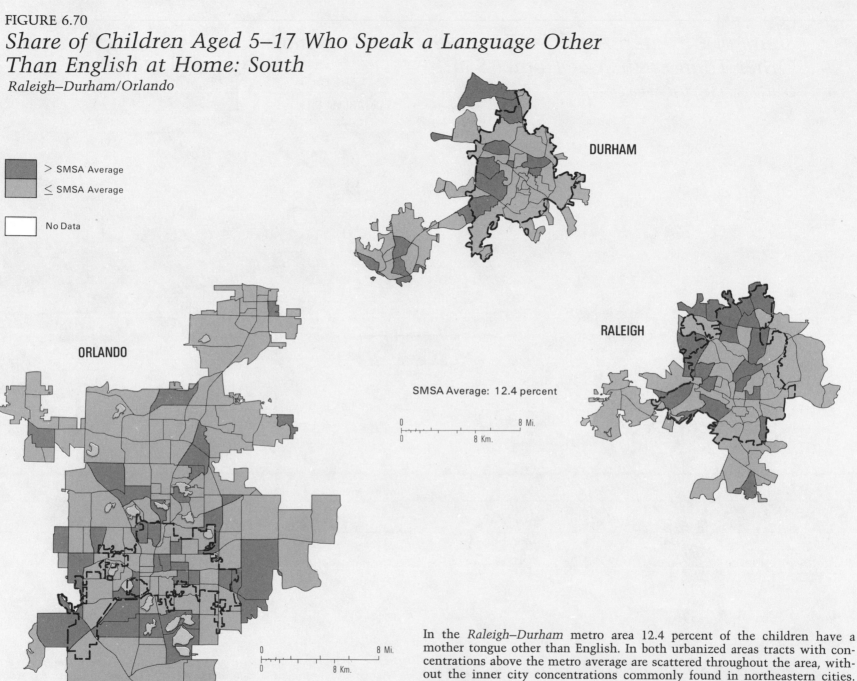

FIGURE 6.70
Share of Children Aged 5–17 Who Speak a Language Other Than English at Home: South
Raleigh–Durham/Orlando

> SMSA Average
≤ SMSA Average
No Data

DURHAM

RALEIGH

SMSA Average: 12.4 percent

0   8 Mi.
0   8 Km.

ORLANDO

0   8 Mi.
0   8 Km.

SMSA Average: 10.5 percent

N

In the *Raleigh–Durham* metro area 12.4 percent of the children have a mother tongue other than English. In both urbanized areas tracts with concentrations above the metro average are scattered throughout the area, without the inner city concentrations commonly found in northeastern cities. The *Orlando* metro area, a region of immigrant settlement, evidently is an even greater center of net domestic in-migration: 10.5 percent of the children have a non-English mother tongue. Most tracts exceeding the metro average are in the central city and adjacent suburbs, but the pattern is fragmented and scattered.

217

FIGURE 6.71

Share of Children Aged 5–17 Who Speak a Language Other Than English at Home: South

Oklahoma City/San Antonio

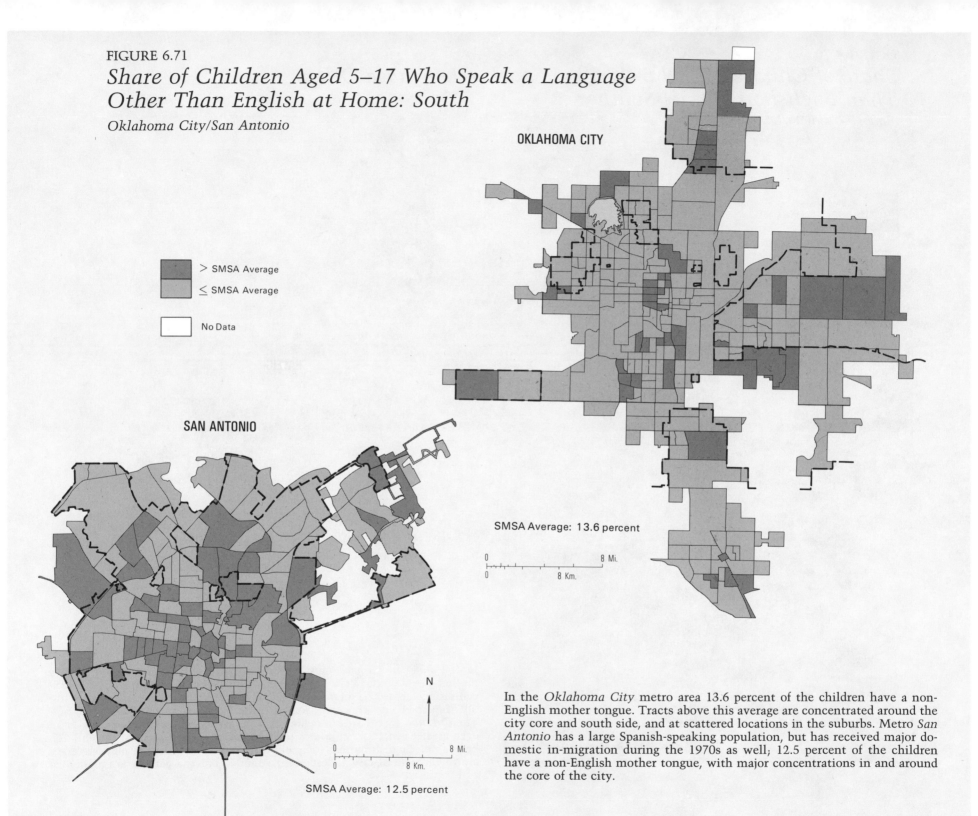

OKLAHOMA CITY

> SMSA Average

≤ SMSA Average

No Data

SMSA Average: 13.6 percent

0   8 Mi.

0   8 Km.

SAN ANTONIO

N

0   8 Mi.

0   8 Km.

SMSA Average: 12.5 percent

In the *Oklahoma City* metro area 13.6 percent of the children have a non-English mother tongue. Tracts above this average are concentrated around the city core and south side, and at scattered locations in the suburbs. Metro *San Antonio* has a large Spanish-speaking population, but has received major domestic in-migration during the 1970s as well; 12.5 percent of the children have a non-English mother tongue, with major concentrations in and around the core of the city.

FIGURE 6.72

Share of Children Aged 5–17 Who Speak a Language Other Than English at Home: South

Birmingham/Memphis

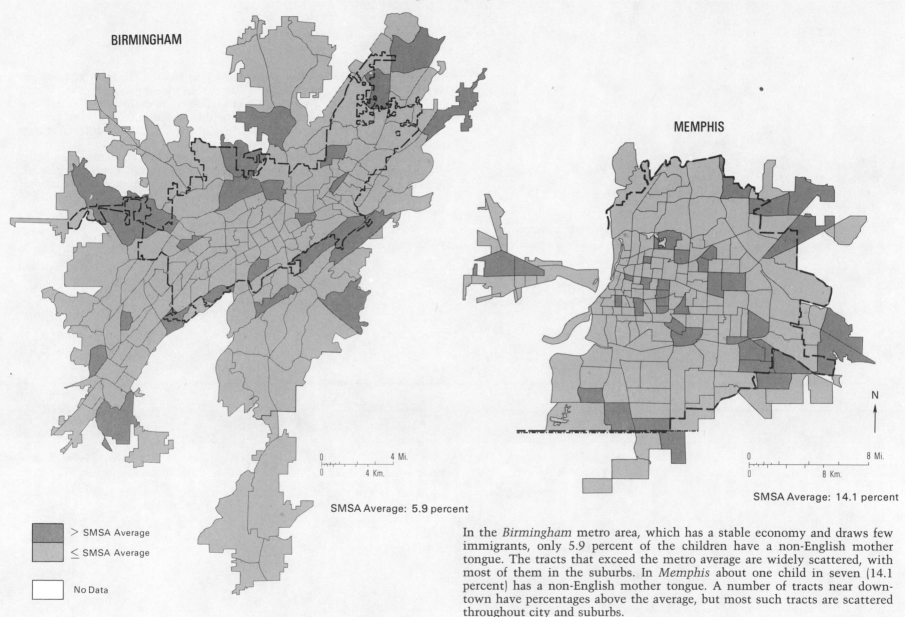

BIRMINGHAM

MEMPHIS

N

0   4 Mi.
0   4 Km.

0   8 Mi.
0   8 Km.

SMSA Average: 5.9 percent

SMSA Average: 14.1 percent

> SMSA Average

≤ SMSA Average

No Data

In the *Birmingham* metro area, which has a stable economy and draws few immigrants, only 5.9 percent of the children have a non-English mother tongue. The tracts that exceed the metro average are widely scattered, with most of them in the suburbs. In *Memphis* about one child in seven (14.1 percent) has a non-English mother tongue. A number of tracts near downtown have percentages above the average, but most such tracts are scattered throughout city and suburbs.

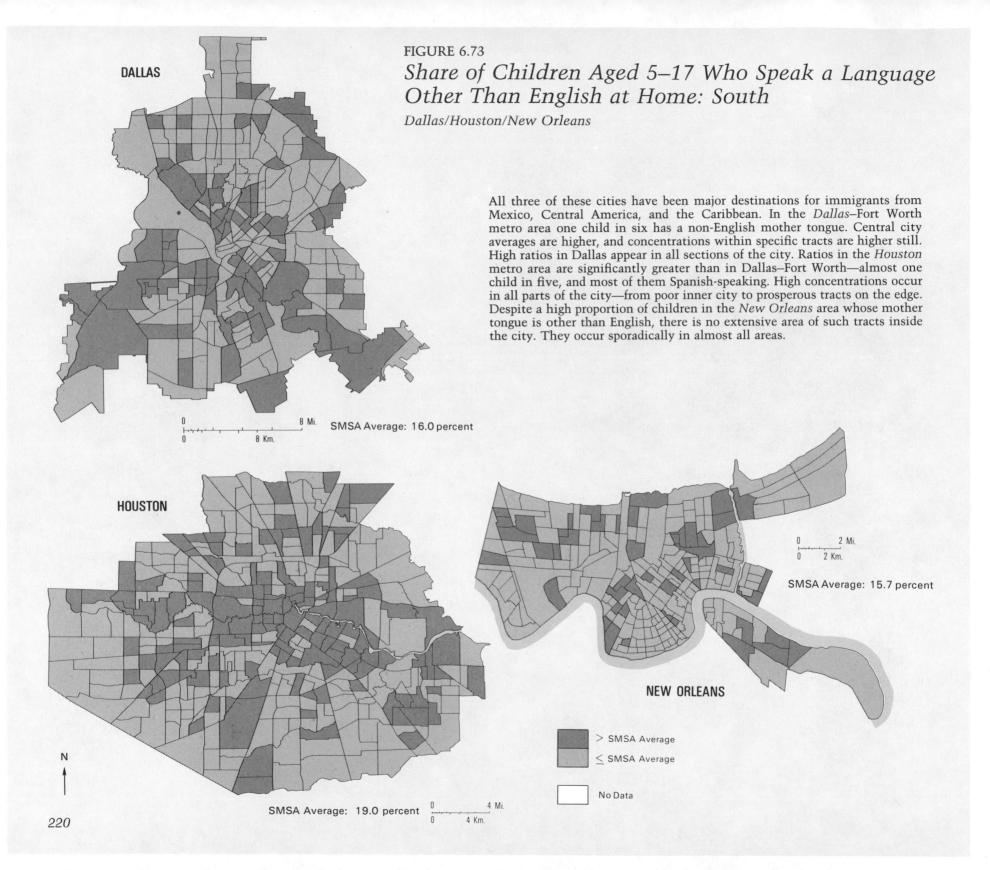

DALLAS

FIGURE 6.73

Share of Children Aged 5–17 Who Speak a Language Other Than English at Home: South

Dallas/Houston/New Orleans

All three of these cities have been major destinations for immigrants from Mexico, Central America, and the Caribbean. In the *Dallas*–Fort Worth metro area one child in six has a non-English mother tongue. Central city averages are higher, and concentrations within specific tracts are higher still. High ratios in Dallas appear in all sections of the city. Ratios in the *Houston* metro area are significantly greater than in Dallas–Fort Worth—almost one child in five, and most of them Spanish-speaking. High concentrations occur in all parts of the city—from poor inner city to prosperous tracts on the edge. Despite a high proportion of children in the *New Orleans* area whose mother tongue is other than English, there is no extensive area of such tracts inside the city. They occur sporadically in almost all areas.

0   8 Mi.

0   8 Km.

SMSA Average: 16.0 percent

HOUSTON

NEW ORLEANS

0   2 Mi.

0   2 Km.

SMSA Average: 15.7 percent

N

▉ > SMSA Average

▨ ≤ SMSA Average

☐ No Data

SMSA Average: 19.0 percent

0   4 Mi.

0   4 Km.

FIGURE 6.74

Share of Children Aged 5–17 Who Speak a Language Other Than English at Home: South

Baltimore/Washington/Miami

In the *Baltimore* metro area fewer than one child in 10 has a non-English mother tongue, but the city map discloses no extensive area of tracts with high proportions—just occasional high points in all parts of the city. The *Washington* pattern looks much like Baltimore's. The overall metro percentage is 10.6 percent in Washington compared with 9.2 in Baltimore, and the above-average tracts occur in a similar widespread pattern at city center, south of the Anacostia River, west of Rock Creek, and even in the heavily black east side. *Miami* has a deserved reputation as a major immigrant destination from Caribbean lands, especially from Cuba. Domestic migration to the Miami area is also high, so the proportion of children with a non-English mother tongue remains about one in 10, but the total number rises rapidly—and in all parts of the city.

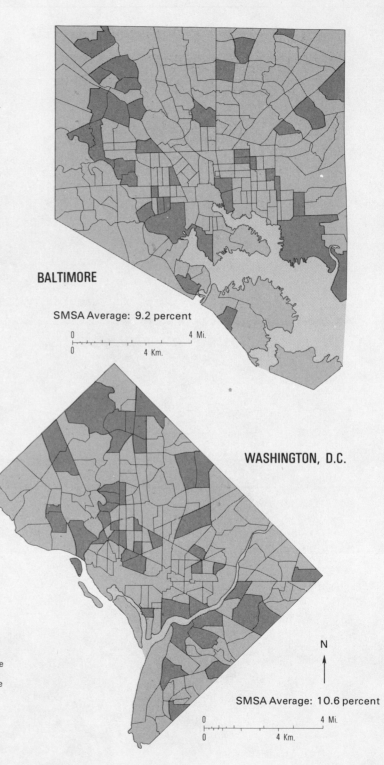

BALTIMORE

SMSA Average: 9.2 percent

0 — 4 Mi.
0 — 4 Km.

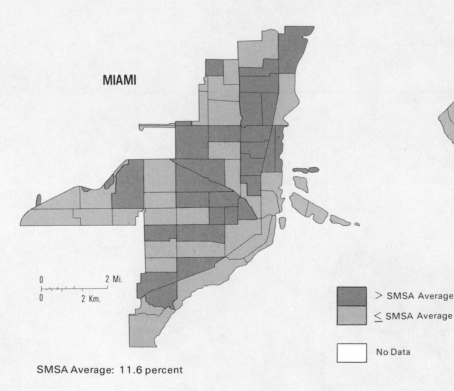

MIAMI

0 — 2 Mi.
0 — 2 Km.

SMSA Average: 11.6 percent

> SMSA Average
≤ SMSA Average
No Data

WASHINGTON, D.C.

N

SMSA Average: 10.6 percent

0 — 4 Mi.
0 — 4 Km.

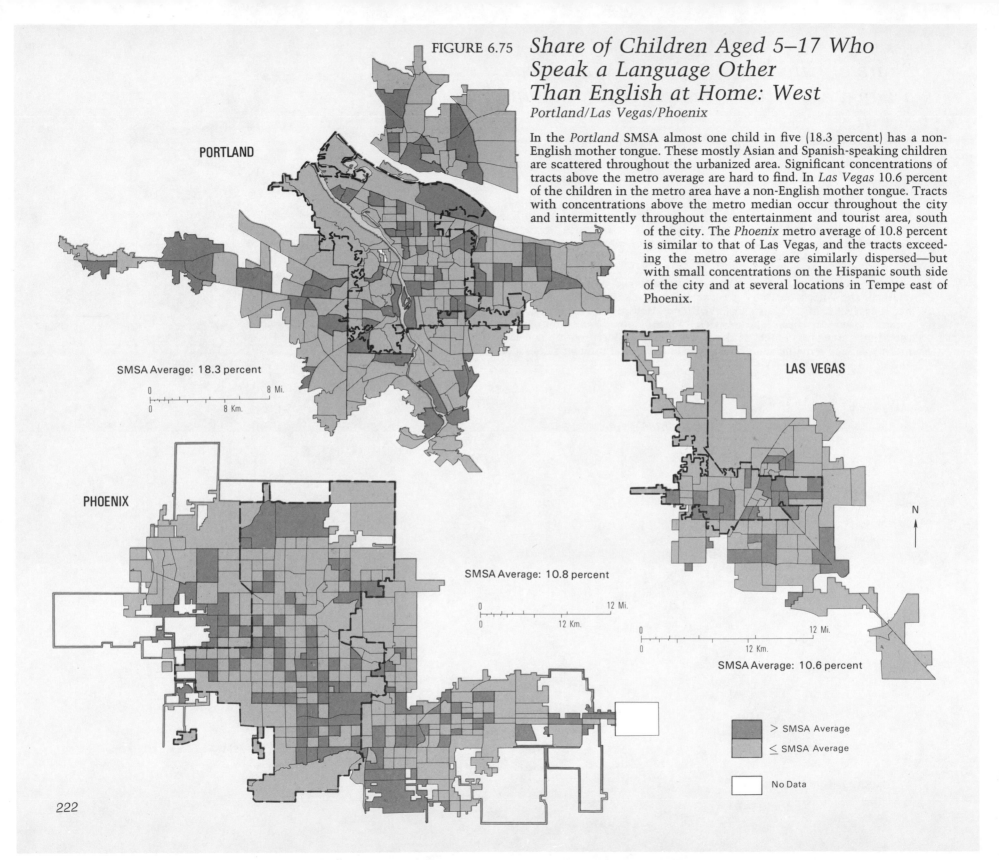

FIGURE 6.75 *Share of Children Aged 5–17 Who Speak a Language Other Than English at Home: West*
Portland/Las Vegas/Phoenix

In the *Portland* SMSA almost one child in five (18.3 percent) has a non-English mother tongue. These mostly Asian and Spanish-speaking children are scattered throughout the urbanized area. Significant concentrations of tracts above the metro average are hard to find. In *Las Vegas* 10.6 percent of the children in the metro area have a non-English mother tongue. Tracts with concentrations above the metro median occur throughout the city and intermittently throughout the entertainment and tourist area, south of the city. The *Phoenix* metro average of 10.8 percent is similar to that of Las Vegas, and the tracts exceeding the metro average are similarly dispersed—but with small concentrations on the Hispanic south side of the city and at several locations in Tempe east of Phoenix.

PORTLAND

SMSA Average: 18.3 percent

0 ——— 8 Mi.
0 ——— 8 Km.

LAS VEGAS

N

PHOENIX

SMSA Average: 10.8 percent

0 ——— 12 Mi.
0 ——— 12 Km.

0 ——— 12 Mi.
0 ——— 12 Km.

SMSA Average: 10.6 percent

> SMSA Average

≤ SMSA Average

No Data

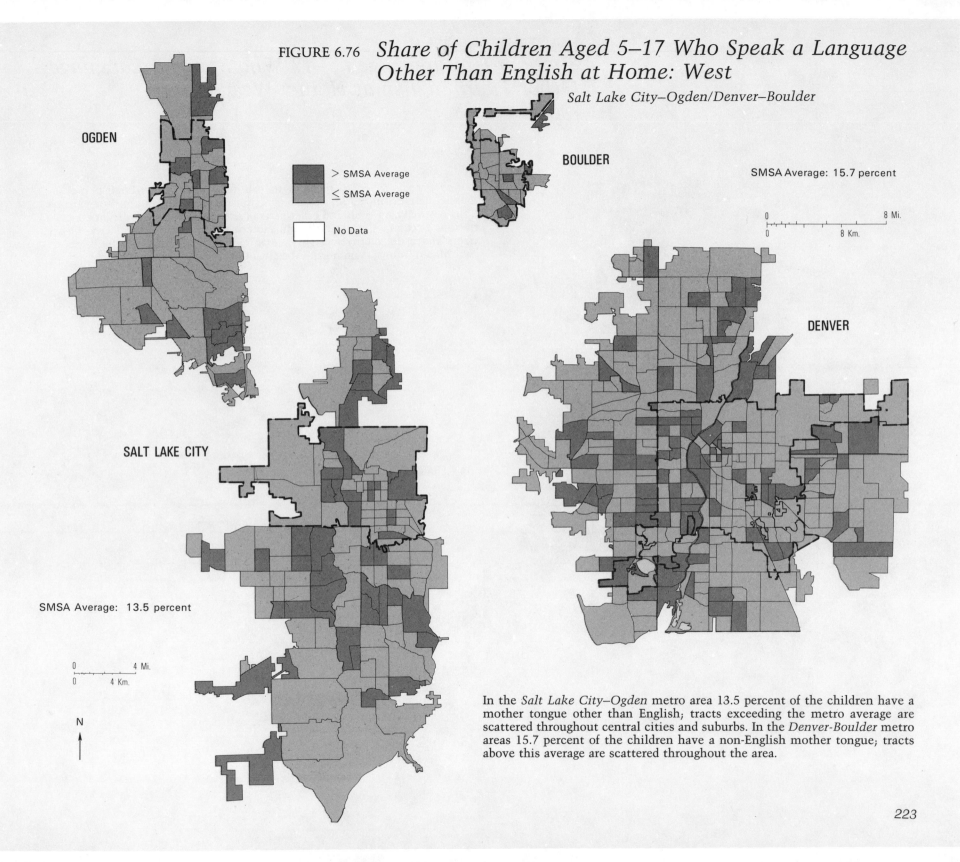

FIGURE 6.76 *Share of Children Aged 5–17 Who Speak a Language Other Than English at Home: West*

Salt Lake City–Ogden/Denver–Boulder

OGDEN

BOULDER

> SMSA Average

≤ SMSA Average

No Data

SMSA Average: 15.7 percent

0   8 Mi.

0   8 Km.

DENVER

SALT LAKE CITY

SMSA Average: 13.5 percent

0   4 Mi.

0   4 Km.

N

In the *Salt Lake City–Ogden* metro area 13.5 percent of the children have a mother tongue other than English; tracts exceeding the metro average are scattered throughout central cities and suburbs. In the *Denver–Boulder* metro areas 15.7 percent of the children have a non-English mother tongue; tracts above this average are scattered throughout the area.

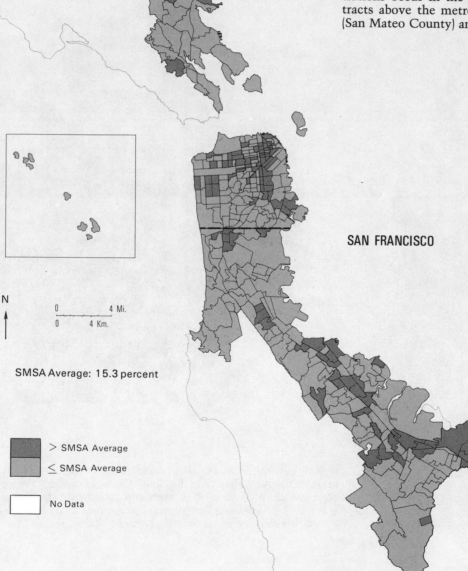

FIGURE 6.77

Share of Children Aged 5–17 Who Speak a Language Other Than English at Home: West

San Francisco

In *San Francisco* 15.3 percent of the children have a non-English mother tongue. The urbanized area is a major immigration destination for persons from Pacific Basin lands and other parts of Latin America. Significant concentrations occur in the northern and eastern parts of the central city. Other tracts above the metro average are scattered throughout the suburbs south (San Mateo County) and north (Marin County) of the city.

SAN FRANCISCO

N

0   4 Mi.

0   4 Km.

SMSA Average: 15.3 percent

> SMSA Average

≤ SMSA Average

No Data

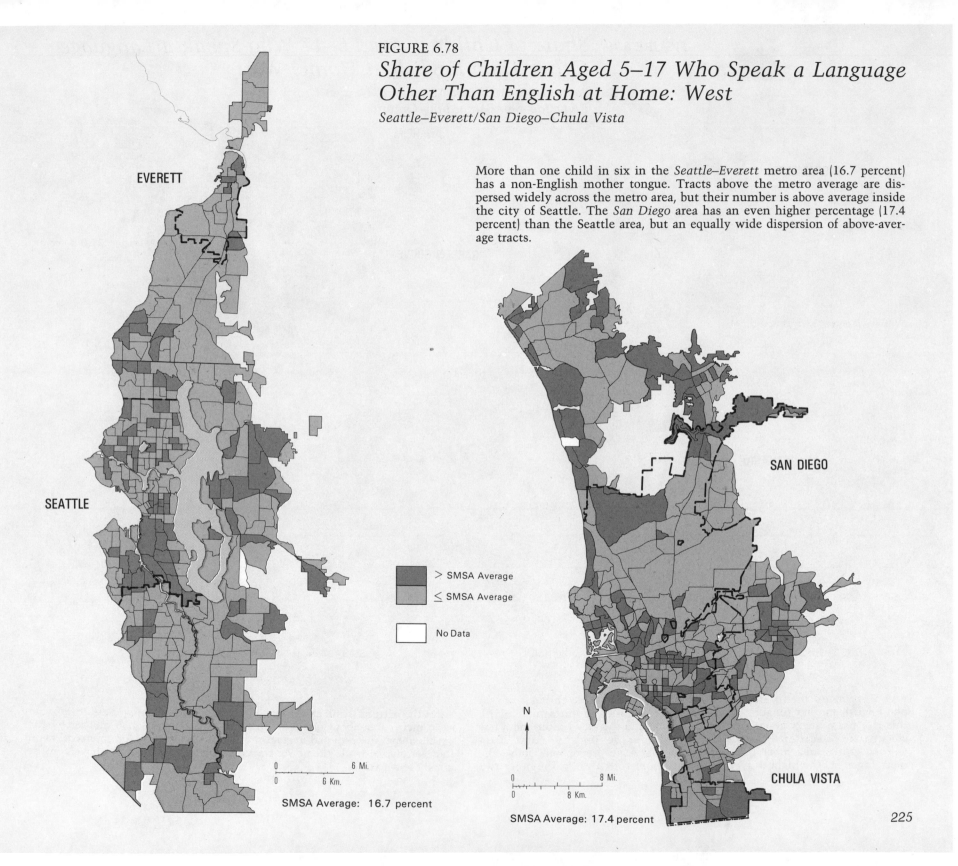

FIGURE 6.78

Share of Children Aged 5–17 Who Speak a Language Other Than English at Home: West

Seattle–Everett/San Diego–Chula Vista

EVERETT

SEATTLE

More than one child in six in the *Seattle–Everett* metro area (16.7 percent) has a non-English mother tongue. Tracts above the metro average are dispersed widely across the metro area, but their number is above average inside the city of Seattle. The *San Diego* area has an even higher percentage (17.4 percent) than the Seattle area, but an equally wide dispersion of above-average tracts.

SAN DIEGO

CHULA VISTA

> SMSA Average

≤ SMSA Average

No Data

0   6 Mi.

0   6 Km.

SMSA Average: 16.7 percent

N

0   8 Mi.

0   8 Km.

SMSA Average: 17.4 percent

225

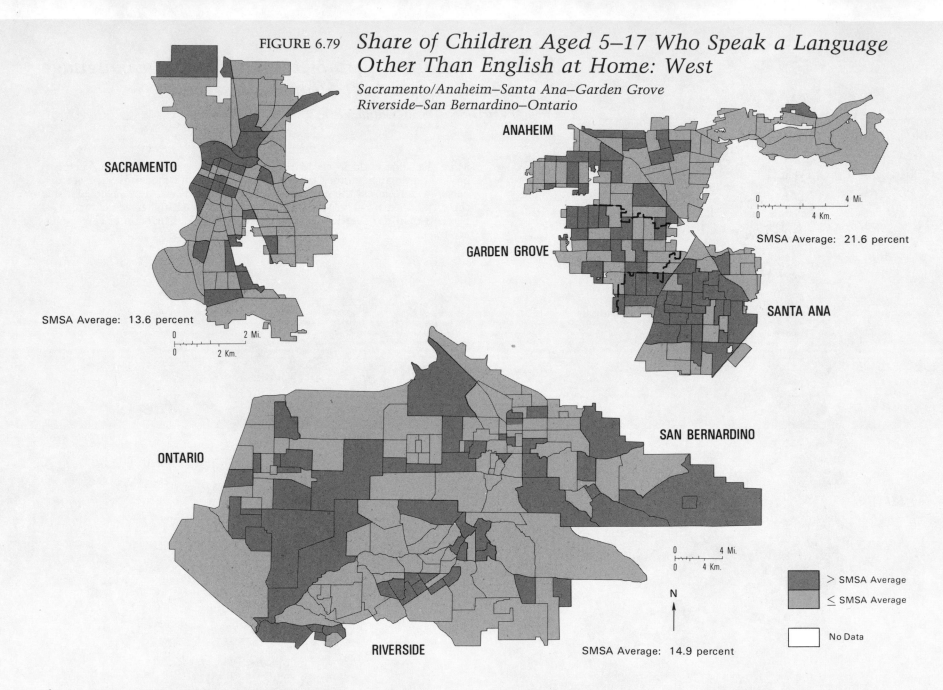

FIGURE 6.79 *Share of Children Aged 5–17 Who Speak a Language Other Than English at Home: West*

Sacramento/Anaheim–Santa Ana–Garden Grove Riverside–San Bernardino–Ontario

SACRAMENTO

SMSA Average: 13.6 percent

0 2 Mi.
0 2 Km.

ANAHEIM

GARDEN GROVE

SANTA ANA

0 4 Mi.
0 4 Km.

SMSA Average: 21.6 percent

ONTARIO

SAN BERNARDINO

RIVERSIDE

0 4 Mi.
0 4 Km.

N

SMSA Average: 14.9 percent

> SMSA Average

≤ SMSA Average

No Data

The *Sacramento* metro area has a moderate proportion of children with a non-English mother tongue. Unlike many other cities in our sample of 19, this city has a heavy concentration in and around the city center and a few concentrations scattered elsewhere in the city. In the *Anaheim–Santa Ana–Garden Grove* area most tracts in Santa Ana have proportions above the metro average, the highest average in our sample of cities. In the other two cities the pattern is mixed throughout. In the *Riverside–San Bernardino–Ontario* metro area about one child in seven has a non-English mother tongue. Tracts above the national average are concentrated in older core sections of the metro area, while the newer tracts on the edge of the cities have conspicuously fewer tracts.

Single-Unit Housing Within Urbanized Areas

The geographic distribution of the various types of housing options plays a central role in determining where different kinds of households live. The main distinctions in housing type are in terms of value and of housing units per unit area, or density. The housing stock in most urban areas contains a full range of housing units arrayed by value and located at different densities.

Because most housing in American cities was built during the last century, a period of steadily improving mobility, the residential densities of new construction have typically been lower than the densities of earlier housing, and consumers like it that way. Most households prefer low-density to high-density housing, with preferences for type of unit dictated by considerations of costs compared with income, household size, and household composition.

Because of the ways that we built housing through the decades, the smaller, older, and cheaper units are usually in the inner city, while newer, more expensive, and larger units are closer to the outer edges of the urbanized area. Family households with children usually adjust their budgets to obtain the extra interior room and exterior yard space they feel they need for a growing family. After children grow up and leave, the empty-nester parents are slow to contract their housing consumption by moving to a smaller unit. It is sometimes hard to predict if children once gone will stay away, and it is easier to store a house full of possessions than to decide what must go when moving to smaller quarters.

Zoning laws vigorously protect single-unit housing areas as the locations on the urban landscape that have the highest social value. In these areas a sense of control by owner occupants enhances the stability of the area. Before 1970, when many suburban areas were almost entirely filled with single-unit houses, the contrast between city, with its mixed housing stock, and suburb was greater than it is today. The suburban apartment boom, which started in the late 1960s, diversified the housing stock of many suburbs.

Renter households that aspire to owner occupancy usually prefer single-unit housing. A disproportionate share of owner-occupied housing is single-unit housing. In recent decades most owner occupants in single-unit housing have realized significant asset appreciation from their houses. City neighborhoods and suburban communities with high proportions of single-unit houses are generally areas that are in demand by families, which in turn is a factor in their continued stability.

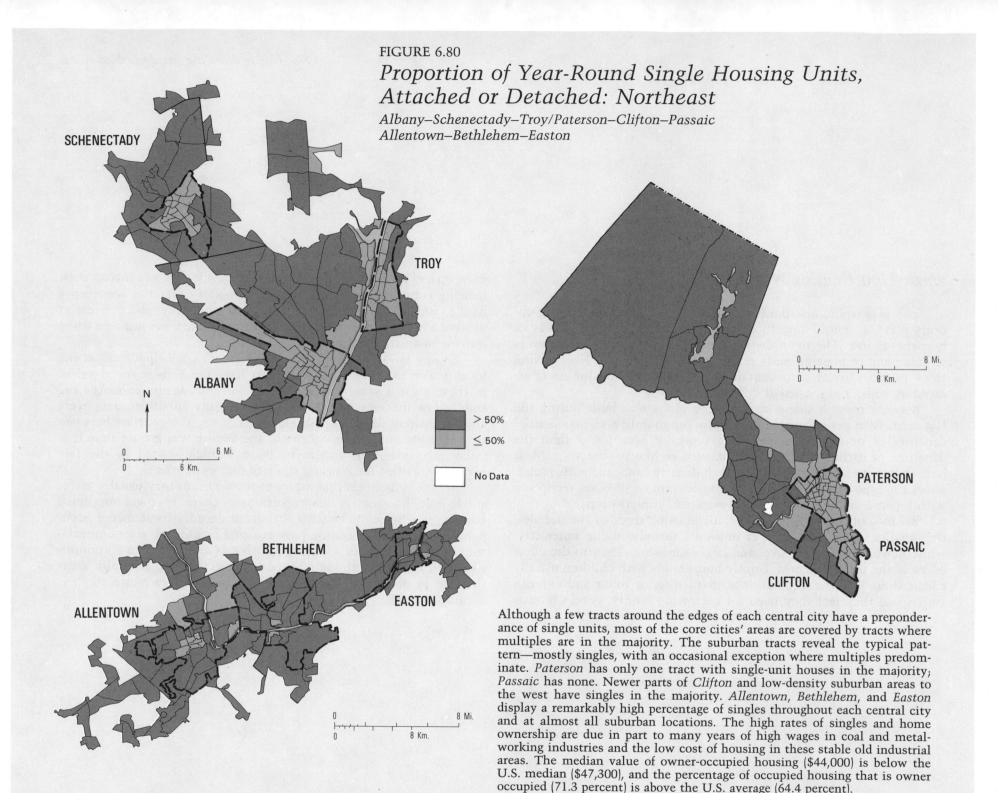

FIGURE 6.80

Proportion of Year-Round Single Housing Units, Attached or Detached: Northeast

Albany–Schenectady–Troy/Paterson–Clifton–Passaic
Allentown–Bethlehem–Easton

SCHENECTADY

TROY

ALBANY

N

> 50%

≤ 50%

No Data

0   6 Mi.

0   6 Km.

PATERSON

PASSAIC

CLIFTON

0   8 Mi.

0   8 Km.

BETHLEHEM

EASTON

ALLENTOWN

0   8 Mi.

0   8 Km.

Although a few tracts around the edges of each central city have a preponderance of single units, most of the core cities' areas are covered by tracts where multiples are in the majority. The suburban tracts reveal the typical pattern—mostly singles, with an occasional exception where multiples predominate. *Paterson* has only one tract with single-unit houses in the majority; *Passaic* has none. Newer parts of *Clifton* and low-density suburban areas to the west have singles in the majority. *Allentown, Bethlehem,* and *Easton* display a remarkably high percentage of singles throughout each central city and at almost all suburban locations. The high rates of singles and home ownership are due in part to many years of high wages in coal and metal-working industries and the low cost of housing in these stable old industrial areas. The median value of owner-occupied housing ($44,000) is below the U.S. median ($47,300), and the percentage of occupied housing that is owner occupied (71.3 percent) is above the U.S. average (64.4 percent).

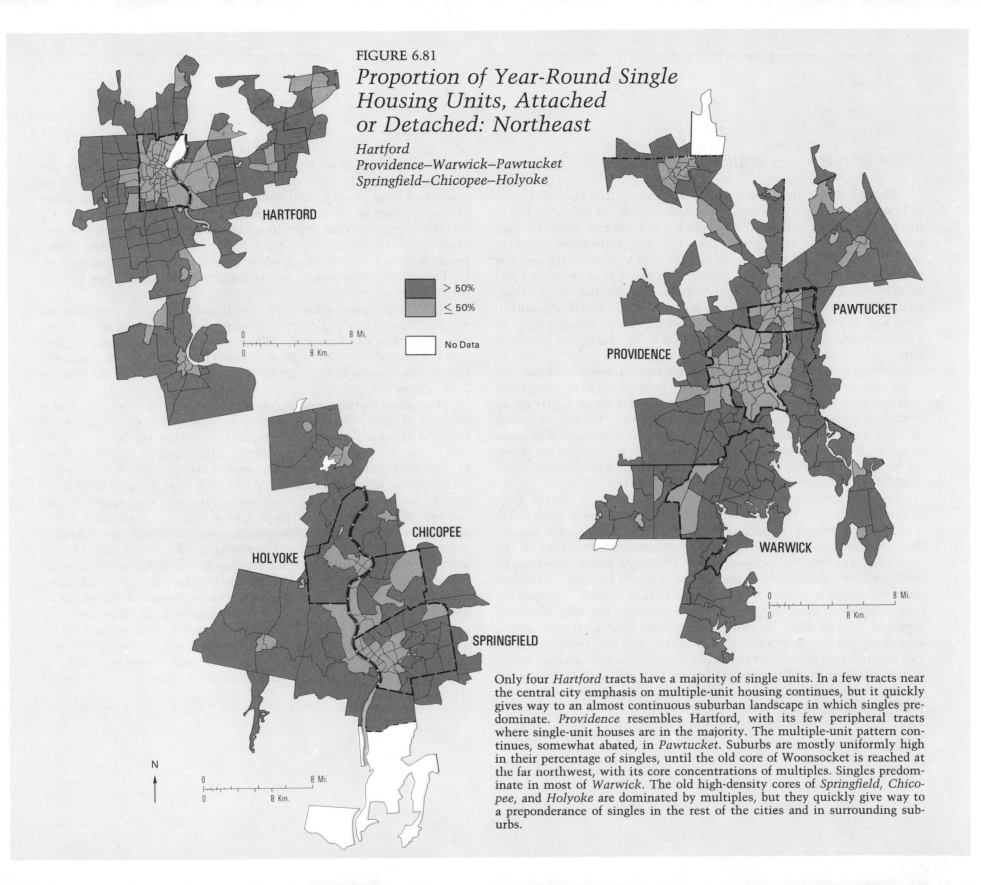

FIGURE 6.81

Proportion of Year-Round Single Housing Units, Attached or Detached: Northeast

Hartford
Providence–Warwick–Pawtucket
Springfield–Chicopee–Holyoke

HARTFORD

> 50%

≤ 50%

No Data

0   8 Mi.

0   8 Km.

PAWTUCKET

PROVIDENCE

WARWICK

0   8 Mi.

0   8 Km.

CHICOPEE

HOLYOKE

SPRINGFIELD

N

0   8 Mi.

0   8 Km.

Only four *Hartford* tracts have a majority of single units. In a few tracts near the central city emphasis on multiple-unit housing continues, but it quickly gives way to an almost continuous suburban landscape in which singles predominate. *Providence* resembles Hartford, with its few peripheral tracts where single-unit houses are in the majority. The multiple-unit pattern continues, somewhat abated, in *Pawtucket*. Suburbs are mostly uniformly high in their percentage of singles, until the old core of Woonsocket is reached at the far northwest, with its core concentrations of multiples. Singles predominate in most of *Warwick*. The old high-density cores of *Springfield*, *Chicopee*, and *Holyoke* are dominated by multiples, but they quickly give way to a preponderance of singles in the rest of the cities and in surrounding suburbs.

Single-Unit Housing Within Central Cities

In most urban areas the density of housing—that is, the number of housing units per unit area—has been controlled by the value of the land at the time the housing was built. Land that carries a high price offers valuable accessibility properties and environmental amenities. When city land is cheap, it can be used extravagantly and low densities are the result. When land is expensive, it is conserved and used in small amounts per dollar value of construction on it. Thus, an expensive lot by the ocean, on a lake, or on a hill with a beautiful view will support either one or two very expensive housing units or a large number of smaller units, each on a less expensive parcel of land.

Zoning practice in older cities generally followed land-use patterns that already were in place. If a city grew faster than transit and road systems could be installed in the late nineteenth and early twentieth centuries, the shortage of buildable lots in the face of strong demand drove up land prices and encouraged developers and builders to put up housing at high densities on narrow lots. Chicago neighborhoods from the 1920s are a good example. Baltimore's row house neighborhoods from the 1840s are another example.

In some cities the growth fell far short of projections and of what the road and transit systems could handle. The result was large cheap lots and low-density residential construction. Minneapolis and St. Paul are good examples. Twin Cities streetcar entrepreneurs, on the basis of rapid population growth in the 1880s and 1890s, projected an urbanized area population of one million persons by 1920—and then built the streetcar system to accommodate such growth. The population expansion never matched the projections, but the expanded streetcar system added so much developable land to the urbanized area that land prices dropped to low levels, and the Twin Cities region became one of the lowest-density large metro areas in the United States, with single-unit detached housing in many areas where the zoning allows doubles and multiples. But zoning provided only a ceiling to densities—not a floor.

In the old metro areas of the Northeast, and occasionally in the Midwest and South, the location of the central city boundary is an artifact of local history. As urbanized areas expanded in population and areal extent at the end of the nineteenth century and in the early twentieth century, state legislatures in urbanizing areas acted to prevent reapportionment of political power and to curtail the cities' power to annex peripheral suburban areas into their jurisdictions. After boundaries were frozen, suburbanization continued, but beyond the city limits.

In the new metro areas of the South and West some states—most notably Texas—enabled cities to keep expanding their borders to enclose suburban developments. When this expansion occurs, it puts into the central city part or all of the new housing stock that in other metro areas can be found only in first-tier or second-tier suburbs, or even farther out.

The maps in this section describe the tracts in 1980 that had a majority of their housing in single-unit (attached or detached) structures. In urban real estate markets, and in popular sentiment, single-unit, owner-occupied housing is higher priced and more desirable on average than rental housing. Cities that boast a healthy proportion of their housing stock in singles have an easier time hanging onto community leadership that might otherwise disappear to narrow, provincial and illiberal suburbs. Cities that have significant numbers of single-unit houses scattered throughout many neighborhoods have a greater proportion of property-tax-paying residents and diverse outlooks represented in city and metro political debates. Single-unit houses have larger households, on the average, and more children than do housing units in multiple structures. Balanced communities have a wide range of economic activities to support them and a diverse assortment of housing options—old and new, large and small, expensive and modestly priced, high density and low density—for residents to live regardless of their financial circumstances, tastes, or stage of life. These maps portray the variety present among the 19 cities.

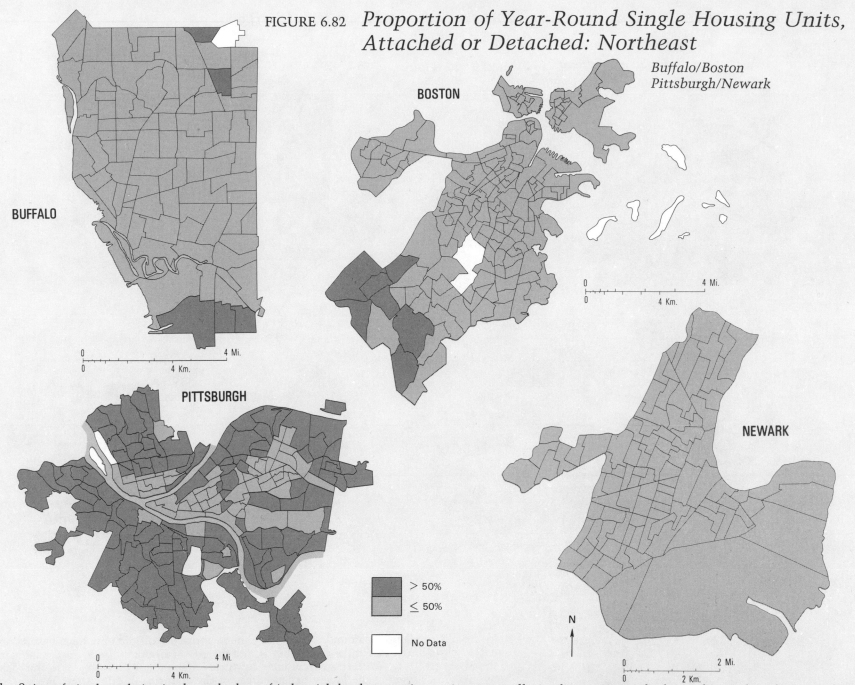

FIGURE 6.82 *Proportion of Year-Round Single Housing Units, Attached or Detached: Northeast*

Buffalo/Boston
Pittsburgh/Newark

BOSTON

BUFFALO

PITTSBURGH

NEWARK

> 50%

≤ 50%

No Data

N

The fixing of city boundaries in the early days of industrial development in *Buffalo* and population expansion means that only in a few tracts on the edge of the city do single units predominate. Suburbanization in *Boston* was channeled southwestward on a highly confined site between the Charles River to the west and Boston Harbor to the east. High demand and limited supply drove prices so high that the land area was actually extended into the Harbor and Back Bay, but high densities have resulted throughout the old area, dropping eventually in the streetcar suburbs to the south and west and in the auto-oriented suburbs beyond. Continuous prosperity for many decades and extensive transit systems serving downtown and the industrial developments along the river and stream valleys in the hilly *Pittsburgh* area have led to substantial development in single-unit housing. Extraordinary development pressure surrounding the *Newark* and greater New York area leaves no tract in the city where single-unit housing predominates.

231

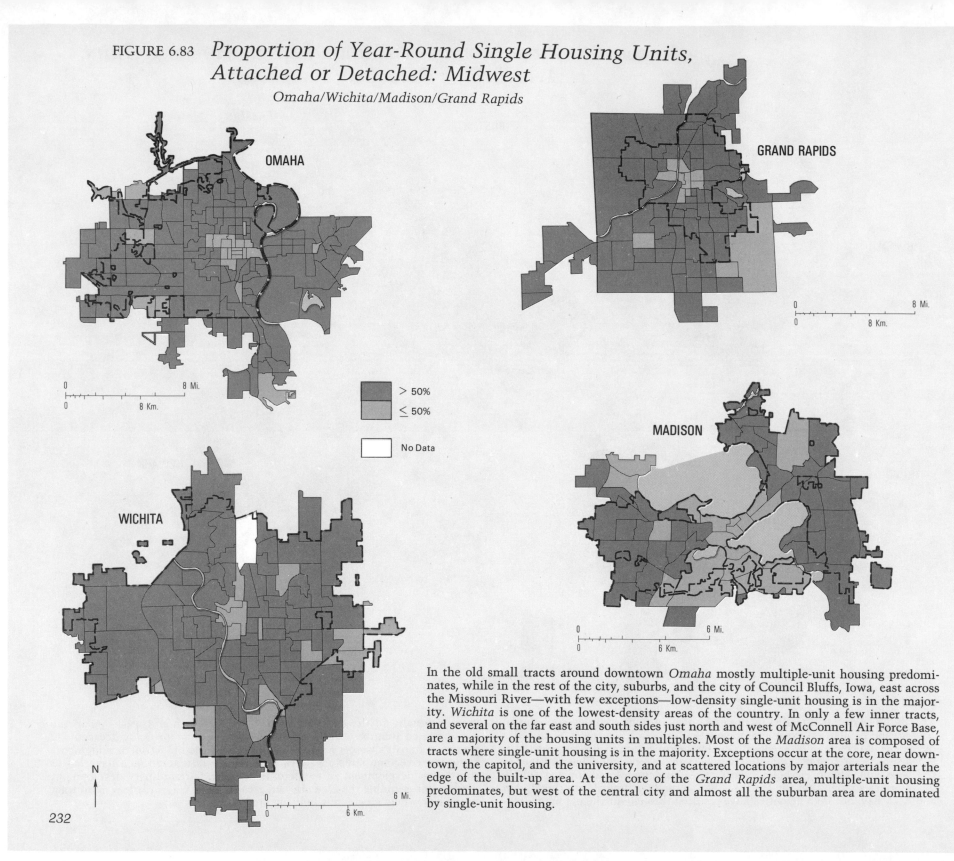

FIGURE 6.83 *Proportion of Year-Round Single Housing Units, Attached or Detached: Midwest*

Omaha/Wichita/Madison/Grand Rapids

OMAHA

GRAND RAPIDS

0   8 Mi.

0   8 Km.

> 50%

≤ 50%

No Data

MADISON

0   6 Mi.

0   6 Km.

WICHITA

N

0   6 Mi.

0   6 Km.

In the old small tracts around downtown *Omaha* mostly multiple-unit housing predominates, while in the rest of the city, suburbs, and the city of Council Bluffs, Iowa, east across the Missouri River—with few exceptions—low-density single-unit housing is in the majority. *Wichita* is one of the lowest-density areas of the country. In only a few inner tracts, and several on the far east and south sides just north and west of McConnell Air Force Base, are a majority of the housing units in multiples. Most of the *Madison* area is composed of tracts where single-unit housing is in the majority. Exceptions occur at the core, near downtown, the capitol, and the university, and at scattered locations by major arterials near the edge of the built-up area. At the core of the *Grand Rapids* area, multiple-unit housing predominates, but west of the central city and almost all the suburban area are dominated by single-unit housing.

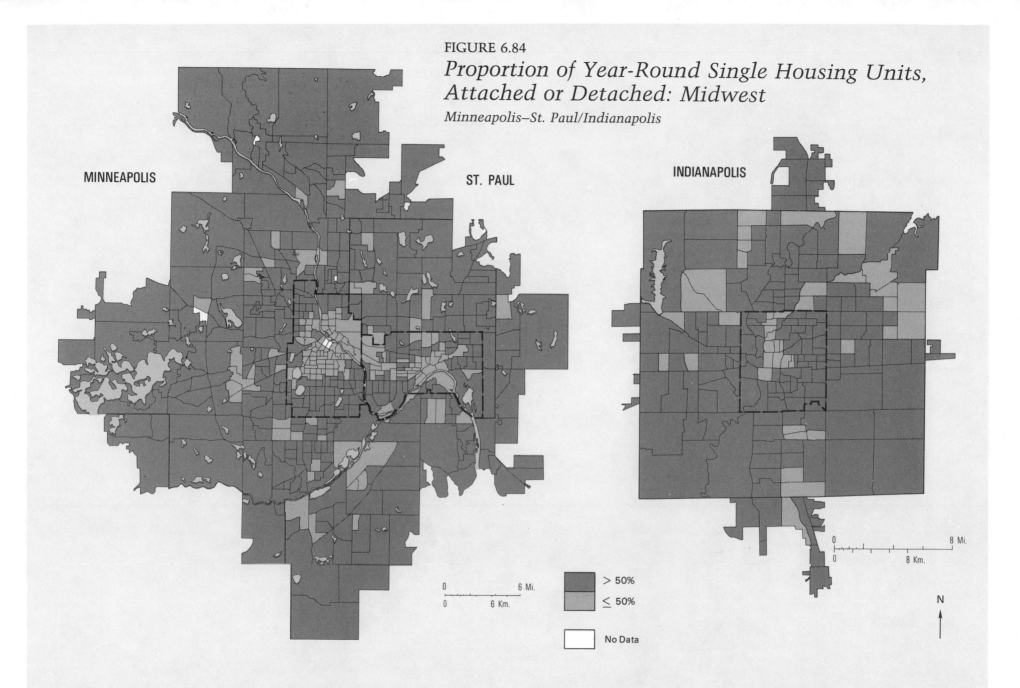

FIGURE 6.84

Proportion of Year-Round Single Housing Units, Attached or Detached: Midwest

Minneapolis–St. Paul/Indianapolis

MINNEAPOLIS

ST. PAUL

INDIANAPOLIS

0   8 Mi.

0   8 Km.

0   6 Mi.

0   6 Km.

> 50%

≤ 50%

No Data

N

The inner half of *Minneapolis* and the inner third of *St. Paul* are dominated by multiple-unit housing. Outside the core singles predominate throughout Minneapolis; St. Paul is more mixed. Suburban areas are dominated by singles, but tracts emphasizing multiples occur sporadically in every sector. The core tracts and extensions north of city center in *Indianapolis* are dominated by multiples. In most of the city's tracts single-unit housing predominates, as in the suburbs. Areas with a majority of multiples are scattered throughout the suburbs.

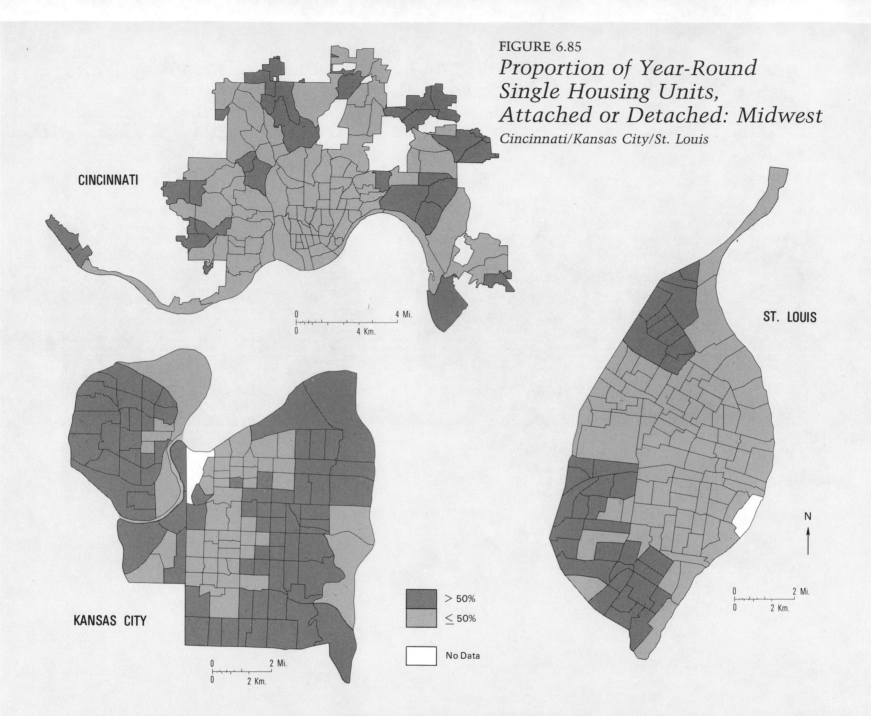

FIGURE 6.85

Proportion of Year-Round Single Housing Units, Attached or Detached: Midwest

Cincinnati/Kansas City/St. Louis

CINCINNATI

KANSAS CITY

ST. LOUIS

N

> 50%

≤ 50%

No Data

0   4 Mi.
0   4 Km.

0   2 Mi.
0   2 Km.

0   2 Mi.
0   2 Km.

Cincinnati has only a minority of tracts where single-unit housing predominates—but those areas are in most parts of the city, which is a good sign of stability. In *Kansas City*, Kansas, almost all tracts contain predominantly single-unit housing. Kansas City, Missouri, has a large sector of multiples south of downtown, and another smaller thrust to the east, but most of the city area is covered by mainly single-unit tracts. *St. Louis* had its city limits fixed in the nineteenth century and so failed to capture some of the suburban areas that have developed since 1872. The result is that singles predominate in only a few tracts—in the far south and southwest and the far northwest.

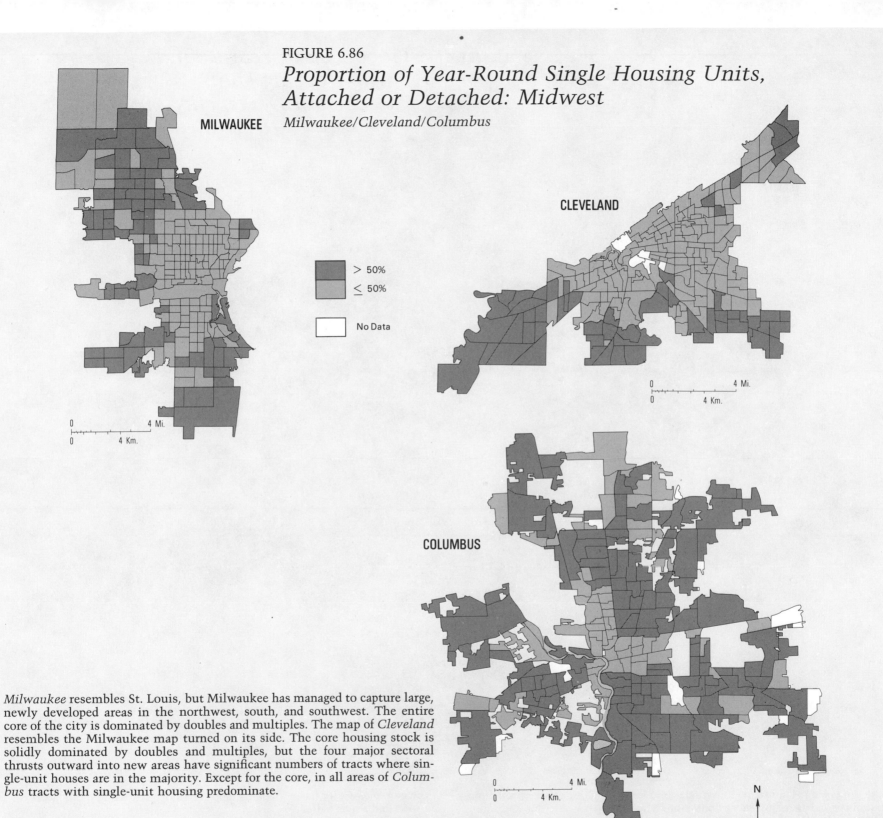

FIGURE 6.86
Proportion of Year-Round Single Housing Units, Attached or Detached: Midwest
Milwaukee/Cleveland/Columbus

MILWAUKEE

CLEVELAND

COLUMBUS

> 50%

≤ 50%

No Data

Milwaukee resembles St. Louis, but Milwaukee has managed to capture large, newly developed areas in the northwest, south, and southwest. The entire core of the city is dominated by doubles and multiples. The map of *Cleveland* resembles the Milwaukee map turned on its side. The core housing stock is solidly dominated by doubles and multiples, but the four major sectoral thrusts outward into new areas have significant numbers of tracts where single-unit houses are in the majority. Except for the core, in all areas of *Columbus* tracts with single-unit housing predominate.

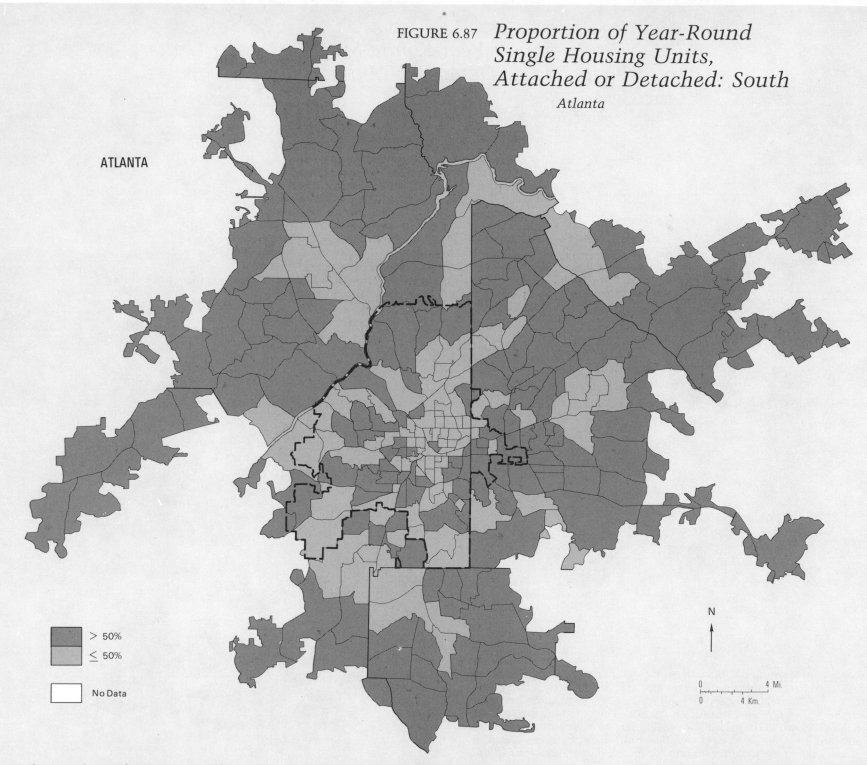

FIGURE 6.87 *Proportion of Year-Round Single Housing Units, Attached or Detached: South*

Atlanta

ATLANTA

> 50%

≤ 50%

No Data

N

0   4 Mi.

0   4 Km.

In the sprawling *Atlanta* region single-unit houses predominate throughout the suburbs, with major exceptions along the northwest corridor and along the fashionable Peachtree corridor to the north-northeast of city center. Most of the core of the city has a preponderance of multiples, as do many areas on the west and south sides.

FIGURE 6.88

Proportion of Year-Round Single Housing Units, Attached or Detached: South

Raleigh–Durham/Orlando

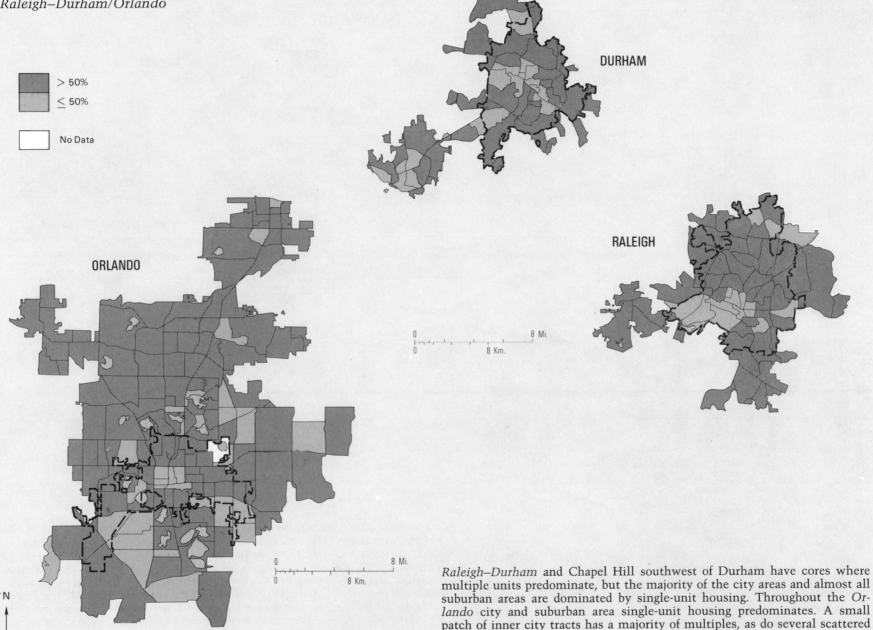

> 50%

≤ 50%

No Data

DURHAM

ORLANDO

RALEIGH

0   8 Mi.

0   8 Km.

0   8 Mi.

0   8 Km.

N

Raleigh–Durham and Chapel Hill southwest of Durham have cores where multiple units predominate, but the majority of the city areas and almost all suburban areas are dominated by single-unit housing. Throughout the *Orlando* city and suburban area single-unit housing predominates. A small patch of inner city tracts has a majority of multiples, as do several scattered suburban locations along main corridors to the northeast, southeast, and southwest.

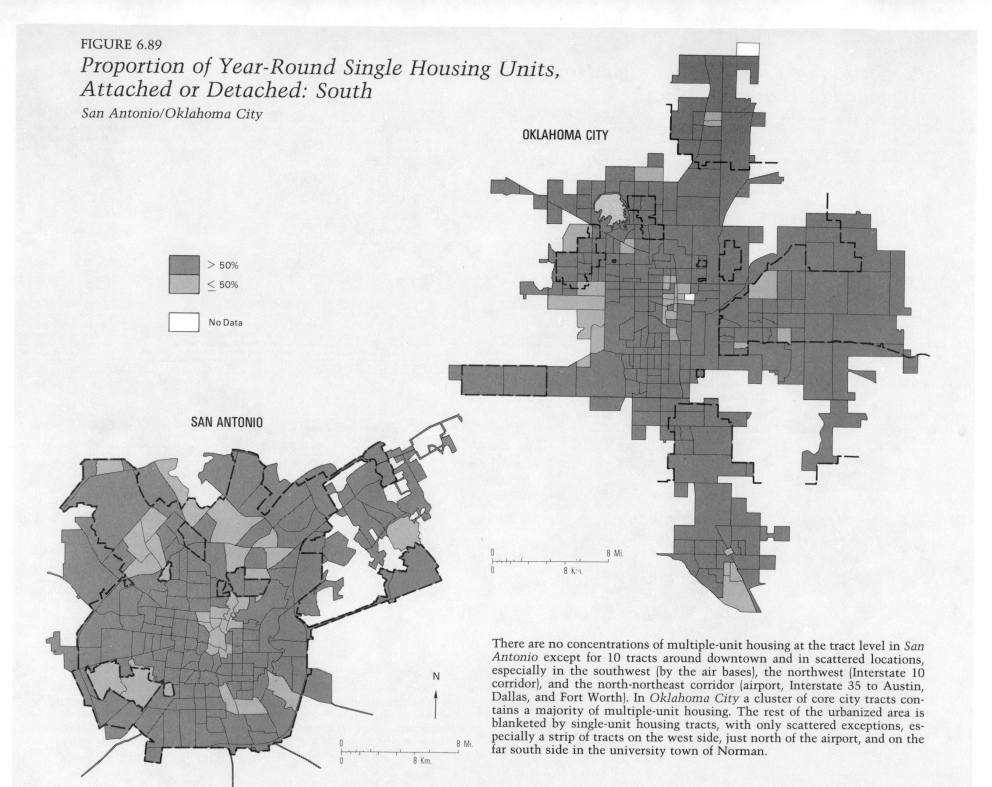

FIGURE 6.89
Proportion of Year-Round Single Housing Units, Attached or Detached: South
San Antonio/Oklahoma City

OKLAHOMA CITY

> 50%

≤ 50%

No Data

SAN ANTONIO

N

0 ———— 8 Mi.

0 ———— 8 Km.

0 ———— 8 Mi.

0 ———— 8 Km.

There are no concentrations of multiple-unit housing at the tract level in *San Antonio* except for 10 tracts around downtown and in scattered locations, especially in the southwest (by the air bases), the northwest (Interstate 10 corridor), and the north-northeast corridor (airport, Interstate 35 to Austin, Dallas, and Fort Worth). In *Oklahoma City* a cluster of core city tracts contains a majority of multiple-unit housing. The rest of the urbanized area is blanketed by single-unit housing tracts, with only scattered exceptions, especially a strip of tracts on the west side, just north of the airport, and on the far south side in the university town of Norman.

FIGURE 6.90

Proportion of Year-Round Single Housing Units, Attached or Detached: South

Birmingham/Memphis

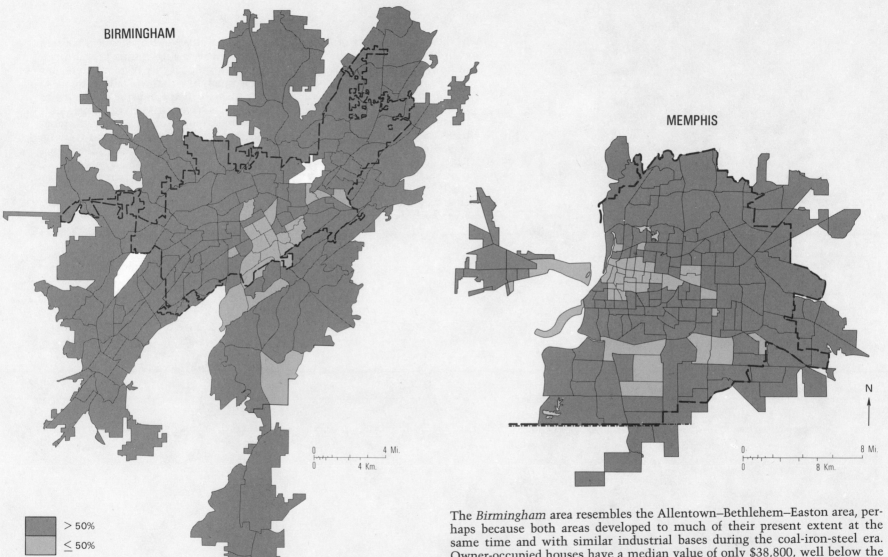

BIRMINGHAM

MEMPHIS

N

> 50%

≤ 50%

No Data

The *Birmingham* area resembles the Allentown–Bethlehem–Easton area, perhaps because both areas developed to much of their present extent at the same time and with similar industrial bases during the coal-iron-steel era. Owner-occupied houses have a median value of only $38,800, well below the U.S. average, but were above the national average of all occupied units at 67.6 percent. A small core of inner city tracts is dominated by multiple-unit housing, but in almost all other areas single-unit housing predominates. An extensive old high-density core of *Memphis* is dominated by multiple-unit housing, but almost everywhere else in the city, as well as in the suburbs, single-unit housing is in the majority.

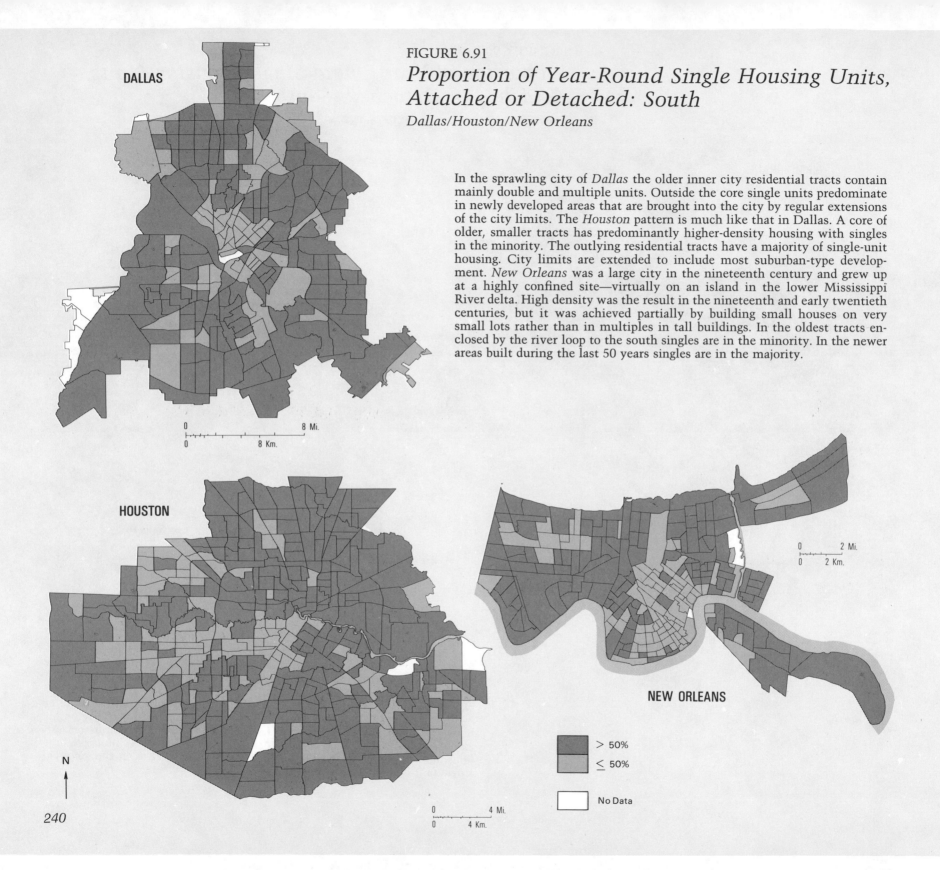

DALLAS

FIGURE 6.91

Proportion of Year-Round Single Housing Units, Attached or Detached: South

Dallas/Houston/New Orleans

In the sprawling city of *Dallas* the older inner city residential tracts contain mainly double and multiple units. Outside the core single units predominate in newly developed areas that are brought into the city by regular extensions of the city limits. The *Houston* pattern is much like that in Dallas. A core of older, smaller tracts has predominantly higher-density housing with singles in the minority. The outlying residential tracts have a majority of single-unit housing. City limits are extended to include most suburban-type development. *New Orleans* was a large city in the nineteenth century and grew up at a highly confined site—virtually on an island in the lower Mississippi River delta. High density was the result in the nineteenth and early twentieth centuries, but it was achieved partially by building small houses on very small lots rather than in multiples in tall buildings. In the oldest tracts enclosed by the river loop to the south singles are in the minority. In the newer areas built during the last 50 years singles are in the majority.

```
0                    8 Mi.
0                    8 Km.
```

HOUSTON

NEW ORLEANS

```
0      2 Mi.
0      2 Km.
```

N

> 50%

≤ 50%

No Data

```
0        4 Mi.
0        4 Km.
```

FIGURE 6.92

Proportion of Year-Round Single Housing Units, Attached or Detached: South

Baltimore/Washington/Miami

Like New Orleans, inner city old *Baltimore* built at high densities, but did so with row houses rather than with small singles or with duplexes and apartment houses. Today, the single attached house dominates the city center except for a few tracts at the edge of downtown. Outside the core throughout the city singles continue to predominate, but conventional detached singles are the rule. In *Washington* single-unit housing predominates in many tracts west of Rock Creek, in outlying parts of northern and northeastern Washington, and in a few tracts in the southeastern part of the city. A core of high-density tracts in *Miami* is surrounded by a ring of predominantly singles; the patterns are mixed at the edge.

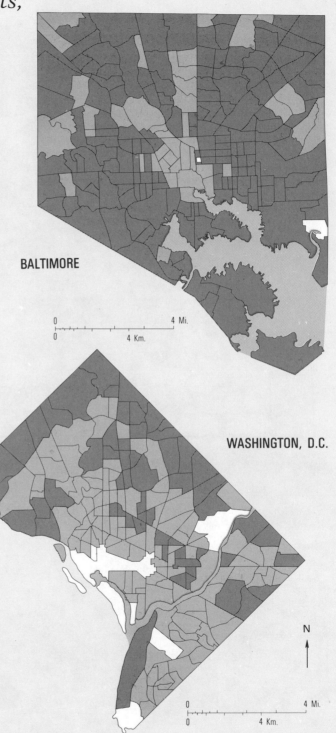

BALTIMORE

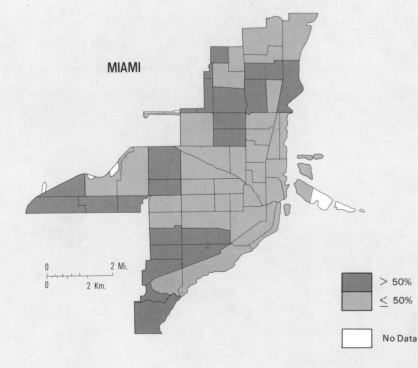

MIAMI

WASHINGTON, D.C.

> 50%

≤ 50%

No Data

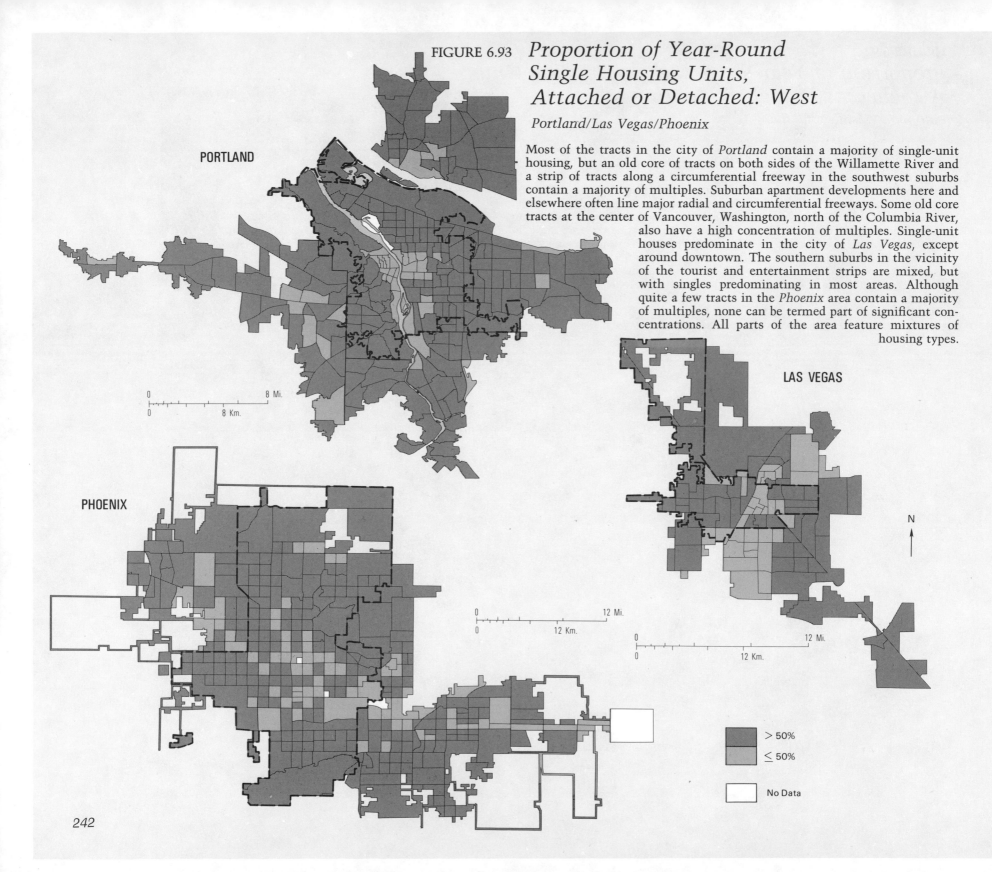

FIGURE 6.93 *Proportion of Year-Round Single Housing Units, Attached or Detached: West*

Portland/Las Vegas/Phoenix

PORTLAND

Most of the tracts in the city of *Portland* contain a majority of single-unit housing, but an old core of tracts on both sides of the Willamette River and a strip of tracts along a circumferential freeway in the southwest suburbs contain a majority of multiples. Suburban apartment developments here and elsewhere often line major radial and circumferential freeways. Some old core tracts at the center of Vancouver, Washington, north of the Columbia River, also have a high concentration of multiples. Single-unit houses predominate in the city of *Las Vegas*, except around downtown. The southern suburbs in the vicinity of the tourist and entertainment strips are mixed, but with singles predominating in most areas. Although quite a few tracts in the *Phoenix* area contain a majority of multiples, none can be termed part of significant concentrations. All parts of the area feature mixtures of housing types.

LAS VEGAS

0 ___ 8 Mi.
0 ___ 8 Km.

PHOENIX

0 ___ 12 Mi.
0 ___ 12 Km.

N

0 ___ 12 Mi.
0 ___ 12 Km.

> 50%

≤ 50%

No Data

242

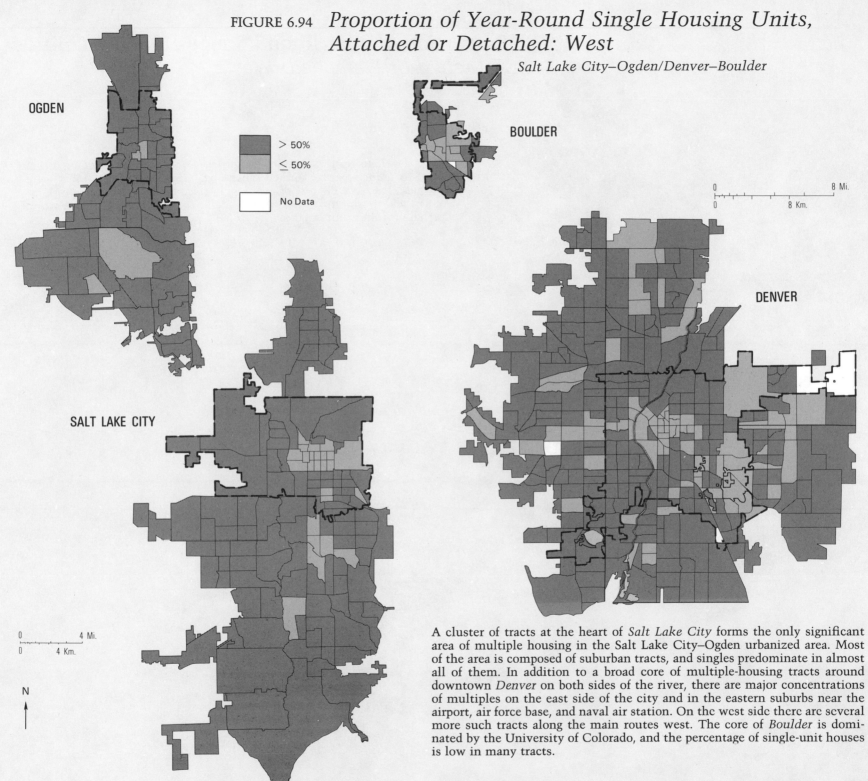

FIGURE 6.94 *Proportion of Year-Round Single Housing Units, Attached or Detached: West*

Salt Lake City–Ogden/Denver–Boulder

OGDEN

BOULDER

> 50%

≤ 50%

No Data

DENVER

SALT LAKE CITY

0   4 Mi.

0   4 Km.

N

0   8 Mi.

0   8 Km.

A cluster of tracts at the heart of *Salt Lake City* forms the only significant area of multiple housing in the Salt Lake City–Ogden urbanized area. Most of the area is composed of suburban tracts, and singles predominate in almost all of them. In addition to a broad core of multiple-housing tracts around downtown *Denver* on both sides of the river, there are major concentrations of multiples on the east side of the city and in the eastern suburbs near the airport, air force base, and naval air station. On the west side there are several more such tracts along the main routes west. The core of *Boulder* is dominated by the University of Colorado, and the percentage of single-unit houses is low in many tracts.

243

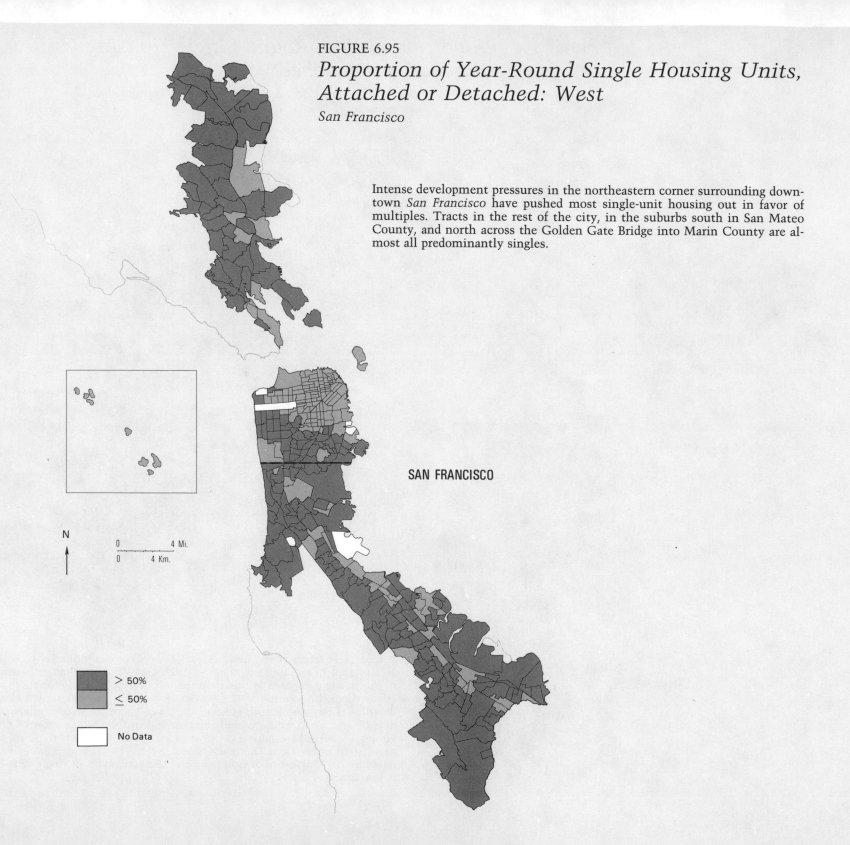

FIGURE 6.95

Proportion of Year-Round Single Housing Units, Attached or Detached: West

San Francisco

Intense development pressures in the northeastern corner surrounding downtown *San Francisco* have pushed most single-unit housing out in favor of multiples. Tracts in the rest of the city, in the suburbs south in San Mateo County, and north across the Golden Gate Bridge into Marin County are almost all predominantly singles.

SAN FRANCISCO

N

0   4 Mi.

0   4 Km.

> 50%

≤ 50%

No Data

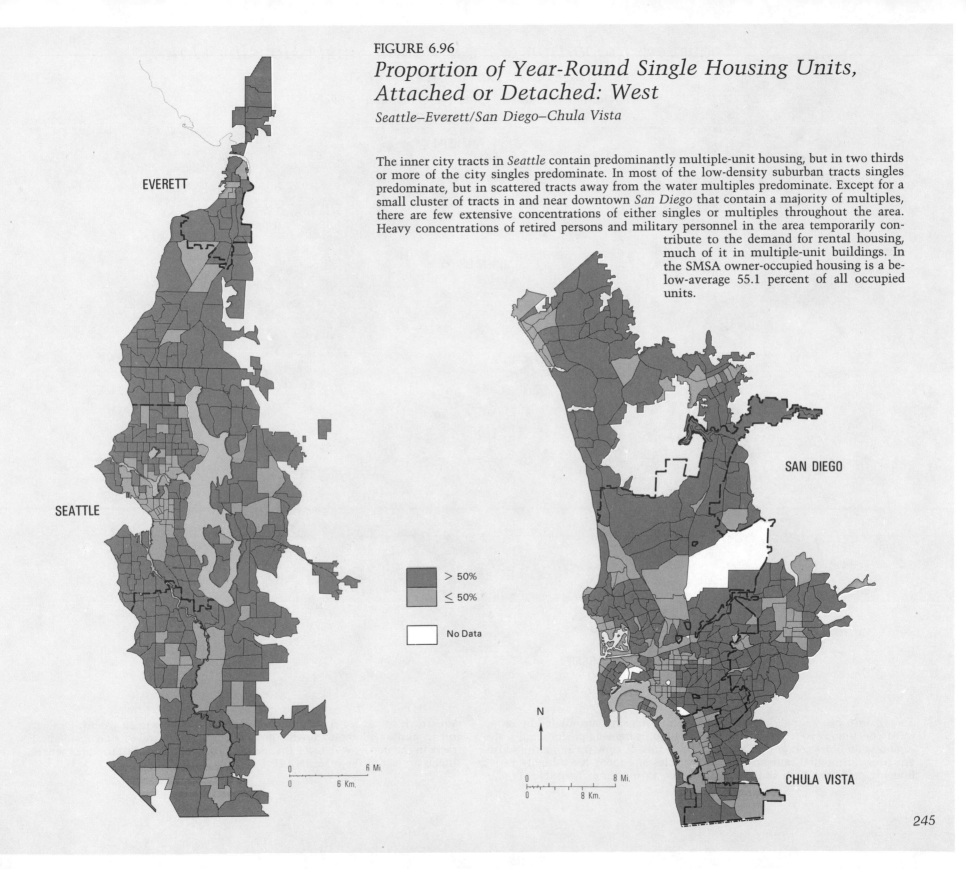

FIGURE 6.96

Proportion of Year-Round Single Housing Units, Attached or Detached: West

Seattle–Everett/San Diego–Chula Vista

The inner city tracts in *Seattle* contain predominantly multiple-unit housing, but in two thirds or more of the city singles predominate. In most of the low-density suburban tracts singles predominate, but in scattered tracts away from the water multiples predominate. Except for a small cluster of tracts in and near downtown *San Diego* that contain a majority of multiples, there are few extensive concentrations of either singles or multiples throughout the area. Heavy concentrations of retired persons and military personnel in the area temporarily contribute to the demand for rental housing, much of it in multiple-unit buildings. In the SMSA owner-occupied housing is a below-average 55.1 percent of all occupied units.

EVERETT

SEATTLE

SAN DIEGO

CHULA VISTA

> 50%

≤ 50%

No Data

N

0   6 Mi
0   6 Km.

0   8 Mi.
0   8 Km.

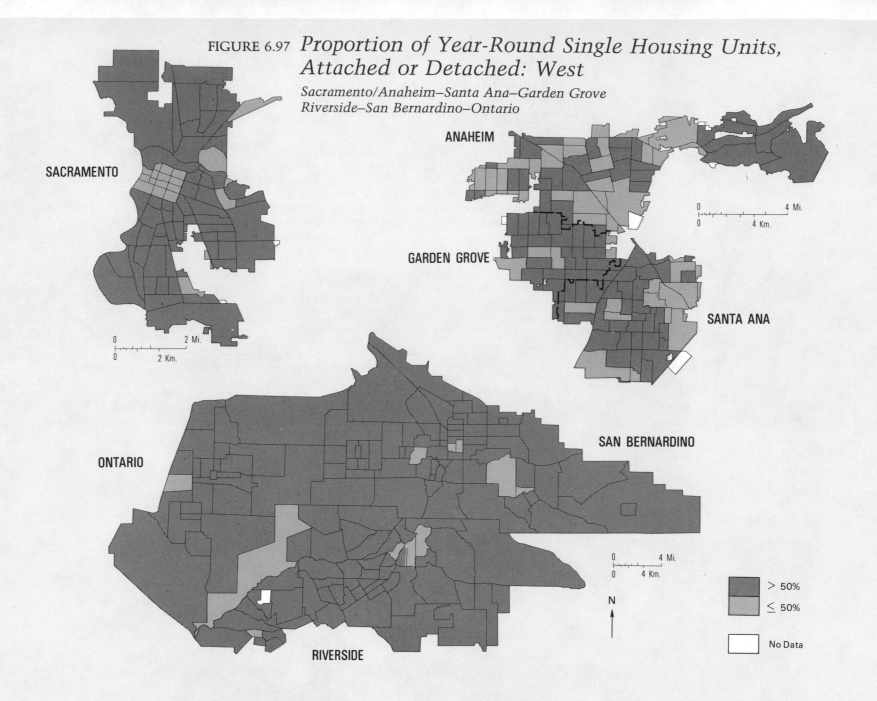

FIGURE 6.97 *Proportion of Year-Round Single Housing Units, Attached or Detached: West*
Sacramento/Anaheim–Santa Ana–Garden Grove
Riverside–San Bernardino–Ontario

Sacramento has a single core of high-density housing surrounded by an almost continuous zone of tracts where single-unit housing predominates. *Anaheim* is an older center by California standards. It grew up along the southern transcontinental railroad into Los Angeles and today has a highly varied housing map with high and low densities occurring throughout. Newer *Garden Grove* and *Santa Ana* have had most of their growth in recent decades, and in almost all tracts singles predominate. It is hard to find residential tracts in the new, low-density *Riverside–San Bernardino–Ontario* area where singles are not in the majority.

New Housing Units in the Central City, 1979–March 1980

Almost all new housing units built in recent decades have been erected on new land in suburban settings. Some new housing has been built on former railroad, port, and obsolete industrial land or placed in central city neighborhoods on land cleared of a former residential use. The new housing is often built at densities higher than the obsolete housing it replaces. School buildings, warehouses, and factory buildings have been rehabilitated and converted to residential use.

Since 1970 a significant amount of new housing has been built in or near the downtown of cities, occasionally as one element in a development program that includes several functions: hotels, shops, offices, housing, and so forth. Some houses, apartment buildings, condominiums, and other structures stand alone as separate private and publicly sponsored projects. Sometimes the new housing is the result of major building rehabilitation, renovation, or occasionally a historic preservation project in the oldest part of town, which is usually the core.[37]

Houses built one or two at a time can succeed in the suburbs, but within the built-up central city new residential development must be on a sufficiently large scale in order to succeed. Housing provides a bundle of services: a structure and dwelling place; the social and physical environment of the neighborhood; and accessibility to various sections of the urban area. If a residential development takes place on a sufficiently large scale—say, 10 acres or more—it can create its own physical and social environment. Then, if it is well situated with respect to accessibility, it can succeed. If a new development on the edge of the built-up area or near the core is located in a sector of the urban area that has been traditionally favored by the elite, then it is much easier to establish a social environment that promotes success of the development.

In developments on the edge of the built-up area, large parcels of land are usually available for housing. In inner city redevelopment, small parcels are usually the only ones available. Complex development projects and financial deals involving inner city land acquisition for housing often favor large buildings on small parcels. Profits can be greater for a given amount of entrepreneurial and management effort on a large downtown project than on a small one. Land acquisition for a single parcel is easier than for multiple parcels, so costly delays can be controlled during the land acquisition phase of development.

In the 1970s the suburbs got most of the new housing, but the central city and the downtown area got a share. The developments in the inner city got more attention than the suburban developments because they were visually more interesting and easier for the press to cover. In the context of post–World War II suburban residential trends through the 1960s, the downtown developments were unexpected and frequently triggered conflict—and media attention is drawn to conflict.

[37]See S. B. Laska and Daphne Spain, eds., *Back to the City: Issues in Neighborhood Renovation* (New York: Pergamon, 1980); John Mercer and D. A. Phillips, "Attitudes of Homeowners and the Decision to Rehabilitate Property," *Urban Geography* 2, no. 3 (1981): 216–36; and D. D. Rosenthal, ed., *Urban Revitalization* (Beverly Hills, CA: Sage, 1980).

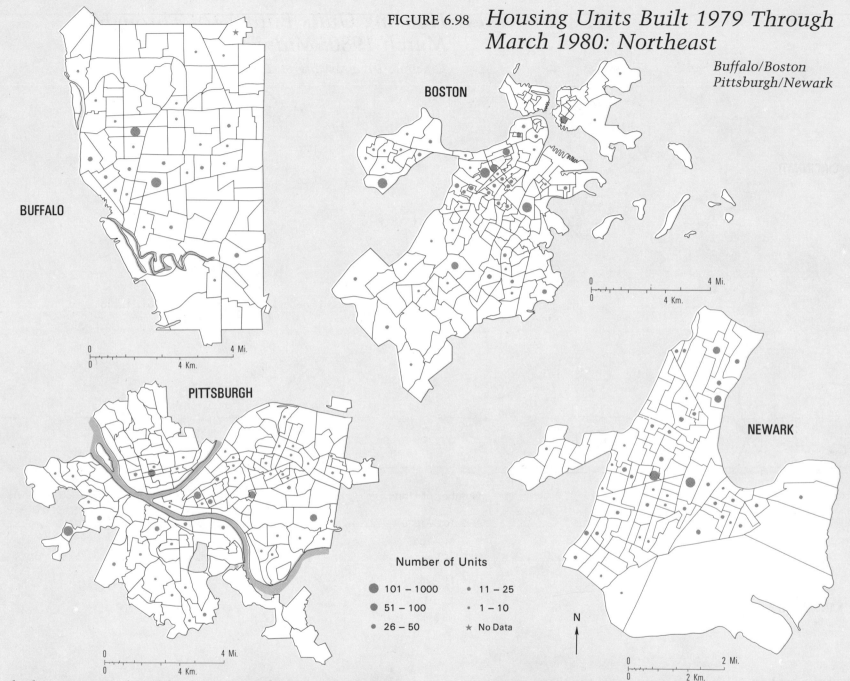

FIGURE 6.98 *Housing Units Built 1979 Through March 1980: Northeast*

Buffalo/Boston
Pittsburgh/Newark

BOSTON

BUFFALO

PITTSBURGH

NEWARK

Number of Units

- 101 – 1000
- 51 – 100
- 26 – 50
- 11 – 25
- 1 – 10
- ★ No Data

N

In the large majority of *Buffalo* tracts no new housing construction took place. Two tracts near downtown gained over 100 units each. The pattern of new housing in the city of *Boston* resembles Buffalo's. Most development occurred near the core. Three tracts gained more than 100 new units, and one over 200. Most had none or fewer than 10. In one tract in western *Pittsburgh* over 100 new housing units were built, and in eastern Pittsburgh another 100.

A few projects were developed near downtown, but the pattern of inner city concentration seen in Buffalo and Boston is absent here. Most tracts had none or fewer than 10 new units. New units reported in many *Newark* tracts suggest steady but perhaps insufficient renewal of the city's housing stock. In two tracts near city center over 100 new units were built, and a few scattered tracts had one to several dozen.

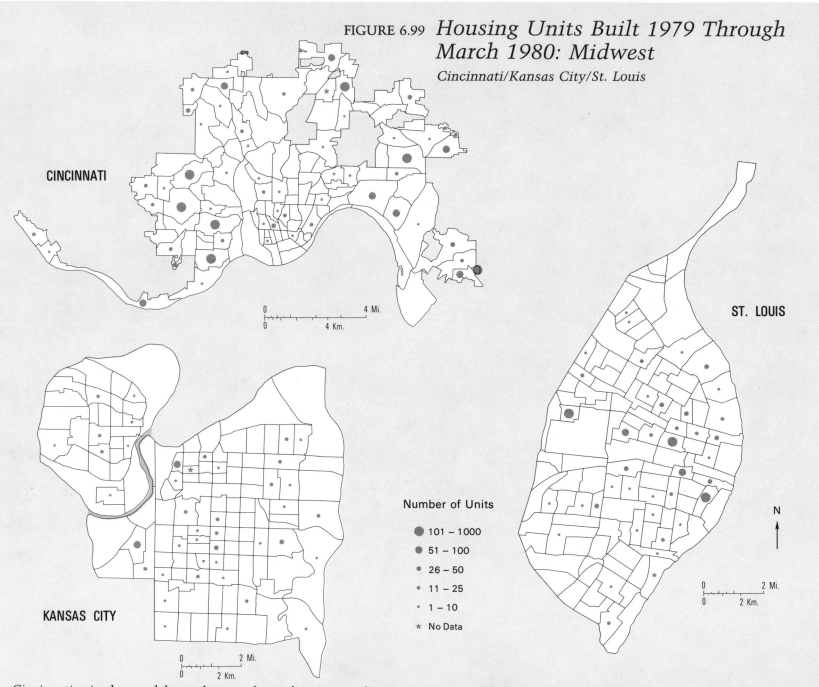

CINCINNATI

ST. LOUIS

KANSAS CITY

Number of Units

● 101 – 1000
● 51 – 100
● 26 – 50
· 11 – 25
. 1 – 10
★ No Data

N

Cincinnati gained several large clusters of new housing on the west side, with over 150 new units each in two tracts and over 200 in a third tract. Significant numbers of new units were built in various locations on the east and north sides, but almost no new construction occurred in the old core-city tracts. One tract near downtown *Kansas City*, Missouri, gained almost 100 new housing units, and a peripheral tract in Kansas City, Kansas, over 50.

Other tracts in both cities had few or none. The same was true in *St. Louis*. In several tracts close to downtown a total of about 500 new housing units were added, and in another western tract west of Forest Park by Washington University, almost 200. Elsewhere, new construction was extremely limited or nonexistent.

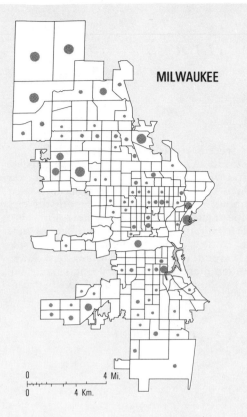

MILWAUKEE

FIGURE 6.100

Housing Units Built 1979 Through March 1980: Midwest

Milwaukee/Cleveland/Columbus

CLEVELAND

Number of Units

- 101 – 1000
- 51 – 100
- 26 – 50
- 11 – 25
- 1 – 10
- ★ No Data

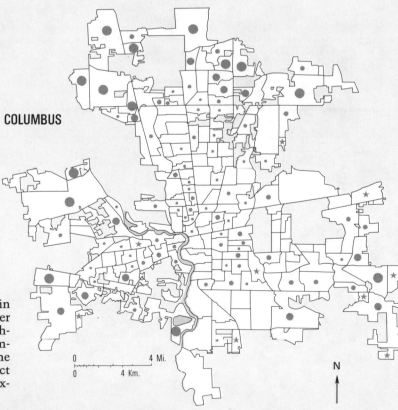

COLUMBUS

Significant amounts of new housing construction occurred in *Milwaukee* in the vigorous northwest sector where the eight leading tracts gained over 1,500 new units. New units near city center were scarce, except for the high-amenity location near the lake. In the quiet and stable south side small numbers of new units were added at many locations. Except for one tract on the eastern edge of downtown with 180 new units, and another west-side tract on the lake with 164, the new housing construction in *Cleveland* was extremely sparse.

N

251

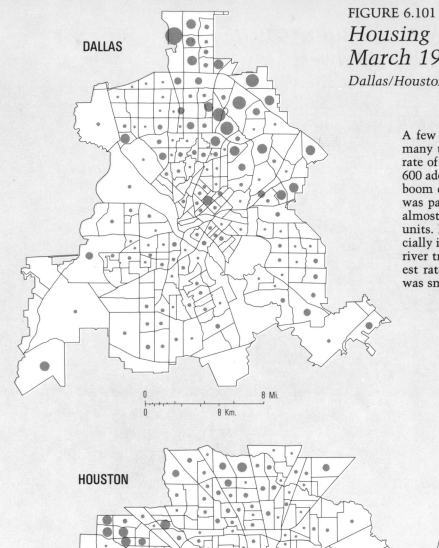

DALLAS

0 ——— 8 Mi.
0 ——— 8 Km.

FIGURE 6.101
Housing Units Built 1979 Through March 1980: South
Dallas/Houston/New Orleans

A few hundred new housing units were added to core tracts in *Dallas* and many thousands were built on the north and east sides. There was a modest rate of construction on the south and west sides as well, with a peak of over 600 added to one peripheral tract there. *Houston* was one of the nation's great boom cities of the 1970s, and new housing construction throughout the city was part of the result. The west-side tracts gained the most new units, but almost all tracts in all parts of the city gained significant numbers of new units. In *New Orleans* a significant number of units were constructed, especially in the newly developing northeastern, western, and southeastern downriver tracts. The old, historic, and often protected inner city tracts had modest rates of new construction, but the number of units added to each tract was small.

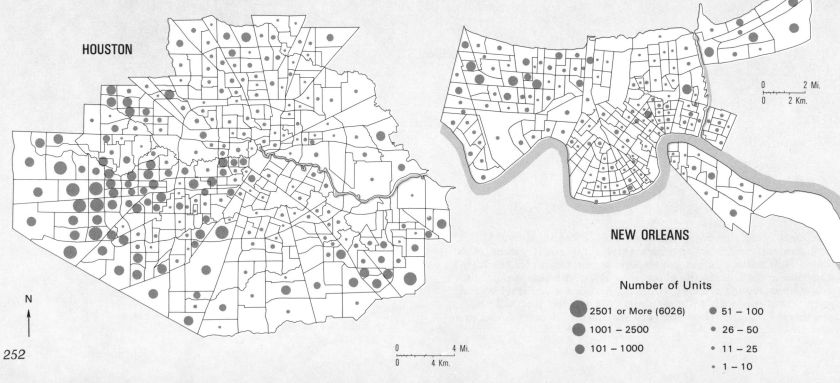

HOUSTON

N

0 ——— 4 Mi.
0 ——— 4 Km.

0 ——— 2 Mi.
0 ——— 2 Km.

NEW ORLEANS

Number of Units

- 2501 or More (6026)
- 1001 – 2500
- 101 – 1000
- 51 – 100
- 26 – 50
- 11 – 25
- 1 – 10

FIGURE 6.102
Housing Units Built 1979 Through March 1980: South

Baltimore/Washington/Miami

Scattered development and redevelopment projects in *Baltimore* added over 100 new housing units to each of seven tracts, but the core tracts in general gained little new housing, like most tracts elsewhere in the city. New housing construction occurred throughout the city of *Washington* and was especially intense around the core and in tracts to the north, east of Rock Creek. The largest increment was at the northeastern edge behind the National Arboretum. In *Miami* new housing construction was significant in all parts of the city, but was intense in tracts by the ocean just north and south of downtown.

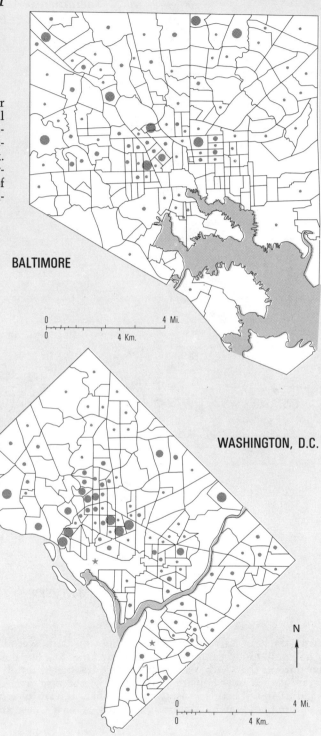

BALTIMORE

0 ——— 4 Mi.
0 ——— 4 Km.

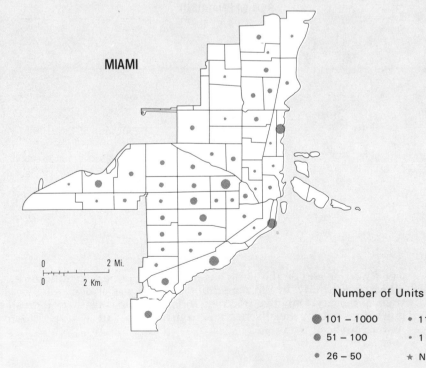

MIAMI

0 ——— 2 Mi.
0 ——— 2 Km.

WASHINGTON, D.C.

N

0 ——— 4 Mi.
0 ——— 4 Km.

Number of Units

● 101 – 1000   • 11 – 25

● 51 – 100   · 1 – 10

● 26 – 50   ★ No Data

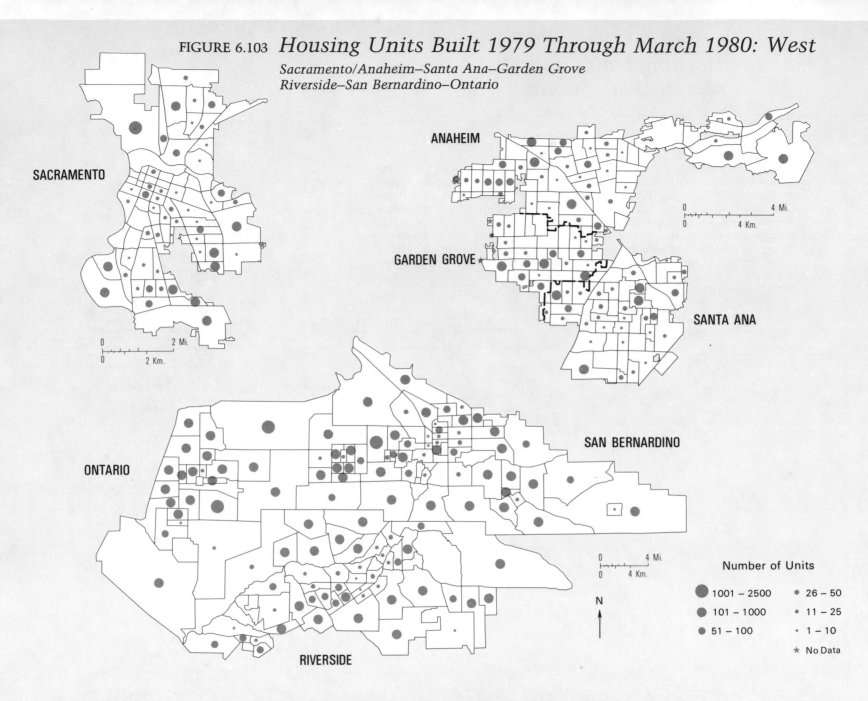

FIGURE 6.103 *Housing Units Built 1979 Through March 1980: West*
Sacramento/Anaheim–Santa Ana–Garden Grove
Riverside–San Bernardino–Ontario

SACRAMENTO

ANAHEIM

GARDEN GROVE ★

SANTA ANA

ONTARIO

SAN BERNARDINO

RIVERSIDE

N

Number of Units

- 1001 – 2500
- 101 – 1000
- 51 – 100
- 26 – 50
- 11 – 25
- 1 – 10
- ★ No Data

In half the core tracts of *Sacramento* no new housing units were built, and in the other half only modest numbers, from a few units to a few dozen, were built. Farther out, on the south, east, and north sides, construction was vigorous. *Anaheim* gained new housing in all parts of the city, as did *Garden Grove* and *Santa Ana*. There seems to be little bias toward or against the downtowns and old cores (which are not very old by East Coast standards).

The *Riverside* area on the south had new construction at significant levels in all parts of the city. In *San Bernardino* building was also vigorous in all districts of the city. Only two tracts in *Ontario* had no construction. In all three cities core tracts generally had new construction, but at levels lower than newer peripheral tracts.

Changes in Median Values of Housing in the Central City, 1970–1980

Suburban areas around central cities and upper-middle-class sub-markets within cities and suburbs enjoyed above-average housing price appreciation in the 1970s and received a disproportionate share of the new construction during the decade. New housing is usually higher priced than existing housing; and when it is built in an area it not only raises the median housing values for that reason, but also pulls up values of lower-priced houses, which become more attractive when located near higher-priced properties.[38]

Middle- and upper-middle-class households accrued significant untaxed capital gains on their houses in the 1970s, and those gains lowered significantly (sometimes to zero or lower) their real after-tax housing costs. Above-average disposable household income in mid-dle- and upper-middle-class neighborhoods and a high average propensity to spend, based in part on the steadily enhanced wealth position of the homeowner, contribute to a strong tax base in the area; a healthy, vigorous, and attractive business environment that people enjoy living near and using; and good practices of tending the physical and scenic infrastructure of the area. In a circular and cumulative process, attractive upper-middle-class neighborhoods are created, oc-cupied, and maintained. Renters like to live in these areas and will do so if they can afford to and leave if they cannot. Above-average housing price advances in such neighborhoods usually force many renters out even if zoning permits them. Owners are insulated from above-average value increases—they actually benefit from them—whereas renters enjoy no such protection, except in the rare case where rents are kept well below market levels by local rent control ordinances.

Where are these prized locations? Usually in one or two suburban sectors that lie beyond the central city neighborhoods that enjoyed that high status at an earlier time. Occasionally a central city will retain some neighborhoods that compete effectively with the more desirable and exclusive suburbs. If and when the central cities suc-ceed in the competition—as they have in Seattle, San Francisco, St. Paul, Minneapolis, New Orleans, Miami, and some others—they can retain a significant share of the metro leadership and put that leader-ship to work on their behalf. If a central city cannot, the leadership eventually abandons it for the suburbs, leaving a core city with a much-diminished capacity to dictate the terms of its future as a place to live, work, and recreate.

In the maps that follow we calculated the ratio: median value of owner-occupied housing in the SMSA in 1980 compared with the same measure in 1970. For each SMSA this ratio was a threshold. The lowest values occurred in Buffalo (2.22), Boston (2.35), Cleveland (2.36), and Newark (2.56), where growth in the 1970s was slow, which meant that appreciation of values from market forces was muted, and the slow pace of new construction raised average prices very little.

At the other extreme, rapid rates of new construction combined with inflationary pressures on existing housing stock pushed the 1980/1970 metro ratios to high levels in Houston (3.72), Anaheim–Santa Ana–Garden Grove (3.93), Riverside–San Bernardino–Ontario (3.68), and Sacramento (3.62). Baltimore's ratio was 3.38, but part of the explanation for this high ratio is the overlap of its suburbs with those from Washington, which received large volumes of expensive new housing in the 1970s.

Once each metro area's average rate of change was established, each 1980 central city tract was examined to see how its median housing value changed between 1970 and 1980 compared with the rate of metro change.

If a tract's boundaries changed only slightly between 1970 and 1980, we ignored the changes. Medians are estimates for the tract area and are relatively stable with respect to minor boundary shifts, which generally do not affect the median much.

In only two tracts in *Buffalo* did median housing values rise faster in the 1970s than the metro ratio ($39,700/$17,900 = 2.22), and those tracts were near downtown, presumably with only a few owner-occupied units. One had some new construction during the decade; the other could have lost some of its lowest-value housing, which would have raised its median. *Boston* was subject to intense development pressure around the harbor and downtown area in the 1970s. Comparing the Boston map of new housing with this map ▶

---

[38] See J. R. Follain and S. Malpezzi, "Estimates of Housing Inflation for 39 SMSAs: An Alternative to the Consumer Price Index," *Annals of Regional Science* 14, no. 3 (1980): 41–56.

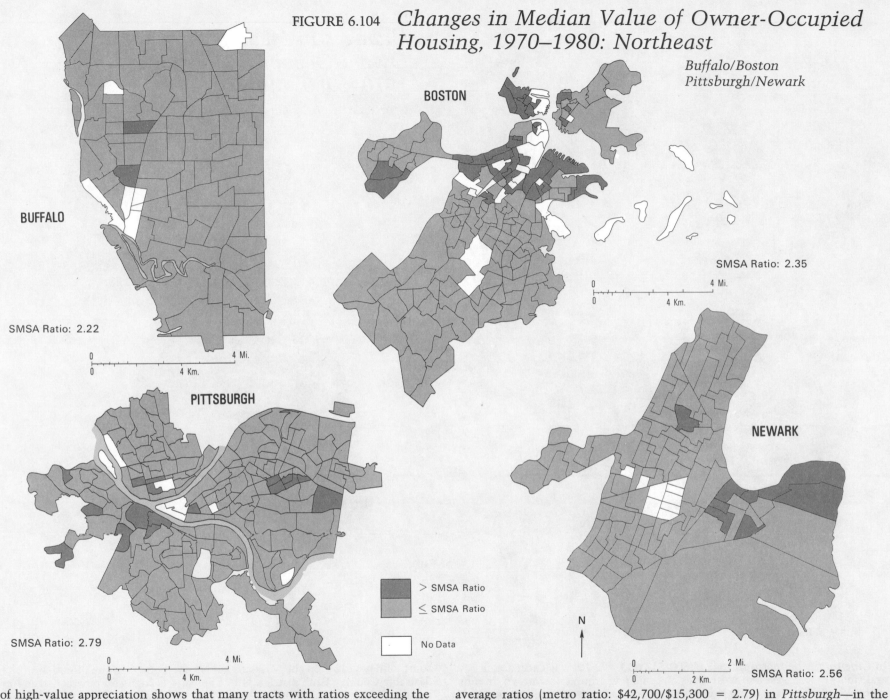

FIGURE 6.104 *Changes in Median Value of Owner-Occupied Housing, 1970–1980: Northeast*

Buffalo/Boston
Pittsburgh/Newark

BOSTON

SMSA Ratio: 2.35

0   4 Mi.

0   4 Km.

BUFFALO

SMSA Ratio: 2.22

0   4 Mi.

0   4 Km.

PITTSBURGH

SMSA Ratio: 2.79

0   4 Mi.

0   4 Km.

NEWARK

> SMSA Ratio

≤ SMSA Ratio

N

No Data

0   2 Mi.

0   2 Km.

SMSA Ratio: 2.56

of high-value appreciation shows that many tracts with ratios exceeding the metro ratio ($56,000/$23,800 = 2.35) had no new construction in 1979 and early 1980, suggesting that perhaps the rise in many tracts is due more to market forces of demand against fixed (or diminished) supply and less to recent new construction. The tracts that showed high ratios may have gained expensive new housing in the early 1970s.[39] There are a few tracts of above-

average ratios (metro ratio: $42,700/$15,300 = 2.79) in *Pittsburgh*—in the traditionally exclusive areas east of downtown, on the high bluffs south of the rivers, and a few new redevelopment areas north of the river and west of downtown. The only high ratios in *Newark* (metro ratio: $72,400/$28,300 = 2.56) are a few tracts east of downtown by Newark Bay and the main road into Manhattan via the Holland Tunnel. Tracts with high ratios are often different from those with new housing in 1979 and later.

[39]See M. Edel and E. Sclar, "The Distribution of Real Value Changes: Metropolitan Boston, 1870–1970," *Journal of Urban Economics* 2 (1975): 366–87.

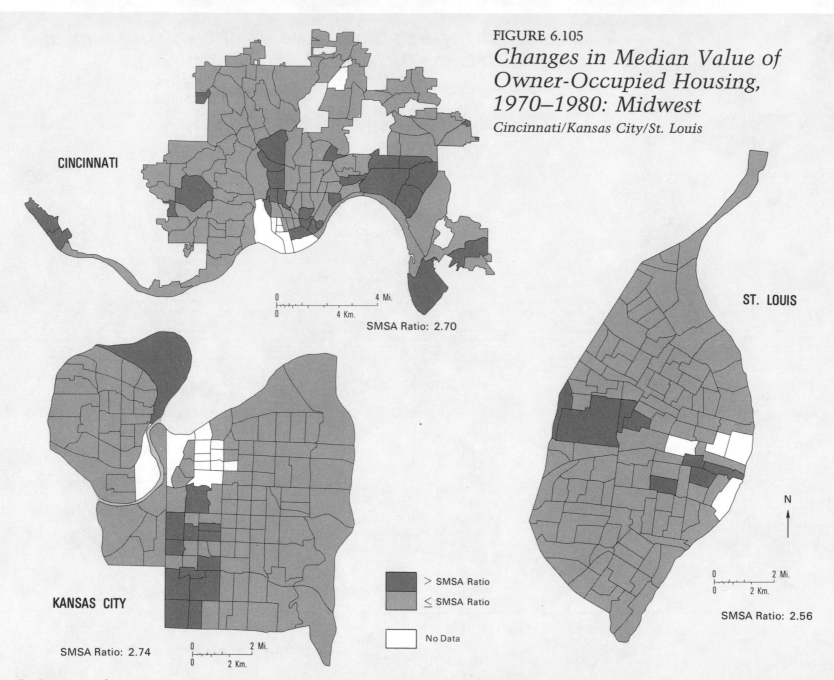

FIGURE 6.105

Changes in Median Value of Owner-Occupied Housing, 1970–1980: Midwest
Cincinnati/Kansas City/St. Louis

CINCINNATI

0   4 Mi.
0   4 Km.

SMSA Ratio: 2.70

ST. LOUIS

N

0   2 Mi.
0   2 Km.

SMSA Ratio: 2.56

> SMSA Ratio

≤ SMSA Ratio

No Data

KANSAS CITY

SMSA Ratio: 2.74

0   2 Mi.
0   2 Km.

In *Cincinnati* the metro ratio ($47,500/$17,600 = 2.70) was exceeded in several tracts on the east and west sides and in a few around downtown. In most cases where the tract ratios were high, there had been new construction in 1979 and later, but not enough to move the median significantly. It is more likely that new housing was built in attractive areas where demand was strong, which raised the ratio. The metro ratio in the *Kansas City* area ($43,500/$15,900 = 2.74) was exceeded in a number of tracts on the sector south of downtown on the Missouri side of the border, in the direction of the desirable Country Club district, where demand is high and new construction apparently is easily absorbed at good prices. The only tracts in *St. Louis* that achieved high ratios (metro ratio: $41,800/$16,300 = 2.56) were west of St. Louis University and around Forest Park, and just southwest of downtown. The entire metro area has been losing population, and most of the central city has had a hard time maintaining its attractiveness and desirability.

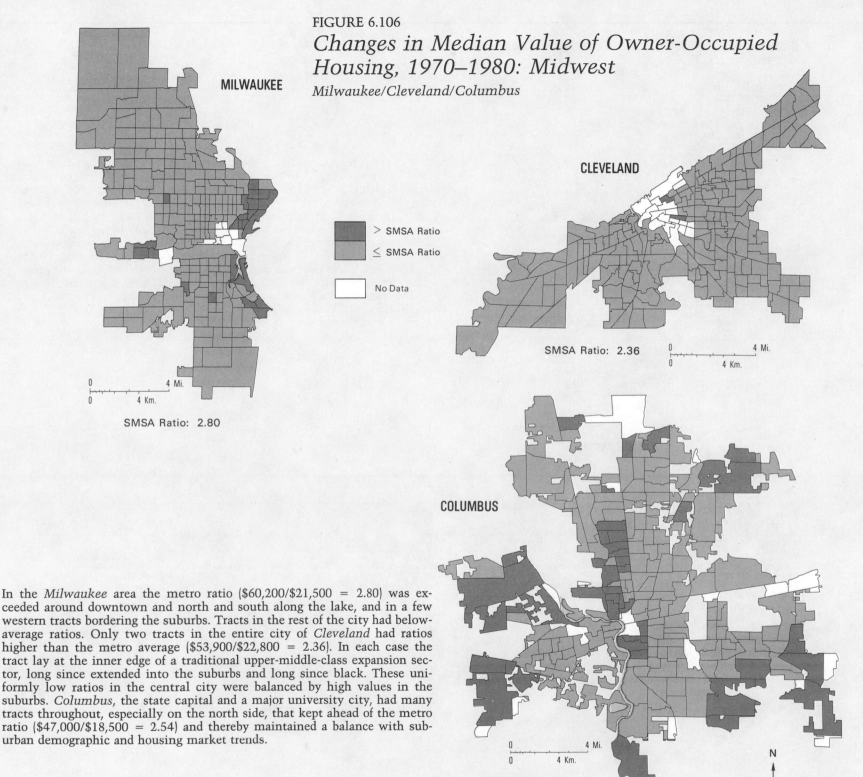

FIGURE 6.106

Changes in Median Value of Owner-Occupied Housing, 1970–1980: Midwest
Milwaukee/Cleveland/Columbus

MILWAUKEE

CLEVELAND

> SMSA Ratio

≤ SMSA Ratio

No Data

SMSA Ratio: 2.36

SMSA Ratio: 2.80

COLUMBUS

SMSA Ratio: 2.54

In the *Milwaukee* area the metro ratio ($60,200/$21,500 = 2.80) was exceeded around downtown and north and south along the lake, and in a few western tracts bordering the suburbs. Tracts in the rest of the city had below-average ratios. Only two tracts in the entire city of *Cleveland* had ratios higher than the metro average ($53,900/$22,800 = 2.36). In each case the tract lay at the inner edge of a traditional upper-middle-class expansion sector, long since extended into the suburbs and long since black. These uniformly low ratios in the central city were balanced by high values in the suburbs. *Columbus*, the state capital and a major university city, had many tracts throughout, especially on the north side, that kept ahead of the metro ratio ($47,000/$18,500 = 2.54) and thereby maintained a balance with suburban demographic and housing market trends.

259

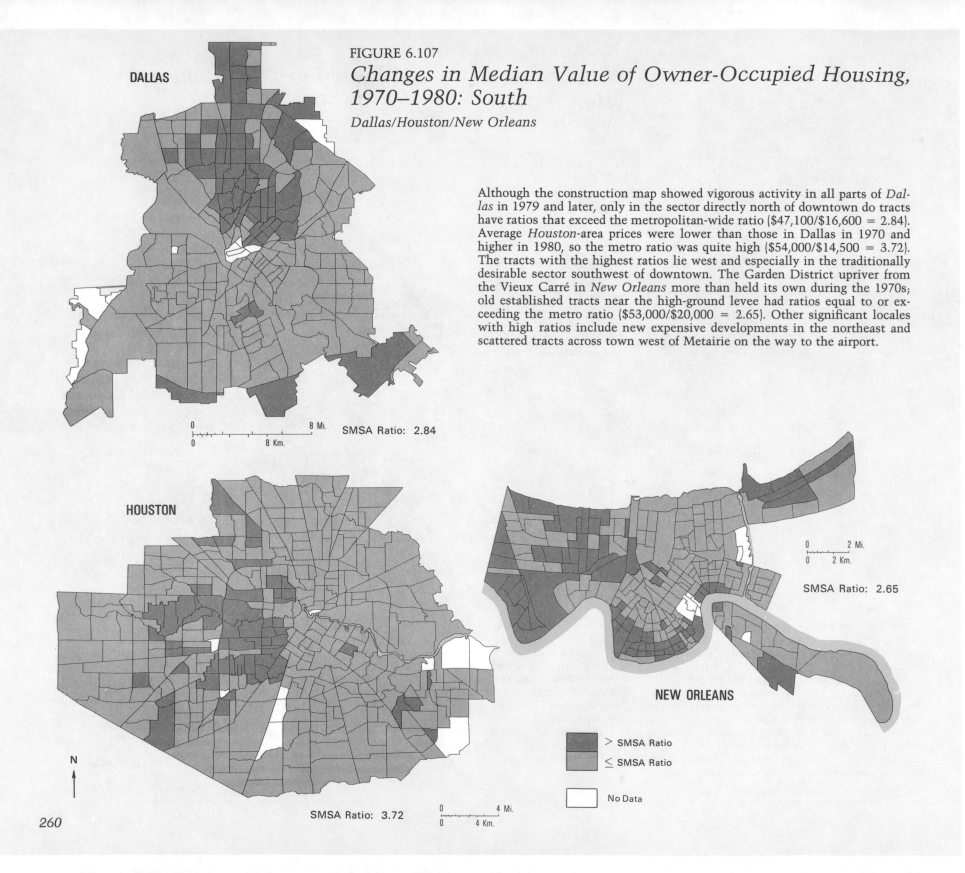

FIGURE 6.107
Changes in Median Value of Owner-Occupied Housing, 1970–1980: South
Dallas/Houston/New Orleans

DALLAS

Although the construction map showed vigorous activity in all parts of *Dallas* in 1979 and later, only in the sector directly north of downtown do tracts have ratios that exceed the metropolitan-wide ratio ($47,100/$16,600 = 2.84). Average *Houston*-area prices were lower than those in Dallas in 1970 and higher in 1980, so the metro ratio was quite high ($54,000/$14,500 = 3.72). The tracts with the highest ratios lie west and especially in the traditionally desirable sector southwest of downtown. The Garden District upriver from the Vieux Carré in *New Orleans* more than held its own during the 1970s; old established tracts near the high-ground levee had ratios equal to or exceeding the metro ratio ($53,000/$20,000 = 2.65). Other significant locales with high ratios include new expensive developments in the northeast and scattered tracts across town west of Metairie on the way to the airport.

0   8 Mi.
0   8 Km.

SMSA Ratio: 2.84

HOUSTON

0   2 Mi.
0   2 Km.

SMSA Ratio: 2.65

NEW ORLEANS

N

> SMSA Ratio

≤ SMSA Ratio

No Data

SMSA Ratio: 3.72

0   4 Mi.
0   4 Km.

FIGURE 6.108

Changes in Median Value of Owner-Occupied Housing, 1970–1980: South

Baltimore/Washington/Miami

An old pattern of residential desirability emerged in *Baltimore* as tracts from the inner harbor, downtown, and north in a wedge to the city's edge defined a pattern where ratios exceeded the metro ratio ($51,400/$15,200 = 3.38). In *Washington*, intense demand for housing inside the District escalated prices in most areas, except south of the Anacostia River, above the metro ratio ($79,900/$28,200 = 2.83). In the city of *Miami* ratios were higher on the south side than on the north side or along the waterfront (metro ratio: $54,700/$19,000 = 2.88).

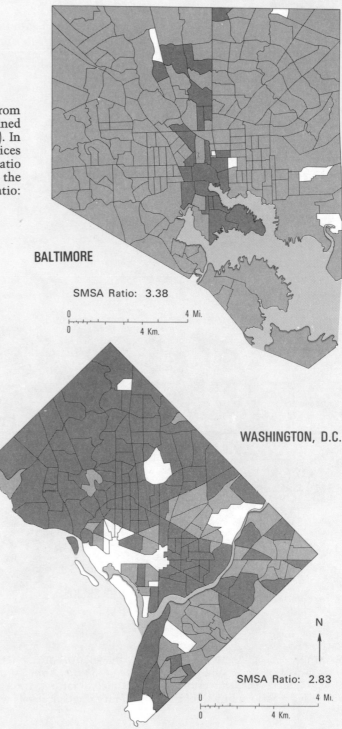

BALTIMORE

SMSA Ratio: 3.38

0   4 Mi.
0   4 Km.

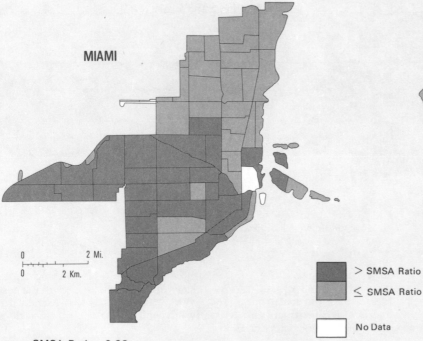

MIAMI

0   2 Mi.
0   2 Km.

SMSA Ratio: 2.88

> SMSA Ratio

≤ SMSA Ratio

No Data

WASHINGTON, D.C.

N

SMSA Ratio: 2.83

0   4 Mi.
0   4 Km.

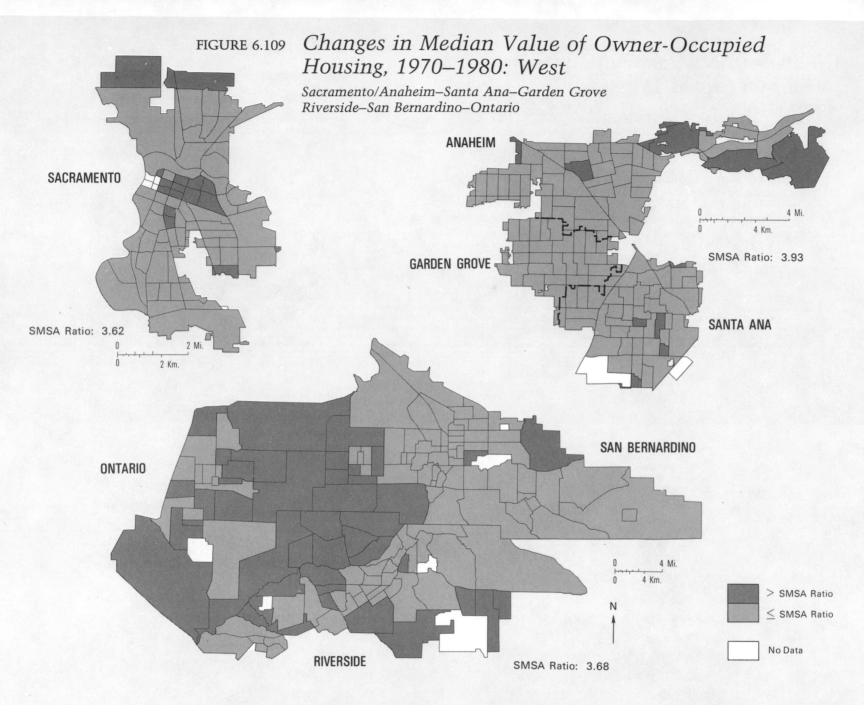

FIGURE 6.109 *Changes in Median Value of Owner-Occupied Housing, 1970–1980: West*

Sacramento/Anaheim–Santa Ana–Garden Grove
Riverside–San Bernardino–Ontario

SACRAMENTO

SMSA Ratio: 3.62

0   2 Mi.

0   2 Km.

ANAHEIM

GARDEN GROVE

SANTA ANA

0   4 Mi.

0   4 Km.

SMSA Ratio: 3.93

ONTARIO

SAN BERNARDINO

0   4 Mi.

0   4 Km.

N

RIVERSIDE

SMSA Ratio: 3.68

■ > SMSA Ratio

■ ≤ SMSA Ratio

□ No Data

In *Sacramento* the ratio was highest around the downtown and the state capitol and low elsewhere, except a few fringe tracts by the suburbs (metro ratio: $64,800/$17,900 = 3.62). The suburbs of *Anaheim–Santa Ana–Garden Grove* stayed well above the exceptionally high metro ratio ($106,800/$27,200 = 3.93), leaving ratios in most of the central city tracts at levels well below the average. Only a few scattered tracts in Anaheim and Santa Ana bucked the trend of central city tracts. In the *Riverside–San Bernardino–Ontario* area the metro ratio ($64,700/$17,600 = 3.68) was exceeded in the large low-density tracts and generally fell well below the metro ratio in the small, dense, inner city tracts.

Elementary School Children in Nonpublic Schools

It is widely held that the elementary school opportunities available in a city and its neighborhoods are significant factors in a family's willingness to live there if they have or soon will have elementary-school-age children.[40] The Bureau of the Census defines "elementary school" as including grades 1 through 8 and "high school" as including grades 9 through 12. In 1980 there were 51.1 million children in public school at all levels and 9.2 million (15 percent of the total) in private schools, which includes parochial schools owned and operated by various religious organizations and private nonsectarian schools. In recent years the public-private mix has changed. In 1985 public school enrollments were down 3 percent from 1980 to 49.6 million, while private school enrollments were up 2 percent to 9.4 million. Public elementary school enrollments declined from 24.3 million to 23.7 million, while private elementary school enrollments slipped from 3.7 million to 3.6 million.[41]

These averages reveal little about the link between schooling and housing because national average figures hide the considerable regional variability in the use of nonpublic schools in the United States. They are most common in the Northeast, where 24 percent of elementary school pupils attend them (3.6 million of 14.9 million in 1981) and least common in the South, where only 13 percent (2.6 million of 20.8 million) attend.

In the West 18 percent attend nonpublic elementary schools (2.4 million of 13.5 million), and in the Midwest 20 percent (4.7 million of 23.4 million). Private and parochial schools are often located in central cities, and an increasing percentage of their pupils are nonwhite. In 1960 nonpublic elementary pupils were 96.4 percent white; in 1970, 93.3 percent white; and by 1982, 89.5 percent white.[42]

Inside central cities the proportion of neighborhood elementary children attending nonpublic schools varies sharply from place to place, from almost zero in some tracts to well over half in others. Some are children of devout members of church congregations, who use parochial schools for religious instruction in addition to general education. Some parents use nonpublic schools because the curriculum, the classmates, or the special cachet of a nonpublic school are attractive. Some parents may elect to send their children to nonpublic schools to separate them from others of different race, class, or ethnic background, or to join with others like themselves in a neighborhood school that seems to parents to be locally controlled, client-oriented, and eager to accept their children. There are also differences in nonpublic school attendance that attach to ethnic origins. German-Americans, for example, have favored parochial schools far more than have

[40]See John S. Adams and Kathleen Molnar Brown, "Public School Goals and Parochial School Attendance in Twenty American Cities," in John S. Adams, ed., *Urban Policymaking and Metropolitan Dynamics. A Comparative Geographical Analysis* (Cambridge, MA: Ballinger, 1976), pp. 219–55.

[41]U.S. Bureau of the Census, *Statistical Abstract of the United States, 1984*, p. 134.

[42]U.S. Bureau of the Census, *Statistical Abstract of the United States, 1984*, pp. 136, 140. See also Karl E. Taeuber, "Demographic Perspectives on Housing and School Segregation," *Wayne Law Review* 21, no. 3 (March 1975): 833–50.

Italian-Americans.[43] Whatever the mix of motivations, the availability of nonpublic school options in central cities helps to stabilize family populations who might otherwise choose to move away in order to exercise school choice in educating their children.

The maps that follow portray the large differences from city to city and neighborhood to neighborhood in the availability and use of nonpublic elementary schools. Schooling is one of the most important services that accompany the housing bundle and the last of the features examined in our comparative map series. Some nonpublic schools are supported in part by endowments that were supplied by benefactors through the years. The parochial schools are usually supported almost entirely by tuition supplemented by support from the parishes to which they are attached. In some inner city low-income and minority neighborhoods certain religious organizations and congregations supply school personnel to make alternative school options available to families who could not otherwise exercise school choice for their children. To the degree that housing choice is also school choice for families with school-age children, the availability of choice in schooling has some influence on families' decisions to stay or to leave a neighborhood. At present, the heavy use of nonpublic elementary schools in certain cities may mean that classrooms are more homogeneous with respect to religion, social class, ethnicity, race, income, or other traits than they might otherwise be, but it is

likely that this outcome is balanced by neighborhoods that remain more heterogeneous than they would be if school choices were unavailable.

In Pittsburgh almost one elementary school child in three attended nonpublic schools in 1980, with Boston, New Orleans, and Buffalo close behind. At the other end of the distribution were southern and western cities like Houston, Anaheim–Santa Ana–Garden Grove, and Riverside–San Bernardino–Ontario (Table 6.5).

TABLE 6.5

Proportion of Central City Elementary School (Grades 1-8) Children Who Attended Nonpublic Schools in 1980 in 19 Sample SMSAs

MIDWEST		NORTHEAST	
Cincinnati	22.2%	Boston	28.6%
Cleveland	22.5	Buffalo	26.4
Columbus	14.1	Newark	13.1
Kansas City	15.9	Pittsburgh	32.9
Milwaukee	27.4		
St. Louis	24.3		
WEST		SOUTH	
Anaheim–Santa Ana–		Baltimore	15.5
Garden Grove	10.3	Dallas	12.0
Riverside–San Bernardino–		Houston	9.2
Ontario	10.3	Miami	17.3
Sacramento	12.4	New Orleans	27.3
		Washington	15.5

SOURCE: U.S. Bureau of the Census, 1980 Census of Population, *Census Tracts*, table P-9.

---

[43]Kathleen Mary Molnar, *"Nonpublic Schools and Neighborhood Stability: Geographic Considerations for Public Policy in Education,"* doctoral dissertation, University of Minnesota, 1976; and Andrew M. Greeley and Peter H. Rossi, *The Education of Catholic Americans* (Chicago: Aldine, 1966).

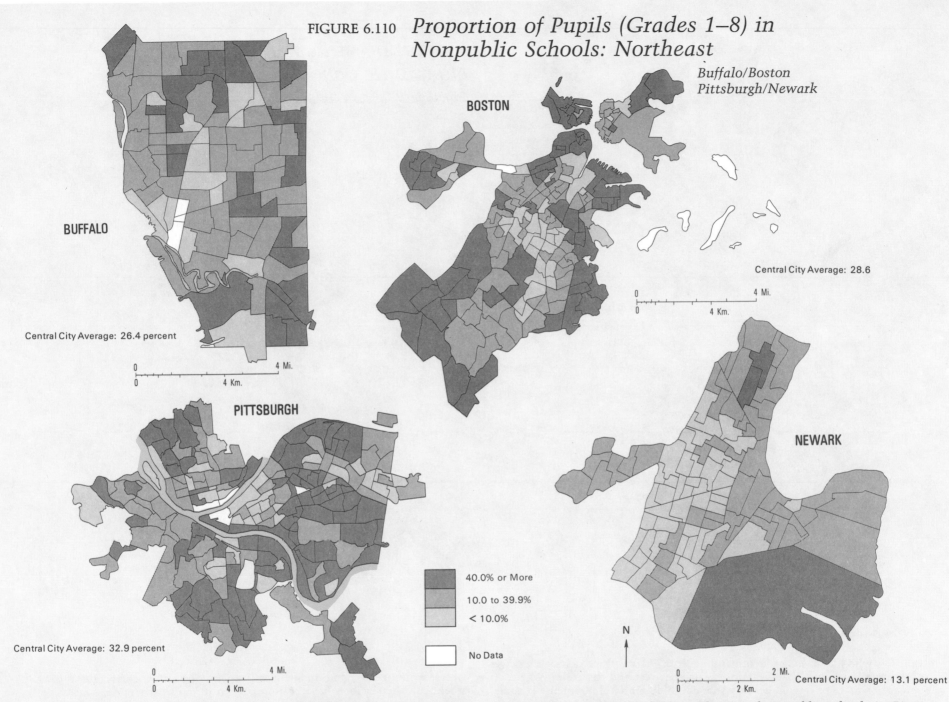

FIGURE 6.110 *Proportion of Pupils (Grades 1–8) in Nonpublic Schools: Northeast*

Buffalo/Boston
Pittsburgh/Newark

BOSTON

BUFFALO

Central City Average: 28.6

Central City Average: 26.4 percent

PITTSBURGH

NEWARK

Central City Average: 32.9 percent

40.0% or More

10.0 to 39.9%

< 10.0%

No Data

N

Central City Average: 13.1 percent

In the large majority of *Buffalo* tracts the proportion of elementary school children who attend nonpublic schools is either moderate (10.0 to 39.9 percent) or high (40 percent or more). The wedge of traditionally middle-class tracts from downtown to the northern suburbs is especially high, as are tracts on the far southside. Nonpublic, and especially Roman Catholic, parochial schools have been important throughout *Boston* for many decades. A trough of low tracts extends south-southwest of downtown—an area formerly middle-class Protestant, then immigrant Jewish, and recently black. The propor-

tion of elementary school children who attend nonpublic schools in *Pittsburgh* has historically been among the nation's highest, with a large number of tracts in almost all parts of the city exceeding 40 percent. Black tracts immediately east of downtown are low in the use of nonpublic schools. The newer and wealthier parts of *Newark* on the west and east sides tend to make above-average use of nonpublic schools, while poorer and minority areas throughout the central area of the city are below average.

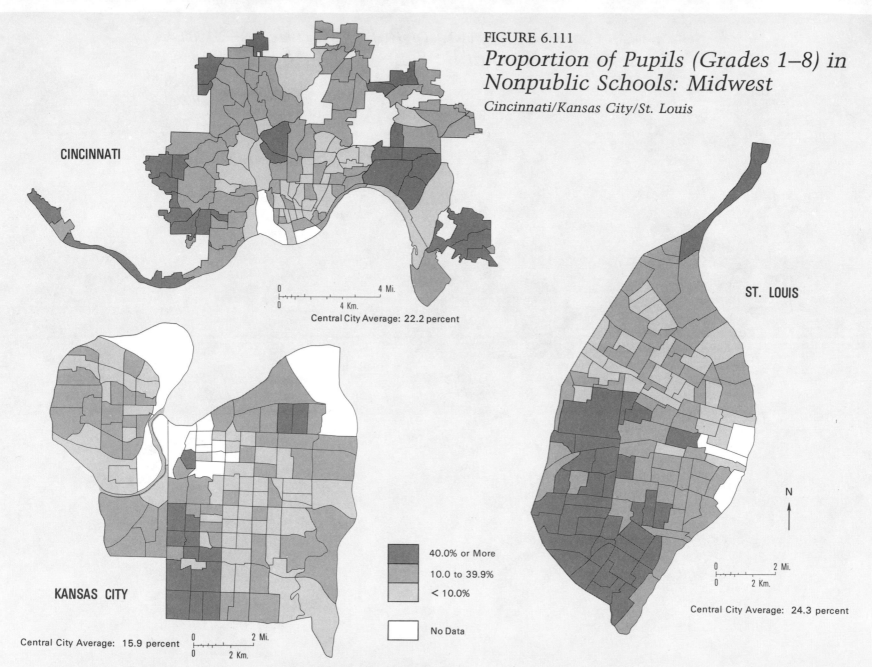

FIGURE 6.111

Proportion of Pupils (Grades 1–8) in Nonpublic Schools: Midwest
Cincinnati/Kansas City/St. Louis

CINCINNATI

0 ——— 4 Mi.
0 ——— 4 Km.
Central City Average: 22.2 percent

ST. LOUIS

N

0 ——— 2 Mi.
0 ——— 2 Km.
Central City Average: 24.3 percent

KANSAS CITY

Central City Average: 15.9 percent
0 ——— 2 Mi.
0 ——— 2 Km.

40.0% or More

10.0 to 39.9%

< 10.0%

No Data

Families who live in lower-income inner city *Cincinnati* make much less use of nonpublic schools than do families on the west and east sides, where 40 percent or more of the elementary school children attend nonpublic schools. In *Kansas City*, Kansas, low and moderate rates of nonpublic schooling predominate. The same is true in most parts of Kansas City, Missouri, on the east side, where the only high rates occur in the traditionally high-income sector south of downtown. Most of south-side *St. Louis* has traditionally been white, working-class and middle-class, of Catholic and Lutheran immigrant stock. Parochial schools have been important in most parts of the south side. The northwest sector traditionally housed the upper-middle-class business and merchant classes, who moved farther out west and northwest to be replaced by blacks, many of whom were Catholics from Louisiana. Today the north-side tracts provide only modest support for nonpublic schools.

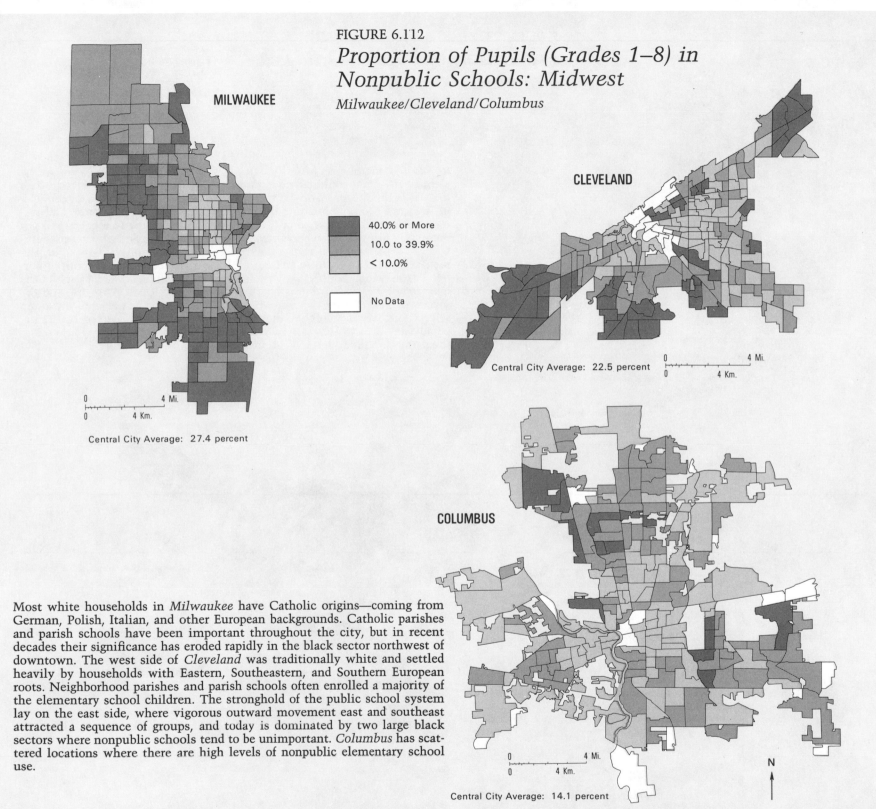

FIGURE 6.112
Proportion of Pupils (Grades 1–8) in Nonpublic Schools: Midwest
Milwaukee/Cleveland/Columbus

MILWAUKEE

CLEVELAND

COLUMBUS

40.0% or More

10.0 to 39.9%

< 10.0%

No Data

0   4 Mi.
0   4 Km.

Central City Average: 27.4 percent

Central City Average: 22.5 percent

0   4 Mi.
0   4 Km.

Central City Average: 14.1 percent

N

Most white households in *Milwaukee* have Catholic origins—coming from German, Polish, Italian, and other European backgrounds. Catholic parishes and parish schools have been important throughout the city, but in recent decades their significance has eroded rapidly in the black sector northwest of downtown. The west side of *Cleveland* was traditionally white and settled heavily by households with Eastern, Southeastern, and Southern European roots. Neighborhood parishes and parish schools often enrolled a majority of the elementary school children. The stronghold of the public school system lay on the east side, where vigorous outward movement east and southeast attracted a sequence of groups, and today is dominated by two large black sectors where nonpublic schools tend to be unimportant. *Columbus* has scattered locations where there are high levels of nonpublic elementary school use.

267

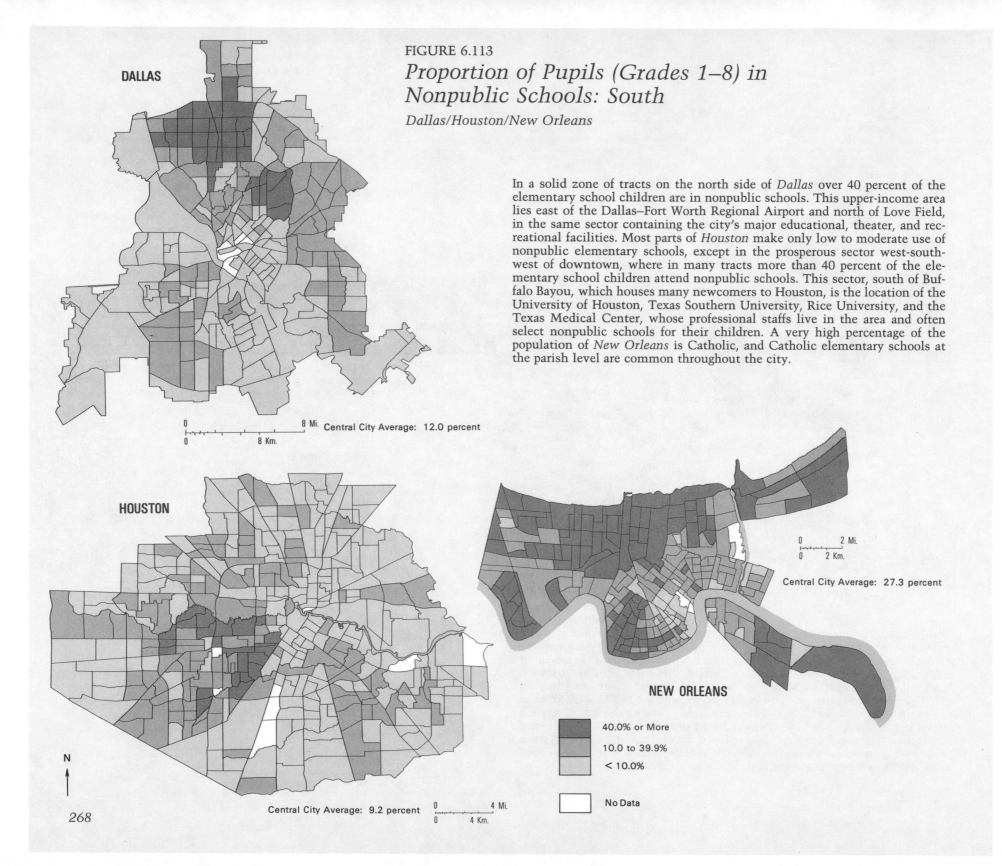

DALLAS

FIGURE 6.113
Proportion of Pupils (Grades 1–8) in Nonpublic Schools: South
Dallas/Houston/New Orleans

In a solid zone of tracts on the north side of *Dallas* over 40 percent of the elementary school children are in nonpublic schools. This upper-income area lies east of the Dallas–Fort Worth Regional Airport and north of Love Field, in the same sector containing the city's major educational, theater, and recreational facilities. Most parts of *Houston* make only low to moderate use of nonpublic elementary schools, except in the prosperous sector west-southwest of downtown, where in many tracts more than 40 percent of the elementary school children attend nonpublic schools. This sector, south of Buffalo Bayou, which houses many newcomers to Houston, is the location of the University of Houston, Texas Southern University, Rice University, and the Texas Medical Center, whose professional staffs live in the area and often select nonpublic schools for their children. A very high percentage of the population of *New Orleans* is Catholic, and Catholic elementary schools at the parish level are common throughout the city.

0   8 Mi. Central City Average: 12.0 percent
0   8 Km.

HOUSTON

NEW ORLEANS

0   2 Mi.
0   2 Km.

Central City Average: 27.3 percent

N

40.0% or More

10.0 to 39.9%

< 10.0%

No Data

Central City Average: 9.2 percent

0   4 Mi.
0   4 Km.

268

FIGURE 6.114

Proportion of Pupils (Grades 1–8) in Nonpublic Schools: South

Baltimore/Washington/Miami

Since colonial times *Baltimore*, like New Orleans, has been one of the few southern cities with a significant Catholic population and extensive parochial school system. In addition, Baltimore attracted many European immigrants during the past century while most southern cities were too underdeveloped industrially to do so. The scattered tracts with high proportions of elementary school children in nonpublic schools are a legacy of both eras of Baltimore history. Nonpublic elementary schools thrive in *Washington*, where they tend to be more private than parochial, and create difficult competition for the local public school system. They are especially significant west of Rock Creek Park, around the capitol, and in southeastern Washington north of the Anacostia River. In only a few tracts in *Miami* are high proportions of elementary school children in nonpublic schools. The most likely clientele for nonpublic schools is the large Hispanic population, which appears uninterested or lacks the financial resources to support nonpublic schools.

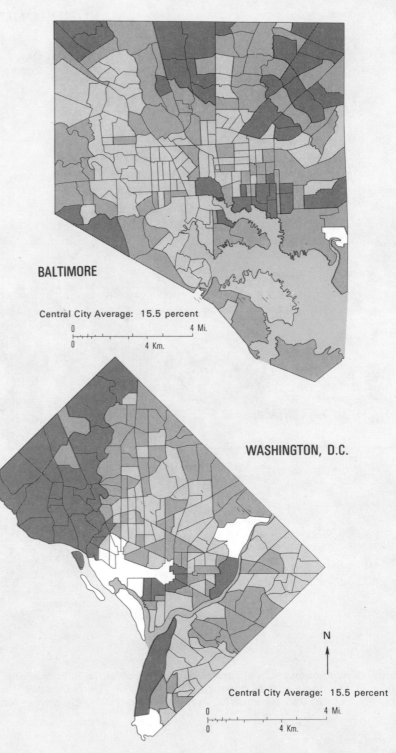

BALTIMORE

Central City Average: 15.5 percent

0   4 Mi.

0   4 Km.

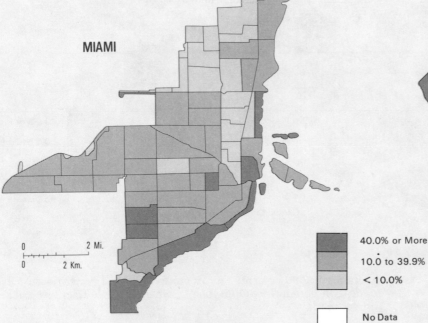

MIAMI

0   2 Mi.

0   2 Km.

Central City Average: 17.3 percent

WASHINGTON, D.C.

N

40.0% or More

10.0 to 39.9%

< 10.0%

No Data

Central City Average: 15.5 percent

0   4 Mi.

0   4 Km.

FIGURE 6.115 *Proportion of Pupils (Grades 1–8) in Nonpublic Schools: West*

Sacramento/Anaheim–Santa Ana–Garden Grove
Riverside–San Bernardino–Ontario

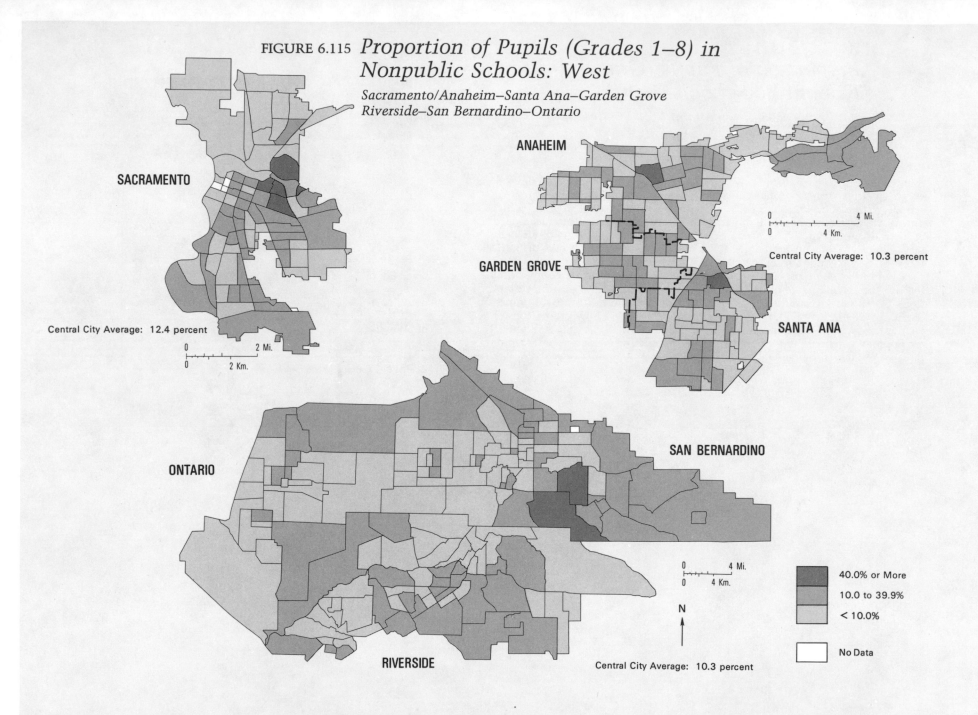

SACRAMENTO

Central City Average: 12.4 percent

0   2 Mi.
0   2 Km.

ANAHEIM

GARDEN GROVE

SANTA ANA

0   4 Mi.
0   4 Km.

Central City Average: 10.3 percent

ONTARIO

SAN BERNARDINO

RIVERSIDE

0   4 Mi.
0   4 Km.

N

Central City Average: 10.3 percent

40.0% or More

10.0 to 39.9%

< 10.0%

No Data

Nonpublic elementary school enrollments are uncommon in *Sacramento*, except in a few tracts east of downtown. In only one *Anaheim* tract—in the large, prosperous, and fast-growing area—have nonpublic elementary enrollments reached 40 percent. An essentially identical pattern occurs in the *Riverside–San Bernardino–Ontario* area, where a single tract has reached the 40 percent mark.

7

CONTINUING HOUSING ISSUES AND PUBLIC POLICY RESPONSES

THE PRECEDING chapters discussed the private and public meanings of housing in the United States—shelter against the elements; a storage place for possessions; a private refuge from the world; a form of savings; an inflation hedge; a status symbol; a ticket into a school district and a set of community services; a tax base for local governments; a source of livelihood for developers, builders, financiers, insurers, furnishers, agents, building trades workers, materials suppliers; and on and on. Attention focused mainly on the role of housing in society, on the housing stock and how it changes, on the demand for housing and the forces driving demand; and on patterns of housing use nationwide and in selected metropolitan housing markets and submarkets. This concluding chapter examines inefficiencies and other defects in the American system of housing, persistent public policy issues that involve housing, and the ways that have been devised to define and correct our nation's housing problems.[1]

Current Housing Problems

At the outset we need to ask: Is there really a housing problem or, what would be worse, a housing crisis?[2] During the 1970s American mass media proclaimed one housing crisis after another. But pub-

---

[1]There is a large literature recounting the public policy questions that persist in the U.S. housing realm. Some are descriptive, some analytical, and most favor vigorous public response at each government level. A few favor minimal governmental intervention and a freer play of market forces. For a representative sample of recent publications, see George Sternlieb, James Hughes, et al., *America's Housing: Prospects and Problems* (New Brunswick, NJ: Center for Urban Policy Research, Rutgers University, 1980); Roger Montgomery and Dale Rogers Marshall, *Housing Policy for the 1980s* (Lexington, MA: Lexington Books, 1980); Irving H. Welfeld, *America's Housing Problem: An Approach to Its Solution* (Washington, DC: American Enterprise Institute, 1973); and Jon Pynoos, Robert Schafer, and Chester W. Hartman, eds., *Housing Urban America*, 2nd ed. (New York: Aldine, 1980), which contains a comprehensive bibliography. Most general treatments of housing and housing policy display little sensitivity

to the uniquely geographical character of housing in its neighborhood settings and the ways that housing policy in its global concerns must ultimately play itself out in real neighborhood settings. For an important geographical treatment of housing in cities, see Larry S. Bourne, *Internal Structure of the City: Readings on Urban Form, Growth, and Policy* (New York: Oxford University Press, 1982). The sheer complexity of housing and its many links to other elements in the society and economy invite analysts to contrive new methods of policy analysis. For an especially innovative and successful effort, see Frank de Leeuw and Raymond J. Struyk, *The Web of Urban Housing: Analyzing Policy with a Market Simulation Model* (Washington, DC: Urban Institute, 1975). For another view of neighborhood and ecological policy analysis, see Peter D. Salins, *The Ecology of Housing Destruction: Economic Effects of Public Intervention in the Housing Market* (New York: New York University Press, for the International Center for Economic Policy Studies, 1980). Sometimes policy statements focus on a single issue: John Gender and Steven Gordon, *The Housing Needs of Non-Traditional Households*, U.S. Department of Housing and Urban Development, (Washington, DC: U.S. Government Printing Office, 1980).

[2]Based on John F. Kain, "America's Persistent Housing Crises: Errors in Analysis and Policy," American Academy of Political and Social Science, *Annals* 465 (January 1983); 136–48. It would be easier to argue housing policy issues if the nature of regional and metropolitan housing markets were better understood. See F. E. Case, "Construction and Real Estate Market Interrelationships," *Annals of Regional Science* 1, no. 1 (1967): 143–51; Harry B. Wolfe, "A Model of the San Francisco Housing Market," *Socio-Economic Planning Science* 1 (1967): 71–95; R. S. Conway and C. T. Howard, "A Forecasting Model for Regional Housing Construction," *Journal of Regional Science* 20(1981): 1–10; and P. T. Chinloy, "An Empirical Model of the Market for Resale Homes," *Journal of Urban Economics* 7 no. 3 (1981): 279–92.

lic concern over these crises tended to dissolve as dispassionate research demonstrated that the crisis claims had been exaggerated. The studies disclosed that housing conditions steadily improved after World War II, that the improvement came about because of a rapid growth in per capita and household incomes, that direct government housing programs made only small contributions, and that government programs were both inequitable and inefficient. As postwar housing improved in quantity and quality, the proportion of households living in substandard housing dropped, and housing problems of poor people were increasingly understood as poverty problems rather than housing problems. Evaluations of housing problems and policies argued for reductions in housing subsidies for middle- and low-income households, a shift away from production-oriented programs, and more reliance on cash grants and vouchers for low-income households to enable them to acquire suitable housing. The consensus, then, identified no crisis, but there were a series of continuing problems, and policy debates over what to do about them.

Problems for the House Builders[3]

At the end of World War II, pent-up housing demand from both the Depression and the war years and favorable government action—especially better financing and aggressive highway building—helped to promote a boom in house construction. A new kind of enterprise called the merchant builder brought together all the elements of house construction and sales, from land acquisition to consumer finance and marketing.

Housing starts declined somewhat in the late 1950s and 1960s from their immediate postwar highs and then rose to all-time highs in the 1970s. Dozens of merchant builders sought to expand their scale of operations, some of them even dreaming of creating truly national operations. The inflation of the 1970s and the entry into the housing market of persons born during the postwar baby boom helped fuel an enormous volume of housing starts, resale transactions, and merchant builder profits. But after 1979, business was sharply down and profits were severely constrained.[4] By the mid-1980s, demand and supply conditions facing the builders resembled those of the 1960s.

The constraints on the builders have led to a housing stock used more intensely—with sharing of units, subdividing of existing units, and so on. New houses of the 1980s are smaller and built at higher densities, as townhouses and in multistory buildings. More young households are renters and will stay renters longer than was typical in the early postwar decades.

It is more accurate to portray the 1980s as a time of difficult and sometimes painful transition rather than as a crisis for builders. Money for housing in the 1980s is more expensive than it was in the 1970s, but if it is sufficient for national production averaging about 1.5 million units per year during the decade, the construction industry as a whole will be operating close to optimal efficiency.[5]

Making Sure That There Is Enough Money for Housing[6]

During the late 1970s, mortgage interest rates rose to a 1981 peak above 18 percent, inflation seemed almost out of control, and the nation's mortgage finance and delivery system was seriously disrupted. Yet the deregulation of depository institutions allowed the thrifts and other mortgage lenders to fight back. They had to charge high market rates for their loans, but they now could pay savers enough to attract a continuous flow of new money to finance mortgage lending. As a result the mortgage finance industry found itself in a period of transition in the 1980s, offering new types of mortgage instruments and trying to identify new sources of reasonably priced money for mortgages. Although not much used, the nation's private pension funds are one major source which can buy mortgage-backed securities through the secondary mortgage market. By the mid-1980s their total share of mortgage asset holdings had not changed much. The relaxation of federal regulations so that pension funds can be invested in mortgages opened an important door to increasing the volume of money available for housing, which would help contain the cost of that money.

Mortgage revenue bonds have been another important source of

[3]Based on Ned Eichler, "Homebuilding for the 1980s: Crisis or Transition?" American Academy of Political and Social Science, *Annals* 465 (January 1983): 35–44.

[4]See Stephan R. Seidel, *Housing Costs and Government Regulation*, (New Brunswick, NJ: Center for Urban Policy Research, 1978).

[5]Eichler, op. cit., p. 43.

[6]Based on Mark J. Riedy, "Where Will the Money Come From?" American Academy of Political and Social Science, *Annals* 465 (January 1983): 14–20. For a critical analysis of how financial institutions in recent decades have loaned mortgage money in ways that helped some classes of urban neighborhoods while hurting the interests of persons in other neighborhoods, see Calvin P. Bradford and L. S. Rabinowitz, "The Urban-Suburban Disinvestment Process: Consequences for Older Neighborhoods," American Academy of Political and Social Science, *Annals* 422 (1975): 77–86.

subsidized new money for housing.[7] They were introduced in the 1970s when there was strong demand for tax-exempt securities, which drove tax-exempt interest rates below their usual levels relative to taxable bonds. But this demand is cyclical. As it declines, tax-exempt interest rates will rise, reducing the incentive for municipalities to issue bonds and providing less advantage to home buyers whose mortgages are financed by bonds. The issuance of mortgage revenue bonds drives up the rate on state housing finance agency bonds, relative to other tax-exempts, and competes with mortgage-backed securities, particularly in the portfolios of savings institutions. To the extent that they compete, there is little increase in the supply of mortgage funds.

Congress intended that revenue bonds be used to finance utilities and industrial development that contributed to a community's economic base. Federal guidelines restrict how they can be used. As the use of the bonds has broadened to finance service employment facilities, such as offices and hotels, and housing, localities have come into conflict with the federal government. Tax-exempt mortgage revenue bonds were advocated as a means of increasing homeownership among middle-income families, but at the end of the 1970s they did not seem to be achieving that objective, at least in Chicago, the first city for which detailed data became available. Moreover, the income redistributive consequences of the bonds appeared to be perverse because they subsidized families in the upper half of the income distribution.

Some cities issued bonds in order to attract and retain middle- and upper-income households. Evidence indicated that suburbanites are probably not induced to return to the city in greater numbers than normally occurs, although there are some conflicting data. But even if central cities were successful in attracting high-income households, suburban jurisdictions could issue bonds as well, offsetting the cities' advantage. Insofar as the cities are successful in attracting higher-income families, they may drive up the price of lower-income housing and displace relatively low-income households.

Mortgage revenue bonds cannot provide as deep a subsidy and are not as flexible as other targeted subsidy programs. If cities have the option of issuing either tax-exempt or subsidized taxable bonds, the tax-exempts appear to be preferable because they have about the same impact on housing markets at a lower revenue loss to the federal government. As a housing subsidy, taxable bonds would be quite similar to several current and recent mortgage interest subsidy programs.

Controlling Inflation—Whose Interests Are Affected?

Inflation during the 1960s and especially the 1970s generated large wealth transfers among the various groups involved in the housing process.[8] The biggest shift has been the gain by mortgage borrowers at the expense of lenders and savers. Homeowners did not profit as uniformly as is widely believed because much of their gain depended on house price inflation, and rates of inflation varied widely within each metropolitan housing market and from one region of the country to another.

Landlords have generally experienced sharp declines in net operating incomes. Their expenses rose with inflation, but their ability to raise rents ran into competition from abundant opportunities for owner occupancy on the part of their higher-income tenants.

The cycles of residential construction since the early 1970s reveal the destabilizing impact of inflation. Residential construction grew substantially faster than gross national product in real terms in the early 1970s but fell behind between 1976 and 1980. When changes in the value of the entire housing stock are compared with those for the nonresidential capital stock in the 1960s and 1970s, one can discern no favorable influence of inflation on the housing sector. In fact, the average annual percentage growth in the net value of the private housing stock dropped in the 1970s compared with the 1960s. Meanwhile, relative gains of nonresidential capital in the two decades exceeded those of housing.

The growth of residential mortgage debt accounted for 33 percent of the total nonfederal government debt increase in the 1970s compared with 25 percent in the 1960s. It equaled 54 percent of the growth of long-term debt in the 1970s compared with 47 percent in the 1960s. Thus, the larger share of housing in the nonfederal total debt meant that business borrowers, along with state and local governments, were pinched for funds in a national capital market that seemed to favor housing. The disproportionate growth of residential mortgage debt reflected a circle of cumulative causation involving

---

[7]Discussion based on John A. Tuccillo and John C. Weicher, *Local Mortgage Revenue Bonds: Economic and Financial Impacts* (Washington, DC: Urban Institute, 1979), pp. v–vi. See also George E. Peterson and Brian Cooper, *Tax Exempt Financing of Housing Investment* (Washington, DC: Urban Institute, 1979), and a related discussion in chapter 4 above.

[8]Based on Leo Grebler, "Inflation: A Blessing or a Curse?" American Academy of Political and Social Science, *Annals* 465 (January 1983): 21–31.

cheap mortgage money, house price inflation, associated rises in loan amounts per house, and the homebuying binge. Lending policies of mortgage lending institutions on the whole did not resist inflationary forces. Credit expansion without equivalent real capital expansion is one of the notable and ultimately unsustainable maladjustments during inflation, as capital values are redistributed according to one's access to and use of mortgage credit and depending on the rates of inflation that affect the mortgage properties. Capital value is redistributed from owners of lower-priced houses, who incur capital losses on houses that lose value prematurely in real terms, to owners of newer high-priced houses, who realize an untaxed capital gain when their properties advance in value at above-average rates.

During inflation, buyers tend to acquire houses as large and as high in quality as they can in order to maximize value appreciation. Builders respond by erecting houses larger than would be demanded in the absence of the speculation motive, perpetuating the cycle. When stable times return, the illusion of inflation dividends fades, and the quantity of housing consumed tends to correspond more closely to households' needs. Builders are thereby encouraged to provide a broader mix of options, including subdivision of existing large units.

Renewed inflation would lead to rent increases and political pressure in some quarters for rent control ordinances. Judging from the counties and jurisdictions with rent control ordinances in force, supplies of private rental housing would tend to diminish sharply. Governments would have to become the main supporters of rental construction, but their own fiscal difficulties during inflation would limit the subsidies they could offer. In general, rent control perpetuates shortages of rental housing, halts most building of new rental units, discourages many owners from maintaining existing buildings in good condition, and speeds up the deterioration of the existing stock. Those who already occupy rental units receive a benefit that they do not pay for; and others who desire to rent and who are willing to pay market rates find that units are in short supply. Since demand for rental units can exceed supply by a wide margin under strict rent control regimes, access to units that become vacant would increasingly be reserved for prospective tenants willing to make under-the-table lump-sum payments, a practice common in countries with prolonged rent control. Thus, one of the best housing policies, with respect to inflationary effects, is a policy that leads to stable price levels, accompanied by the widespread expectation that prices will remain stable into the indefinite future.

The State of Rental Housing

In the early 1980s there was not yet a rental housing shortage, but one was thought possible, especially in the fast-growth areas of the United States.[9] Rental housing accommodates about a third of all households, with eight rental units in nine provided by private landlords.

Moves in the late 1970s and early 1980s of many better-off renter households to owner status have changed the composition of the renter group to higher percentages of low- and moderate-income households. The percentage rise in residential rental levels has lagged behind living cost increases for 20 years up through the 1970s. But then homeownership became more difficult just as unusually large numbers of new households entered the housing market, driving up rents especially in fast-growing areas of the country. Developers responded to higher rents by building large numbers of new units. The result is that in 1983, 1984, and 1985 the Consumer Price Contract Rent Index rose faster than consumer prices generally—and the national rental vacancy rate was near a 10-year high in 1986, with vacancy rates the highest and having risen the most in the Sunbelt.

Experience in other Western democracies demonstrates that government responses to housing shortages and rising rents often take the form of expanding publicly subsidized housing, rather than allowing the private sector to meet the need for more rental housing. Their response is politically easier than ending rent controls, allowing rents to rise high enough to lure private developers back into producing sufficient numbers of new units and providing rental assistance programs to needy households. If the federal government were to respond to a future pressure to do something about rental housing shortages by subsidizing more public housing, the private rental inventory might shrink fast, as it has in the United Kingdom. In 1947, 61 percent of all British housing consisted of privately owned rental units.

---

[9] Based on Michael Sumichrast, "A Five Year Housing Forecast," and Anthony Downs, "The Coming Crunch in Rental Housing," American Academy of Political and Social Science, *Annals* 465 (January 1983): 45–57; 76–85. See also F. G. Mittelbach et al., "The Role of Removals from the Inventory in Regional Housing Markets," *Annals of Regional Science* 4, no. 1 (1970): 38–48; R. E. Grieson, "The Supply of Rental Housing: Comment," *American Economic Review* 63 (1973): 433–36; and Larry S. Bourne, "Housing Supply and Housing Market Behavior in Residential Development," in David T. Herbert and Ronald J. Johnston, eds., *Spatial Processes and Form*, Social Areas in Cities, vol. 1 (New York: Wiley, 1976).

At the end of the 1970s such units constituted only about 11 percent of all units.[10]

One way to avoid a major expansion of publicly subsidized and operated housing—which is less desirable and more expensive for all income groups, including the poor, than rentals furnished by the private market—would be a combination of a national ban on rent controls and a federal housing voucher entitlement program aimed at low-income renters. Alternatively, rather than preempting state and local sovereignty on the rent control issue, the federal government could say that no federal housing subsidy funds would be available to rent-controlled jurisdictions.

Can Neighborhoods in Trouble Be Helped?

As the nation's cities reached the mid-1980s, two movements in opposite directions could be seen—gentrification of certain inner city neighborhoods and continued suburbanization.[11] Observers of the first movement point to forces of deconcentration that they claim are played out, the high cost of energy, the changing age structure of the population, a rejection of suburban lifestyles, and the trickle of mid-dle-class families into neighborhoods that were written off in the 1950s and 1960s. After a critical mass of new middle-class residents exists in neighborhoods at the center, growth will be self-sustaining, it is said.

Another more persuasive group holds that if middle- and upper-income households had nothing to return to in the 1960s, they have even less reason to return a quarter of a century later. The vast majority of suburban residents in the labor force work in the suburbs. And with few exceptions only a small percentage of the central city housing stock in most metro areas can appeal to today's affluent suburbanites. Unless metro employment in general recentralizes, which it shows no signs of doing, households will not, and gentrification will remain confined almost entirely to selected areas adjacent to reasonably healthy downtowns.

While conflicts brew between central city and suburban interests, additional controversy exists within cities between housing program managers and neighborhood housing activists. Recent emphasis on community development and citizen participation has broadened the base of participation in program implementation and occasionally in policy formulation. The Neighborhood Housing Services Program began in 1973 and the Community Development Block Grant Program in 1974. The Community Reinvestment Act dates from 1975, the National Neighborhood Policy Act from 1977, and the Neighborhood Self-Help Development Act from 1978.

The emphasis on neighborhood investment and neighborhood-based organizations arises from a belief that some of the desirable features of small-town environments can be duplicated in cities through appropriately small-scale residential setting. Face-to-face contacts and knowing one's neighbors are thought to lead to mutual support networks and to enhanced political influence by residents on behalf of neighborhood interests.

The main reason that neighborhood and community development issues are politically charged is that these activities intend the empowerment of the poor, the minorities, and the disenfranchised from the city. The importance of the neighborhood idea is closely tied to the idea of decentralizing power to these groups, and housing programs have been part of the apparatus of power sharing at the neighborhood level.

Cities vary significantly with respect to their degree of governmental decentralization. Seattle and Birmingham, for example, have been models of citizen participation in housing and community development programs. In other cities the typical situation is tight con-

---

[10]Joel F. Brenner and Herbert M. Franklin, *Rent Control in North America and Four European Countries* (Washington, DC: Potomac Institute, 1977), quoted in Downs, "The Coming Crunch in Rental Housing," fn. 9, p. 85.

[11]Based on William G. Grigsby and Thomas C. Corl, "Declining Neighborhoods: Problem or Opportunity," and Lynne Beyer Sagalyn, "Mortgage Lending in Older Urban Neighborhoods: Lessons from Past Experience," Academy of Political and Social Science, *Annals* 465 (January 1983): 86–97; 98–108. Neighborhoods change because people move in and out of them, those who remain change, structures get old and deteriorate, new construction modifies old landscapes, government action forces change, and for other reasons. The nature of the forces bringing about neighborhood change as well as questions about their legitimacy trigger scholarly as well as policy debate. See Anthony Downs, "Key Relationships Between Urban Development and Neighborhood Change," *Journal of the American Institute of Planning* 45, no. 4 (1979): 462–72; Donald C. Dahmann, "Assessments of Neighborhood Quality in Metropolitan America," *Urban Affairs Quarterly*, 20, no. 4 (June 1985): 511–35; William A. V. Clark and Eric G. Moore, eds., *Residential Mobility and Public Policy* (Beverly Hills, CA: Sage, 1980); J. K. Brueckner, "Residential Succession and Land-Use Dynamics in a Vintage Model of Urban Housing," *Regional Science and Urban Economics* 10 (1981): 225–40; Martin T. Cadwallader, "Neighborhood Evaluation in Residential Mobility," *Environment and Planning A* 11 (April 1979): 393–401; Michael J. Dear, "Abandoned Housing," in John S. Adams, ed., *Urban Policymaking and Metropolitan Dynamics: A Comparative Geographical Analysis* (Cambridge, MA: Ballinger, 1976), pp. 59–99; Mary Ingels, John Kavaliunas, and Arthur Spilkia, *Housing Data Resources: Indicators and Sources of Data for Analyzing Housing and Neighborhood Conditions* (Washington, DC: U.S. Government Printing Office, 1980); and Anthony Downs, *Neighborhoods and Urban Development* (Washington, DC: Brookings Institution, 1981).

trol from the mayor's office. Another barrier to decentralization is lack of leadership and interest in many of the neighborhoods that need help the most.

One of the principal goals of neighborhood activism in Chicago was the elimination of discriminatory mortgage lending in low-income and minority neighborhoods. In April 1982 the President's Commission on Housing issued its final report, with recommendations based on the belief that the housing sector can work most efficiently to deliver services at lower cost if government involvement is minimized. Reduced government involvement in residential credit markets could affect the flow of credit into urban neighborhoods through changing policy regarding the volume of FHA-insured home mortgage loans or regulations aimed at eliminating redlining—the Home Mortgage Disclosure Act and the Community Reinvestment Act. FHA-insured mortgages have been an important source of credit in urban areas, especially in neighborhoods undergoing racial transition. These two federal laws, by requiring financial institutions to disclose the details of the amounts and locations of their mortgage-lending activities and by creating incentives to evaluate lending procedures and to provide credit in old and poor neighborhoods, have sought to step up the flow of mortgage funds to these areas and thereby slow down and possibly halt neighborhood decline.[12]

Housing for the Poor

Housing accommodations for the poor in the United States depend almost entirely on the private housing economy, a situation rare among the major industrial countries.[13] For the most part this system has yielded good results during the post–World War II era. Shelter provisions for the poor improved steadily during this period.

Direct publicly owned housing plays a relatively minor role in housing for the poor—only 1.3 million out of 88 million units were publicly owned and operated as of 1980. About 4 million low- and moderate-income households, only 5 percent of the nation's 80 million households, received some form of direct housing subsidy in 1980.

State and municipal housing aid grew in importance in the 1970s and 1980s, but the total is small and spread among a variety of income groups.

Housing for the poor, then, has not been a very significant goal of public policy in the postwar era, yet significant volumes of housing units of steadily higher quality have been provided to the poor as a result of other policies that favored high rates of new construction for middle- and upper-income households. As the affluent households moved up to better housing, the used housing trickled down to the poor. Eventually the worst housing was withdrawn from the stock. We lose about 1 percent of the housing inventory each year this way. Thus, although a relatively small proportion of record production levels was targeted directly to America's poverty population, their housing improved markedly as a consequence of the filtering process. The policy debate for years has centered on how much politically expedient subsidy should go to middle- and upper-income homeowners, recognizing that significant indirect housing benefits trickle down to the poor, and how much subsidy should go directly to the poor in the form of housing allowances or vouchers, rent subsidies, low-interest loans for house purchase, and publicly built and operated housing. For most of the postwar era, the decision at all levels of government has favored direct and indirect assistance to the affluent, significant trickle-down housing benefits for the poor, and only modest direct housing assistance programs for the poor.

The future success of this mix of approaches, and especially the much-maligned filtering process, is uncertain because of the breakdown of the traditional political housing alliance, the stagnation of real incomes among the middle classes, the growing number of people below the poverty level, and a housing finance system that since the passage of the Depository Institutions Deregulation and Monetary Control Act of 1980 is subject to full market forces and credit competition for the first time since the New Deal.

Within this new political and economic environment, housing wants and needs of the middle class are issues of greater political potency than are the housing needs of the poor. Yet without the ref-

---

[12]Calvin P. Bradford and Paul Schersten, *A Tool for Community Capital: Home Mortgage Disclosure Act 1985 National Survey*, Working Paper (Minneapolis: Hubert H. Humphrey Institute of Public Affairs, University of Minnesota, 1985).

[13]Based on George Sternlieb and James W. Hughes, "Housing the Poor in a Post-Shelter Society," American Academy of Political and Social Science, *Annals* 465 (January 1983): 109–22. For reviews of various programs focused on housing programs for low-income households, and the Experimental Housing Allowance Program of the 1970s, see Jon Erickson and Charles Wilhelm, eds., *Housing the Homeless* (Piscataway, NJ: Center for Urban Policy Research, 1985); Joseph Friedman and Daniel H. Weinberg, *The Great Housing Experiment*, Urban Affairs Annual Reviews, vol. 24 (Beverly Hills, CA: Sage, 1983); Ira S. Lowry, "The Housing Assistance Supply Experiment: An Overview," Regional Science Association, *Papers* 37 (1976): 21–30; C. Peter Rydell, "Supply Response to the Housing Allowance Program," *International Regional Science Review* 5, no. 2 (1980): 119–38; Raymond J. Struyk, *A New System for Public Housing: Salvaging a National Resource* (Washington, DC: Urban Institute, 1980); *Development Without Displacement II (A Theme for the 1980s)*, "Closing the Low Income Housing Gap: The Case for Affordable Housing" (Chicago: Chicago Rehab Network, 1981); and Robert Orvis Bixby, "Small Town Public Housing: A Geographic Analysis and Case Study," doctoral dissertation, University of Minnesota, 1985.

ormation of a broad-based housing constituency—of consumers, producers, materials suppliers, transportation and finance interests, building trades, and others with a direct stake in high-volume, high-quality, low-cost housing production—continued steady improvement in the shelter available for the poor is unlikely in the 1980s and beyond.

Local Growth Controls and the Housing Process[14]

Almost all the laws that govern the land development and house building processes are passed and enforced at the local—usually municipal—level. In the first postwar building boom years starting in 1945 residential developments in the suburbs were carried out with a minimum of regulation. Houses were built, sold, and occupied, while new and inexperienced suburban governments were saddled with the job of providing streets, water and sewer systems, schools, parks, police and fire protection, and other general government functions carried out at city hall. The huge external costs associated with this sprawling suburban development free-for-all began to be totaled in the 1950s, so that between the mid-1960s and the mid-1970s communities across the country had begun tightening their control over land development and house building. They intended to slow down rapid growth that was engulfing them or to create more order and community control over a process that had become chaotic and expensive.

In some cases local governments changed laws at a single stroke by adopting comprehensive growth management ordinances. More typically, they put in place one at a time a series of review procedures and permit requirements that produced striking cumulative effects—raising the up-front cost of new housing and slowing down the devel-

opment and building processes.[15] The stated rationales for the new requirements included protecting farmland and local environmental quality; stretching out the development process so that communities would receive a range of housing types and households of different ages; permitting capital improvements to be added in an orderly, efficient, and fiscally sound manner; and forcing developers, builders, and their customers to pay the full marginal cost of their new housing units, rather than passing on part of these extra costs to old residents through extension of average cost pricing of municipal services to newly arrived households.

Regardless of the valid rationales for imposing community control over the development process, they have had the effect of limiting the options available to some housing consumers, both directly, in terms of first-time occupants, and indirectly, in constraining production in the initial phase of the filtering process. Since households that desire to move into a specific suburban community live elsewhere, they usually are not organized as a political force and they arrive on the scene too late to influence the key decisions about their houses and neighborhoods. Moreover, it is widely held that development controls that raise the cost of suburban housing have disproportionate impact on lower-middle-income households, among whom minority households are heavily represented. To the extent that the controls slow down or stop the entry of low-income or low-wealth households into suburban communities, they exclude disproportionate numbers of minority households.

The Civil Rights Act of 1968 declared that "it is the policy of the United States to provide . . . for fair housing." Title VIII of this act, known as the Fair Housing Act, holds it "unlawful to discriminate against any person in the . . . sale or rental of a dwelling . . . because of race, color, religion, sex, or national origin."[16] But whereas the language and intent of the law are clear, progress toward the stated goal has been slow. Racial discrimination continues, and residential patterns remain highly segregated by race, class, income, and wealth. The recent acceleration of black suburbanization has not much altered these patterns as central city segregated neighborhoods are rep-

[14]Based in part on Bernard J. Frieden, "The Exclusionary Effect of Growth Controls," American Academy of Political and Social Science, *Annals* 465 (January 1983): 123–35. See also Urban Land Institute, *Fair Housing and Exclusionary Land Use: Historical Overview, Summary of Litigation and a Comment with Research Bibliography* (Washington, DC: Urban Land Institute, 1974); John F. Kain and John M. Quigley, *Housing Markets and Racial Discrimination: A Microeconomic Analysis* (New York: National Bureau of Economic Research, 1975); Paul N. Courant and John Yinger, *On Models of Racial Prejudice and Urban Residential Structure* (Madison: Institute for Research on Poverty, University of Wisconsin, 1975); Trudy P. McFall, "Fair Share Housing: The Twin City Story," *Planning*, vol. no. 42 (August 1977): 22–25; and Ann M. Shafor and Roberta E. Longfellow, *Fair Share Housing: A Bibliography* (Chicago: Council of Planning Librarians, 1980).

[15]See Fred P. Bosselman and David Callies, *The Quiet Revolution in Land Use Control*, prepared for the Council on Environmental Quality (Washington, DC: U.S. Government Printing Office, 1972); and Fred P. Bosselman, Duane A. Feurer, and Charles L. Siemon, *The Permit Explosion: Coordination of the Proliferation* (Washington, DC: Urban Land Institute, 1976).

[16]42 U.S. Code, sections 3601–3619, discussed in Robert W. Lake, "Changing Symptoms, Constant Causes: Recent Evolution of Fair Housing in the United States," *New Community* 11 (Spring 1984): 206–13.

licated in suburban settings. As a result, blacks experience lower rates of home ownership and occupy lower-quality housing than whites even after controlling for socioeconomic characteristics and household composition.[17]

Almost all programs that are designed and launched to help resolve these thorny policy issues require support and cooperation from local governments and their agencies. Yet a review of the intent of the Housing Assistance Plan, created by the landmark Housing and Community Development Act of 1974, and the actual Housing Assistance Plan process as designed and deployed by the U.S. Department of Housing and Urban Development through the end of the 1970s, found problems at the local level, where people actually live and where the housing process operates.[18] The review found that local governments and HUD together deserve good marks for attempting to ensure that assisted housing resources are shared equitably among competing groups, especially in the provision of assistance to families (as opposed to elderly households). Much less satisfactory, however, was the matching of the delivery strategy—that is, the mix of new construction, rehabilitation, and lease of existing units—with local market conditions. In some cases the HUD area office was too active a partner of the community in designing the strategy; yet even when HUD's role was appropriate, the guidance provided was inadequate to define the boundaries under which local planning should occur. Thus, both the guidance and forms work against truly effective coordination of housing resources. Moreover, once the local housing assistance plan is completed with all its weaknesses, it usually is not followed in the ultimate distribution of housing subsidy resources by HUD, in part because of production pressures and in part because of the activities of state housing agencies. These problems constitute strong disincentives to local governments to invest the necessary resources—of both staff and the political executive—to develop solid housing assistance plans.

Inclusionary Housing Programs

It is widely conceded that post–World War II housing policies in the United States produced steady and significant improvements in the housing stock, but did little to provide low- and moderate-income housing opportunities in a manner that promoted social and economic integration of society. Municipalities often adopted "exclusionary" zoning and development control ordinances that had as a direct and intended consequence, or as an indirect and unintended result, the exclusion of low-income and minority populations. "Inclusionary zoning ordinances" and "inclusionary housing programs" began in California and New Jersey as controversial elements of land use and housing policy. Under these policies and related laws, developers must provide, as a condition of project approval, or are given incentives to provide, low- and moderate-income housing as part of or in conjunction with their proposed development projects. These initiatives have strong advocates and have met with some success, but they have raised serious questions of law, public policy, and economic soundness that have yet to be answered.[19]

Summary and Conclusions

We have reviewed the persistent housing-related issues in the United States in recent times.[20] They center on how to make housing markets more efficient and more equitable; stabilizing production for the producers as well as consumers; upgrading the quality of new housing and maintaining the existing stock in good condition; making sure that there is a steady flow of money to finance construction and purchase of housing; controlling inflation; making sure that renters avoid a market crunch in the 1980s; helping neighborhoods avoid trouble; and making sure that poor and minority households get the help they need to obtain decent housing at an affordable price. With regard to the last and perhaps the most intractable long-term issue—that of the needs of the poor—housing programs do not confront the causes of impoverishment, but they try to ameliorate some of poverty's consequences.

The multiplicity of purposes in housing programs for the poor is matched by a multiplicity of available tools. Rents can be lowered

[17]Lake, "Changing Symptoms," p. 206; John R. Logan and Mark Schneider, "Racial Segregation and Racial Change in American Suburbs, 1970–1980," *American Journal of Sociology* 89 (January 1984): 874–88; and Suzanne M. Bianchi, Reynolds Farley, and Daphne Spain, "Racial Inequalities in Housing: An Examination of Recent Trends," *Demography* 19 (February 1982): 37–51.

[18]Discussion based on Raymond J. Struyk, *Saving the Housing Assistance Plan: Improving Incentives to Local Governments* (Washington, DC: Urban Institute, 1979).

[19]See Alan Mallach, *Inclusionary Housing Programs* (New Brunswick, NJ: Center for Urban Policy Research, 1984); and M. Bruce Johnson, ed., *Resolving the Housing Crisis: Government Policy, Decontrol and the Public Interest*, Pacific Studies in Public Policy (Cambridge, MA: Ballinger, 1982).

[20]For a major bibliography of the principal housing publications of the 1960s and early 1970s, see Virginia Paulus, *Housing: A Bibliography, 1960–1972* (New York: AMS Press, 1974). For an account of one of the most useful and complete data systems describing the U.S. housing stock, its settings, and its use, with considerable geographical detail, see John M. Goering, *Housing in America: The Characteristics and Uses of the Annual Housing Survey*, U.S. Department of Housing and Urban Development (Washington, DC: U.S. Government Printing Office, 1979).

through supply-side subsidies or households can be provided—directly or through payments on their behalf to landlords—with additional funds to enable them to pay required rents (demand-side subsidies), or both. On the supply side there can be up-front capital grants, covering part of or all construction costs (including federal purchase of a privately originated mortgage); below-market interest rate on the mortgage, through a direct federal loan, payment of part or all of the interest and amortization for private financing, or financing based on tax-exempt bonds; tax savings through rapid depreciation; federal requirements for matching local or state contributions, directly or through property tax abatement; and contributions toward maintenance and operating costs.[21]

On the demand side there can be general income assistance to low-income families, not specifically designated for housing, but usable for rent if the family desires; income assistance, some or all of which is earmarked for rent or housing payments; and payments on behalf of tenants to owners, in housing units of the tenants' choosing, with or without requirements of minimum quality standards.

These methods of lowering the rent or housing cost burden are not mutually exclusive; combinations exist. Each method, if used alone, has implications for the depth of subsidy that can be attained and the income group that can be served.

There are disparate views on a host of other housing issues: whether it is efficient to promote rental housing construction by means of shallow subsidies; how to induce owners of multifamily rental housing to maintain and rehabilitate this stock without wholesale economic displacement of the present tenants; whether it is possible to stimulate new home construction without simply substituting for housing that would have been built anyway; how to moderate the sharp cyclical swings in construction and sales of housing; what the appropriate methods are for reducing construction costs; what incentives would lead to efficient space utilization in the existing inventory of housing; and how to reduce racial segregation and discrimination in housing.[22]

Some of the most important decisions affecting housing are not known as "housing policy." Changes in tax laws, legislation permitting the transformation of financial institutions, and shifts in welfare programs all have profound effects on levels of investment and con-

sumption of housing. The actions of the Federal Reserve Board may have wider consequences for housing activity than those of the Secretary of Housing and Urban Development. Good housing is one of the prizes that a wealthy society can offer its citizens. How much each household and group gets is partly a matter of private market decisions, but it is also shaped by public policies.[23]

Appendix

The Effect of Publicly Sponsored Housing Programs on Housing Demand and Supply

The federal government has tried to influence housing consumption patterns of low-income households ever since the 1930s.[24] We have already discussed ways that financial institutions and tax policies have molded the structure of housing demand and patterns of housing consumption. Let us now review significant federal programs that have been sources of flux in housing demand and in patterns of housing use.

In his 1971 message to Congress on housing policy President Richard Nixon asked for an expansion of the Department of Housing and Urban Development's Experimental Housing Allowance Program (EHAP): ". . . to make decent housing available for all low-income families without the housing project stigma, the loss of freedom of choice and the inordinately high cost of current programs."[25] Housing allowances and rent certificates have been advocated since the 1930s. The Taft subcommittee hearings on postwar housing policy, and discussions that preceded the 1949 Housing Act, contained debates for

---

[21]Based on Grace Milgram, "Housing the Urban Poor: Urban Housing Assistance Programs," in *Housing: A Reader*, prepared by the Congressional Research Service, Library of Congress (Washington, DC: U.S. Government Printing Office, 1983), pp. 114–17.

[22]Morton J. Schussheim, "Housing: An Overview," in Milgram, "Housing the Urban Poor," pp. 23–24.

[23]Ibid.

[24]See J. Paul Mitchell, ed., *Federal Housing Policy and Programs: Past and Present*, (Piscataway, NJ: Center for Urban Policy Research, 1985); Henry J. Aaron, *Shelter and Subsidies: Who Benefits from Federal Housing Policies?* (Washington, DC: Brookings Institution, 1972); Barry G. Jacobs. *Guide to Federal Housing Programs* (Washington, DC: Bureau of National Affairs, 1982); Ira S. Lowry, *Experimenting with Housing Allowances. Executive Summary: The Final Comprehensive Report of the Housing Assistance Supply Experiment* (Santa Monica, CA: Rand Corporation, 1982); Raymond J. Struyk, Neil Mayer, and John A. Tuccillo, *Federal Housing Policy at President Reagan's Mid-Term* (Washington, DC: Urban Institute Press, 1983); Edgar O. Olsen, "Housing Programs and the Forgotten Taxpayer," *Public Interest*, vol. no. 66 (Winter 1982): 97–109; Roberta Drews, *Federal Subsidies for Public Housing: Issues and Options*, U.S. Congress, Congressional Budget Office (Washington, DC: U.S. Government Printing Office, 1983); U.S. General Accounting Office, *Block Grants for Housing: A Study of Local Experiences and Attitudes* (Washington, DC: U.S. Government Printing Office, 1983); and Daniel J. Elazar, "Restructuring Federal Housing Programs: Who Stands to Gain?" *Publius* 6, no. 2 (1976): 75–94.

[25]Richard M. Nixon, President's Message to Congress on Housing Policy, September 19, 1971.

and against rent certificates for the poor. The committee concluded that rent certificates would be degrading to recipients, that they would not add to the housing supply, that they would deter participation of private enterprise, and that there would be no way to limit the program.

A shift in housing policy toward housing allowances occurred in the Housing and Urban Development Act of 1965 with the rent supplement program, which established the principle of income-related subsidies to tenants in privately owned housing. A second program of the same law (Section 23) enabled local housing authorities to lease privately owned housing and sublease it to low-income households at rents they could afford, a program that was later transformed into the Section 8 program.

In 1967–68 the President's Committee on Urban Housing (the Kaiser Committee) devoted special attention to housing allowances and recommended an experiment to test their effects.[26] In the EHAP that followed in Kansas City, Wilmington, Delaware, and 10 other cities, two ideas were tested: (1) that the best way to help families who needed better housing was to give them money that they could use on their own and (2) that the best way to learn how a new approach would work was to conduct a large-scale social experiment. An underlying theoretical reason for a housing allowance experiment was the belief that incentives should be created to encourage households to allocate more of their total income to housing than they might without the incentives. The argument is that housing is an important merit good and that society should place a greater value on the housing of the poor than the poor themselves would, because spillover effects of slum housing create health and safety hazards, and minimum shelter requirements are essential for childrearing and health standards.[27] Another rationale for the EHAP was unhappiness with traditional standardized housing programs for the poor, which focused on production of new buildings that were then rented to the poor at below-market rates.

In the demand portion of the EHAP, the research focused on the extent to which eligible households participated, on changes in housing expenditures, and on the choices people made with respect to location and quality of housing and their satisfaction with those choices. The experimental housing allowance was designed as a housing gap payment formula. Under the formula 25 percent of the family's adjusted gross income was assumed to be allocated for housing. The difference between it and estimated local annual cost of adequate rental housing appropriate for their family size and composition was the amount paid to the family as their housing allowance. Program participants were required to live in housing that met minimum standards, and the allowance they collected could not exceed the actual rent they paid.

The experiment was based on the elemental idea that the poor cannot afford decent housing. The government should therefore determine what the poor can afford (that is, establish a rent-income ratio) and the cost of decent housing (rent level for adequate housing), and then pay the difference. The problem according to critics is that there is no single "right" rent in a complex metropolitan housing market.[28]

Before the housing allowance experiment, many thought that increases in the disposable incomes of poor families would lead to a nearly proportional increase in their housing expenditures. However, the income elasticity of housing outlays in the EHAP (that is, the percentage change in housing expenditures compared with the percentage change in disposable income) was about .19 for renters. Families who receive housing allowances were free to decide how much of this payment to spend for additional housing, and they did not raise their rent outlays very much. Federal officials expected the typical family to move to better accommodations and to spend most of its subsidy as higher rent. What happened was that most families stayed where they were, made minor repairs to meet program standards, and used the payments to free their own funds for nonhousing expenditures.[29]

[26]Dowell Myers, "Housing Allowances, Submarket Relations and the Filtering Process," *Urban Affairs Quarterly* 11 (December 1975): 216; Arthur P. Solomon, "Housing Allowances and National Objectives," in *Housing in the Seventies*, Working Paper, no. 2 (Washington, DC: U.S. Department of Housing and Urban Development, 1976); and U.S. Department of Housing and Urban Development, *Experimental Housing Allowance Program: Conclusions, the 1980 Report* (Washington, DC; U.S. Government Printing Office, 1980).

[27]Arthur P. Solomon and Chester G. Fenton, "The Nation's First Experience with Housing Allowances: The Kansas City Demonstration," *Land Economics* 50 (1974): 213.

[28]There is no single "right" rent because there is no single housing market in a metro area. See Risa I. Palm, "Spatial Segmentation of the Urban Housing Market," *Economic Geography* 54, no. 3 (July 1978): 210–21; and A. C. Brummell, "A Test of Spatial Submarkets in Urban Housing," *Canadian Journal of Regional Science* 4, no. 1 (1981): 89–112.

[29]Kevin Kajer, "Housing Allowances and the Experimental Housing Allowance Program," unpublished report, Humphrey Institute of Public Affairs, University of Minnesota, June 1985.

The Rise and Decline of Mortgage Revenue Bonds to Finance Low- and Moderate-Income First-Time House Buyers

Local governments in the 1970s often subsidized mortgage lending by selling tax-free bonds to investors and lending the proceeds at below-market interest rates to low- and moderate-income first-time house buyers. Since the interest on the bonds was free of federal income tax and often free of state income tax as well, the investors were willing to pay high prices for the bonds and accept below-market interest payments. The result was lower-cost mortgage loans for qualified borrowers. Payments on the mortgages were earmarked for interest payments to the bond holders and eventual retirement of the bonds.

These mortgage revenue bonds seemed like a good idea to their promoters and the borrowers who were helped, but the U.S. General Accounting Office concluded that they were a costly way to finance housing purchases compared with the benefits created and compared with other means of providing the same assistance to house buyers. It was shown that the public purpose objective of subsidizing low- and moderate-income households to buy houses was not generally achieved and that specifying purchase price and income limits was ineffective in targeting benefits. Although this program was politically popular, there was a significant federal tax loss; thus, the Mortgage Subsidy Bond Tax Act of 1980 attempted to restrict the use of these instruments, but the volume of single-family mortgage revenue bond issues in 1984 and 1985 exceeded that of any previous year.[30]

The Allocation of Housing Assistance Funds to Urban and Rural Counties

In the early 1980s HUD worked within a statutory authority to establish a "Fair Share" formula to allocate housing assistance funds on a county-by-county basis. The formula was used to allocate about 80 percent of new Section 8 and Public Housing money in each fiscal year, with the remainder allocated by HUD discretion.

Each county's need for housing assistance was calculated as a percentage of total U.S. need under the Fair Share formula using six criteria: total county population, poverty population, dwelling units lacking complete plumbing, overcrowded housing units, shortfall in the number of vacant units below a 6 percent vacancy rate, and renter households with one or more housing problems. Each of HUD's approximately 40 field offices received a Fair Share allocation of money, which was then subdivided into allocation areas within the office's jurisdiction. After the Fair Share formula determined the funding for each allocation area, local communities prepared Housing Assistance Plans (HAPs) in conjunction with their applications for Community Development Block Grant Funds, specifying the proportion of funds that would be devoted to each of nine user groups, based on three categories of household (elderly, family, and large family) and three kinds of housing (new, rehabilitated, and existing). The HUD area office determined the allocation among the nine groups for rural areas lacking a housing Assistance Plan and not participating in the Community Development program.[31]

In addition to HUD's Fair Share allocations of housing assistance money, the Farmers' Home Administration has provided housing assistance funds to states based on need, using a formula that considers rural population, poverty, substandard housing, and housing cost. The state FmHA offices, in turn, allocate funds to the counties and substate areas for the single-family homeownership and home repair programs.[32]

The objectives of these programs are to lower the cost of standard housing for protected classes of households and to enhance the quality of housing available to low- and moderate-income households. Program administrative rules steer the funds to geographical areas that have the largest numbers and the greatest relative concentrations of poorly housed people. The hope has been that public subsidies will stimulate demand for higher-quality housing for the poor and expand the supply of standard housing for needy households at the locations where they want to live.

[30]George E. Peterson and Brian Cooper, *Tax Exempt Financing of Housing Investment* (Washington, DC: The Urban Institute, 1979); James A. Verbrugge, *Tax-Exempt Bonds for Single Family Housing: An Evaluation of State Housing Finance Agency and Local Government Programs* (Chicago: U.S. League of Savings Institutions, 1979); U.S. Congress, House Committee on Banking, Finance and Urban Affairs, *Tax Exempt Bonds for Single Family Housing* (Washington, DC: U.S. Government Printing Office, 1979); Cynthia Francis Gensheimer and Martha J. Smith, *The Mortgage Subsidy Bond Tax Act of 1980*, U.S. Congress, Congressional Budget Office (Washington, DC: U.S. Government Printing Office, 1982); and Susannah E. Calkins, "The Home Mortgage Revenue Bonds Controversy," *Publius* 10, no. 1 (Winter 1980): 111–18; and U.S. General Accounting Office, *The Costs and Benefits of Single Family Mortgage Revenue Bonds*, Preliminary Report (Washington, DC: U.S. Government Printing Office, 1983).

[31]Iric Nathanson, *Housing Needs of the Rural Elderly and the Handicapped*, U.S. Department of Housing and Urban Development (Washington, DC: U.S. Government Printing Office, 1980), pp. 20–21.
[32]Ibid., p. 21.

Publicly Assisted Rental Housing

Conventional public housing, the oldest of the federal housing assistance programs, enables public housing agencies to build, acquire, manage, lease, and own housing units occupied by low-income households.

Under the conventional public housing program, local public housing agencies (PHAs) develop, own, and operate low-rent public housing projects financed through the sale of tax-exempt bonds. Debt service on these bonds is paid by the federal government under annual contributions contracts (ACC) for up to 40 years. Construction is normally financed through the sale of tax-exempt project notes of the PHA, backed by a federal guarantee.

In the early years federal contributions were limited to the amounts required to amortize the full capital costs of the projects. However, operating subsidies became necessary as operating expenses increased and maximum rents were limited to 25 percent of the tenant's adjusted income. The 1979 Housing Authorization Bill authorized that operating subsidies could still be paid after the original annual contributions contracts had expired, so long as the project continued to serve low-income families. Additional contributions have been made available in recent years to amortize the costs of modernizing older public housing projects.

At the end of the 1970s, there were 267,000 nonmetro public housing units, with 92,000 (34 percent) devoted to families, 156,000 (59 percent) to elderly, and 19,000 (7 percent) to nonelderly handicapped.[33] The 156,000 devoted to the nonmetro elderly constituted 26 percent of the U.S. total of 584,000 public housing units occupied by elderly. The 19,000 nonmetro nonelderly households in public housing were 18 percent of the nation's total of 106,000.

Under Section 202, HUD has provided long-term direct loans at .5 percent above the federal borrowing rate to nonprofit organizations to build new housing or substantially rehabilitate housing for the low-income elderly and for the handicapped.

The original Section 202 program provided loans at a 3 percent interest rate. This original program was considered very successful financially, producing approximately 45,000 units during its 10 years of operation, with only one foreclosure, but it was phased out in favor of construction financed by Section 236. Since 1975, Section 202 financing has been provided in tandem with Section 8 rental assistance.

[33]Nathanson, *Housing Needs*, p. 12.

An important aspect of the revised Section 202 program is that all projects receive the benefits of leased housing assistance payments under the Section 8 program, which means that eligible tenants will not pay more than 25 percent of their incomes for rent.

To guarantee their availability on approval of the financing, reservations for Section 8 funds are set aside at the time a Section 202 reservation is made. Tenants in Section 202 housing built before 1975 must meet income limits set by HUD. Section 8 income limits—set at 80 percent of the area median—usually apply for projects built since 1975. By law 20 to 25 percent of Section 202 funds must be used in nonmetropolitan areas. At the start of 1980 rural elderly Section 202 and Section 8 loan reservations applied to about 9,000 units.[34]

Through the Section 515 program the Farmers Home Administration provides direct loans to private, public, and non-profit organizations that provide rental housing for the elderly, the handicapped, and low- and moderate-income families. Funds can be used to build new housing or to buy and rehabilitate existing housing. Section 515 can be used in tandem with HUD's Section 8 program. At the start of the 1980s over 65,000 of the 192,000 Section 515 rural units were occupied by elderly households.[35]

HUD's Section 8 program became the agency's major housing assistance program of the later 1970s and early 1980s. It provided subsidies to owners of new, rehabilitated, or existing housing occupied by low-income tenants. Under the Section 8 new construction program, assistance has been provided to rental households living in dwellings newly constructed under prior commitment from the Department of Housing and Urban Development. HUD pays owners the difference between the contract rent established by agreement with HUD and the payment made by the household. The household locates its own apartment in an eligible structure and is accepted by the landlord, who verifies its income. The household pays between 15 and 25 percent of its income, depending on income and household size.

Except for projects specifically built for the elderly and the handicapped, the only eligibility criterion is income. Preference is to be given to families who occupy substandard housing or who are involuntarily displaced from their current residences.

[34]Ibid., pp. 12–13. See also Raymond J. Struyk, Sue A. Marshall, and Larry J. Ozanne, *Housing Policies for the Urban Poor* (Washington, DC: Urban Institute, 1978); and Raymond J. Struyk, *A New System for Public Housing: Salvaging a National Resource* (Washington, DC: Urban Institute, 1980).
[35]Nathanson, *Housing Needs*, p. 14.

The maximum income, set by HUD in each market area, is generally 80 percent of the local median for four-person families, up to 100 percent of median for families of eight persons or more, and down to 50 percent of median for one-person households. Thirty percent of assisted households must be of very low income—that is, below 50 percent of median, adjusted for household size. Approximately two fifths of households in the country were potentially eligible.

Rather than provide direct financing for new or rehabilitated housing, HUD guarantees a subsidy for a specified number of units in the project for the life of the contract, which can run from 15 to 40 years.

In the Section 8 new construction program the subsidy has been tied to the housing unit; in the existing housing program the subsidy generally follows the tenant recipients as long as they qualify. Under the Section 8 Existing Housing and Moderate Rehabilitation Program rental assistance is given to households that are certified by a public housing agency (PHA) for units in existing structures. The PHA, authorized to provide housing, issues certificates through a HUD allocation system. Each certified family finds its own apartment—which can be the one in which it currently resides—in the private market at no more than the fair market rent. The owner has to agree to participate and to meet HUD requirements. The apartment also has to meet HUD-established standards.

The existing housing program includes a moderate rehabilitation program. This program is administered by public housing agencies, which select proposals from owners in such a way as to promote one of three objectives: freedom of housing choice and spatial deconcentration of assisted housing, prevention of displacement of lower-income families in neighborhoods undergoing private revitalization, and neighborhood preservation and revitalization. A minimum expenditure of $1,000 per unit is required. The upper limit on expenditures is to be controlled by the fair market rents, which are set at 120 percent of the existing housing rent schedule for the area. By the mid-1980s the Section 8 program for New and Substantially Rehabilitated Units was being phased out.

At the start of 1980, new and substantially rehabilitated nonmetro units under the Section 8 program totaled 189,000. Of these, 106,000 (56 percent) went to elderly households (head or spouse aged 62 or older). The nonmetro elderly units were 26 percent of the 414,000 Section 8 elderly units nationwide. Section 8 contracts in existing housing covered 32,000 nonmetro elderly households, or 29 percent of the 112,000 nonmetro totals, and 15 percent of the nationwide total of 212,000 elderly units.

Section 235 provided homebuying assistance to low- and moderate-income families. Direct cash subsidy payments were made by HUD to reduce mortgage interest costs to as low as 4 percent under the revised Section 235 program—1 percent under the original and 5 percent from 1976 to January 1978. The homeowner had to contribute at least 20 percent of adjusted gross income toward monthly mortgage payments, insurance, and tax payments on the house.

The original Section 235 program was suspended in January 1973, and a revised Section 235 program was implemented in early 1976. The program is now essentially defunct.

The Section 236 Rental Housing Assistance Program was a major source of new rental housing from 1969 to 1973. Since then the government has been phasing out new construction under this program, with only a handful of projects built in the early 1980s under earlier commitments. Subsidies continue, however, on behalf of some half a million tenant households that occupy Section 236 housing built in prior years.

Mortgage interest reduction payments are made by the federal government to the lender on behalf of the owner of qualified multifamily housing. The Housing and Community Development Act of 1974 authorized additional rental housing assistance—deep subsidies—to be provided on behalf of low-income tenants whose rental charges exceed 25 percent of income and required that 20 percent of tenants in a project be of such a low income.

Rural and Elderly Housing Assistance Programs

The Farmers Home Administration's rental assistance program parallels Section 8. FmHA pays owners of rental housing the difference between 25 percent of the tenant's income and a basic rent level approved for the project. The program can be used in tandem with FmHA's Section 515 Loan Program. By 1980, 40,000 units were in the program, but the proportion occupied by elderly or handicapped is unknown.

HUD's Section 235 program for assistance payments for homeownership gives mortgage interest subsidies to households whose adjusted gross income is less than 95 percent of the area's median. FmHA's Section 502 program makes direct loans (with interest rates as low as 1 percent) to low- and moderate-income households who cannot obtain loans elsewhere. The program started in 1965 and by the beginning of 1980 over 42,000 loans had been provided to the rural elderly. FmHA Section 502 loans can be used to repair and renovate single-family housing.

FmHA Section 504 loans can be made to very low income home-owners to remove hazards to their health and safety (water supply, septic systems, roof repairs, heating systems, storm windows and doors, structural defects). Since 1977 Section 504 funds have been used to make over 15,000 direct grants to persons aged 62 and over. HUD's Community Development Block Grant Program, enacted in 1974, supports activities principally aimed at benefiting low- and moderate-income people, including housing rehabilitation loans and grants. Nonmetro communities under 50,000 can apply for funds from a 20 percent set-aside for nonmetro areas.[36]

[36]See James P. Zais et al., *Housing Assistance for Older Americans: The Reagan Prescription* (Washington, DC: Urban Institute Press, 1982); and Stephen M. Golant, *The Residential Location and Spatial Behavior of the Elderly*, Research Paper no. 143 (Chicago: Department of Geography, University of Chicago, 1972).

TABLE A1.1

Housing Units, by States, 1940–1980

	Number of Units					Percentage Change by Decade				
State	1940	1950	1960	1970	1980	1940–50	1950–60	1960–70	1970–80	1940–80
Alabama	708,043	843,857	967,466	1,120,239	1,467,374	19.2%	14.6%	15.8%	31.0%	107.2%
Alaska	22,414	33,072	67,193	90,827	162,825	47.6	103.2	35.2	79.2	626.4
Arizona	147,079	240,750	415,834	585,751	1,110,558	63.7	72.7	40.9	89.6	655.1
Arkansas	520,613	575,163	586,552	675,620	898,593	10.5	2.0	15.2	33.0	72.6
California	2,340,373	3,590,660	5,465,870	7,000,174	9,279,036	53.4	52.2	28.1	32.6	296.5
Colorado	354,660	436,226	594,522	757,835	1,194,253	23.0	36.3	27.5	57.6	236.7
Connecticut	488,543	611,162	818,544	981,603	1,158,884	25.1	33.9	19.9	18.1	137.2
Delaware	75,567	97,013	143,725	180,233	238,611	28.4	48.2	25.4	32.4	215.8
District of Columbia	185,128	229,738	262,641	278,327	276,984	24.1	14.3	6.0	-0.5	49.6
Florida	590,451	952,131	1,776,961	2,527,596	4,378,691	61.3	86.6	42.2	73.2	641.6
Georgia	796,715	966,672	1,170,039	1,470,754	2,028,350	21.3	21.0	25.7	37.9	154.5
Hawaii	90,830	120,606	165,506	216,538	334,235	32.8	37.2	30.8	54.4	268.0
Idaho	152,835	188,328	223,533	244,623	375,127	23.2	18.7	9.4	53.3	145.4
Illinois	2,280,826	2,671,647	3,275,799	3,702,449	4,319,672	17.1	22.6	13.0	16.7	89.4
Indiana	1,005,952	1,232,314	1,503,148	1,730,496	2,091,795	22.5	22.0	15.1	20.9	107.9
Iowa	726,654	811,912	905,295	964,293	1,131,299	11.7	11.5	6.5	17.3	55.7
Kansas	545,721	625,148	740,335	789,735	954,906	14.6	18.4	6.7	20.9	75.0
Kentucky	729,206	820,141	925,572	1,064,826	1,369,125	12.5	12.9	15.0	28.6	87.8
Louisiana	619,233	777,672	978,452	1,150,950	1,548,419	25.6	25.8	17.6	34.5	150.0
Maine	260,659	311,441	364,617	397,182	501,093	19.5	17.1	8.9	26.2	92.2
Maryland	500,156	689,116	934,552	1,249,814	1,590,907	37.8	35.6	33.7	25.7	214.1
Massachusetts	1,221,252	1,400,185	1,690,998	1,890,400	2,208,146	14.7	20.8	11.8	16.8	80.8
Michigan	1,519,378	1,971,842	2,548,792	2,957,303	3,589,912	29.8	29.3	16.0	21.4	136.3
Minnesota	773,042	918,434	1,119,271	1,276,552	1,612,960	18.8	21.9	14.1	26.4	108.7
Mississippi	557,246	609,329	628,945	699,178	911,627	9.3	3.2	11.2	30.4	63.6
Missouri	1,140,493	1,268,354	1,491,397	1,673,638	1,988,915	11.2	17.6	12.2	18.8	74.4

TABLE A1.1 (*continued*)

State	Number of Units					Percentage Change by Decade				
	1940	1950	1960	1970	1980	1940–50	1950–60	1960–70	1970–80	1940–80
Montana	177,443	194,256	233,310	246,603	328,465	9.5	20.1	5.7	33.2	85.1
Nebraska	387,368	417,245	472,950	515,530	624,829	7.7	13.4	9.0	21.2	61.3
Nevada	36,770	56,515	101,623	172,558	339,949	53.7	79.8	69.8	97.0	824.5
New Hampshire	158,044	190,563	224,440	280,962	386,381	20.6	17.8	25.2	37.5	144.5
New Jersey	1,223,887	1,501,473	1,998,940	2,388,689	2,772,149	22.7	33.1	19.5	16.1	126.5
New Mexico	145,642	199,706	281,976	326,108	507,513	37.1	41.2	15.7	55.6	248.5
New York	4,032,460	4,633,806	5,695,880	6,299,684	6,867,638	14.9	22.9	10.6	9.0	70.3
North Carolina	820,888	1,058,367	1,322,957	1,642,015	2,274,737	28.9	25.0	24.1	38.5	177.1
North Dakota	162,881	175,769	194,597	204,235	258,772	7.9	10.7	5.0	26.7	58.9
Ohio	1,977,693	2,402,565	3,041,151	3,466,688	4,108,105	21.5	26.6	14.0	18.5	107.7
Oklahoma	647,485	715,691	815,685	939,564	1,237,040	10.5	14.0	15.2	31.7	91.1
Oregon	369,811	524,003	622,853	744,784	1,083,285	41.7	18.9	19.6	45.4	192.9
Pennsylvania	2,618,056	3,036,494	3,581,877	3,927,206	4,596,431	16.0	18.0	9.6	17.0	75.6
Rhode Island	203,469	244,147	286,757	317,689	372,672	20.0	17.5	10.8	17.3	83.2
South Carolina	458,899	557,672	678,379	815,309	1,153,709	21.5	21.6	20.2	41.5	151.4
South Dakota	179,744	194,573	216,449	225,417	276,997	8.3	11.2	4.1	22.9	54.1
Tennessee	742,030	921,837	1,084,365	1,301,490	1,747,422	24.2	17.6	20.0	34.3	135.5
Texas	1,804,884	2,393,828	3,153,127	3,830,091	5,549,352	32.6	31.7	21.5	44.9	207.5
Utah	147,291	200,554	262,670	315,765	490,006	36.2	31.0	20.2	55.2	232.7
Vermont	106,362	121,911	136,307	165,211	223,199	14.6	11.8	21.2	35.1	109.8
Virginia	659,787	901,483	1,168,913	1,493,939	2,020,941	36.6	29.7	27.8	35.3	206.3
Washington	590,439	809,701	1,009,519	1,221,931	1,689,450	37.1	24.7	21.0	38.3	186.1
West Virginia	459,725	544,075	574,357	597,266	747,810	18.3	5.6	4.0	25.2	62.7
Wisconsin	897,719	1,055,843	1,288,620	1,472,322	1,863,897	17.6	22.0	14.3	26.6	107.6
Wyoming	76,868	92,086	113,096	116,323	188,217	19.8	22.8	2.9	61.8	144.9

NOTES: Except for Massachusetts, Montana, Nevada, New Hampshire, South Carolina, Utah, West Virginia, and Wyoming, the 1970 count has been revised since publication of the 1970 census reports.

The 1950 figure for Alaska represents occupied housing units.

SOURCE: U.S. Bureau of the Census, *General Housing Characteristics: U. S. Summary*, pp. 1–13.

DEFINITIONS AND EXPLANATIONS OF SUBJECT CHARACTERISTICS

General

The 1980 census was conducted primarily through self-enumeration. The principal vehicle for obtaining a response was, therefore, the questionnaire and its accompanying instruction guide. See Appendix 4 for a facsimile of the census questionnaire. Furthermore, census takers were instructed, in their telephone and personal-visit interviews, to read the questions directly from the questionnaire.[1]

Population Characteristics Pertaining to the Housing Census

Household

A household includes all the persons who occupy a housing unit. The measure "persons per household" is obtained by dividing the

---

[1]Based on U.S. Bureau of the Census, 1980 Census of Housing, vol. 1, *General Characteristics of Housing Units* (Washington, DC: U.S. Government Printing Office, 1982), pp. B1–B7. The first U.S. Census of Housing was conducted in 1940. For historical data on U.S. housing, see U.S. Bureau of the Census, *Historical Statistics of the United States: Colonial Times to 1970*, Bicentennial edition, 2 vols. (Washington, DC: U.S. Government Printing Office, 1975). See especially: chap. N, "Construction and Housing."

number of persons in households by the number of households (or householders).

Relationship to Householder

The data on relationship to householder were derived from answers to question 2, which was asked of all persons in housing units.

Householder: One person in each household is designated as the "householder." In most cases this is the person or one of the persons in whose name the home is owned or rented, and who is listed in column 1 of the census questionnaire. If there is no such person in the household, any adult household member could be designated as the "householder." Two types of householders are distinguished: a family householder and a nonfamily householder. A family householder is a householder living with one or more persons related to him or her by birth, marriage, or adoption. The householder and all persons in the household related to him or her are family members. A nonfamily householder is a householder living alone or with nonrelatives only.

Spouse: A person married to and living with a householder. This category includes persons in formal marriages as well as persons in common-law marriages.

Child: A son, daughter, stepchild, or adopted child of the householder regardless of the child's age or marital status. The category excludes sons-in-law and daughters-in-law. "Own" children are sons and daughters, including stepchildren and adopted children, of the householder who are single (never married) and under age 18. "Related" children in a family include own children and all other persons (except the spouse of the householder) under age 18 in the household, regardless of marital status, who are related to the householder by birth, marriage, or adoption.

Other relative: Any person related to the householder by birth, marriage, or adoption who is not shown separately in the particular table (for example, "spouse," "child," "brother or sister," or "parent").

Nonrelative: Any person in the household not related to the householder by birth, marriage, or adoption. Roomers, boarders, partners, roommates, paid employees, wards, and foster children are included in this category.

Unrelated Individual

An unrelated individual is (1) a householder living alone or with nonrelatives only, (2) a household member who is not related to the householder, or (3) a person living in group quarters who is not an inmate of an institution.

Family

A family consists of a householder and one or more other persons living in the same household who are related to the householder by birth, marriage, or adoption. All persons in a household who are related to the householder are regarded as members of his or her family.

Group Quarters

All persons not living in households are classified by the Bureau of the Census as living in group quarters. Two general categories of persons in group quarters are recognized:

Inmates of institutions: Persons under care or custody in institutions at the time of enumeration are classified as "patients or inmates" of an institution regardless of their length of stay in that place and regardless of the number of people in that place. Institutions include homes, schools, hospitals, or wards for the physically and mentally handicapped; hospitals or wards for mental, tubercular, or chronic disease patients; homes for unmarried mothers; nursing, convalescent, and rest homes for the aged and dependent; orphanages; and correctional institutions.

Other: This category includes all persons living in group quarters who are not inmates of institutions. Rooming and boardinghouses, communes, farm and nonfarm workers' dormitories, convents or monasteries, and other living quarters are classified as "other" group quarters if there are 9 or more persons unrelated to the person listed in column 1 of the questionnaire; or if 10 or more unrelated persons share the unit. Persons residing in certain other types of living arrangements are classified as living in "other" group quarters regardless of the number or relationship of people in the unit.

School Enrollment

The data on school enrollment were derived from answers to questions 8, 9, and 10. Persons are classified as enrolled in school if they reported attending a regular school or college at any time between February 1, 1980, and the time of enumeration. Regular schooling is defined as nursery school, kindergarten, elementary school, and schooling which leads to a high school diploma or college degree.

Elementary school, as defined here, includes grades 1 through 8, and high school includes grades 9 through 12. In general, a public school is defined as any school which is controlled and supported primarily by a local, state, or federal government agency.

Language Spoken at Home and Ability to Speak English

The data on language spoken at home and ability to speak English were derived from answers to questions 13a, b, and c. Persons who responded in question 13a that they spoke a language other than English at home were asked to report which language they spoke (question 13b) and how well they could speak English (question 13c). Languages were coded using a detailed classification of languages. Ability to speak English was reported as one of four categories: "Very well," "Well," "Not well," or "Not at all."

The questions were intended to measure the extent to which non-English languages were currently being spoken in the United States and the number of persons who felt that their English ability was limited. The questions were not intended to determine which language was a person's main language, or whether a person was fluent in the non-English language that he or she reported. Therefore, persons who reported speaking a language other than English may have also spoken English at home and they may have been more fluent in English than in the non-English language.

Residence in 1975

The data on residence in 1975 were derived from answers to questions 15a and 15b. Residence on April 1, 1975, is the usual place of residence 5 years before enumeration. The number of persons who were living in a different house in 1975 is somewhat less than the total number of moves during the 5 years. Some persons in the same house at the two dates had moved during the 5-year period but by the time of enumeration had returned to their 1975 residence. Other persons who were living in a different house had made one or more intermediate moves. For similar reasons, the number of persons living in a different county or a different SMSA understates the number of these kinds of moves.

Data on residence in 1975 are based on approximately one half of the full census sample. Therefore, figures in tabulations involving residence in 1975 may differ from tabulations based on the full sample. For example, the number of persons aged 5 and over from residence in 1975 tabulations may not agree with other tabulations by age.

Central Business District (CBD) or Downtown

A central business district (CBD) is an area of very high land valuation characterized by a high concentration of retail businesses, service businesses, offices, theaters, and hotels, and by high traffic flow. CBDs consist of one or more whole census tracts, and have been defined only in SMSA central cities and other SMSA cities with populations of 50,000 or more. CBDs are designated by local Census Statistical Area Committees in consultation with the Census Bureau. Some eligible cities do not have a CBD because they chose not to participate in the CBD delineation program. In order to be counted as working in the CBD, a respondent had to provide enough information

to allow the workplace to be coded to the census tract level. Since some respondents did not do this, the number of persons shown to be working in the CBD is usually understated by an unknown amount.

Income in 1979

The data on income in 1979 were derived from answers to questions 32 and 33. Information on money income received in the calendar year 1979 was requested from persons aged 15 and over. "Total income" is the algebraic sum of the amounts reported separately for wage and salary income; nonfarm net self-employment income; farm net self-employment income; interest, dividend, royalty, or net rental income; Social Security or Railroad Retirement income; public assistance or welfare income; and all other income. The figures represent the amount of income received regularly before deductions for personal income taxes, Social Security, bond purchases, union dues, Medicare deductions, and so on.

There may be differences between the census data on income in 1979 used in this book and similar data shown in the *Summary Characteristics for Governmental Units and Standard Metropolitan Statistical Areas*, PHC80-3, and in the Supplementary Reports, *Advance Estimates of Social, Economic, and Housing Characteristics*, PHC80-S2. Any such differences are a result of errors corrected after the release of the earlier PHC80-3 and the PHC80-S2 reports.

Poverty Status in 1979

Families and unrelated individuals are classified as being below or above the poverty level based on income in 1979 using a poverty index that provides a range of income cutoffs or "poverty thresholds" varying by size of family, number of children, and age of the family householder or unrelated individual. The poverty thresholds used in the 1980 census differ slightly from those used in the 1970 census, which took into account the same three factors as well as sex of the family householder or unrelated individual and farm-nonfarm residence. In addition, for the 1980 census the thresholds by size of family were extended from 7 persons or more to 9 persons or more. The income cutoffs are updated each year to reflect the change in the Consumer Price Index. The poverty threshold for a family of four was $7,412 in 1979; thresholds by size of family are shown below.

Size of Family	Threshold
1 person	$3,686
Under age 65	3,774
Age 65 and over	3,479
2 persons	4,723
Householder under age 65	4,876
Householder age 65 and over	4,389
3 persons	5,787
4 persons	7,412
5 persons	8,776
6 persons	9,915
7 persons	11,237
8 persons	12,484
9 persons or more	14,812

There may be slight differences between the census data on poverty status in 1979 used in this book and similar data shown in the *Summary Characteristics for Governmental Units and Standard Metropolitan Statistical Areas*, and in the Supplementary Reports, *Advance Estimates of Social, Economic, and Housing Characteristics*, a result of errors in the income data which were corrected after the release of the PHC80-3 and the PHC80-S2 reports.

Poverty status is determined for all persons except inmates of institutions, persons in military group quarters and in college dormitories, and unrelated individuals under age 15. For a detailed explanation of the poverty definition, see "Characteristics of the Population Below the Poverty Level: 1980," *Current Population Reports*, series P-60, no. 133.

Housing Characteristics

Comparability with Other Census Bureau Housing Data

In addition to the decennial censuses of housing, the Bureau of the Census conducts several periodic and current surveys. Two periodic national surveys are conducted in conjunction with the decennial census of housing: The Components of Inventory Change Survey, which provides data on the sources of the current inventory and the disposition of a previous inventory between two points in time and furnishes housing characteristics data on the various components such as new construction, other additions, demolitions, other losses, conversions, and mergers; and the Residential Finance Survey, which

obtains data on the financing of nonfarm homeowner and rental properties, as well as on the characteristics of mortgages, properties, and owners. Current surveys include the American Housing Survey (formerly the Annual Housing Survey), which provides information on the size and composition of the housing inventory and related topics for the nation and selected standard metropolitan statistical areas; and two quarterly surveys—the Housing Vacancy Survey and the Survey of Market Absorption of Apartments—which obtain, respectively, data on selected characteristics of vacant and occupied units and on the percentage and characteristics of new apartments which are absorbed nationally and regionally 3, 6, 9, and 12 months after completion. The construction statistics program of the Bureau of the Census also conducts various current surveys to obtain housing-related data such as housing starts and completions, characteristics of new one-family homes, and residential alterations and repairs.

Similar concepts and definitions were used for the 1980 decennial census and the surveys described above. Thus, data from the 1980 Census of Housing are generally comparable to current surveys and previous censuses.

Living Quarters

Living quarters are classified in the census as either housing units or group quarters. Usually, living quarters are in structures intended for residential use (for example, a one-family home, apartment house, hotel or motel, boarding house, mobile home, or trailer). However, living quarters may also be in structures intended for nonresidential use (for example, the room in a warehouse where a night guard lives), as well as in boats, tents, vans, and so on.

Housing units: A housing unit is a house, an apartment, a group of rooms, or a single room, occupied as separate living quarters or, if vacant, intended for occupancy as separate living quarters. Both occupied and vacant housing units are included in the housing unit inventory except that boats, tents, vans, caves, and the like are included only if they are occupied as someone's usual place of residence. Vacant mobile homes are included, provided they are intended for occupancy on the site where they stand.

Group quarters: Group quarters are any living quarters that are not classified as housing units. There are two types of group quarters: institutional and noninstitutional.

Rules for hotels, rooming houses, and similar places: Occupied rooms or suites of rooms in hotels, motels, and similar places are classified as housing units only when occupied by permanent residents, that is, persons who consider the hotel as their usual place of residence or who have no usual place of residence elsewhere.

Year-round housing units: Data on housing characteristics in the 1980 census reports are limited to year-round housing units; that is, all occupied units plus vacant units available or intended for year-round use. Vacant units intended for seasonal occupancy and vacant units held for migratory labor are excluded because of the difficulty of obtaining reliable data on their characteristics.

Occupancy and Vacancy Characteristics

Occupied housing units: A housing unit is classified as occupied if it is the usual place of residence of the person or group of persons living in it at the time of enumeration, or if the occupants are only temporarily absent; for example, away on vacation.

Persons in occupied housing units: "Persons in occupied housing units" is the total population less those persons living in group quarters. "Persons per occupied housing unit" is computed by dividing the population living in housing units by the number of occupied housing units.

Vacant housing units: A housing unit is vacant if no one is living in it at the time of enumeration, unless its occupants are only temporarily absent.

Type of vacant unit: Vacant housing units are classified as either "seasonal or migratory" or "year-round." "Seasonal" units are intended for occupancy during only certain seasons of the year.

Vacancy status: Year-round vacant units are subdivided according to their vacancy status as follows: "For sale only"; "For rent"; "Rented or sold, awaiting occupancy"; "Held for occasional use"; and "Other vacant." If a vacant year-round unit does not fall into any of the classifications, it is classified as "Other vacant." For example, this category includes units held for settlement of an estate, for occupancy by a caretaker or janitor, and for personal reasons of the owner.

Tenure: A housing unit is "owner occupied" if the owner or co-owner lives in the unit, even if it is mortgaged or not fully paid for. All other occupied units are classified as "renter occupied," including units rented for cash rent and those occupied without payment of cash rent.

Condominium housing units: A condominium involves ownership that enables a person to own an apartment or house in a development of similar units and to hold a common or joint ownership in common areas, hallways, entrances, elevators, and so forth. The owner has a deed to the individual unit and, very likely, a mortgage on the unit. A condominium housing unit need not be occupied by the owner to be counted as such.

Comparability with 1970 census condominium housing unit data: In 1970 owner-occupied cooperatives and condominium housing units were identified together. The 1980 census identifies only condominium housing units.

Race of householder: The data on race of householder were derived from answers to question 4, for the person listed on column 1 of the census questionnaire.

The concept of race as used by the Census Bureau reflects self-identification by respondents; it does not denote any clear-cut scientific definition of biological stock. Since the 1980 census obtained information on race through self-identification, the data represent self-classification by people according to the race with which they identify. In this book, data are presented for housing units classified by the race of the householder.

For persons who could not provide a single response to the race question, the race of the person's mother was used. If a single response could not be provided for the person's mother, the first race reported by the person was used. This is a modification of the 1970 census procedure in which the race of the person's father was used.

The category "White" includes persons who indicated their race as white, as well as persons who did not classify themselves in one of the specific race categories listed on the questionnaire but entered a response such as Canadian, German, Italian, Lebanese, or Polish. In the 1980 census, persons who did not classify themselves in one of the specific race categories but marked "Other" and/or wrote in entries such as Cuban, Puerto Rican, Mexican, or Dominican were included in the "Other" race category.

The category "Black" includes persons who indicated their race as black or Negro as well as persons who did not classify themselves in one of the specific race categories listed on the questionnaire, but reported entries such as Jamaican, Black Puerto Rican, West Indian, Haitian, or Nigerian.

The categories "American Indian," "Eskimo," and "Aleut" include persons who classified themselves as such in one of the specific race categories. In addition, persons who did not report themselves in one of the specific race categories but entered the name of an Indian tribe were classified as American Indian.

In this book, the category "Asian and Pacific Islander" includes persons who indicated their race as Japanese, Chinese, Filipino, Korean, Vietnamese, Asian Indian, Hawaiian, Guamanian, or Samoan.

The category "Other" includes Asian and Pacific Islander groups not listed separately (for example, Cambodian, Laotian, Pakistani, Fiji Islander) and other races not included in the specific categories listed on the questionnaire.

Comparability with 1970 census data on race of householder: Differences between 1980 and 1970 census counts by race seriously affect the comparability for certain race groups. First, a large number of Spanish-origin persons reported their race differently in the 1980 census from what they reported in the 1970 census; this difference in reporting has a substantial impact on the counts and comparability for the "White" and "Other" populations. A much larger proportion of the Spanish-origin population in 1980 than in 1970 reported their race as "Other." Second, in 1970 most persons who marked the "Other" race category and wrote in a Spanish designation such as Mexican, Venezuelan, Latino, and so forth, were reclassified as "White." In 1980 such persons were not reclassified but remained in the "Other" race category. As a result of this procedural change and the differences in reporting by this population, the proportion of the Spanish-origin population classified as "Other" race in the 1980 census was substantially higher than that in the 1970 census. Nationally, in 1970 only 1 percent of the Spanish-origin persons were classified as "Other" race and 93 percent as "White." In 1980, 40 percent of Spanish-origin persons reported their race as "Other" and only 56 percent reported "White." As a consequence of these differences, 1980 population and housing unit totals for "White" and "Other" are not comparable with corresponding 1970 figures.

The 1980 count for the Asian and Pacific Islander population reflects a high level of immigration during the 1970s as well as a number of changes in census procedures which were developed, in part, as a result of this high level of immigration. The number of Asian and Pacific Islander categories listed separately on the 1980 census questionnaire was expanded over that in 1970 to include four additional groups: Vietnamese, Asian Indian, Guamanian, and Samoan. Asian Indians were classified as "White" in 1970 but were included in the

"Asian and Pacific Islander" category in 1980. The Vietnamese, Guamanian, and Samoan populations were included in the "Other" race category in the 1970 census but were included in the "Asian and Pacific Islander" category in 1980.

In addition, in 1980 data were collected separately for Hawaiians and Koreans in all states, but in 1970 data for the two groups were not collected for Alaska.

Comparability between 100 percent and sample data by race of householder: The data for race of householder shown in this book may differ from comparable figures shown in certain other 1980 census reports. Some of the data in this book are based on 100 percent tabulations and some are based on a sample. Differences between 100 percent and sample data are the result of sampling variability, nonsampling error, and an additional edit and review performed on the sample questionnaires. During the sample processing the responses in the race question underwent more extensive review and edit than performed during the previous processing stages. Additional efforts were made to assign write-in entries to specific race categories and to resolve inconsistent and incomplete responses. The impact of this further work varied substantially by racial group and by geographic area, but it is generally negligible. Information now available indicates that, since the effects of the additional review and edit were generally limited and rather varied, the 100 percent tabulations for the United States and for each state are usually the preferable source for data on racial groups. In the case of distributions for subjects covered on a sample basis only (for example, units in structure, mortgage status and selected monthly owner costs, gross rent, and so forth), and data for the total Asian and Pacific Islander population, the sample figures from which the cross-tabulations in Chapter 5 were derived are the only data available and should be used within the context of the sampling variability associated with them.

Spanish/Hispanic origin of the householder: The data on Spanish/Hispanic origin or descent of householder were derived from answers to question 7, for the person in column 1 of the census questionnaire.

Persons of Spanish origin or descent are those who classified themselves in one of the specific Spanish-origin categories listed on the questionnaire—as Mexican, Puerto Rican, or Cuban—as well as those who indicated that they were of other Spanish/Hispanic origin. Persons reporting "other Spanish/Hispanic" origin are those whose origins are from Spain or the Spanish-speaking countries of Central or South America, or they are Spanish-origin persons identifying themselves generally as Spanish, Spanish-American, Hispano, Latino, and so forth. Origin or descent can be viewed as the ancestry, nationality group, lineage, or country in which the person or person's parents or ancestors were born before their arrival in the United States. Persons of Spanish origin may be of any race. In this book data are presented for housing units classified by the Spanish origin of the householder.

Limitations of the data on householders of Spanish/Hispanic origin: A preliminary evaluation study of the reporting in the 1980 census item on Spanish origin indicated that there was misreporting in the Mexican origin category by white and black persons in certain areas. The study results showed evidence that the misreporting occurred in the South (excluding Texas), the Northeast (excluding the New York City area), and a few states in the Midwest region. Also, results based on available data suggest that the impact of potential misreporting of Mexican origin in the 1980 census is severe in those portions of the above-mentioned regions where the Spanish-origin population is generally sparse. However, 1980 census data on the Mexican-origin population or total Spanish-origin population, at the *national* level, are not seriously affected by the reporting problem. For a more detailed discussion of the evaluation of the Spanish-origin item, see the 1980 census Supplementary Reports, *Persons of Spanish Origin by State: 1980*, PC80-S1-7.

Comparability between 100 percent and sample data on householders of Spanish/Hispanic origin: The data on householders of Spanish/Hispanic origin shown in this book may differ from comparable figures shown in other 1980 census reports. Differences between findings based on the 100 percent counts and on sample data are the result of sampling variability, nonsampling error, and more extensive edit procedures for the Spanish-origin item on the sample questionnaires. Since the effects of the extensive edit performed during the sample processing were generally limited, the 100 percent tabulations are usually the preferable source for data on householders of Spanish origin. In the case of distributions for subjects covered on a sample basis only, the sample figures are the only data available and should be used within the context of the sampling variability associated with them. A description of the sample data for Spanish-origin groups, sample processing, sampling variability, and so forth, appears in Characteristics of the Population, *General Social and Economic Characteristics*, PC80-1-C.

Comparability with 1970 census data on householders of Spanish origin: The 1980 figures on householders of Spanish origin are not directly comparable with 1970 Spanish-origin totals because of a num-

ber of factors, namely, overall improvements in the 1980 census, better coverage of the population, improved question design, and an effective public relations campaign by the Census Bureau with the assistance of national and community ethnic groups. These efforts undoubtedly resulted in the inclusion of a sizable but unknown number of persons of Hispanic origin who are in the country in other than legal status.

Housing Utilization Characteristics

Persons: All persons occupying the housing unit are included. These persons include not only occupants related to the householder but also any lodgers, roomers, boarders, partners, roommates, wards, foster children, and resident employees who share the living quarters of the householder.

Rooms: The intent of the question on rooms is to count the number of whole rooms used for living purposes, which includes living rooms, dining rooms, kitchens, bedrooms, finished recreation rooms, enclosed porches suitable for year-round use, and lodgers' rooms. Excluded are strip or pullman kitchens, bathrooms, open porches, balconies, halls, half-rooms, utility rooms, unfinished attics or basements, or other unfinished space used for storage. A partially divided room is a separate room only if there is a partition from floor to ceiling.

Persons per room: "Persons per room" is a derived measure obtained by dividing the number of persons in each occupied housing unit by the number of rooms in the unit.

Bedrooms: The number of bedrooms in the unit is the count of rooms used mainly for sleeping, even if also used for other purposes. Rooms reserved for sleeping, such as guest rooms, even though used infrequently, are counted as bedrooms. On the other hand, rooms used mainly for other purposes, even though used also for sleeping, such as living rooms with a sofa bed, are not considered bedrooms. A housing unit consisting of only one room, such as a one-room efficiency apartment, is classified, by definition, as having no bedroom.

Kitchen facilities: A unit has complete kitchen facilities when it has all of the following: (1) an installed sink with piped water, (2) a range or cookstove, and (3) a mechanical refrigerator. All kitchen facilities must be located in the structure, but they need not be in the same room. Quarters with only portable cooking equipment are not considered as having a range or cookstove. An icebox is not considered to be a mechanical refrigerator.

Structural Characteristics

Year structure built: "Year structure built" refers to when the building was first constructed, not when it was remodeled, added to, or converted. For a houseboat or mobile home or trailer, the manufacturer's model year is assumed to be the year built. The figures shown in this report relate to the number of units in structures built during the specified periods and in existence at the time of enumeration.

Units in structure: A structure is a separate building that either has open space on all sides or is separated from other structures by dividing walls that extend from ground to roof. In the determination of the number of units in a structure, all housing units, both occupied and vacant, were counted. The statistics are presented for the number of housing units in structures of specified type and size, not for the number of residential buildings. Included in the count of mobile homes or trailers are units classified as boats, tents, vans, and so forth.

Plumbing facilities: The category "Complete plumbing for exclusive use" consists of units which have hot and cold piped water, a flush toilet, and a bathtub or shower inside the housing unit for the exclusive use of the occupants of the unit. "Lacking complete plumbing for exclusive use" includes those conditions when (1) all three specified plumbing facilities are present inside the unit, but are also used by another household; (2) some but not all the facilities are present; or (3) none of the three specified plumbing facilities is present.

Comparability with 1970 census plumbing facilities data: In 1970 there were separate questions on the presence of hot and cold piped water, a bathtub or shower, and a flush toilet. In 1980 these three items were combined into a single question on plumbing facilities. In addition, the facilities must be inside the housing unit rather than inside the structure as in 1970.

Units at address: The data are presented for 1 unit, 2-to-9 units, and 10 units or more at an address. Data are also presented for mobile homes or trailers. On the long-form sample questionnaire, answers to question H13, "units in structure," provided the data on the number of housing units in structures of specified size. Care should be taken in using "units at address" as a proxy for "units in structure" because some multiunit buildings have more than one street address.

Equipment and Fuels

Air conditioning: Air conditioning is defined as the cooling of air by a refrigeration unit. It does not include evaporative coolers, fans, or blowers which are not connected to a refrigeration unit; however, it does include heat pumps. A central system is an installation that airconditions a number of rooms. A system with individual room controls is a central system.

Vehicles available: Data for this item refer to the number of households with vehicles available at home for the use of the members of the household. Included in this item are passenger cars, pickup trucks, small panel trucks of one-ton capacity or less, as well as station wagons, company cars, and taxicabs kept at home for the use of household members.

Telephone in housing unit: A unit is classified as having a telephone if there is a telephone in the living quarters. Units where the respondent uses a telephone located inside the building but not in the respondent's living quarters are classified as having no telephone.

Financial Characteristics

Value: Value is the respondent's estimate of how much the property (house and lot) or condominium unit would sell for, if it were for sale. For vacant units, value is the price asked for the property.

Value and price asked are tabulated separately for certain kinds of housing units. Value statistics are presented for "specified owner-occupied" housing units and "specified vacant for sale only" housing units. These "specified" housing units include only one-family houses on less than 10 acres without a commercial establishment or medical office on the property. Mobile homes, trailers, boats, tents, or vans occupied as a usual residence, and owner-occupied noncondominium units in multifamily buildings are also excluded from the value tabulations.

Mortgage status and selected monthly owner costs: The data are presented for "specified owner-occupied" housing units. The data exclude owner-occupied condominium housing units, mobile homes, trailers, boats, tents, or vans occupied as a usual residence, as well as owner-occupied noncondominium units in multifamily buildings. Selected monthly owner costs are the sum of payments for mortgages, deeds of trust, or similar debts on the property; real estate taxes; fire and hazard insurance on the property; utilities (electricity, gas, and water); and fuels (oil, coal, kerosene, wood, and so forth).

Household income in 1979 by selected monthly owner costs as percentage of income: The selected monthly housing costs is expressed as a percentage of monthly household income (total household income in 1979 divided by 12). The percentage is presented for the same owner-occupied units for which selected monthly owner costs was tabulated; thus, the statistics reflect the exclusion of certain owner-occupied units. The percentage was computed separately for each unit and was rounded to the nearest whole number. Units occupied by households that reported no income or a net loss constitute the category "Not computed."

Contract rent: Contract rent is the monthly rent agreed to, or contracted for, regardless of any furnishings, utilities, or services that may be included. The statistics on rent are tabulated for "specified renter-occupied" housing units which include renter-occupied housing units except one-family houses on 10 or more acres. Respondents were asked to report rent only for the housing unit enumerated and to exclude any rent paid for additional units or for business premises.

This report presents data only on median contract rent, without any tabulation by rent categories. Medians for contract rent are rounded to the nearest dollar. In computing median contract rent, units reported as "No cash rent" are excluded.

Gross rent: The statistics on rent are tabulated for "specified renter-occupied" housing units. The computed rent termed "gross rent" is the contract rent plus the estimated average monthly cost of utilities (electricity, gas, and water) and fuels (oil, coal, kerosene, wood, and so forth) if these are paid for by the renter (or paid for the renter by someone else) in addition to rent. Gross rent is intended to eliminate differentials that result from varying practices with respect to the inclusion of utilities and fuels as part of the rental payment. The estimated costs of water and fuels are reported on a yearly basis but are converted to monthly figures in the computation process. Renter units occupied without payment of cash rent are shown separately as "No cash rent" in the tabulations. This report presents data on medians for gross rent rounded to the nearest dollar. In computing median gross rent, units reported as "No cash rent" are excluded.

Household income in 1979 by gross rent as percentage of income: The gross rent is expressed as a percentage of monthly household income (total household income in 1979 divided by 12). The percentage is presented for the same renter-occupied units for which gross rent was tabulated; thus, the statistics reflect the exclusion of certain renter-occupied units. The percentage was computed separately for each unit and was rounded to the nearest whole number. Units for which no cash rent is paid and units occupied by households that reported no income or a net loss constitute the category "Not computed."

Overview

Public use microdata samples are computer tapes that contain records for a sample of housing units, with information on the characteristics of each unit and the people in it. In order to protect the confidentiality of respondents, the Census Bureau excludes identifying information from the records. Within the limits of the sample size and geographic detail provided, these tapes permit users with special needs to prepare virtually any tabulations of the data they may desire.

Three separate public use microdata samples are available, each representing 5 percent or 1 percent of the population and housing of the United States:

1. A sample, 5 percent, identifying all states and various subdi-

visions within them, including most counties with 100,000 or more inhabitants

2. B Sample, 1 percent, identifying all metropolitan territory and most SMSAs individually, and groups of counties elsewhere

3. C Sample, 1 percent, identifying regions, divisions, and most states by type of area (urban/rural)

Three 1-in-1,000 samples are also prepared, one each extracted from the A, B, and C samples. The data tables in Chapter 5 are based on the 1-in-1,000 A sample.

NOTE: Based on U.S. Bureau of the Census, Census of Population and Housing, 1980: Public Use Microdata Samples, Technical Documentation (Washington, DC: U.S. Government Printing Office, 1983).

This leaflet shows the content of the two questionnaires being used in the 1980 Census of Population and Housing. See the explanatory notes on page 2.

Please fill out this official Census Form and mail it back on Census Day, Tuesday, April 1, 1980

1980 Census of the United States

If the address shown below has the wrong apartment identification, please write the correct apartment number or location here:

D0	A1	A2	A4	A5	A6

A message from the Director, Bureau of the Census . . .

We must, from time to time, take stock of ourselves as a people if our Nation is to meet successfully the many national and local challenges we face. This is the purpose of the 1980 census.

The essential need for a population census was recognized almost 200 years ago when our Constitution was written. As provided in Article I, the first census was conducted in 1790 and one has been taken every 10 years since then.

The law under which the census is taken protects the confidentiality of your answers. For the next 72 years — or until April 1, 2052 — only sworn census workers have access to the individual records, and no one else may see them.

Your answers, when combined with the answers from other people, will provide the statistical figures needed by public and private groups, schools, business and industry, and Federal, State, and local governments across the country. These figures will help all sectors of American society understand how our population and housing are changing. In this way, we can deal more effectively with today's problems and work toward a better future for all of us.

The census is a vitally important national activity. Please do your part by filling out this census form accurately and completely. If you mail it back promptly in the enclosed postage-paid envelope, it will save the expense and inconvenience of a census taker having to visit you.

Thank you for your cooperation.

Your answers are confidential

By law (title 13, U.S. Code), census employees are subject to fine and/or imprisonment for any disclosure of your answers. Only after 72 years does your information become available to other government agencies or the public. The same law requires that you answer the questions to the best of your knowledge.

Para personas de habla hispana

(For Spanish-speaking persons):
SI USTED DESEA UN CUESTIONARIO DEL CENSO EN ESPAÑOL llame a la oficina del censo. El número de teléfono se encuentra en el encasillado de la dirección.

O si prefiere, marque esta casilla ☐ y devuelva el cuestionario por correo en el sobre que se le incluye.

U.S. Department of Commerce
Bureau of the Census
Form D-61

Please continue ➚

How to fill out your Census Form

Page 1

See the filled-out example in the yellow instruction guide. This guide will help with any problems you may have.

If you need more help, call the Census Office. The telephone number of the local office is shown at the bottom of the address box on the front cover.

Use a black pencil to answer the questions. Black pencil is better to use than ballpoint or other pens.

Fill circles "O" completely, like this: ●

When you write in an answer, print or write clearly.

Make sure that answers are provided for everyone here.

See page 4 of the guide if a roomer or someone else in the household does not want to give you all the information for the form.

Answer the questions on pages 1 through 5, and then starting with pages 6 and 7, fill a pair of pages for each person in the household.

Check your answers. Then write your name, the date, and telephone number on the back page.

Mail back this form on Tuesday, April 1, or as soon afterward as you can. Use the enclosed envelope; no stamp is needed.

Please start by answering Question 1 below.

Question 1

List in Question 1

• Family members living here, including babies still in the hospital

• Relatives living here

• Lodgers or boarders living here

• Other persons living here

• College students who stay here while attending college, even if their parents live elsewhere

• Persons who usually live here but are temporarily away (including children in boarding school below the college level)

• Persons with a home elsewhere but who stay here most of the week while working

Do Not List in Question 1

• Any person away from here in the Armed Forces.

• Any college student who stays somewhere else while attending college.

• Any person who usually stays somewhere else most of the week while working there.

• Any person away from here in an institution such as a home for the aged or mental hospital.

• Any person staying or visiting here who has a usual home elsewhere.

1. **What is the name of each person who was living here on Tuesday, April 1, 1980, or who was staying or visiting here and had no other home?**

_____
_____
_____
_____
_____
_____
_____
_____
_____
_____
_____

Note
If everyone here is staying only temporarily and has a usual home elsewhere, please mark this box ☐.

Then please:
• answer the questions on pages 2 through 5 only, and
• enter the address of your usual home on the back page.

Please continue ➚

Page 2

Here are the QUESTIONS ↓	These are the columns for ANSWERS ⟶ Please fill one column for each person listed in Question 1.	PERSON in column 1	PERSON in column 2	PERSON in column 3	PERSON in column 4	PERSON in column 5	PERSON in column 6
		Last name / First name / Middle initial	Last name / First name / Middle initial	Last name / First name / Middle initial	Last name / First name / Middle initial	Last name / First name / Middle initial	Last name / First name / Middle initial

QUESTIONS ASKED OF ALL HOUSEHOLDS

2. How is this person related to the person in column 1?

Fill one circle.

If "Other relative" of person in column 1, give exact relationship, such as mother-in-law, niece, grandson, etc.

- Column 1: START in this column with the household member (or one of the members) in whose name the home is owned or rented. If there is no such person, start in this column with any adult household member.
- Columns 2–6: If relative of person in column 1:
  - ○ Husband/wife   ○ Father/mother
  - ○ Son/daughter   ○ Other relative
  - ○ Brother/sister

  If not related to person in column 1:
  - ○ Roomer, boarder   ○ Other nonrelative
  - ○ Partner, roommate
  - ○ Paid employee

3. Sex Fill one circle.
- Each column: ○ Male   ○ Female

4. Is this person —

Fill one circle.
- ○ White   ○ Asian Indian
- ○ Black or Negro   ○ Hawaiian
- ○ Japanese   ○ Guamanian
- ○ Chinese   ○ Samoan
- ○ Filipino   ○ Eskimo
- ○ Korean   ○ Aleut
- ○ Vietnamese   ○ Other — Specify
- ○ Indian (Amer.)   Print tribe →

5. Age, and month and year of birth

a. Print age at last birthday.
b. Print month and fill one circle.
c. Print year in the spaces, and fill one circle below each number.

- a. Age at last birthday
- b. Month of birth: ○ Jan.—Mar. ○ Apr.—June ○ July—Sept. ○ Oct.—Dec.
- c. Year of birth

6. Marital status

Fill one circle.
- ○ Now married   ○ Separated
- ○ Widowed   ○ Never married
- ○ Divorced

7. Is this person of Spanish/Hispanic origin or descent?

Fill one circle.
- ○ No (not Spanish/Hispanic)
- ○ Yes, Mexican, Mexican-Amer., Chicano
- ○ Yes, Puerto Rican
- ○ Yes, Cuban
- ○ Yes, other Spanish/Hispanic

QUESTIONS ASKED OF SAMPLE HOUSEHOLDS

8. Since February 1, 1980, has this person attended regular school or college at any time? Fill one circle. Count nursery school, kindergarten, elementary school, and schooling which leads to a high school diploma or college degree.
- ○ No, has not attended since February 1
- ○ Yes, public school, public college
- ○ Yes, private, church-related
- ○ Yes, private, not church-related

9. What is the highest grade (or year) of regular school this person has ever attended?

Fill one circle.

If now attending school, mark grade person is in. If high school was finished by equivalency test (GED), mark "12."

- Highest grade attended:
  - ○ Nursery school   ○ Kindergarten
  - Elementary through high school (grade or year)
    1 2 3 4 5 6 7 8 9 10 11 12
    ○ ○ ○ ○ ○ ○ ○ ○ ○ ○ ○ ○
  - College (academic year)
    1 2 3 4 5 6 7 8 or more
    ○ ○ ○ ○ ○ ○ ○ ○
  - ○ Never attended school – Skip question 10

10. Did this person finish the highest grade (or year) attended?

Fill one circle.
- ○ Now attending this grade (or year)
- ○ Finished this grade (or year)
- ○ Did not finish this grade (or year)

CENSUS USE ONLY   A. ○ 1 ○ N ○ ○

EXPLANATORY NOTES

This leaflet shows the content of the 1980 census questionnaires. The content was determined after review of the 1970 census experience, extensive consultation with many government and private users of census data, and a series of experimental censuses and surveys in which various alternatives were tested.

Two questionnaires are being used in the census:

One questionnaire, called the "short form," contains only those questions which are asked of all housing units/households. These questions are shown on pages 1, 2, and 3 of this leaflet.

The other questionnaire contains all of the "short form" questions plus additional questions as specified on this leaflet, which are asked of only a sample of housing units/households. Please note that population questions 11 to 33 (on pages 6 and 7) are repeated for each person in the household on separate pairs of facing pages not reproduced here.

Questionnaires are assigned to housing units/households on a random basis. An instruction guide accompanies each questionnaire to help the householder complete it.

For additional information about the 1980 Census, please write to the Director, Bureau of the Census, Washington, D.C. 20233.

QUESTIONS ASKED OF ALL HOUSEHOLDS

Page 3

PERSON in column 7

Last name

First name — Middle initial

If relative of person in column 1:

O Husband/wife
O Son/daughter
O Brother/sister
O Father/mother
O Other relative

If not related to person in column 1:

O Roomer, boarder
O Partner, roommate
O Paid employee
O Other nonrelative

O Male — O Female

O White
O Black or Negro
O Japanese
O Chinese
O Filipino
O Korean
O Vietnamese
O Indian (Amer.) *Print tribe* →
O Asian Indian
O Hawaiian
O Guamanian
O Samoan
O Eskimo
O Aleut
O Other — *Specify*

a. Age at last birthday

b. Month of birth

O Jan.—Mar.
O Apr.—June
O July—Sept.
O Oct.—Dec.

c. Year of birth 1

1 ● | 8 O 9 O | 0 O 1 O 2 O 3 O 4 O 5 O 6 O 7 O 8 O 9 O | 0 O 1 O 2 O 3 O 4 O 5 O 6 O 7 O 8 O 9 O

O Now married
O Widowed
O Divorced
O Separated
O Never married

O No (not Spanish/Hispanic)
O Yes, Mexican, Mexican-Amer., Chicano
O Yes, Puerto Rican
O Yes, Cuban
O Yes, other Spanish/Hispanic

O No, has not attended since February 1
O Yes, public school, public college
O Yes, private, church-related
O Yes, private, not church-related

Highest grade attended:

O Nursery school — O Kindergarten

Elementary through high school *(grade or year)*
1 2 3 4 5 6 7 8 9 10 11 12
O O O O O O O O O O O O

College *(academic year)*
1 2 3 4 5 6 7 8 or more
O O O O O O O O

O Never attended school—*Skip question 10*

O Now attending this grade *(or year)*
O Finished this grade *(or year)*
O Did not finish this grade *(or year)*

CENSUS USE ONLY — A. O I | O N | O O

If you listed more than 7 persons in Question 1, please see note on back page.

H1. Did you leave anyone out of Question 1 because you were not sure if the person should be listed — *for example, a new baby still in the hospital, a lodger who also has another home, or a person who stays here once in a while and has no other home?*

O Yes — *On the back page give name(s) and reason left out.*
O No

H2. Did you list anyone in Question 1 who is away from home now — *for example, on a vacation or in a hospital?*

O Yes — *On the back page give name(s) and reason person is away.*
O No

H3. Is anyone visiting here who is not already listed?

O Yes — *On the back page give name of each visitor for whom there is no one at the home address to report the person to a census taker.*
O No

H4. How many living quarters, occupied and vacant, are at this address?

O One
O 2 apartments or living quarters
O 3 apartments or living quarters
O 4 apartments or living quarters
O 5 apartments or living quarters
O 6 apartments or living quarters
O 7 apartments or living quarters
O 8 apartments or living quarters
O 9 apartments or living quarters
O 10 or more apartments or living quarters

O This is a mobile home or trailer

H5. Do you enter your living quarters —

O Directly from the outside or through a common or public hall?
O Through someone else's living quarters?

H6. Do you have complete plumbing facilities in your living quarters, that is, hot and cold piped water, a flush toilet, and a bathtub or shower?

O Yes, for this household only
O Yes, but also used by another household
O No, have some but not all plumbing facilities
O No plumbing facilities in living quarters

H7. How many rooms do you have in your living quarters?
Do not count bathrooms, porches, balconies, foyers, halls, or half-rooms.

O 1 room
O 2 rooms
O 3 rooms
O 4 rooms
O 5 rooms
O 6 rooms
O 7 rooms
O 8 rooms
O 9 or more rooms

H8. Are your living quarters —

O Owned or being bought by you or by someone else in this household?
O Rented for cash rent?
O Occupied without payment of cash rent?

H9. Is this apartment (house) part of a condominium?

O No
O Yes, a condominium

H10. *If this is a one-family house —*

a. Is the house on a property of 10 or more acres?

O Yes — O No

b. Is any part of the property used as a commercial establishment or medical office?

O Yes — O No

H11. *If you live in a one-family house or a condominium unit which you own or are buying —*

What is the value of this property, that is, how much do you think this property (house and lot or condominium unit) would sell for if it were for sale?

Do not answer this question if this is —

- A mobile home or trailer
- A house on 10 or more acres
- A house with a commercial establishment or medical office on the property

O Less than $10,000
O $10,000 to $14,999
O $15,000 to $17,499
O $17,500 to $19,999
O $20,000 to $22,499
O $22,500 to $24,999
O $25,000 to $27,499
O $27,500 to $29,999
O $30,000 to $34,999
O $35,000 to $39,999
O $40,000 to $44,999
O $45,000 to $49,999
O $50,000 to $54,999
O $55,000 to $59,999
O $60,000 to $64,999
O $65,000 to $69,999
O $70,000 to $74,999
O $75,000 to $79,999
O $80,000 to $89,999
O $90,000 to $99,999
O $100,000 to $124,999
O $125,000 to $149,999
O $150,000 to $199,999
O $200,000 or more

H12. *If you pay rent for your living quarters —*

What is the monthly rent?

If rent is not paid by the month, see the instruction guide on how to figure a monthly rent.

O Less than $50
O $50 to $59
O $60 to $69
O $70 to $79
O $80 to $89
O $90 to $99
O $100 to $109
O $110 to $119
O $120 to $129
O $130 to $139
O $140 to $149
O $150 to $159
O $160 to $169
O $170 to $179
O $180 to $189
O $190 to $199
O $200 to $224
O $225 to $249
O $250 to $274
O $275 to $299
O $300 to $349
O $350 to $399
O $400 to $499
O $500 or more

FOR CENSUS USE ONLY

A4. Block number

0 0 0 / 1 1 1 / 2 2 2 / 3 3 3 / 4 4 4 / 5 5 5 / 6 6 6 / 7 7 7 / 8 8 8 / 9 9 9

A6. Serial number

0 0 0 0 / 1 1 1 1 / 2 2 2 2 / 3 3 3 3 / 4 4 4 4 / 5 5 5 5 / 6 6 6 6 / 7 7 7 7 / 8 8 8 8 / 9 9 9 9

B. Type of unit or quarters

Occupied
O First form
O Continuation

Vacant
O Regular
O Usual home elsewhere

Group quarters
O First form
O Continuation

For vacant units

C1. Is this unit for —

O Year round use
O Seasonal/Mig. — *Skip C2, C3, and D.*

C2. Vacancy status

O For rent
O For sale only
O Rented or sold, not occupied
O Held for occasional use
O Other vacant

C3. Is this unit boarded up?

O Yes — O No

D. Months vacant

O Less than 1 month
O 1 up to 2 months
O 2 up to 6 months
O 6 up to 12 months
O 1 year up to 2 years
O 2 or more years

E. Indicators

1. O O Mail return
2. O O Pop./F

O O

F. Total persons

0 0 0 / 1 1 1 / 2 2 2 / 3 3 3 / 4 4 4 / 5 5 5 / 6 6 6 / 7 7 7 / 8 8 8 / 9 9 9

Page 4

QUESTIONS ASKED OF SAMPLE HOUSEHOLDS

H13. Which best describes this building?
Include all apartments, flats, etc., even if vacant.

O A mobile home or trailer
O A one-family house detached from any other house
O A one-family house attached to one or more houses
O A building for 2 families
O A building for 3 or 4 families
O A building for 5 to 9 families
O A building for 10 to 19 families
O A building for 20 to 49 families
O A building for 50 or more families
O A boat, tent, van, etc.

H14a. How many stories (floors) are in this building?
Count an attic or basement as a story if it has any finished rooms for living purposes.

O 1 to 3 — *Skip to H15*
O 4 to 6
O 7 to 12
O 13 or more stories

b. Is there a passenger elevator in this building?

O Yes — O No

H15a. Is this building —

O On a city or suburban lot, or on a place of less than 1 acre? — *Skip to H16*
O On a place of 1 to 9 acres?
O On a place of 10 or more acres?

b. Last year, 1979, did sales of crops, livestock, and other farm products from this place amount to —

O Less than $50 (or None)
O $50 to $249
O $250 to $599
O $600 to $999
O $1,000 to $2,499
O $2,500 or more

H16. Do you get water from —

O A public system *(city water department, etc.)* or private company?
O An individual drilled well?
O An individual dug well?
O Some other source *(a spring, creek, river, cistern, etc.)*?

H17. Is this building connected to a public sewer?

O Yes, connected to public sewer
O No, connected to septic tank or cesspool
O No, use other means

H18. About when was this building originally built? *Mark when the building was first constructed, not when it was remodeled, added to, or converted.*

O 1979 or 1980
O 1975 to 1978
O 1970 to 1974
O 1960 to 1969
O 1950 to 1959
O 1940 to 1949
O 1939 or earlier

H19. When did the person listed in column 1 move into this house (or apartment)?

O 1979 or 1980
O 1975 to 1978
O 1970 to 1974
O 1960 to 1969
O 1950 to 1959
O 1949 or earlier
O Always lived here

H20. How are your living quarters heated?
Fill one circle for the kind of heat used most.

O Steam or hot water system
O Central warm-air furnace with ducts to the individual rooms *(Do not count electric heat pumps here)*
O Electric heat pump
O Other built-in electric units *(permanently installed in wall, ceiling, or baseboard)*
O Floor, wall, or pipeless furnace
O Room heaters with flue or vent, burning gas, oil, or kerosene
O Room heaters without flue or vent, burning gas, oil, or kerosene *(not portable)*
O Fireplaces, stoves, or portable room heaters of any kind
O No heating equipment

H21a. Which fuel is used most for house heating?

O Gas: from underground pipes serving the neighborhood
O Gas: bottled, tank, or LP
O Electricity
O Fuel oil, kerosene, etc.
O Coal or coke
O Wood
O Other fuel
O No fuel used

b. Which fuel is used most for water heating?

O Gas: from underground pipes serving the neighborhood
O Gas: bottled, tank, or LP
O Electricity
O Fuel oil, kerosene, etc.
O Coal or coke
O Wood
O Other fuel
O No fuel used

c. Which fuel is used most for cooking?

O Gas: from underground pipes serving the neighborhood
O Gas: bottled, tank, or LP
O Electricity
O Fuel oil, kerosene, etc.
O Coal or coke
O Wood
O Other fuel
O No fuel used

H22. What are the costs of utilities and fuels for your living quarters?

a. Electricity
$ ________ .00 OR
Average monthly cost
O Included in rent or no charge
O Electricity not used

b. Gas
$ ________ .00 OR
Average monthly cost
O Included in rent or no charge
O Gas not used

c. Water
$ ________ .00 OR
Yearly cost
O Included in rent or no charge

d. Oil, coal, kerosene, wood, etc.
$ ________ .00 OR
Yearly cost
O Included in rent or no charge
O These fuels not used

H23. Do you have complete kitchen facilities? *Complete kitchen facilities are a sink with piped water, a range or cookstove, and a refrigerator.*

O Yes — O No

H24. How many bedrooms do you have?
Count rooms used mainly for sleeping even if used also for other purposes.

O No bedroom
O 1 bedroom
O 2 bedrooms
O 3 bedrooms
O 4 bedrooms
O 5 or more bedrooms

H25. How many bathrooms do you have?
A complete bathroom is a room with flush toilet, bathtub or shower, and wash basin with piped water.
A half bathroom has at least a flush toilet or bathtub or shower, but does not have all the facilities for a complete bathroom.

O No bathroom, or only a half bathroom
O 1 complete bathroom
O 1 complete bathroom, plus half bath(s)
O 2 or more complete bathrooms

H26. Do you have a telephone in your living quarters?

O Yes — O No

H27. Do you have air conditioning?

O Yes, a central air-conditioning system
O Yes, 1 individual room unit
O Yes, 2 or more individual room units
O No

H28. How many automobiles are kept at home for use by members of your household?

O None
O 1 automobile
O 2 automobiles
O 3 or more automobiles

H29. How many vans or trucks of one-ton capacity or less are kept at home for use by members of your household?

O None
O 1 van or truck
O 2 vans or trucks
O 3 or more vans or trucks

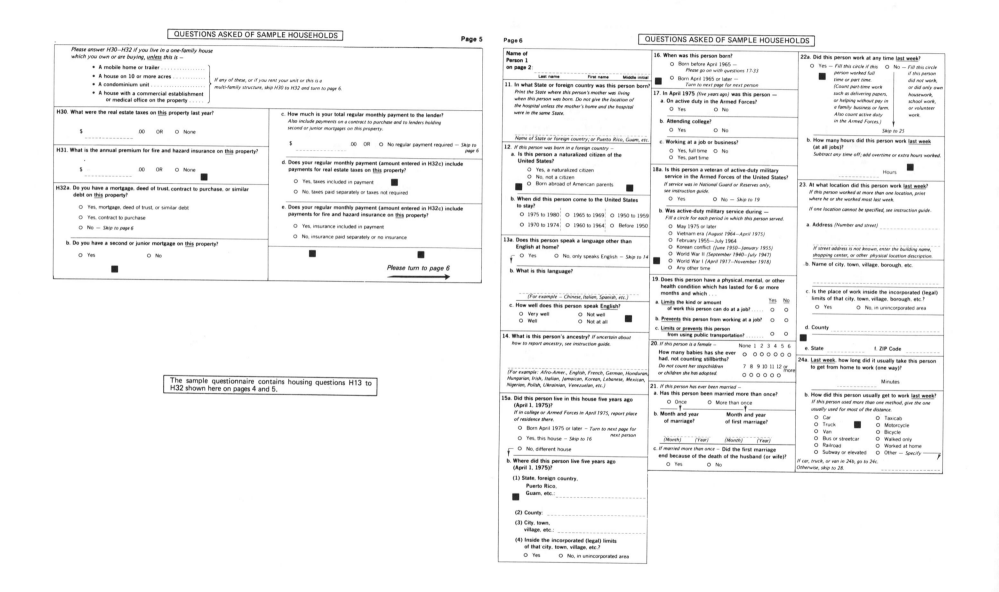

Please answer H30–H32 if you live in a one-family house which you own or are buying, unless this is –

- • A mobile home or trailer . . . .
- • A house on 10 or more acres . . . .
- • A condominium unit . . . .
- • A house with a commercial establishment or medical office on the property . . . . .

If any of these, or if you rent your unit or this is a multi-family structure, skip H30 to H32 and turn to page 6.

H30. What were the real estate taxes on this property last year?

$ _____ .00   OR   ○ None

H31. What is the annual premium for fire and hazard insurance on this property?

$ _____ .00   OR   ○ None

H32a. Do you have a mortgage, deed of trust, contract to purchase, or similar debt on this property?

○ Yes, mortgage, deed of trust, or similar debt
○ Yes, contract to purchase
○ No – *Skip to page 6*

b. Do you have a second or junior mortgage on this property?

○ Yes   ○ No

c. How much is your total regular monthly payment to the lender?
Also include payments on a contract to purchase and to lenders holding second or junior mortgages on this property.

$ _____ .00   OR   ○ No regular payment required – *Skip to page 6*

d. Does your regular monthly payment (amount entered in H32c) include payments for real estate taxes on this property?

○ Yes, taxes included in payment
○ No, taxes paid separately or taxes not required

e. Does your regular monthly payment (amount entered in H32c) include payments for fire and hazard insurance on this property?

○ Yes, insurance included in payment
○ No, insurance paid separately or no insurance

Please turn to page 6

The sample questionnaire contains housing questions H13 to H32 shown here on pages 4 and 5.

Name of Person 1 on page 2:

Last name   First name   Middle initial

11. In what State or foreign country was this person born?
Print the State where this person's mother was living when this person was born. Do not give the location of the hospital unless the mother's home and the hospital were in the same State.

Name of State or foreign country; or Puerto Rico, Guam, etc.

12. If this person was born in a foreign country –
a. Is this person a naturalized citizen of the United States?

○ Yes, a naturalized citizen
○ No, not a citizen
○ Born abroad of American parents

b. When did this person come to the United States to stay?

○ 1975 to 1980   ○ 1965 to 1969   ○ 1950 to 1959
○ 1970 to 1974   ○ 1960 to 1964   ○ Before 1950

13a. Does this person speak a language other than English at home?

○ Yes   ○ No, only speaks English – *Skip to 14*

b. What is this language?

(For example – Chinese, Italian, Spanish, etc.)

c. How well does this person speak English?

○ Very well   ○ Not well
○ Well   ○ Not at all

14. What is this person's ancestry? *If uncertain about how to report ancestry, see instruction guide.*

(For example: Afro-Amer., English, French, German, Honduran, Hungarian, Irish, Italian, Jamaican, Korean, Lebanese, Mexican, Nigerian, Polish, Ukrainian, Venezuelan, etc.)

15a. Did this person live in this house five years ago (April 1, 1975)?
If in college or Armed Forces in April 1975, report place of residence there.

○ Born April 1975 or later – *Turn to next page for next person*
○ Yes, this house – *Skip to 16*
○ No, different house

b. Where did this person live five years ago (April 1, 1975)?

(1) State, foreign country, Puerto Rico, Guam, etc.: _____

(2) County: _____

(3) City, town, village, etc.: _____

(4) Inside the incorporated (legal) limits of that city, town, village, etc.?

○ Yes   ○ No, in unincorporated area

16. When was this person born?

○ Born before April 1965 –
  Please go on with questions 17-33
○ Born April 1965 or later –
  Turn to next page for next person

17. In April 1975 (five years ago) was this person –
a. On active duty in the Armed Forces?

○ Yes   ○ No

b. Attending college?

○ Yes   ○ No

c. Working at a job or business?

○ Yes, full time   ○ No
○ Yes, part time

18a. Is this person a veteran of active-duty military service in the Armed Forces of the United States?
If service was in National Guard or Reserves only, see instruction guide.

○ Yes   ○ No – *Skip to 19*

b. Was active-duty military service during –
Fill a circle for each period in which this person served.

○ May 1975 or later
○ Vietnam era (August 1964–April 1975)
○ February 1955–July 1964
○ Korean conflict (June 1950–January 1955)
○ World War II (September 1940–July 1947)
○ World War I (April 1917–November 1918)
○ Any other time

19. Does this person have a physical, mental, or other health condition which has lasted for 6 or more months and which . . .

	Yes	No
a. Limits the kind or amount of work this person can do at a job?	○	○
b. Prevents this person from working at a job?	○	○
c. Limits or prevents this person from using public transportation?	○	○

20. If this person is a female –
How many babies has she ever had, not counting stillbirths?
Do not count her stepchildren or children she has adopted.

None 1 2 3 4 5 6
○ ○ ○ ○ ○ ○ ○

7 8 9 10 11 12 or more
○ ○ ○ ○ ○ ○

21. If this person has ever been married –
a. Has this person been married more than once?

○ Once   ○ More than once

b. Month and year of marriage?   **Month and year of first marriage?**

(Month) (Year)   (Month) (Year)

c. If married more than once – Did the first marriage end because of the death of the husband (or wife)?

○ Yes   ○ No

22a. Did this person work at any time last week?

○ Yes – *Fill this circle if this person worked full time or part time. (Count part-time work such as delivering papers, or helping without pay in a family business or farm. Also count active duty in the Armed Forces.)*
○ No – *Fill this circle if this person did not work, or did only own housework, school work, or volunteer work.*
                                    Skip to 25

b. How many hours did this person work last week (at all jobs)?
Subtract any time off; add overtime or extra hours worked.

_____ Hours

23. At what location did this person work last week?
If this person worked at more than one location, print where he or she worked most last week.

If one location cannot be specified, see instruction guide.

a. Address (Number and street)

If street address is not known, enter the building name, shopping center, or other physical location description.

b. Name of city, town, village, borough, etc.

c. Is the place of work inside the incorporated (legal) limits of that city, town, village, borough, etc.?

○ Yes   ○ No, in unincorporated area

d. County

e. State   **f. ZIP Code**

24a. Last week, how long did it usually take this person to get from home to work (one way)?

_____ Minutes

b. How did this person usually get to work last week?
If this person used more than one method, give the one usually used for most of the distance.

○ Car   ○ Taxicab
○ Truck   ○ Motorcycle
○ Van   ○ Bicycle
○ Bus or streetcar   ○ Walked only
○ Railroad   ○ Worked at home
○ Subway or elevated ○ Other – Specify

If car, truck, or van in 24b, go to 24c. Otherwise, skip to 28.

QUESTIONS ASKED OF SAMPLE HOUSEHOLDS	Page 7

Page 8

The sample questionnaire also contains population questions 11 to 33, shown here on pages 6 and 7. These questions appear on pairs of facing pages of the sample form (i.e., 6 and 7, 8 and 9, etc.) for each person in the household. Note that questions 17 to 33 do not apply to persons under 15 years of age.

c. When going to work last week, did this person usually —
- ○ Drive alone — *Skip to 28*
- ○ Share driving
- ○ Drive others only
- ○ Ride as passenger only

d. How many people, including this person, usually rode to work in the car, truck, or van last week?
- ○ 2   ■ ○ 4   ○ 6
- ○ 3   ○ 5   ○ 7 or more ■

After answering 24d, skip to 28.

25. Was this person temporarily absent or on layoff from a job or business last week?
- ○ Yes, on layoff
- ○ Yes, on vacation, temporary illness, labor dispute, etc.
- ○ No

26a. Has this person been looking for work during the last 4 weeks?
- ○ Yes   ○ No — *Skip to 27*

b. Could this person have taken a job last week?
- ○ No, already has a job
- ○ No, temporarily ill
- ○ No, other reasons *(in school, etc.)*
- ○ Yes, could have taken a job ■

27. When did this person last work, even for a few days?
- ○ 1980   ○ 1978   ○ 1970 to 1974
- ○ 1979   ○ 1975 to 1977   ○ 1969 or earlier } *Skip to 31d*
- ○ Never worked

28—30. Current or most recent job activity
Describe clearly this person's chief job activity or business last week. If this person had more than one job, describe the one at which this person worked the most hours. If this person had no job or business last week, give information for last job or business since 1975.

28. Industry
a. For whom did this person work? *If now on active duty in the Armed Forces, print "AF" and skip to question 31.*

_____
(Name of company, business, organization, or other employer)

b. What kind of business or industry was this?
Describe the activity at location where employed.

_____
(For example: Hospital, newspaper publishing, mail order house, auto engine manufacturing, breakfast cereal manufacturing)

c. Is this mainly — *(Fill one circle)*
- ○ Manufacturing ■   ○ Retail trade
- ○ Wholesale trade   ○ Other — *(agriculture, construction, service, government, etc.)*

29. Occupation
a. What kind of work was this person doing?

_____
(For example: Registered nurse, personnel manager, supervisor of order department, gasoline engine assembler, grinder operator)

b. What were this person's most important activities or duties?

_____
(For example: Patient care, directing hiring policies, supervising order clerks, assembling engines, operating grinding mill)

30. Was this person — *(Fill one circle)*

Employee of private company, business, or
  individual, for wages, salary, or commissions ...... ○ ■

Federal government employee .... ○
State government employee .... ○
Local government employee *(city, county, etc.)* ...... ○

Self-employed in own business,
professional practice, or farm —
  Own business not incorporated .... ○
  Own business incorporated .... ○

Working without pay in family business or farm ...... ○

31a. Last year (1979), did this person work, even for a few days, at a paid job or in a business or farm?
- ○ Yes ■   ○ No — *Skip to 31d*

b. How many weeks did this person work in 1979?
Count paid vacation, paid sick leave, and military service.

_____ Weeks

c. During the weeks worked in 1979, how many hours did this person usually work each week?

_____ Hours

d. Of the weeks not worked in 1979 (if any), how many weeks was this person looking for work or on layoff from a job?

_____ Weeks

32. Income in 1979 —
Fill circles and print dollar amounts.
If net income was a loss, write "Loss" above the dollar amount.
If exact amount is not known, give best estimate. For income received jointly by household members, see instruction guide.

During 1979 did this person receive any income from the following sources?
If "Yes" to any of the sources below — How much did this person receive for the entire year?

a. Wages, salary, commissions, bonuses, or tips from all jobs ... *Report amount before deductions for taxes, bonds, dues, or other items.*
- ○ Yes ➤ $ _____ .00
- ○ No   *(Annual amount — Dollars)*

b. Own nonfarm business, partnership, or professional practice ... *Report net income after business expenses.*
- ■ Yes ➤ $ _____ .00
- ○ No   *(Annual amount — Dollars)*

c. Own farm ... *Report net income after operating expenses. Include earnings as a tenant farmer or sharecropper.*
- ○ Yes ➤ $ _____ .00
- ○ No   *(Annual amount — Dollars)*

d. Interest, dividends, royalties, or net rental income ... *Report even small amounts credited to an account.*
- ○ Yes ➤ $ _____ .00
- ○ No   *(Annual amount — Dollars)*

e. Social Security or Railroad Retirement ...
- ○ Yes ➤ $ _____ .00
- ○ No   *(Annual amount — Dollars)*

f. Supplemental Security (SSI), Aid to Families with Dependent Children (AFDC), or other public assistance or public welfare payments ...
- ○ Yes ➤ $ _____ .00
- ○ No   *(Annual amount — Dollars)*

g. Unemployment compensation, veterans' payments, pensions, alimony or child support, or any other sources of income received regularly ...
Exclude lump-sum payments such as money from an inheritance or the sale of a home.
- ■ Yes ➤ $ _____ .00
- ○ No   *(Annual amount — Dollars)*

33. What was this person's total income in 1979?
Add entries in questions 32a through g; subtract any losses.
$ _____ .00
(Annual amount — Dollars)
If total amount was a loss, write "Loss" above amount.
OR ○ None

Please Make Sure You Have Filled This Form Completely

For persons who answered in Question 1 that they are staying here only temporarily and have a usual home elsewhere, enter the address of usual home here:

House number	Street or road	Apartment number or location
City		County
State		ZIP Code

For Answers to Questions H1, H2, and H3:

H1. Name of person(s) left out and reason:

_____
_____

H2. Name of person(s) away from home and reason away:

_____
_____

H3. Name of visitor(s) for whom there is no one at the home address to report the person to a Census Taker:

_____
_____

NOTE
If you have listed more than 7 persons in Question 1, please make sure that you have filled the form for the first 7 people. Then mail back this form. A Census Taker will call to obtain the information for the other people.

1 Check to be certain you have:
- Answered Question 1 on page 1.
- Answered the questions on page 2 about the people in your household.
- Answered the questions on page 3 about your house or apartment.
- Answered Questions H13 through H32 on pages 4 and 5.
- Fill a pair of pages for each person listed on pages 2 and 3. That is, pages 6 and 7 should be filled for the Person in column 1; pages 8 and 9 for the Person in column 2, etc.

Please notice we need answers to questions 17 through 33 for every person born before April 1965 even though they may not seem to apply to the particular person.

For example, you may have forgotten to fill all the necessary circles on work or on income for a teenager going to school, or a retired person. To avoid our having to check with you to make sure of the answer, please be certain you have given all the necessary answers.

2 Write here the name of the person who filled the form, the date the form was completed, and the telephone number on which the people in this household can be called.

Name _____

Date _____

Telephone Number _____

3 Then fold the form the way it was sent to you. Mail it back in the enclosed envelope. The address of the U.S. Census Office appears on the front cover of this questionnaire. Please be sure that before you seal the envelope the address shows through the window. No stamp is required.

Thank you very much.

☆ U.S. GOVERNMENT PRINTING OFFICE: 1979—659-502

GENERAL ENUMERATION PROCEDURES AND DATA ACCURACY

Enumeration

Usual Place of Residence

In accordance with census practice dating back to the first U.S. census in 1790, each person enumerated in the 1980 census was counted as an inhabitant of his or her "usual place of residence," which is generally construed to mean the place where the person lives and sleeps most of the time. This place is not necessarily the same as the person's legal residence or voting residence. In the vast majority of cases, however, the use of these different bases of classification would produce substantially the same statistics, although there might be appreciable differences for a few areas.

Detailed information on residence rules is given in the 1980 Census of Population, *Characteristics of the Population: Number of Inhabitants*, PC80-1-A.

Accuracy of the Data

Introduction

Some data in this book are based on complete-count data and other data are based on the 1980 census sample. Estimates can be expected to vary from the complete-count result because they are subject to two basic types of error—sampling and nonsampling. The sampling error in the data arises from the selection of persons and housing units to be included in the sample. The nonsampling error is the result of all other errors that may occur during the collection and processing phases of the census. Nonsampling error, therefore, affects both the complete-count data and the sample data.

Sample Design

While every person and housing unit in the United States was enumerated on a questionnaire that requested certain basic demographic information (for example, age, race, relationship), a sample of persons and housing units was enumerated on a questionnaire that requested additional information. The basic sampling unit for the 1980 census was the housing unit, including all occupants. For persons living in group quarters, the sampling unit was the person. Two sampling rates were employed. In counties, incorporated places, and minor civil divisions estimated to have fewer than 2,500 persons (based on precensus estimates), one half of all housing units and persons in group quarters were to be included in the sample. In all other places, one sixth of the housing units or persons in group quarters were sampled. The purpose of this scheme was to provide relatively more reliable estimates for small places. When both sampling rates were taken into account across the nation, approximately 19 percent of the nation's housing units were included in the census sample.

Errors in the Data

Census data based on a sample may differ somewhat from complete-count figures that would have been obtained if all housing units, persons within those housing units, and persons living in group quarters had been enumerated using the same questionnaires, instructions, enumerators, and so forth. The deviation of a sample estimate from the average of all possible samples is called the sampling error. The standard error of a survey estimate is a measure of the variation among the estimates from the possible samples and thus is a measure of the precision with which an estimate from a particular sample approximates the average result of all possible samples. The sample estimate and its estimated standard error permit the construction of interval estimates with prescribed confidence that the interval includes the average result of all possible samples.

In addition to the variability that arises from the sampling procedures, both sample data and complete-count data are subject to nonsampling error. Nonsampling error may be introduced during each of the many extensive and complex operations used to collect and process census data. For example, operations such as editing, reviewing, or handling questionnaires may introduce error into the data.

Nonsampling error may affect the data in two ways. Errors that are introduced randomly will increase the variability of the data and should therefore be reflected in the standard error. Errors that tend to be consistent in one direction will make both sample and complete-count data biased in that direction. For example, if respondents consistently tend to underreport their income, the resulting counts of households or families by income category will be skewed toward the lower income categories. Such biases are not reflected in the standard error.

Control of Nonsampling Error

As mentioned above, nonsampling error is present in both sample and complete-count data. If left unchecked, this error could introduce serious bias into the data, the variability of which could increase dra-

matically over that which would result purely from sampling. While it is impossible to completely eliminate nonsampling error from an operation as large and complex as the 1980 census, the Bureau of the Census attempted to control the sources of such error during the collection and processing operations. The primary sources of nonsampling error and the programs instituted for control of this error are described below. The success of these programs, however, was contingent upon how well the instructions were actually carried out during the census. To the extent possible, both the effects of these programs and the amount of error remaining after their application will be evaluated.

Undercoverage: It is possible for some housing units or persons to be entirely missed by the census. This undercoverage of persons and housing units can introduce biases into the data. Several extensive programs that were developed to focus on this important problem are explained below.

1. The Postal Service reviewed mailing lists and reported housing unit addresses which were missing, undeliverable, or duplicated in the listings.

2. The purchased commercial mailing list was updated and corrected by a complete field review of the list of housing units during a precanvass operation.

3. A record check was performed to reduce the undercoverage of individual persons in selected areas. Independent lists of persons, such as driver's license holders, were matched with the household rosters in the census listings. Persons not matched to the census rosters were followed up and added to the census counts if they were found to have been missed.

4. A recheck of housing units initially classified as vacant or nonexistent was utilized to further reduce the undercoverage of persons.

Respondent and enumerator error: The person answering the questionnaire or responding to the questions posed by an enumerator could serve as a source of error by offering incorrect or incomplete information. To reduce this source of error, questions were phrased as clearly as possible based on precensus tests, and detailed instructions for completing the questionnaire were provided to each housing unit. In addition, respondents' answers were edited for completeness and consistency and followed up as necessary.

The enumerator may misinterpret or otherwise incorrectly record information given by a respondent, may fail to collect some of the information for a person or housing unit, or may collect data for housing units that were not designated as part of the sample. To control these problems, the work of enumerators was carefully monitored. Field staff were prepared for their tasks by using standardized training packages which included experience in using census materials. A sample of the households interviewed by enumerators for nonresponse was reinterviewed to control for the possibility of data for fabricated persons being submitted by enumerators. Also, the estimation procedure was designed to control for biases that would result from the collection of data from housing units not designated for the sample.

Processing error: The many phases of processing the census represent potential sources for the introduction of nonsampling error. The processing of the census questionnaires includes the field editing, follow-up, and transmittal of completed questionnaires; the manual coding of write-in responses; and the electronic data processing. The various field, coding, and computer operations undergo a number of quality control checks to ensure their accurate application.

Nonresponse: Nonresponse to particular questions on the census questionnaire allows for the introduction of bias into the data, since the characteristics of the nonrespondents have not been observed and may differ from those reported by respondents. As a result, any allocation procedure using respondent data may not completely reflect this difference either at the element level (individual person or housing unit) or on the average. Some protection against the introduction of large biases is afforded by minimizing nonresponse. In the census, nonresponse was substantially reduced during the field operations by the various edit and follow-up operations aimed at obtaining a response for every question. Characteristics for the nonresponse remaining after this operation were allocated by the computer using reported data for a person or housing unit with similar characteristics. The allocation procedure is described in more detail below.

Editing of Unacceptable Data

The objective of the processing operation is to produce a set of statistics that describes the housing inventory and population as accurately and clearly as possible. To meet this objective, certain unacceptable entries were edited.

In the field, questionnaires were reviewed for omissions and certain inconsistencies by a census clerk or an enumerator and, if nec-essary, a follow-up was made to obtain missing information. In addition, a similar review of questionnaires was done in the central processing offices. As a rule, however, editing was performed by hand only when it could not be done effectively by machine.

As one of the first steps in editing, the configuration of marks on the questionnaire column was scanned electronically to determine whether it contained information for a person or a housing unit or merely spurious marks. If the column contained entries for at least two of the basic characteristics (relationship, sex, race, age, marital status, Spanish origin), the inference was made that the marks represented a person. In cases in which two or more basic characteristics were available for only a portion of the people in the unit, other information on the questionnaire provided by an enumerator was used to determine the total number of persons. Names were not used as a criterion of the presence of a person because the electronic scanning did not distinguish any entry in the name space.

If any characteristic for a person or a housing unit was still missing when the questionnaires reached central processing, they were supplied by allocation. Allocations, or assignments of acceptable codes in place of unacceptable entries, were needed most often when there was no entry for a given item or when the information reported for a person or housing unit on that item was inconsistent with other information for the person or housing unit. As in previous censuses, the general procedure for changing unacceptable entries was to assign an entry for a person or housing unit that was consistent with entries for other persons or units with similar characteristics. Thus, a person who was reported as a 20-year-old son of the householder, but for whom marital status was not reported, was assigned the same marital status as that of the last son processed in the same age group. The assignment of acceptable codes in place of blanks or unacceptable entries enhances the usefulness of the data.

The editing process for complete-count data also includes another type of correction; namely, the assignment of a full set of characteristics for a person or a housing unit. When there was indication that a housing unit was occupied but the questionnaire contained no information for all or most of the people, although persons were known to be present or when there was no information on the housing unit, a previously processed household was selected as a substitute, and the full set of characteristics for each substitute person or housing unit was duplicated. These duplications fall into two classes: (1) "substitution for mechanical failure," for example, when the questionnaire page was not properly microfilmed, and (2) "substitution for noninterview," for example, when a housing unit was indicated as occupied but the occupants or housing unit characteristics were not listed on the questionnaire.

Specific tolerances were established for the number of computer allocations and substitutions that would be permitted. If the number of corrections was beyond tolerance, the questionnaires in which the errors occurred were clerically reviewed. If it was found that the errors resulted from damaged questionnaires, from improper microfilming, from faulty reading by the computer of undamaged questionnaires, or from other types of machine failure, the questionnaires were reprocessed.

Bibliography

Aaron, Henry J. *Shelter and Subsidies: Who Benefits from Federal Housing Policies?* Washington, DC: The Brookings Institution, 1972.

Abler, Ronald F.; John S. Adams; and Ki-Suk Lee *A Comparative Atlas of America's Great Cities: Twenty Metropolitan Regions.* Minneapolis: University of Minnesota Press, 1976.

Adams, John S. "Residential Structure of Midwestern Cities." *Annals*, Association of American Geographers 60:1(1970):37–62.

——— "The Meaning of Housing in America." *Annals*, Association of American Geographers 74:4(1984):515-26.

———, ed. *Contemporary Metropolitan America*, 4 vols. Cambridge, MA: Ballinger, 1976.

———, ed. *Urban Policy Making and Metropolitan Dynamics: A Comparative Geographical Analysis.* Cambridge, MA: Ballinger, 1976.

———, **and James D. Fitzsimmons** "Planning for the Geography of Metropolitan America." In Charles M. Christian and Robert A. Harper, eds., *Modern Metropolitan Systems.* Columbus, OH: Charles E. Merrill, 1982, pp. 457–80.

Alonso, William *Location and Land Use: Toward a General Theory of Land Rent.* Cambridge, MA: Harvard University Press, 1964.

Aronovici, Carol *Housing the Masses.* New York: Wiley, 1939.

Bernhardt, Arthur D. *Building Tomorrow: The Mobile/Manufactured Housing Industry.* Cambridge, MA: M.I.T. Press, 1980.

Berry, Brian J. L., and Donald C. Dahmann *Population Redistribution in the United States in the 1970s.* Washington, DC: National Academy of Sciences, 1977.

Berry, Brian J. L., and John D. Kasarda *Contemporary Urban Ecology.* New York: Macmillan, 1977.

Beyer, Glenn H. *Housing: A Factual Analysis.* New York: Macmillan, 1965.

——— *Housing and Society.* New York: Macmillan, 1965.

———, **and J. Hugh Rose** *Farm Housing.* New York: Wiley, 1957.

Bianchi, Suzanne; Reynolds Farley; and Daphne Spain "Racial Inequalities in Housing: An Examination of Recent Trends." *Demography* 19 (1982):37–51.

Birch, David L. *America's Housing Needs: 1970–1980.* Cambridge, MA: M.I.T. and Harvard University Press, 1973.

Birch, Eugenie Ladner, ed. *The Unsheltered Woman: Women and Housing in the 1980s.* New Brunswick, NJ: Center for Urban Policy Research, 1985.

Borchert, John R. "American Metropolitan Evolution." *Geographical Review* 57:3(1967):301–22.

——— "America's Changing Metropolitan Regions." *Annals*, Association of American Geographers 62:2(1972):353–73.

Bourne, Larry S. *The Geography of Housing.* New York: Wiley, 1981.

——— *Internal Structure of the City: Readings on Urban Form, Growth, and Policy.* New York: Oxford University Press, 1982.

Bradbury, Katharine L., and Anthony Downs, eds. *Do Housing Allowances Work?* Washington, DC: The Brookings Institution, 1981.

———; **and Kenneth A. Small** *Urban Decline and the Future of American Cities.* Washington, DC: The Brookings Institution, 1982.

Burns, Leland S., and Leo Grebler *The Housing of Nations.* New York: Wiley, 1977.

Cadwallader, Martin T. "Neighborhood Evaluation in Residential Mobility." *Environment and Planning A* 11 (1979):393–401.

——— "A Unified Model of Urban Housing Patterns, Social Patterns, and Residential Mobility." *Urban Geography* 2:2(1981):115–30.

Christian, Charles M., and Robert A. Harper *Modern Metropolitan Systems.* Columbus, OH: Charles E. Merrill, 1982.

Clark, William A. V., and Lun A. Anoka "Life Cycle and Housing Adjustment as Explanations of Residential Mobility." *Urban Studies* 20 (1983):47–57.

Clark, William A. V., and Martin T. Cadwallader "Location Stress and Residential Mobility." *Environment and Behavior* 5 (1973):29–41.

Clark, William A. V., and Eric G. Moore, eds. *Residential Mobility and Public Policy.* Beverly Hills, CA: Sage, 1980.

Colean, Miles L., and The Housing Committee of the Twentieth Century Fund *American Housing: Problems and Prospects.* New York: Twentieth Century Fund, 1944.

Cooper, Clare *The House as Symbol of Self.* Working Paper No. 120. Berkeley, CA: Institute of Urban and Regional Development, University of California, 1971.

Dahmann, Donald C. "North–South Differences in Housing and the Housing and Community Development Act of 1977." *Journal of the American Real Estate and Urban Economics Association* 7 (Summer 1979):230–42.

——— *Housing Opportunities for Black and White Households: Three Decades of Change in the Supply of Housing.* Washington, DC: U.S. Government Printing Office, 1982.

——— "Racial Differences in Housing Consumption During the 1970s: Insights from a Components of Inventory Change Analysis." *Urban Geography* 4:3(1983):203–22.

——— "Assessments of Neighborhood Quality in Metropolitan America." *Urban Affairs Quarterly* 20:4(1985):511–35.

Dear, Michael J., and Jennifer R. Wolch *Landscapes of Despair: From Deinstitutionalization to Homelessness.* London: Policy Press/Basil Blackwell, 1986.

de Leeuw, Frank, and Raymond J. Struyk *The Web of Urban Housing: Analyzing Policy with a Market Simulation Model*. Washington, DC: The Urban Institute, 1975.

Downs, Anthony *Opening Up the Suburbs: An Urban Strategy for America*. New Haven, CT: Yale University Press, 1973.

—— "Key Relationships Between Urban Development and Neighborhood Change." *Journal of the American Institute of Planning* 45:4(1979):462–72.

—— "Too Much Capital for Housing." *The Brookings Bulletin* 17:1(Summer 1980):4.

—— *Neighborhoods and Urban Development*. Washington, DC: The Brookings Institution, 1981.

—— *Rental Housing in the 1980s*. Washington, DC: The Brookings Institution, 1983.

—— *The Revolution in Real Estate Finance*. Washington, DC: The Brookings Institution, 1985.

——, **and Katharine Bradbury, eds.** *Energy Costs, Urban Development and Housing*. Washington, DC: The Brookings Institution, 1984.

Drury, Margaret J. *Mobile Homes: The Unrecognized Revolution in American Housing*. New York: Praeger, 1972.

Easterlin, Richard A. *Birth and Fortune: The Impact of Numbers on Personal Welfare*. New York: Basic Books, 1980.

Erickson, Jon, and Charles Wilhelm, eds. *Housing the Homeless*. New Brunswick, NJ: Center for Urban Policy Research, 1986.

Federal National Mortgage Association *Housing Finance in the Eighties: Issues and Options*. Washington, DC: Federal National Mortgage Association, 1981.

Firey, Walter *Land Use in Central Boston*. Cambridge, MA: Harvard University Press, 1947.

Fitzsimmons, James D.; John S. Adams; and David J. Borchert "Recent U.S. Population Redistribution: A Geographical Framework for Change in the 1980s." *Social Sciences Quarterly* 61 (1980):485–507.

Florida, Richard L., ed. *Housing and the New Financial Markets*. New Brunswick, NJ: Center for Urban Policy Research, 1986.

Follain, James R.; Larry Ozanne; and Verna M. Alburger *Place to Place Indexes of the Price of Housing: Some New Estimates and a Comparative Analysis*. Washington, DC: The Urban Institute, 1979.

Frieden, Bernard J., and Arthur A. Solomon *The Nation's Housing: 1975 to 1985*. Cambridge, MA: Joint Center for Urban Studies, 1977.

Friedman, Joseph, and Daniel H. Weinberg *The Economics of Housing Vouchers*. Orlando, FL: Academic Press, 1979.

—— *The Great Housing Experiment*. Urban Affairs Annual Reviews, Vol. 24. Beverly Hills, CA: Sage, 1983.

Gellen, Martin *Accessory Apartments in Single Family Housing*. New Brunswick, NJ: Center for Urban Policy Research, 1985.

Gender, John, and Steven Gordon *The Housing Needs of Non-Traditional Households*. U.S. Department of Housing and Urban Development. Washington, DC: U.S. Government Printing Office, 1980.

Goedert, Jeanne E., and John L. Goodman, Jr. *Indicators of the Quality of U.S. Housing*. Washington, DC: The Urban Institute, 1977.

Golant, Stephen M., and James P. Zais *The Residential Location and Spatial Behavior of the Elderly*. Research Paper No. 143. Chicago: University of Chicago, Department of Geography, 1972.

Goodman, John L., Jr. "Local Residential Mobility and Family Housing Adjustments." In James N. Morgan, ed., *Five Thousand American Families: Patterns of Economic Progress*, Vol. 2. Ann Arbor: Institute for Social Research, University of Michigan, 1974, pp. 79–105.

—— "Housing Consumption Disequilibrium and Local Residential Mobility." *Environment and Planning* 11:2(1974):175–83.

Gries, John M., and James Ford, eds. *The President's Conference on Home Building and Home Ownership*. Washington, DC: U.S. Government Printing Office.

Hancock, Judith Ann, ed. *Housing the Elderly*. New Brunswick, NJ: Center for Urban Policy Research, 1986.

Handlin, David P. *The American House: Architecture and Society, 1815–1915*. Boston, MA: Little, Brown, 1979.

Hanson, Royce *The Evolution of National Urban Policy 1970–1980: Lessons from the Past*. Committee on National Urban Policy, National Research Council. Washington, DC: National Academy Press, 1982.

—— *Perspectives on Urban Infrastructure*. Washington, DC: National Academy Press, 1984.

Hanushek, Eric A., and John M. Quigley "The Dynamics of the Housing Market: A Stock Adjustment Model of Housing Consumption." *Journal of Urban Economics* 6:1(1979):90–111.

Hart, John Fraser *The Look of the Land*. Englewood Cliffs, NJ: Prentice-Hall, 1975.

——, **ed.** *Regions of the United States*. New York: Harper & Row, 1972.

Harvey, David *Social Justice and the City*. Baltimore, MD: Johns Hopkins University Press, 1973.

Hayden, Dolores *Redesigning the American Dream: The Future of Housing, Work and Family Life*. New York: Norton, 1984.

Holleb, Doris "Housing and the Environment: Shooting at Moving Targets." *Annals*, American Academy of Political and Social Science 453 (1981):180–222.

Hombs, Mary Ellen, and Mitch Snyder *Homelessness in America: A Forced March to Nowhere*. Washington, DC: Committee for Creative Non-Violence, 1982.

Howenstine, E. Jay *Housing Vouchers: A Comparative International Analysis*. New Brunswick, NJ: Center for Urban Policy Research, 1986.

Hoyt, Homer *The Structure and Growth of Residential Neighborhoods in American Cities*. Washington, DC: Federal Housing Administration, 1939.

Hughes, James W., and George Sternlieb *The Dynamics of America's Housing*. New Brunswick, NJ: Center for Urban Policy Research, 1987.

Kain, John F., and John M. Quigley "Measuring the Value of Housing Quality." *Journal of the American Statistical Association* 65 (1970):532–48.

Lake, Robert W. *The New Suburbanites: Race and Housing in the Suburbs*. New Brunswick, NJ: Center for Urban Policy Research, 1981.

Leven, Charles L., and others *Neighborhood Change: Lessons in the Dynamics of Urban Decay*. New York: Praeger, 1976.

Listokin, David, ed. *Housing Rehabilitation: Economic, Social and Policy Perspectives*. New Brunswick, NJ: Center for Urban Policy Research, 1983.

——; **Lizabeth Allewelt; and James J. Nemeth** *Housing Receivership and Self-Help Neighborhood Revitalization*. New Brunswick, NJ: Center for Urban Policy Research, 1985.

Little, James T. "Residential Preferences, Neighborhood Filtering, and Neighborhood Change." *Journal of Urban Economics* 3 (1976):68–81.

Long, Larry *Black Movers to the Suburbs: Are They Moving to Predominantly White Neighborhoods?* Washington, DC: Bureau of the Census, Center for Demographic Studies, 1980.

Lowry, Ira S. "The Housing Assistance Supply Experiment: An Overview." *Papers*, Regional Science Association 37 (1976):21–30.

—— *Experimenting with Housing Allowances. Executive Summary: The Final Comprehensive Report of the Housing Assistance Supply Experiment.* Santa Monica, CA: The Rand Corporation, 1982.

McAlester, Virginia, and Lee McAlester *A Field Guide to American Housing.* New York: Knopf, 1985.

McCarthy, Kevin F. "The Household Life Cycle and Housing Choice." *Papers*, Regional Science Association 37 (1976):55–80.

Mallach, Alan *Inclusionary Housing Programs: Policies and Practices.* New Brunswick, NJ: Center for Urban Policy Research, 1984.

Mandelker, Daniel R., and Roger Montgomery, eds. *Housing in America: Problems and Perspectives.* Indianapolis: Bobbs-Merrill, 1973.

Meyer, David R. *Spatial Variations in Black Urban Households.* Research Paper No. 129. Chicago: Department of Geography, University of Chicago, 1970.

Michaelson, William H. *Man and His Urban Environment: A Sociological Approach.* Reading, MA: Addison-Wesley, 1976.

—— *Environmental Choice, Human Behavior, and Residential Satisfaction.* New York: Oxford University Press, 1977.

Milgram, Grace "Housing the Urban Poor: Urban Housing Assistance Programs." In *Housing: A Reader.* Prepared by the Congressional Research Service, Library of Congress, for the 98th Congress, 1st Session. Committee Print 98-5. Washington, DC: U.S. Government Printing Office, 1983, pp. 114–38.

Mitchell, J. Paul, ed. *Federal Housing Policy and Programs: Past and Present.* New Brunswick, NJ: Center for Urban Policy Research, 1985.

Montgomery, Roger, and Dale Rogers Marshall *Housing Policy for the 1980s.* Lexington, MA: Lexington Books, 1980.

Morris, Earl W., and Mary Winter *Housing, Family, and Society.* New York: Wiley, 1978.

Murdie, Robert A. *Factorial Ecology of Metropolitan Toronto, 1951–1961: An Essay on the Social Geography of the City.* Research Paper No. 116. Chicago: Department of Geography, University of Chicago, 1969.

Muth, Richard F. "The Demand for Non-Farm Housing." In A. C. Harberger, ed., *The Demand for Durable Goods.* Chicago: University of Chicago Press, 1960.

—— *Cities and Housing: The Spatial Pattern of Urban Residential Land Use.* Chicago: University of Chicago Press, 1969.

—— "The Allocation of Households to Dwellings." *Journal of Regional Science* 18 (1978):159–78.

Nathanson, Iric *Housing Needs of the Rural Elderly and Handicapped.* U.S. Department of Housing and Urban Development Report, HUD-PDR-633. Washington, DC: U.S. Government Printing Office, 1980.

Olsen, Edgar "A Competitive Theory of the Housing Market." *American Economic Review* 59 (1969):612–22.

Palm, Risa I. "Spatial Segmentation of the Urban Housing Market." *Economic Geography* 54:3(1978):210–21.

—— *The Geography of American Cities.* New York: Oxford University Press, 1981.

——, **and others** *Home Mortgage Lenders, Real Property Appraisers and Earthquake Hazards.* Program on Environment and Behavior, Monograph #38. Boulder, CO: Institute of Behavioral Science, University of Colorado, 1983.

Perin, Constance *Everything in its Place: Social Order and Land Use in America.* Princeton, NJ: Princeton University Press, 1977.

Perry, Clarence A. *Housing for the Machine Age.* New York: Russell Sage Foundation, 1939.

Peterson, George E., and Brian Cooper *Tax Exempt Financing of Housing Investment.* Washington, DC: The Urban Institute, 1979.

President's Committee on Urban Housing *A Decent Home.* Washington, DC: U.S. Government Printing Office, 1969.

Pynoos, Jon; Robert Schafer; and Chester W. Hartman, eds. *Housing Urban America*, 2nd ed. New York: Aldine, 1980.

Ratcliff, Richard U.; Daniel B. Rathbun; and Junia H. Honnold *Residential Finance, 1950.* New York: Wiley, 1957.

Rees, Philip H. "Concepts of Social Space: Toward an Urban Social Geography." In Brian J. L. Berry and Frank E. Horton, eds., *Geographic Perspectives on Urban Systems, with Integrated Readings.* Englewood Cliffs, NJ: Prentice-Hall, 1970.

—— *Residential Patterns in American Cities: 1960.* Research Paper No. 189. Chicago: Department of Geography, University of Chicago, 1979.

Rose, Harold M. *Black Suburbanization: Access to Improved Quality of Life or Maintenance of the Status Quo?* Cambridge, MA: Ballinger, 1976.

Roseman, Curtis C. "Living in More Than One Place: Second Homes in the United States, 1970 and 1980." *Sociology and Social Research* 70:1(1985):63–7.

Rosen, Kenneth T. *Seasonal Cycles in the Housing Market: Patterns, Costs, and Policies.* Cambridge, MA: M.I.T. Press, 1979.

Rossi, Peter *Why Families Move.* New York: Free Press, 1955.

Savings and Loan Fact Book '80 Chicago: United States League of Savings Associations, 1980.

'82 Savings and Loan Sourcebook Chicago: United States League of Savings Associations, 1982.

Schmidman, Frank, and Jane A. Silverman *Housing, Supply and Affordability.* Washington, DC: Urban Land Institute, 1983.

Schussheim, Morton J. *The Modest Commitment to Cities.* Lexington, MA: D. C. Heath, 1974.

—— "Housing: An Overview." In *Housing: A Reader.* Prepared by the Congressional Research Service, Library of Congress, for the 98th Congress, 1st Session. Committee Print 98-5. Washington, DC: U.S. Government Printing Office, 1983, pp. 1–31.

Schwartz, Barry, ed. *The Changing Face of the Suburbs.* Chicago: University of Chicago Press, 1976.

Seidel, Stephan R. *Housing Costs and Government Regulation.* New Brunswick, NJ: Center for Urban Policy Research, 1978.

Smith, Wallace F. *Housing: The Social and Economic Elements.* Berkeley: University of California Press, 1970.

——— "Housing in America." *The Annals*, American Academy of Political and Social Science 465 (1983): 9–13.

Social Science Panel, Advisory Committee to the Department of Housing and Urban Development, National Academy of Sciences–National Academy of Engineering. *Freedom of Choice in Housing: Opportunities and Constraints.* Washington, DC: National Academy of Sciences, 1972.

Speare, Alden, Jr.; Sidney Goldstein; and William H. Frey *Residential Mobility and Metropolitan Change.* Cambridge, MA: Ballinger, 1974.

Sternlieb, George R. "The Evolution of Housing and Its Social Compact." *Urban Land* 41 (December 1982):17–20.

——— *Patterns of Development.* New Brunswick, NJ: Center for Urban Policy Research, 1986.

———, **and James W. Hughes** "Housing the Poor in a Post-Shelter Society." *The Annals*, American Academy of Political and Social Science 465 (1983):109–22.

———, **and others** *America's Housing: Prospects and Problems.* New Brunswick, NJ: Center for Urban Policy Research, 1980.

Struyk, Raymond J.; Susan A. Marshall; and Larry J. Ozanne *Housing Policies for the Urban Poor.* Washington, DC: The Urban Institute, 1978.

Swan, Craig "A Model of Renter and Owner Occupied Housing." *Journal of Urban Economics* 16 (1984):297–316.

Twentieth Century Fund *American Housing: Problems and Prospects.* New York: Twentieth Century Fund, 1944.

U.S. Bureau of the Census *The Coverage of Housing in the 1980 Census.* 1980 Census of Population and Housing. Evaluation and Research Reports, PHC 80-E1. Washington, DC: U.S. Government Printing Office, 1985.

U.S. Congressional Budget Office *Homeownership: The Changing Relationship of Costs and Incomes, and Possible Federal Roles.* Washington, DC: U.S. Government Printing Office, 1977.

——— *Housing Assistance for Low- and Moderate-Income Families.* Washington, DC: U.S. Government Printing Office, 1977.

——— *Federal Housing Policy: Current Programs and Recurring Issues.* Washington, DC: U.S. Government Printing Office, 1978.

——— *Federal Housing Assistance: Alternative Approaches.* Washington, DC: U.S. Government Printing Office, 1982.

U.S. Department of Housing and Urban Development *Housing in the Seventies: Working Papers,* 2 vols. Washington, DC: U.S. Government Printing Office, 1976.

——— *Final Report of the Task Force on Housing Costs.* Washington, DC: U.S. Government Printing Office, 1978.

——— *A Guidebook: Home Mortgage Disclosure Act and Reinvestment Strategies.* Washington, DC: U.S. Government Printing Office, 1979.

——— *Measuring Racial Discrimination in American Housing Markets: The Housing Market Practices Survey.* Washington, DC: U.S. Government Printing Office, 1979.

——— *Problems Affecting Low-Rent Public Housing Projects: A Field Study.* Washington, DC: U.S. Government Printing Office, 1979.

——— *The Role of the Real Estate Sector in Neighborhood Change.* Washington, DC: U.S. Government Printing Office, 1979.

——— *The Conversion of Rental Housing to Condominiums and Cooperatives: A National Study of Scope, Courses and Impacts,* 4 vols. Washington, DC: U.S. Government Printing Office, 1980.

——— *A Guidebook for Using Home Mortgage Disclosure Data for Community Development and Maintenance.* Washington, DC: U.S. Government Printing Office, 1980.

——— *The Land Use and Urban Development Impacts of Beltways,* 3 vols. Washington, DC: U.S. Government Printing Office, 1980.

——— *Regional Housing Mobility Programs: A Guidebook for the Promotion of Housing Opportunities.* Washington, DC: U.S. Government Printing Office, 1980.

U.S. National Commission on Neighborhoods *People, Building Neighborhoods: Final Report.* Washington, DC: U.S. Government Printing Office, 1979.

U.S. National Commission on Urban Problems (The Douglas Commission) *More Than Shelter: Social Needs in Low- and Moderate-Income Housing.* Research Report No. 8. Washington, DC: U.S. Government Printing Office, 1968.

U.S. National Housing Policy Review *Housing in the Seventies.* Washington, DC: U.S. Government Printing Office, 1974.

U.S. President's Commission on Housing *The Report of the President's Commission on Housing.* Washington, DC: U.S. Government Printing Office, 1982.

U.S. President's Committee on Urban Housing (The Kaiser Commission) *A Decent Home.* Washington, DC: U.S. Government Printing Office, 1969.

Vance, James E., Jr. "The American City: Workshop for a National Culture." In John S. Adams, ed., *Contemporary Metropolitan America*, Vol. 1. Cambridge, MA: Ballinger, 1976, pp. 1–49.

——— *This Scene of Man: The Role and Structure of the City in the Geography of Western Civilization.* New York: Harper & Row, 1977.

Weicher, John C.; Lorene Yap; and Mary S. Jones *Metropolitan Housing Needs for the 1980s.* Washington, DC: Urban Institute Press, 1982.

Welfeld, Irving H. *America's Housing Problem: An Approach to Its Solution.* Washington, DC: American Enterprise Institute, 1973.

Wheaton, William L. C.; Grace Milgram; and Margi Ellin Meyerson, eds. *Urban Housing.* New York: Free Press, 1966.

Wilson, John Oliver *After Affluence: Economics to Meet Human Needs.* San Francisco: Harper & Row, 1980.

Winnick, Louis, and Ned Shilling *American Housing and Its Use: The Demand for Shelter Space.* New York: Wiley, 1957.

Wolch, Jennifer R. "The Residential Location of the Service Dependent Poor." *Annals*, Association of American Geographers 70 (1980):330–41.

——— "The Location of Service Dependent Households in Urban Areas." *Economic Geography* 57 (1981):52–67.

Wood, Edith Elmer *Recent Trends in American Housing.* New York: Macmillan, 1931.

——— *Introduction to Housing: Facts and Principles.* Washington, DC: U.S. Government Printing Office, 1940.

Wright, Gwendolyn *Building the Dream: A Social History of Housing in America.* New York: Pantheon, 1981.

Name Index

Subject Index

Boldface numbers refer to figures and tables.